CW00919628

THE AEROSPACE ENCYCLOPEDIA OF
AIR WARFARE
Volume 2
1945 to the present

THE AEROSPACE ENCYCLOPEDIA OF

AIR WARFARE

Volume 2

1945 to the present

Editors:
Chris Bishop
Soph Moeng

Aerospace Publishing Ltd
AIRtime Publishing Inc.

Published by
Aerospace Publishing Ltd
179 Dalling Road
London W6 OES
England

Published under licence in USA and Canada by
AIRtime Publishing Inc.
10 Bay Street
Westport, CT 06880
USA

First published 1997

Aerospace ISBN: 1 874023 88 3
AIRtime ISBN: 1-880588-26-9

Distributed in the UK, Commonwealth and Europe by
Airlife Publishing Ltd
101 Longden Road
Shrewsbury SY3 9EB
England
Telephone: 01743 235651
Fax: 01743 232944

Distributed to retail bookstores in the USA and Canada by
AIRtime Publishing Inc.
10 Bay Street
Westport, CT 06880
USA
Telephone: (203) 838-7979
Fax: (203) 838-7344

US readers wishing to order by mail, please contact
AIRtime Publishing Inc. toll-free at
1 800 359-3003

Publisher: Stan Morse

Editor: Chris Bishop

Editorial contributors: David K Donald
Robert F. Dorr
John Heathcott
Jon Lake
Daniel March
Soph Moeng

Sub Editors: Claire Alexander
Karen Leverington
Chris Chant

Designers: Charlotte Cruise
Hilary Speller

Artists: Chris Davey
Keith Fretwell
Mark Rolfe
John Weal
Keith Woodcock
Iain Wyllie

Colour reproduction:
Universal Graphics
Singapore

Printed in Italy

WORLD AIR POWER JOURNAL is published quarterly and provides an in-depth analysis of contemporary military aircraft and their worldwide operators.

WINGS OF FAME is a sister journal on the subject of historic and classic military aircraft.

Filled with extensive colour photography, superb technical illustration and featuring comprehensive information on variants and colour schemes, WORLD AIR POWER JOURNAL and WINGS OF FAME are available by subscription from:

(UK, Europe and Commonwealth)

Aerospace Publishing Ltd
FREEPOST
PO Box 2822
London W6 OBR
Telephone: 0181-740 9554
Fax: 0181-746 2556
(no stamp needed within the UK)

(USA and Canada)

AIRtime Publishing Inc.
Subscription Dept
10 Bay Street
Westport, CT 06880
USA
Telephone: (203) 838-7979
Fax: (203) 838-7344
Toll-free order number in USA:
1 800 359-3003

CONTENTS

THE COLD WAR

The dominant military feature of the half century since the end of World War II was the undeclared war of nerves known as the Cold War. Two inimical cultural and political systems, centred on the military might of the United States of America and the Union of Soviet Socialist Republics, drew a large part of the world into their respective blocs. But the key to the rivalry was in the five decades of titanic military confrontation between NATO and the Warsaw Pact, the heart of which was across the 'Iron Curtain' which divided Europe between East and West soon after the fall of Hitler.

The Iron Curtain Descends

1945-1948

Left: Douglas C-54 Skymasters from US- and European-based units participated in the Berlin Airlift. The type's high speed and 10-tonne capacity made it the work-horse of the operation, while its modern nosewheel configuration gave it excellent crosswind tolerance.

Below: A pair of Spitfire FR.Mk XIVs of No.II (AC) Squadron take-off from Wunstorf, an operational airfield also used as a crucial Airlift hub.

Three months before the defeat of Germany, Churchill, Roosevelt and Stalin met at Yalta to discuss the division of the post-War world into 'spheres of influence'. Stalin mistrusted his Western Allies, believing that they wanted to destroy the USSR. He hoped to achieve security by neutralising bordering nations and believed that Germany should be crippled to prevent German militarism from ever resurfacing. The Yalta Treaty became the basis of the peace with Germany, and the USSR was promised 55 per cent of German reparations and a sphere of influence which encompassed all of Eastern Europe. Germany surrendered in May 1945 and was divided into four zones administered by the victorious Allies, including France.

German rehabilitation

Soon after the war the USA and Britain came to the view that Germany should be rehabilitated to play a full part in the economic recovery of Europe. The Anglo-American zones were merged, soon joined by the French. The combined Western zone established a federal government, but in the east the USSR continued to act independently. Berlin, split into four zones and controlled jointly by all four 'Allied' powers, was 160 km (100 miles) inside the Soviet zone, and Stalin felt the four-power presence to be anomalous after the unilateral creation of a virtually independent Germany by the West. Consequently, he began placing stringent controls on surface travel to Berlin from the West. On 31 March 1948 the Soviets announced that road traffic into Berlin would be subject to inspection. The West refused to abide by this unilateral decision and cancelled all surface transportation except food and freight trains. At midnight on 18 June the Soviets formally banned all passenger traffic and followed this on 24 June by stopping food trains.

Air supply

The Western powers decided to keep West Berlin supplied by air, at least while negotiations proceeded. It was calculated that 2000 tonnes of food and essential supplies would be needed each day to maintain the 2.5 million inhabitants, and a full-scale Airlift was mounted to defeat the blockade.

Since the war Allied transport fleets had been run down, but what remained mobilised immediately for the Airlift. By 29 June the whole of RAF Transport Command's 64 aircraft Dakota fleet was based in RAF Germany, reinforced by aircrews from Australia, New Zealand and South Africa. By 1 July the Dakotas had been joined by the RAF's Yorks and Hastings and two Coastal Command Sunderland squadrons. The RAF's entire home-based transport fleet was committed to Operation 'Plainfare', supplemented by British civil aircraft, including Haltons, Lancastrians and converted Halifax, Lancaster and Liberator bombers. Under Operation 'Vittles', the USAF provided 102 C-47s and began mobilising a fleet of C-54 Skymasters, most of them based in the USA. It was very soon realised that the load estimate was far too low, and that at least 4000 tonnes of coal, food and other essentials would be needed daily in order to stockpile supplies before winter, which would inevitably disrupt air traffic. It was soon apparent that the

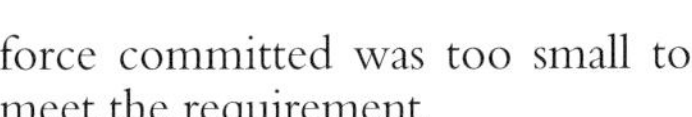

force committed was too small to meet the requirement.

The early achievements of the RAF and USAF were impressive, with over 2000 tonnes flown into Berlin daily in July, and average daily figures of 3839 tonnes and 4600 tonnes in September and October. Meanwhile, the USAF Military Air Transport Service provided eight squadrons of C-54s, which could carry 10 tonnes of freight and weren't as maintenance-intensive as the smaller Dakotas.

Reorganisation

The deployment of the Skymasters coincided with the arrival of a new commander, Major-General William H. Tunner, who set about organising the Airlift more efficiently, getting maximum utilisation from his most-effective resources, using a smaller number of the larger aircraft. On 15 October the RAF and USAF operations were merged officially into a Combined Airlift Task

Left: An RAF Wunstorf Air Traffic Controller signals to a taxiing Dakota with an Aldis Lamp, at the height of the Airlift.

Below: P-80s of the 62nd Fighter Squadron, 56th Fighter Group, lined up at an RAF airfield, en route to Germany during the Berlin crisis.

Post-war air power

While civilians at home still regarded Stalin as 'Uncle Joe', the West's valiant Ally against Hitler, Allied forces at the front line soon realised that the USSR's hostility and suspicion of the West could result in another war. The USSR had an entirely different approach in its zone of occupation, and Europe soon coalesced into two hostile blocks. By 1947, Churchill could declare at Fulton, Ohio, that an 'Iron Curtain' divided the continent.

Lockheed P-80
This Lockheed P-80A of the 62nd Fighter Squadron, 56th Fighter Group, was one of those re-deployed to Europe to reinforce US Forces in the face of rising tension, alongside B-29 bombers. The P-80 was the USAF's first jet fighter, and its deployment was an indication of the seriousness of the situation.

Ilyushin Il-10 Shturmovik
The tactical air forces which supported Zhukov's drive to Berlin soon formed the backbone of a massive Soviet military presence in the Soviet zone of Germany. Il-2s and -10s were the force's main ground-attack aircraft.

Hawker Tempest II
Based first at Fassberg, and then at Gutersloh, the Tempest II's of No. 33 Squadron were deployed to RAF Gatow in Berlin to show an RAF presence over the former enemy capital. The Tempest formed the backbone of the RAF's contribution to BAFO in the immediate post-war period.

Above: Avro Yorks of RAF Transport Command were the unsung heroes of the Airlift, with an 8/9-tonne payload which could include extremely bulky loads, unlike the 10-tonne capacity C-54 or the lightweight 3-tonne capacity C-47.

Force (Provisional). The USAF C-47s were soon replaced by 300 C-54s, gathered from various sources. The importance of the RAF's contribution declined steadily, the Dakotas and Yorks completely vacating Celle and Fassberg, moving farther from Berlin to make way for the C-54s. The four-hour cycle on which the Airlift was based placed the RAF's aircraft at a disadvantage, as they often missed their 'slot' in the next cycle because they were used to transport bulky cargo, passengers and exported manufactured goods, which required longer to load and unload.

The Soviet 16th Air Army had 3,000 combat aircraft, including Yak-3 and La-5FN fighters. When these began buzzing the heavily-laden transport aircraft, the USAF reacted by deploying two groups of B-29 Superfortresses to British bases and a wing of P-80 jet fighters to Furstenfeldbruck. This Allied commitment increased tension, but demonstrated that intimidation would gain nothing.

At the peak of the Airlift aircraft took off and landed at Gatow and Tempelhof airports every 90 seconds, and aircraft remained on the ground at Berlin for an average of only 30 minutes. The Airlift brought in almost one tonne of supplies per Berliner, and had continued around the clock, seven days a week, except briefly during November 1948. Altogether 1586530 tonnes of coal, 92282 tonnes of fuel and 538016 tonnes of

Greek Civil War 1944-1949

During World War II Greece had been occupied by the Nazis after a very brief campaign, which ended with a humiliating British defeat at Crete. In Greece, as in other occupied countries, there had been a small but active resistance movement, dominated by the Communists. At the end of the war Greece was placed in the UK's sphere of influence, and the British immediately re-established the Greek monarchy and re-equipped and revitalised the nation's armed forces. The Royal Hellenic air force received large numbers of war surplus aircraft from the RAF, mostly drawn from the Desert Air Force. They included Oxfords, Ansons, Austers, Dakotas (which were used as bombers), Harvards, Beaufighters, Spitfires and Wellingtons. The Communist guerrillas were unwilling to exchange Nazi oppression for reactionary monarchist rule, and rose against the new government. The Civil War was won eventually by the monarchists, who had begun to receive substantial military aid from the USA. This included aircraft to supplement those supplied by the UK and comprised C-47s, T-6 Texans and L-5 Grasshoppers.

To his credit, Stalin made no attempt to gain control of any territory not allocated at Yalta, even stopping his troops at the Greek border during the revolutionary struggle, when intervention could easily have drawn Greece into the Communist orbit. In similar compliance with the Yalta conference, Stalin withdrew his forces from those areas of Berlin which were to be occupied by the Western Allies, just as the UK and the USA withdrew from Czechoslovakia and the east of Germany.

Royal Air Force Dakotas drop paratroopers near Athens at the end of World War II. British and American support ensured the Greek monarchists would win the civil war with the communists.

Above: A No. 201 Squadron Sunderland unloads supplies on Berlin's Lake Havel. Two RAF Coastal Command Sunderland squadrons participated, easing the strain on West Berlin's crowded airfields by flying from Hamburg's Finkenwarder to Lake Havel.

food, a total of 2325809 tonnes of supplies, had been airlifted in. The USSR realised that it could not starve Berlin into submission and the blockade was lifted at one minute past midnight on 12 May 1949. Despite this the Airlift continued until September, building up stocks in case surface links were cut again. Germany came to be seen as a valuable Ally in the fight against Soviet aggression and the Federal Republic of Germany was formally established on 21 September 1949, marking the division of Europe.

West Germany was accepted into NATO and her armed forces armed with American equipment to bring it up to operational readiness standards against the Soviet block and to take its part in the Cold War which was just beginning.

Left: Douglas C-54 Skymasters and C-47 Skytrains formed the backbone of the USAF's transport effort during the Berlin Airlift. The C-54s were fast and efficient, but could not carry the bulkier, more awkward loads, which went by C-47, Dakota or by Avro York.

Operating Routes of the Berlin Airlift

Schleswigland
Lubeck
Fuhlsbuttel
Finkenwarder
Fassberg
Celle
Wunstorf
Buckeburg
Lake Havel
Tegel
Gatow
Tempelhof
BRITISH ZONE
RUSSIAN ZONE
AMERICAN ZONE
Rhein Main
Wiesbaden
BEACON
COMBINED RAF/USAF BASES
RAF BASES
USAF BASE
TRACKS TO BERLIN
TRACKS FROM BERLIN

Above: The complexity of the operation to keep Berlin supplied by air was further complicated by the different speeds of the participating aircraft. The slow Yorks and C-47s often needed longer to fly to and from Berlin, and to load and unload than the four-hour blocks allocated.

Berlin Airlift transports

The Berlin Airlift transported 2325809 tonnes of cargo into the city, including 1586530 tonnes of coal, and 538016 tonnes of food. Liquid fuels (primarily oil) made up another 92282 tonnes, all of this being carried by British civil aircraft. The RAF carried 17 per cent of the total tonnage, while British civil carriers accounted for another 6.3 per cent. The USAF accounted for the lion's share, however.

Douglas C-54 Skymaster
The C-54 provided the backbone of the Berlin Airlift (with a peak total of 200 aircraft committed) and the system of time blocks for participating aircraft was optimised around the C-54's performance characteristics, even though this led to other, slower types sometimes missing their slots.

Handley Page HP.70 Halton I
The Halton I was essentially a civilianised transport derivative of the wartime Halifax bomber. BOAC's Haltons (and civilianised Halifax bombers operated by other companies) were pressed into service on the Airlift.

Avro Lancaster III
Hastily civilianised Lancasters were pressed into service on the Airlift. There were accidents, some caused by the intensive operations in what were often poor conditions. This aircraft was written-off in 1948.

Strategic Air Command

1946-1955

Boeing B-47 Stratojets provided SAC with its first truly modern jet bomber. Some 2,102 were delivered, equipping 43 bomb wings of the 2nd, 8th and 15th Air Forces. The aircraft was also used in the strategic reconnaissance, electronic warfare and weather reconnaissance roles, and served until late-1965 in its primary role. Here, six B-47Es stage a flypast.

Above left: Strategic Air Command's badge of a mailed fist holding lightning bolts and an olive branch graphically summed up the underlying philosophy of 'peace through strength'.

The philosophy of deterring aggression by a world power with the threat of immediate and devastating retaliation became a reality the moment the two opposing world political blocs acquired nuclear weapons. For over 40 years, the mainstay of the Western world's airborne nuclear deterrent was the USAF's Strategic Air Command (SAC), a force of long-range bombers constantly deployed between bases throughout the world.

Long after SAC was founded under General George C. Kenney on 21 March 1946, US Air Force officers coined the motto 'peace is our profession'. In fact, once SAC got underway with a mere six combat groups of B-29 Superfortresses – and a handful of Mk III bombs similar to the plutonium weapon that had razed Nagasaki – no one was thinking of peace. For men and machines, the daily regimen consisted of rehearsal for war.

In the newly unfolding Cold War, atomic bombs were seen simply as a new kind of weapon. The US tested them repeatedly. (On 1 July 1946, a B-29 dropped a Nagasaki-type bomb on 73 ships lying off Bikini atoll in the western Pacific.) The knowledge that the increasingly belligerent Soviet Union was also developing nuclear weapons – the first was detonated in 1949 – gave impetus to the rapid expansion and modernisation of SAC. East-West tensions also prompted the USAF to treat SAC's members as an elite fighting force. General Curtis E. LeMay, who followed Kenney and shaped the SAC of the 1950s, hyped the special duties of his men with everything from colourful scarves to spot promotions for top performers.

Above: The monstrous B-36 was designed during World War II as an intercontinental bomber able to hit targets in Germany or Japan from US bases. It went on to become the mainstay of SAC's long-range nuclear bomber force during the service's formative years.

Left: The Boeing B-50 was an interim replacement for the B-29. It was originally designated B-29D, and redesignated in order to win funding at a time when B-29s were delivered straight to storage. These are B-50Ds of the 15th AF (identified by the circle tail marking).

Above: The USAF's new Strategic Air Command initially controlled only six B-29-equipped bomb wings. The type had a relatively brief life in SAC service, although converted KB-29s served as tankers after the basic model had been phased out by bomb squadrons.

B-36 Peacemaker: SAC's 'Big Stick'

The first B-36As were delivered to the USAF in the summer of 1948, and by the end of the year the aircraft was able to fly an unrefuelled dummy attack from Carswell AFB in Texas to Pearl Harbor on Hawaii, dropping an inert 4536-kg (10,000-lb) bomb in the sea. The 13036-km (8,100-mile) raid went undetected by local defences. The type equipped 10 bomb wings and served to 1959.

Convair B-36A
Left: The first B-36s equipped two heavy bomb groups (the 7th and 11th) of the Eighth Air Force at Carswell AFB. Most wore three-digit 'Buzz numbers', with a BM prefix.

Convair B-36J
Right: A host of improvements were fitted to the B-36 during its production life. Underwing pods with four J47 turbojets were introduced with the B-36D, along with snap-action bomb-doors. The B-36H introduced a new bomb sight, and from 1954, B-36s were lightened to improve speed and altitude performance.

The concept of airborne nuclear deterrent was evolved between 1947 and 1950, and spurred the development of newer, bigger strategic bombers for the expected nuclear war with the Soviet Union.

The B-29, which had proven so effective against Japan during World War II, was downgraded from 'very heavy' to 'heavy' to 'medium' bomber status as it was replaced by the B-50, the B-47 Stratojet and the thundering B-36 Peacemaker.

Below: During the Korean War B-29s were tasked with precision attacks against bridges. One of the weapons tested was the annular-finned, radio-controlled Tarzon. However, it proved unsuccessful in service and only three were ever dropped.

Although its development had begun even before the US entry into World War II, the giant Convair B-36 was just right for the early Cold War era – a powerful, six-engined behemoth with a 70.10-m (230-ft) wing span, a bomb bay large enough to hold a Nash Rambler automobile, and no fewer than 16 20-mm cannons arrayed from nose to tail on the silvery cigar of its fuselage. When four wingtip jet engines were added, the B-36 became the biggest, farthest-reaching nuclear bomber in the sky. Crews routinely flew 12-hour missions. Flying in the RB-36 reconnaissance versions, they were aloft for up to 22 hours.

Hydrogen weapons

Strategic Air Command also filled its expanding bomber groups with the B-50, a much-improved bomber based on the B-29 with greatly enhanced crew comforts. When hydrogen bombs were added to the arsenals of both sides in the 1950s, 'mediums' like the B-50 had difficulty handling new and enormous nuclear bombs like the Mk 15 Zombie. The B-50 soldiered on heroically but its contribution as a front-line bomber was limited to a span of a few years.

The veteran B-29 was the only big bomber recalled to action for the 1950-53 Korean War. The sad truth was that the Pentagon assigned a lower priority to Korea than to the expected nuclear war with Moscow. Thus, stateside SAC bases operated B-50 bombers, C-124 Globemaster II transports (used to haul nuclear weapons), and

Above: SAC was responsible for conducting strategic reconnaissance, as well as for bombing. RB-29s, RB-50s (as seen here), RB-47s and RB-36s were among the strategic bombers converted for this vital role. Numerous overflights of the Soviet Union were conducted by these types during the early days Cold War.

Convair B-36D Peacemaker
This B-36D of the 326th Bomb Squadron (Heavy), seen dropping a Mk 17 bomb, was built as a B-36B. It was converted to B-36D configuration by the addition of underwing jet engine pods, and other improvements.

Hydrogen bomb
The B-36's primary mission was intercontinental nuclear strike against targets deep within the Soviet Union for which it carried the monster Mk 17 hydrogen thermonuclear bomb. This weighed a massive 21 tonnes and measured 7.3 m (24 feet) in length.

Above: Operation 'Longstride' in August 1953 saw the deployment of 31st FEW F-84Gs to Morocco in a demonstration of long-range escort capability. The aircraft flew directly from Turner AFB, Georgia, refuelling in flight from SAC KB-29s, and supported by a C-74.

Above: Republic F-84F Thunderstreak fighter-bombers were assigned to SAC for long-range escort fighter duties, replacing straight-winged F-84Ds, Es and Gs. SAC's first escort fighter was the F-82 Twin Mustang.

the B-47 jet bomber, while all of these aircraft were withheld from the Korean commitment.

At any given time, SAC never had more than 205 of the giant B-36s (of 383 built). To build a US strategic force in the kind of numbers that would guarantee victory over the Soviet Union, LeMay and the Pentagon relied heavily on the B-47, a radical bomber different in almost every respect from every bomber before it. The B-47 was fighter-like in its appearance and configuration, with swept-back wings and podded turbojet power.

Although difficult to fly and almost impossible to bail out of, the B-47 was the most potent bomber of the early-1950s and was seen as such a threat to the USSR that Stalin ordered countermeasures. At the height of SAC's strength, nearly 2,000 B-47s formed the vanguard of the strategic bombing force – gradually, B-29s and later B-36s and B-50s were phased out as the 1960s approached – and the nuclear arsenal to equip them grew to tens of thousands of warheads. The 21-tonne Mk 17 hydrogen bomb became the American giant of nuclear bombs, and SAC crews carried them on airborne alert.

In the 1940s and 1950s, SAC operated fighter escort squadrons, beginning with the twin-boom F-82 Twin Mustang and culminating with the swept-wing F-84F Thunderstreak. LeMay was furious when his 27th Fighter Escort Group (with straightwing F-84D/E Thunderjets) was commandeered to participate in Korean fighting: he demanded his fighters back, got them, and bolstered them with improved, straightwing F-84Gs.

SAC's dedicated fighter pilots faced the grim prospect of a one-way journey into horror if nuclear war actually came. Their courage was beyond question, but the

Above: The North American RB-45 Tornado was a successful stop-gap in the strategic recce role. A handful of USAF RB-45s were used for radar mapping of IP-to-target runs inside Russia, flown by RAF crews.

Right: The FICON mix of GRB-36F and RF-84K entered service briefly with the 99th SRW and 91st SRS in 1955. The RF-84K parasite was intended to extend the combination's reconnaissance range.

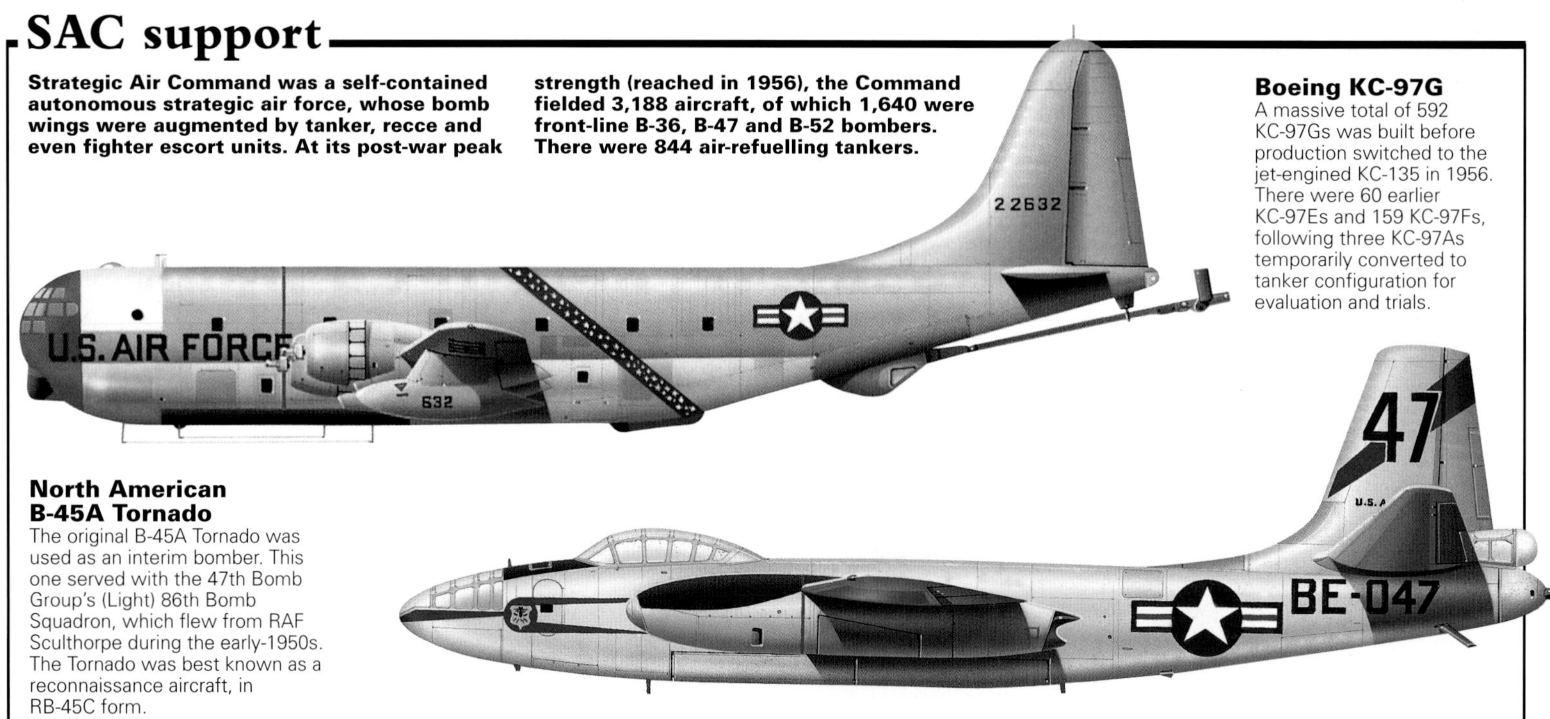

SAC support

Strategic Air Command was a self-contained autonomous strategic air force, whose bomb wings were augmented by tanker, recce and even fighter escort units. At its post-war peak strength (reached in 1956), the Command fielded 3,188 aircraft, of which 1,640 were front-line B-36, B-47 and B-52 bombers. There were 844 air-refuelling tankers.

Boeing KC-97G
A massive total of 592 KC-97Gs was built before production switched to the jet-engined KC-135 in 1956. There were 60 earlier KC-97Es and 159 KC-97Fs, following three KC-97As temporarily converted to tanker configuration for evaluation and trials.

North American B-45A Tornado
The original B-45A Tornado was used as an interim bomber. This one served with the 47th Bomb Group's (Light) 86th Bomb Squadron, which flew from RAF Sculthorpe during the early-1950s. The Tornado was best known as a reconnaissance aircraft, in RB-45C form.

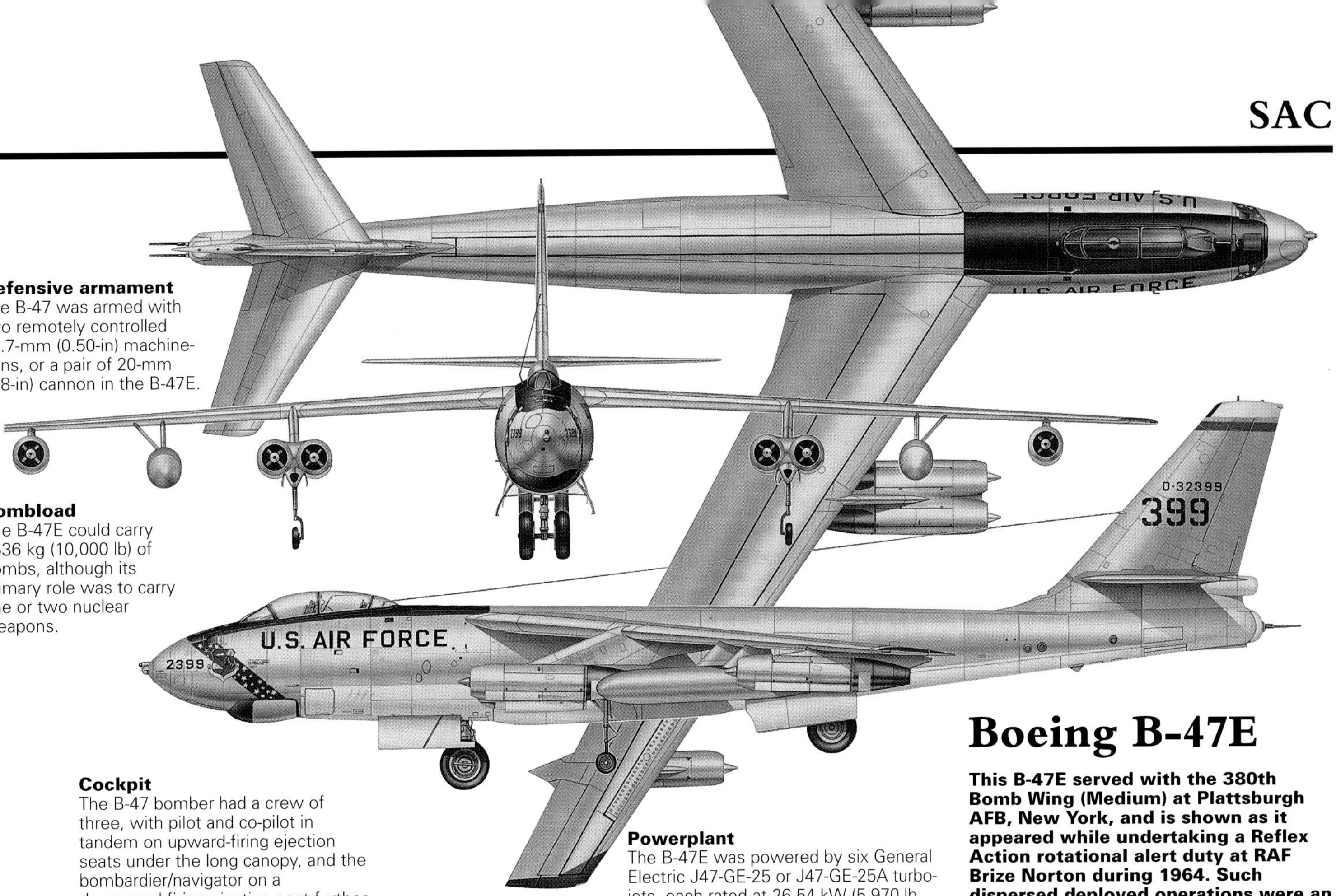

Defensive armament
The B-47 was armed with two remotely controlled 12.7-mm (0.50-in) machine-guns, or a pair of 20-mm (0.8-in) cannon in the B-47E.

Bombload
The B-47E could carry 4536 kg (10,000 lb) of bombs, although its primary role was to carry one or two nuclear weapons.

Cockpit
The B-47 bomber had a crew of three, with pilot and co-pilot in tandem on upward-firing ejection seats under the long canopy, and the bombardier/navigator on a downward-firing ejection seat further forward in the nose. Some of the later reconnaissance versions carried three additional crew members in a capsule in the former bomb bay.

Powerplant
The B-47E was powered by six General Electric J47-GE-25 or J47-GE-25A turbojets, each rated at 26.54 kW (5,970 lb st), or 32 kW (7,200 lb st) on take-off, with water injection. The engines were underslung from the high aspect-ratio wing in low-drag nacelles.

Boeing B-47E

This B-47E served with the 380th Bomb Wing (Medium) at Plattsburgh AFB, New York, and is shown as it appeared while undertaking a Reflex Action rotational alert duty at RAF Brize Norton during 1964. Such dispersed deployed operations were an integral part of SAC's operating procedures during the early-1960s, reducing vulnerability to a first strike by enemy missiles or bombers.

fighter jocks never won the heart of their leader. When swept-wing RF-84K Thunderflash reconnaissance aircraft went aloft as 'parasites' operating from the bays of B-36 bombers, LeMay was sceptical. The general told everybody within earshot that "fighters are fun but bombers are important." In the late-1950s, LeMay was unwilling to invest in newer, faster fighters – SAC operated the F-101A Voodoo only briefly – and the fighter escort force was abandoned.

Tanker support

In one way, the most important SAC aircraft of the era was the inflight-refuelling tanker: the prop-driven KC-97 Stratofreighter and the epoch-making, jet-propelled KC-135 Stratotanker gave the bombers worldwide reach. Tankers literally revolutionised air warfare, and the world has not been the same since.

Under the aegis of General Curtis LeMay, SAC reached the peak of its strength in 1956 when its aircraft inventory totalled 3,188 (247 B/RB-36, 97 B-52, 254 RB-47, 1,306 B-47, 16 RB-57, 51 C-124, 750 KC-97, 74 KB-29, 366 F-84, 57 RF-84F/K). SAC was never to see such numbers again. But the challenge persisted. Introduction of the B-52 Stratofortress – armed with thermonuclear weapons of unprecedented power – on 29 June 1955, followed by the image of Nikita Khruschev pounding his shoe on the table during a United Nations debate, augered a new era in the Cold War.

Above: Carrying a Bell GAM-63 Rascal missile under the starboard wingroot, the YDB-47E Stratojet refuels from a KC-97 tanker. The Rascal represented an early attempt to provide SAC's bombers with a stand-off missile capability.

Below: SAC refined and honed its capability with exercises and competitions. Here, B-47s are lined up on the ramp at at Barksdale AFB waiting to participate in SAC's sixth annual bombing and navigation competition, in August 1954.

Birth of NATO and the Warsaw Pact

1948–1956

Europe's division into two armed camps began soon after VE-Day. Retaining only the minimum of troops necessary to police their sectors of defeated Germany, the Western Allies ran down their forces with all possible speed, from five million to one million within 12 months. The Soviet Union, still establishing communism in the territories from which it had ejected the Nazis, made no such reduction.

Suspicious of the West's 'delay' in launching D-Day, fearful of a Western/German alliance against him, and wary of an ideological 'Trojan horse' in the generous American offers of reconstruction aid to Europe, Josef Stalin kept the Red Army at some five million troops. As countries that were once Western oriented were forced into the Soviet bloc and Berlin was almost lost to a communist siege, the West drew its own conclusions from the Soviet refusal to demobilise. Its first steps towards a defence against Stalin's armies were taken in March 1948 with formation of the Western Union (the UK, France, Belgium, the Netherlands and Luxembourg).

The Western Union

The new alliance had hardly been organised before talks began on extension of the Western Union with US and Canadian elements. This followed a US Senate resolution of 11 June 1948 which allowed the country to associate itself in peacetime with 'such regional and other collective arrangements as are based on continuous and effective self-help and mutual aid, and as affect its national security'. Like God, the USA was advertising its willingness to help those who help themselves.

By the time the North Atlantic Treaty was signed in Washington on 4 April 1949, Denmark, Iceland, Italy, Norway and Portugal had joined the seven founder nations. Later were to come Greece and Turkey (both in 1952), West Germany (in 1955) and Spain (in 1982). All endorsed a broad declaration of peaceful co-operation and willingness to solve disputes without re course to arms, but it was the fifth of the Treaty's 14 component articles which contained the most vital assertion: 'The Parties agree that an armed attack against one or more of them in Europe or North America shall be considered an attack against them all . . .' No aggressor could say that he had not been warned.

NATO takes shape

Not until the start of the Korean War in June 1950 did NATO begin to take the form by which it is now recognised. On 2 April 1951 (two years after the North Atlantic Treaty had been signed), Allied Command Europe became operational under the former liberator of Western Europe, General Dwight Eisenhower. Simultaneously Allied Air Forces Central Europe was established with Lieutenant General Lauris Norstad as its first commander-in-chief. It was only now that NATO began to rearm with US jet aircraft through the Mutual Defense Assistance Program, starting with a handful of Republic F-84E Thunderjets. By 1952, the F-84G model was arriving in Europe in its hundreds, and the air forces of Belgium, Denmark, France Italy, the Netherlands, Norway and

Above: Lockheed's F-80 Shooting Star entered service in the last months of World War II, though it saw no combat. Although outclassed by later designs, it was the US Air Force's primary air combat fighter on the establishment of NATO in March 1948.

Below: Built in huge numbers, the Ilyushin Il-10 was the main Soviet ground attack aircraft in the early post-war years. Rugged and hard-hitting, it was also to equip the Czechoslovak and many other Warsaw Pact air forces.

Right: Britain's Gloster Meteor was one of the world's first operational jet fighters, and was a standard NATO fighter in the early years. Belgium acquired more than 240 of the type, building many aircraft under licence at Avions Fairey.

Early Cold War jets

The first combat jets had entered service in 1944, and marked a great leap forwards in capability. Many of the wartime designs were to serve with distinction into the 1960s, but within five years they were to be outclassed by a new generation of fighting machines, incorporating advanced aerodynamics and with vastly superior performance.

Mikoyan-Gurevich MiG-15

Right: Designed using captured German research data, and powered by an unlicensed copy of the Rolls Royce Nene turbojet, the MiG-15 was a serious challenge to NATO. It could outperform every western fighter except the North American F-86 Sabre.

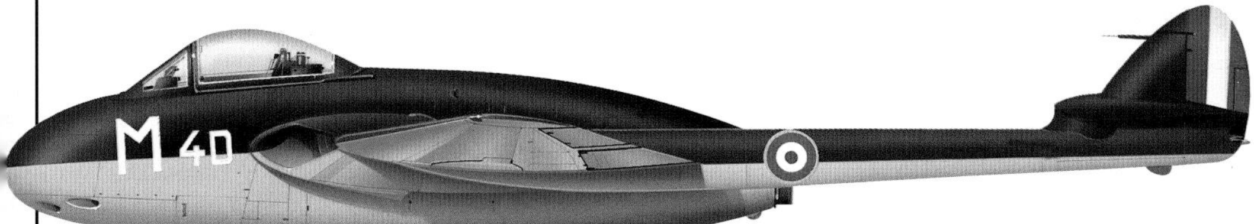

de Havilland Vampire

Left: First flown in 1943 and entering service in 1945, the British-designed de Havilland Vampire was instrumental in re-establishing France's war-ravaged aviation industry. More than 430 examples of the type were license-built by SNCASE at its factory in Marseille in the early 1950s.

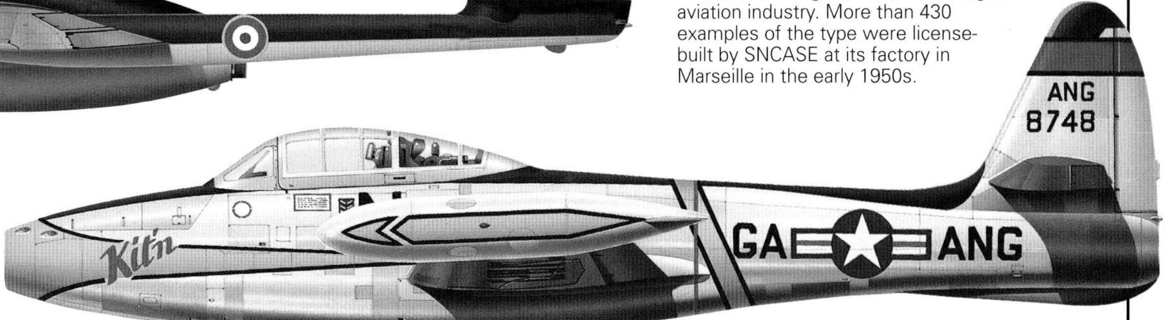

Republic F-84G Thunderjet

Although designed as a fighter, the straight-winged F-84 never had the performance of its swept-wing rivals. However, it found its forte as a tough ground attack aircraft, and more than 2,000 were delivered to NATO's emerging air forces as well as to the US Air Force and the Air National Guard.

Portugal were soon transformed. Later, Greece and Turkey qualified for receipt of the ubiquitous Thunderjet, and more went to southern Europe as the swept-wing F-84F Thunderstreak and its reconnaissance configured RF-84F Thunderflash variant were supplied to the central area. The F-86 Sabre was a rare sight in Europe during the Korean War, though Canadian-built examples served with RCAF units and the RAF before they were redistributed to Italy, Greece, Turkey and West Germany. In May 1953, Fiat of Italy obtained a licence to produce the limited all-weather F-86K interceptor for European use by the local air force as well as by France, the Netherlands, Norway and West Germany.

Behind what was already coming to be known as the 'Iron Curtain', the Soviet Union viewed with continued misgivings the movement towards the reunification of Germany, and then with growing alarm the plans for its re-armament by the Western powers. Though Stalin had died in 1953, his policies were maintained in large measure by the leaders who followed, and one of their greatest priorities was to prevent West Germany from rearming. Attempts were made by the new administration in Moscow to secure the broader ideal of a demilitarised Europe – apart, that is, from the

EUROPE'S GREAT DIVIDE

Any trust the victorious Allies might have felt after the end of the war in Europe soon changed to suspicion as two mutually antagonistic power blocs were established. In Winston Churchill's inimitable words, an Iron Curtain had descended across the centre of Europe. On one side, the war-weary but free democratic states of Western Europe were backed by the military, political and industrial muscle of the United States of America. On the other side, Eastern Europe fell under the heavy hand of the Soviet Union, which exercised control by installing puppet governments backed by the ever-present threat of military intervention. The Red Army's victory in the Great Patriotic War had not been followed by an appreciable stand-down of Soviet forces, and it was to counter this huge military potential that NATO was set up.

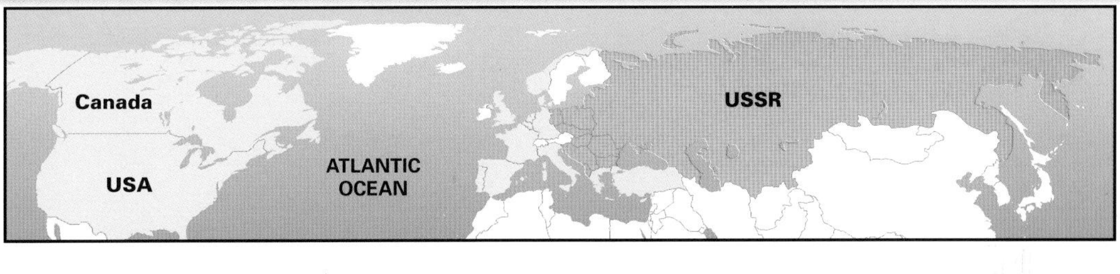

Left: *F-84Gs of the Netherlands air force fly in formation. Not a great performer, the Thunderjet was nevertheless of great value to NATO through the 1950s, being tough, easy to maintain, reliable and available in numbers.*

Above: Germany became a full NATO member in 1955, and soon become a major force on the Central Front. A key item in the Luftwaffe's inventory was the Republic F-84F, 450 of which served between 1956 and 1969.

Left: Lavochkin La-5FN fighters of the 1st Czechoslovak Fighter Regiment are seen in Germany at the end of World War II. Units like this which fought alongside the Soviets were to form the core of post-war East European air forces, armed almost exclusively with Soviet equipment.

territories occupied by Soviet forces in 1945. This one-sided disarmament did not appeal to NATO, and so plans for German membership went ahead. In a remarkable attempt to render the North Atlantic Treaty impotent, the USSR suggested on 31 March 1954 that it might be prepared to join NATO, a proposal which was firmly rejected by the UK, France and the USA a month later. West Germany became a member of NATO on 5 May 1955, and with its efforts thwarted, the USSR organised the signing of a counter declaration in Warsaw just nine days later.

THE WARSAW PACT

This Treaty of Friendship, Mutual Assistance and Co-operation (known for short as the Warsaw Pact) between Moscow and its client states of Albania, Bulgaria, Czechoslovakia, East Germany, Hungary, Poland and Romania was dedicated only to the defence of European territory, and thus excluded the central and eastern Soviet Union. Though NATO loosely refers to the Warsaw Pact as its counterpart, the Eastern alliance merely formalised bilateral treaties already in being and later modified by status-of-forces agreements with Poland, East Germany, Romania and Hungary in 1956-7 and with Czechoslovakia in 1968.

The Warsaw Pact had some propaganda value – it was formed after NATO and could declared as a 'response to capitalist aggression.' In all practical terms, however, it made no difference to the strategic situation, save that between 5 and 14 May 1955 the last hope for a reversal of the European arms build-up was lost. The Soviet Union continued to dictate the pace of rearmament in its territories, and if any of its signatories briefly took heart from the Warsaw Pact's declaration of 'non-interference in their internal affairs', illusions were dispelled by the Soviet invasion of Hungary only 18 months later.

From May 1955, the two sides in the Cold War were neatly defined as NATO versus the Warsaw Pact, and those whose task it is to make the man in the street understand strategic matters were able to draw different-sized ranks of blue soldiers and red soldiers to depict the balance of forces. At the time, though, the head-counting exercise had temporarily lost its point, for the era of the nuclear bomber and intercontinental missile was at hand.

Laft: One of the classic fighters of all time, the MiG-15 was designated 'Fagot' under the new NATO reporting system, and was standard Warsaw Pact equipment through the 1950s and 1960s. Built in huge numbers in the Soviet Union, it was also manufactured in Poland and Czechoslovakia. These Polish LIM-2s are versions of the more powerful MiG-15bis, which first flew in 1949.

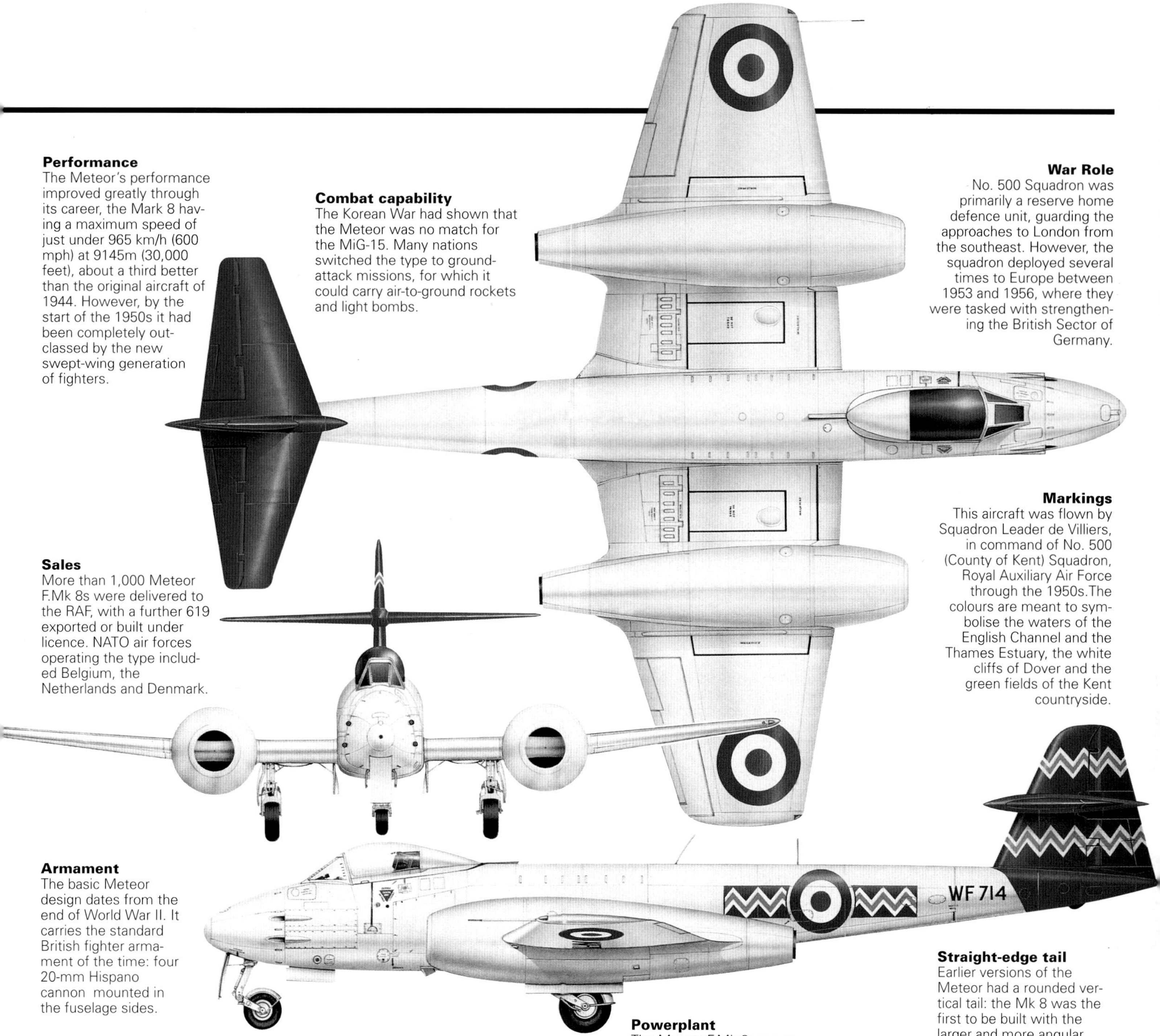

Performance
The Meteor's performance improved greatly through its career, the Mark 8 having a maximum speed of just under 965 km/h (600 mph) at 9145m (30,000 feet), about a third better than the original aircraft of 1944. However, by the start of the 1950s it had been completely outclassed by the new swept-wing generation of fighters.

Combat capability
The Korean War had shown that the Meteor was no match for the MiG-15. Many nations switched the type to ground-attack missions, for which it could carry air-to-ground rockets and light bombs.

War Role
No. 500 Squadron was primarily a reserve home defence unit, guarding the approaches to London from the southeast. However, the squadron deployed several times to Europe between 1953 and 1956, where they were tasked with strengthening the British Sector of Germany.

Sales
More than 1,000 Meteor F.Mk 8s were delivered to the RAF, with a further 619 exported or built under licence. NATO air forces operating the type included Belgium, the Netherlands and Denmark.

Markings
This aircraft was flown by Squadron Leader de Villiers, in command of No. 500 (County of Kent) Squadron, Royal Auxiliary Air Force through the 1950s.The colours are meant to symbolise the waters of the English Channel and the Thames Estuary, the white cliffs of Dover and the green fields of the Kent countryside.

Armament
The basic Meteor design dates from the end of World War II. It carries the standard British fighter armament of the time: four 20-mm Hispano cannon mounted in the fuselage sides.

Gloster Meteor F.Mk 8

The world's first operational jet fighter (beating the Messerschmitt 262 into regular squadron service by a matter of days), the Gloster Meteor was the mainstay of the Britain's fighter force in the postwar years, and continued to serve with reserve units through the 1950s. It was sold to more than a dozen nations.

Powerplant
The Meteor F.Mk 8 was an attempt to squeeze the maximum performance out of the airframe without major modification: it was powered by uprated Rolls-Royce Derwent 8 turbojets each delivering 15.57 kN (3,500 lb st).

Straight-edge tail
Earlier versions of the Meteor had a rounded vertical tail: the Mk 8 was the first to be built with the larger and more angular tailplane depicted here. Designed to decrease high-speed buffeting, the redesign was only marginally successful.

Above: Apart from uniform and insignia, Warsaw Pact air forces were indistinguishable from those of the Soviet Union. These Polish pilots flew Soviet tactics in Soviet aircraft, and in time of war would have been under Soviet command.

Right: By 1956 the Cold War lines in Europe had been drawn, and the World War II-era equipment which had equipped both sides had been replaced by advanced new designs. These are Ilyushin Il-28 'Beagle' bombers of the Soviet air force .

Cold War over the Ocean

1945-1970

The end of World War II left both the USA and Britain with the massive navies with which they had undertaken the convoy war in the Atlantic, and the island-hopping drive to Japan. Aircraft-carriers had played a major role, but now had little to do. Large numbers of ex-Royal Navy and ex-US Navy carriers were retired: some were placed in mothballs, and others were sold or given to friendly nations to allow them to develop their own naval air arms.

Before carrier aviation could wither entirely, the Korean War broke out, and both British and American aircraft carriers played a major part in the campaign, primarily in the ground-attack role. The war allowed carrier aviation to be properly funded, and prompted renewed effort in research, development and operational analyses.

New tensions

The world was a very different place at the end of the Korean War, with the Cold War suddenly very real. The chances of additional conflicts (perhaps proxy struggles like Korea) seemed very real. The need to keep open the sealanes to Europe and Japan became apparent as the USSR raced to build a blue water navy, laying emphasis on creating a powerful submarine fleet.

The US Navy commissioned a new class of modern aircraft-carriers, laying the keel of the 60000 tonne USS *Forrestal* in July 1952. These ships were truly modern aircraft carriers, incorporating the British-developed angled flight deck and steam catapult from the start, and capable of carrying giant air wings. Moreover, the very role of the carrier was expanded. Wartime carriers had been little more than floating fighter airfields, providing escort and air-defence fighters and light-attack aircraft, sometimes with a rudimentary anti-submarine capability. The new carriers were designed from the start to project power, with complements which would include powerful long-range attack and strike aircraft, as well as fighters and fighter-bombers. With the introduction of nuclear-armed Douglas A-3 Skywarriors (and later, briefly, A-5 Vigilantes), aircraft-carriers took on a semi-strategic role, and were integrated into SIOP.

Growing threat

Their new importance made the carriers inviting targets for Russia's expanding submarine fleet, and older aircraft-carriers were hastily modified and modernised to serve as dedicated ASW carriers, equipped with ASW helicopters and aircraft. These were then deployed to screen attack carrier groups against the growing Soviet submarine threat. This threat was probably over-estimated initially, with expectations that the USSR would deploy cloned Type XXI U-boats in massive numbers for a 'Battle of the Atlantic'-type war against Allied shipping. In fact, post-war Soviet submarine development was less ambitious. Although lessons were learned from captured U-boat technology, early post-war submarines were evolved from wartime boats, with relatively minor improvements and built in relatively small numbers.

The growth of the Soviet navy

Above: Britain's RAF Coastal Command (absorbed by Strike Command from 1968) fielded a fleet of Avro Shackletons for maritime patrol and anti-submarine operations. This one is a tricycle undercarriage-equipped MR.Mk 3, and served with No. 206 Squadron.

Below: Soviet maritime patrol forces retained flying-boats for longer than most Western nations. The Beriev Be-12 'Mail' seen here did not enter service until the mid-1960s (replacing the piston-powered Be-6) and remains in service in small numbers to this day.

Above: The Canadair Argus was designed as an indigenous replacement for the Avro Lancaster in the ASW role. It used the wing and empennage of the Bristol Britannia, mated to a new ASW equipment-packed fuselage and four Wright R-3350 piston engines.

Left: The backbone of the US Navy's ASW force for the early years of the Cold War was the Lockheed P2V (later designated P-2) Neptune. It was gradually superseded by the P-3 Orion from the early-1960s.

Worldwide ASW

Even before submarines took over the strategic nuclear strike role, they posed a great risk to naval surface ships and to the convoys on which each superpower would have relied in the event of war. When submarines became the means by which nuclear war could have been fought, their detection (and protection from enemy submarines) brought ASW aircraft a new importance.

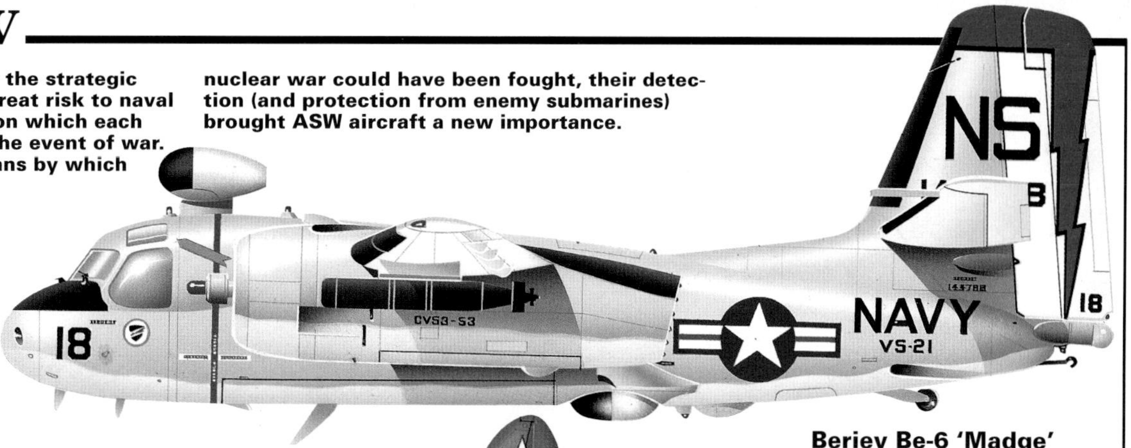

Grumman S-2E Tracker

The Tracker first entered service with the US Navy in 1954 and was the first dedicated carrierborne ASW aircraft to combine hunter/killer roles in one airframe. Fifteen countries around the world operated Trackers with some still in use today. This S-2E served with VS-21, 'Fighting Redtails' aboard USS *Kearsarge*.

Beriev Be-6 'Madge'

The Beriev Be-6 served from about 1951 until the mid-1960s, when it was replaced by the turbine-engined (but otherwise quite similar) Be-12. Small numbers remained in use well into the 1970s. MAD equipment was installed in an extended tail sting during the late-1950s or early-1960s.

Avro Shackleton

The Shackleton was a dedicated maritime derivative of the Avro Lincoln, which had itself been developed from the Lancaster. The Shackleton formed the backbone of the RAF's ASW force until the early-1970s. This early MR.Mk 1 served with No. 120 Squadron during 1954.

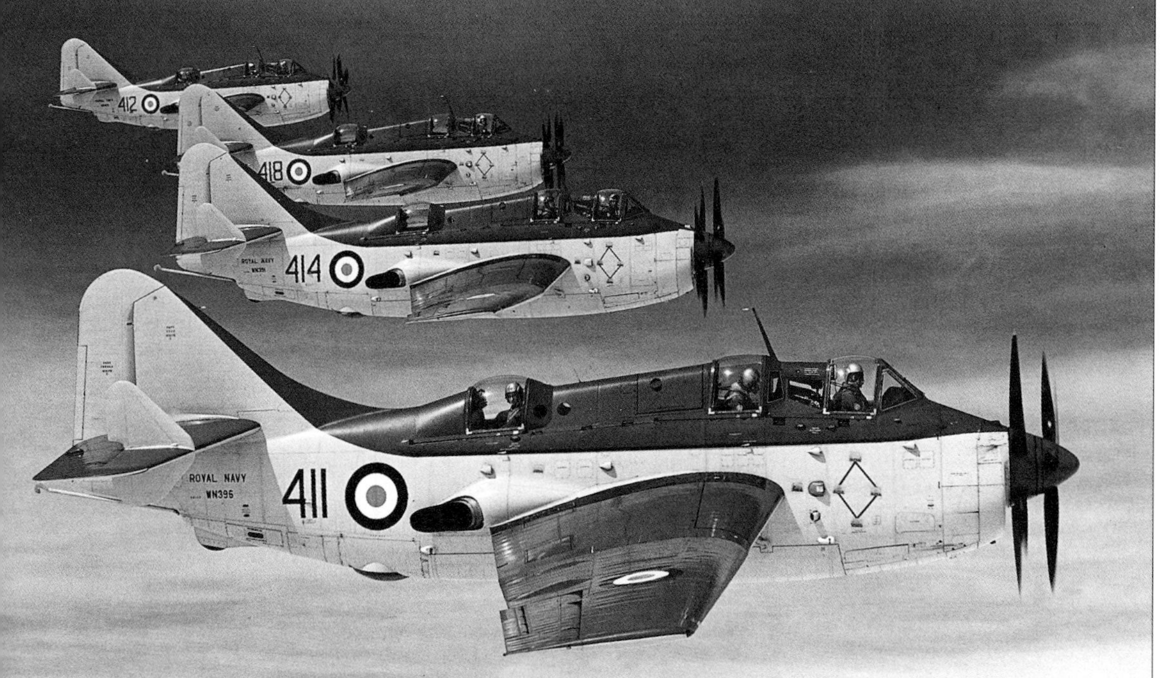

Left: It was impossible to cover the world using only land-based ASW aircraft, and several nations made extensive use of carrierborne ASW aircraft to cover mid-ocean gaps and to provide ASW coverage for groups of warships. Britain's carriers embarked the Fairey Gannet.

(and fear of its growth) necessitated more constant coverage of the entire oceans than could be achieved using a handful of isolated aircraft-carrier groups, and at the same time that carrier aviation was revolutionised America was developing a new generation of land-based long-range patrol aircraft. They were intended to be able to operate in both the maritime patrol role, keeping tabs on Soviet surface vessels, and also in the ASW role, monitoring the movement of Soviet submarines and engaging them if it ever became necessary. In retrospect, aircraft like the Martin Marlin flying-boat can be seen to have represented a dead-end in patrol/ASW aircraft development, although they were effective enough by the standards of the time. More important were developments in ASW radar and in active and passive sonar, as well as in the deployment of new systems, most notably MAD (Magnetic Anomaly Detectors) which could detect changes to the earth's magnetic field caused by the presence of a large steel submarine. Such equipment was fitted to versions of the Lockheed P-2 Neptune, the Avro Shackleton and Canadair Argus.

The introduction of nuclear submarines with teardrop hulls, capable of sustaining high underwater speeds, presented a challenge to ASW forces, which also had to react to reductions in noise levels and advances in tactics and countermeasures. In the late-1950s, the first ballistic missile-carrying submarines were deployed, and the number of submarines and submarine-launched missiles grew exponentially, driving progressive improvements in ASW aircraft and equipment.

Right: Westland Wessex HAS Mk 1 was one of the first dedicated ASW helicopters. It was fitted with dipping sonar and could carry torpedoes or depth charges and operated from Royal Navy Destroyers and anti-submarine cruisers. This Wessex HAS Mk 1 is from No. 737 Squadron, Portland, Dorset.

ELINT, Spies and Ferrets

1948-1960

Left: The lead taken by the West in jet propulsion allowed aircraft such as the North American RB-45 Tornado to undertake limited cross-border incursions. However, it was not long before the Soviet defences developed the ability to ward off these unwelcome flights.

Below: At the end of World War II the principal US long-range reconnaissance aircraft was the Boeing F-13, a camera-equipped modification of the standard B-29 bomber. Redesignated as the RB-29 after the war, the aircraft continued in the role for many years, providing sterling service during the Korean War. The aircraft also began to acquire a Sigint (signals intelligence) mission, which was passed on successively to the similar RB-50, the RB-47 and then finally the RC-135 converted transport.

There was one highly secret aspect of the Cold War which merits being called a war in its own right, a struggle taking place at sea, on the ground, in the air, and even in space. There has been a large cast of supporting countries – the UK, West Germany, Libya, Syria and others – but for half a century it was primarily a superpower rivalry. It cost at least 170 lives, but its proponents claimed to have prevented conflicts of far greater magnitude, perhaps even the ultimate conflagration. It is the secret war of electromagnetic reconnaissance.

Below: Early attempts to take photographs behind the Iron Curtain were undertaken by a specialist unit, the 91st SRS. It used US RB-45C aircraft, crewed by RAF personnel and repainted in RAF national insignia. Here four are seen at RAF Sculthorpe.

Right: From its earliest days, the Canberra was in great demand for risky high-altitude reconnaissance missions. Some time in 1953 or 1954, a PR.Mk 3 similar to this aircraft is believed to have photographed the Soviet missile test site at Kapustin Yar at the request of the USAF.

As the Cold War arrived in the late 1940s, the West (and particularly the Americans) felt an urgent need to update their information on possible targets behind the Iron Curtain. There was virtually no up-to-date intelligence on such matters: early SAC target lists were almost exclusively based on German wartime intelligence and operational reports. But the bombers needed more accurate en-route navigational information to get them to the targets. Therefore, photo-reconnaissance Boeing RB-

US ferrets

As the iron Curtain descended across Europe, reconnaissance aircraft from both sides began a long vigil across the borders and around the peripheries of NATO and the Warsaw Pact. The vast majority of missions involved converted maritime patrol aircraft, transports and bombers being used for electronic intelligence gathering missions. Several US aircraft were shot down.

Lockheed P2V Neptune
The Neptune was the US Navy's standard maritime patrol platform, but was also used for electronic surveillance missions.

Boeing RB-29 Superfortress
The RB-29 was principally a camera platform, but was also used for Sigint flights. The RAF also used the type (known as the Washington) for Sigint work around the WarPac borders.

29 Superfortresses equipped with rudimentary World War II-era radar receiving and jamming equipment set out from the UK on lengthy radar reconnaissance missions around and occasionally over Communist territory.

By the end of the Korean War, the B-50 upgrade of the Superfortress had supplanted the RB-29 in Strategic Air Command's line-up. Over 40 RB-50E/F/G models served with the 55th Strategic Reconnaissance Wing, which went on to claim an almost unbroken post-war lineage of 'ferret' operations.

Jet reconnaissance

The B-29 and B-50 were followed closely into the UK by RB-45Cs, a dedicated reconnaissance version of the the North American Tornado four-jet bomber. This performed photo-reconnaissance missions which often penetrated far behind Iron Curtain borders despite the aircraft's vulnerability to interception by the MiG-15 then coming into service. However, the Tornado's ceiling could be pushed to 13716m (45,000 ft), and its range was extended by very large wingtip tanks and by the routine 'top-ups' it received from accompanying KB-29 tanker aircraft before it entered hostile territory. In this way the RB-45C stood a chance of outrunning the opposition, and there are no recorded instances of an RB-45 coming to grief over Eastern Europe.

The same is true of the B-36, Convair's monster six-engined intercontinental bomber. This had found a reconnaissance application as the RB-36, with two of its four large bomb bays converted to carry 14 cameras. Late-model aircraft with four auxiliary turbojets could reach the same altitude as the RB-45, but they were very slow cruisers. Twelve of the massive aircraft were converted to become motherships for the Republic RF-84K Thunderstreak jet in the extraordinary FICON (FIghter CONveyor) programme: the single-seat reconnaissance fighter was carried aloft in a semi-recessed position inside the B-36 bomb bay until the target area was reached, when it was released for a low-level photographic penetration before climbing back up to the mothership for a free ride home.

Above: Designed as a patrol aircraft in competition with the Lockheed Neptune, the Martin Mercator saw most service in its P4M-1Q form. This was widely used on electronic intelligence missions, serving with the US Navy's main Sigint units, VQ-1 and 2.

Below: A pair of Republic RF-84F Thunderflashes refuel from a KB-29 tanker. Tactical aircraft such as the Thunderflash were on occasion used for short cross-border penetration missions to gather vital photographic intelligence.

The advent of the RB-45 should have decreased the vulnerability of Elint aircraft, but they too were no match for the faster MiG-15, and were forced into night time operations that were distinctly unsuccessful. Tactical reconnaissance aircraft such as the Douglas RB-26 and Lockheed RF-80 had similar problems in Korea.

More often than not, it was the Elint aircraft rather than the photographic types which proved vulnerable to interception, despite their shallower incursions into Iron Curtain territory. They were generally based on larger and slower patrol and bomber types, the only aircraft capable of lifting the heavy weight and bulk of the early intercept receivers. But the nature of the mission also made them uniquely vulnerable: in order to gain meaningful intelligence they had to stimulate the opposition into turning on their radars. This entailed dangerous 'cat and mouse' games as the ferret aircraft endeavoured to get itself 'painted' by search and tracking radars. Subsequently, they hoped to monitor any communications between ground-station controllers and the fighters scrambled to intercept – while avoiding those same fighters. Furthermore, the rudimentary nature of early Elint equipment meant that missions often had to be repeated to improve or amplify the data originally returned to the ground for analysis.

Even before the formation of NATO in 1949, the UK was developing close links with the USA in the field of airborne reconnaissance. A formal intelligence-sharing agreement was signed in 1948, the same year that SAC B-29s were first deployed to the UK (during the Berlin crisis). The British had much to offer: they had pioneered airborne Elint and ECM during

World War II, and had retained a nucleus of such experience in the Central Signals Establishment at Watton. Their front-line photo reconnaissance platform in the early post war years was the de Havilland Mosquito, which had a 5794-km (3,600-mile) range and a 11125m (36,500-ft) ceiling, characteristics which led to their employment over eastern Europe until the MiG threat became too great.

CANBERRA PENETRATIONS

The Mosquito was succeeded by the English Electric Canberra, one of the world's first jet bombers. The Canberra was fast enough and could fly high enough to make it difficult for the MiG-15s to make an intercept, and was used for a number of missions deep into the Soviet Union – missions which remain classified more than 40 years later.

In 1951 No. 192 Squadron was re-formed with modified Avro Lincoln B.Mk 2 aircraft to concentrate on the gathering of Elint. When the USA loaned the RAF a fleet of B-29 bombers (renamed the Washington by the British), a few went to this squadron to supplement the unpressurized Lincolns. The British were the first to confirm that the Soviets had developed AI (airborne intercept) radar when they brought back a 20-second recording of the 'Scan Odd' system. Later, British airborne and land-based radars first discovered the existence of Soviet ECM and LORAN systems.

In return, the UK gained access to US photo-reconnaissance operations. American RB-45Cs based at Sculthorpe in the UK acquired British roundels and some British flight crews, although they were never officially on RAF strength. Later, British pilots trained on the Lockheed U-2 which subsequently appeared at Watton.

Meanwhile, the US services had steadily expanded their airborne surveillance fleets, concentrating increasingly on peripheral ferret missions. That such flights made some deliberate incursions into hostile territory seems obvious now, but at the time they were routinely denied. If the Soviets managed to bring down a ferret and chose to publicize the event, the incursion was put down to 'navigational error'. By the end of 1959, at least 12 US spy flights had been shot down, and not all of them were 'over international waters', to use the time-honoured phrase.

NAVY LOSSES

US naval aircraft had featured in six of the 12 losses. Four of them were Lockheed P2V Neptunes flying from Japanese or Alaskan bases. The long range of this anti-submarine aircraft was particularly well suited to the routine eavesdropping mission. However, the Navy had specialized snoopers as well and at first used the Consolidated PB4Y Privateer, based on the wartime B-24 bomber.

On 8 April 1950, one of these aircraft became the first casualty in the undeclared reconnaissance 'war' when it was shot down by four fighters 'in the Baltic Sea' according to the US authorities, or '23 kilometres [14 miles] inland over Latvia' in the Soviet version. It had taken off from Wiesbaden in West Germany and was due to land at Copenhagen in Denmark. The dictates of geography have made the Baltic a key and continuing area of interest for the peripheral reconnaissance mission.

The Privateer gave way to the Martin P4M Mercator, a twin-piston and twin-jet aircraft designed for maritime patrol. Only 21 were built, but between 1950 and 1960 these found useful employment as 'ferrets'. One Mercator was shot down by Chinese fighters off Wenchow in August 1956. It was operated by Navy squadron VQ-1, which had been set up in the previous year as the US Navy's first dedicated ECM unit.

In the late 1950s the US Navy ferret mission went to sea when the carrier-capable Douglas A-3 Skywarrior came into service. The five-seat RA-3B photo-reconnaissance aircraft was followed closely by the seven-seat EA-3B for Elint work, in which role several examples served until 1991 with VQ-1 and its sister squadron in the Atlantic Fleet, VQ-2. It was the heaviest-ever carrier aircraft, and latterly concentrated on interception of signals and radar emissions from Soviet naval vessels.

In SAC, the reconnaissance trio of RB-36, RB-45 and RB-50 began to give way in 1954 to the Boeing RB-47, and no fewer than five wings of dedicated reconnaissance Stratojets were established to

Above: Relatively large numbers of the RB-47E were produced, this being a photo-reconnaissance version of the Stratojet bomber. Its primary purpose was to map the approaches to Soviet targets to aid planning nuclear bombing raids.

Below: This Consolidated PB4Y Privateer served with VP-26, a long-established intelligence gathering unit of the US Navy. This squadron was the first to lose an aircraft to Soviet fighters when a Privateer was shot down in April 1950.

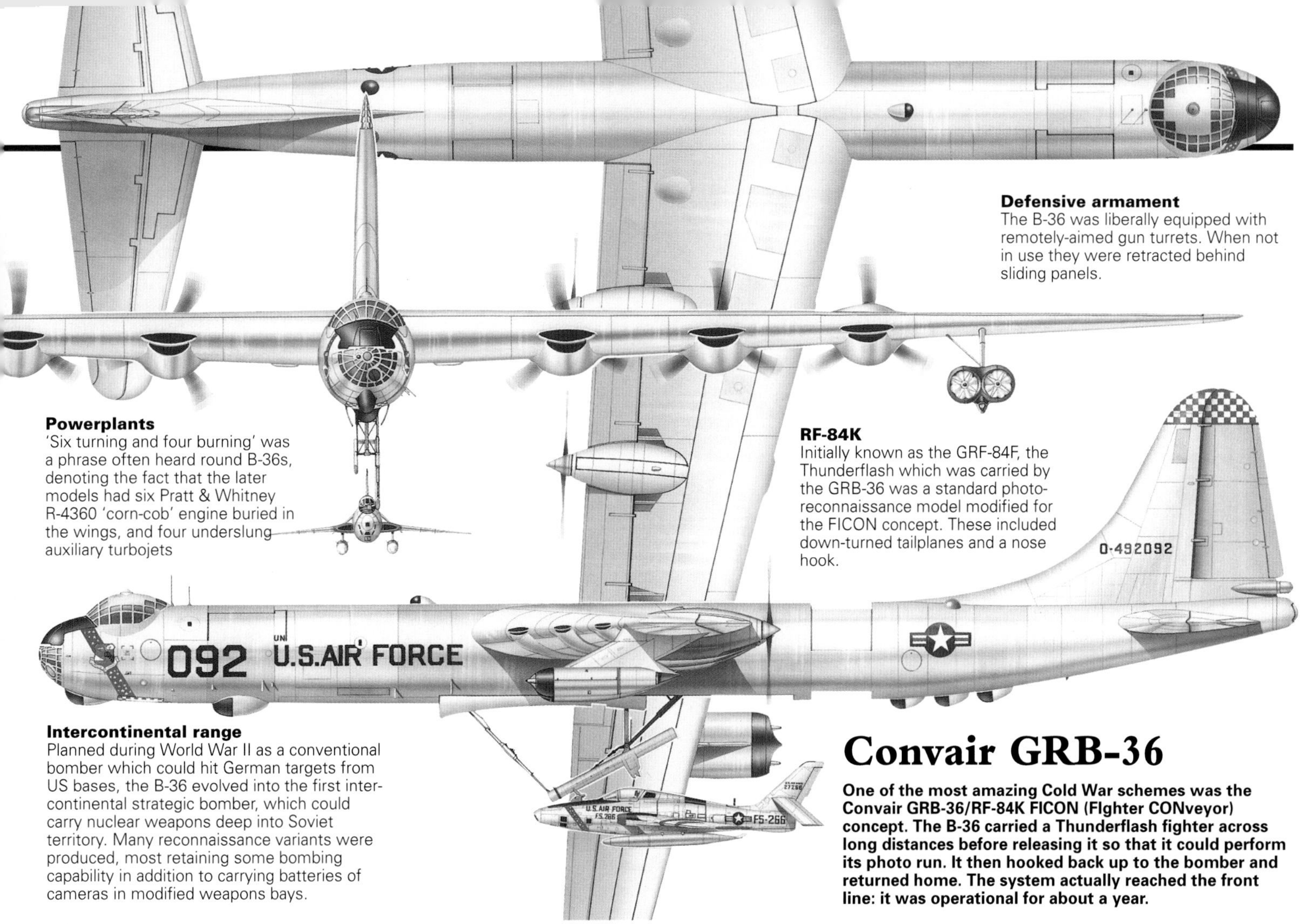

Defensive armament
The B-36 was liberally equipped with remotely-aimed gun turrets. When not in use they were retracted behind sliding panels.

Powerplants
'Six turning and four burning' was a phrase often heard round B-36s, denoting the fact that the later models had six Pratt & Whitney R-4360 'corn-cob' engine buried in the wings, and four underslung auxiliary turbojets

RF-84K
Initially known as the GRF-84F, the Thunderflash which was carried by the GRB-36 was a standard photo-reconnaissance model modified for the FICON concept. These included down-turned tailplanes and a nose hook.

Intercontinental range
Planned during World War II as a conventional bomber which could hit German targets from US bases, the B-36 evolved into the first inter-continental strategic bomber, which could carry nuclear weapons deep into Soviet territory. Many reconnaissance variants were produced, most retaining some bombing capability in addition to carrying batteries of cameras in modified weapons bays.

Convair GRB-36

One of the most amazing Cold War schemes was the Convair GRB-36/RF-84K FICON (FIghter CONveyor) concept. The B-36 carried a Thunderflash fighter across long distances before releasing it so that it could perform its photo run. It then hooked back up to the bomber and returned home. The system actually reached the front line: it was operational for about a year.

operate the 250-strong fleet. The majority of them were RB-47E camera-ships with a new suite of 11 cameras and improved photoflash bombs, but there was also a renewed emphasis on radar photography to provide accurate data for the penetrating bomber fleet. A smaller number of RB-47H and ERB-47H models served with the 55th SRW. The latter carried the Melpar ALD-4 Elint system which was originally planned to be underslung on the Convair B-58. The equipment and its three operators were housed in an enormous pod.

One of these aircraft, flying out of Brize Norton, England, was shot down by two Soviet MiGs in the remote northern waters of the Barents Sea on 1 July 1960. Two of the six-man crew survived and were taken prisoner.

Left: In its own right the B-36 was a very capable reconnaissance craft. It could reach altitudes unattainable by the early MiGs, and carried a huge sensor payload. Specially stripped 'featherweight' versions were produced for extreme altitude performance.

The nearby Kola and Kanin peninsulas housed the Soviet navy's main northern bases as well as numerous IRBM sites and bomber airfieids. The area had been scheduled for attention two months earlier on 1 May by a U-2 overflight from Pakistan that would subsequently land in Norway. But the U-2 never reached its northern objective, since it was shot down by an SA-2 missile near Sverdlovsk .

The U-2 and RB-47 incidents in 1960 marked a turning point in the reconnaissance Cold War, and not only because President Kennedy had to promise to cease overflights of the Soviet Union in order to get the two SAC crewmen back (U-2 pilot Francis Gary Powers was released a year later in exchange for a Soviet spy held in the USA).

This was a period when technological advances made a significant impact on the science of electronic intelligence gathering. 1960 was also the year when the USA achieved its first success with reconnaissance satellites, an event matched by the Soviets three years later. And the secret war expanded still further, since the Soviet Union was now adapting its long-range bombers to the stage where it felt able to send them out on increasingly wide-ranging reconnaissance missions.

Below: The workhorse of the Sigint fleet for much of the Cold War was the Boeing RB-47H (and similar ERB-47H). Their many dangerous missions included flying directly at Soviet defences in an attempt to make them power up, only turning away at the last moment.

SAC: The B-52 Years

1956-1970

Left: Boeing's B-52 Stratofortress first flew on 15 April 1952, and entered service with Strategic Air Command in June 1955. In a stunning demonstration of the type's unmatched strategic capability, these three B-52Bs took off from Castle AFB in California on 16 January 1957, returning 45 hours and 19 minutes later after flying non-stop around the world.

Below: The medium-range Convair B-58 Hustler was the B-52's supersonic counterpart. Entering service in 1960, it had phenomenal performance, but it was a complex, costly machine. After a ten-year career the B-58 was retired, mainly for economic reasons

From the time the B-52 Stratofortress arrived in the mid-1950s, Strategic Air Command (SAC) was immersed in a new phase of the Cold War. SAC, quite naturally, was controlled by men who had flown B-17s and B-29s in World War II, who had shaped strategic air power, and who saw the long-range bomber as salvation for the West in the face of the Soviet nuclear threat. But by the 1960s the 'bomber generals' dominated the entire US Air Force.

Former SAC boss Curtis E. LeMay served as USAF chief of staff between 1961 and 1965. LeMay was the force behind the manned bomber as the linchpin of American policy. He swaggered and smoked his trademark cigar, insisting that aircraft on the flight line could not catch fire from it because "They wouldn't dare". LeMay often said the Air Force needed three things, "the bomber, the bomber, and the bomber". Less visible was Gen. Bernard A. Schriever, who quietly led a revolution to win the Air Force over to the coming ICBM (intercontinental ballistic missile). But the B-52, not the ICBM, symbolised everything SAC was doing.

American policy went under different names. The strategy of containment (1947-52) aimed to prevent any encroachment across any border by the Soviets or their allies. Containment was replaced in the Eisenhower years (1953-61) by a policy of massive retaliation. This meant, as a White House aide put it, that "if the Soviets stick their head up anywhere, they're going to get sledgehammered." The slightest act of aggression would be met with a nuclear response, aimed not at Soviet bases but at cities.

SAC no longer had as many people or aircraft as in the previous decade, but in 1963 it still boasted 271,672 men and 2,424 warplanes including 32 heavy bomb wings and three aerospace wings equipped with the B-52. Apart from reconnaissance assets and two medium bomb wings with the B-58 Hustler, SAC also possessed 41 air refuelling squadrons, nearly all equipped with the KC-135 Stratotanker.

On 16 October 1963, a B-58 of the 305th Bomb Wing at Bunker Hill AFB, Indiana dashed from Tokyo to London in an elapsed time of eight hours 35 minutes (plus a few seconds), averaging 1,510 km/h (938 mph), a record for the 12,920-km (8,030-mile) journey. However, by the end of the 1960s, the B-58 was on its way out of inventory, but the manned bomber was not. With the B-52 out of production and expected to need replacement by the end of the 1960s, the USAF invested $5 billion into the Mach 3 B-70 Valkyrie – only to cancel the B-70 programme after flight testing was well

Above: Signs that the bomber could become vulnerable to enemy defences had SAC looking at a number of unmanned nuclear delivery systems. The Northrop SM-62 Snark was a bomber-sized cruise missile with a 10000-km(6,215 mile) range which pioneered many of the advanced avionics and guidance techniques used today. It was operational from 1957 to 1961.

Left: The reason that early cruise missiles were abandoned was that ballistic missiles offered so much more. Atlas was the West's first true ICBM, becoming operational in 1960 with SAC's 564th Strategic Missile Squadron at Warren AFB, Wyoming. Atlas could deliver a 3-megaton warhead over a range of more than 16000 km (10,000 miles).

Above: A total of 744 B-52s were built between 1952 and 1961. Few could have foreseen that the last of these titanic machines would still be flying nearly half a century after the first, or that they would outlast Strategic Air Command itself.

advanced. Plans to retire the B-52 proceeded anyway.

MISSILE DOMINANCE

On 21 April 1964, SAC passed a milestone: the number of ICBMs on alert surpassed the number of bombers on ground alert. Titan II and Minuteman ICBMs were increasing in number, and most of the massive force of six-jet B-47s had been retired.

Belatedly, Secretary of Defense Robert S. McNamara replaced the policy of assured destruction with a policy of flexible response, which included the previously unthinkable concept of limited nuclear war. If the Soviets obliterated Chicago, the United States would flatten Magnitogorsk – but the response would be proportionate and might not lead to an all-out exchange.

In 1965, the US launched a build-up in Vietnam and B-52s began flying conventional bomb mission against the Viet Cong. But much of SAC's focus stayed on the number of nuclear weapons in the world, which now exceeded 50,000. The majority, about 30,000 were American. The Soviets had 20,000 warheads, and a handful were kept elsewhere by Britain and France. Nuclear war between the two superpowers was still being taken more seriously than limited war in Asia – even by an administration which had flexible response at the root of its doctrine.

At the height of the Cold War, bombers stood alert not merely on runways but in the air. B-52s were aloft 24 hours a day, with live hydrogen bombs in their bays. Only elite crews flew these 'Chrome Dome' missions. It was taken for granted that it was safe to fly around with 'The Bomb' on board. Even as the United States began its relentless descent into the Vietnamese quagmire, airborne alert missions pressed on.

NUCLEAR ACCIDENTS

In January 1966, a B-52 collided with a KC-135 during a refuelling and both crashed near Palomares, Spain. There were four survivors and seven fatalities. Radioactive material was released when the TNT triggers of two of the four weapons aboard the B-52 exploded on impact. All but one of the hydrogen bombs was recovered immediately. The search for the lost weapon took two months and was concluded at a water depth of 870m (2,850 feet) in the Mediterranean World attention was glued on Palomares until 7 April when the missing weapon was recovered, using an experimental submersible.

Oddly the Palomares incident did not bring an end to aircraft flying with nuclear weapons on board during peacetime – but a second nuclear mishap, where bombs were lost in a Greenland B-52 crash, did. 'Chrome Dome' missions ended. Bombers still stood nuclear alerts, armed and ready to launch at short notice, but on the ground.

McNamara planned to retire a major part of the SAC bomber force by 1971, but plans were changed when control of the White House shifted in January 1969. Richard Nixon's advisers kept the B-52 alive and invested in the FB-111 'Aardvark' as an interim part of the SAC arsenal, but the dominance of the bomber was becoming past tense, as ICBMs and submarine-launched missiles became more important.

SAC in the 60s

Although numbers of aircraft deployed had fallen from their peak in the early 1950s, Strategic Air Command was still the world's most powerful strike force in the 1960s. SAC operated 17 B-52 wings divided between the 8th Air Force headquartered in Louisiana and the 15th Air Force with headquarters in California. To this they could add two wings of B-58s and over 700 KC-135 tankers.

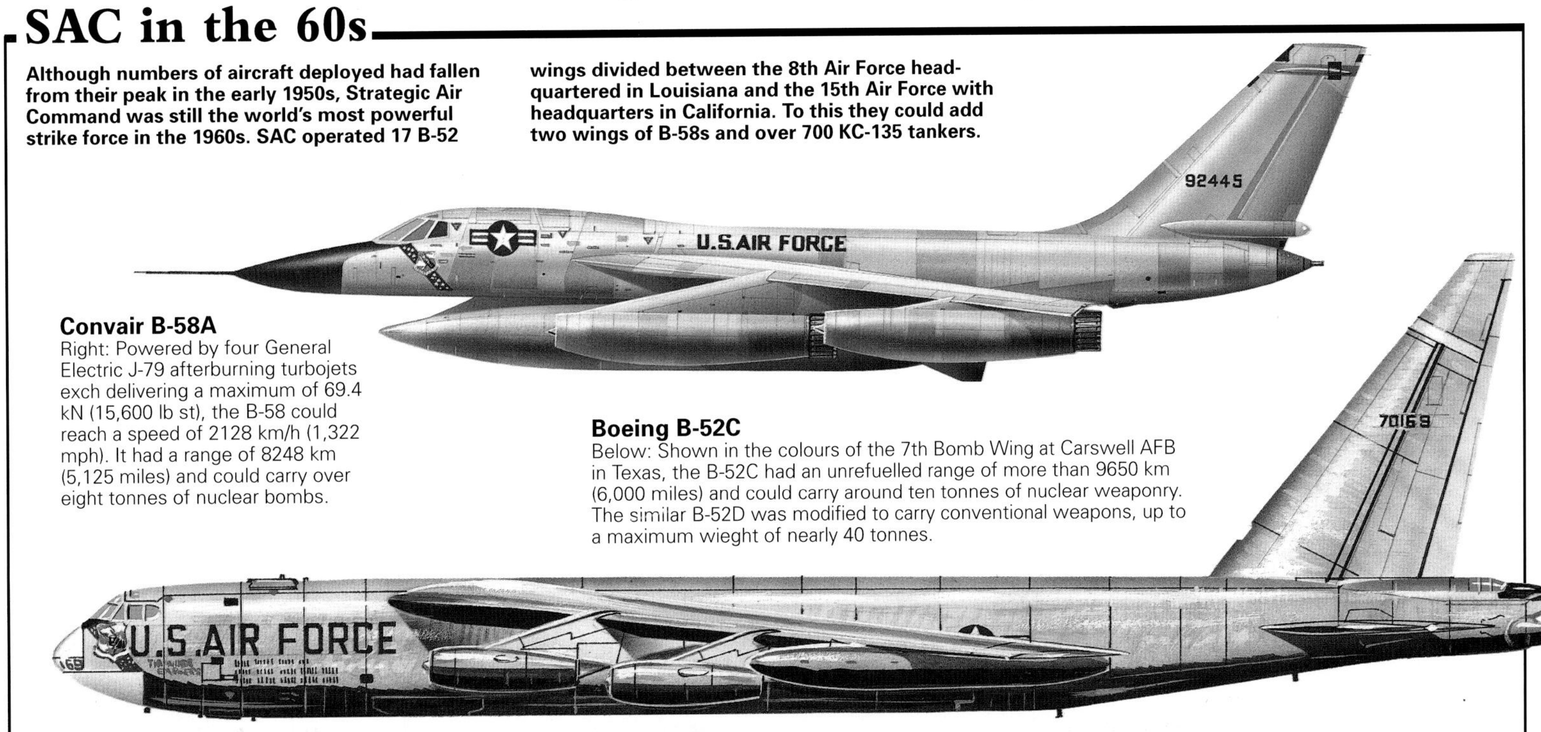

Convair B-58A
Right: Powered by four General Electric J-79 afterburning turbojets exch delivering a maximum of 69.4 kN (15,600 lb st), the B-58 could reach a speed of 2128 km/h (1,322 mph). It had a range of 8248 km (5,125 miles) and could carry over eight tonnes of nuclear bombs.

Boeing B-52C
Below: Shown in the colours of the 7th Bomb Wing at Carswell AFB in Texas, the B-52C had an unrefuelled range of more than 9650 km (6,000 miles) and could carry around ten tonnes of nuclear weaponry. The similar B-52D was modified to carry conventional weapons, up to a maximum wieght of nearly 40 tonnes.

The Cold War

Britain's V-Force

1951-1975

Although not normally privy to the secrets of the American wartime atomic bomb, the UK, by the participation of its scientists in the production of the weapon in the USA, was favourably equipped to undertake the development of its own atomic bomb after the war. Although an aircraft such as the Lincoln would have been capable of carrying a 'tailored' atomic bomb (but over much shorter distances than the American B-29), the British Air Staff decided to embark on a programme aimed at equipping Bomber Command with large jet-powered bombers, and issued a number of very advanced requirements shortly after the end of the war. Fortunately, the world has been spared any demonstration of the true credibility of these aircraft in their role of nuclear-armed deterrents.

In 1947 the Chiefs of Staff declared their belief that the possession of "weapons of mass destruction ...would be the most effective deterrent to war itself." The die was cast for the issue of Operational Requirement OR.229. This was

Above: A Vulcan B.Mk 1 leads Mk 1 versions of the other two V-Bombers: Valiant off its port wing and Victor off the starboard side. All three were conceived as strategic nuclear bombers, relying on speed and high-altitude performance to evade interception.

Right: A Vulcan crew scramble to their waiting aircraft. The V-Force trained intensively to be able to be airborne and en route to their targets before hostile bombers or missiles could wipe out their bases. It was an Armageddon scenario.

Below: This early Vulcan B.Mk 1 of the Waddington wing is still in the overall silver finish applied to the very earliest V-Bombers. That was soon replaced by a high-gloss white intended to reflect the 'flash' of an atomic explosion.

Right: Third of the V-Bombers was the Handley Page Victor, ordered into production as an insurance policy against failure of the revolutionary Vulcan. It proved faster than the Vulcan, and carried a larger bombload, but few were purchased.

From high-level to stand-off

During its long life, the V-Force dramatically changed its procedures and tactics, embracing quick-reaction alerts, operations from dispersed sites, and a switch to low-level operations. Perhaps most crucially, it adopted a stand-off weapon, allowing aircraft to attack targets without having to penetrate the heaviest defences. Blue Steel was to have been replaced by the US Skybolt, but this was cancelled.

Vickers Valiant B.Mk 1
The Valiant was ordered as an interim aircraft, pending the introduction of the more advanced Vulcan and Victor. When these aircraft were available in sufficient numbers, Valiants were switched to the tactical role (and assigned to SACEUR) and some were converted for reconnaissance and tanker duties, before fatigue problems prompted their early retirement.

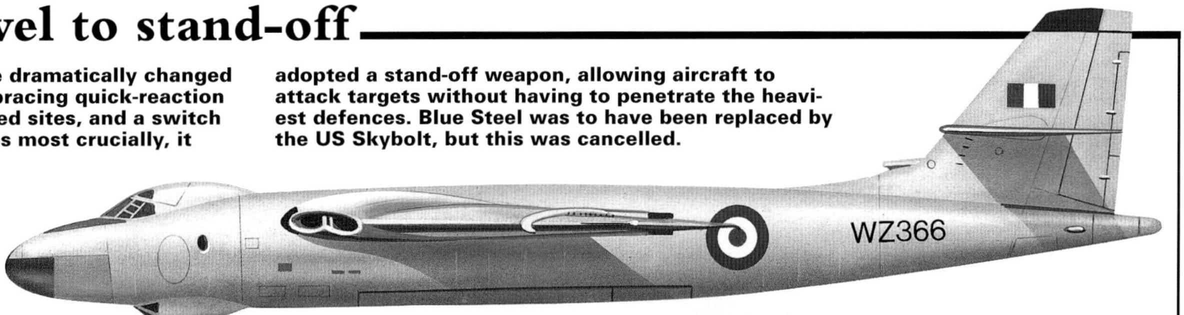

Avro Vulcan B.Mk 2
A Vulcan B.Mk 2 of No. 9 Squadron. The second generation of V-Bombers was designed with enhanced high-altitude performance and improved electronic countermeasures equipment, but the entire concept of high-level penetration was then rendered obsolete by advances in SAM technology.

Handley Page Victor B.Mk 2(BS)
With the switch to low-level penetration, the V-Bombers adopted camouflage (like this Blue Steel-armed Victor of the Wittering Wing). Only 57 Blue Steel missiles were procured.

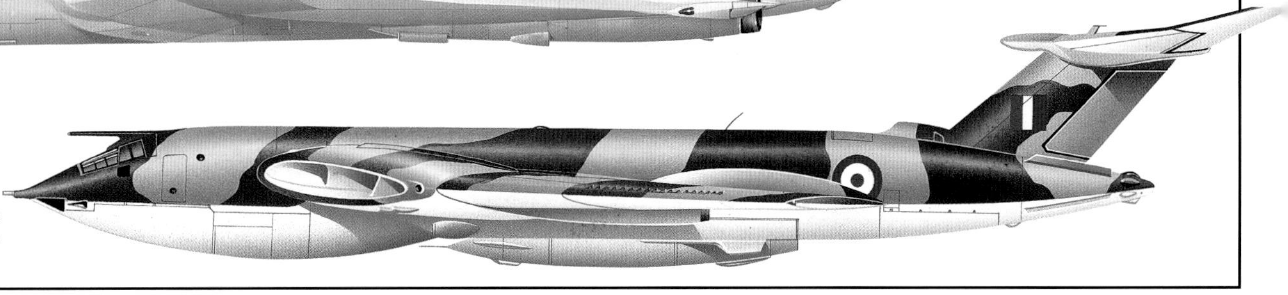

for a four-jet Lincoln replacement capable of delivering a 4536-kg (10,000-lb) nuclear device, while flying at 500 kt and 13716 m (45,000 ft), with a still air range of 5633 km (3,500 miles). The performance figures were later adjusted to require a still air range of 8047 km (5,000 miles), and an over-target ceiling of 15420 m (50,000 ft). These figures, it was emphasised, were minimums, and it was hoped that they would be handsomely exceeded. The resulting specification B.35/46 also called for a high degree of manoeuvrability, and blind-bombing capability using H2S. First of the new bomber specifications, B.14/46, which brought forth the Short Sperrin, proved abortive largely through overestimated bomb dimensions hopelessly compromising the design. Shortly afterwards a follow-up requirement,

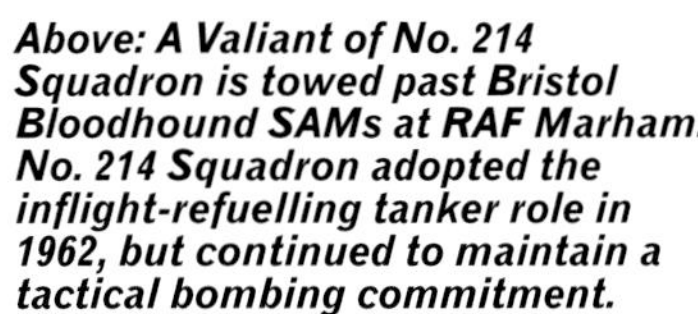

Above: A Valiant of No. 214 Squadron is towed past Bristol Bloodhound SAMs at RAF Marham. No. 214 Squadron adopted the inflight-refuelling tanker role in 1962, but continued to maintain a tactical bombing commitment.

Right: The requirement for the V-Bombers was issued in 1946, and called for a jet bomber which would have the speed and altitude performance of the Canberra (which was too small to carry contemporary nuclear weapons, until the development of small tactical devices during the 1950s), yet which would exceed the range of the piston-engined Lincoln. The V-Bombers were designed around the dimensions of Britain's first indigenous bomb, the Blue Danube, a plutonium-based weapon first tested in October 1952. This weapon was replaced by the megaton-yield Yellow Sun from 1958. Even in their initial form, the V-Bombers had a long enough radius of action to attack targets well east of Moscow, or to reach Moscow via circuitous routes which kept them clear of the heaviest defences. V-Bombers could have attacked Moscow and then recovered to bases in the Mediterranean, and the options increased when inflight refuelling was introduced. The adoption of Blue Steel added little to maximum range, but Skybolt's greater reach would have made a significant difference.

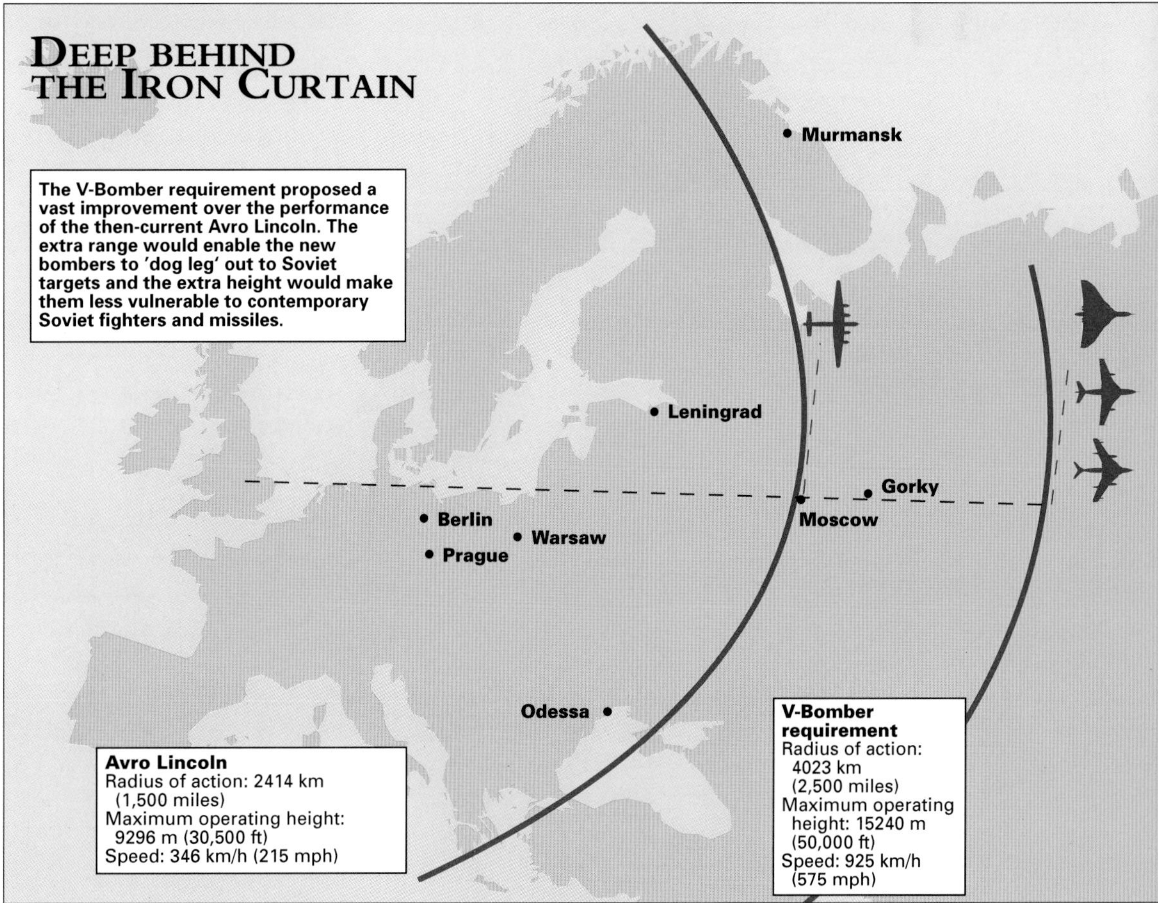

***Left:* The V-Force maintained its QRA aircraft at four-minute readiness, 24 hours a day, cutting reaction time to two minutes with the introduction of runway-edge ORPs and simultaneous engine starting.**

***Above:* This Valiant wears the low-level camouflage adopted by the V-Force during the mid-1960s with the switch to low-level ops. They proved fatal to the Valiant, causing unexpected fatigue.**

B.35/46, proved more promising and, with a new specification issued in 1947, provided the basis on which the UK's nuclear bombing force was to be founded: B.35/46 was updated in 1948 by B.9/48.

The first of the new generation of V-Bombers, the Vickers Valiant, was flown on 18 May 1951 and entered service with No. 138 Squadron in February 1955. Meanwhile, the UK had detonated its first nuclear device in the Monte Bello Islands off the northwestern coast of Australia. On 11 October 1956 Valiants of No. 49 Squadron took part in trials at Maralinga, Australia, when an aircraft captained by Squadron Leader E. J. G. Flavell dropped the first British atomic bomb; on 15 May the following year, in Operation 'Grapple', another No. 49 Squadron Valiant dropped the first British hydrogen bomb over Christmas Island in the Pacific.

BRITAIN'S V-BOMBER BASES

V-BOMBERS AT SUEZ

In the meantime, Valiants of Nos 138, 148, 207 and 214 Squadrons had been deployed to Luqa, Malta, for operations against Egypt during the Suez campaign, the first V-Bombers to drop 'conventional' bombs in anger. In 1965 Valiants were found to be suffering from metal fatigue in the main wing spars and were withdrawn from service. Their last duties with Bomber Command included those operated as inflight-refuelling tankers, all members of the V-Force being

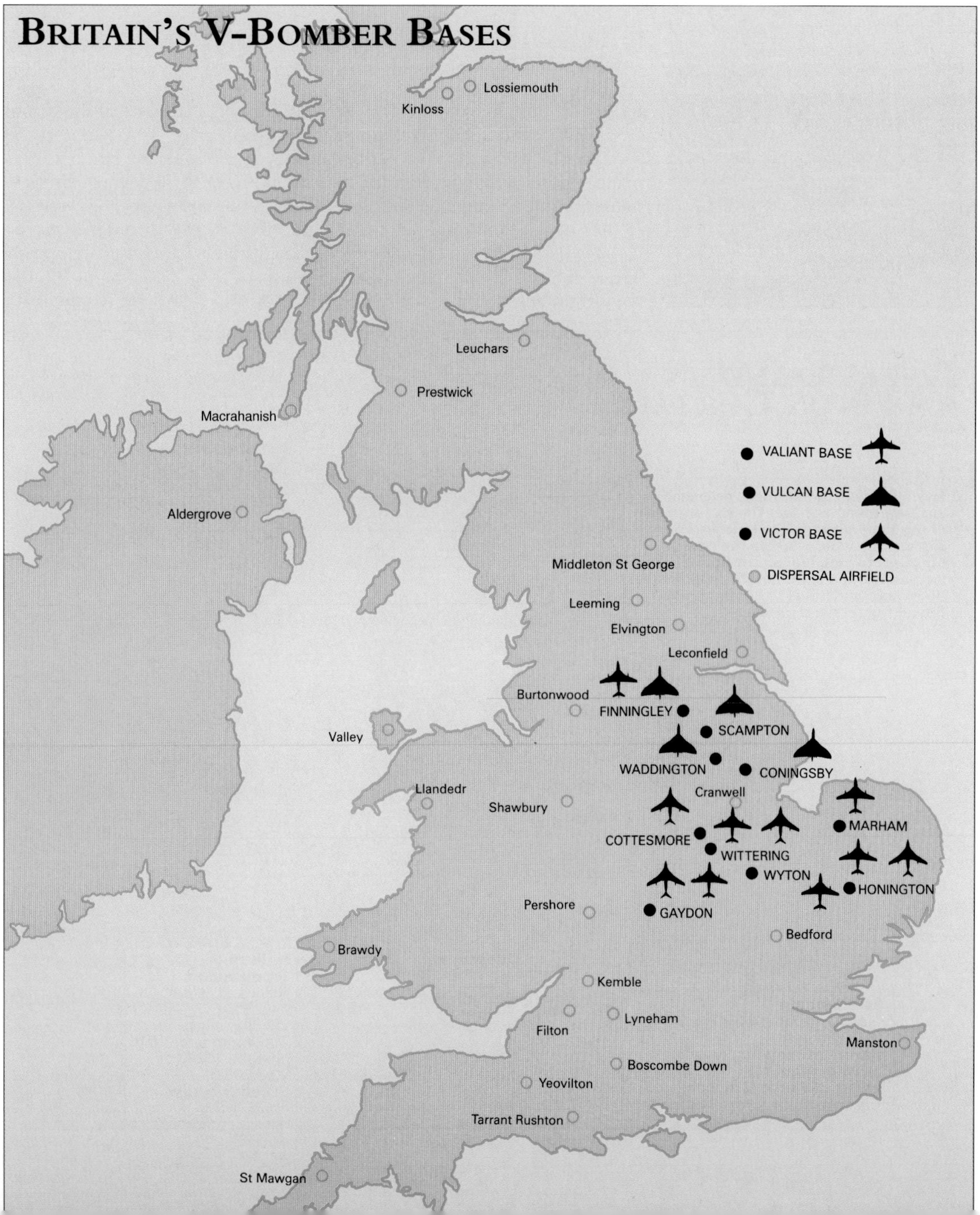

***Left:* At the height of its capability, in late-1962, the V-Force's strategic nuclear deterrent numbered 15 squadrons, with two wings of three Vulcan B.Mk 2 squadrons (Nos 9, 12 and 35) at Coningsby, and Scampton (Nos 27, 83 and 617), and a three-squadron wing of B.Mk 1As (Nos 44, 50 and 101) at Waddington. Cottesmore had two squadrons of Victor B.Mk 1s (Nos 10 and 15), Honington two Victor B.Mk 1A squadrons (Nos 55 and 57), and Wittering two Victor B.Mk 2 squadrons (Nos 100 and 139). These were augmented by three SACEUR-assigned Valiant tactical strike/bomber squadrons (Nos 49, 148 and 207) at Marham, and four more Valiant tanker, ECM and recce units (Nos 90, 214, 18 and 543), based at Marham, Honington, Finningley and Wyton. V-Bomber OCUs were based at Finningley and Gaydon. The strike Valiants carried US weapons, which also equipped four Canberra squadrons based in Germany. A similar 'dual-key' nuclear force consisted of 60 Thor missiles, each with a 2414-km (1,500-mile) range and a 1-megaton warhead.**

Left: A Valiant B(K).Mk 1 of No. 90 Squadron refuels a Vulcan B.Mk 1A from the Waddington Wing (probably No. 617, which was the first to practice refuelling operations).

Below: Each of the V-Bombers carried strike cameras for bomb damage assessment, and each spawned a dedicated strategic reconnaissance derivative. First was the Valiant B(PR).Mk 1 which equipped No. 543 Squadron from July 1955.

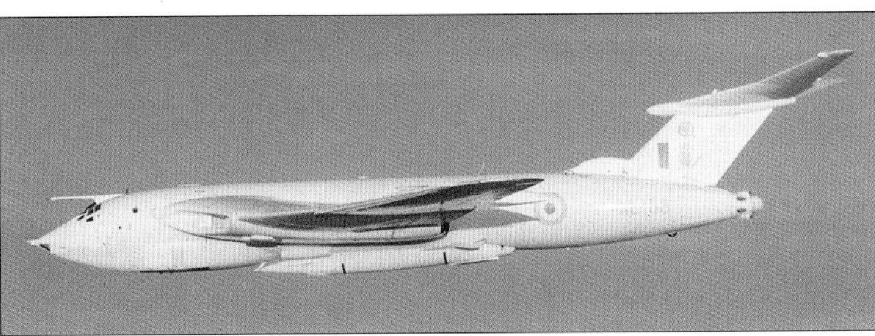

Above: In addition to anti-flash white paint, the V-Bombers also had national insignia toned down to pastel shades to avoid them becoming 'hot spots' on the skin. This is a Victor B.Mk 2(BS).

given inflight-refuelling facility.

Next of the V-Force trio to fly was the Avro Vulcan, on 30 August 1952. This, the most impressive of all the bombers, was a large delta-wing aircraft originally powered by Avon and then Sapphire turbojets, but in production by two-spool Olympus engines which eventually produced about 88.97-kN (20,000-lb) thrust. Production of the Vulcan was very modest, only 45 Mk 1s and 68 Mk 2s (with bigger wings and elevons) being built.

Long-lived Vulcan

By means of a number of life-extension expedients, however, this force remained in a service for almost 30 years, serving in turn as high- and low-level bombers, stand-off bombers, reconnaissance aircraft and ultimately as tankers. During that period they equipped nine RAF squadrons at Coningsby, Cottesmore, Finningley, Honington, Scampton and Waddington in the UK, and at Akrotiri in Cyprus between 1969 and 1975. Most of the Vulcan B.Mk 2s were adapted to carry the Avro Blue Steel stand-off nuclear missile, but plans to

QRA: 24-hour readiness

Ten Class One airfields were developed for the V-Force, each with a minimum 2745-m (9,000-ft) runway, hardstandings for at least 16 aircraft, and the ability to withstand aircraft weights of up to 90720 kg (200,000 lb). They were Coningsby, Cottesmore, Finningley, Gaydon, Honington, Marham, Scampton, Waddington, Wittering and Wyton. Another 27 were later upgraded to handle dispersed flights of V-Bombers, with runway ORPs, crew quarters and refuelling facilities.

Above: Scampton-based Vulcans make a stream take-off after scrambling from their runway-edge ORP. Four Vulcans could be airborne and en route to their targets within two minutes of the order to scramble.

Above: Operational Readiness Platforms (ORPs) were built at the V-Bomber bases, and at other airfields nominated as potential homes for dispersed flights of Vulcans or Victors in time of war.

Right: Even the reconnaissance specialists practiced QRA. Here, the crew of a No. 543 Squadron Valiant scramble for a QRA take-off.

V-Force weapons of war

Above: The Vulcan and Victor could perform conventional bombing duties with clips of seven 454-kg (1,000-lb) bombs. The Vulcan could drop three clips, while the Victor bomb bay accommodated five.

Above: A Victor drops its maximum bombload of 35 454-kg (1,000-lb) GP bombs. The Avro Vulcan, by comparison, could carry only 21 of these weapons. A normal V-Force load was a single huge nuclear weapon.

Below: Seventy-two Vulcans (each with two Skybolt missiles) were to have replaced 144 V-Bombers each carrying a single Blue Steel or free-fall bomb. Skybolt was selected in place of the Blue Steel Mk 2.

Below: A Blue Steel missile on its AEC Mandator waits to be lowered onto the trolley which will take it forward under the belly of the waiting Vulcan B.Mk 2. Blue Steel entered service in 1962.

The first nuclear weapon for the V-Force was the Blue Danube, a 7.3-m (24-ft) long, 1.5-m (5-ft) diameter monster weighing about 4990 kg (11,000 lb). In 1958, Finningley and Scampton received 12 interim Violet Clubs, essentially Green Grass hydrogen bomb warheads in the Blue Danube case. The Green Grass warhead was subsequently fitted in a new casing to create the Yellow Sun Mk 1. From 1958 the Waddington Vulcans, the Honington Victors and the Marham Valiants received US-made Mk 5 weapons under Project E; the Waddington wing later gained Yellow Sun. Yellow Sun Mk 2 used a Red Snow Mk 2 warhead similar to that of the Blue Steel missile.

equip the aircraft with the American Skybolt missile were aborted by cancellation of that programme, and the nuclear deterrent passed to the Polaris submarine force. Despite its great bulk the Vulcan was classed as a medium bomber, capable of carrying up to 21 454-kg (1,000-lb) iron bombs or a 4536-kg (10,000-lb) Blue Steel. Although employed out of context as a global nuclear deterrent, the Vulcan's last operation was the most spectacular when two aircraft were deployed to attack the Falkland Islands in 1982 during the illegal occupation by Argentine forces; in successive sorties from Ascension Island, these aircraft attacked Port Stanley airfield with 454-kg (1,000-lb) bombs and a radar installation with anti-radiation missiles.

Victor

Third of the V-Bombers was the Handley Page Victor with crescent wing, an aircraft that took so long to develop that by the time it entered service in 1958 it was already obsolescent in a world of surface-to-air missiles and Mach 2+ interceptors. Fifty-five Mk 1s and Mk 1As were produced, as well as 34 Mk 2s, so small a quantity that their unit cost was considered inordinately high. As with the Vulcan, their vulnerability at altitude resulted in a change of role to low-level bombing, equipped with Blue Steel missiles, while the last eight aircraft were completed as strategic reconnaissance aircraft for service with No. 543 Squadron at Wyton. Although capable of carrying 35 454-kg (1,000-lb) iron bombs (14 more than the Vulcan), the true value of the Victor was to be as a tanker for the other aircraft of the V-Force, Nos 55 and 57 Squadrons at Marham (as well as No. 543 Squadron) being the last surviving operational units in existence. Victor bombers served with nine RAF squadrons.

Whether or not a force of V-Bombers, of which fewer than 50 were ever combat-capable simultaneously, constituted a credible deterrent (to which the independent French Force de Frappe might in certain circumstances be added) will for ever remain unknown. Yet while these forces have been combined with the might of American land-, sea- and air-based nuclear deterrent, nuclear war has remained a spectre... and no more.

From bomber to tanker

The premature grounding of the Valiant fleet left the RAF without tankers. Plans for the conversion of redundant Victor B.Mk 1s to tanker configuration were already in hand, with a prototype Victor tanker having flown early in 1964. The programme was expedited in order to provide a replacement for the Valiant tankers, and six bombers were hastily fitted out as two-point tankers as Victor B(K).Mk 1As. The first of 24 three-point tanker K.Mk 1s (with new tanks in the former bomb bay) followed in November 1965. The Victor K.Mk 1s were limited by their lack of thrust, and were eventually replaced by tanker conversions of the B.Mk 2.

Victor K.Mk 2

The contract to convert Victor B.Mk 2s was awarded to Hawker Siddeley in 1970, a slap in the face which 'finished off' the ailing Handley Page.

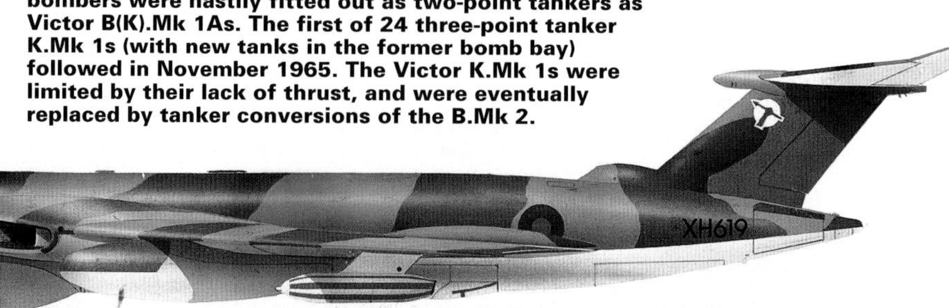

Radar
The main H2S Mk 9A radar was augmented from July 1965, when the RAF ordered 165 General Dynamics TFRs, whose radome was housed in a small pimple on the tip of the nose, below the inflight-refuelling probe. This worked in conjunction with the altimeters to generate simple 'up' and 'down' commands in the cockpit.

Wing
The original Vulcan design had a simple delta planform, but a kinked, drooped outerwing leading edge – the so-called Phase 2 wing – was soon added to reduce buffet at high Mach numbers. This was further refined to become the Phase 2C wing with a more pronounced kink and rounder tips, used on the B.Mk 2.

Vulcan colours
Anti-flash white was adopted during 1958, and toned-down national markings followed in the early-1960s. The switch to low-level operations brought about the introduction of disruptive pattern camouflaged top surfaces. Radomes were overpainted and undersurfaces turned light-grey during the mid-1970s, and from 1977 some aircraft received a wraparound camouflage, extending over the undersides, for participation in US exercises.

Powerplant
The Avro Vulcan B.Mk 2 was powered by a quartet of Bristol Siddeley Olympus turbofans. The Scampton Wing standardised on aircraft with the BO 16 Olympus 201, while Waddington used the later machines, fitted with BO 121 Olympus 301s. The Olympus 201 provided 75.65 kN (17,000 lb st) of thrust while the 301 was rated at 89 kN (20,000 lb st). Forty-five Vulcan B.Mk 2s were powered by the original engine.

Avro Vulcan B.Mk 2

XM600 was one of the aircraft assigned to No. 617 Squadron at RAF Scampton during the mid-1970s. The squadron then used WE177B free-fall laydown nuclear weapons in its primary tactical strike role for SACEUR, but also had a secondary conventional bombing role, and a secondary maritime radar reconnaissance commitment.

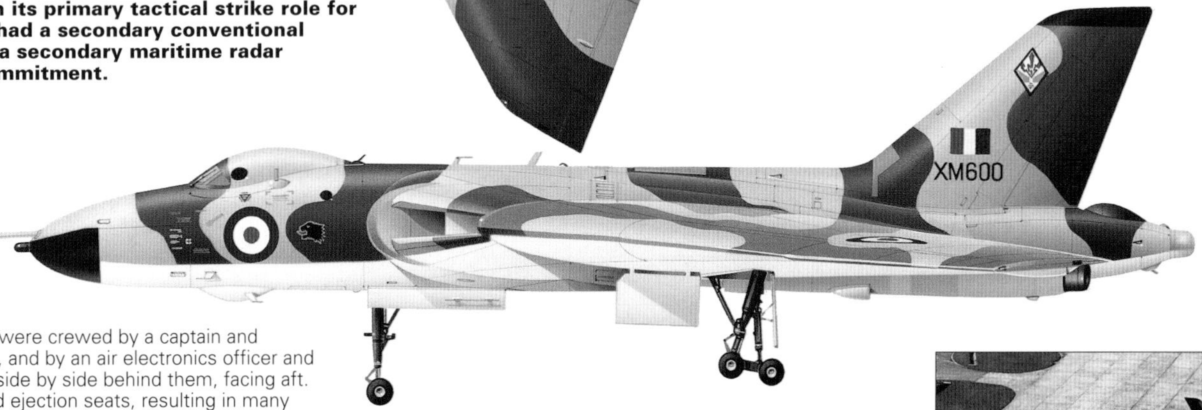

XM600

Crew
The RAF's V-Bombers were crewed by a captain and co-pilot sitting forward, and by an air electronics officer and two navigators sitting side by side behind them, facing aft. Only the two pilots had ejection seats, resulting in many rear crew deaths when aircraft got into difficulties.

Left: Four Victors operated alongside No. 543 Squadron's Valiants from 1958, operating in the radar recce role. Seven B.Mk 2s were subsequently converted for reconnaissance duties to replace No. 543's Valiants from early-1966.

Right: Vulcan B.Mk 2s at RAF Akrotiri, where Nos 9 and 35 Squadrons formed a tactical strike wing from January 1969 until January 1975, operating primarily in support of CENTO. They were equipped with conventional and WE 177B nuclear bombs.

Cold War Air Defences

1950-1960

***Left:** The Northrop F-89 Scorpion guarded the farthest reaches of the North American continent in the 1950s. Not particularly fast, it was distinguished by long range, a powerful airborne intercept radar and a sophisticated (for the time) fire-control system. It was also the first fighter to carry nuclear-tipped air-to-air weapons.*

***Below:** The Gloster Javelin was the first twin-engined, delta wing jet to enter service. It was also the first British warplane designed from the outset as an all-weather interceptor, integrating airframe, radar and missiles as a single weapons system. Although offering much greater capability than the Meteors it replaced, the Javelin was difficult to keep serviced .*

To most military personnel, the Cold War was a time of endless training for a war which never came. But there was one group of airmen who went head-to-head with their potential enemies for real. Day in, day out, air defence and interceptor pilots both East and West took to the air against intruders, weapons live and ready to shoot if called upon.

NATO in its early days had one vital raison d'être: to counter the forcible conversion of Western Europe to communism by the might of the Soviet Union.

World War II had shown that control of the air was vital to any land campaign, and any move by the thousands of Soviet and Warsaw Pact tanks on the Central Front would have been preceded by an all-out air assault, with the main aim of knocking out NATO air defences. Europe may be small as continents go, but at the height of the Cold War it presented a very wide variety of problems when it came to air defence.

Germany was on the Iron Curtain front line. Major Soviet air bases were only a few minutes flying time from the country's industrial heartland, and the defence of Germany was a key pillar of NATO strategy. German interceptors served alongside aircraft from Belgium, the Netherlands, Denmark, the United Kingdom, France, the USA and Canada. They were kept on a high state of alert, ready to launch against intruding bombers at a moment's notice.

Britain, on the other hand, was the linchpin of NATO's plans for reinforcement across the Atlantic, and her fighters were charged with intercepting bombers far out over the ocean. Soviet long-range maritime aircraft probed the defences regularly, and fighters on quick-reaction alert went up to investigate contacts daily. Subsonic Javelins in the 1950s gave way in RAF service to supersonic Lightnings and Phantoms in the 1960s.

Other NATO countries, particularly those on NATO's flanks bordering directly with the Soviet Union had problems peculiar to their own geographical locations. The wastes of northern Norway commanded the Arctic while Turkey bottled up the Soviet Black Sea Fleet. Both were key Soviet targets and had to be defended.

And for the first time, the United States itself was under threat. Although politically worlds apart, the USA and the Soviet Union were very close geographically. It does not look that way in an atlas, but a polar projection shows that North America is not too far from Eurasia across the Arctic Ocean.

In the 1950s, the American military regarded an attack by Soviet nuclear-armed bombers as a real and imminent prospect. In the Pentagon and in the Canadian Defence Ministry, these officers

***Left:** Entering service only five years after the Javelin, the English Electric Lightning offered a whole new order of performance. Capable of more than two and a half times the speed of sound, it was one of the fastest-climbing interceptors ever built.*

Lightning Interceptor

Britain's postwar lead in jet aircraft design did not last long: it had been overhauled by both the USA and the USSR by the early 1950s. But the gap was closed to some extent with the entry into service of the English Electric Lightning, the fastest British fighter ever. Although the Lightning's radar was primitive by modern standards, and its cockpit an ergonomic nightmare, in 1960 a missile-armed, radar-equipped single-seater with an early computerised fire control system was state of the art.

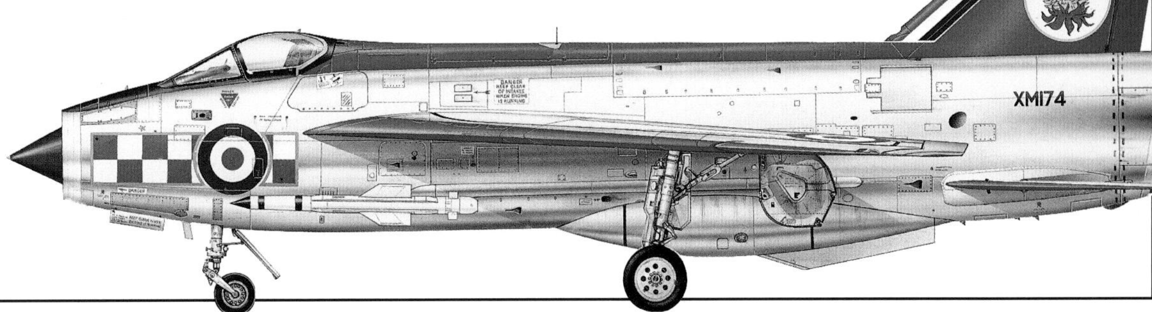

Lightning F.Mk 1A
Right: Seen in the colours of No.56 Squadron RAF, which in 1960 was the second squadron to equip with the type, the F.Mk 1A differed from the original fighter in that it had provision for inflight refuelling. This gave the short-legged Lightning the ability to deploy long distances non-stop.

faced a challenge without precedent – a likely onslaught by air that might wreak such ghastly destruction, even the recently-won World War II would seem a footnote by comparison. In 1951, intelligence analysts estimated that Moscow would soon be able to "deliver a sufficient number of atomic bombs to cause over one hundred detonations in the United States". This estimate was premature but within a decade it became real and multiplied. At the height of the Cold War, the number of nuclear warheads in the Soviet arsenal was measured not in the hundreds but in the tens of thousands.

Air Defense Command

The primary defender of the USA was the fledgling Air Defense Command, or ADC, which had been founded on 21 March 1946. In 1947, the year the US Air Force broke off from the Army to become an independent service, Winston Churchill warned of an 'Iron Curtain' falling over the communist nations. By 1949, the Soviets had exploded their first atomic device and ADC grew from a 'paper' command to being the operator of a few twin-engine Northrop F-61C Black Widow night fighters. Expansion with Lockheed F-80 Shooting Stars followed, but by 1951 these relatively slow straight-winged machines were being superseded by the swept-wing, state-of the art North American F-86 Sabre.

But single-seat day fighters could only do part of the job. A number of new all-weather fighters were developed to equip ADC's growing fighter-interceptor squadrons. All-weather was the new term for radar-equipped interceptors that could function by day or by night and in adverse conditions (though

Right: The Lockheed F-94 was one of the first radar-equipped jet interceptors. Based on the T-33 trainer, the F-94 equipped more than 24 squadrons of the US Air Defense Command. Aircraft were maintained on three-minute alert, ready to intercept hostile bombers.

Polar Watch

Although the USA and the USSR might have seemed a long way apart to the transatlantic traveller of the time, in fact the two superpowers were close neighbours – as long as you were flying over the North Pole. The prospect of hordes of nuclear bombers attacking across the virtually unpopulated Arctic waste was one of the great fears of the Cold War warriors, and the United States and Canada expended a great deal of money and resources on developing a system which would give adequate warning of a surprise Soviet attack. The tripwire initially consisted of chains of radar stations stretching across the continent, to which was added the BMEWS ballistic missile early warning system as the threat changed from aircraft bombs to missile-borne warheads.

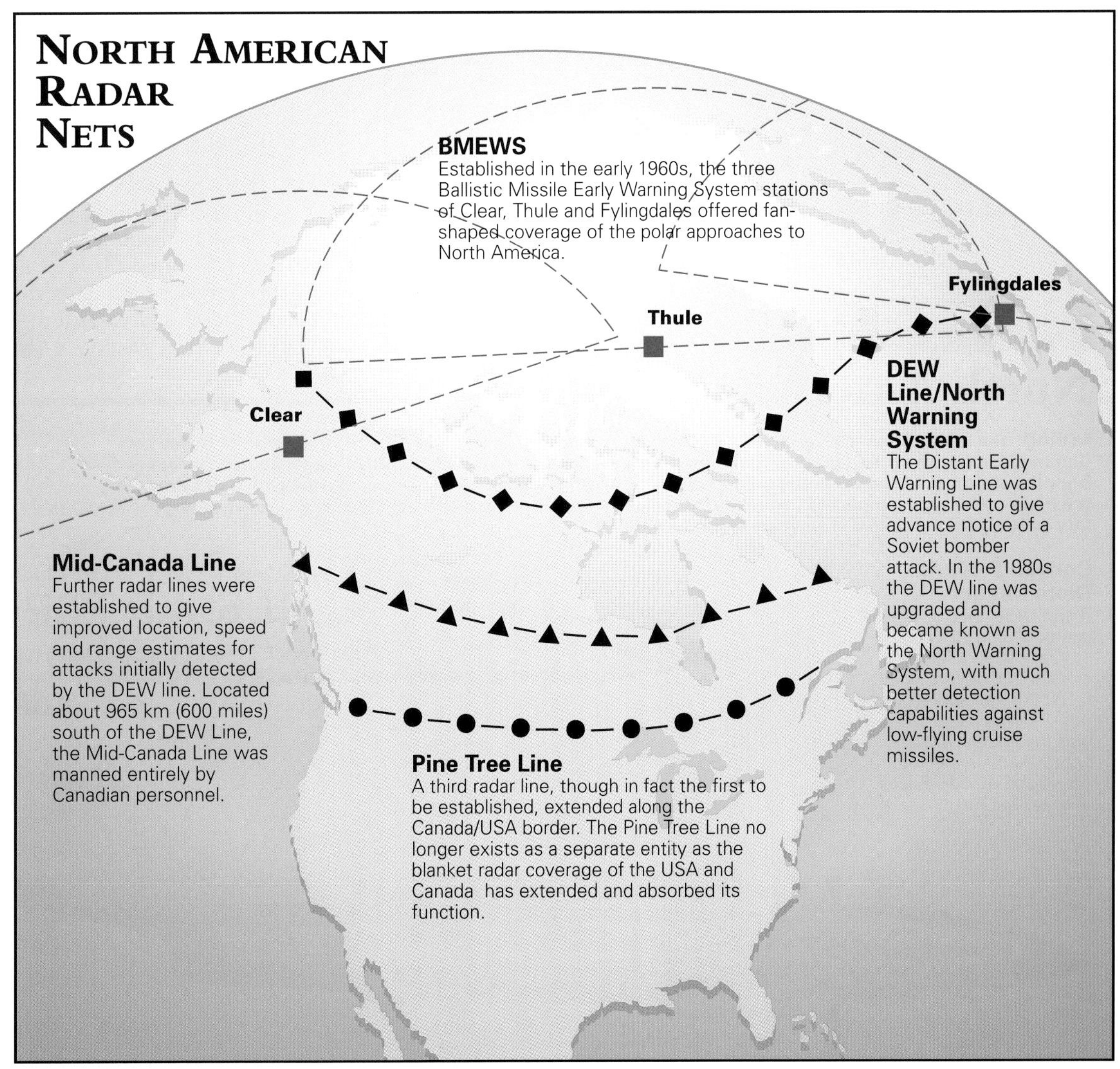

Left: A McDonnell F-101B Voodoo fires an AIR-2 Genie rocket. Designed to disrupt large bomber formations, the unguided Genie had a 1.5 kiloton nuclear warhead with a 500m (1,640 ft) lethal blast radius and could seriously damage targets at up to 1000m (3,300 ft). The missile had a range of only 10 km (6.2 miles), so the launch aircraft had to pull a very tight turn after launch to escape the blast.

the term was misleading; they could fly in some adverse weather but not all). In the USAF, the squadrons which flew them were called Fighter Interceptor Squadrons, or FISs, pronounced 'fizzes'.

The North American F-86D Sabre, Northrop F-89 Scorpion, and Lockheed F-94 (nicknamed Starfire in its F-94C variant only) were a trio of 'interim' warplanes tailored to carry airborne radar, guns, and rocket projectiles. Crews were trained to scramble against incoming bombers and to intercept them as far as possible from their targets – at best, north of the Arctic circle and far from vulnerable cities.

With the 1957 establishment of the joint US/Canadian North American Air Defense Command (NORAD), the Canadian Avro CF-100 Canuck joined the fighter-interceptor forces arrayed towards the north. They practised radar-guided Ground Control Intercept (GCI) missions throughout the 1950s while planners in Washington and Ottawa searched for more advanced interceptors. Their work was characterised in a booklet of the era in which ADC attempted to coin the acronym DIID (Detect, Identify, Intercept, and Destroy) but this jargon for the air defence mission never caught on.

Right: The North American F-86D was a bomber destroyer. It carried no guns, being armed with 24 2.75-in (70-mm) 'Mighty Mouse' unguided high explosive rockets fired from a ventral tray.

Below: The 1950s saw the Soviet bomber threat made manifest with the massive Tupolev Tu-95 'Bear', a long-range heavy bomber with awesome range. US fighters based on Iceland regularly intercepted 'Bears' over the Atlantic.

Weapons systems

By 1954 the USAF had begun to develop an interceptor using an integrated 'weapons system' approach that would produce the aircraft and its military capability simultaneously. The result was the Convair F-102 Delta Dagger (the nickname was not applied until more than a decade after the type was in service), which overcame early developmental problems to become an effective interceptor. It was joined in ADC squadrons – as well as Air National Guard squadrons, dedicated to the ADC mission – by the McDonnell F-101B Voodoo, a huge, powerful aircraft which was difficult to fly but which, when used properly, could bring enormous firepower into an engagement with bombers.

In Canada in mid-1950s, work progressed on the Avro CF-105 Arrow, a giant, delta-winged interceptor which offered bright hopes for the future of the Canadian aircraft industry and would give

North American defenders

NORAD, the North American Aerospace Defense Command, controls air and ground elements drawn from the air forces of the US and Canada. One of the more enduring examples of Canadian/US military collaboration, NORAD is 40 years old. It was created in 1957 at a time when the threat posed by Soviet long-range bombers was perceived as being on the increase, with the possibility of a devastating surprise attack over the Pole.

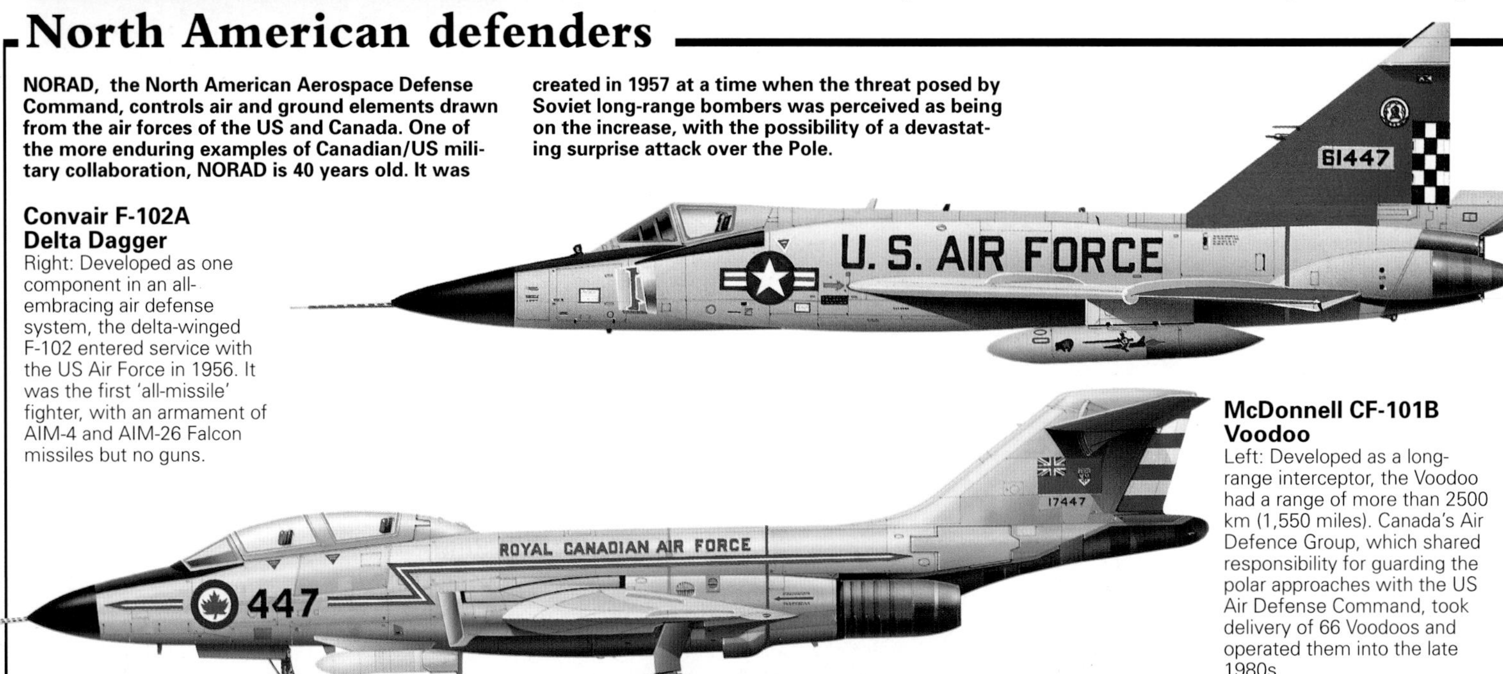

Convair F-102A Delta Dagger

Right: Developed as one component in an all-embracing air defense system, the delta-winged F-102 entered service with the US Air Force in 1956. It was the first 'all-missile' fighter, with an armament of AIM-4 and AIM-26 Falcon missiles but no guns.

McDonnell CF-101B Voodoo

Left: Developed as a long-range interceptor, the Voodoo had a range of more than 2500 km (1,550 miles). Canada's Air Defence Group, which shared responsibility for guarding the polar approaches with the US Air Defense Command, took delivery of 66 Voodoos and operated them into the late 1980s.

Radar
The APG-40 was one of the best airborne radars of its time, with a detection range of around 80 km (50 miles) for bomber-sized targets and a lock-on range of about 8 km.

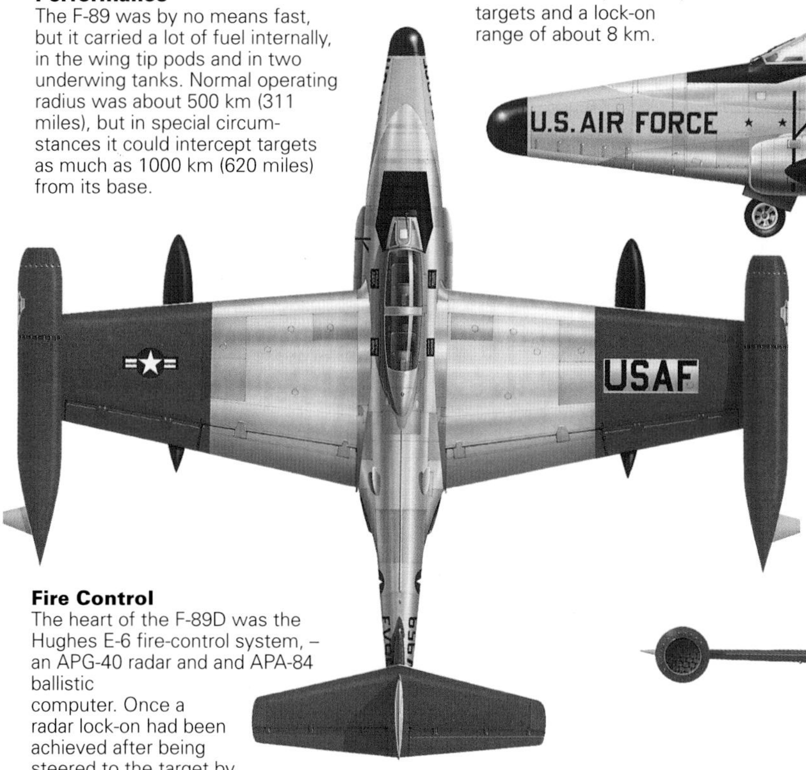

Performance
The F-89 was by no means fast, but it carried a lot of fuel internally, in the wing tip pods and in two underwing tanks. Normal operating radius was about 500 km (311 miles), but in special circumstances it could intercept targets as much as 1000 km (620 miles) from its base.

Northrop F-89D Scorpion

With 682 built, the F-89D was the most numerous variant of the Scorpion. This example is seen in the markings of th 59th Fighter Interceptor Squadron, based at Goose Bay Airport in Labrador. The high-visibility markings were designed to help search and rescue forces in case of accident and were standard for aircraft operating over the uninhabited wastes beyond the Arctic Circle.

Fire Control
The heart of the F-89D was the Hughes E-6 fire-control system, – an APG-40 radar and and APA-84 ballistic computer. Once a radar lock-on had been achieved after being steered to the target by ground control, the E-6 provided steering inputs to the autopilot and could fire the rockets automatically when in range.

Weapons
The F-89 carried a total of 104 'Mighty Mouse' folding finned high-explosive rockets. The 2.75-in (70-mm) unguided weapons were launched from the huge wingtip pods, and could be fired in one, two or three salvos.

NORAD the capability to meet Soviet bombers as far away as the North Pole. Five Arrows underwent a flight test programme launched in 1958, but the huge white aircraft was doomed to political and technical woes. It never entered production, and Canada eventually acquired American-built CF-101B Voodoos instead.

The ultimate interceptor was the Convair F-106 Delta Dart, which eventually reached 14 ADC squadrons and was described by one pilot as "the pure thoroughbred of fighter airplanes".

To help the Cold War era's expanding fighter-interceptor force in its grim job of parrying a bomber strike, NORAD developed a DEW (Distant Early Warning) Line of ground radar stations running from Greenland to Alaska, all pointed north. Approaching bombers would be detected by ground-based radar, then ground controllers would track the bombers and direct fighters to the intercept. The fighter pilot would receive short, voice instructions ("Your target is at 30 degrees, altitude 20, speed 430") intended to get him within range to use his own radar. Voice-directed Ground Controlled Intercepts (GCI) were replaced in the late 1950s with the SAGE (Semi-Automatic Ground Environment) System which 'flew' an interceptor to its target via automatic pilot, the pilot taking over only when it was time to fire. SAGE was used until the late 1970s when improved, secure communication made it possible again to use voice transmissions to vector an interceptor toward its target.

When NORAD came into being during the summer of 1957,

Above: Scattered across thousands of kilometres of some of the most inhospitable terrain on the planet, the DEW Line radar stations were vital components in the detection of aircraft penetrating North American air space from the north.

Below: An F-102 pilot's view of a Soviet 'Bear'. This is a peacetime scene: in combat, the fighter would never have come within range of the bomber's guns, but would have engaged from a distance with AIM-4 Falcon missiles.

Left: The Yakovlev Yak-25 was the Soviet equivalent to the American F-89, although it appeared somewhat later. Given the NATO reporting name of 'Flashlight', it was a two-seat, twin-jet all-weather interceptor which first flew in 1953. Around 1,000 were produced before production ended in 1959.

Below: Although a number of dedicated radar-equipped all-weather fighters were produced by the Soviet Union, by far the bulk of the air defence force was provided by day fighters. Some, like the MiG-19PM seen here, were modified with an all-missile armament and radar in the intake fairing.

the USA and Canada had more than 1,000 aircraft dedicated to air defence, a force level which was maintained until well into the 1960s, when it was acknowledged that the manned bomber had been supplanted by the ICBM as the vehicle most likely to be employed as a nuclear weapon delivery system in future.

Thereafter the respective interceptor fleets entered a period of decline, which had a devastating effect on overall force strength. Some idea of the impact of this contraction can be gleaned from the fact that by the mid-1970s the ADC had fallen to just six squadrons (all equipped with the Convair F-106A Delta Dart) ably supported by a rather larger number of second-line Air National Guard units flying the McDonnell F-101B Voodoo and F-102A Delta Dagger as well as some F-106s.

ADC had been renamed Aerospace Defense Command in January 1968, but continued to serve as the combat arm of NORAD. On 1 October 1979, its resources were transferred to Tactical Air Command which took over most of its functions, and, on 31 March 1980, ADC was disbanded.

The interceptor force remained at the ready, however. In the 1980s, years of neglect were reversed, prompted in part by Soviet deployment of cruise missile-armed bombers, and the old fighter types were replaced by modern F-15s, F-16s and CF-18s, well able to deal with any threat.

View from the East

The world looked very different to the fighter pilots on the other side of the Iron Curtain. Russia has always been paranoid about invaders – with some justification, as a cursory glimpse of history shows. From the Mongols of the 13th century to the Germans of the 20th, the country has repeatedly been ravaged by intruding powers, most of whom have had to be thrown back at fearful cost to the Russian people.

To prevent the recurrence of the German invasion of 1941, the Voyska Protivo-Vozdushnoy Oborony (V-PVO, or Air Defence Troops) was established. Directly responsible to the minister of defence, V-PVO handled all ground and air-based defensive systems and at its peak had a strength of more than 500,000 personnel.

As air defence needs changed, so too did the Air Defence Troops, adding the Zenith Rocket Troops (Zenityye Raketnyye Voyska) with their 10,000 surface-to-air missile (SAM) launchers; Radio-Technical Corps (Radioteknicheskiye Voyska) to operate the vast and comprehensive detection and communications network with its 5,000 radars; Anti-Space Defence (Protivokosmicheskaya Oborona); and Anti-Rocket Defence (Protivoraketnaya Oborona) to defend against ballistic missile attack.

Manned interceptors were flown by a further section of the Voyska PVO, designated Aviation of Air Defence (Aviatsiya PVO). For much of its existence, Air Defence Aviation was autonomous on a national scale, and was organised into several air defence zones with-

Right: The Tupolev Tu-28 'Fiddler' entered service in the 1960s. This huge fighter had a range of more than 3000 km (1,865 miles) and was designed for patrolling the vast expanses of the northern Soviet Union. It carried four AA-5 'Ash' medium-range missiles which came in both semi-active radar and infra-red homing versions.

Right: The transonic Yak-28P 'Firebar' entered service in the mid-1960s. It bore a resemblance to the preceding Yak-25, but had better radar and was considerably faster.

Below: The MiG-25 'Foxbat' is the world's fastest fighter. Developed in the 1960s to intercept the abortive B-70 Valkyrie, production continued even after the American bomber's cancellation. It is capable of sustained speeds of Mach 2.8, with Mach 3 (3200 km/h/2,000 mph) available for short periods.

Soviet Interceptors

The Soviet air defence force was vastly larger than its American equivalent all through the Cold War. The bulk of the numbers was made up with standard tactical fighters, but many hundreds of specialised all-weather interceptors were also deployed, making up in numbers what they may have lacked in sophisticated avionics when compared to the best of the West.

Yakovlev Yak-25
Left: The Yak-25 'Flashlight' was very much a product of the 1950s, with a speed of around 1100 km/h (685 mph) and a range of around 2700 km (1,675 miles).

Sukhoi Su-15 'Flagon'
Right: Standard Soviet single-seat interceptor from the 1960s through to the 1980s, the Su-15 was blisteringly fast though relatively short-ranged. It was an Su-15 which shot down Korean Air Lines' Flight 007 in 1983.

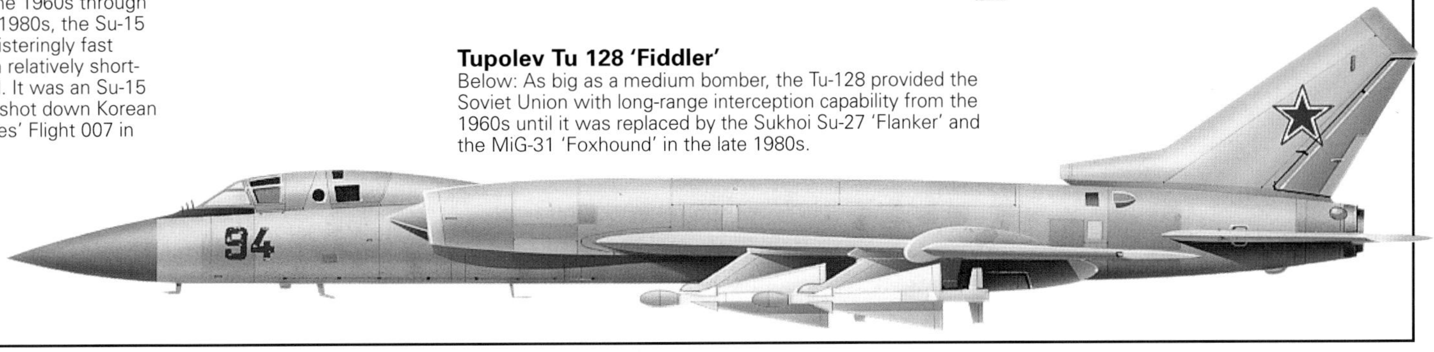

Tupolev Tu 128 'Fiddler'
Below: As big as a medium bomber, the Tu-128 provided the Soviet Union with long-range interception capability from the 1960s until it was replaced by the Sukhoi Su-27 'Flanker' and the MiG-31 'Foxhound' in the late 1980s.

in each of the Soviets' 20 Military Districts.

Soviet jets were always on alert during the Cold War, ready to scramble to intercept NATO spy flights at a moment's notice. Pilots stood on alert at bases across two continents, from the Kola peninsula on the Norwegian border to Cape Dezhnev just across from Alaska.

Willingness to shoot

Unlike Western intercepts, which generally picked up intruding bombers far out to sea and were content with shepherding the intruders away from forbidden air space, Soviet fighters were much more ready to shoot. In several dozen incidents, NATO spyplanes – or aircraft suspected of being spyplanes – were shot down. More disturbingly, the Soviets also showed their willingness to shoot down civil airliners straying into forbidden airspace – culminating in the destruction of a Korean Air Lines Boeing 747 with the loss of more than 300 passengers.

In the early days of the Cold War, the V-PVO depended upon large numbers of the standard day fighters of the time such as the MiG-15 and MiG-17. As with the USA's Air Defense Command, however, it began to receive specialised aircraft more suited to its requirements. Some, like the radar-equipped MiG-19PM, were modifications of existing tactical aircraft. But these, while they had the performance to catch hostile bombers, lacked range, and range is a prerequisite in dealing with the vast expanses of the Soviet Union.

The Soviet Union's sheer size presents unique challenges to those tasked with the defence of her borders. Fighters designed to operate across the immense distances involved need good long-range performance, and the ability to carry and deliver air-to-air weaponry at beyond visual range.

The first radar-equipped all-weather jet fighter was the Yak-25, a twin-engined machine which appeared in the 1950s. It was succeeded by the transonic Yak-28. Serving alongside the Yaks were a series of delta-winged Sukhoi machines, starting with the Su-9 and Su-11. These evolved into the very fast Su-15 'Flagon', which served into the 1990s.

For very long-range intercepts, standard equipment through the 1960s and 1970s was the massive Tu-128 'Fiddler' – as big as a medium bomber. The amazing Mach 3-capable Mikoyan MiG-25 'Foxbat' was developed in the 1960s as a counter to the threat of the USAF's abortive B-70 Valkyrie bomber. Short on range, the MiG-25 was developed into the very long-range MiG-31 'Foxhound' currently in service with the Russian air force.

Right: Rocket-assisted Su-15 'Flagons' streak skywards on an air defence exercise. The Soviet air defence system was not there for show: dozens of aircraft were shot down for intruding into Soviet air space by accident or design.

Aerial intelligence: the U-2 years

1956-1965

***Left:** All of the overflights performed by the U-2 were undertaken by CIA aircraft with CIA or RAF pilots. The USAF also received the aircraft, using them for high-altitude sampling missions to catch nuclear fall-out from Soviet bomb tests.*

***Below:** The early-generation U-2s were steadily modified to encompass the electronic intelligence mission, which assumed massive importance after the Powers shoot-down. This is a U-2C, fitted with an uprated J75 engine for improved performance, dorsal spine housing extra equipment and 'sugar-scoop' jetpipe to deter heat-seeking missiles.*

Lockheed's U-2, the most famous of all spyplanes, was created out of a growing American realisation that the USA was simply not going to get enough Soviet intelligence from conventional means. The controlled world of communist society was not going to yield up its secrets to infiltrated agents, and the growing size and capability of Soviet air defences would shield all except their border areas from intelligence-gathering aerial intruders. Unless, that is, they could fly above the reach of those defences

Balloons had been tried from 1953 onwards, taking advantage of the prevailing eastward-flowing jetstreams in the upper atmosphere to traverse the Soviet Union with underslung cameras: clearing Soviet Asia, such balloons received radio commands from Japan to eject their photographic payloads. However, the system was distinctly unreliable: not only was the exact course of flight at the mercy of the elements, but the balloon's internal pressure had to be controlled in order to maintain the desired flight level. This often failed to happen and the the Soviets retrieved a number of the balloons and cameras.

'OPEN SKIES'

In July 1955 at the Geneva summit conference President Eisenhower proposed an 'Open Skies' policy, in order to reduce the growing tension and arms race between the superpowers. The proposal (for mutual and agreed aerial reconnaissance) appears rather naive today, but it has been in de facto operation since the mid-1960s as a result of the use of reconnaissance satellites by both countries. In the 1950s, however, it was rejected by the Soviet Union.

Three days before that rejection, on 1 August 1955, the top-secret Lockheed U-2 spyplane, built for and operated by the Central Intelligence Agency, had taken to the air for the first time. A year later, the type had embarked on an overflight programme which would take it deep into the Soviet heartland to photograph airfields and missile sites, and listen to radar defences and missile telemetry.

The U-2 could cruise at an unassailable 21335 to 24385m (70,000-80,000 ft) thanks to its incredible glider-type wing and its unique weight-saving design. Early flights were mounted from West Germany, and covered northern and western areas of the Soviet Union, and almost immediately discovered that Soviet bomber development and production was nowhere near as advanced as had been thought.

ICBM WATCH

In 1957 attention switched to the south as the Soviets began to test medium- and intercontinental-range ballistic missiles from Kapustin Yar near Volgograd and from the new cosmodrome misleadingly named Baikonur by the Soviets, (it is actually situated 320 km (200 miles) south of that city). The first pictures of Kapustin Yar had been brought back in 1953 by a photo-reconnaissance Canberra of the RAF, though the aircraft had been badly shot up by the Soviet defences, and since that time there had been no new information. But since the U-2 flew well above the service ceiling of the defending MiGs it could be used to find out what was happening.

***Below:** While its ceiling of more than 24385m (80,000 ft) kept the high-flying U-2 out of range of hostile MiGs, it was just possible that new SAMs might reach that height. The CIA had realised this at least two years before the Powers incident, and had already instigated the follow-on SR-71 programme.*

A detachment moved to Turkey and conducted more overflights, as well as a much larger number of peripheral missions, cruising across Turkey and Iran, using their great height to monitor the cosmodromes visually and electronically to detect signs of impending rocket launches. Another U-2 detachment was based in Japan, to cover the growing military developments in Soviet Asia.

The whole policy of overflights and intelligence gathering missions changed dramatically in 1960. An electronics-packed Boeing RB-47, flying out of Brize Norton, England, was shot down by two Soviet MiGs in the remote northern waters of the Barents Sea on 1 July 1960. Two of the six-man crew survived and were taken prisoner.

The nearby Kola and Kanin peninsulas house the Soviet navy's main northern bases, as well as IRBM sites and bomber airfields. The area had been scheduled for attention two months earlier on 1 May by a U-2 overflight from Pakistan that would take in several sites across the Soviet Union, with the intention to land in Norway. But the U-2, flown by Francis Gary Powers, never reached its northern objective, since it was shot down by an SA-2 missile near Sverdlovsk.

Right: Dominating the instrument panel of the U-2 was the circular driftsight. This was connected to a periscope on the underside of the nose so that the pilot could see the world below.

Nikita Khrushchev was able to turn the U-2 incident of 1 May 1960 into a powerful propaganda weapon. The Soviet leader stage managed a walk-out from the Paris summit meeting only a fortnight after the aircraft was brought down. Perhaps he was exacting revenge for the four-year U-2 operation, during which a surprisingly small number of direct overflights had assured US policy makers that Khruschev's oft-repeated boasts about Soviet strategic missile and aircraft superiority were groundless.

PHOTO-ANALYSIS

For instance, a classic example of the photo-interpreters' art had occurred in the previous year with a U-2 mission over the Tyuratam cosmodrome. From the large size of the aperture seen in photos of the base of the launch pad, analysts were able to deduce that the Soviets were still using auxiliary rockets to boost their intercontinental-range missile - which was hardly an advance on existing US missiles then nearing operational status, and was almost certainly not a deployable, operational system.

The U-2 and RB-47 incidents marked a turning point in the reconnaissance Cold War, and not only because President Kennedy had to promise to cease overflights of the Soviet Union in order to get the two SAC crewmen back (U-2 pilot Francis Gary Powers was released a year later in exchange for a Soviet spy held in the USA).

1960 was also the year when the USA achieved its first success with reconnaissance satellites, to be followed by the Soviets three years later. Advances in missile technology meant that flying at very high altitude was no longer a guarantee

US spyplanes

Naturally it was the United States which led the way in developing new aircraft for intelligence gathering. Most were conversions of existing aircraft, using transports or bombers for the Sigint mission, which required the carriage of heavy equipment and numerous operators. In addition to the U-2, the high-altitude Sigint/photography mission was also undertaken by the RB-57 Canberra.

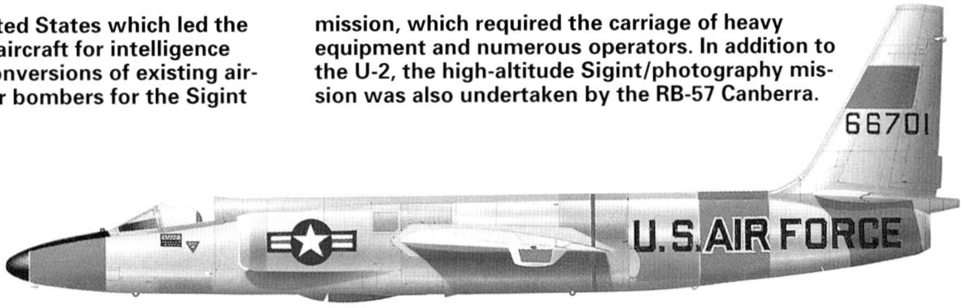

Lockheed RB-69A
Below left: A little-known variant of the US Navy's P-2 Neptune, the B-69 was used for secret missions around the fringes of Soviet and WarPac territory in the late 1950s and early 1960s. Its primary function was the collection of SIGINT and ELINT about Soviet radar systems and air defence networks.

Lockheed U-2A
Above right: Aircraft 56-6701 is typical of the U-2 fleet, having been recorded in at least 11 different colour schemes and equipment configurations since its early days with the CIA. It is seen here as it appeared soon after transfer to the US Air Force at Edwards AFB Later it was modified as a U-2B and then a U-2C, with a long dorsal 'canoe' and many special sensor fits.

General Dynamics B-57F
Left: Standard Canberras and Martin RB-57Ds (with extended wings) were widely used for high-altitude reconnaissance, but neither could match the extraordinary RB-57F, which had new outsize wings and auxiliary turbojets.

Boeing RB-47H
Right: The Sigint-dedicated Stratojet was covered in antennas to serve its onboard systems. Four 'Crows' (electronic warfare officers) were crammed into the swollen converted bomb bay to operate the equipment.

The U-2 Incident

The National Air and Space Administration's press release of May 5 1960 began prosaically enough. "One of our U-2 research planes, in use since 1956 in a continuing program to study high-altitude meteorological conditions, has been missing since 9 o'clock Sunday morning when its pilot reported that he was having oxygen difficulties over Lake Van, Turkey."

NASA went on say, amongst other things, that the aircraft was based at Incirlik in Turkey, that it carried air sampling equipment, that the pilot was a civilian employee of NASA, and that if he had blacked out, the automatic pilot would have kept the plane on a northeasterly course.

The story was almost completely fabricated. A U-2 had in fact been lost, but far from being over the Lake Van area of Turkey, it had been close to the town of Sverdlovsk, deep inside the Soviet Union. This was indeed to the northeast of the position reported by NASA, but the aircraft had been nowhere near Turkey. Neither had it been anything to do with NASA.

At 0626 on the morning of 1 May 1960, Francis Gary Powers took off from Peshawar in Pakistan. The U-2 he was flying belonged to the Central Intelligence Agency, and his mission was to photograph Soviet missile facilities at Tyuratam, going on to spy on what was believed to be a new long-range missile site at Plesetsk. From there he would recover to the Norwegian base at Bodo, having completed the first spy flight clear across the USSR.

The flight had not gone well: Powers was experiencing difficulties with the autopilot, the weather was not favourable, and he was drifting off course.

Through his drift sight, Powers had seen numerous Soviet fighters trying to intercept, and later evidence showed that many missiles had been fired to no effect. But three hours and 27 minutes into the flight, Powers felt an explosion which ripped the tail from his aircraft. He has been hit by an SA-2 'Guideline' missile, apparently at a height of 20000m (nearly 68,000 feet). There is some debate about this figure – the Soviets agreed with Powers' estimate, but evidence has been collected that for at least part of the flight the U-2 was several thousand feet lower.

Whatever the truth of the matter, there were two incontrovertible facts. Powers had not been able to trigger the destruct mechanism. The Soviets salvaged the wreckage, including its intelligence gathering equipment and now had hard evidence that the American spyflights were real. Perhaps more importantly, the flight showed that modern surface-to-air missiles meant that altitude was no longer a guarantee of safety, prompting a complete change in the way all air forces looked at war in the air.

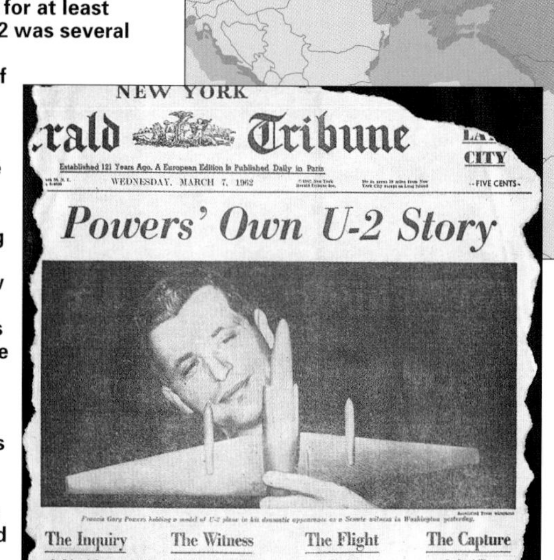
NEW YORK
.rald Tribune
Established 121 Years Ago. A European Edition Is Published Daily in Paris
WEDNESDAY, MARCH 7, 1962
CITY
FIVE CENTS

Powers' Own U-2 Story

The Inquiry | The Witness | The Flight | The Capture

***Above:* Powers' flight would have been the first complete crossing of the Soviet Union by a spy plane, but the route chosen would have left the U-2 with no fuel reserve at the end of the flight.**

***Left:* Francis Gary Powers was tried by a Soviet court and convicted of spying. He spent two years in jail before being exchanged on 10 February 1962 for the KGB agent Rudolf Abel.**

of safety. The headlong pace of electronic development was making a significant impact on the science of electronic intelligence-gathering

Radar advances in the 1950s led to the early side-looking airborne radar (SLAR) type, which had obvious application to stand-off, over-the-border reconnaissance. The first airborne reconnaissance craft to use a SLAR may have been the mysterious and little-known Lockheed/US Air Force RB-69A. This was a conversion of seven US Navy P2V Neptunes carried out in 1954. A podded SLAR was carried on each side of the rear fuselage, and the aircraft also had a number of other radomes and Elint sensors. They were deployed to Europe and Japan for a time before being reconfigured as standard US Navy Neptunes.

***Left:* Seen flying in company with a standard RB-57A Canberra is a Martin RB-57D. This was the first stretched-wing model and it performed useful peripheral Sigint work in Europe. It was also used by the CIA for intelligence flights over mainland China.**

Their replacement was the Martin RB-57D, a big-wing development of the US version of the English Electric Canberra. This aircraft had been a rival to the U-2 for the CIA contract: although losing, it did receive a limited production order from the US Air Force. It was flown by the same SAC reconnaissance wing that operated a number of U-2As for secondary high-altitude duties – although not for the most sensitive missions, which were the province of the CIA. Some of the RB-57Ds had camera systems, but others had a SLAR faired neatly into the underside of the wing root. They too were flown from Europe and Japan, but suffered wing fatigue problems and were withdrawn from front-line reconnaissance use in 1960.

However, three years later some of them were further modified by General Dynamics with even bigger wings and turbofan engines to make the RB-57F, which was now virtually unrecognisable from the original Canberra. A US-based squadron of the aircraft had sampling of the upper atmosphere as its primary role, taking over from SAC U-2s. It should not be forgotten that minute particles of fall-out from Soviet and Chinese nuclear tests, captured on filter paper by such flights, could subsequently be analysed in laboratories to provide valuable clues to the nuclear capabilities of those countries.

LOOKING OVER THE FENCE

But other RB-57Fs went abroad, to Rhein Main, Germany and Yokota, Japan, to resume border surveillance duties. One of the German-based aircraft was shot down over the Black Sea in 1965 by a Soviet SAM. Two RB-57Fs were supplied to the Pakistan air force under CIA auspices - their Peshawar base was convenient for monitoring test sites in Soviet Kazakhstan. In the 1965 Indo-Pakistan war, one of them was nearly shot down by an example of the first SA-2 SAMs supplied to India: it was an Elint flight, trying to determine the fre quency and precise location of Amritsar radar.

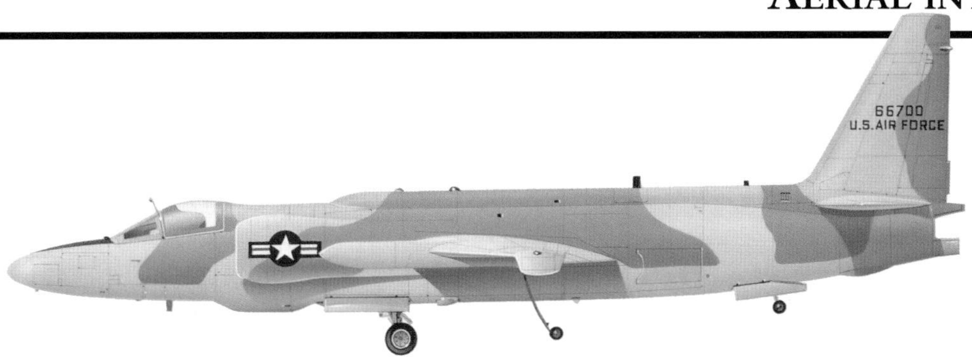

Undercarriage
The U-2 was fitted with a unique undercarriage arrangement, consisting of a central mainwheel which took most of the aircraft's weight, and a small tailwheel with solid tyres. Lateral stability for take-off came from wing-mounted pogo wheels, which dropped away when the aircraft launched. On landing, the U-2 tipped gently on to wingtip skids.

Camouflage
The unusual two-tone grey camouflage adopted by the Pave Onyx/Pave Nickel aircraft had more to do with politics than tactical considerations. Most U-2s wore an all-black scheme as that was what was most effective when the aircraft was at high altitude. However, the black scheme carried with it sinister overtones, and the UK government did not want to draw unwarranted attention to the aircraft which it had allowed to operate from its territory.

Defence
Apart from its extreme operational altitude, the U-2 had little in the way of defenses. Radar receivers provided some warning of impending missile attack, while the System 20 (mounted on the starboard wing trailing edge) was an infra-red detection unit. Some jamming equipment was fitted.

Sensor carriage
U-2s could carry a sizeable sensor payload. The largest items were accommodated in the Q-bay, directly behind the cockpit, and in the nose section. A smaller E-bay was located in the lower fuselage aft of the Q-bay. U-2Cs introduced slipper pods on the wings for further sensor carriage. Additional antennas for Elint/Comint systems were often seen sprouting from the lower fuselage and along the spine.

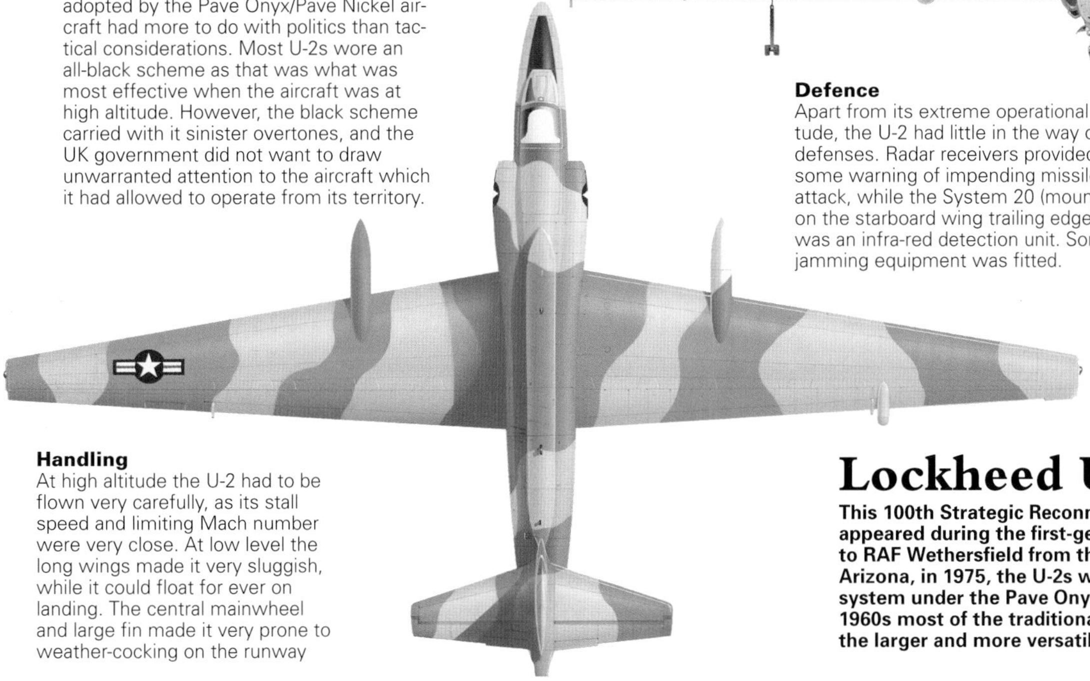

Handling
At high altitude the U-2 had to be flown very carefully, as its stall speed and limiting Mach number were very close. At low level the long wings made it very sluggish, while it could float for ever on landing. The central mainwheel and large fin made it very prone to weather-cocking on the runway

Lockheed U-2C

This 100th Strategic Reconnaissance Wing U-2C is depicted as it appeared during the first-generation U-2's final active deployment. Sent to RAF Wethersfield from the 100th's base at Davis-Monthan AFB, Arizona, in 1975, the U-2s were involved in testing a new radar location system under the Pave Onyx/Pave Nickel programmes. From the late 1960s most of the traditional U-2 missions had been undertaken using the larger and more versatile U-2R second-generation aircraft.

The RB-57F could sustain 22250 m (73,000 ft) in a lightly-loaded condition. The ceiling of British Canberras in the reconnaissance role was much lower, ranging from 15240 m (50,000 ft) for the 1953-vintage PR.Mk 3 model to about 18288 m (60,000 ft) for the PR.Mk 9 in 1959, which had a modified wing root. In between were the PR.Mk 7 and a few long-radome B.Mk 6s for Elint work.

Electronic intelligence was growing in importance, but even though the equipment now being introduced was generally fitted with advanced new filters, the ever-increasing amount of data being returned was beginning to swamp the analysis labs. The move from analog to digital systems promised greater discrimination and automation but was only part of the solution, the other being to perform more of the analysis in real-time by flying greater numbers of Elint system operators.

Left: Much of Britain's contribution to the NATO reconnaissance effort was handled by the Canberra. No. 192/51 Sqn flew Sigint 'specials' while several squadrons used high-altitude photo-platforms like the PR.Mk 7 seen here.

ELINT AIRLINERS

This called for the use of roomier transport-type aircraft. The British took the lead in 1957 when three de Havilland Comet C.Mk 2 jets were allocated to No. 192 Squadron. The RAF's premier Elint squad ron was renumbered No. 51 in the following year, and continued to fly the Comets into the early 1970s, when they were replaced by three specially-modified Nimrods. In the interim, the squadron moved from Watton to Wyton, where it joined the RAF's other long-range reconnaissance outfit, No. 543 Squadron. This unit flew the Vickers Valiant B(PR).Mk 1 followed by the Handley Page Victor SR.Mk 2. The converted V bombers housed large cameras in the bomb bay, but were primarily engaged on radar reconnaissance of the potential approaches to enemy territory for the V-bomber force.

The US Air Force put 13 Elint specialists plus equipment into the Lockheed Hercules and the Soviets promptly shot one of them down when it intruded into Armenia. Some reports claimed that the Soviets had 'lured' the Hercules over the border by altering the power or beam configurations of their two nearby radio beacons to resemble two beacons on the Turkish side.

The US Navy put an even greater number of operators aboard its Lockheed EC-121M Elint aircraft: 31 were on board the example that was shot down by the North Koreans in 1969. These lumbering old Super Constellation conversions were replaced by 1975 with the EP-3E variant of the Lock heed Orion patrol plane, which also had a large crew complement: 15 for the mission, plus reliefs, plus flight crew.

CUBAN MISSILE CRISIS

1962

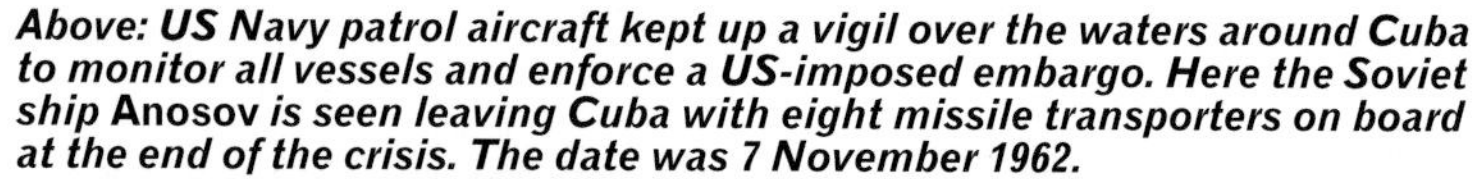

Above: US Navy patrol aircraft kept up a vigil over the waters around Cuba to monitor all vessels and enforce a US-imposed embargo. Here the Soviet ship **Anosov** *is seen leaving Cuba with eight missile transporters on board at the end of the crisis. The date was 7 November 1962.*

It seemed inevitable that the tension between the superpowers would lead to a crisis, with the world on the brink of nuclear war. But the crisis, when it came, did not involve Berlin as many had expected. Instead, it erupted in America's back yard.

The corrupt Batista regime had been in power in Cuba, less than 145 km (90 miles) from the coast of Florida, since 1952. Resistance to Batista centred on the revolutionary movement led by exiled Fidel Castro, who landed at Las Coloradas in Oriente with 81 men. Castro's guerrillas had popular support, and by the end of the 1958 Batista had fled, leaving the liberators to form a new government in Havana. It aligned itself firmly with the Soviet Union, and many of Castro's opponents fled to Florida.

By the time John F. Kennedy took office, a CIA-sponsored plan to overthrow Castro was under way. Supported by various transport aircraft and ex-USAF B-26 bombers painted in false Cuban markings, with communications handled by an old PBY Catalina, more than 1,400 Cuban exiles landed at at Bahia de Cochinos (Bay of Pigs) at 0530 on 17 April 1961. After some small success, the invaders were thrown back ignominiously, leaving 120 exiles dead and 1,200 taken. A few evaded capture and trickled back to the USA.

It was against a background of humiliation over the Bay of Pigs incident and tensions over the building of the Berlin Wall that Kennedy faced his toughest trial. Cuba had requested more arms from the USSR to protect herself against the continuing threat of US interference. By August 1962 the CIA was aware of significant arms shipments, and on 22 August Director John McCone advised the president of the presence of large missiles on the island.

Below: Shot on 4 November, this picture shows the Mariel port facility, complete with four missile transporters (top left), four fuel trailers (bottom left) and a series of oxidiser trailers (right). This kind of photography came courtesy of RF-8s or RF-101s working at low level.

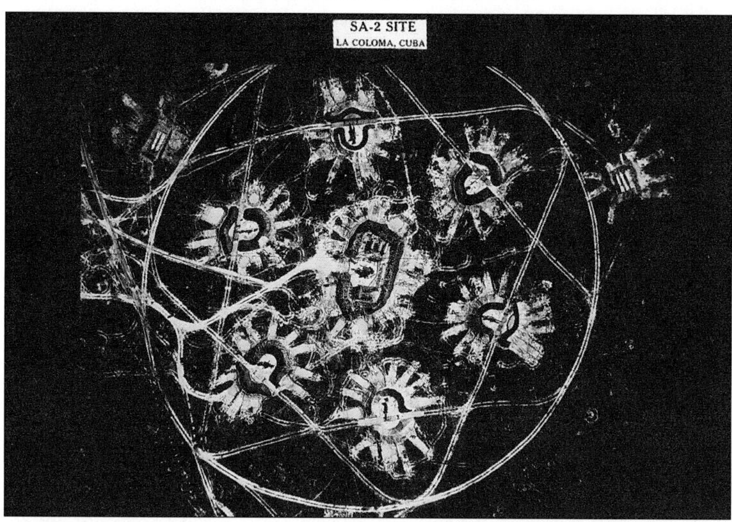

Above: The characteristic pattern is that of an SA-2 surface-to-air missile site, first seen on Cuba by the camera of a high-flying U-2. The placement of SAM defences was the first sign that something worth defending was to arrive in Cuba imminently, sparking the Missile Crisis.

MORE RECONNAISSANCE

Agency Lockheed U-2 flights over Cuba were stepped up, and USN and USAF patrol and reconnaissance aircraft paid special attention to Soviet shipping. A U-2 flight from McCoy AFB on 29 August photographed two SA-2 sites on Cuba, with six more under construction. Photo interpreters became anxious when it was realised that the layout was similar to that of surface-to-air missile (SAM) sites associated with the protection of strategic missile bases in the Soviet Union. On 4 September Kennedy warned Khrushchev that the USA would not tolerate the siting of offensive weapons on Cuba; Khrushchev replied by saying that the Soviet Union had no need to place such weapons in the Caribbean. But just four days later a Lockheed P-2 Neptune of VP-44 photographed the freighter *Omsk* heading for Havana with large oblong canisters on the decks. U-2

Above: Workhorse of the low-level mission over Cuba was the McDonnell RF-101 Voodoo. Relying on speed and surprise for its defence, it was very successful in maintaining a steady flow of photographs to the US command.

flights were again stepped up.

Reconnaissance flights showed more construction work, and on 10 October the USAF 4080th SRW formally assumed responsibility for overflights from the CIA, using Agency U-2E variants equipped with electronic countermeasures equipment. The overt reason for the transfer to the USAF was the threat from SA-2 missiles, but in fact the CIA was not in good odour with the authorities after the Bay of Pigs fiasco and numerous intelligence errors over Berlin.

On 14 October Major Steve Heyser flew a U-2 over Cuba for just six minutes, during which time he took 928 pictures of two sites at San Cristobal and Sagua la Grande. Processed on the following day the photographs were rushed to President Kennedy on 16 October. They clearly showed SS-4 'Sandal' medium-range ballistic missile (MRBM) sites in an advanced state of preparation. Low-level reconnaissance flights by McDonnell RF-101Cs of the 29th TRS revealed more missile sites at Guanajay and Remedios.

The Soviet Union was applying pressure to gain concessions over Berlin and possibly the removal of 45 Jupiter and 60 Thor IRBMs from Italy, Turkey and England. On 22 October a 'quarantine' (blockade) of Cuba was announced. Strategic Air Command was put on full alert and its bombers dispersed to civilian airports whilst naval vessels raced to the Caribbean to enforce the blockade. Air Defense and Tactical Air Commands moved units south to Florida. The US base at Guantanamo Bay on Cuba was reinforced with a garrison of 8,000 US Marines and sailors and Task Force 135 was established to defend the base; ships in the force included the carriers USS *Enterprise* (CVN-65) and USS *Independence* (CVA-62). The quarantine was enforced by units of Task Force 136, which comprised 180 vessels including the carrier USS *Essex* (CVS-9) with two units of Grumman S2F-1 Trackers.

Left: The US Navy's contribution to the tactical reconnaissance effort was handled by the Vought RF-8As of VFP-62, although they flew from bases in Florida rather than carrier decks. Marine squadron VMCJ-2 also flew photo-Crusaders on missions over Cuba.

Soviets back down

Khrushchev wrote to Kennedy on 26 October accepting the American terms for the removal of offensive weapons, which by now included 44 Ilyushin Il-28 bombers being as sembled at San Julian, but only in exchange for American removal of the Jupiter missiles, which in fact Kennedy had previously ordered.

On 27 October the tension increased as Major Anderson was shot down by an SA-2 and killed on an overflight of naval installations at Banes. Early the following day Soviet intercontinental ballistic missiles (ICBMs) came to full alert as another U-2 inadvertently but embarrassingly overflew the Chukostkiy Peninsula at the eastern tip of Siberia.

At 1000 on 28 October the crisis ended as the Soviets agreed to dismantle the missiles under inspection. But the Il-28s were still being assembled and the quarantine was not lifted until 20 November, by which time the Soviets had agreed to their removal. The first aircraft departed Cuba in crates on 15 December aboard the freighter *Kasimov*.

During the period from 14 October to 6 December the USAF flew 102 U-2 sorties over Cuba, but low-flying aircraft were able to supervise the operation with a versatility unmatched by more remote observation. The following year the superpowers agreed to instal the 'hot-line' telephone link, and as further evidence of the thaw in relations a nuclear test-ban agreement was signed in August.

Cuba's ageing air force

The Communist state of Cuba was only three years old when the Missile Crisis loomed, and it had not yet received fighters from the Soviet Union. The air force relied on a handful of aircraft which were left over from the days of the Batista regime. Later the island state was the recipient of MiG-17s and MiG-21s from the Soviet Union, posing a further threat to the US dominance over the Caribbean region.

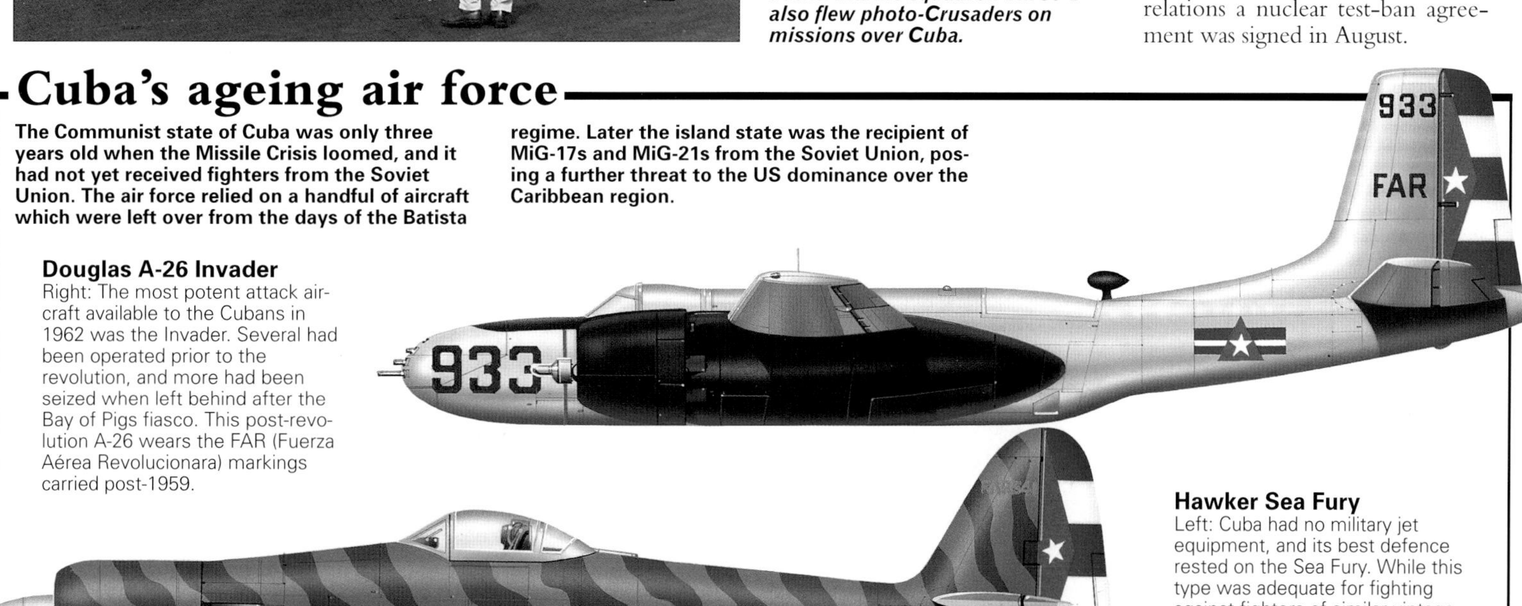

Douglas A-26 Invader

Right: The most potent attack aircraft available to the Cubans in 1962 was the Invader. Several had been operated prior to the revolution, and more had been seized when left behind after the Bay of Pigs fiasco. This post-revolution A-26 wears the FAR (Fuerza Aérea Revolucionara) markings carried post-1959.

Hawker Sea Fury

Left: Cuba had no military jet equipment, and its best defence rested on the Sea Fury. While this type was adequate for fighting against fighters of similar vintage which abounded in the region even in the early 1960s, it was clearly no match for US types.

Central Front Confrontation

1965-1990

For four decades, the world stood poised on the brink of nuclear destruction as the competing world views of the United States and the Soviet Union brought them into Cold War conflict. The most obvious manifestation of superpower rivalry came in the heartland of Europe, where the two titanic military alliances they headed faced each other with the most powerful concentration of military force the world has ever seen.

Fortunately for the human race, Europe's Central Front never exploded into battle, but the Cold War rivalry between NATO and the armies of the Warsaw Pact was still the dominant influence on military technology in the second half of the 20th Century. Weapons development, which had boomed through the 1950s, advanced with even more dizzying speed through the 1960s and 1970s. And while one side in the conflict decided to apply the new technology to an older type of war, the other began to grope to whole new concept of battle.

Whilst the West devoted considerable effort towards divining the minute details of Soviet intentions and capabilities, intelligence analysts were fully aware of the basic plan of any future assault on the Free World. Not only were the broad tactics known, but also the precise date of their origin: 22 June 1941.

It was on this day more than half a century ago that Hitler invaded his former ally, the Soviet Union. The Luftwaffe established massive air superiority above the advancing German army and shattered its counterpart in the air and on the airfields. These tactics almost annihilated the air and land forces of the Soviet Union and left no doubt in

Above: The opening rounds of any war on the Central Front would have involved mass attacks on airfields. Although NATO had a technological superiority, the Warsaw Pact had numbers on its side. Low-level fighter-bombers such as the MiG-27 were available in abundance.

Below: Soviet attackers like this Sukhoi Su-7 'Fitter' were crude by comparison with their Western counterparts, but might well have been devastatingly effective, since they could have overwhelmed NATO defences by sheer weight of numbers.

Right: Although it was the nuclear threat which held sway over the Central Front, the menace of chemical and biological warfare was never far away. Here a MiG-21 is seen spraying water during a chemical warfare trial.

Below: Warsaw Pact forces were well-versed in the art of airborne assault, and large numbers of Mil Mi-8s were available. Unlike NATO's assault helicopters, Soviet Mi-8s carried heavy armament to put down suppressive fire.

Threat from the East

Forward-based in the Warsaw Pact countries, the Soviet Union possessed a mighty armada of attack aircraft, ranging from close support types to nuclear bombers. NATO could not hope to defend itself against an all-out attack, and so a pre-emptive tactical nuclear strike against WarPac airfields was the only practical means of defence.

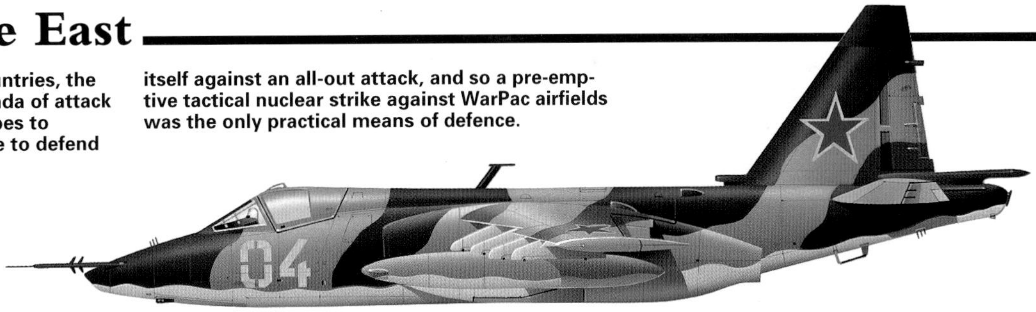

Sukhoi Su-25 'Frogfoot'
Right: Forged in battle over Afghanistan, the Su-25 could carry a heavy weapons load, and was ideal for close support and helicopter escort operations. Most were forward deployed in East Germany, located close to the potential front-line.

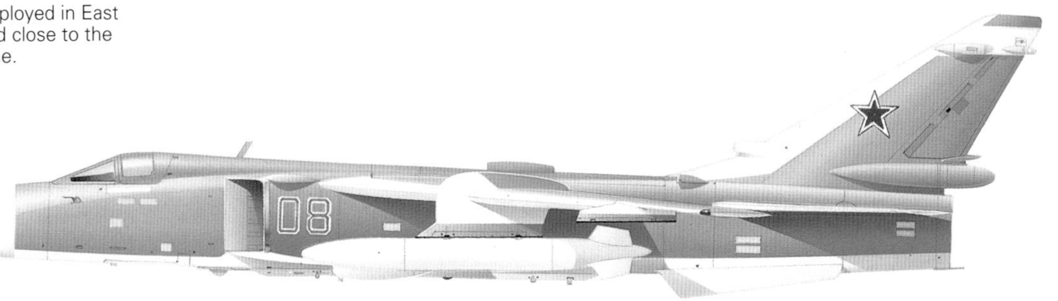

Sukhoi Su-24 'Fencer'
Left: WarPac's equivalent of the F-111 or Tornado, the Su-24 regiments were based in eastern East Germany and western Poland. From these bases they would have struck deep into NATO territory, hitting airfields and other key installations.

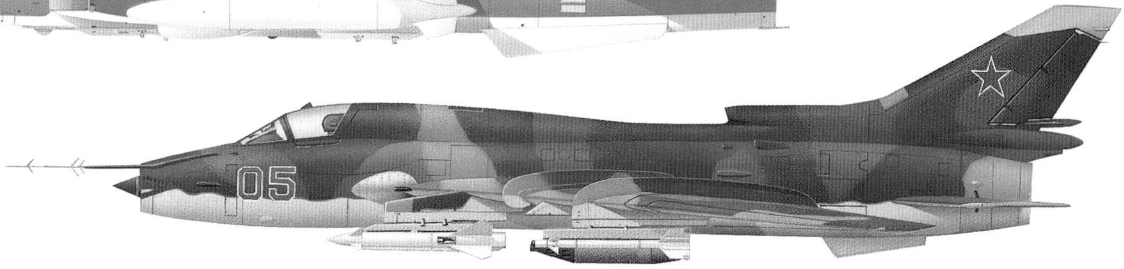

Sukhoi Su-17 'Fitter'
Right: A variable-geometry version of the earlier Su-7, the Su-17 was a far more capable attacker, offering limited precision-guided missile capability. Two regiments were in East Germany, with others further back from the front-line.

Above: The Su-25 was the Soviet answer to the A-10, but it was considerably faster (although not as capable), rendering it less vulnerable over the Central Front battlefield. Most Soviet attack aircraft had rough-field capability.

the minds of post-war Soviet planners that Blitzkrieg was by far the most effective form of assault.

Should the Warsaw Pact have marched against Western Europe in a war of conventional or limited NBC (Nuclear, Biological and Chemical) weaponry, it would have had the aggressor's privilege of choosing the time of attack. Again, there was no secret about timing: it would have been on, or shortly before a weekend or holiday, unless the build-up of diplomatic tension had lasted long enough to allow NATO forces to be placed on full alert. The Soviet Union also vowed publicly that no battles were be fought on its own territory, meaning that conflict would have taken place on Western European ground or that of its Warsaw Pact allies.

According to Soviet doctrine: 'the offensive is the basic form of combat action. Only by a resolute attack conducted at great tempo and in great depth is the destruction of the enemy achieved.'

As the Soviet armies moved forward, the main role for air power would have been the elimination of threats before they could materialise, or countering them before they are able to press home an attack. Strike bombers like the Sukhoi Su-24 'Flanker' were tasked with penetrating enemy defences to destroy key military targets such as command and control centres, airfields and runways. Other tactical aircraft – in the early days MiG-15s, 17s and Sukhoi-7s, succeeded by much more advanced types such as MiG-27s and Su-22s – would have ranged the rear areas, destroying enemy reserves, cutting lines of communication and supply and blocking reinforcements.

Provision of the air assets for these operations was the responsibility of Frontal Aviation (Frontovaya Aviatsiya) a component of the Soviet air forces, whose aircraft were assigned to Frontal Air Armies under the control of the local army group commander. Originally intended to provide a defensive umbrella over the troops advancing beneath, by the late 1960s Frontal Aviation's role was changing.

Quality and Quantity

Having usefully employed the 1970s period of 'detente' with the West to build up Frontal Aviation, the Soviet Union by the 1980s had a powerful tactical air arm at its disposal. Optimised for support of an advancing army and with the additional capability to attack targets well behind the battle line, Frontovaya Aviatsiya was by its size and composition an overtly offensive force optimised to emulate the spectacular success of the Blitzkrieg form of attack.

By the early 1980s, Frontal Aviation operated some 5,000 fixed-wing aircraft and 3,250 helicopters, up to 70 per cent of which were based in Eastern Europe (including the westernmost military districts of the Soviet Union).

The Soviets were great believers in confusing the enemy, and parachute attacks played a big part in their plans. Airborne troops were tasked with causing confusion behind the lines as well as with seizing port facilities and key airfields, where they could be reinforced by sea or by air.

Although air units could inflict considerable damage on the enemy, their main purpose in a combined arms offensive was to prepare for the main attack of fast-moving armoured forces supported by ground-attack aircraft and heavy artillery.

Right: One of the most feared weapons in the land war was the Mil Mi-24 'Hind' armed assault helicopter. Its heavy weapon load, including anti-tank missiles, made it a powerful gunship, while its internal cabin could be used to carry up to eight troops. 'Hinds' were based throughout East Germany, flying alongside Mi-8s in assault regiments.

Left: Mass procurement of US types by the European NATO nations went some way to redressing the imbalance of numbers. The Republic F-84F was the standard ground attack platform for many years, able to carry tactical nuclear weapons.

Above: Reforger exercises demonstrated the speed with which US forces could be deployed to Europe in time of tension. However, the deployment was mainly by sea, and would not have been quick enough to help in the face of a full-scale surprise attack.

These assaults would have been pressed in army strength or larger along several axes. Speed was considered to be of the essence, so while the main punch of the assault was provided by armoured forces, paratroopers and heliborne assault troops supported by gunship helicopters and close-support aircraft would have provided the mobile element in the attack.

Meanwhile, fast-moving flanking forces were intended to go round the main enemy force, either to attack from the side or the rear, or to cut the enemy's lines of communication. The deployment of large numbers of assault helicopters and helicopter gunships in the 1970s meant that such attacks could then have been pressed home much faster than with land- or vehicle-based troops.

Soviet planning expected that all elements of an attack would work very closely together. The main assault troops were supported by large numbers of artillery pieces. Once they were engaged, however, their most flexible and responsive weapon was close air support, provided by the ground-attack fighters of Frontal Aviation and by the army's own helicopter gunships.

Skill and Technology

Hopelessly outnumbered by Warsaw Pact forces in the tank equation, the NATO allies relied on skill and technology to redress the balance. Highly trained aircrew and state-of-the-art aircraft, electronics and weapons produced very impressive displays of anti-tank firepower, but they were themselves vulnerable. The big question for western planners was 'will enough of our weapons platforms survive WarPac's initial strikes and the massive Soviet battlefield air defence system to be able to stop an endless torrent of enemy tanks?'

And it could really have been a torrent. In the early 1980s there were some 25,000 main battle tanks stationed in Central Europe, of which 18,000 were east of the Iron Curtain. Outnumbered 2.5 to 1, NATO's 7,000 battle tanks also faced 10,200 helicopter- or vehicle-mounted anti-tank guided weapon systems.

European strategy on the central front took several forms. Germany played a key role, in spite of some initial French reservations. Despite some indifference from its people West Germany's government set about forming fighting services in the mid-1950s. Re-born in September 1956, the Luftwaffe was the subject of such a large build-up that a mere four years later it included 62,000 personnel, 375 Republic F-84F Thunderstreaks in five wings, 108 RF-84F Thunderflashes in two wings and 225 North American F-86 Sabres in three wings, plus training, transport and support units. An early priority was to obtain more modern equipment. Lockheed offered a multi-role version of the Starfighter, and with new avionics and a sizzling Mach 2 capability, the F-104G Super Starfighter was adopted for fighter-bomber, nuclear strike and reconnaissance duties as well as in its original role. F-104s also armed Belgium, Canada, Denmark, Greece, Italy, the Netherlands, Norway and Turkey.

The second major plank in NATO's defences was the commitment of large American forces to European defence. The North American F-100 Super Sabres, McDonnell F-101 Voodoos and Douglas B-66 Destroyers of the late 1950s gave way to McDonnell Douglas F-4 Phantoms, General Dynamics F-111s and General Dynamics F-16 Fighting Falcons.

Regular deployment exercises were also held for US-based units. The most impressive of these was the 'Reforger' (REinforcement of FOrces in GERmany) series which included a massive airlift of units over the Atlantic, although it must be remembered that, Lockheed C-141 StarLifters and C-5 Galaxies notwithstanding, the major resupply in wartime would be by sea.

Canadian contribution

Canada, too, with its particular affiliations to the UK and France, was represented in Europe. Most of the 200 CF-104 Starfighters obtained for what was then the Royal Canadian Air Force replaced European-based Canadair/North

Left: Following the F-84F as NATO's principal strike platform was the Lockheed F-104 Starfighter, which also undertook the fighter and reconnaissance missions. West Germany was the largest user, with four wings dedicated to nuclear strike, two for reconnaissance, two for maritime strike and two for interception.

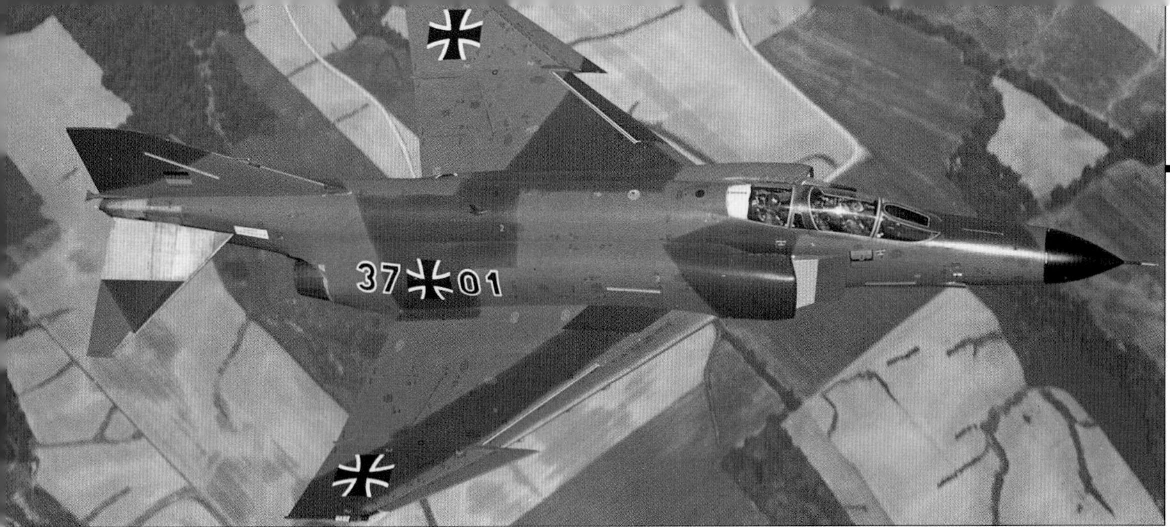

Left: *In the face of huge numbers, NATO could respond only by increasing capability. The F-4 Phantom was an advanced interceptor, but those purchased by West Germany were hampered by the political decision to carry only short-range Sidewinder missiles.*

Below: France's Dassault Mirage IIIC was a potent interceptor which was later evolved into the multi-role Mirage IIIE.

Above: Canada maintained a strong presence in the 4ATAF area with CF-104 Starfighters. The Canadian aircraft were optimised for nuclear strike, carrying a single US-owned B57 weapon which was held under a dual-key arrangement.

American F-86 Sabres and Canadair CF-100 Canucks from 1962 onwards, and were themselves replaced by McDonnell Douglas CF-18 Hornets.

France was a major component of NATO at the start of the supersonic era and contributed tactical fighters to the 4th Allied Tactical Air Force as well as discharging its obligations under the four-power air traffic agreement covering access to Berlin. French pioneering in high-speed flight found its reward in the Mirage III, which entered service in 1962 as a Mach 2 fighter bomber and interceptor. Forming the backbone of French tactical and air defence commands, the Mirage III found a ready export market (mostly outside NATO) and was joined in 1964 by a scaled-up, twin engine bomber version, designated Mirage IVA.

By 1966, France had a nuclear deterrent (popularly termed the Force de Frappe) which restored what was seen to be its status in the world. In March 1966, President de Gaulle announced that France was leaving NATO. The country main-

USAF in Europe

The cornerstone of NATO's defence in Central Europe were the United States Air Forces in Europe (USAFE). Fighters, fighter-bombers and reconnaissance platforms were based in sizeable numbers in West Germany and France (until 1964) as part of the 4th ATAF, backed up by longer-range nuclear bombers in the United Kingdom, which never really lost its tag of being the Americans' permanent aircraft-carrier off the coast of Europe. Additional USAFE assets guarded the Southern Flank, being based in Spain and Italy.

Left: Qualitatively superior to their Soviet counterparts, USAFE tactical aircraft were flown by well-trained and highly-motivated crews. European-based aircraft were regularly bolstered by transatlantic deployments. This quartet of F-100Cs is seen over a German city.

Below left: The F-4E Phantom became the backbone of USAFE during the 1970s. It could fly the fighter and strike roles with equal ease. This machine is from the Ramstein-based 86th TFW.

Below: Two wings of General Dynamics F-111s were stationed in England. These were central to NATO's Follow-on Forces Attack concept of deep (nuclear) interdiction.

Nato Anti-tank helicopters

*Above: For the British the Westland Lynx AH.Mk 1 was available for anti-armour missions, armed with eight **TOW** missiles. It also had a capacious cabin, allowing it to reposition Milan anti-tank teams.*

*Above: Demonstrating its ability to hide in the vegetation (made safer by its shrouded fenestron tail rotor) this Aérospatiale SA 342 Gazelle is armed with four **HOT** anti-tank missile tubes.*

*Below: West Germany's Heeresflieger adopted the MBB BO105 as its PAH-1 anti-armour helicopter. Six **HOT** missiles could be carried and the type was also a useful scout.*

*Below: King of the anti-armour helicopters was the Bell AH-1 Cobra, armed with eight **TOWs**. The type had originated as a pure gunship for close support, but matured as an anti-tank weapon.*

Faced with a huge disparity in tank numbers, NATO rapidly seized on the specialist anti-armour helicopter as a means of restoring some parity. Naturally the US Army led the way, deploying large numbers of Bell AH-1 Cobras (augmented by AH-64 Apaches in the final years of the Cold War). The employment of anti-armour helicopters was intended to bottle up the Warsaw Pact armoured thrusts in key chokepoints, enabling other weapon systems to be brought to bear on the halted columns. After the Cold War, most Western military officers privately questioned whether anything short of a massive, pre-emptive tactical nuclear strike could have halted the Red Army.

tained a residual presence on the North Atlantic Council, but did not participate in the Defence Planning Committee.

On the other side of the English Channel, the UK did at least appear to be adding forces to NATO, although this was only a reassignment of units already in being. The UK was vital to NATO as the rear depot for assembling forces and holding reserves in the event of a European war. Having special responsibilities outside Europe, the UK retained certain elements under national control, but assigned RAF Strike Command in its entirety to NATO in April 1975. As such, the remainder of the UK's combat aircraft joined those of RAF Germany under NATO stewardship. RAFG, equipped with Hunters and Canberras at the start of the 1960s, progressively re-equipped with V/STOL Harriers, Jaguars, F-4 Phantoms and Tornadoes.

Benelux Co-operation

Smaller nations of NATO continued to assign the bulk of their armed forces to mutual defence. This was particularly true of the central area represented by Belgium, Luxembourg and the Netherlands. The Belgium and the Netherlands even had a joint pilot-training programme until they selected different Republic F/RF-84 replacements in the late 1960s: Dassault Mirage 5s and Canadair/Northrop NF-5As respectively. Both then elected to license produce F-16 Fighting Falcons as a Starfighter follow-on.

Denmark and Norway, too,were Fighting Falcon customers, but instead of adding depth to the Central Front, they were on the exposed Northern Flank. Their armed forces were small, for which reason they were likely to have been one of the main deployment areas for NATO's Allied Command Europe Mobile Force (AMF).

Approved by the NATO Council in September 1961, the AMF was established as a multi-national, variable-content force ready to be sent at short notice to any threatened area. It was seen to have the deterrent effect of stressing the unity of NATO and the central theme that 'an armed attack against one [is] an attack against all'. Often termed the 'NATO Fire Brigade', the AMF regular mounted training exercises involving the armed services of all members.

Britain's 'Jump-jet'

The fact that airfields would be high on the list for attack on Day One of any central European war vexed military commanders on both sides of the Iron Curtain. While WarPac invested heavily in dispersed-base operations, with all key infrastructure being mobile and with highway strips ready prepared, NATO toyed with vertical take-off as a means of continuing the war when there were no airfields left. The Harrier was the only practical outcome of this line of thinking.

Hawker Siddeley Harrier

Right: Developed with the Central Front in mind, the Harrier was designed to operate from woods, supermarket car parks or literally anywhere it could find cover and a flat place to land and take off. Three squadrons (including No. 20, illustrated) were deployed to West Germany, based close to the front-line

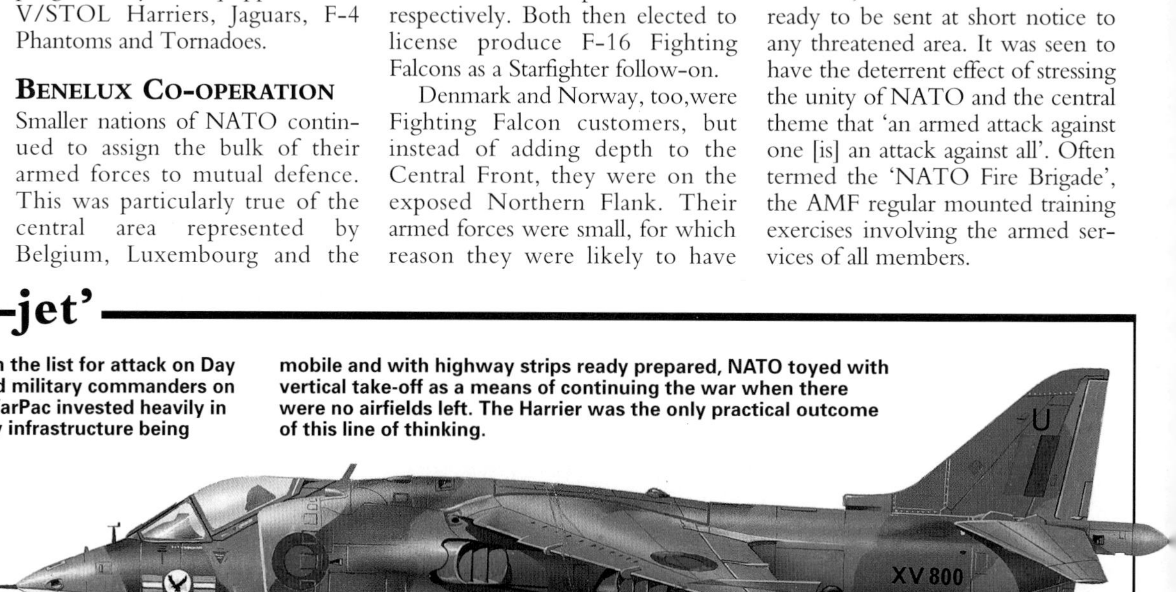

Fairchild A-10A

Although officially christened the Thunderbolt II, the A-10 was known universally as the 'Warthog'. Its mission was primarily anti-armour, and a six-squadron wing was established in the UK, each squadron having a forward operating location in West Germany. A-10 pilots regularly flew from the FOLs, becoming familiar with the landmarks that they would encounter if they ever had to go to war.

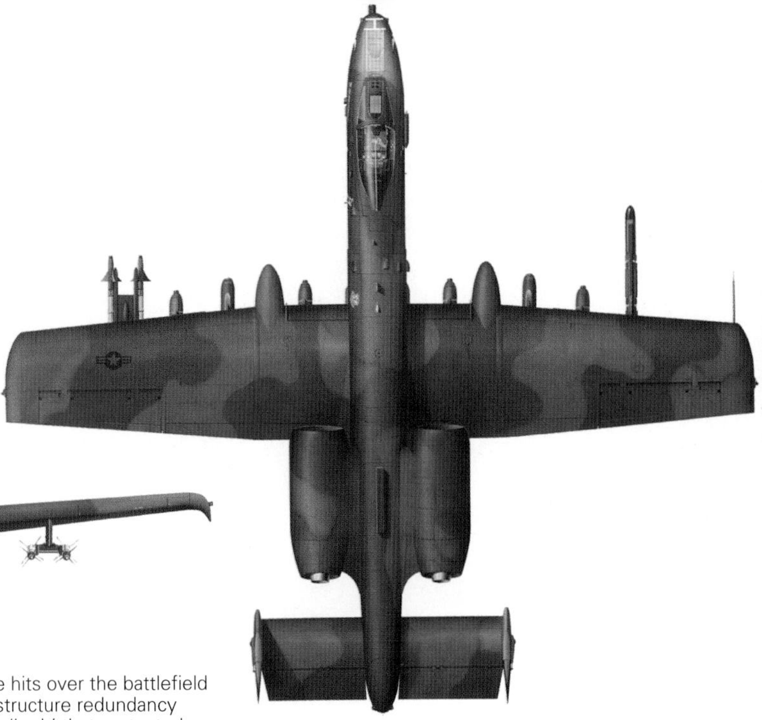

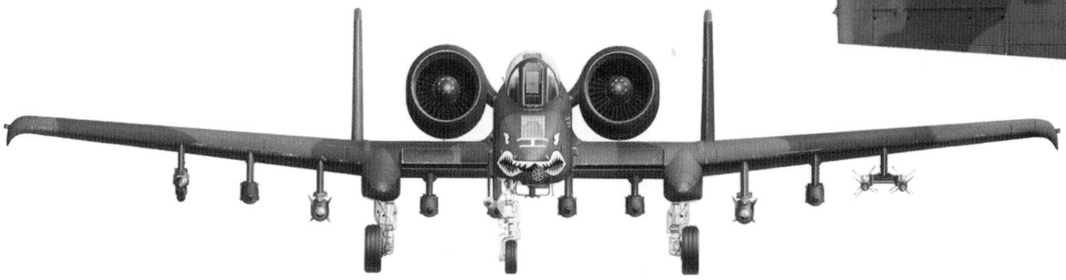

Manoeuvrability
Relatively large and slow, the A-10 relied on rapid jinking and low-level agility for its defence. The aircraft was designed with neutral stability and large control surfaces to make it highly responsive to any control inputs.

Survivability
The A-10 was expected to sustain groundfire hits over the battlefield and was designed accordingly. System and structure redundancy were key features, as was the huge titanium 'bath' that protected the pilot and the ammunition.

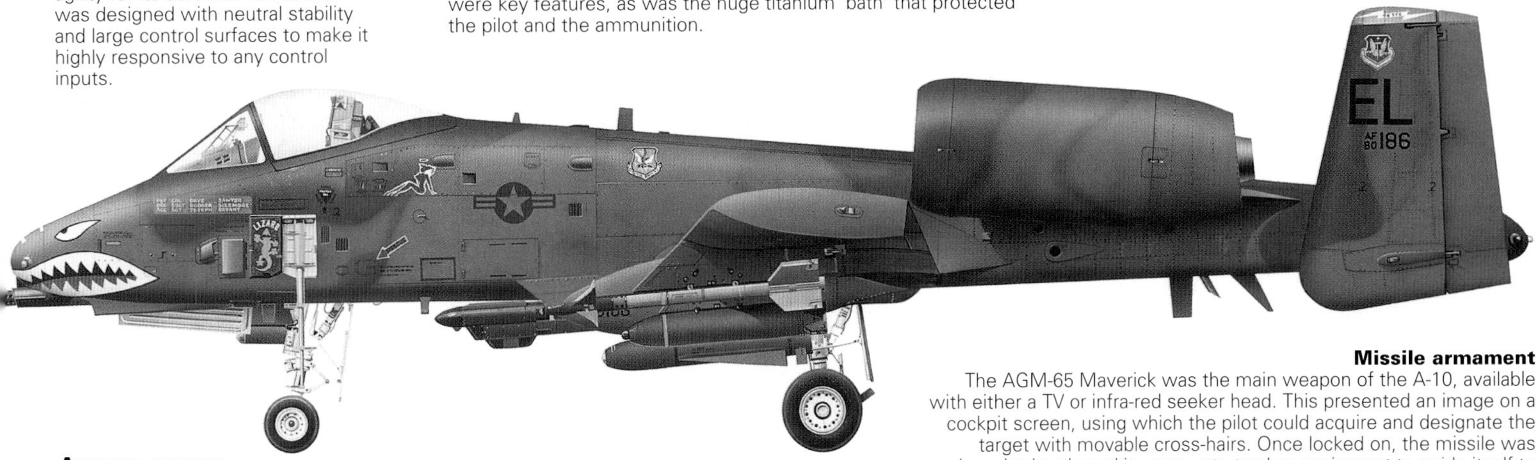

Missile armament
The AGM-65 Maverick was the main weapon of the A-10, available with either a TV or infra-red seeker head. This presented an image on a cockpit screen, using which the pilot could acquire and designate the target with movable cross-hairs. Once locked on, the missile was launched and used its own auto-tracker equipment to guide itself to the target. This allowed the A-10 to take evasive action as soon as the missile had been launched.

Avenger cannon
The weapon with which the A-10 was most associated was its massive General Electric GAU-8/A cannon. This was fitted with seven 30-mm barrels and fired depleted uranium (non-radioactive) rounds of great density, interspersed with high explosive. The gun itself was mounted slightly offset to port, so that the firing barrel was on the aircraft's centreline. Firing at up to 4,200 rounds per minute, the gun could easily decelerate the aircraft alarmingly if used for too long a burst.

***Above and left:* NATO forces evaluated and occasionally ran exercises in dispersed operations, using autobahns as runways, but never embraced the concept the way WarPac units did. Even runway lighting at Soviet bases was truck-mounted so that it could move to a nearby highway strip at a moment's notice.**

***Right:* The business end of an A-10 is dominated by the GAU-8/A cannon. This powerful weapon could out-range light AAA guns, but in most cases 'Hog' pilots preferred to tackle targets with the longer-ranged Maverick missile.**

Spies in the skies

1965-1992

Left: Many might have thought the U-2's career had come to an abrupt end in 1960 when Francis Gary Powers was shot down over Sverdlovsk, but the type continues to be vital to US intelligence-gathering capability. In the mid-1960s the U-2R was developed, essentially a new, much larger design utilising only the engine and general layout of its predecessor. Seeing action in Vietnam, the Middle East and during the Gulf War, the U-2R is still highly prized for its ability to produce Comint, Elint and radar imagery from high-altitude.

Below: Illustrating the type of reach the U-2R's sensors can provide is this image of San Francisco Bay taken by a NASA-operated ER-2 (a derivative of the U-2R).

Modern reconnaissance has split into two main areas of activity. Strategic reconnaissance is designed to help create the 'big picture' for high commands and national authorities, while tactical reconnaissance is dedicated to providing operational and tactical information for ground forces.

Intelligence comes in three varieties. Humint (human intelligence) is the stuff of spy novels with agents in target countries gathering a wide variety of information, but which has little to do with spy aircraft.

Imagery involves obtaining photographic, infra-red, or radar images of particular areas. Aircraft and satellites are the major means of obtaining such information. Lastly, the vast field of Sigint (signals intelligence) covers communications intelligence, electronic intelligence and telemetry intelligence, among others.

SHEDDING LIGHT

In peace or war, good intelligence is vital. Without it you are like a man searching for a black cat in a darkened room: you know it is there, somewhere, but finding it will be down to blind chance. Reconnaissance is the light which enables you to do the job.

The basic and oldest-established form of reconnaissance involves making images of a target area. In the old ballooning days it involved a man with a pencil and paper making sketches of enemy fortifications, but soon aircraft were carrying cameras into the skies. Today, the camera shooting black-and-white film is still an important reconnaissance tool, although it is a far cry from the ones you would use to take your holiday snaps. Long focal lengths, high-technology optics and superfine film mean that a satellite in orbit can take a pictures with a

High Flyers

Apart from the two SR-71As which were returned to service in 1996, the USAF's U-2 is the only high-altitude reconnaissance platform in service today. The modular payload carriage, illustrated by this U-2EPX (a cancelled US Navy maritime patrol variant), provides the U-2 with great versatility. Imaging sensors include the ASARS-2 radar and SYERS camera, either of which can be carried in the nose. The former produces picture-quality radar images, and now includes a moving-target function for spotting vehicles on the move. The SYERS is a very long focal length optical sensor recording data electronically rather than on film. A wide-band Comint and Elint system is usually carried to provide synergistic multi-sensor coverage across long distances. Data can be downlinked to ground stations for real-time analysis, or uplinked via the Senior Span equipment (carried in a dorsal fairing) to satellites for global relay. In the 1990s the fleet was re-engined, raising the designation to U-2S.

Right: When designing the U-2R, Lockheed engineers made the aircraft easier to land than its predecessors, although it still takes a skilled pilot. Visible in this view is the rear-view mirror for checking if the aircraft is pulling a contrail, and the underfuselage glass dome for the driftsight optics.

resolution of 7.6 cm (3 in) from ranges of 240 km (150 miles). It's not quite reading someone's newspaper from orbit, but you can probably read the headlines.

Other sensors used to produce imagery include infra-red and video cameras, and radar systems. Modern synthetic aperture radars can produce images of almost photographic quality, and can do so through thick cloud or in the dead of night. Television cameras are also used to transmit information via satellite to ground stations, where intelligence officers can watch the scene below in real time, as it happens.

ELECTRONIC SPYING

Sigint (signals intelligence) is a vast and ever-growing area of reconnaissance, covering the gathering of information across the whole of the electromagnetic spectrum. It splits into a variety of different forms, dealing with deliberate and accidental transmissions. Comint, or communications intelligence, is quite simply eavesdropping on a potential opponent's radio traffic. Many countries have specialised Comint aircraft, sucking up information across all wavebands, and recording them for later analysis.

Of course, much of the information gathered is in code, so the Comint community works closely with the code-breakers. Telint (telemetry intelligence) is a specialised form of Comint, involving the interception of guidance data transmitted between missiles and ground control during tests. Analysis of the data can give precise details of the missile's performance, which is useful information to have when you are negotiating arms treaties.

The primary purpose of a strategic reconnaissance system is to enable national command authorities to assess the military capacity of a target nation during peacetime, and to continue such a task if war breaks out. This kind of operation, carried out continuously over long periods of time, is more properly known as surveillance. Strategic reconnaissance platforms need to gather information about as wide an area as possible in a single pass, so they have in the past tended to be high-altitude craft such as the Lockheed U-2 and the amazing Lockheed SR-71.

Conceived of in 1959 as a U-2 successor, the SR-71 flies faster than Mach 3 at over 30000 m (nearly 100,000 ft), and is in many

Right: First seeing service in 1968 over Vietnam, the Lockheed SR-71 is the world's fastest air-breathing aircraft, combining this performance with an even greater operational altitude than that of the U-2. The type has been used in all of the world's hot-spots.

Above: Both U-2 (illustrated) and SR-71 aircrew wear David Clark pressure suits to protect them in the event of cockpit depressurisation at altitude. The suits are fully sealed, with an orange-coloured outer covering to protect them.

Right: The Lockheed Skunk Works was responsible for both the U-2 and SR-71. Here the ASARS-2 radar development U-2R flies in a rare formation with the resident Palmdale test SR-71A. Both types serve operationally with the 9th Reconnaissance Wing at Beale AFB, California.

respects still ahead of its time. Its first employment was probably by the CIA over China in its pre-series A-12 guise. In the early 1960s the 'Bamboo Curtain' was even more tightly closed than the 'Iron Curtain' and the USA especially wanted to extend its knowledge of what was going on at the Chinese nuclear weapons test sites in deepest Inner Mongolia. The A-12 first flew in 1962, and a few subsequently operated from Okinawa until replaced by SR-71s in 1968. Overflights of China ceased in 1971 when the Sino-American rapprochement began. By this time, control of such reconnaissance assets had passed from the CIA to Strategic Air Command.

In spite of the fact that the 'Blackbird' was not seriously threatened by interception from either aircraft or missiles, it was not used to penetrate Soviet airspace like its predecessor, instead flying its missions along the Soviet border and probing deep with its long-range sensors.

WATCH ON CUBA

The U-2 remains an important platform. CIA U-2s had continued to monitor Cuba and China after being withdrawn from Soviet overflights in 1960, playing a major part in the Cuban missile crisis. U-2 operations over China were mounted from Taiwan using a mix of American and Nationalist Chinese pilots, six of whom were lost to communist air defences, despite the provision of ever-more sophisticated ECM devices on the fragile bird.

The Chinese also bagged a number of US Air Force reconnaissance drones starting in 1964, when a squadron from the SAC U-2 wing moved to the Far East for the first operational deployment of such craft. The 'Lightning Bug' was a development of the Ryan Firebee drone, and had been initiated by the Pentagon as an alternative U-2 replacement. Launched from the modified DC-130 Hercules, the drone flew high altitude photo-runs over southern and eastern China, to be recovered (in theory) by helicopters over friendly territory. Despite their successes, the drones had to fight a US Air Force bureaucracy which heavily favoured manned systems.

SCALED-UP DRAGON

The U-2R was an improved and scaled-up version of the original aircraft, introduced in 1968. It eventually took over the Elint monitoring task out of Osan and also played its part in Vietnam. One was sent to Akrotiri in 1970 to monitor an Israel-Egypt ceasefire, returning after the 1973 Yom Kippur War to perform similar duties on a semi-permanent basis.

Nowadays the bulk of the intelligence used in strategic planning comes from satellites. These look for a wide range of signs of military expansion, from major troop movements or the setting-up of new missile batteries to militarily significant economic changes, such as factories producing ammunition going on to a three-shift, 24-hour production schedule.

The boundary between strategic and tactical reconnaissance is a little blurred. In general, tactical reconnaissance is carried out on behalf of the battlefield commander, and is usually provided by variants of current high-performance aircraft. But strategic systems can also be used for tactical purposes. The TR-1 was a version of the U-2 put back into production in the 1980s to provide battlefield commanders with information, though it has since reverted to the U-2 designation. And SR-71s have made Mach 3 high-altitude reconnaissance flights to check out hostile defences before US military actions in the 1980s, in places like Grenada, Libya and Panama.

The first Soviet airframe which was entirely dedicated to reconnaissance in this period was the Yakovlev design known to NATO as 'Mandrake'. Probably designated Yak-26, this 20500-m (67,255-ft) altitude aircraft utilised a Yak-25 fuselage married to a long, high-aspect ratio wing (as on the U-2). It was in service by 1963 and was reported over the Mediterranean and West Asia. It was replaced by

Above: During the Vietnam War the 100th SRW made widespread use of Ryan AQM-34 drones to gain photographs and Elint data over North Vietnam. The drones were launched from Hercules and recovered by Sikorsky CH-3 helicopters. This aircraft was the high-time drone with 68 missions.

Below: The Yakovlev Yak-25RD 'Mandrake' was the Soviet equivalent of the Martin RB-57D. It was a long-winged version of the Yak-25 fighter, and was used on some high-altitude missions in the Middle East. The aircraft could not match the U-2 for altitude or range capability.

Elint platforms

While high-flying U-2s and SR-71s captured the public's imagination, it was the Sigint aircraft which were the intelligence workhorses of the Cold War, flying daily missions around the Soviet Union and its allies recording and analysing electronic signals. The 55th Strategic Reconnaissance Wing was the premier USAF Sigint unit, exchanging its Boeing RB-47Hs for Boeing RC-135s in the 1960s. These veterans are still very much in service today, their onboard equipment having been continuously updated in response to developments in air defence systems and communications networks.

Boeing RC-135V Rivet Joint

The large internal capacity and excellent range/load performance made the C-135 tanker/transport an obvious choice for a Sigint platform. Eight RC-135Vs and six similar RC-135Ws are currently in service, augmented by a pair of RC-135Us used for more specialist work.

The Sigint suite of the RC-135 is served by large aerials under the fuselage and by batteries of side-facing antennae arranged in cheek fairings. In addition to the flight crew, the RC-135 carries about 17 equipment operators and inflight maintenance technicians.

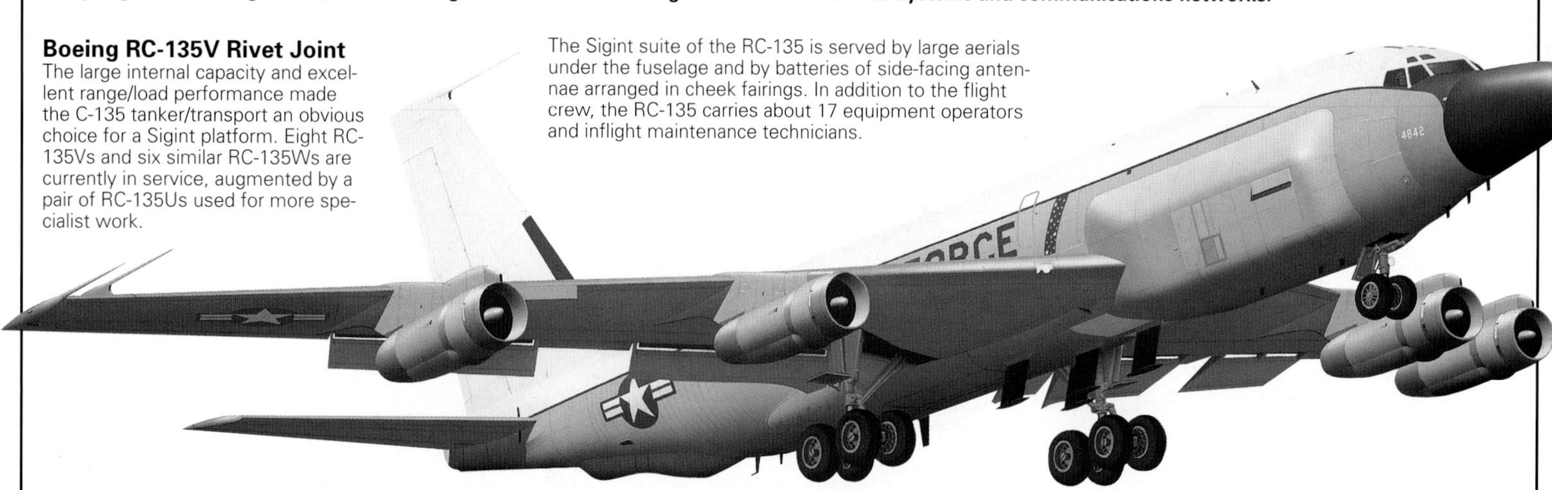

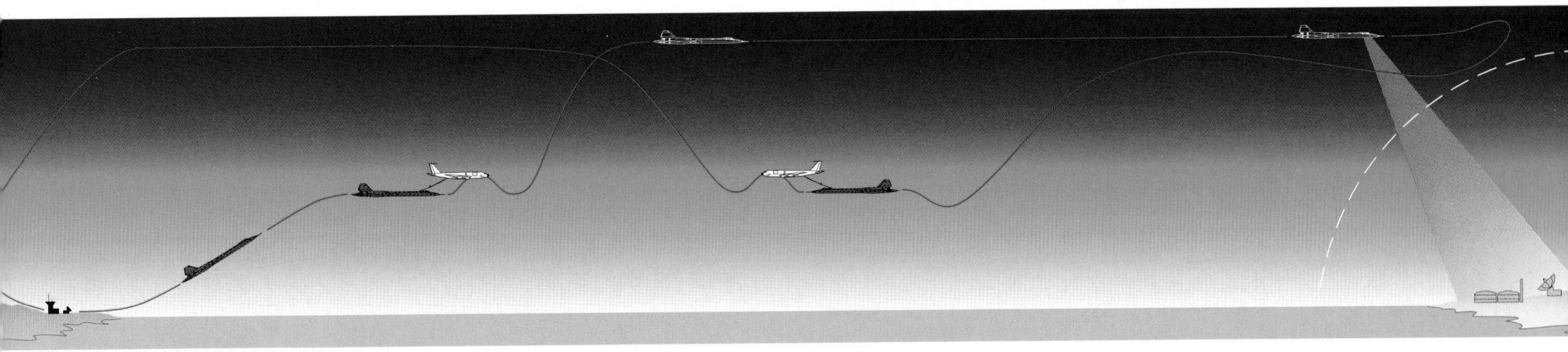

Blackbird mission

Even now, long after most of the fleet has retired, the targets, tactics and results of SR-71 missions remain highly classified. However, the US Air Force allowed its fliers to talk about other areas of their job. Major Duane Noll (pilot) and Major Tom Veltri (Reconnaissance Systems Officer) were one such crew.

"You'll always hear pilots talk about having to look in two or three places at one time," Major Noll said, "but here we have about six or seven things at one time and you're continually scanning the cockpit. In addition to the standard jet instruments we have an inlet system which incorporates another six or eight dials.

"When Tom gets in the sensitive area, he really goes to work. He not only has the cameras, but also the other sensors, the ECM gear and the repeater flight instruments. It's Tom's airplane in the sensitive area. I take off, I get the gas and get him to the target. From that point it's his mission."

Operating so close to unfriendly territory requires precise navigation to avoid embarrassing and potentially dangerous penetrations of hostile airspace. The main unit was the Northrop astro-inertial navigation system, which has a star-tracker peering through a small window behind the cockpit. Major Veltri explained the main problem:

"Because we can only hold 35° of bank, the airplane turns very slowly at supersonic speeds. We're talking about 200 miles to do a 360° turn. Quick turns are out of the question at Mach 3, so you have to keep a close check that everything is running to plan."

Even though the SR-71 was largely unassailable at its operating height and speed, it undoubtedly carried counter-measures, though details on ECM gear were classified. It was chased many times, but was never caught. Nevertheless, on paper it could have been intercepted by a well-placed MiG-25 'Foxbat' or by some of the large Soviet SAMs. As a result, it did not fly over hostile airspace, but used its great altitude and advanced equipment to peer deep into a target area from beyond any national borders.

The US Air Force would not discuss the SR-71's sensors, except for saying that they 'could survey 100,000 square miles [nearly 260000 km²] in one hour'. But it is probably accurate to propose that they fell into three main areas: radar, optical and electronic.

The optical and radar sensors tend to be of the long range oblique type, directed sideways. Black and white photography is still a favourite medium, and the cameras carried by the SR-71 had large magnifications and ultra high resolution for the best possible interpretation. Side-looking radars were particularly good at spotting military installations and armoured formations.

Sigint (signals intelligence) gathering was the third discipline performed by the SR-71, and is considered one of great importance in today's electronic battlefield. Sigint sensors are even more classified than the radars and cameras, and can perform many tasks. The most common is the identification, location and 'fingerprinting' of hostile radars.

Above: A typical SR-71 mission shows the aircraft refuelling soon after take-off to top off its tanks before 'going hot' for its sensor pass on the target area. The aircraft then has to descend for another refuelling to enable it to reach its base safely. The aircraft usually stays outside hostile airspace, using its altitude to peer many miles inside the target territory. During overflights, the great speed keeps it safe from SAMs

Performance
The SR-71 is restricted in normal operations to Mach 3.2, but the aircraft can go faster. Its predecessor, the single-seat A-12 'Cygnus', was lighter and marginally faster, being clocked at Mach 3.56 although it was restricted in operations to Mach 3.3. The A-12 could also sustain an altitude of 27430m (90,000 ft) with ease.

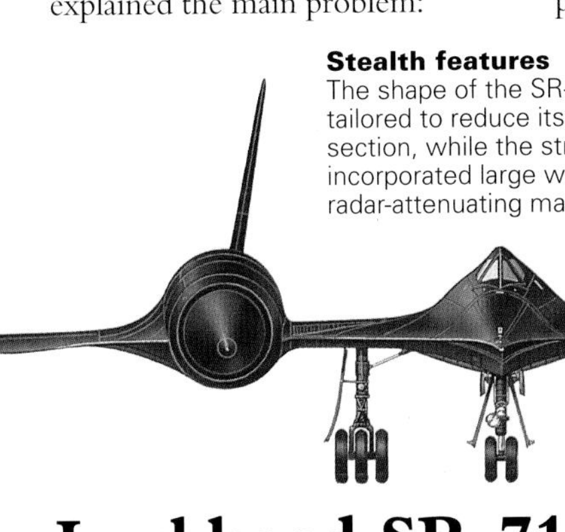

Stealth features
The shape of the SR-71 was tailored to reduce its radar cross-section, while the structure incorporated large wedges of radar-attenuating material.

Powerplant
Power came from two Pratt & Whintey J58 bleed-bypass turbojets. These featured huge moveable inlet spikes.

Lockheed SR-71A

A total of 32 SR-71s was built, of which three were twin-stick trainers. Of these usually only six to ten were ever in active service at one time, based at Beale in the USA, Mildenhall in England and Kadena on Okinawa. Among the most notable missions were those launched from Kadena to photograph Iran.

Sensor carriage
Sensors were mounted in interchangeable nose sections (ASARS-1 radar or panoramic cameras) or in a series of bays along the fuselage bays (close-look Technical Objective cameras). Elint equipment could also be carried.

Blackbird areas of operation

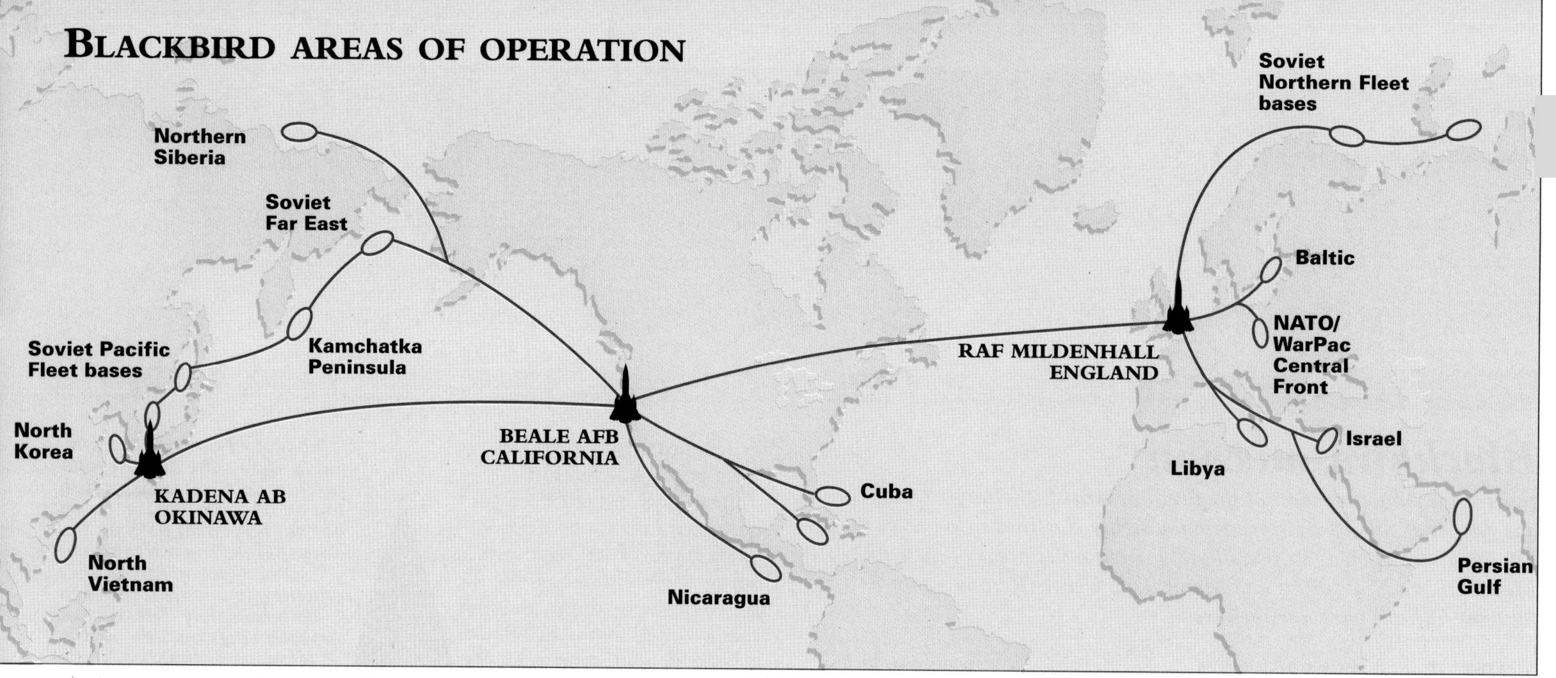

Above: From its three bases worldwide, the SR-71 could easily reach all of the normal trouble spots, and with planning could be expected to visit anywhere else. At Beale the aircraft launched regularly on 'Clipper' sorties around Cuba, and was also used briefly over Nicaragua. From Mildenhall the SR-71 regularly covered the German border, Baltic Sea and North Cape, and ventured into the Mediterranean when required. The Kadena-based 'Habus' plied their trade along the Pacific Rim, targeting Vietnam, China, North Korea and the Soviet Far East. The longest missions were those flown from Kadena to the Persian Gulf, and by aircraft launching from the eastern US seaboard to the Suez canal zone. The latter provided intelligence to the Israelis during the Yom Kippur war, and had to be flown from the US as the UK denied the use of its bases.

Above: The Soviets developed the MiG-25R 'Foxbat-B' as a high- and fast-flying camera ship. Capable of Mach 3.2 for a short burst, the type flew missions over Israel from Egyptian bases. Later SLAR- and Elint- equipped versions were developed.

Below: This Sigint-gatherer is an RC-135D, originally used by the 6th Strategic Wing in Alaska on missions aimed against the Soviet Far East. These aircraft were occasionally deployed to Kadena to augment the Vietnam War effort which was mostly flown by RC-135Ms.

the Mikoyan Gurevich MiG-25R 'Foxbat', which is considered to be an excellent reconnaissance aircraft by Western analysts, even if its interceptor version was downgraded in esteem after one was flown to Japan by a defecting pilot in 1976. The 'Foxbat' first appeared in Egypt during 1970, and it proceeded to defeat Israeli attempts at interception during supersonic, high-altitude runs down the Suez Canal and off the Israeli coast. It also flew unopposed over Iran. The 'Foxbat-B' carries cameras and a small SLAR: the 'Foxbat-D' sacrifices the cameras for a larger SLAR. Top altitude for both models is in the order of 26800 m (87,925 ft) – only the SR-71 routinely flies higher.

Elint (electronic intelligence) is a specialised and very important form of Sigint. Elint aircraft are equipped with highly sensitive receivers tuned to the frequencies of the radar defences of a potential enemy. Their task is the recording and analysis of enemy signals in order to work out the best ways to jam or evade the radar net. Most of the time they stay well clear of the enemy borders, but occasionally they will press in close to set the enemy defences in motion. This provides a wealth of intelligence, on subjects like the sensitivity and range of the defence network and the speed of reaction of its interceptors.

Electronic C-135

A few US Air Force Boeing KC-135 tankers were modified with a SLAR system in 1962, but in 1965 the custom-built RC-135 version of the Model 707 transport was introduced. This aircraft has been the major platform for SAC's Elint collection activities ever since, and has been progressively modified with ever more sophisticated sensors and signal processing equipment. Eleven Elint specialists were carried, and the flight crew was augmented by a relief pilot and a second navigator, essential for the long-endurance, along-the-border flying in remote areas undertaken by these aircraft

At the height of the Cold War the RC-135s operated by the 55th Strategic Reconnaissance Wing flew from their home base at Offutt, and from detachments at Mildenhall in England, Athens in Greece and Kadena in Okinawa. In addition, Eielson AB Alaska and Shemya in the Aleutians have housed a few other exotic Elint conversions of the KC-135.

Naval EW platforms

US Navy shore-based Elint duties are performed by a dedicated variant of the Lockheed P-3 Orion, while carrier-borne duties were performed in succession by variants of the Douglas Skyknight, the Douglas Skywarrior, and most recently by the Lockheed Viking. Britain replaced its electronic warfare Comets in the 1970s with three British Aerospace Nimrod R.Mk 1s, which were supplemented by reconnaissance-dedicated variants of the Handley-Page Victor and the Avro Vulcan. Sweden, France, and Germany also used converted airliners, bombers, or long-range maritime patrol aircraft as electronic listening platforms.

By contrast, the Soviet Union did not follow the trend towards the utilisation of transport airframes as Elint platforms until the mid-1970s, when versions of the Antonov An-12 and Ilyushin Il-18 were first noted. They were also about ten years behind the West in embarking upon routine, long-range reconnaissance bomber probes of opposing defences. In high-altitude supersonic reconnaissance they were also some years in arrears. These delays were largely the result of deficiencies in the Soviets' airframe and electronics technology – never admitted, sometimes uncovered by reconnaissance, and yet still often only realised in the West by hindsight.

Of course, this time-lag was not so crucial when one considers that the equivalent of much of the intelligence that the West was painstakingly ferreting out from behind the Iron Curtain was available to the Soviets for the price of an unclassified electronics handbook or a good road map. Their own atlases deliberately displaced cities and other prominent features in order to con fuse the West.

Above: Blessed with enormous range capability, the Tupolev Tu-95RT 'Bear-D' snooped around Western navies, fingerprinting the radar fits of NATO vessels. The aircraft also had an over-the-horizon missile targeting role.

Right: Tu-16 'Badgers' in various configurations were widely used on Sigint and general reconnaissance flights. But most of their attentions were for maritime targets, although they regularly probed NATO air defence systems.

Bomber conversions

The trio of long-range bombers which the Soviets developed in the 1950s began to make their first appearances in international airspace towards the end of that decade. They were the Myasishchev M-4, Tupolev Tu-16 and Tupolev Tu-95, otherwise known to NATO as the 'Bison', 'Badger' and 'Bear'.

'Badger-D' models with enlarged nose radar and three additional ventral areas began flying Elint missions against US radars in the Pacific. The 'Badger-E' with large cameras in the bomb bay and nose made its first appearance in 1963, followed closely by the 'Badger-F' with pylon-mounted Elint pods under each wing.

The workhorse type was undoubtedly the 'Bear', which first entered service in 1956 and was still in production 35 years later. Its very long unrefuelled radius enabled it to be employed on flights of over 20 hours duration. The 'Bear-E' was a photographic platform, but the major Elint version was the 'Bear-D' which was mainly flown by the Soviet naval air force. First seen in 1967, this version has flown non-stop from the Murmansk area via the Iceland-UK gap to Cuba or Conakry in the West African state of Guinea. Alternatively, it has flown down the eastern side of the UK inviting interception from RAF fighters before turning back north, or perhaps east and into the Baltic. Another regular run was from Ukrainian airfields, across the Black Sea and through the Bosphorus for a Mediterranean patrol, perhaps continuing southwards to land in Aden or Somalia. They also probed US defences from Alaska to Pearl Harbor, often operating from the US-built facility at Cam Ranh Bay in Vietnam.

Soviet intelligence gatherers

Unlike the West, the Soviet Union did not have a string of bases surrounding its potential enemy, and relied mainly on long-range roving patrols over international waters and non-aircraft means to gather its intelligence. A handful of bases (notably in Angola, Guinea, Cuba, Vietnam and Yemen) provide the long-range 'Bears' with some global destinations to head for.

Ilyushin Il-20 'Coot'

Left: This conversion of the Il-18 airliner performed a Sigint/radar reconnaissance role. It carried a large side-looking radar under the fuselage, and optical sensors in the fuselage side fairings. An extensive Elint suite onboard allowed sophisticated radar fingerprinting.

Tupolev Tu-95RT

Below: Equipped with a massive search radar under its belly, the Tu-95RT was used to find and track Western warships. It also had electronic listening equipment for identification and analysis of maritime air defence and other systems.

Anti Submarine Warfare

1970 - 1996

The Tupolev 'Bear' had phenomenal range, and was used by the Soviet navy for maritime patrols worldwide. But closer to home it was also tasked with hunting down Western hunter-killer submarines.

If World War III had ever broken out, it is most likely that the opening shots would have been fired in the icy waters of the North Atlantic, the Norwegian Sea and the Arctic Ocean.

Soviet naval forces had a major problem. If they were to interfere with NATO's transatlantic lifeline in time of war, they had to get out into the Atlantic. But to do that, they had to get from their bases in the Baltic, the Black Sea and the far north of the Soviet Union through geographical 'choke points', where NATO would be waiting.

The primary route was via the 'GIUK Gap': the 300 km (185 mile)-wide Denmark Strait between Greenland and Iceland, and the 800 km (500 miles) of sea between Iceland, the Faroe Islands and Britain.

Even in peacetime, maritime aircraft patrolled the GIUK Gap constantly, and the movement of every Soviet vessel passing into or out of the Atlantic was carefully monitored and plotted. ASW crews were among the few NATO personnel

Right: Britain's Lynx is one of the fastest and most capable light naval helicopters currently in service. It is carried by many NATO destroyers and frigates as their principal ASW weapon.

Anti-sub Helicopters

The development of the helicopter has changed many aspects of warfare, and nowhere is that more true than at sea. ASW helicopters armed with dipping sonar, sonobuoys, depth charges and lightweight homing torpedoes have extended both the sensor and weapons range of surface combatants from the visual horizon out to 100 km (60 miles) and more.

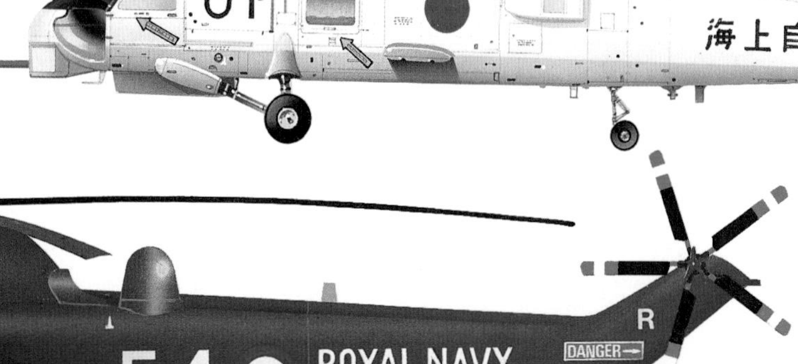

Sikorsky SH-60 Sea Hawk
Right: Developed from the US Army's UH-60 Blackhawk utility helicopter, the Sea Hawk is used aboard vessels from frigate size right up to the largest US Navy supercarrier. It can be used for transport, rescue, and for light anti-shipping strikes with air-to-surface missiles as well as for ASW. It is used by Japan and Australia in addition to the US Navy

54 ROYAL NAVY XV658 054

Westland Sea King
Seen here in its earlier days with the Royal Navy, the British-built variant of the long-serving Sikorsky Sea King is a sophisticated submarine hunter. It is equipped with a sea-search radar, advanced electronic systems, sonobuoys and a dipping sonar capable of being deployed more than 200 m (655 feet) beneath the surface of the ocean.

High-tech Hunters

The ocean is a big place, and a submerged submarine is not easy to find. Successful maritime reconnaissance and anti-submarine aircraft need to be able to cover vast distances in their patrols, combining incredibly long endurance with the ability to use very advanced sensors and avionics and to deliver a wide range of weaponry.

BAe Nimrod MR.Mk 2

Left: Based on the pioneering Comet airliner, the Nimrod entered service in 1969. Thanks to its jet engines it can make very fast transits to its assigned patrol area: once there it can shut down one or two engines and loiter at low speed for up to 12 hours.

Lockheed P-3C Orion

Right: Developed from the Lockheed Electra turboprop airliner, the Orion is the US Navy's primary land-based ASW and maritime patroller, and is used by another 14 nations including Norway. Like the Nimrod, it can shut down engines for economy, enabling the P-3 to stay in the air for more than 17 hours. The current P-3C model is packed with advanced avionics, and can carry more than nine tonnes of weapons and sensors.

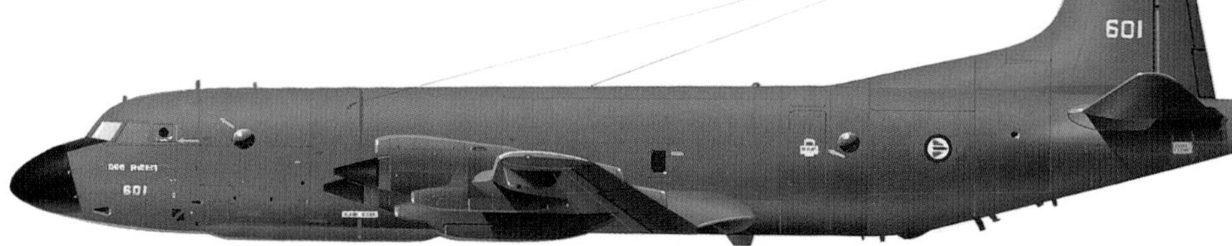

Tupolev Tu-142 'Bear-F'

Below: First flown as a strategic bomber in the early 1950s, and still in production more than four decades later, the 'Bear' has been produced in many versions. The 'Bear-D' is a maritime patroller and intelligence gatherer; the similar 'Bear-F' seen here adds anti-submarine warfare capability

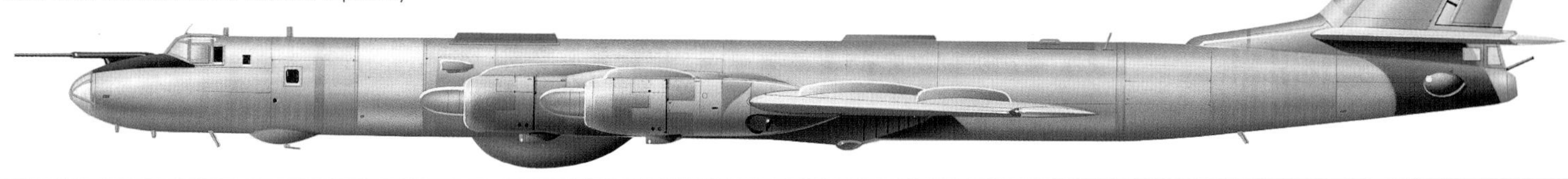

who carried out their war roles for real, with live weapons.

The Soviet threat was multi-layered. Missile-armed aircraft like the long-range Tupolev 'Bear' bomber were one part of the web, along with missile cruisers and destroyers on the surface. But the major threat came from the huge Soviet submarine force. Primitive, noisy and short-ranged in the early post-war years, by the 1980s the Red Fleet was fielding some of the largest, fastest and most sophisticated boats ever built.

A surfaced submarine is an easy target for any aircraft, but once it has slipped beneath the waves it presents a uniquely challenging problem. In every other military field you can rely on visual, radar or infra-red techniques to detect and home-in on targets, but under the sea, except for some special cases, you have to rely on sound. But it is impossible for an aircraft flying through the air to detect sound directly through the barrier of the ocean's surface. It cannot dip a hydrophone into the water like a helicopter, a surface ship or a submarine. Without some kind of sound-sensing device, it has to rely on MAD Magnetic Anomaly Detection) gear, or radar.

Detection by sound

The solution to the problem is the sonobuoy. Sonobuoys are expendable acoustic systems, ejected from the aircraft as it flies over the surface of the ocean. These send data via radio to the aircraft overhead, which can then use homing torpedoes or nuclear depth charges to attack any target revealed.

Orions of the Royal Norwegian Air Force based at Andøya were the first to react to any movement of Soviet submarines from their bases on the Kola Peninsula. First warning would probably have come from the SOSUS line of underwater sensors stretching from Norway to Spitzbergen.

Iceland was the hinge upon which NATO'S efforts to 'bottle up' the Soviet fleet depended. US Navy P-3s based at Keflavik flew missions over the Denmark Strait and over the gap between Iceland and the Faroes. Even in peacetime, America kept an Orion squadron active on the island, with smaller detachments at bases in Britain and Norway.

Britain's Nimrod maritime patrol aircraft flew out of bases in the north of Scotland and in the far south-west of England. The Scottish-based aircraft were part of the NATO ASW force assigned to closing the GIUK Gap.

Typically, Nimrods would mount search patrols up to 1600 km (1,000 miles) from home, at which range they could stay on station for more than six hours. With aerial refuelling the aircraft could stay on patrol for as long as 18 hours, crew fatigue being a limiting factor on the length of missions.

Above: Modern ASW aircraft like the P-3 can be datalinked to specialised ASW vessels like the FFG-7-class frigate, creating an ASW team of great efficiency. Both platforms are in service with the USA, Spain and Australia.

Right: The Atlantique 2 is the latest variant of the Franco-German Atlantic. Currently in service with France's Aeronavale, the Atlantique 2 carries state-of-the-art avionics and ASW weapons.

SAC's Last Years

1970-1992

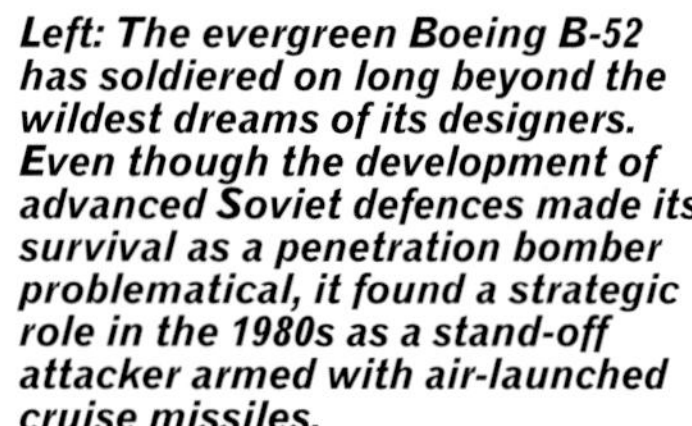

Left: The evergreen Boeing B-52 has soldiered on long beyond the wildest dreams of its designers. Even though the development of advanced Soviet defences made its survival as a penetration bomber problematical, it found a strategic role in the 1980s as a stand-off attacker armed with air-launched cruise missiles.

As the Cold War continued relentlessly into the 1970s and 1980s, the surest way for a Strategic Air Command (SAC) officer to be proven wrong was to develop a schedule to put the B-52 out to pasture. At various times, planners drew up itineraries which would fly the last Stratofortress to the boneyard in 1968, or 1975, or 1984. None of the target dates was reached. It never happened, even while exploring new technologies and looking at future bombers

Just as the B-52 refused to go away, the second candidate named as its replacement also refused to disappear. A decade after the failed XB-70, the Rockwell B-1A was developed to replace the Stratofortress. The XB-70 Valkyrie of the early 1960s was doomed when the advent of the surface-to-air missile forced bombers from high to low altitude. Modifications enabled the B-52 to adjust to this change in the conduct of warfare, but the XB-70 was intended to fly at great heights and was not amenable to being modified.

The second attempt to groom an replacement for the B-52 began with a request to American industry dated 3 November 1969. Rockwell received the nod with a 5 June 1970 contract to build five (later reduced to four) Rockwell B-1A Advanced Manned Strategic Aircraft (AMSAs). The first all-white B-1A flew at Palmdale, California on 23 December 1974.

Stop-start program

On 30 June 1977, President Jimmy Carter cancelled B-1A development. In part because of the difficulty of developing a heavy bomber to replace the B-52, SAC began to operate two combat wings of General Dynamics FB-111A swing-wing strike aircraft, based on the F-111 used by tactical units. The FB-111A remained in service until the early 1990s.

Carter's hope to reduce the Cold War arms race did not outlast his term in office. In October 1981, President Ronald Reagan revived plans for the Rockwell bomber – in effect, rendering Carter's decision void. The US Air Force demanded significant changes in the original design, and announced in September 1981 that it would order 100 B-1Bs with improved avionics, structure, and engine inlets, now designated B-1B. A new flight program began on 23 March 1983.

In the free-spending 1980s when Ronald Reagan routinely referred to the Soviet Union as the 'Evil Empire', enormous amounts were spent on incredibly ambitious projects including an improved Intercontinental Ballistic Missile (ICBM) and the Strategic Defense Initiative: the 'Star Wars' missile defence. Many Pentagon officers regarded the prospect of nuclear war with Moscow as real, imminent, and more important than smaller conflicts around the globe – just as their predecessors had done three decades earlier. The top brass in the 1980s did not have the means to make SAC as large as it had been in the 1950s, but they did have a way to put the Strategic Air Command on the cutting edge of technology. Their shining hope was the stealthy Advanced Technology Bomber, which emerged from years of secrecy as the Northrop B-2 Spirit flying wing. The B-2's main mission was to attack 'mobile, relocatable targets' not easy to engage with ICBMs – that is, rail-

Left: The MGM-118A Peacekeeper, previously known as the MX missile, was the ultimate SAC ICBM. It carried up to 10 independently targeted manoeuvring re-entry vehicles, each accurate to within 120 m (130 yards) after a flight of 11000 km (6,835 miles).

Below: The General Dynamics FB-111 was a long-range version of the swing-wing tactical bomber. Armed with AGM-69 SRAM nuclear missiles, it was designed to race in ahead of the main bomber force to destroy key nodes in the Soviet air defence network.

Left: An evolution of the original Mach 2 B-1A, the B-1B is a highly sophisticated low-level penetrator able to carry massive weapons loads at transonic speeds.

way-based ICBMs – with nuclear bombs and stand-off weapons.

High-tech future

To those who knew, the B-2 was the future of SAC. The Air Force would procure 132 of them to equip a dozen squadrons in five combat wings, scattered among SAC's many air bases. The very public and highly publicised Rockwell B-1B was, in the view of these men, merely an 'interim' weapon until the B-2 arrived.

One strong argument for the B-2 is its flexibility. Unlike an ICBM, the B-2 can be 'flushed' – that is, deployed in an airborne alert pattern or even started towards its target, but it is still possible for the aircraft to be recalled. And unlike a submarine-launched ballistic missile, it is extremely accurate against mobile targets, including rail-mounted ICBMs.

While the USAF publicly promoted the B-1B and secretly developed the B-2, the first B-1B was ceremoniously delivered to SAC at Offutt AFB, Nebraska on 27 July 1985. The first operational B-1Bs went to the 96th Bomb Wing at Dyess AFB, Texas. One hundred B-1Bs were manufactured. Today, the USAF is upgrading them and shifting their duties so that most can now carry out conventional bombing missions.

The 1990s were a time of global change. In 1991, the world was treated to the sight of the ageless B-52 Stratofortress bombing Saddam Hussein's Republican Guards during the Gulf War. Among these were missions with C-ALCMs (Conventional warhead Air-Launched Cruise Missiles).

With the Berlin Wall being torn down, the Soviet Union fragmenting, and US attention shifting to trouble spots in the Persian Gulf, Somalia and Bosnia, the stealthy B-2 was suddenly very visible. One officer said it stood out like a sore thumb – not only because of its amazing cost but also for having capabilities which were inappropriate and unnecessary for the times.

In a dramatic move reflecting the changing world order, President George Bush ordered a stand-down of all US nuclear alert forces on 28 September 1991. For the first time in nearly half a century, bombers no longer waited at the ready with thermonuclear weapons in their bays.

Striving toward a strength of 40 combat wings in the free-spending 1980s, the USAF went into the 1990s expecting to operate with only 17 combat wings. The B-2 stealth bomber, which in many ways seemed the epitome of everything SAC represented, was never to serve in SAC at all.

The end of an era

Reflecting a new world without a Soviet Union, a world in which the 'hot' war of the 1990s had been Operation Desert Storm, Strategic Air Command went out of business on 1 June 1992. On that date, SAC's bomber wings were merged with stateside tactical air units to create a new Air Combat Command (ACC) headquartered at Langley AFB, Virginia. Since then, the tankers formerly operated by SAC have been reassigned to Air Mobility Command (AMC) at Scott AFB, Illinois.

Above: Designed for Strategic Air Command, but entering service after the reorganisation of the US Air Force which saw its dissolution, The Northrop B-2 'stealth' bomber is the most advanced and most expensive warplane ever built.

Right: As newer bombers have come on line to take up the strategic mission, the 70-odd surviving B-52H aircraft have been freed for more conventional roles. These include very long-range maritime operations.

Cruise carrier

Universally known throughout the B-52 community as the 'Cadillac', the 'H' model introduced significant enhancement of the veteran bomber's load/range performance, crew comfort and weapons delivery capability. The 70 or so remaining aircraft, most being much older than the crews which fly them, are set to remain in service well into the 21st century, giving the B-52 over half a century of front line use.

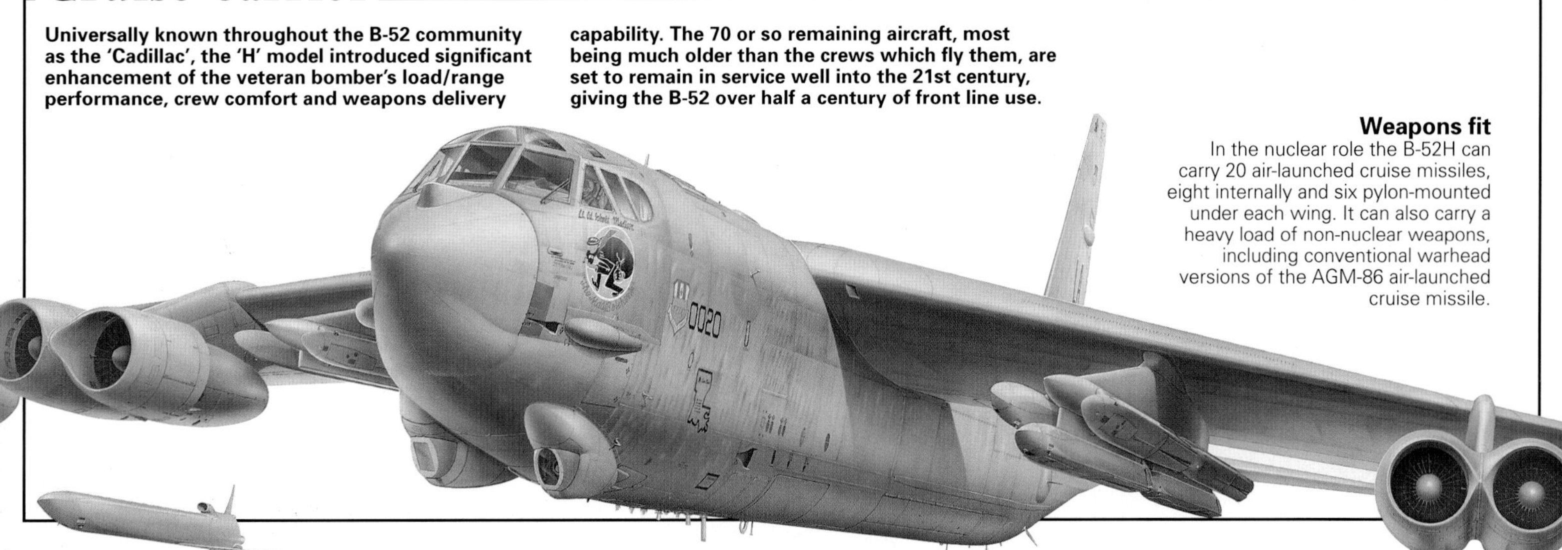

Weapons fit

In the nuclear role the B-52H can carry 20 air-launched cruise missiles, eight internally and six pylon-mounted under each wing. It can also carry a heavy load of non-nuclear weapons, including conventional warhead versions of the AGM-86 air-launched cruise missile.

Last Cold War Defenders

1980-1993

Left: To this day the F-15 Eagle rules the roost as the arguably the world's best fighter. USAF aircraft are deployed to Europe, Alaska and the Far East as the spearhead of the Western air defences. F-15s from CONUS bases regularly practise deployments to regions such as the Middle East.

Above: Elderly fighters such as the F-4 Phantom have kept apace with modern fighter development with update programmes. While little can be done with the airframes other than life extension, radar and weapon system capability can be dramatically enhanced. This is a Luftwaffe F-4F.

By the end of the 1980s, the nature of the Cold War had altered. Perestroika and Glasnost had dramatically changed the structure and outlook of the Soviet Union, bringing the possibility of some kind of rapprochement with the West. Even so, fighter interceptors remained on the alert all over the world. From the Far East and Siberia to the North Sea and Alaska, over Scandinavia and Alaska, pilots sat ready to take off at a moment's notice. Their mission was to locate, deter, and if necessary destroy hostile aircraft penetrating defended airspace.

The quickest reactions were required along the boundary between East and West, most importantly the Central Front in Germany.

Intercepts fell into a number of categories. The primary threat was seen as aircraft from East Germany or Czechoslovakia detected by radar approaching or crossing the border. A rapid reaction was required to counter such a threat, for there was always the chance that these might have been the advance echelons of a pre-emptive strike against the West. However, navigational errors are much more likely causes of unintentional border crossings, and it was essential that the fighter pilot, whether flying and American F-15 Eagle, a Dutch F-16 or a German F-4 should divine the intentions of any intruder.

Obviously a weapon-carrying strike aircraft which showed no signs of turning back would have required swift action on the part of the fighter. All air defence interceptors carried live weapons for use in the last resort. However, the analysis of intent is of prime importance during this phase of the mission: the destruction of an aircraft that accidentally violated West German airspace would have had serious diplomatic and military repercussions. An inadvertent border crossing in peacetime requires a different reaction, and the hope was that the presence of the NATO fighter would be enough to make it turn back, though warning shots might have been required.

FACING WARPAC

By far the majority of scrambles were to the aid of Western aircraft that strayed near the border. Warsaw Pact defences were just as ready for action as those in the West, but they were far more likely to shoot than their NATO counterparts. Once the aircraft under investigation had been declared safe, or shepherded away from danger, the fighters were free to return to base.

Yet though it was never exer-

Left: In the interceptor role the F-15 uses its quick-start capability and enormous power to react rapidly to any potential threat. In Europe the F-15 stood 'Zulu' alert at Bitburg, covering the 4 ATAF region which encompassed the southern half of West Germany.

Below: The General Dynamics F-16A was a new breed of fighter: supremely agile in a dogfight, but just as capable in the attack role. The purchase of F-16s by Belgium, Denmark, the Netherlands and Norway dramatically enhanced European air defences.

NATO Interceptors

In northern Europe NATO directly faced the cream of the Warsaw Pact air forces, and deployed large numbers of interceptors to meet the expected threat from the East. USAF F-15s and RAF Phantoms stood alert in Germany, while the RAF also patrolled the northern waters from where a bomber attack was most likely to have come.

Panavia Tornado ADV
The dedicated fighter version of the Tornado was an RAF-specific design with a primary mission of maritime air defence. It was expected to loiter a long way from land and then destroy bombers as they approached Europe from the Arctic Ocean. This aircraft is an F.Mk 2 from 229 OCU, the training unit.

McDonnell Douglas F-15
USAF Europe was an early recipient of the F-15, and at the peak of the force had a three-squadron wing at Bitburg in West Germany, augmented by the 32nd TFS (illustrated) based at Soesterberg (Camp New Amsterdam) in the Netherlands.

cised, their reason for being was to counter the strike from the east. The constant nagging thought that the next alert warning might have sounded for a force of 'Fencers' or 'Backfires' instead of a lost light plane ensured that everyone in the air defence community applied 100 per cent effort and concentration. As 'games' go, none was more serious than that played by the men on air defence alert.

Maritime Air Defence

Further away from the potential front line, fighters faced very different problems, even if the mission to intercept, identify and if necessary destroy intruders was basically the same. Island nations like Britain and Japan would have had more warning of attack, and aimed to mount their intercepts far out to sea. Norwegian and British fighters together with US interceptors on Iceland were tasked with preventing Soviet bombers from getting out into the Atlantic, while the defence of the United States and Canada was aimed at stopping attacks over the pole and across Alaska.

Britain was typical of the air defence regions which NATO established. It was a prime Warsaw Pact target during the Cold War, being NATO's vital rear depot and collecting point for men and supplies, as well as being the base for a third of the Alliance's combat aircraft. As a result, the RAF's responsibility was both to protect the citizens of the United Kingdom and to keep NATO's supply lines open.

The UK Air Defence Region covers nearly 10 million km^2 (4 million sq miles) around Britain's coasts, from the English Channel and the North Sea round via the Shetlands and Faeroes out into the Atlantic almost as far as Iceland. Such a huge area requires continual vigilance to patrol.

But vigilance is not enough in the modern world of fast, cruise missile-armed, low-flying bombers. In the 1980s British defences were upgraded to cope with the new threat. It was a far-reaching programme, involving the introduction of the Tornado F.Mk 3 interceptor, the Boeing Sentry AWACS airborne early warning system, new mobile ground radars, new command and control centres hardened against nuclear attack, expanded missile defences, increased weapons stocks, increasing the number of interceptors available by arming Hawk trainers with AIM-9 Sidewinders, and developing a

Above: Although the major confrontation between East and West was in Europe, it was a world-wide phenomenon. This Alaskan-based F-15 has intercepted a Soviet 'Bear' over the North Pacific.

Below: In the 1980s the RAF introduced the Mixed Fighter Force concept, which envisaged the use of Tornado F.Mk 3s as a 'mini-AWACS'. The Tornado's long-range Foxhunter radar enabled its navigator to vector radarless but Sidewinder-armed Hawk trainers on to hostile targets.

Below: To further its ability to detect airborne intruders from the East NATO turned to the Boeing E-3 AWACS, which in addition to the USAF was purchased by the RAF, France and a joint NATO force .

Left: Based loosely on the MiG-25, the MiG-31 'Foxhound' replaced the Tu-128 as the Soviet Union's main long-range interceptor. Using radar and weapons technology reputedly derived from that employed by the F-14, the MiG-31 could travel across vast distances in the Soviet north and shoot down intruders at extreme range.

highly computerised nationwide command and communications network to improve battle management.

Literally hundreds of Soviet reconnaissance flights were intercepted in the last years of the Cold War, from the North Sea to the North Slope of Alaska. The crews of Soviet 'Bears' and 'Badgers' became accustomed to seeing a Phantom, Tornado, Tomcat or Eagle appear on their wing to escort them out of sensitive areas or to keep them clear of NATO exercises.

But the increase in capability was not confined to NATO. In many ways, the Soviet Union had an even more impressive defensive network, and it was a network which it was not afraid to use in anger. Over the years, more than 20 American aircraft – ranging from U-2 spyplanes to transports straying off course – were shot down over or around the Soviet Union. However, this readiness to open fire has led to tragedy, most notably in the 1983 destruction of an off-course Korean Air Lines Boeing 747, destroyed over Sakhalin island in 1983, which cost the lives of all 269 passengers and crew.

In the 1980s a profound upgrading programme transformed Soviet air defence forces, the V-PVO, in part because of failings revealed in the KAL shoot down. Responsible for all ground- and air-based defensive systems, the V-PVO was reorganised in its last Soviet years. It was divided into three huge air defence zones, comprising Urals-Western Siberia; Eastern Siberia-Transbaikal; and South Urals-Volga. Only the Moscow Air Defence district survived from before.

V-PVO Force

In the late 1980s the V-PVO had a strength of over 1,250 aircraft These included around 500 Sukhoi Su-15 'Flagons', MiG-25 'Foxbats' and Yakovlev Yak-28 'Firebars' from earlier generations of fighters. Competent enough to intercept high-level intruders, they (or more accurately, their radars) were much less capable against low-level threats.

However, the introduction into service of long-range interceptors like the Mikoyan MiG-31 'Foxhound' and the Sukhoi Su-27 'Flanker' gave the Soviets a new generation of fighters whose superb performance was matched by advanced new radars and some of the best air-to-air weaponry in the world.

In addition to the dedicated air defence aircraft, the Soviets could call on around 2,000 tactical interceptors from Frontal Aviation. Fighters like the swing-wing MiG-23 'Flogger' were perfectly adequate for some kinds of air defence,

Above: The Su-27 'Flanker' represented a major advance in Soviet fighter capability, and its ability to escort bombers from their home bases all the way to targets as far west as the UK posed NATO real problems.

Right: In the final years of the Cold War NATO would have found itself facing the very manoeuvrable MiG-29 over the German battlefield. By the time of the reunification of Germany, the type was the most numerous in the 16th Air Army.

Soviet Interceptors

Traditionally tied wholly to cumbersome ground controlled intercept systems and procedures, Soviet interceptors were slowly freed from these shackles during the 1980s as weapon systems became more capable. A greater accent was placed on manoeuvrability and performance, allowing a well-flown MiG-29 or Su-27 to match the West's F-15 and F-16. Weapons development also proceeded apace, capitalising in the Soviet Union's acknowledged lead in many areas of missile technology. At the same time, force numbers remained high compared to NATO.

Sukhoi Su-15 'Flagon'
Right: Representative of the 'old school' of Soviet interceptors, the Su-15 had exceptional speed and altitude performance, long-range missiles and a crude yet powerful radar. Interceptor operations were virtually always flown under tight ground control.

Sukhoi Su-27 'Flanker'
Left: One of NATO's most unpleasant surprises of the 1980s was the appearance of the phenomenally agile and fast-climbing Su-27, attended by a subtle change to more autonomous operations. Able to fly escort or intercept missions at very long range, the Su-27 also carried up to 10 missiles, including both radar- and IR-guided versions of the capable R-27/AA-10 'Alamo'.

The destruction of KAL 007

At 0326 (local time) on the morning of 1 September 1983, Major Vassily Kasmin, an experienced Soviet fighter pilot, launched two deadly AA-3 'Anab' missiles from the underwing pylons of his Sukhoi Su-15 'Flagon-F' interceptor. His target was a Boeing 747 of Korean Airlines, with 29 crew and 240 passengers aboard.

"I am closing in on the target, am in lock-on. Distance to the target 8 [hundred metres]."

With these words, Major Kasmin, on the instructions of ground control, pronounced the death sentence on 269 people.

"I have executed the launch." Two seconds later he added, "The target is destroyed. I am breaking off the attack"

The shoot down of flight KE 007, on the last leg of a scheduled passenger service from New York to Seoul, has been the subject of violent controversy in the years since the tragedy.

One of the few undoubted facts is that the airliner was more than 400 km (250 miles) north of of its planned route, taking it from the safety of international airspace into the highly dangerous skies over some of the most sensitive military installations in the Soviet Union.

Flown by an experienced crew under Captain Chun Byung In, KE 007 took off from Alaska at 1250 GMT, about 30 minutes late. It began to deviate from its planned track almost immediately. The 747 was 19 km (12 miles) north of its assigned route by the time it reached Bethel, the first waypoint.

About one hour later a small blue light would have illuminated on the instrument panel, indicating that the big Boeing was being observed on radar. Chun may have believed that he was being tracked by an American radar based in the Aleutians, but the truth was more sinister. The monolithic Soviet air defence organisation was already treating the 747 as a potential hostile, initially referring to the radar blip as an RC-135 spyplane, and later simply as 'the target'.

At 1600 another KAL aircraft relayed a message that KE007 was passing the Neeva waypoint. In fact the straying Jumbo was 240 km (150 miles) further north, about to enter Soviet airspace, and heading straight for the Kamchatka Peninsula 645 km (400 miles) ahead. Moments later a USAF RC-135 electronic intelligence-gathering aircraft crossed in front of the Korean aircraft, leading to later claims by the Soviets that there had been a deliberate rendezvous.

As the Boeing flew over the Kamchatka Peninsula six Soviet MiG-23 'Flogger' fighters were apparently scrambled, but not until the last moment, and they failed to intercept the airliner. As they crossed the west coast the co-pilot made a radio call, reporting that they were passing waypoint Nippi. By this time they were actually 250 miles further north. Less than an hour ahead lay the island of Sakhalin, where Soviet fighters were already being prepared to intercept the intruder.

At 1742 GMT, the Soviet fighter controllers scrambled a Sukhoi Su-15TM 'Flagon-F', flown by Major Kasmin, followed by three MiG-23 'Floggers'.

According to Major Kasmin, he flew several close passes by the 747, and fired four bursts of tracer shells past the nose all without response before making his final, fatal attack.

Nobody knows why the big airliner was so far off course. It is very unlikely to have been a spy flight. It could have been an instrument error, although with three sophisticated inertial navigation systems it seems unlikely. Pilot error is possible, even with such an experienced flight crew, especially if erroneous data had been fed into the navigation system. It could have been a simple case of mistaken identity by a rigid, inflexible Soviet air defence system which only saw an American spyplane intruding into highly restricted military airspace.

But whatever the cause, the destruction of KE 007 was a tragic illustration of the Cold War threat implicit in the words printed onto every air chart of the region:

"WARNING: aircraft infringing on Non-Free Flying Territory may be fired on without warning."

After reportedly firing warning cannon shots across the bow of the KAL 747, the Su-15TM of Major Kasmin positioned behind the airliner to fire the two K-8 missiles which destroyed the aircraft. The tragedy illustrated just how rigid the Soviet air defence system was, and how closely controlled from the ground Soviet interceptors were.

but with the introduction of tactical 'Flankers' and superb dogfighters like the MiG-29 'Fulcrum' battlefield intercept capability also increased dramatically.

To this should be added the potent missile net. SAM production in the mid-1980s peaked at about 50,000 missiles per year, providing for replacement of the obsolete SA-1 and augmentation of the ageing SA-2 and SA-3s. Giant SA-5s provide long-range defence (up to 300 km/185 miles) and the SA-10 and SA-12 were brought into service. The former, a Mach 6 weapon, was claimed to be effective against the cruise missiles which formed one pillar of the West's deterrence, whilst the SA-12 will engage a target at any height from 30 to 30500 m (100 to 100,000 ft) up to 100 km (62 miles) from its launcher.

Right: Until recently elderly interceptors like this Su-15 played an important part in the defence of the Soviet Union/CIS. Although not able to deal with modern low-level attackers, they were deployed in areas where they would only be likely to face NATO's bombers.

Post-Soviet Conflicts

1991-1996

The collapse of the Soviet Union and the Communist Party after the failure of the hardline coup of August 1991 set in train a series of destructive conflicts on the fringes of the old Soviet empire. The successor states in the Caucasus have used the vast arsenals left behind by withdrawing Red Army troops to fight a series of vicious wars. These conflicts have yet to run their course.

ARMENIA AND AZERBAIJAN

The first Caucasus conflict of the post-Soviet era actually slightly predated the end of the Soviet Union. Since 1989 tension had been high between Armenia and Azerbaijan over the disputed enclave of Nagorny-Karabakh, which was inside the borders of Muslim Azerbaijan but had a largely Christian Armenian population. The two newly independent states inherited much of the Soviet military materiel on their territory and set about forming national armies and air forces. Ex-Soviet MiG-21s, Sukhoi Su-25s, Mil Mi-8s and Mil Mi-26s were used by both sides as they struggled to gain control of the enclave. Until they were able to drive a land corridor through to Nagorny-Karabakh, the Armenians relied on a fleet of ex-Aeroflot Mi-8s to ferry supplies into their garrison and bring out refugees.

Below: The end of the Warsaw Pact has seen the huge Soviet military machine formerly in place in Easern Europe pulled back to Russia. Many like this Mil Mi-24 'Hind' have exchanged the Cold War for a bitter struggle in the breakaway republic of Chechnya.

GEORGIA

Next to fall victim to war was the Republic of Georgia on the Black Sea Coast. Like its southern neighbours, Georgia was riven by political and ethnic disputes. The centre of opposition to the Georgian government was the region of Abkhazia, which had long wanted independence. With covert Russian backing the Abkhazians rose in revolt during September 1993 and besieged the Georgian garrison in the region's capital, Sukhumi. Georgian Air Force Su-25 jets intervened to rocket Abkhazian troops to little effect. The Georgians then tried to resupply their troops by air but the Abkhazians shot down several airliners using SA-7 Strela missiles. This forced the Georgians to retreat from the region and call for a halt to the fighting. A Russian and UN peacekeeping mission then moved to monitor the ensuing ceasefire.

Above: Helicopters have played a major part in the wars which have raged through the Caucasus since the collapse of the Soviet Union. The newly independent states all have access to former Soviet aircraft left on their territory, and most of the fighting men have some heliborne training from their days as Soviet conscripts.

Below: More advanced weaponry is a little more problematical, as the smaller states do not have the infrastructure to maintain and support the former Soviet fast jets left in their possession on the withdrawal of the Soviet Army. Even so, MiG-21s have seen combat in the fighting between Armenia and Azerbaijan.

CHECHNYA

Russian forces withdrew from the Chechen capital Grozny in late 1991, leaving behind a whole division's worth of arms and equipment, including a large contingent of Aero L.39 Albatross training jets. The region's citizens then set about killing each other in a series of blood feuds.

In December 1994 the Russians decided to re-establish their control of the breakaway region. Russian air force Sukhoi Su-24s and Su-25s spearheaded the assault destroying the L-39s and a number of Mi-8s at Grozny airport. The bombers used laser-guided weapons and older 'iron' bombs to destroy their targets at the airport before reaching out to hit 'strategic' locations throughout the Chechen Republic. Television footage of the raids indicates that the Russian air strikes were far from accurate and as a result many civilians were killed and injured.

With air supremacy assured, Russian army aviation Mil Mi-24 assault helicopters and armed Mi-8s then swept ahead of tank columns entering Chechnya, hitting bridges, arms dumps and other targets with AT-6 Shturm guided missiles and unguided rockets. Western journalists reported that the Russians con-

centrated on hitting civilian cars, which were designated 'terrorist' supply vehicles.

At least two more squadrons of Mi-24s and two squadrons of Mi-8s, plus a flight of Mil Mi-26 heavy-lift helicopters, were drafted into the Caucasus region to support the Russian ground forces attempting to seize Grozny. The Chechens put up fanatical resistance to the Russian invaders who were thus unable to take the Chechen capital until mid-January.

Russian helicopter gunships were involved in every aspect of the operation, in spite of bad weather that forced them to fly under ceilings of less than 100 m (330 feet) and in visibility of under 1,000 metres (1,095 yards). In the brutal street fighting the Chechens used heavy machine guns and SA-7 missiles to target Russian helicopters, downing several. Shot down crews captured by the Chechens were shown no mercy.

Russian Mi-8s were in great demand to airlift the thousands of Russian casualties from frontline positions to field hospitals at the main Russian supply bases located just beyond the Chechen borders. The massive Mi-26s were used to airlift ammunition to artillery batteries blasting Chechen positions.

For the next 18 months the Chechens waged a determined guerrilla war against the Russians, including hijacking civilian passenger aircraft and staging a number of high-profile hostage takings, the most notable being the seizure of hundreds of civilians at Kizlyar in January 1996. The Russians tried to free these hostages, the bungled rescue attempt involving Mi-24s strafing the village. These attacks culminated in the dramatic Chechen offensive that allowed them to retake Grozny from the Russians in July 1996.

The Russians unleashed their helicopter gunships again, but the Chechens were well dug-in among the ruins of the city. The failure of the Russian offensive to clear out the rebels from the city forced Boris Yeltsin to send former paratroop commander General Alexander Lebed as a trouble-shooting envoy, with instructions to negotiate a peaceful solution.

Below: The USSR's answer to the Tornado and the F-111, the Sukhoi Su-24 'Fencer' was used to deliver precision-guided weapons against Chechen targets. Results were mixed to say the least: eyewitness accounts said that Russian bombs caused many civilian casualties.

Below: Designed for a European war which never was, the Sukhoi Su-25 'Frogfoot' has been used extensively in the fighting between and within the former Soviet Republics. It was one of the main strike weapons supporting the Russian army in Chechnya.

Yugoslavia falls apart

1991-1993

Left: The shooting down of a Yugoslav Air Force Gazelle helicopter over Slovenia in June 1991 brought the simmering cauldron which was post-Tito Yugoslavia to the boil. The ensuing civil war was the most bitter to have been fought in Europe since World War II.

On the early evening of 27 June 1991 a Federal Yugoslav air force (JRV) SA.341 Gazelle carrying a cargo of bread was trying to find a landing site in the Slovenian capital Ljubljana when a heat seeking SA-7 Strela missile zoomed up from a city street. The helicopter exploded in mid-air, showering the city with hot burning debris. This was the first aircraft to be lost in action during the bloody break up of Yugoslavia and the emergence of the new states of Slovenia, Croatia and Bosnia-Herzegovina.

SLOVENIA

Serbian strongman Slobodan Milosevic and the Federal Yugoslav military (JNA) high command reacted swiftly to the Slovenian declaration of independence with a massive military intervention. Tank columns headed into the small country, with the intention of seizing border crossing points. Federal ground attack aircraft, including SOKO J-1 Jastrebs, G-4M Super Galebs, J-22 Oraos and MiG-21s, swooped ahead of the ground troops, attacking civil aircraft at Ljubljana airport and border posts on the Austrian and Italian frontiers. But the Slovenian Territorial Defence Force (TDF) was well armed, trained and motivated. Its volunteer militiamen held their ground, cut the Federal troops' supply lines and then waited for them to surrender. Although Mil Mi-8 transport helicopters and Gazelles landed small parties of airborne troops in vain attempts seize key points, by 7 July the Federal authorities threw in the towel and agreed to an European Community peace effort. Slovenia was free.

Attention now switched to Croatia, Yugoslavia's second largest and richest republic. The JRV was in a state of crisis because of the Croat 'war of barracks' campaign, which saw thousands of federal troops besieged in their garrisons throughout Croatia. But Milosevic and his Serb nationalist supporters were not going to let the country go without a serious fight.

By the autumn the JRV had managed to pull back enough men and equipment to bases in Bosnia (Bihac, Banja Luka, Tuzla and Sarajevo) and into Serbia (Novi Sad, Vrasc and Sombor), as well as Udbina in the largely Serb-populated Krajina region of Croatia, to begin operations in earnest against the Croats.

WAR IN CROATIA

In September a state of open war existed between Croatia and Serbia along a 1600-km (1,000-mile) front, with the JRV striking at targets deep inside Croatia. MiG-21s made sweeps over the Croat capital Zagreb and on 7 October launched a precise attack on the presidential palace, using AGM-65 Maverick infra-red guided missiles. Croatian President Franjo Tudjman was only a few feet away from the impact area, but survived.

The main emphasis of the JRV offensive was in Eastern Slavonia, where Croat troops were putting up strong resistance to Serb offensives across the Danube. From August onwards, JRV jets made daily strikes against the city of Vukovar, which became known as the 'Stalingrad of the Balkans'. It held out for 100 days, until in

Above: On the face of it, the Serb-dominated federal forces had all of the advantages, controlling as they did the bulk of the former Yugoslav Air Force. Among the aircraft at its command was the Yugoslav/ Romanian-designed SOKO J-22 Orao ground-attack jet.

Left: Although long past its best days as a front-line fighter, the MiG-21 'Fishbed' was still vastly more capable than anything the breakaway states of Slovenia, Croatia and Bosnia-Herzegovina could hope to offer in opposition.

Federal MiG-21

One of the classic jet fighters of the post-war years, the Soviet-built MiG-21 served in vairly large numbers with the Yugoslav air force. Over 110 aircraft equipped eight interceptor squadrons and were Yugoslavia's first line of defence until the arrival of a squadron of MiG-29s in 1987. Most survivors were used for ground-attack duties in the early stages of the Balkan war.

MiG-21bis

Right: First entering service in 1972, the MiG-21bis was an improved version of the long-serving Soviet fighter. Although fast and fairly agile at high speed, by the 1990s it was beginning to look somewhat archaic, with its poor radar, lack of long-range weaponry and almost cripplingly short range.

November the starved defenders surrendered. Serb soldiers then massacred hundreds of their prisoners.

Aircraft losses

Some 46 JRV aircraft and helicopters were lost in the bloody conflicts with Slovenia and Croatia. The JRV's lamentable air campaign culminated in January 1992 with the destruction over Croatia of a white painted Agusta-Bell AB.206 . The Italian helicopter was being operated on behalf of the European Community Monitoring Mission.

Newly independent Croatia found itself without an air force in the summer of 1991 after the JRV spirited away almost all its aircraft back to Bosnia and Serbia. The Croat paramilitary Special Police had a small air arm with a handful of Bell 206 and 212 helicopters, along with a couple of Mi-8s. A handful of MiG-21 pilots of Croat origin defected from the JRV with their aircraft but these were soon lost in action.

Lacking modern munitions, the new Croat air force (HRZ) had to resort to rough and ready improvisations to take the war to the Serbs. Antonov An-2 biplanes were pressed from parachute clubs into military service, first dropping supplies to besieged Vukovar and then becoming bombers. Recycled explosives were used to fill old oil drums or gas cylinders to create Croatia's first indigenously manufactured aircraft ordnance. It is not thought that the improvised weapons killed many Serbs, but they certainly raised morale among the Croats.

The Serb-Croat war burnt itself out in the spring of 1992 and an uneasy three-year peace was maintained under the supervision of the United Nations Protection Force (UNPROFOR).

The Croats used this time to rebuild their army and air force, shopping in the international arms markets for more than 20 MiG-21s, 40 Mil Mi-8s and 15 Mil Mi-24 'Hind' attack helicopters.

In August 1995 they launched a major attack against the Serbs, seizing almost all the territory lost in the 1991 war. Croat helicopters delivered commandos behind enemy lines and HRZ MiGs flew scores of close air support and interdiction missions. Serb jets that tried to intervene suffered to Croat air defences, two aircraft being lost.

Below: As with most modern wars, much of the most important aerial work has been done by helicopters. Federal forces made some airborne assaults using Mil Mi-8 'Hips' early in the invasion of Slovenia, but they had little effect against the highly motivated and relatively well-trained Slovenian militia.

Below: Croatia acquired two MiG-21MFs and a MiG-21bis when their pilots defected from the Federal air force. One was lost in action, but they have since been joined by 20 more bought from Ukraine.

Bosnia

1992-1997

***Left:** NATO's initial involvement in the Balkans was primarily a watching brief. Naval forces and Boeing E-3 AWACS aircraft monitoring the skies and seas around the region in order to prevent shipments of arms to the embattled former Yugoslav republics. However, it soon became clear that a simple embargo was doing nothing to control the warring factions.*

***Below:** The airport of the Bosnian capital of Sarajevo was the focus of an international relief effort designed to provide aid to the hundreds of thousands of refugees displaced by the war. Surrounded by mountains and within range of a variety of weaponry, it proved to be a perilous destination for United Nations relief flights.*

NATO air forces first became involved in the former Yugoslavia in the summer of 1992, when the alliance decided to dispatch naval units to the Adriatic Sea. Their task was to enforce the United Nations arms embargo against the now independent republics formerly part of the Federal Socialist Republic of Yugoslavia.

The air component of this operation consisted of Boeing E-3A Sentry AWACS radar surveillance aircraft, of the multi-national NATO Airborne Early Warning Force (NAEWF) to provide top cover for alliance ships. At the same time, individual NATO countries made available tactical transport aircraft to fly humanitarian aid into the besieged capital of Bosnia-Herzegovina.

The Sarajevo airlift was run by the UN High Commissioner for Refugees (UNHCR) and continued until January 1996, flying some 12,951 sorties into the city with the loss of one Italian aircraft to an anti-aircraft missile. More than 50 aircraft were hit by ground fire while making the dangerous approach to the city's single runway airport.

In February 1993 the humanitarian airlift was expanded by the United States, France and Germany to include air drops of aid to besieged Bosnian enclaves. This operation involved some 2,828 sorties up to August 1994.

The continuing escalation of the Bosnian conflict in the autumn of 1992 forced the international community to increase its 'crisis management' efforts to contain and limit the war. In October 1992 the UN imposed a 'No Fly Zone' (NFZ) for military aircraft over Bosnia and the NAEWF extended its scope of operations to include monitoring this zone, with E-3 aircraft flying tracks over the Adriatic and Hungary. The latter move was the first time NATO air forces had operated over the territory of a former Warsaw Pact state.

USE OF FORCE APPROVED

Bosnia's warring factions showed total disregard for the NFZ and amid the Srebrenica crisis in March 1993, it was agreed by the international community that NATO airpower would be used to enforce the flight ban. American, British, Dutch, French and Turkish fighter aircraft based in Italy and on aircraft carriers in the Adriatic, under the command of NATO's 5th Allied Tactical Air Force (5 ATAF), were instructed to enforce the NFZ.

On 12 April 1993 NATO aircraft began Operation Deny Flight which saw around the clock fighter combat air patrols over Bosnia to stop the warring factions using combat aircraft.

Fighter operations were controlled by very strict rules of engagement (ROE) to prevent any politically damaging incidents. Only aircraft actively engaged in combat missions could be engaged by the NATO aircraft; other aircraft could only be warned to land or buzzed at high speed to force them

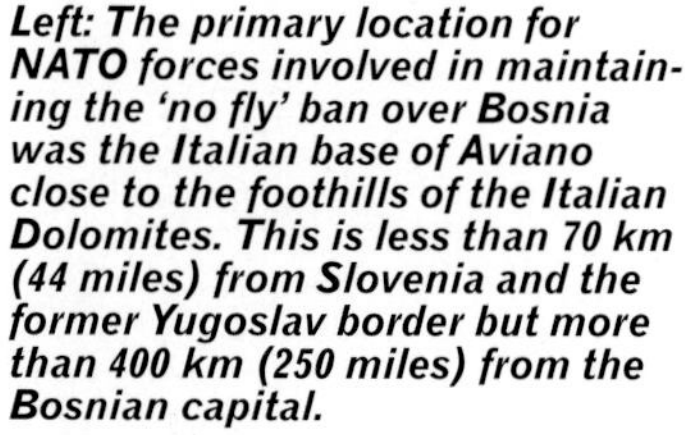

***Left:** The primary location for NATO forces involved in maintaining the 'no fly' ban over Bosnia was the Italian base of Aviano close to the foothills of the Italian Dolomites. This is less than 70 km (44 miles) from Slovenia and the former Yugoslav border but more than 400 km (250 miles) from the Bosnian capital.*

***Above:** The bulk of the most dangerous flying in the war zone was done by transport pilots from the USA, France, Britain and Italy among others. C-130 Hercules and C.160 Transalls flew more than 2,000 humanitarian sorties a year between 1991 and 1996, often in the face of hostile gunfire and even surface-to-air missile attack.*

Peacekeeping helicopters

As it has so often shown in the last three decades, the helicopter has become an essential part of modern military operations. That is much or perhaps even more true for the assorted UN and NATO forces – involving troops from 14 NATO and as many as 18 non-NATO armies – trying to keep the peace in the former Yugoslavia as it has been in any war of the 1990s.

Above: A Norwegian Bell 412 'Huey' comes in to land at the Croatian port of Split in the spring of 1995. It has just flown a mission in support of embattled and besieged ***UNPROFOR*** *observers in Bosnia.*

Above: A Ukrainian Mil Mi-8 'Hip' makes a casualty evacuation flight. Bosnia was the region in which former Warsaw Pact troops first operated under the same command as their former ***NATO*** *opponents.*

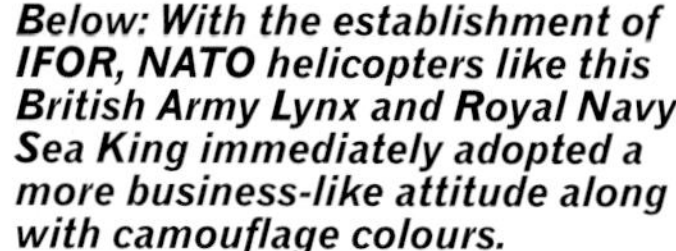

Below: White painted ***UNPROFOR*** *helicopters like this French Super Puma were often the sole means of access to the vital airport at Sarajevo when gunfire closed the runway to conventional traffic.*

Below: With the establishment of ***IFOR, NATO*** *helicopters like this British Army Lynx and Royal Navy Sea King immediately adopted a more business-like attitude along with camouflage colours.*

to land. While the warring factions made great use of helicopters for resupply missions, they generally did not employ their fighter aircraft, though when Serb bombers attacked targets in central Bosnia in February 1994 USAF Lockheed Martin F-16 Fighting Falcons intercepted them and shot them down.

The next major infringements of the NFZ took place during November 1994 around Bihac, when Serb fighters based in Croatia – outside the NFZ – were making brief dashes across the border to bomb Bosnian positions in the enclave. NATO fighters could not stop the Serb aircraft because the ROE said they could not engage outside Bosnian airspace. This led to the famous NATO airstrike on Serb held Udbina airbase in Croatia on 21 November 1994, which cratered the runway to stop the Serb air force taking off.

Further major infringements took place in the summer and autumn of 1995, when Croat and Serb air forces tried to support their armies fighting in north west Bosnia. NATO fighters protected by heavy suppression of enemy air defence (SEAD) forces made large sweeps to force the Serbs and Croats to land.

The vulnerability of UN peacekeeping troops to Serb reprisals made the issue of air strikes the subject of much political infighting in the world's capitals, with the US

Above: British light carriers in the Adriatic served as platforms both for Sea Harrier fighters and Sea King helicopters, the latter being extensively used as transports during the United Nations phase of the peacekeeping operation.

Left: With an air wing of 85 modern combat aircraft, including three or four squadrons of the versatile F/A-18 Hornet, the ***US*** *Navy carriers patrolling in the Adriatic provided the single most powerful and most immediately available* ***NATO*** *force in the Bosnian region.*

Above: France's contribution to the Bosnian peacekeeping effort includes some 10,000 troops together with carrier-based air power and Armée de l'Air Mirage F1CR reconnaissance fighters, air-defence Mirage 2000Cs and multi-role Mirage 2000Ns in Italy.

Below: Turkey provided a unit of licence-built Lockheed F-16Cs as part of NATO's Operation Deny Flight, enforcing the no-fly zone over Bosnia. Here one of the Turkish aircraft approaches a USAF KC-135 tanker while on a combat air patrol.

keen to use airpower and the Europeans more cautious. Stuck in the middle of this high level political dogfight, were the troops of the UN Protection Force (UNPROFOR) and the airmen of 5 ATAF.

In June 1993, the international community agreed to provide UNPROFOR with close air support (CAS) if its troops came under attack, so 5 ATAF was allowed to start flying CAS aircraft over Bosnia on a daily basis to be ready to strike if UN troops came under fire. However, in what came to be known as the 'dual key' arrangement, they could only act if the UN Secretary General himself agreed. One month later NATO's new strike capability was used to issue an ultimatum to the Serbs to withdraw from Mount Igman overlooking Sarajevo.

During 1994 the international community agreed to make UNPROFOR's posture and ROE more robust, giving its new commander, Lt Gen Sir Michael Rose, the green light to use airpower against the warring factions' artillery sites around Sarajevo. All heavy weapons within a 32-km (20-mile) exclusion zone were to be placed under UN control or face air attack. This set the agenda for the coming year, with a series of crises developing around the Bosnian capital over the control of Serb heavy weapons. Twice General Rose called in air strikes against weapons not in control points.

In April 1994 CAS was used twice against Serb troops attacking Gorazde in eastern Bosnia after British Special Air Service troops came under fire and one was killed. A further heavy weapon exclusion zone was then established around the town to deter more Serb attacks.

Following the Udbina air strike in November 1994 and subsequent NATO attacks on Serb anti-aircraft sites, the Serbs escalated the conflict by taking more than 300 UN troops hostage around Sarajevo. The international community backed down and refused to call the Serbs' bluff. NATO air operations were dramatically scaled down and the Serbs released their hostages.

Next spring a repeat of the hostage crisis occurred when General Rose's successor, Lt Gen Rupert Smith, ordered two NATO air strikes on a weapons dump outside Sarajevo after Serbs forcibly removed artillery from a UN collection point. Again the UN and NATO was ordered to back down by the international community in order to secure the release of the 300 UN peacekeepers held hostage by the Serbs. During this crisis USAF F-16 pilot Capt Scott O'Grady was shot down over west-

Right: Captain Scott O'Grady arrives at Frankfurt after his dramatic rescue by Marine Corps helicopters. O'Grady's F-16 had been shot down by a surface-to-air missile, but he managed to evade Serbian forces searching for him.

Targets for attack

None of the sides fighting in Bosnia showed any great respect for past agreements, but history seems to have cast the Bosnian Serbs as the most disruptive force in the region. The only way for NATO to persuade them to hold to their agreements was to use force. NATO had flown some ground attack missions earlier in the war, but it was Operation Deliberate Force in 1995 which persuaded them to pull back from their siege of Sarajevo. Carried out at the end of August, large scale attacks delivered more than 1,000 bombs – the majority precision-guided – against key Serb positions. The ferocity and deadly accuracy of the strikes against anti-aircraft and communications sites convinced everybody involved that NATO was through with playing games.

Left: A communications facility high in the hills between Sarajevo and the Serb stronghold of Pale lies shattered and in ruins after being subject to the surgical sledgehammer of NATO precision-guided weapon attacks.

Above: The deadly efficiency of Operation Deliberate Force persuaded the Bosnian Serbs to pull heavy artillery and surface-to-air missiles back from Sarajevo. This collection of anti-aircraft equipment was part of the withdrawal.

British Aerospace Sea Harrier FA.2

Latest incarnation of the long-serving Harrier V/STOL fighter to enter service, the Sea Harrier FA.Mk 2 made its combat debut over Bosnia in August 1994. It was flown by No. 899 Squadron, the Fleet Air Arm's Operational Evaluation Unit, from the deck of HMS *Invincible.*

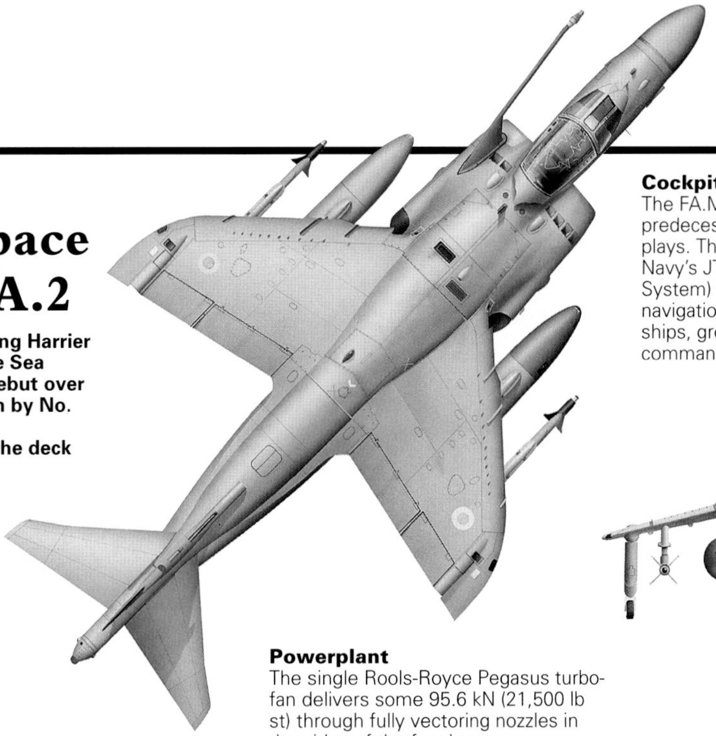

Cockpit
The FA.Mk 2's cockpit retains the head-up display of its predecessor, with two new multi-function cockpit displays. The fighter is currently being integrated with the US Navy's JTIDS (Joint Tactical Information Distribution System) which can securely transfer communications, navigation and targeting data between aircraft, surface ships, ground units and airborne, ground-based and naval command and control systems.

Air-to-surface weapons
With a maximum weapons load of more than 3600 kg (7,935 lb), the Sea Harrier FA.Mk 2 can deliver guided and unguided bombs, air-to-surface rockets, Sea Eagle anti-ship missiles or ALARM anti-radar missiles.

Powerplant
The single Rools-Royce Pegasus turbofan delivers some 95.6 kN (21,500 lb st) through fully vectoring nozzles in the sides of the fuselage.

Radar
The GEC-Marconi Blue Vixen multi-mode radar offers all-weather look-down/shoot-down capability, multiple target engagement and enhanced surface target acquisition.

Air-to-air weapons
The FA.Mk 2 can carry four AIM-120 AMRAAM missiles, or two AMRAAMs and four AIM-9 Sidewinders, The fuselage pylons can be replaced by two 30-mm Aden cannon pods.

ern Bosnia by an SA-6 SAM.

Further humiliation was heaped on the UN and NATO in July when their political masters called off air operations in support of the Dutch garrison defending the UN safe area at Srebrenica after UN troops were again taken hostage by the Serbs.

In July 1995 the UN and NATO were authorised by the London Conference to begin preparations for widespread offensive air action against the Bosnian Serbs if the safe areas came under attack again. To clear the decks and prevent further hostage taking UN troops were withdrawn from the enclaves of Gorazde and Zepa in August.

A 30 August mortar attack on Sarajevo was the trigger for 5 ATAF to launch Operation Deliberate Force. Some 300 NATO aircraft were involved, flying strike, fighter, SEAD, reconnaissance, combat search and rescue, air-to-air refuelling, transport and liaison missions over a period of two weeks.

Deliberate Force

In the course of Operation Deliberate Force NATO aircraft and UN artillery from the Rapid Reaction Force destroyed key Bosnian Serb air defence sites, command posts, communications towers, ammunition depots, bridges, surface-to-air missile batteries and artillery batteries.

Some 708 precision-guided weapons and 300 'iron' bombs were used during the air offensive, along with 13 Tomahawk cruise missiles fired from a US Navy cruiser in the Adriatic. Under the weight of this highly accurate bombardment, which was eating away at their prized military assets, the Bosnian Serbs gave in to UN demands for free access to Sarajevo and pulled back all their heavy guns from the city. Serb commanders had finally seen what NATO and the UN could do when aroused, and they did not like the result.

Barely a month later Serb, Croat and Bosnian political leaders signed the Dayton peace accords, ending the war and opening the way on 20 December 1996 for NATO to deploy its peace Implementation Force (IFOR) to take over from UNPROFOR.

IFOR troops, now in camouflage rather than UN white, were mandated to enforce vigorously the military provisions of the Dayton accords and ground commanders were free to call in air support without recourse to the cumbersome UN chain of command. 5 ATAF simply became IFOR's air component. Its aircraft continued to police the skies over Bosnia looking for prohibited military air activity; they flew CAS support for IFOR troops being threatened by former warring faction troops and conducted extensive air reconnaissance to look for activity breaching the Dayton accords.

In 1997 IFOR handed over to the new NATO military force, dubbed the Stabilisation Force (SFOR), but 5 ATAF continued going about its business in much the same way as before. NATO fighter and strike aircraft from America, Belgium, Britain, France, Germany, Holland, Italy, Spain and Turkey continue to make daily sweeps over Bosnia to support alliance ground troops.

Left: Ultimately, the major purpose of NATO's intervention in Bosnia was to allow airmen like these members of the USAF Reserve to deliver the aid so necessary to avoid a humanitarian disaster.

ASIA

Conflict in Asia since the end of World War II has been caused by a number of widely varying factors. The Cold War has been a minor contributor to many of the wars, though the first real East/West shooting confrontation fought out in Korea was a notable exception. The liberation struggles which forced the withdrawal of the old imperial powers were a much more common cause of battle, with religion being thrown in as an added irritant in the wars betwen India and Pakistan. But if there is one area which exemplifies war in Asia, it is Indochina. The region has seen more than half a century of colonial, post-colonial, tribal, capitalist and communist struggle, all fought on a foundation of more than a thousand years of local rivalry.

The Dutch East Indies & Indonesia

1945-1963

Left: The P-51D/K Mustang was the primary Dutch fighter and ground-attack aircraft at the outbreak of hostilities in the Dutch East Indies after World War II. This flight (probably from No. 120 or 122 Squadron) is seen over Medan in Sumatra in October 1948. Following the Dutch withdrawal in 1950, the Mustangs were handed over to the fledgling Indonesian air force which operated them until well into the 1970s.

Below: Dutch strike power took the form of two units with B-25D/J Mitchells; No. 18 Squadron based on Kemajoram and No. 16 Sqn at Palembang. Both were tasked with medium bombing and were used extensively between 1946 and 1950.

The Netherlands East Indies were occupied by the Japanese during World War II. On liberation the Dutch expected that power would be restored to them, though the indigenous Indonesians had been promised independence by the Japanese during the closing stages of the war. Sukharno, the nationalist leader, declared independence on 17 August 1945, three days after the Japanese surrender.

The area was under British control, and they found themselves opposed by freed Dutch POWs and internees, and by the republicans, who naturally suspected that the two European colonial nations would co-operate against their interests. Republican forces began disrupting Britain's POW repatriation operations, forcing the British into an alliance with the Dutch.

RAF aircraft (principally P-47D Thunderbolts, Mosquitoes and Spitfire Mk XIVs) began flying sorties against terrorist positions, usually after dropping warning leaflets. Dutch forces began replacing British units, and local negotiations resulted in an informal agreement that Java and Sumatra would come under the authority of the Indonesians themselves, while the Dutch would share the task of bringing the remaining islands into a federation.

There was a ceasefire in early 1947, and agreement that Indonesia would be a federal united states, with some allegiance to the Netherlands, but the details were sketchy and ceasefire violations increased. The Dutch captured most towns, and interned the nationalist leadership, but growing international pressure and American threats to withdraw aid forced a formal ceasefire on 11 August 1949, and there was a transfer of sovereignty to a new United States of Indonesia (under the released Sukharno) on 27 December 1949.

Indonesian ambitions

The new nation was inherently unstable, encompassing 100 million ethnically and religiously diverse people on 10,000 islands, many of whom had no wish to exchange rule from the Hague for rule from Batavia. Sukharno's ambition to expand Indonesia's territories, coupled with a tolerance of the communists, led to US hostility to his rule, and the CIA supported his opponents when they staged an abortive rebellion in Sumatra and Celebes in February 1958. This support took the form of training, the organisation and payment of mercenaries, and an air force of ex-USAF aircraft including 15 B-26s, a C-54, various C-46s and C-47s, and, according to some sources, a B-29. These were operated fron Manado on the northern tip of Celebes, and one B-26 was shot down during a raid on Ambon on 18 May 1958. An amnesty was offered in 1961, and the rebellion ended.

Sukharno claimed Dutch New Guinea from 1957, on the basis that as a Dutch colony in the Dutch East Indies, it should always have been part of Indonesia. By 1960 he was threatening to take the colony by force of arms, and in response the Dutch deployed No.322 Squadron, with 12 Hawker Hunter F.Mk 4s and two Alouette IIs, to Biak, to augment 12 Neptunes of No.321 Squadron, a similar number of Firefly AS.Mk 4s of No.6 Squadron, and a number of C-47s. An Indonesian invasion fleet arrived on 15 January 1962, covered by F-51D Mustangs and accompanied by a paratroop drop. One landing ship was sunk by a Dutch warship, and negotiations began before the Hunters could intervene. Dutch New Guinea was handed over as West Irian in May 1963.

Below: Indonesia's territorial claims to Dutch New Guinea in 1960 were met by a deployment of Dutch air power when 12 Hunter F. Mk 4 fighters of No. 322 Squadron were sent to Biak. The archer emblem on the fin identifies this F.4 as a Hunter of sister unit No. 323 Squadron.

Below: The heavily-armed B-26 Invader was operated by both the Indonesian air force and anti-government forces. In addition to the eight nose guns, the air force example seen here also carries four rockets and a twin 12.7-mm (0.5-in) gun pod under each wing.

Right: At the time of the Hunters' deployment, the Royal Netherlands air force already had air assets in place in the form of maritime patrol Neptunes and a unit of Firefly naval strike fighters. These flew some operational missions when a limited shooting war broke out in January 1962.

French Indochina

1945-1954

Left: Although handicapped by a lack of range, inadequate ventilation and a restricted view downwards, the F8F Bearcat proved popular and successful in Indochina, able to deliver a wide variety of ordnance and proving fast and agile enough to be a difficult target for ground fire.

Below: Ten squadrons of Bearcats were active in Indochina during the war, three of them operating in the reconnaissance role.

Left: The first US front-line aircraft type in service in Indochina was the Bell P-63C King Cobra, four squadrons of which were supplied from July 1949. These equipped Groupes des Chasse 5 and 6.

The return of French government to Indochina after the ending of Japanese occupation during World War II was followed inevitably by increasing tension created by the Viet Minh, who attempted but failed to wrest control of Hanoi and other cities from the French. However, although the French took the initiative, they never managed to crush the Vietnamese partisans, whose strength steadily increased.

As early as August 1945 the French government had ordered the embarkation of Armée de l'Air units for the Far East and, after the blocking by the USA of use of P-47 Thunderbolts in Southeast Asia, France acquired from the UK a number of Spitfire Mk IXs which arrived at Saigon to join some Spitfire Mk VIIIs (transferred after the departure of RAF No. 273 Squadron from Tan Son Nhut in January 1946) and a few Nakajima Ki-43 'Oscar' fighters seized from the Japanese after the Pacific War.

Close support

The French air forces in Indochina were employed exclusively in the ground supply and support roles as the Viet Minh possessed no combat aircraft. On the other hand, supplied increasingly and almost exclusively by Communist China in the north, the guerrillas became highly proficient in the use of light flak guns of 20-, 23- and 37-mm calibres, weapons that were to take a mounting toll of French aircraft.

The Armée de l'Air in Indochina was initially organised into two tactical groups, TFIN in Tonkin and northern Annam, and TFIS in Cochin-China and southern Annam. In 1950 these were redeployed as three groups, GATAC North for Tonkin, GATAC Central for Annam, and GATAC South for Cochin-China. During the first half of 1947 the French flew a number of Mosquito Mk VI fighter-bombers in the theatre but, although able to reach further over guerrilla-held territory, they were plagued by poor serviceability, their wooden construction proving

Left: The Japanese surrender in Indochina was taken by Britain in the south, and by China in the north. A Vichy French administration had ruled the area until March 1945, when the Japanese proclaimed Vietnamese, independence and interning the French. British forces helped the French re-establish control (including the North, the independent Republic of Vietnam, initially recognised by France). The Viet Minh mounted a guerrilla war from across the Chinese border, and prevented the French from consolidating their position, isolating garrisons which were later over-run. The French lost 6,000 men at Cao Bang (23 walked out alive) and 2,293 dead and 9,000 PoWs at Dien Bien.

Below: The Supermarine Spitfire was France's primary combat aircraft in Indochina in the early years, because the USA blocked the use of more suitable types outside Europe.

Borrowed and blue

The French made extensive use of single-engined fighters and attack aircraft against the Viet Minh. In the early years many of these were Spitfires borrowed and later purchased from the RAF, while the Armée de l'Air also used fighters captured from the Japanese. These were augmented by Aéronavale aircraft, operating from ship and shore bases, with American types used after an embargo was lifted in 1947.

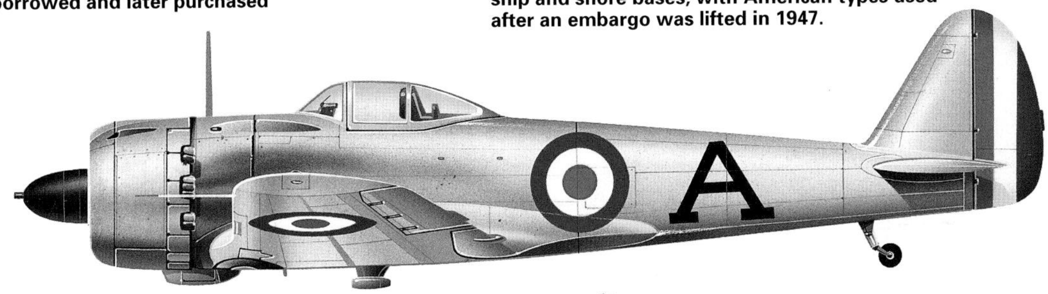

Nakajima Ki-43-11
When Escadron de Chasse 1/7 was sent to Indochina, its pilots arrived before its crated Spitfires. They flew captured ex-Japanese Oscars repainted in French markings.

Curtiss SB2C-5 Helldiver
American hostility to European nations re-establishing their pre-war colonial empires initially led them to ban the use of US combat aircraft in Indochina, forcing the Armée de l'Air to deploy Spitfires and Mosquitoes rather than P-47 Thunderbolts and B-26 Invaders.

Grumman F6F Hellcat
Ex-US Navy Hellcats were used by three Groupes de Chasse of the Armée de l'Air between 1950 and 1953. French navy F6Fs were also deployed from September 1951 aboard the carriers *Arromanches* and *Lafayette*.

Chance Vought AU-1 Corsair
Although operated by French naval pilots, the Chance Vought Corsair flew exclusively from land bases in Indochina. The USA had loaned 25 examples of the type, which were used in the last two years of the war.

unsuitable for prolonged service in the hot, humid conditions.

As the nature of the anti-guerrilla operations underwent change during 1948-49, and the Viet Minh tended to concentrate their forces closer to the distant borders with China, the French made renewed efforts to persuade the Americans to permit the use of US aircraft, at just the moment when the Communists were gaining spectacular victories over the Western-aligned Chinese nationalists. As a result of these overtures the French were able to send about 50 Bell F-63C Kingcobras to Indochina, aircraft which proved well suited to the conditions and demands of the campaign and, indeed, were superi-

Left: Despite the pressing demands of the Korean War, the USA supplied enough B-26 Invaders to equip three bomber squadrons, with another active in the reconnaissance role.

Below: The Consolidated PBY-2 Privateer saw extensive service in the long-range reconnaissance and patrol roles over Indochina. Several were lost to ground fire during the long war.

Left: The Vietnamese Air Force was formed with French aid from June 1951, when a training centre was opened at Nha Trang. The first air observation squadrons with MS.500s was formed in July 1951.

Right: In Indochina GT 1/34 used captured German Ju 52/3ms, but other units, including GT 2/62, GT 2/63, GT 1/64 and GT 3/64 used the French-built equivalent, the Amiot AAC.1 Toucan.

or to the relatively short-range Spitfires. These two aircraft types were in turn joined and eventually replaced by Grumman F8F Bearcats which, although still possessing a disappointing radius of action, were fast and capable of delivering a wide range of ground-support weapons.

Before 1951 the French did not employ bombers as such (other than fighter-bombers with relatively modest loads), simply because the dispersal of the guerrilla forces rendered them almost immune to set-piece bombing. However, during November that year, despite pre-occupation with the war in Korea, the USA supplied sufficient B-26 Invaders to equip two groups, and these aircraft undertook vital and successful bombing and reconnaissance work right up to the end of the campaign.

Air transport played a vital, albeit inconspicuous part in the French operations, the venerable World War II Junkers Ju 52/3m (dubbed the Toucan in the Armée de l'Air) and the C-47 later being joined by a few Bristol Type 170 Freighters and Fairchild C-119s, whose operations were limited to the small number of well-paved air bases. For the evacuation of casualties and movement of prisoners in the forward areas, the French possessed 17 Hiller UH-12 and H-23 light helicopters and 25 Westland-Sikorsky S-51 and S-55 medium helicopters.

Left: French MS.500s were used for directing air strikes and artillery barrages, as well as for liaison flying. The MS.500 was a licensed copy of the German wartime Fieseler Fi 156 Storch.

Aéronavale forces

French naval aviation was involved in the war almost from the start. In October 1945 Flottille 8F arrived in the region with the Consolidated PBY Catalina, being joined soon afterwards by four Japanese Aichi E13A1s of Escadrille 8S. Placed at the disposal of the overall air command in Indochina, the naval air components took part in numerous operations, of which one involved the return of French forces to Tonkin in March 1946. The E13A1s were joined in August 1947 by Supermarine Sea Otters, and shortly after by two flotilles of Douglas SBD Dauntless dive-bombers.

The escalation of the war at the start of the 1950s prompted the Aéronavale to acquire Grumman F6F Hellcats, which were also being introduced by the Armée de l'Air, and Curtiss SB2C Helldivers. Flottille 3F took on charge its first Consolidated PB4Y-2 Privateer, an aircraft which eventually played a major role in the Battle of Dien Bien Phu. In March 1952 Escadrille 8S re-equipped with the Grumman JRF-5 Goose.

In September 1953, the aircraft carrier *Arromanches* arrived to reinforce the naval force with F6Fs, SB2Cs and Vought AU-1 (F4U-7) Corsairs, took part in the Battle of Dien Bien Phu.

This last chapter followed a change in French tactics by General Henri Navarrel, based on the concentration of well-supplied 'honeypot' garrisons within Viet Minh-dominated territory in the north, intended to draw the guerril-

Air transport

The thick jungles of Vietnam made communications difficult, placing a premium on air transport. The Armée de l'Air operated a massive fleet of transport aircraft to support its widespread network of garrisons. As the war in Indochina raged, transport aircraft played an increasingly active role. By the end of the war they were resupplying isolated and besieged garrisons like Dien Bien Phu.

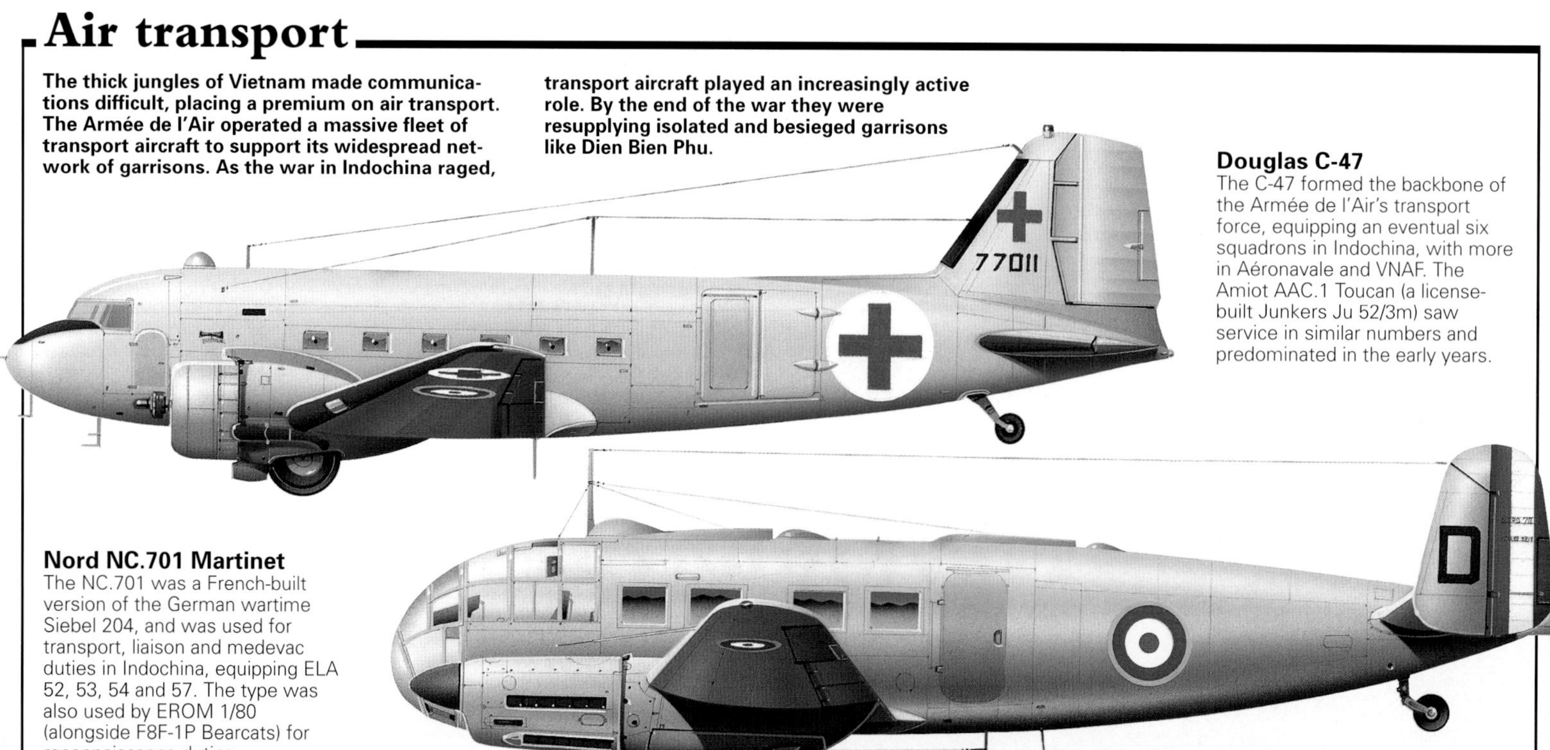

Douglas C-47
The C-47 formed the backbone of the Armée de l'Air's transport force, equipping an eventual six squadrons in Indochina, with more in Aéronavale and VNAF. The Amiot AAC.1 Toucan (a license-built Junkers Ju 52/3m) saw service in similar numbers and predominated in the early years.

Nord NC.701 Martinet
The NC.701 was a French-built version of the German wartime Siebel 204, and was used for transport, liaison and medevac duties in Indochina, equipping ELA 52, 53, 54 and 57. The type was also used by EROM 1/80 (alongside F8F-1P Bearcats) for reconnaissance duties.

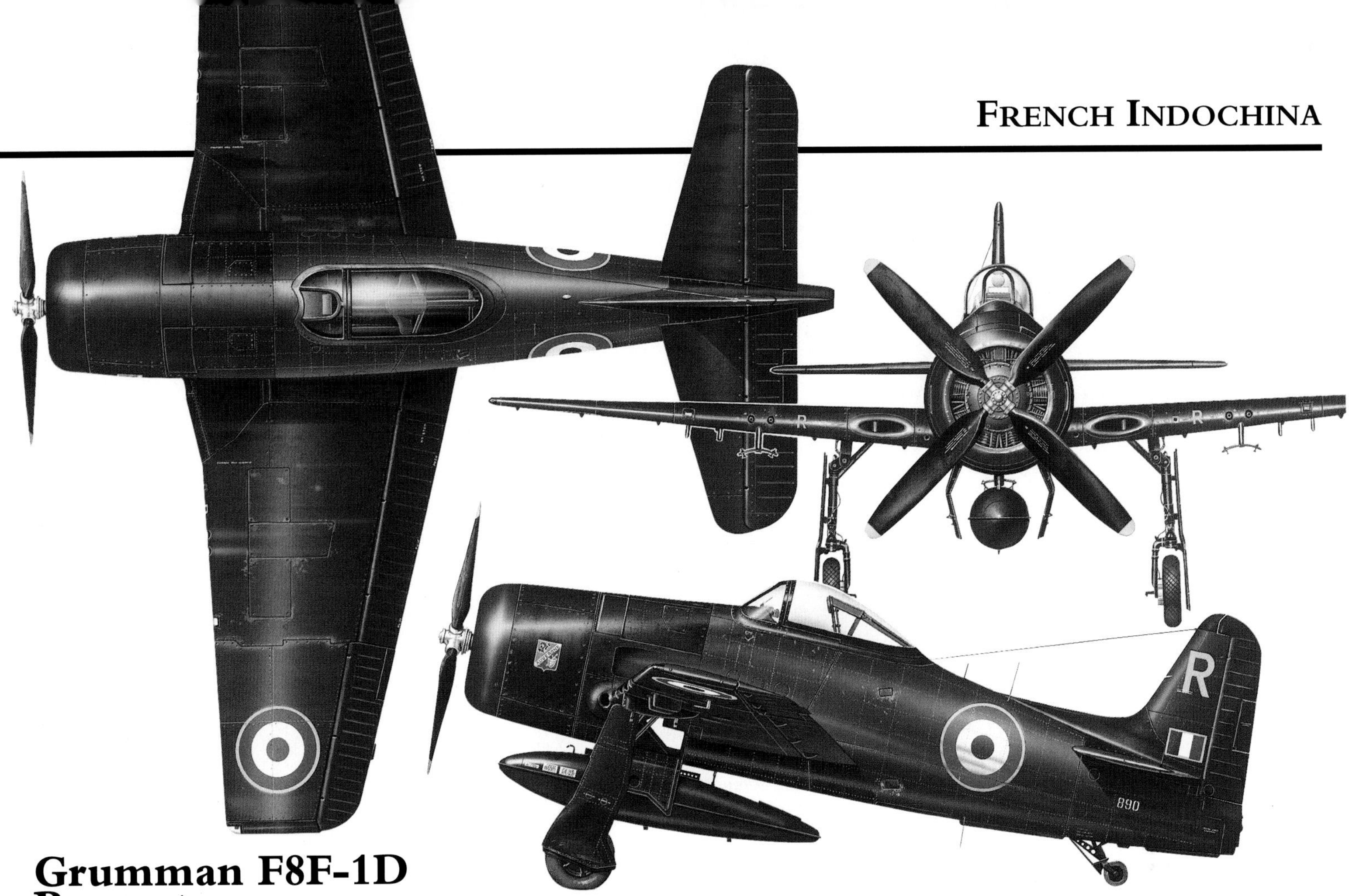

Grumman F8F-1D Bearcat

This F8F-1 wears the insignia and yellow-edged fin flash of Groupe de Chasse 9's and 2nd Escadron, GC 2/9 'Auvergne'. The unit transitioned to the F8F from the F6F-5 Hellcat, and flew mainly from Tan Son Nhut.

The Bearcat in Indochina
The F8F equipped a number of units in Indochina, including GC 1/8 (later GC 1/22), GM 2/8, GC 2/9 'Auvergne') later GC 2/22), GM 2/9 (later GC 2/21), GC 1/21 (later GC 1/22 'Saintagne').

Role
Though designed as a dedicated shipborne air-defence fighter, the F8F found its niche as a land-based fighter/bomber. Some were deployed to Dien Bien Phu, where they were destroyed on the ground.

la forces into open battle. After a number of limited successes by these garrisons, the forces at Dien Bien Phu were totally surrounded by considerable Communist formations, and although constantly reinforced, supported and supplied from the air the French garrison was finally over-run in May 1954. This crushing psychological blow, coming as it did less than 10 years after France had emerged battered from World War II, lent impetus to peace negotiations which were then about to open in Geneva. A cease-fire, which in fact acknowledged defeat of the French throughout Indochina, was agreed on 20 July that year.

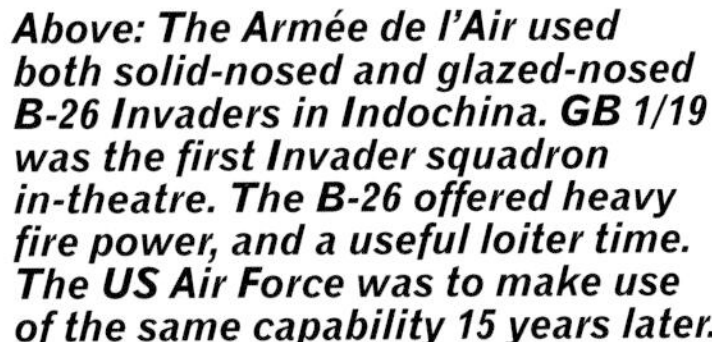

***Above:** The Armée de l'Air used both solid-nosed and glazed-nosed B-26 Invaders in Indochina. GB 1/19 was the first Invader squadron in-theatre. The B-26 offered heavy fire power, and a useful loiter time. The US Air Force was to make use of the same capability 15 years later.*

***Above:** Bearcat pilots of GC 1/22 'Saintogne' brief before a strike mission. The Bearcat's STOL characteristics allowed it to operate from forward airstrips, which compensated for its relatively short range.*

***Below:** Fairchild C-119s were loaned to the French in Indochina and were operated in Civil Air Transport livery, by crews supplied by Claire Chennault. A handful were lost in action.*

Malaya: Operation 'Firedog'

1948-1960

Above: The nuclear bombs dropped on Hiroshima and Nagasaki ended the war before the Hornet could enter service, and the jet age rendered it obsolete for home defence. The RAF's fastest piston-engined fighter found its niche as a fighter-bomber in the Far East. Here a flight of Hornets from No. 45 Squadron flies over Malaya.

There had been an anti-British guerrilla movement in Malaya before the Japanese occupation of 1942, but the British administration then supported this Chinese-led organisation as the only element able to harass and spy on the mutual enemy, Japan. Thus, at the end of the war the British found themselves with a depleted infrastructure of their own but facing a well organised and equipped guerrilla force. Under pressure, but otherwise reluctant to grant independence, the British attempted to shepherd the diverse sultanates and states into a federation under the British flag. The

Left: Bristol Brigands replaced ageing Beaufighters with Nos 45 and 84 Squadrons, but had a short career before they were themselves retired after an alarming spate of structural failures and accidents. Here a Brigand of No. 84 Squadron rockets a terrorist target. The Brigand gave way to the de Havilland Hornet from 1951.

Above: Australia contributed a squadron of long-range Avro Lincoln B.Mk 30 heavy bombers to the war. RAF Lincolns also took part, on temporary deployments from the UK. The Lincolns of No. 1 Squadron, RAAF, were replaced by a squadron of Canberras and two of Sabres in 1958, but by then the war was almost over.

Piston-engined warriors

The harsh climatic conditions, primitive facilities and absence of an enemy air threat allowed the RAF to make use of a number of piston-engined aircraft types in Malaya that would have been considered obsolete in Europe. The Beaufighter, Spitfire, Mosquito and Hornet finished their front-line careers in Malaya, supporting Operation 'Firedog'.

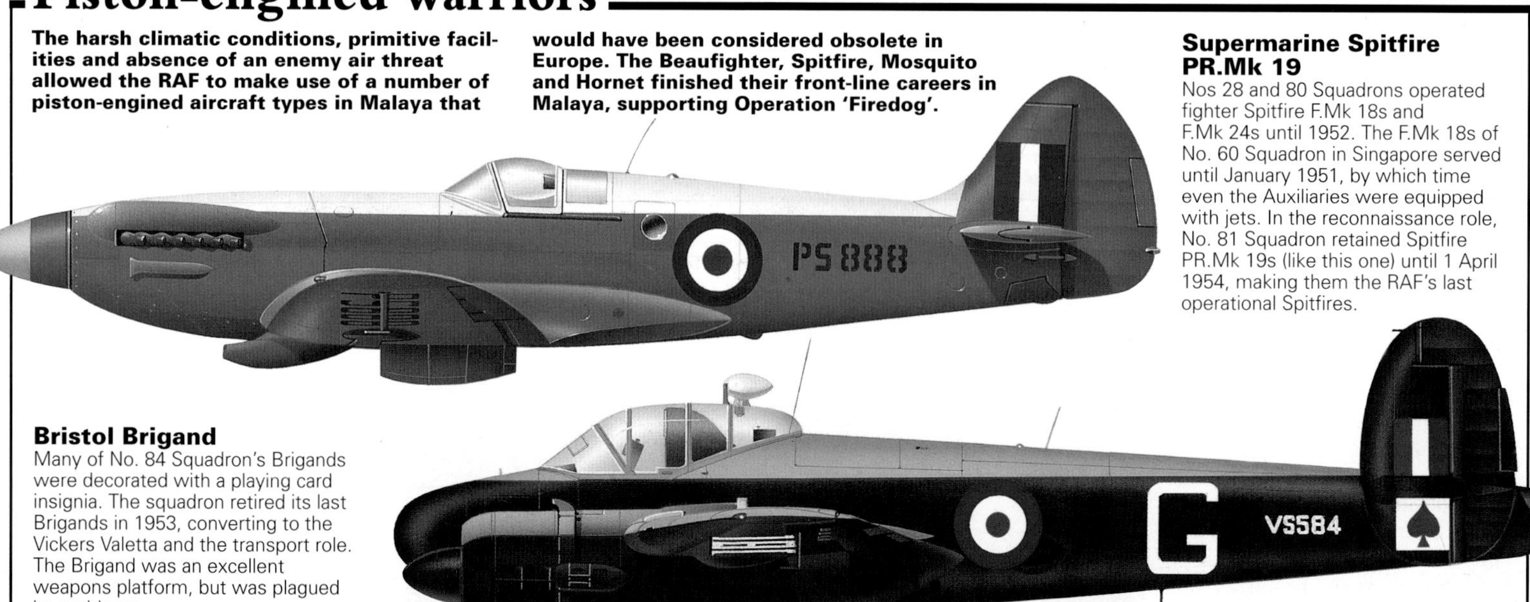

Supermarine Spitfire PR.Mk 19

Nos 28 and 80 Squadrons operated fighter Spitfire F.Mk 18s and F.Mk 24s until 1952. The F.Mk 18s of No. 60 Squadron in Singapore served until January 1951, by which time even the Auxiliaries were equipped with jets. In the reconnaissance role, No. 81 Squadron retained Spitfire PR.Mk 19s (like this one) until 1 April 1954, making them the RAF's last operational Spitfires.

Bristol Brigand

Many of No. 84 Squadron's Brigands were decorated with a playing card insignia. The squadron retired its last Brigands in 1953, converting to the Vickers Valetta and the transport role. The Brigand was an excellent weapons platform, but was plagued by problems.

Above: The RAF Tengah wing shows its teeth, here photographed from a No. 81 Squadron Pembroke. De Havilland Venoms flank an Australian Lincoln of No. 1 Squadron. They were flown by No. 45 Squadron at Butterworth and by No. 60 Squadron, RAF, and No. 14 Squadron, RNZAF at Tengah.

Below: Malaya was mainly a ground war and resupply of the troops was mostly by air as the roads were non-existing. These were mainly paradropped from Dakotas, Valettas and Hastings. Here a RAAF Dakota from No. 38 Squadron is seen returning to Changi after one such drop.

Communist-inspired guerrillas now took on the mantle of freedom fighters and unified all independence-seeking groups behind them against the UK. So started the campaign, generally known as the Malayan Emergency, which lasted until 1962. The military operation in Malaya was known as Operation 'Firedog'.

Forces in-theatre

When the state of emergency was declared in 1948, the RAF deployed a total of eight squadrons of Spitfires, Mosquitoes, Beaufighters and Dakotas at Changi, Seletar and Tengah on Singapore Island, and at Kuala Lumpur in the north. The tropical climate played havoc with the wooden Mosquitoes and these aircraft had to be quickly replaced, along with the Spitfires, the more recently deployed Tempests which could not carry sufficient stores, and the Beaufighter which was becoming obsolete.

In came the Bristol Brigand flown by No. 45 Squadron, and although they could put up impressive displays of attacks with guns, bombs and rockets, it was soon discovered that such techniques had little effect on the loose bands of guerrillas operating 'somewhere' under the triple-canopy rain forest below. Only when Lincolns were deployed from the UK to carry out area bombing did an impression begin to be made. Such deployments were sporadic, since these bombers could not be easily spared from their other duties, but the Royal Australian Air Force contributed Lincolns on a more permanent basis from 1950 onwards. The Brigands ran into serviceability and safety problems and were supplanted by de Havilland Hornets, which were very manoeuvrable and could

Below: The war against the terrorists in Malaya provided the helicopter with a unique opportunity to demonstrate its usefulness for supporting jungle warfare. Whirlwinds of No. 848 Squadron, RN, and No. 155 Squadron RAF were deployed to Malaya.

Below: During the war, Britain had equipped, organised and trained the guerrillas who had resisted the Japanese. These same groups formed the basis of the anti-British guerrilla movement after the war, resisting British attempts to organise the diverse states and sultanates of the area into a Federal Malaysia. Remarkably, the guerrillas attracted little popular support, and the British were able to isolate them in the jungle and defeat them militarily, largely using air power from an extensive network of bases.

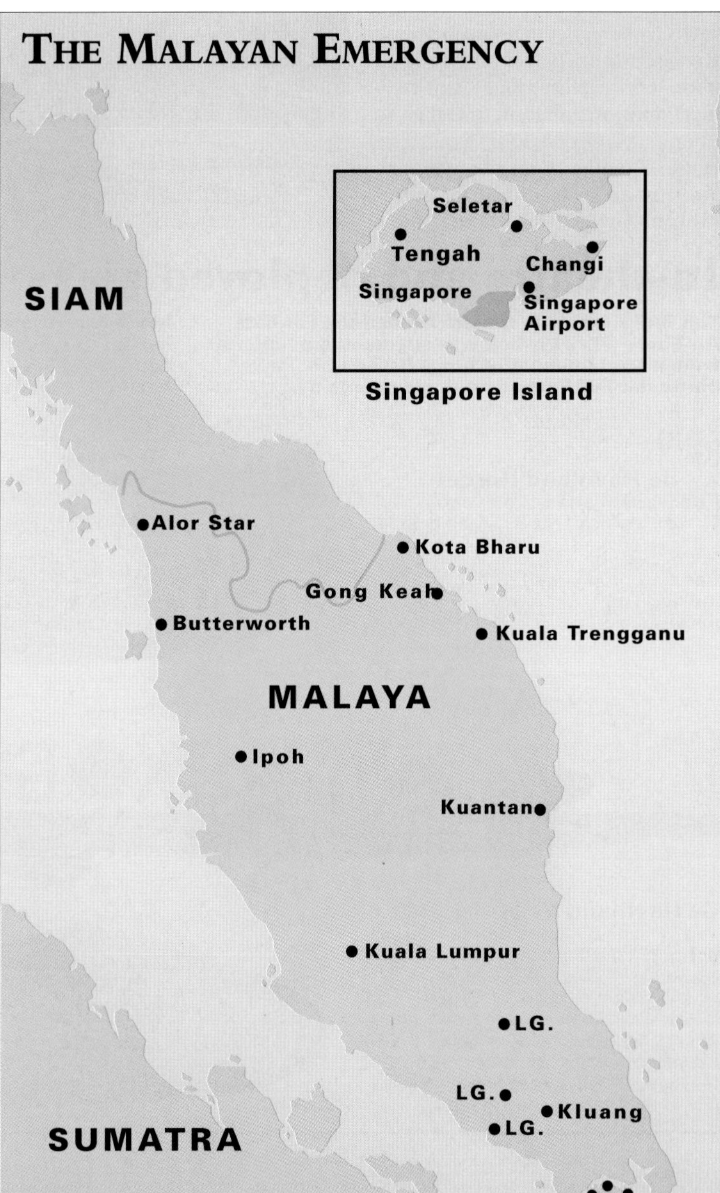

Left: The Westland Dragonfly was essentially a licence-built Sikorsky S-51, though most Dragonflies also used a British Alvis Leonides engine in place of the usual Pratt & Whitney Wasp Junior. A casevac flight was sent to Malaya in 1950, and this became No. 194 Squadron on 1 February 1953.

attack with precision in conditions of bad weather and tricky terrain.

JET AIRCRAFT ARRIVE

By 1953, jet aircraft began to arrive in the form of Vampires and Meteors and, a little later, Venoms and Canberras. Once again, these were found to be unsuitable, with poor serviceability, range and payload, plus an inherent inability to operate slowly at low level. The tangible results of all this offensive air support was minimal, but it probably helped by keeping the insurgents under pressure and on the move.

Of greater importance was the transport effort. Malaya was devoid of good roads and it was a very slow business for the ground troops to make headway through the jungle and plantations. Resupply from the air was often a necessity, and Dakotas, Valettas and later Hastings paradropped essential supplies to the forces in the field while Yorks ferried material around the peninsula. Paratrooping itself was not often employed, since the dropping zones were seldom hospitable, but Malaya saw the world's first extensive use of helicopters and these soon transformed the tactics of the security forces.

ENTER THE DRAGONFLY

Introduced in 1950, the Sikorsky S-51 Dragonfly began to take on casualty evacuation duties, which improved both efficiency and

Below: English Electric Canberras from UK-based Bomber Command squadrons deployed to Butterworth from Binbrook during 1955 and 1956 under Operation 'Mileage'. This Canberra was from No. 101 Squadron. FEAF gained its own Canberras from 1957.

In-theatre and deployed air power

The RAF's forces in-theatre formed the Far East Air Force (FEAF) which was augmented by aircraft from a large number of home-based units. In particular FEAF relied on deployments by home-based Lincoln and Canberra bombers, and had no organic heavy transport capability of its own. It did have its own fighter-bomber, light-bomber, reconnaissance and light-transport units.

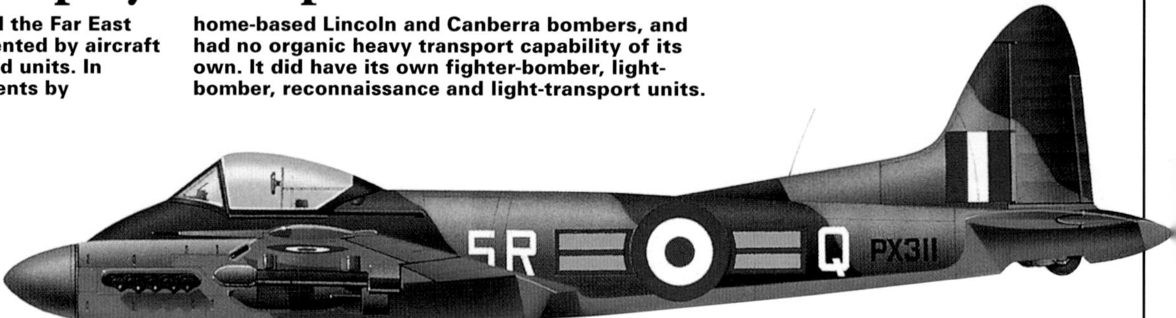

de Havilland Hornet
This Hornet wears the colours and codes of No. 33 Squadron, one of two squadrons using the fast piston-engined fighter in Malaya. Another squadron used the Hornet in Hong Kong.

Avro Lincoln
UK-based Bomber Command Lincolns deployed to Tengah for bombing missions over Malaya under Operations 'Red Lion', 'Musgrave' and 'Bold', between 1947 and 1955.

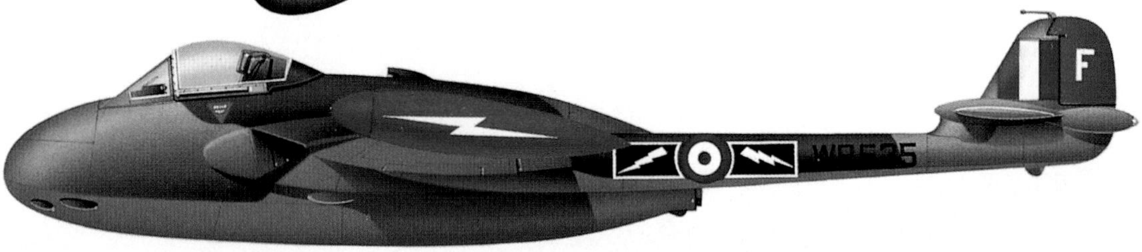

de Havilland Venom FB.Mk 4
This Venom FB.Mk 4 wears the markings of No. 60 Squadron, one of two Venom squadrons at Tengah. Three more Venom squadrons were based in-theatre at Butterworth. The Venom proved a highly effective gun and rocket platform. However, individual airframes were restricted to a few flying hours in-theatre, due to their wooden nose structure.

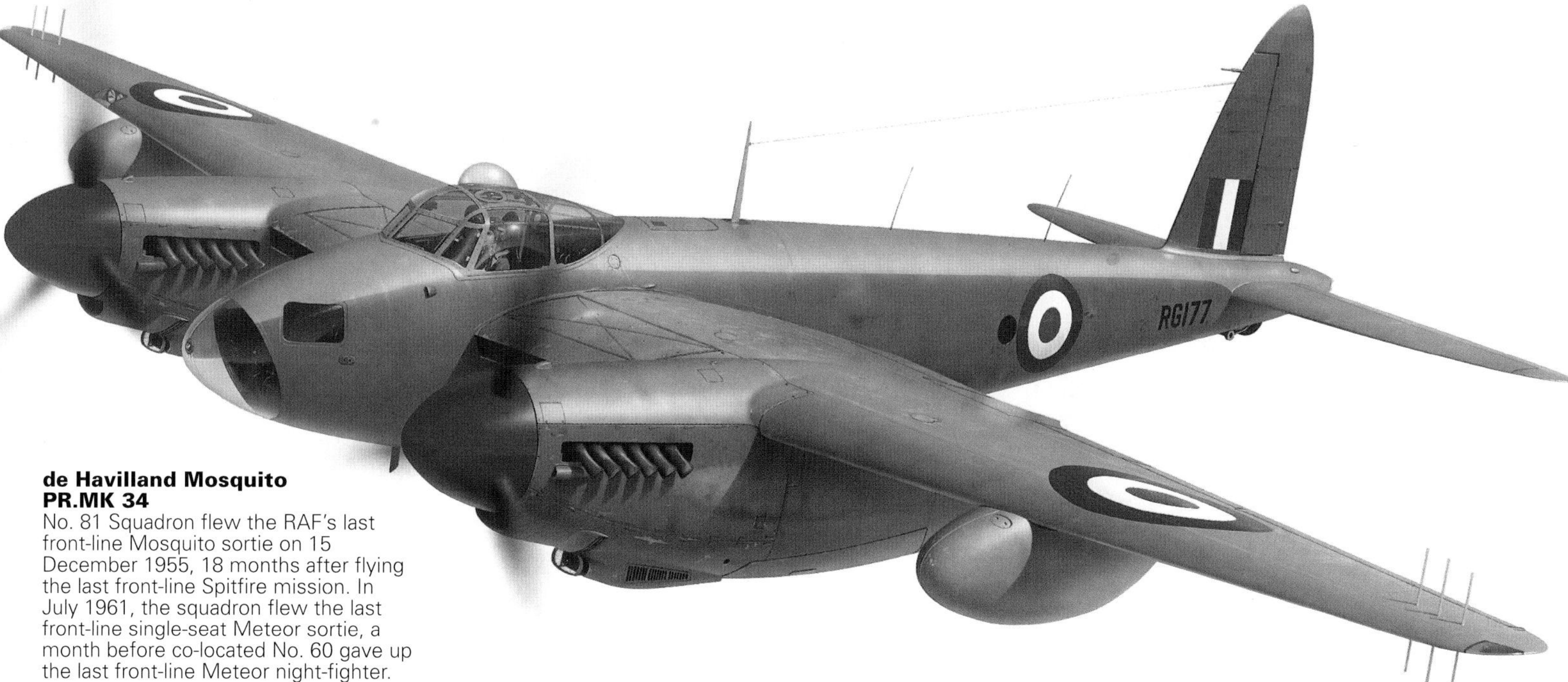

de Havilland Mosquito PR.MK 34
No. 81 Squadron flew the RAF's last front-line Mosquito sortie on 15 December 1955, 18 months after flying the last front-line Spitfire mission. In July 1961, the squadron flew the last front-line single-seat Meteor sortie, a month before co-located No. 60 gave up the last front-line Meteor night-fighter.

morale. By the mid-1950s, Bristol Sycamores and Westland Whirlwinds arrived to undertake assault as well as evacuation sorties. Able to insert up to nine troops into remote areas, they introduced mobility into an otherwise tough, debilitating and painfully slow-moving action. Alongside the helicopters, Auster lightplanes were used to support the observation posts and jungle forts essential to maintaining local security. The Auster AOP.Mk 6 and the later AOP.Mk 9 were able to land and take off in 150 metres (165 yd) and proved to be very useful. Later came the tough Scottish Aviation Pioneer, an aircraft which could carry four passengers instead of the Auster's one and could operate out of airstrips only half the length of those required by the Auster.

Below: The Dragonflys of No. 194 Squadron had established jungle operation techniques so by the time the Bristol Sycamores had arrived in-theatre these lessons could be put to good use. No. 194 Squadron exchanged its Dragonflys for HR.14 Sycamores in October 1954. They are seen here inserting troops into a jungle clearing.

VITAL PHOTO RECCE

Perhaps the most essential air task of all fell to a single squadron which performed superbly throughout Operation 'Firedog'. There was little good mapping of Malaya at the start of the operation and it was impossible to fight the war without this and other vital information. No. 81 Squadron was tasked with photographic reconnaissance of the entire peninsula. Flying a variety of aircraft (Spitfire PR.Mk 19, Mosquito PR.Mk 34, Meteor PR.Mk 10, Pembroke C(PR).Mk 1 and Canberra PR.Mk 7), the squadron unstintingly persevered in its mission and provided vital information for both air strikes and ground operations. It also incidentally flew the last operational sorties of the RAF's Spitfire and Mosquito.

The UK eventually moved towards the grant of independence, fostering the indigenous Malays as the new ruling element. The conflict then took on a racial dimension, with the Chinese isolated against the now unified Malays and British. 'Divide and rule' succeeded and the insurgents fought a losing battle.

Operation 'Firedog' was always a war fought on the ground, but air support in the offensive, transport and reconnaissance roles played a valuable and, maybe, a vital part in the success of the operation.

Above: The Venom proved popular with its pilots and was extensively used in Malaya by both the RAF and Royal New Zealand Air Force. Here a line up of 14 Squadron RNZAF start up for another day's operations from Tengah in 1958.

Right: The RAF's last Avro York was named* Ascalon II*, and served with the FEAF Communications squadron at RAF Changi, Singapore, until its retirement in 1957. It served alongside Dakotas, Valettas, Devons, Pembrokes, Ansons, Harvards, Austers, Vampires, Venoms and Meteors. The aircraft was replaced by a Handley Page Hastings.

Korea: The Early Months

JUNE-OCTOBER 1950

Following some months of intermittent border 'incidents' along the 38th Parallel – the artificial boundary separating North and South Korea that had been established by the United Nations – all-out hostilities began on 25 June 1950. Eight North Korean (Communist) divisions crossed the border in an attempt to achieve a swift conquest of the Republic of Korea (ROK) and impose reunification of the whole country under a single Communist government.

Correctly assessing the almost non-existence of the ROK air force, which comprised no more than 16 unarmed trainers and observation aircraft, the North Korean Air Force (NKAF) possessed a fighter regiment of 70 Yak-9 and La-11s and a ground-attack regiment of 62 Il-10s, all Soviet aircraft of late-World War II vintage. They were

Above: Three Boeing B-29s of the Yokota-based 92nd Bomb Group fly to targets in Korea. B-29s from Guam, forward-deployed to Kadena, actually began bombing operations on 27 June 1950, one day before President Truman formally gave the OK for offensive operations.

Right: An armourer loads up the eight nose-mounted 12.7-mm (0.50-in) calibre machine-guns of a Douglas A-26 Invader of the activated AFRes 452nd Bomb Group, in September 1950. B-26s interdicted targets by day and night.

Left: The British Commonwealth maintained an aircraft-carrier on station off Korea throughout the war. The Australian contribution was provided by HMAS* Sydney*, one of whose Firefly fighter bombers is seen being launched after the carrier had arrived to relieve HMS* Glory*.

Mustangs at war

When war began, F-82 Twin Mustangs based in Japan were the only USAF fighters in the area with sufficient range to fly useful combat missions over Korea. They thus played a large role in the early fighting. Numbers of F-51D Mustangs were returned to service for use in the fighter-bomber role over Korea and some scored air-to-air victories.

F-82G Twin Mustang
This F-82G of the 68th Fighter (All Weather) Squadron, flown by Lt William 'Skeeter' Hudson and Lt Carl Hudson (radar observer), scored the first kill of the war. It occurred over Kimpo airfield, by downing a North Korean Yak-7U coded 'C6'.

F-51D Mustang
This F-51D was the personal aircraft of Major 'Moon' Mullins of the 18th Fighter Bomber Group's 67th Fighter Bomber Squadron, which scored three kills in the Mustang.

Right: When North Korea launched its attack, the South lay outside Truman's protective perimeter, and there were no USAF-based aircraft to cover the evacuation of US civilians. MacArthur solved this by ordering standing patrols by Japan-based F-82G Twin Mustangs.

Below: Grumman F9F-2 Panthers line up on the deck of the USS Leyte (CV-32). The Panther enjoyed some success against North Korean MiGs, but was primarily used in the ground-attack role.

highly effective when no air opposition existed. The North Koreans had not counted, however, on an immediate decision by the UN to resist their aggression by employing all available Western forces under the command of General Douglas MacArthur.

Few modern American combat aircraft had reached the Far East by mid-1950 and, as USAF C-54s hurriedly evacuated American citizens from Seoul, the South Korean capital, the only combat aircraft immediately available in the theatre (and then in Japan, and not Korea itself) were a small number of short-ranged F-80C Shooting Star jet fighter-bombers and some obsolescent North American F-82 Twin Mustang piston-engined fighters. On 27 June, however, the first jet fighter combat by American fighters occurred when four F-80Cs shot down four NKAF Il-10s, while elsewhere F-82Gs destroyed three Yak-9s. The inability of the ROK ground forces to defend their own territory was such that the Communists made swift progress southwards. Seoul and its airfield at Kimpo fell on 28 June as the South Korean army retreated in disarray. Realising that the immediate need was for ground support from the air, the USAF quickly moved three wings of F-51 Mustangs to the theatre, aircraft which proved excellent in the ground-attack role when armed with rockets and bombs and which equipped South African and Australian volunteer squadrons with the UN forces in Korea. At the same time, the F-80s were assigned the air combat role on occasions of interference by the NKAF.

As the UN command frantically assembled ground forces with which to stem the Communist

Below: A B-29 pilot briefs his crew for a pre-dawn take-off on 17 July 1950, when B-29s were being flung into the war in the tactical bombing role, in an attempt to halt the relentless North Korean advance on the ground. Three B-29 groups were assigned to MacArthur.

Above: Watched by an anti-aircraft gun crew, a B-29 lumbers into the air for an attack against strategic targets in North Korea. Such attacks (against harbours, railway yards, oil depots and steel factories began in August 1950, when fighter-bombers took over the tactical targets.

Right: It is unclear why this North Korean Yak trainer is taxiing with three people and a dog aboard. Presumably some heroic rescue mission was being re-enacted for the camera, but the details are lost.

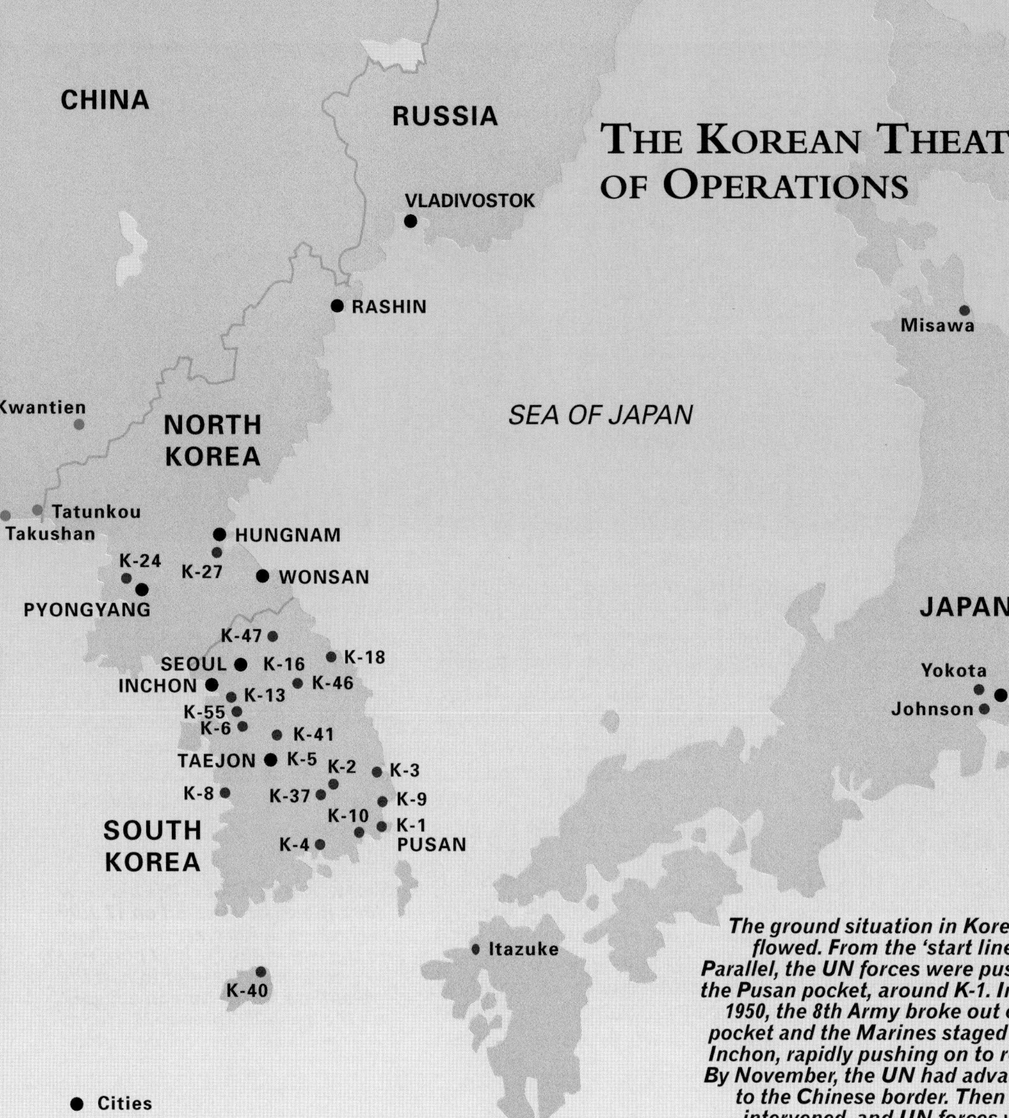

The ground situation in Korea ebbed and flowed. From the 'start line' of the 38th Parallel, the UN forces were pushed back to the Pusan pocket, around K-1. In September 1950, the 8th Army broke out of the Pusan pocket and the Marines staged a landing at Inchon, rapidly pushing on to retake Seoul. By November, the UN had advanced almost to the Chinese border. Then the Chinese intervened, and UN forces were pushed back; by 25 January they had lost Seoul, Inchon, and even Osan. By the end of the war, most territory up to the 38th Parallel was once more in UN hands.

advance, the ROK army having been all but destroyed, USAF strength in the theatre quickly increased. Japan-based B-26 light and B-29 heavy bombers joined aircraft of the US Navy in frequent raids on North Korean industrial targets as well as the key supply routes to the south. By September all but a small area around Pusan in the extreme southeast had been over-run by the invaders, and almost all operations by the UN air forces had to be launched from the US Navy's carriers at sea or from Japan. In the nick of time the advance was halted, as much by exhaustion among the Communist forces as by the relentless air attacks on their supply lines. This exercise of growing UN air superiority was to be the key to the entire war.

The UN air effort became

Above: Although dominated by the USA, the UN effort in Korea was a multinational one. South Africa contributed its No. 2 Squadron 'Flying Cheetahs', initially equipped with F-51Ds, subsequently replacing them with F-86F Sabres.

Below: Peasants duck as a Lockheed F-80 of the 9th FBS, 49th FBG takes off from Itazuke. In this 'bankers war', F-80 pilots lived in luxury, going to war in the morning before returning home for a leisurely round of golf, dinner and a beer in the O club.

Below: Armourers race to load their F4U Corsairs aboard the Philippine Sea *(CV-47), the second USN carrier on the scene in Korea after the* Valley Forge. *An old-fashioned straight-deck carrier, CV-47 embarked four fighter squadrons; VF-113 and VF-114 had F4Us.*

***Left:* These Corsairs of the US Marine Corps' VMF-214 'Blacksheep' flew from the USS *Sicily* on 3 August 1950 to record the first USMC strikes of the Korean War. The squadron subsequently operated from shore bases and played a major part in the defence of the Pusan pocket.**

genuinely multinational on 5 September, when South Africa committed its No. 2 Squadron to the fight. America's main wartime Ally was already involved, along with another Dominion air force. Britain had already joined the fray, sending the aircraft carrier HMS *Triumph* (whose aircraft flew strikes from 3 July), while Australia committed the Japan-based No. 77 Squadron from 26 June.

On 15 September MacArthur launched a powerful amphibious assault at Inchon, 160 km (100 miles) up the west coast of Korea, gaining (on account of poor Communist intelligence) total surprise. Inchon itself fell that same day, and Seoul was retaken within three days of the landings, along with the vital airfield at Kimpo. Supported from the air by aircraft from the fast carriers *Philippine Sea*, *Valley Forge* and *Boxer*, the escort carriers *Bandoeng Strait* and *Sicily* and the Royal Navy's *Triumph*, the landings were co-ordinated with a break-out from the Pusan perimeter, and in a short time the invading Communist army was being systematically decimated.

Air support for Marines

Vought F4U Corsairs, Douglas AD-4 Skyraiders and Grumman F9F-2 Panthers of the US Navy and US Marine Corps, joined by Fleet Air Arm Fireflies and Seafires, let loose a storm of gunfire, rockets and bombs in support of US Marines who went ashore at Wolmi Do. Within a couple of days, Kimpo airfield had been recaptured, and a US Marine night-fighter squadron of Grumman F7F-2N Tigercats, together with helicopters and spotter aircraft, were operating from shore bases.

Meanwhile, US Army forces from the 8th Corps 'holed up' at Pusan broke out of the pocket, and began advancing against the North Koreans with great success.

By the end of September scarcely any organised Communist forces remained at large south of the 38th Parallel. This return to the status quo might well have brought the Korean War to an end after only

***Above:* Designed for World War II but too late to see action, the Grumman F7F Tigercat made its combat debut with the Marine Corps over Korea, where it served as a night fighter.**

***Below:* Operations in Korea were hard on men and machines. Here an F-51D flown by 1st Lt David L Gray of the 16th Fighter Bomber Wing makes a wheels-up landing. His Mustang had been damaged by enemy anti-aircraft fire while on a close support mission for United Nations ground troops.**

Northern combatants

When the war began, the South Korean air force consisted of 13 spotter planes and three T-6 Texans. The North Koreans were considerably better equipped, with an estimated 60 Il-2 and Il-10 Shturmoviks and more than 70 single-engined fighters, principally Yakovlev Yak-3s and Yak-7s. The NKAF also had a significant support and training element.

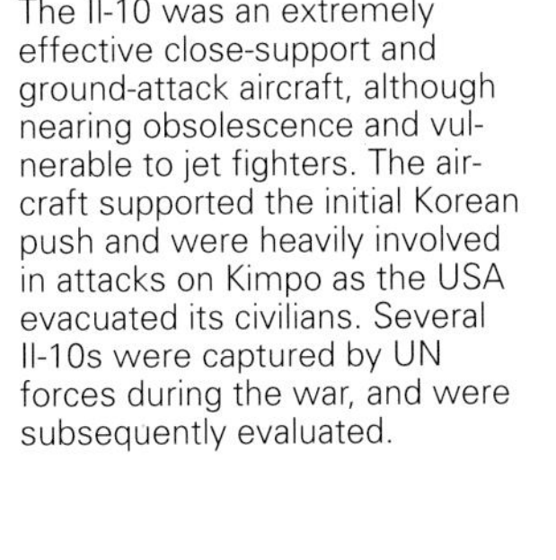

Ilyushin Il-10 Shturmovik
The Il-10 was an extremely effective close-support and ground-attack aircraft, although nearing obsolescence and vulnerable to jet fighters. The aircraft supported the initial Korean push and were heavily involved in attacks on Kimpo as the USA evacuated its civilians. Several Il-10s were captured by UN forces during the war, and were subsequently evaluated.

Yakovlev Yak-3
The Yak-3 was arguably the best Soviet fighter of the war, and in skilled hands was more than a match for the Mustang. Fortunately, North Korean pilots were inexperienced and poorly trained, and they expected negligible fighter opposition.

three months' fighting, together with a return to the negotiating table, had not Communist China intervened with threats of armed intervention in support of the North Koreans. Reconnaissance carried out by the Japan-based B-29s confirmed a substantial build-up of Chinese military forces immediately behind the North Korean borders with China and an increase in activity by Chinese MiG-15 jet fighters just north of the Yalu river.

Right: *Grumman F9F Panthers prepare to launch aboard a wooden-decked US Navy carrier. They are almost certainly aircraft from VF-51 aboard the* **Valley Forge**, *two of which scored the US Navy's first air combat kills of the Korean War.*

It was at this moment that General MacArthur made clear his intention to occupy the whole of North Korea, in contrast to the UN's stated objective of simply restoring partition of the two states on the 38th Parallel. UN forces finally crossed the 38th Parallel on 1 October to begin the 'liberation' of North Korea. Wonsan fell on 10 October, and elements of the 1st US Cavalry entered Pyongyang on 19 October. Some believed that the war would be over by Christmas, but crossing the pre-war border had made active intervention by Communist China inevitable, in turn necessitating a long struggle.

Below: *This Ilyushin Il-10 Shturmovik was one of three captured and later evaluated by the US Air Force. After the initial North Korean invasion, its air force played little real part in the fighting.*

Below: *Douglas AD-4 Skyraiders from VA-55 aboard* **Valley Forge** *rocket North Korean positions during September 1950. It is probably during operations in support of the Marine Corps landings at Inchon, which turned the tide of the war.*

Navy and Marine Corps participation

The Marine Corps played a major role in the Korean air war, deploying to Korea and operating from Japanese bases from August 1950, in defence of the Pusan pocket. The aircraft's task for most of the war was direct support of USMC troops, but they also flew night interdiction, reconnaissance, transport, medevac and night-fighter sorties.

Grumman F7F Tigercat

VMF(N)-513 was shore-based in Japan when war broke out, equipped with a mix of night-fighter Tigercats and F4U-5N Corsairs. The squadron was immediately committed to the fighting as night intruders, transferring to a carrier in the wake of the Inchon landing. They replaced the similarly equipped and newly-arrived VMF(N)-542, which went ashore to Kimpo, then Wonsan then Yonpo.

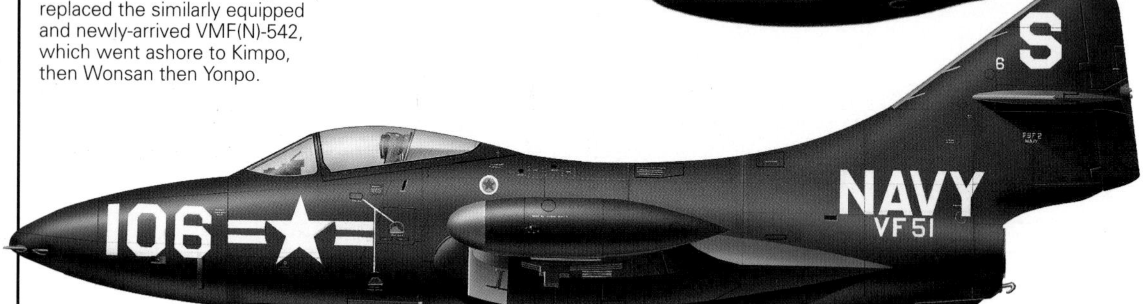

Grumman F9F-2 Panther

This F9F of VF-51 aboard the *Valley Forge* was the aircraft used by Lt Leonard Plog to score the Navy's first kill of the Korean War, a Yak-9 on 3 July 1950. His wingman downed another during the same mission. As they steamed to Korea, the *Valley Forge* and *Philippine Sea* each carried two F9F and two F4U fighter squadrons, with AD-4 Skyraiders for attack duties.

Sikorsky HO3S-1

The US Marine Corps used the HO3S-1 for aerial resupply, medevac and light-observation duties with a number of squadrons. The US Navy's HU-1 used the type for plane guard duties, with a number of detached flights aboard US Navy carriers.

Above: Robert Dewald of the 35th FBS was one of three squadron pilots to score a victory in a single engagement on 27 June 1950. Flight leader Captain Ray Schilleref and Dewald each claimed a single Il-10, and Lt Robert E. Wayne downed the other two.

Fighting fighter-bombers

The 8th Fighter Bomber Group had re-equipped with F-80Cs just before the Korean War, and used these aircraft until they received back their old F-51Ds (still in storage on the other side of their airfield). Before they did so, the 35th and 36th Fighter Bomber Squadrons flew air-defence sorties covering the evacuation, scoring many air combat victories over the North Korean Yaks and Shturmoviks. Here, Captain Robert McKee of the 36th FBS describes a mission flown on 19 July.

"I was flying as No. 3 in a flight of four F-80s, 20 miles northeast of Taejon. We were informed by radio that four Yaks were strafing and bombing the airfield. Nos 1 and 2 started towards the action, and we moved to cover them from above and behind. At approximately 12,000 ft the No. 2 man spotted four Yak-9s in formation, headed north at about 6,000 ft. Lead still did not see them, so the No. 2 took over the No. 1 slot. We remained about 2,000 ft above them. As we got in behind the enemy and were discovered, two Yaks on our left made a sharp turn to the left and down. The two on the right turned right and up.

"At this time I noticed my lead pull straight up. Our No. 2 man hit the enemy element that had turned left and down. My element went after the other two Yaks. I used my gyro sight and closed in on the lead ship and started to fire at 15-20-degree angle off, slightly above him and at about 1,000-ft range. My hits were clustered around the engine, cockpit and left wingroot.

"Suddenly there was a fair-sized explosion around the wingroot and he began trailing grey-white smoke, with a small fire on the bottom side of the wing. I broke off the attack by breaking high and to the left, trying to spot the Nos 1 and 2 who had taken the other element.

"Completing a quick 360-degree turn, I came in on another Yak-9. As I opened fire from zero angle-off and approximately 900 ft, I observed hits on both wingroots and the rear of the cockpit."

The formation was credited with downing three of the Yak-9s, with victories being assigned to McKee, 1st Lt Charles W. Wurster and 2nd Lt Elwood A. Kees. The following day, pilots from the same squadron downed two more Yak-9s, but these were the last kills for the next 103 days.

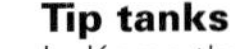

Tip tanks
In Korea the F-80's original teardrop-shaped 625-litre (165-US gal) tank was quickly replaced by the 757-litre (200-US gal) Misawa tank, produced in Japan by adding a new cylindrical centre-section.

Lockheed F-80C

This 35th FBS F-80C was used on 17 July by Captain Francis B. Clark to score a victory over a North Korean Yak-9. This was two days before the engagement described above.

Armament
The F-80C had a concentrated package of six 12.7-mm (0.50-in) Colt-Browning M2/M3 machine-guns in the nose, with 300 rounds per gun. With no lead-computing gunsight, the F-80 was not an ideal dogfighter, however.

Powerplant
The prototype P-80 was powered by a British Halford turbojet, which went on to become the de Havilland Goblin, but later aircraft used the indigenous Allison J33. The initial J33-GE-9 was rated at 17.11 kN (3,850 lb st), while the 17.77-kN (4,000-lb st) GE-11 was introduced from the 30th aircraft. Later aircraft used the 23.11-kN (5,200-lb st) J33-A-21.

Korea: Chinese Invasion

1950 - 1951

Whatever efforts might have been made by the UN to gainsay General MacArthur's hawkish ambitions, the matter was rendered academic when on 1 November 1950 an American F-80C was shot down by Chinese AA guns firing into Korean airspace from across the Yalu river. In another incident the pilots of some UN F-51s reported being fired on by MiG-15s which then made off towards Chinese territory.

Above: As UN forces advanced toward the China border, winter closed in. Rarely seen sunlight here drenches Napalm Nan, an F-51D Mustang of the 39th FBS/18th FBW carrying 454-kg (1,000-lb) bombs and 127-mm (5-in) HVAR rockets.

Right: The Lockheed F-80 Shooting Star was no match for the MiG-15 in a dogfight, but it was a lethal fighter-bomber. This aircraft is heavily laden with napalm tanks for an air-to-ground strike on intervening Chinese troops.

Pyongyang falls

By now American forces had advanced deep into North Korea, their intention (now sanctioned by the UN) being ostensibly to 'secure peace throughout the Korean peninsula'. The North Korean capital, Pyongyang, had fallen to them on 19 October, and already the USAF had begun to run down its strength in the theatre. At the moment of intervention by the Chinese jets the UN air forces in the Korean theatre comprised three F-51 wings, two of F-80Cs, two of B-26s and three of B-29s.

No further pretence at non-intervention was made by the Chinese as, on 3 November, their forces swarmed across the Yalu. An American division was forced hurriedly to retreat to protect its supply lines as the powerful US Navy Carrier Task Force 77 sailed north to launch heavy strikes against the

Below: The Douglas B-26 Invader (which had been designated A-26 during World War II) stood out as a night intruder which stalked and attacked all kinds of North Korean targets, from front-line soldiers to railway marshaling yards.

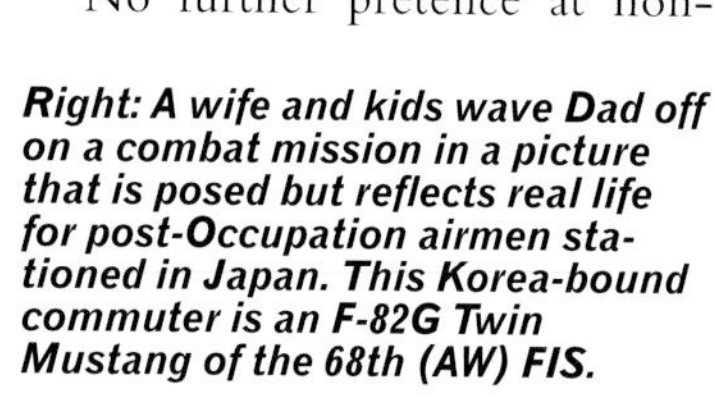

Right: A wife and kids wave Dad off on a combat mission in a picture that is posed but reflects real life for post-Occupation airmen stationed in Japan. This Korea-bound commuter is an F-82G Twin Mustang of the 68th (AW) FIS.

Ground attackers

Straight-wing victor
Right: F-84E-25-RE Thunderjet 51-493 flown by 1st Lt Jacob Kratt, Jr, of the 27th Fighter Escort Wing. Kratt was straight-wing champion of the air duels over Korea: he shot down two MiG-15s and a Yak-3.

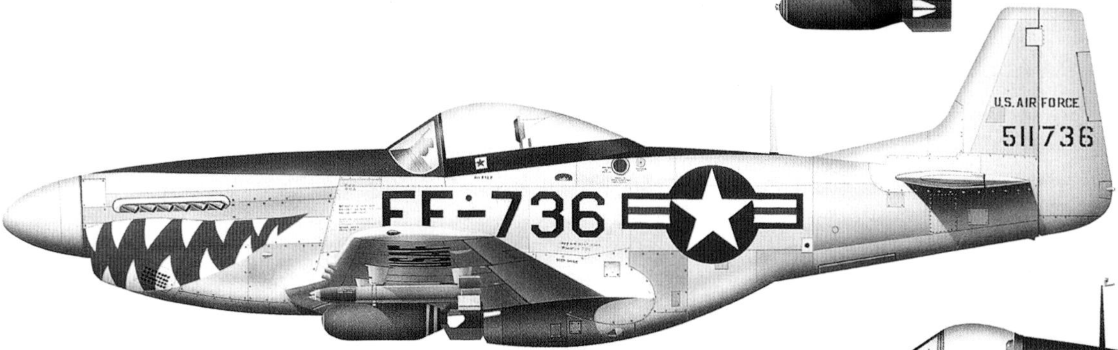

Glessner's Yak Killer
Left: Flying this Dallas-built F-51D-30-NT Mustang (45-11736), 1st Lt James Glessner of the 12th FBS/18th FBG racked up an aerial victory over a North Korean Yakovlev Yak-9 on 2 November 1950, just as China was entering the Korean War.

MiG-killing Corsair
Right: Captain Jesse Folmar of Marine squadron VMA-312 'Checkerboards' shot down a MiG-15 on 10 September 1952 while flying this F4U-4B, but was then shot down himself and rescued.

Chinese crossing the Yalu. At first the MiG-15 pilots simply trailed their coats over Korea in efforts to tempt American aircraft into Chinese airspace, but on 8 November a section of four of the communist jets ventured too far and were boxed in by four F-80s - in the first all-jet air combat in history. Lieutenant Russell J. Brown, USAF, shot down a MiG-15 which crashed just 185 m (200 yards) inside Korean territory. On the following day a US Navy F9F Panther pilot flying off the deck of the USS *Philippine Sea* also downed a Chinese MiG. But it was not all one-way traffic: on 10 November Chinese jets shot down a B-29 heavy bomber.

By the end of the month a quarter of a million Chinese troops were in the field in Korea. The war had certainly entered a new phase.

Forced to accept that the appearance of the modern Soviet-designed MiG-15, which with transonic performance was far superior all of the fighters then equipping the UN forces, and that the F-80 pilots could not reasonably be expected to match the new enemy fighters, the decision was quickly taken to send to Korea a wing of North American F-86A Sabres, then the latest fighters in service with the USAF. Early in December the Sabre-equipped 4th Fighter Interceptor Wing arrived at Kimpo airfield. At about the same time the 27th Fighter Escort Wing, with Republic F-84D Thunderjets, also arrived in the war theatre.

Veteran pilots

Although the numbers were not large, many of the newly-arrived American fighter pilots were World War II veterans with considerable flying and combat experience, whereas US intelligence had revealed that the Korean and Chinese pilots were much younger and lacked such experience. It was felt that the new fighters were easily enough to restore UN air supremacy.

The first brushes with enemy jets were inconclusive, but on 22 December eight F-86s fought 15 MiG-15s and shot down six. Further combats were not immediately possible because of the advance by communist ground forces threatening Kimpo, and the Sabres were moved southwards out

Below: The MiG-15 was a devastating surprise to United Nations commanders when first spotted by Allied pilots on 1 November 1950. These MiG-15s lined up in China would have been vulnerable to attack, but for political reasons no US air strike ever came.

Right: F-86A Sabres of Lt Col John C. Meyer's 4th Fighter Group line the pierced-steel ramp surface at Kimpo. Wingtip-to-wingtip parking invites attack, but apart from nocturnal 'nuisance' raids, the North Koreans and Chinese never struck at the Sabre force.

Left: F-84E Thunderjets of the 27th Fighter Escort Wing hurtle skyward carrying light ordnance. The 27th was led by Col Donald Blakeslee, the famed World War II ace. In its hands, the Thunderjet evolved into a lethal fighter-bomber.

Above: This MiG pilot lowered his gear after falling into the crosshairs of a sharpshooting Sabre pilot. At times, gun-camera film showed wheels down because US fliers strayed into the crowded air space above Manchurian airfields.

of danger. Now based far from the MiGs' patrol areas they were unable to stay long enough to enjoy long patrol sorties. By the same token, however, the communist advance southwards also moved out of range of the MiGs which remained firmly based around Antung beyond the Yalu.

It was this relative difficulty in providing air cover with jet aircraft for the UN forces that lent importance to the work of the carrier-borne strike aircraft of the US Navy and Royal Navy (the latter contributing the carriers HMS *Theseus*, *Glory* and *Ocean*, which took turns on station with HMAS *Sydney* of the Royal Australian Navy).

NAVAL AIR POWER

Task Force 77 had supported the Inchon landings early in the war with three 'Essex' class carriers, the Royal Navy's HMS *Triumph* and two escort carriers, flying aircraft which varied from jet-powered Grumman F9F Panthers through the piston-powered Douglas AD Skyraider to the World War II vet-

Left: The 'checkertails' tell us that these F-86E Sabres belong to the 51st Fighter Interceptor Wing, the second outfit to operate the Sabre in pitched duels over MiG Alley. The F-86E model introduced an 'all-flying' horizontal tail.

Left: The 'alert' pad at Kimpo where F-86A Sabre fighters belonging to 1st Lt Martin J. Bambrick (foreground) and Capt Robert J. Love of the 4th FIW are poised for action, powered-up, and ready. In the background, another Sabre rides a pillar of black exhaust smoke as it lifts off for a mission to MiG Alley. Not visible but certainly somewhere nearby are Bambrick, who later got one MiG kill flying another Sabre and Love, whose ship was named 'Bernie's Bo'. Love, who was an air racing figure in later years, was the 11th jet ace on the American side.

eran Vought F4U Corsair. The two prop-driven machines were to prove exceptionally efficient in the strike role, and the absence of hot jet exhaust meant that they could be flown from the wooden flight decks with which many of the American carriers were still equipped. Indeed a successful attack by torpedo-carrying Skyraiders against the Hwachon dam on 1 May 1951 achieved greater success

Left: The Douglas AD Skyraider was a big, versatile warplane that flew from carrier decks and land bases to challenge the Chinese onslaught. Navy and Marine 'Able Dog' pilots carried an incredible variety of bombs and rockets and delivered them accurately.

Above: The Vought F4U Corsair also flew from land and sea. At the Chosin Reservoir in November 1950, Corsair pilots braved horrendous weather and point-blank Chinese gunfire to provide direct support to Marines battling for survival on the ground.

Prop against Jet

Commander Peter Carmichael was a Royal Navy carrier pilot with World War II experience. Leading a flight of Hawker Sea Fury fighters from the light carrier HMS* Ocean*, he became the first pilot of a British piston-engined aircraft to shoot down a MiG-15, in an encounter on 3 April 1952.

"The first encounter my flight had with the MiGs took place at 0600 on 9 August 1952 near Chinnampo. We had been inland on a spot of rail wrecking between Manchon and Pyongyang, and were patrolling at 3,500 ft (1065 m). My No. 2, Sub-Lieutenant Carl Haines, called up 'MiGs – five o'clock, coming in!' Eight MiGs came at us out of the sun. We all turned towards the MiGs and commenced a 'scissors'.

"It soon became apparent that four MiGs were after each section of two Furies, but by continuing our break turns we presented practically impossible targets. They made no attempt to bracket us.

"One MiG came at me head on. I saw his heavy tracer shells. I fired a burst, then he flashed past me I believe Carl got some hits on him too. This aircraft then broke away and went head on to my Nos 3 and 4, Lieutenants Pete Davies and 'Smoo' Ellis. They were seen to get good hits on one who broke away with smoke coming from him .

"On another occasion a MiG pulled up in front of 'Smoo' with its airbrakes out. He gave it a long burst and noticed hits on the enemy's wings. The aircraft then proceeded northwards at reduced speed with some of the other MiGs in company. Then two more MiGs came head-on towards me, but nothing happened until I saw another down below me, going very slowly, it seemed. I turned into him and closed to 300 yards (275 m), firing all the time.

"I lost sight of him momentarily. I turned and looked over my shoulder and saw an aircraft go into the deck and explode. For one horrible moment I thought it was one of my boys. I called up, 'Tell off' and they all came back, 'Two', 'Three', 'Four'. Over the intercom someone said, 'Wizard, you've got him!'

"The MiG looked a beautiful job – it just seemed to glide through the air, but the MiG pilots didn't observe even the most elementary rules of combat tactics. They didn't even stick together in pairs. Two more got hit before they broke off the engagement. Though I have been credited with shooting down the first MiG, I feel that it was more of a flight effort than an individual one, because the one that crashed had been fired at by all of my flight.

"After our encounter, our boys, who had been somewhat apprehensive of the MiGs, went out looking for trouble. Though the piston-engined Sea Fury is about 200 mph (320 km/h) slower, it can cope as long as the MiG can be seen in time. If the MiG comes in and fights we are confident of the result."

The Helo comes of age

Above: The US Air Force Sikorsky H-5 rescued many downed and wounded men and whisked them to safety using an external casualty litter, shown here.

Above: Always to the fore in exploiting rotary wing technology, the US Marine Corps introduced the Sikorsky HRS-2 nearly three years before the US Army's equivalent H-19 reached Korea.

Below: A US Army Bell H-13 helicopter arrives to carry wounded infantrymen to a MASH, or Mobile Army Surgical Hospital. The Army H-13 also used an external litter.

Below: A US Army Hiller H-23 of the 3rd Helicopter Detachment sets off in March 1951 to collect casualties from the banks of the Han River during the Chinese assault on Seoul.

Korea became the crucible which forged the helicopter. In previous wars, cameo appearances were made by these bizarre machines with their spinning metal blades. Rotary-wing aviation, it was called, and American, British and German forces had flown helicopters by 1945. But in Korea, the helicopter reached maturity and supplanted the fixed wing aircraft in search and rescue duty. The first battlefield rescue in 1950 by a battered, short-ranged Sikorsky H-5 led to training, tactics, and equipment that employed vertical take-off and landing more effectively. By war's end, all military branches were using bigger, better machines like the Sikorsky H-19 (the Marine Corps' HRS).

than previous raids by B-29 heavy bombers (and a commando-style attack by US Rangers), so depriving the Communists of the ability to adjust river levels to suit their own troop movements during their build-up for their spring offensive.

The preparation for this offensive included considerable strengthening of the Communist air forces, principally with the established Yak-9s, La-lls, Il-10s and Tu-2s from the Soviet Union, but also with a few MiG-9 fighters. Meanwhile the 4th Wing's Sabres which had been temporarily moved to Japan while the winter rains flooded their Korean airfields, returned to Korea, now to be based at Suwon. They were not, however, on hand to prevent an attack on 1 March by nine MiG-15s whose pilots made a single firing pass against a formation of 18 B-29s, three of which crashlanded at Taegu.

The tables were turned on 12 April when some 60 MiGs attacked 48 B-29s, escorted by 36 F-84s and 18 F-86s. Three bombers were shot down, but the Americans destroyed 13 of the enemy jets. Notwithstanding this success, it was already becoming clear that the F-84 was no match for the MiG-15, which itself was superior in some performance aspects to the early F-86A Sabre. Only the quality of the American pilots was able to redress the balance.

Bomber 'Ace'

The Boeing B-29 Superfortress bombed North Korean industry and faced the MiG-15 near the Yalu. Some B-29s scored aerial victories. Gunners aboard 'Command Decision,' seen here, were credited with five kills, making the bomber an 'ace.' For the most part, however, the B-29 was vulnerable to the MiG. After MiGs destroyed or damaged a dozen B-29s in October 1951, most daylight raids were ended and the Superfortress – black belly and all – became a creature of the night.

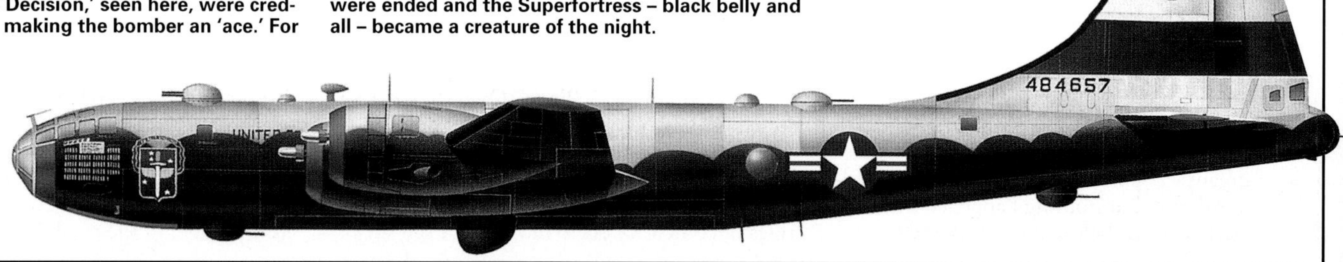

'Command Decision'
Right: The 28th Bomb Squadron, part of the 19th Bomb Group, flew this B-29.

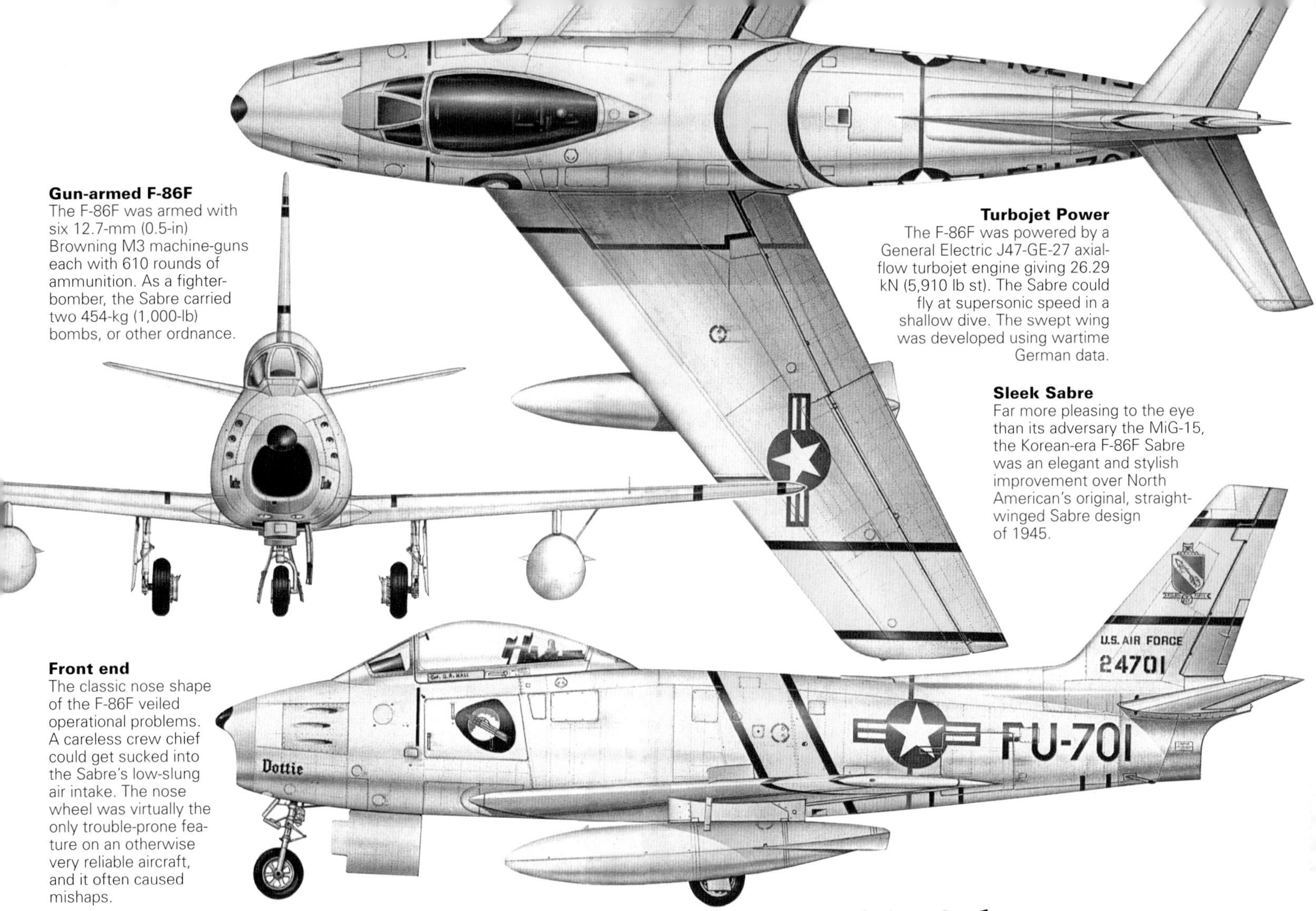

Gun-armed F-86F
The F-86F was armed with six 12.7-mm (0.5-in) Browning M3 machine-guns each with 610 rounds of ammunition. As a fighter-bomber, the Sabre carried two 454-kg (1,000-lb) bombs, or other ordnance.

Turbojet Power
The F-86F was powered by a General Electric J47-GE-27 axial-flow turbojet engine giving 26.29 kN (5,910 lb st). The Sabre could fly at supersonic speed in a shallow dive. The swept wing was developed using wartime German data.

Sleek Sabre
Far more pleasing to the eye than its adversary the MiG-15, the Korean-era F-86F Sabre was an elegant and stylish improvement over North American's original, straight-winged Sabre design of 1945.

Front end
The classic nose shape of the F-86F veiled operational problems. A careless crew chief could get sucked into the Sabre's low-slung air intake. The nose wheel was virtually the only trouble-prone feature on an otherwise very reliable aircraft, and it often caused mishaps.

Famous fighter
More than 9,000 Sabres were built, when naval variants and foreign-built aircraft are included in the total. This made the Sabre the best-known, most popular, and most numerous fighter in the West in the post-World War II era. Many were still in service as late as the early 1980s.

Wing tanks
Standard issue for a patrol to MiG Alley was a pair of finned 200 US gal (757-litre/166.5 Imp gal) fuel tanks beneath the wing. Pilots jettisoned these when combat was imminent, producing an 'aluminum rain'.

F-86F Sabre

'Dottie,' an F-86F-30-NA piloted by Capt. D. R. Hall of the 336th FIS/4th FIW at Kimpo in 1953 was an example of the final wartime version of the Sabre. With its leading-edge slats replaced by a 'hard' leading edge, the late F-86F finally became superior to the MiG-15 in every aspect of flying performance. Compared with the first Sabres, the F model had more power, longer range, and better manoeuvrability.

Left: 'Liza Gal/El Diablo' was an F-86E-10-NA (51-2800) flown by Capt Charles P. Owens of the 4th FIW who narrowly missed 'ace' status by racking up four and one-half aerial victories. Seen at Kimpo in 1953, this fighter was also flown by other Sabre pilots.

Below: Kimpo Air Base, also known as K-14, was a few miles west of Seoul near the Han River. It survives today as South Korea's principal civil airport, located just a few minutes' flying time from the frontier with North Korea.

Korea: The War of the Jets

JULY 1951 - JULY 1953

'Nina II' was the F-86E-10-NA flown by Col John Mitchell who commanded the 51st FIW. Mitchell had flown P-38s in World War II, masterminding the raid that killed Japan's Admiral Yamamoto. In Korea, he bagged two MiG-15s.

The communist spring offensive of 1951 failed in its objective to overrun South Korea and had all but petered out by the end of May, but nevertheless the Chinese intervention had forced the UN to abandon its original aim of unification of North and South. As both sides now attempted to wring the last ounce of propaganda from the military situation, peace talks aimed at securing a truce opened at Kaesong on 10 July 1951, and dragged on for two years.

The hawkish MacArthur was replaced by a slightly more conciliatory General Matthew Ridgeway, but one of the last operations planned before the change of command was an all-out air offensive against the communists' supply lines which, owing to the vulnerability of the railways, depended almost exclusively on the road network. Launched after the failure of the communist offensive, it was given the code name Operation Strangle.

ALL-OUT GROUND ATTACK

All manner of aircraft, from B-26 and B-29 bombers to single-seat F-80s and F-84s – never really a match for the MiG-15 in air-to-air combat, and now being used primarily as fighter-bombers – were used. Alongside aircraft of the US Navy, US Marine Corps, the Royal Navy, the Royal Australian Air Force and the South African Air Force, they started a prolonged offensive against roads, bridges, supply depots and ports, and quickly provoked reaction from the communist MiGs, which remained based in safety beyond the Yalu but which were afforded fairly efficient radar warning of the approach of UN aircraft.

Sabre-versus-MiG combats now became commonplace and the communists quickly became aware that the 4th Fighter Wing was operating out of Suwon, and this prompted a series of nuisance night raids by antiquated Po-2 biplanes against the base. Extremely difficult to counter, these pinprick attacks, with 11-kg (25-lb) fragmentation bombs, caused little damage but their nuisance value was disproportionately high.

The UN bombing offensive, however, did not come up to expectations because of the communist ability to repair damage using huge numbers of impressed labourers. Photo reconnaissance

Above: This Republic F-84E Thunderjet at Taegu shows off its firepower and armament, including 454-kg (1,000-lb) HE bombs, 5-inch High Velocity Aircraft Rockets, and 12.7-mm (0.5-in) Browning M3 machine-guns.

Below: A Lockheed F-80C-10-LO Shooting Star of the 51st FIW carries two 454-kg (1,000-lb) bombs and is ready for a mission while, in the background, two 4th FIW North American F-86 Sabres head aloft toward MiG Alley.

disclosed that the Chinese movement of troops and supplies was almost undiminished. Furthermore, set piece bombing attacks on North Korean cities and major ports met with intense AA fire and the raids were severely restricted by orders to the crews not to overfly neighbouring Chinese territory. Casualties among the big B-29s were fairly high in a force that never exceeded 99 aircraft.

Meanwhile development of an improved version of the Sabre, the F-86E, had gone on apace in the USA, and September brought deliveries of this aircraft to the 4th Wing, by now operating from Kimpo. The communists had also increased their force of MiG-15s by activating a second regiment equipped with the improved MiG-15bis. At once the tempo of air combat increased, and formations of 80 enemy jets were frequently sighted. One of the war's biggest

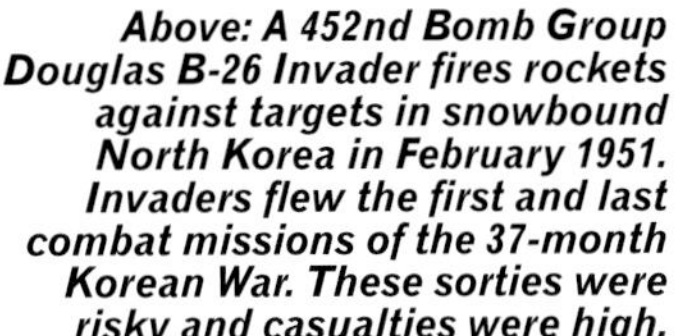

Above: A 452nd Bomb Group Douglas B-26 Invader fires rockets against targets in snowbound North Korea in February 1951. Invaders flew the first and last combat missions of the 37-month Korean War. These sorties were risky and casualties were high.

Below: US forces captured several Ilyushin Il-10 attack aircraft and shipped two of them to Cornell Aero Lab in Ithaca, New York, for study by intelligence experts. This former North Korean Il-10 was returned to flying condition and tested at Wright Field in Ohio.

Above: This photo of a B-29 strike on North Korean supply routes was released in 1951 with a caption that began, 'War is brought home to the communist hordes...' But it was mostly North Korea's manufacturing and transportation industries rather than troops that felt the impact of B-29 raids.

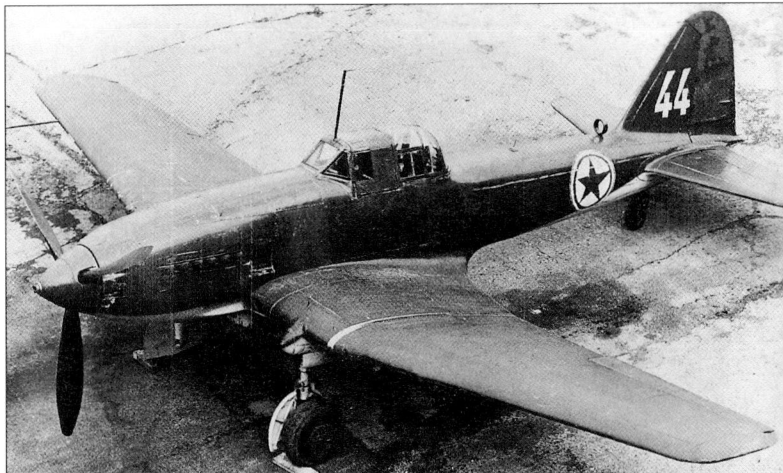

Below: The United Nations brass offered $100,000 to any pilot who would deliver a MiG-15. But when a North Korean flier eventually defected south with this MiG in September 1953 – three months after hostilities had been suspended – he claimed he had 'never heard' of the cash offer.

USAF Fighter and Fighter-Bomber Operations in Korea

Aircraft type	**F-86**	**F-80**	**F-84**	**F-51**	**F-94**	**F-82**
Total sorties	87,177	98,515	86,408	62,607	4,694	1,868
Average theatre inventory	184	270	247	167	56	16
AMERICAN LOSSES						
Air-to-air	78	14	18	10	1	-
Ground fire	19	113	122	172	-	4
Unknown	13	16	13	12	-	-
Total to enemy action	**110**	**143**	**153**	**194**	**1**	**4**
Non-enemy causes	61	96	63	74	6	4
Missing	13	38	33	32	2	3
Non-operational accidents	34	47	56	22	3	6
Non-operational non-committed units	6	49	30	29	16	7
Total losses	**224**	**373**	**335**	**351**	**28**	**24**
Bombs dropped (tons)	7,508	33,266	50,427	12,909	1,222	122
Napalm dropped (tons)	148	8,327	5,560	15,221	-	-
Rockets fired	270	80,935	22,154	183,034	-	1,892
Pilots killed	47	160	98	131	6	23
Pilots missing	65	164	121	133	6	13
Pilots wounded	6	38	11	41	-	1
ENEMY LOSSES						
MiGs destroyed in air	792	6	8	-	1	-
Other enemy aircraft destroyed	18	31	1	9	3	4
Enemy aircraft destroyed on the ground	4	21	-	28	-	-
Total enemy aircraft destroyed	**814**	**58**	**9**	**37**	**4**	**4**
Enemy aircraft probably destroyed	119	37	13	11	-	2
Enemy aircraft damaged	818	57	83	27	2	-

(Taken from USAF Statistical Digest , Fiscal Year 1953.)

Left: The US Air Force assembled these statistics as the war ended to reflect its performance against Chinese and North Korean forces. Later studies indicate that the overall kill ratio may have been somewhat lower, though the F-86 Sabre still established almost total dominance over the communist MiG-15 force.

single combats was fought on 22 October 1951 as eight B-29s, escorted by 55 F-84s and 34 F-86s, were bombing Namsi: suddenly 100 MiGs appeared and boxed-in the escort as 50 others made for the bombers, shooting down three and severely damaging four others. Six MiGs were shot down for the loss of an F-84.

Concerned at the large number of MiGs available to the communists, the USAF now began to withdraw some of the old F-80C Shooting Stars, replacing them with F-84Es, and a second F-84 wing, the 116th, was sent to Korea. The night-fighter F-82s of the 347th All Weather Group were also showing their age (and were of course no match for the MiG-15), and 15 Lockheed F-94 Starfires, a two-seat radar-equipped derivative of the F-80, were despatched to the war. The Starfire proved a disappointment as it lacked an adequate anti-icing system.

Left: Sabres prowl the skies above the Yalu River in the final days of the Korean conflict. By then, the MiG force on the other side of the river had been 'plucked and shorn', as one pilot said. In June and July 1953, USAF Sabre pilots downed about 50 MiGs.

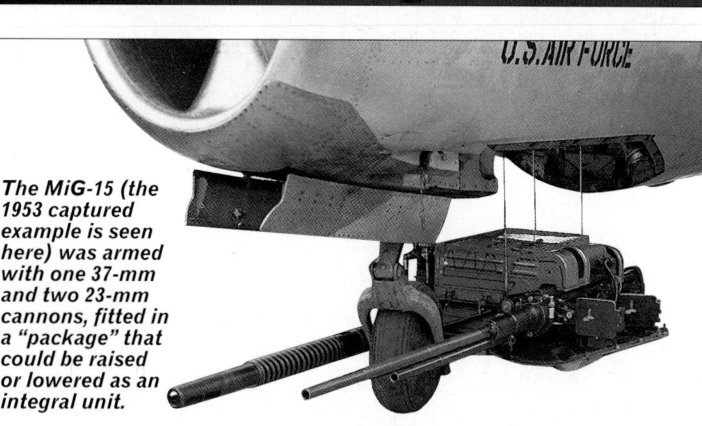

The MiG-15 (the 1953 captured example is seen here) was armed with one 37-mm and two 23-mm cannons, fitted in a "package" that could be raised or lowered as an integral unit.

Below: In spite of the starring role of jets, most of the warplanes that slugged it out in Korean skies were propeller-driven veterans of an earlier era, like this Sea Fury. Speed was less important than the ability to get bombs and rockets on target accurately and consistently.

New F-86 Wing

By the end of 1951 F-86Es were replacing F-80Cs with the 51st Fighter-Interceptor Wing, and the number of MiGs being destroyed rapidly started to rise. At that time the 4th Wing's combat record showed a total of 144 MiG-15s destroyed for the loss in combat of 14 Sabres. The MiG pilots themselves were becoming more aggressive – some indeed were being flown by experienced Soviet pilots,

The US Air Force's Lockheed F-94B (above) and the US Navy's Douglas F3D Skyknight (above right) replaced the North American F-82 in the night-fighting role.

Right: North Korea's Po-2 and Yak-18 biplanes were major targets for these F-82 Twin Mustangs. Often dismissed as 'nuisance' raiders, they nevertheless could inflict serious damage and had to be stopped. Allied night fighters fought them during the nocturnal hours with some success.

Night fighters

The nocturnal hours were often the province of 'Bedcheck Charlie', the irritating North Korean biplanes that kept everybody awake and dished out more real military damage than they were usually credited with. The US Air Force's response was the Lockheed F-94B, often erroneously called the Starfire (the name used for the later F-94C). Navy F4U Corsairs and F3D Skyknights also joined in the chase with some success.

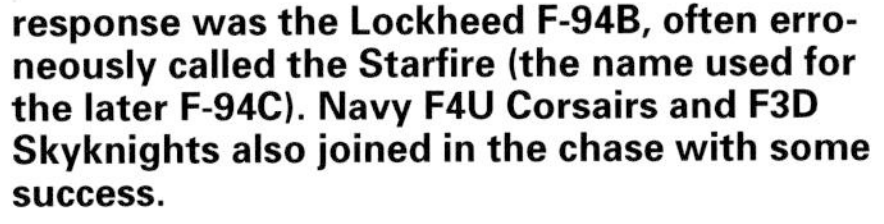

Nocturnal F-94B

Right: Capt Ben L. Fithian and Lt Sam R. Lyons of the 319th FIS scored the first aerial victory for the F-94B on 30 January 1953. The two-seat, tandem F-94B was armed with four 12.7-mm (0.5-in) machine-guns and carried an early air-intercept (AI) radar set. Never intended for air-to-air dogfighting, the F-94 was developed from the F-80 to defend North America from bomber attack.

Ace's Corsair

Left: This F4U-5N Corsair (BuNo. 24453) nicknamed 'Annie Mow' was flown to glory by Lt Guy 'Lucky Pierre' Bordelon, the only American ace in Korea who did not fly the F-86 Sabre. Bordelon shot down four Yakovlev fighters and one Lavochkin in 1953 night actions.

Skyknight Victory

This F3D-2 Skyknight was the mount of Major William Stratton (pilot) and M/Sgt Hans Haglind (radar operator) of squadron VMF(N)-513 'Flying Nightmares'. The Marine duo racked up history's first jet-versus-jet night kill when they downed what was apparently a Yakovlev Yak-15 on 2 November 1952. The Skynight scored more aerial victories in Korea than any other Navy jet.

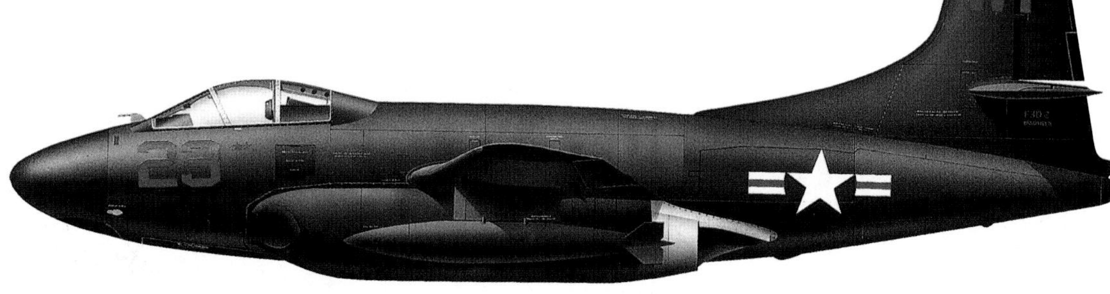

and the improved performance of both fighters resulted in numerous combats taking place above 12190 m (40,000 ft). In March 1952 39 enemy jets were destroyed; the following month the tally rose to 44.

Combat information from Korea had long since filtered through to the Sabre's designers and in June and July 1952 a further-improved Sabre, the F-86F, began to be deployed to the 51st Wing. The F-86F was the first Sabre variant which was superior in all respects to the MiG-15bis, although it was used as much in ground attacks as it was in air combat. By the spring of 1953 there were four wings of F-86s in Korea, and during the last six months of the war these fighters wholly dominated the skies. In May their pilots destroyed 56 enemy jets, and in June no fewer than 77, losing 11 and 23 respectively of their own number.

The death of the Soviet leader, Josef Stalin, on 5 March 1953 instigated a profound change of attitude in the Chinese delegation at the peace talks and, after reversing their previously intransigent demands on such matters as prisoner repatriation, finally agreed to a ceasefire on 27 July 1953.

From an air combat viewpoint the Korean War was interesting in that it was the first major conflict in which large numbers of opposing jet fighters engaged each other and, while it is true that there were a number of high-scoring American Sabre pilots –31-year-old Joseph McConnell of the 51st Wing heading the list with 16 MiG-15s to his credit – the fleeting nature of those all jet combats graphically demonstrated that the age of gun-only armament was rapidly approaching its conclusion. The era of the air-to-air missile was about to dawn.

***Right:* Douglas C-47 Skytrains, C-54 Skymasters and Fairchild C-119 Flying Boxcars of the 315th Air Division (Combat Cargo) flew troops and supplies to United Nations Forces in Korea. The 'Air Bridge' is often forgotten but in many ways was just as important as the combat jets in Korea.**

***Right:* MiG killer Capt. Ralph Parr of the 334th FIS is seen at the controls of this F-86F – which was not his usual assigned aircraft, presumably down for maintenance. The 'F' was the first Sabre which could outfly the MiG-15 in all conditions.**

Sabre Aces

US Far East Air Forces (FEAF) never had more than two fighter wings (4th and 51st FIW) committed to the air campaign along the Yalu River in the trouble zone known as MiG Alley. At times as few as 40 Sabres were combat-ready in all of Korea. Even though they were faced by up to 800 MiG-15s, some flown by seasoned Russian aces, the F-86 prevailed in one of the toughest air campaigns of all time.

MiG-battling 'Butch'

Right: 'Beautious Butch II' was one of several Sabres piloted by Capt Joseph M. McConnell of the 39th FIS/51st FIW at Suwon, Korea. McConnell's MiG kills appear beneath his cockpit as aircraft silhouettes rather than the usual red stars. McConnell scored 16 victories, was shot down and rescued, and went home only to lose his life in a mishap while flying the postwar F-86H Sabre.

Jabara's jet

Left: This F-86A-5-NA Sabre (48-259) was flown by Capt James Jabara during the first of his two Korean combat tours, with the 334th FIS/4th FIW at Kimpo. Jabara became the first US jet ace when he claimed his fifth and sixth MiGs on 20 May 1951. Jabara eventually achieved 15 aerial victories, the second highest score of the Korean War on the US side.

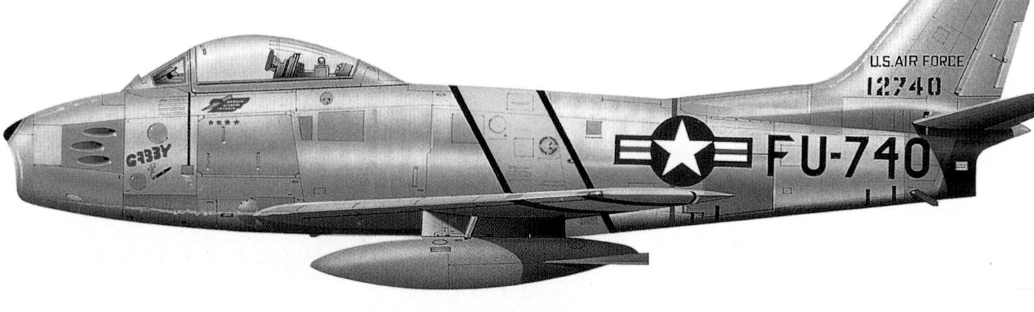

Wing commander

Right: Col Francis S. Gabreski was an ace in two wars, having flown P-47 Thunderbolts in World War II. In Korea, he commanded the 51st FIW and piloted this F-86E-10-NA (51-2740) named 'Gabby'. Like many of the aces, Gabreski flew several aircraft in Korea, and scored some of his 6.5 jet victories in another Sabre nicknamed 'Lady Frances'.

MiG vs. Sabre

Lieutenant Douglas Evans flew F-86 Sabres with the 336th FIS, 4th Fighter Interceptor Wing over Korea. He describes what it was like to fight against MiG-15s, as the dawning jet age took aerial combat into a whole new dimension of speed and performance.

Early in the Korean War, the 4th FIW's Sabres wore black and white identity stripes. These were replaced by a yellow band in late 1951. Powered by a General Electric J47-GE-9 turbojet engine, the early F-86A model depicted here had some deficiencies compared to the MiG-15 but thanks to superior pilot skill it usually prevailed in battle.

"I was really hopped up for the afternoon mission, my 39th in combat in Korea. Charlie Mitson and I took off as numbers Three and Four in Red Flight, the lead flight in the squadron.

"No sooner had we got north of Sinanju and across the Chongchon than we saw gaggles of contrails approaching. I counted 22 MiGs in a squadron formation going by, off to our right, and 16 more further behind, but while my attention was fixed on them Al Simmons, who was Red Flight Leader and who must really have had his eyeballs extended, called eight MiGs right down on the deck. He told off the rest of the squadron to cover us and continue the patrol, and then called 'Red Flight, let's go!'

"Our attack must have come as a complete surprise. When Al fired on them, the MiGs just made a startled break without any discipline to it. I racked around to the left after the nearest two, settled on the leftmost one, and ignored everything else that was going on around me.

"Before I could fire I saw cannon shells come streaking over my right wing. Since I was already in a steep bank, I went over on my back to extend my view a little and saw this second MiG, who had just fired at me, pull up into the clouds. I snapped my attention forward again, just in time to see the first MiG duck into the clouds too. The next moment I was in the clouds myself.

"I didn't have any attention to spare for the instruments; I was too busy staring through the windscreen, trying to get a glimpse of them. There was a moment of darkness, and then the sunlight suddenly hit me in the face. It was about 3,000 ft [915 m], and there were those two MiGs, right under my nose again.

"I horsed the aircraft over and down in a roll that put me right on their tails, steadied the gunsight on the lead MiG, and pressed the trigger. My whole ship shuddered as I let go a blast.

"I wanted a MiG and this guy was it, so on over into the top of a sloppy loop we went, me still hosing him down with tracer and him still shedding pieces of his aircraft and showing more flame.

"After all the pounding and roaring my guns had been doing, I really thought something definite ought to happen. It did. As we headed down toward the cloud again in the backside of the loop, the canopy popped off the MiG and – ha! – out came the pilot like a hopping frog. I let go of the trigger then, and rolled around upright. 'That's what it's like when you have to give up,' I thought to myself."

Above: A sequence of five grainy gun-camera photos taken over the Yalu River shows a MiG-15 succumbing to a Sabre's gunfire. The MiG is hit, the pilot jettisons his canopy, and then he ejects. The Sabre's relatively light machine-gun armament meant that it often took many hits to bring down a MiG.

Left: 1st Lt Douglas Evans of the 4th FIW sits in the cockpit of his F-86A Sabre after a flight to MiG Alley. The V-shaped windscreen was a feature of the F-86A and early F-86E models.

Below: Capt Ken Rapp served alongside Douglas Evans in the 4th FIW. Rapp flew this F-86 Sabre back to Kimpo airfield after having his aileron shot away in a duel with a better-than-average MiG pilot.

China and Taiwan

1945-1996

***Left:** The first F-104s to arrive on Taiwan were USAF fighters sent to bolster the nationalists after the Quemoy confontation in 1958. The Republic of China air force took delivery of 67 ex-US examples in the 1970s, and are now one of the last major users of the type.*

***Below:** The People's Republic of China began licence-building of the supersonic MiG-19 as the J-6 in 1958, but the chaos of the Cultural Revolution meant that production was never steady until the 1970s.*

There were two main power bases in China at the end of World War II. The Soviet Union had liberated Manchuria, and equipped the forces of communist leader, Mao Zedong, which became the People's Liberation Army. Led by Chiang Kai-Shek, the Nationalists were armed and supported by the USA, and they took the surrender of the Japanese forces in the north and in key cities and ports. Talks between the rival Chinese forces broke down as US forces departed in 1946, and the civil war which had been interrupted by Japan's invasion broke out again.

After early successes, by 1947 the Nationalists began to lose their advantage. They lost Peking and Tientsin in January 1949. The People's Republic was founded on 1 October 1949, and the Nationalist forces withdrew to the island of Formosa, establishing a rival Republic of China, now usually known as Taiwan. This has never declared its independence, and each of the rivals officially espouses an eventual reunification under its own leadership.

The outbreak of the Korean War in 1950 played an important part in the development of the Chinese People's Armed Forces Air Force (CPAFAF). In 1950 the CPAFAF had about 150 aircraft including F-51Ds, B-25Cs, C-46s, C-47s, La-11s and Yak-9s. In February the Soviets agreed to deliver the new MiG-15 fighter, and the first deliveries were made in March. The aircraft were first used in Korea in November 1950.

USA supports Taiwan

From 1951, the Nationalists received US support. They were seen as a useful bastion against expansion by (or even the influence of) communist 'Red' China. Taiwan also became a useful strategic base. By 1954 the CNAF operated two wings of Republic F-84Gs, two wings of F-47Ds and one of F-51s; bomber wings still operated the B-24 and B-25. The USA recognized and protected Nationalist China and in return used Taiwan: President Truman sent the US 7th Fleet to the Taiwan Straits at the start of the Korean War, and many secret missions into the mainland operated from Taiwan.

Another, less formal American involvement was with the airline Civil Air Transport, or CAT.

***Right:** By 1954, the Chinese Nationalist air force still had three wings of World War II era F-47s and F-51s together with some B-24 and B-25 bombers. But the most powerful element in the inventory were the two wings of Republic F-84G Thunderjets.*

Founded by General Claire Chennault at the end of World War II, CAT was bought by the CIA in 1950. Used for covert intervention all over East and Southeast Asia, CAT was based on Formosa. CAT supplied the French in Indo-China and spawned further CIA covers including Air America, Southern Air Transport, Air Asia and Asiatic Aeronautical Company. Agents were dropped, but not without risk: between 1951 and 1954, 106 US citizens were killed and 124 captured on covert missions. Many aircraft were lost, including several Boeing B-17s, the last of which flew in 1958.

The Nationalists had retained forces on four offshore islands, Quemoy and Matsu, and the Tachen and Nanchi groups farther north. Mainland pressure on the latter led to withdrawal in January 1954. The US 7th Fleet, covered by F-86Fs of the USAF's 18th FBW, evacuated 17,000 civilians and 25,000 troops. The PLA also turned its attention to Quemoy.

A massive artillery bombardment from the communist naval base at Amoy began on 3 September 1954, and was countered by Nationalist shelling and air raids. Shelling continued intermittently and in August 1958 CNAF RF-84Fs noted a build-up of MiG-17s on bases at Chenghai and Liencheng, followed by a new wave of shelling from 18 August.

On 29 August Peking announced an impending invasion of Quemoy and the liberation of Taiwan. At least four air divisions had moved to bases around Foochow (Nantai, Kaochi, Swatow and Chuhsein) and farther afield at Chienou Tien-ho and Nan Hai.

The CNAF in 1958 comprised 350 aircraft including three wings of F-84Gs, two wings of F-86Fs and one RF-84F squadron. In addi-

***Above:** The American Volunteer Group had flown C-46s in China during World War II, and many were left in the country after 1945. Both sides in the Chinese civil war made use of the capacious transport, with nationalist examples like this flying to Formosa after the communist victory in 1949.*

***Left:** When Chiang Kai-Shek's Nationalists retreated to Formosa and the offshore islands in 1949, they took more than 200 aircraft with them. Included in that number were over 110 North American F-51D Mustangs, which provided the bulk of Taiwan's fighter strength for the next three years.*

Across the Formosa Strait

At their closest, Nationalist and Comminist China are within artillery range of each other. Major clashes over Quemoy island occurred in 1954 and 1958, and the government in Taipei claimed that nearly 400 intruder missions were mounted from the mainland in the eight years between 1963 and 1969.

Nanchang Q-5
Left: Based on the MiG-19 airframe, the Q-5 has been in series production since 1969, and is China's primary ground attack fighter. More than 900 have been delivered to the PLA air force.

McDonnell RF-101C Voodoo
Right: Eight RF-101As were delivered to Taiwan after the 1958 Quemoy fighting. They were used on reconnaissance missions over the mainland: Peking claimed to have shot down two of them in the 1960s.

Right: From 1954 the Nationalist Chinese began exchanging their Republic F-47Ds for Sidewinder-capable North American F-86Fs. By 1958 the two Sabre wings were crucial in maintaining Taiwan's integrity when the People's Republic threatened to invade.

tion the USAF rotated a wing of F-86F Sabres as part of defence commitments agreed in March 1955.

1958 Quemoy crisis

On patrols over the Taiwan Straits Sidewinder-equipped F-86s engaged increasing numbers of MiG-15s and MiG-17s until on 24 September, 10 MiGs were claimed destroyed by a force of 14 Sabres of the 3rd Wing, including four by Sidewinders, the first time that air-to-air guided missiles had been used in combat. Some 31 MiGs were claimed between 14 August and 24 September, for the loss of just two F-86s.

In October the USA increased its commitment to Taiwan with two squadrons of F-100Ds, two of F-104As, one F-101C squadron, one RF-101C squadron, two squadrons of C-130s and one squadron each of B-57s and KB-50s. In addition the US 7th Fleet moved on station: its four aircraft-carriers carried 300 aircraft. In the event there was no major confrontation, although shelling continued, and there was further air fighting when on 5 July 1959 five MiG-17s were destroyed in a 10-minute battle with CNAF Sabres.

A state of cold war continued and the Nationalists claimed to have suffered from 399 mainland raids between 1963 and 1969. The F-104A had made a significant impression on both sides during the Quemoy crisis, but US dissatisfaction during its initial service was reflected by the release of 24 F-104As to Taiwan. These were augmented by further deliveries through MAP to help counter further aggressive Chinese tactics over the disputed Quemoy islands. In 1967, CNAF F-104Gs proved their combat prowess when they shot down two PLAAF MiG-19s from a formation of 12 over Quemoy.

Right: Three-toned green MiG-17s line up on an airfield in Shenyang province. Entering service with the PLA in 1955 and licence-produced as the J-5, it was China's main fighter into the early 1970s.

The CNAF also operated U-2 spyplanes for the CIA. Many overflights of the mainland were made between 1959 and 1974, primarily to monitor the development of China's nuclear weapons programme at Lop Nor and Chiuchuan. Eight aircraft were lost over China. Further clashes have taken place since then, with F-5As and F-5Es predominating.

As relations between Peking and Washington improved Taiwan felt the effect, with restrictions being imposed on delivery of the latest weapons. The thaw in Sino-American relations after the end of the Cultural Revolution became more permanent, and the position of the island republic became more tenuous. The US withdrew its forces from Taiwan in stages from 1974, and began scaling down its military assistance. In 1979, the USA broke off diplomatic relations with Taiwan.

This marked the low point in Taiwan's relations with the USA. Then the Tianenman square massacre focused attention on China's human rights record, and prompted improved relations with the USA, which most recently dispatched warships (including aircraft carriers) when China seemed to be threatening invasion during Taiwan's 1996 presidential elections.

Right: Although the Powers incident was the most famous U-2 shoot-down, it was not the only one. The CNAF operated U-2s for the CIA between 1959 and 1974, and eight aircraft were lost over China.

Vietnam: Early American Involvement

1960 - 1964

The US Air Force's 'Farm Gate' deployment brought the North American T-28 to Vietnam as a low-budget, all-purpose fighter-bomber for Saigon's pilots.

In 1957 the United States, in its role of bastion against what it saw as the insidious, creeping advance of world communism, took over from France the task of training and strengthening the armed forces of South Vietnam. The Vietnamese air force (VNAF) was poorly equipped and trained, despite the fact that the American Military Assistance and Advisory Group (MAAG) had been at work in the country since 1950. The aim of the USA, in line with the 1954 Geneva Protocols, was to achieve unification with North Vietnam by means of democratic elections, but this was compromised from the outset by the uncrossable divide between the communist North and the old Catholic land-owning class which dominated the South. The position was exacerbated by the presence of the Viet Cong, revolutionary insurgents in South Vietnam who were backed by Hanoi.

By the end of the 1950s American advisers in South Vietnam numbered nearly 700, and updating the VNAF accelerated when its F8F Bearcats were replaced by AD-6 Skyraiders. In 1961 the Viet Cong guerrillas staged a show of strength when, supported by increased infiltration from the North, they attacked and cut many of the principal north-south trunk roads.

Special Forces

The newly elected Kennedy administration, though unwilling to involve American forces in formally-declared warfare, redoubled its efforts to train the South Vietnamese in the skills of counter-insurgency. The first US Special Forces units entered the country, ostensibly to provide more training but increasingly being involved in leading active missions against the Viet Cong, and occasionally mounting covert intelligence or sabotage missions against the North.

Above: A South Vietnamese soldier emerges from as US Army Piasecki H-21C helicopter. In the early 1960s, Americans were supposed to be advising, not fighting, but they often joined in.

As the USA supported the South, so the Northern communists were the recipients of large quantities of war materiel from China and the Soviet Union. Some of these supplies were used to bolster the Viet Cong, moving down supply routes through Laos and Cambodia on what became known as the Ho Chi Minh Trail.

The USA responded by supplying US Army Piasecki H-21 helicopters to the South, together with pilots to fly them. American personnel were not supposed to engage in combat missions, though many did. They generally flew with at least one Vietnamese crew member who was ostensibly in command, conveniently creating the fiction that no American units were actually fighting.

Below: The Viet Cong brought their insurgency to the cities. By bombing installations associated with the South Vietnamese government and its US advisers, they unwittingly encouraged Presidents Kennedy and Johnson to send more help to Saigon.

Supply ship sunk

On 2 May 1964 the American aircraft supply ship *Card* was sunk in Saigon harbour by a Viet Cong underwater demolition team while off-loading helicopters. Elsewhere Fairchild C-123 Providers of the USAF were engaged in Operation 'Ranch Hand', stripping large areas of South Vietnamese jungle of foliage by spraying chemicals and thereby depriving enemy infiltrators of their natural camouflage and cover.

On 2 August the same year the American destroyer Maddox was attacked in international waters in the Gulf of Tonkin by Soviet-built torpedo boats, and five nights later it was claimed that the destroyer *Turner Joy* had been similarly attacked. In Washington, President Johnson announced, a 'measured response' to these unprovoked attacks, and US Navy A-1 and A-4 strike aircraft from the carriers *Ticonderoga* and *Constellation* carried out a number of attacks on North Vietnamese bases at Hon Gai and Loc Chao, losing one A-1 and one A-4 to ground fire.

UNDECLARED WAR

This progressive drift to open conflict was not accompanied by a formal declaration of war, but simply escalated by a series of local incidents of growing scale, followed by righteous indignation and retaliation. A guerrilla attack during Christmas Eve 1964 on a hotel used by US officers in Saigon was followed by a mortar attack on Pleiku Air Base which killed eight American personnel. The US Navy again retaliated, this time with Operation Flaming Dart, sending strike aircraft from the carriers *Ranger*, *Hancock* and *Coral Sea* of Task Force 77 against North Vietnamese military targets at Dong Hoi and Vit Thuu. Further Viet Cong mortar attacks on American bases, resulting in numerous casualties, were followed by Flaming Dart II, this time involving USAF as well as US Navy aircraft in strikes against Chanh Hoa and elsewhere.

TROOPS COMMITTED

Open war, involving American ground forces, began on 7 March 1965 when 3,500 US Marines were sent to Da Nang, ostensibly to protect US facilities. Very soon, however, they were in action against the Viet Cong. Within four months the number of American combat troops in Vietnam had grown to 75,000 men; during the next three years this figure was expand enormously to reach over half a million.

Indeed, the nature of the entire war – the absence of a 'front line', the use of guerrilla tactics on a large scale and the underlying ideologies of the combatants – all combined to stretch the endurance of the American fighting men.

Worse, these factors were misunderstood by an ill-informed but powerful pacifist lobby back home in the United States.

Above: The Fairchild C-123 Provider flew 'in-country' airlift and sprayed defoliants, including the infamous Agent Orange.

Below: The Douglas B-26 Invader suffered from wing spar fatigue, but was a superb weapon for jungle and counter-insurgency fighting. Farm Gate's Air Commandos flew hundreds of low-level missions in the B-26.

Watching the Viet Cong

The first American combat aircraft in Vietnam were McDonnell RF-101C Voodoos of the 15th Tactical Reconnaissance Squadron from Kadena. A detachment of four, code-named 'Pipe Stem', arrived at Tan Son Nhut on 18 October 1961.

It happened to be the day the Mekong River overflowed its banks and flooded hundreds of square miles of the countryside. The four RF-101Cs began photographing both the floods and the Viet Cong on 20 October. Another detachment, known as 'Able Mable', flew missions over Laos from Don Muang, Thailand. Captain A. Robert Gould recalled:

"We lived in the Caravelle Hotel, drove our Jeeps to Tan Son Nhut for our 0800 take-off and were back at the hotel by 1500 or 1600 hours. We looked at airfields, bridges, and all the other normal military-type targets. We used French maps over Laos – there were no US maps of sufficient detail."

The McDonnell RF-101C Voodoo was the first USAF warplane in Vietnam, serving from 1961. The camouflage came later, when Voodoos were flying the fastest combat missions of the war.

Confrontation in Borneo

1962-1966

Left: The Hawker Hunter FGA.Mk 9s of No. 20 Squadron based at Tengah in Singapore were the RAF's only in-theatre fighter-bombers. The aircraft were used in the suppression of the initial revolts in Sarawak and Brunei, then against Indonesian armed infiltration and incursion.

Possibly the least known of all post-war RAF operational deployments was that of 1962-64 in Borneo, where neighbouring Indonesia held territorial ambitions following the transfer of independence to North Borneo. The campaign in some respects had much in common with that in Malaya which had only just ended, not least in the similarity of terrain: Borneo, like the Malayan peninsula, is covered with dense jungle with few landmarks of use to navigation. Accurate maps were scarce and, on account of frequent and fairly regular tropical rainstorms, flying was impossible except for about six hours daily between mid-morning and mid-afternoon.

In very broad terms the campaign may be divided into three overlapping phases, namely the suppressing of Indonesian-inspired rebellions in Brunei and Sarawak, the subsequent deployment of units of the Far East Air Force (FEAF) to Borneo to counter Indonesian-trained terrorist infiltrators crossing the 1610-km (1,000-mile) border with Kalimantan, and wider-ranging operations to counter Indonesian air sorties across the border and the despatch of Indonesian raiding parties to Malaya itself.

Right: The Gloster Javelins of Nos 60 and 64 Squadrons at RAF Tengah played their part during the confrontation, maintaining a permanent detachment at Kuching and another at Labuan. Great care was taken to describe the conflict as a 'confrontation' and not a war, and there have been suggestions that kills went unclaimed to avoid inflaming the situation.

RAF forces on hand

The FEAF had undergone considerable modernisation since the signing of the SEAC Defence Treaty of 1954. The RAF component comprised a squadron (No. 20) of Hunter FGA.Mk 9s at Tengah, Singapore, together with Javelin FAW.Mk 9s of No. 60 Squadron and Canberra B.Mk 2s of No. 45 Squadron. Also in Malaya were RAF Canberra PR.Mk 7s, Shackleton MR.Mk 2s and a variety of transport aircraft. At the RAAF base at Butterworth were two CAC Sabre squadrons and No. 2 Squadron RAAF with Canberras, and a Canberra squadron (No. 75) of the RNZAF, also at Tengah. In addition it had become standard RAF training practice to send small detachments of conventionally-armed V-bombers to the Far East for short periods.

Immediately after news of the rebellions in Brunei and Sarawak was received on 8 December 1962, Hastings, Beverleys and Valetta transports began delivering troops to Brunei town, its airfield having been secured from the rebels by

Above: Whereas the Whirlwind could carry eight passengers, the Belvedere could carry 18, and could also lift much heavier underslung loads. Two squadrons of Belvederes served in Borneo, and proved invaluable.

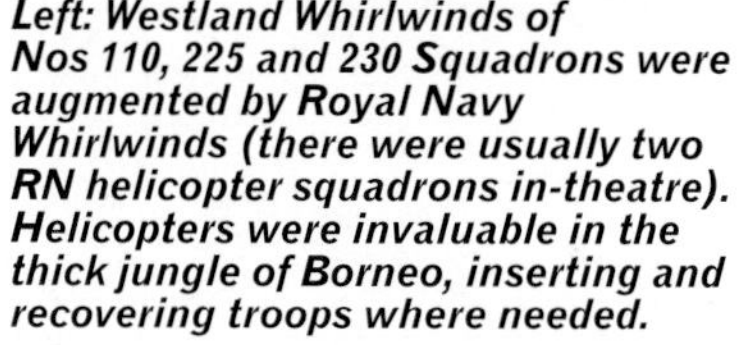

Left: Westland Whirlwinds of Nos 110, 225 and 230 Squadrons were augmented by Royal Navy Whirlwinds (there were usually two RN helicopter squadrons in-theatre). Helicopters were invaluable in the thick jungle of Borneo, inserting and recovering troops where needed.

Confrontation in the air

Indonesia had a well-equipped modern air force, but tended to use older, piston-engined types for incursions into Sarawak, Sabah (North Borneo) and Brunei. They proved difficult to intercept, and air activity was generally limited to ground attack, transport and patrol missions. Some helicopters and light aircraft were downed by ground fire.

Mikoyan-Gurevich MiG-17
Indonesia's MiG-17 and MiG-21 fighters were not committed to action, to the disappointment of the RAF's Hunter and Javelin pilots. Piston-engined Mustangs flew some sorties over Borneo, but avoided interception. This aircraft wears the markings of No. 11 Squadron, then based at Iswahjudi.

Hawker Hunter FGA.Mk 9
The Hunter FGA.Mk 9 was a dedicated fighter-bomber, optimised for use in hot-and-high conditions. The Hunters of No. 20 Squadron flew numerous attacks against Indonesian infiltrators, mainly using their four 30-mm (1.2-in) cannon and underwing rockets.

Tupolev Tu-16
The Tu-16s of Indonesia's Nos 41 and 42 Squadrons at Kemajoram and Iswahjudi flew a number of provocative feints towards Singapore, being intercepted and escorted away by based Javelins. The Indonesian Tu-16s were missile-carrying 'Badger-Bs'.

Gurkha troops who were landed first. A single Britannia flew troops to the nearby island of Labuan. Within a fortnight, 3,200 troops had been delivered, together with 113 vehicles and supporting weapons and stores, and the rebellion in Sarawak put down. Joining the airlift had been an RAAF C-130A Hercules and an RNZAF Bristol Freighter, as well as RAF Shackletons of No. 205 Squadron. On arrival in Borneo the troops were moved forward by Beverleys and Pioneers and by Sycamore helicopters; also employed were the big twin-rotor Bristol Belvedere helicopters of No. 66 Squadron.

The rebellion in Brunei was being sustained by neighbouring Indonesia, and to restore the situation in the area British forces were tasked with isolating and mopping up the rebel bands, a task which involved airlifting troops to the oilfield at Seria and the airstrip at Anduki, the former being successfully undertaken by the short-field Twin Pioneers of No. 209 Squadron and the latter by a single Beverley (which was fired on by the rebels but suffered only negligible damage).

The rebellions having failed,

***Above:** Nos 845, 846 and 848 Squadrons aboard the HMS Albion and HMS Bulwark operated a mix of Whirlwind HAS.Mk 7s, Wessex HAS.Mk 1s and Wessex HU Mk 5s, like the aircraft illustrated. These helicopters augmented RAF Whirlwinds and Belvederes in the troop transport role. The British and allied forces in Borneo used helicopters extensively, which allowed the rapid reinforcement of remote outposts, and the insertion of troops to exactly where they were required. Light Army Air Corps helicopters were also deployed.*

***Left:** Labuan became the RAF's operational hub in Borneo, its flight lines accommodating a wide variety of aircraft types. Visible in this photo are Beverley and Twin Pioneer transports, as well as Javelin interceptors and Canberra bombers. Labuan was an offshore island, and was thus easy to protect against infiltration, offering the RAF a secure base for its aircraft.*

Left: No. 14 Squadron operated MiG-21Fs from Kemajoram. They were the most sophisticated aircraft in the AURI inventory. These fighters were not involved in the operations over Borneo, but were held back for the defence of Indonesia itself.

Below: No. 1 Squadron used a mix of P-51 Mustangs, B-25 Mitchells and B-26 Invaders, while No. 21 Squadron used B-25s and B-26s. Both units were based at Pontianak, from where they flew occasional low-level incursions over Sarawak and North Borneo.

Indonesia began infiltrating guerrilla forces across the border, to counter which the security forces established a number of strongpoints near to the known crossing points. These tiny garrisons were to be sustained wholly from the air, a task which caused a number of new squadrons to be deployed to Borneo, in particular Nos 103, 110 and 230 with the new Westland Whirlwind Mk 10 helicopter.

In a general widening of the conflict Indonesia greatly increased its cross-border incursions, even starting to send F-51 Mustangs into Borneo airspace, aircraft that were particularly difficult to counter as they were able to outmanoeuvre the big Javelins and were virtually immune from the RAF's heat-seeking missiles on account of their piston engines. The RAF V-bomber force supplied a detachment to the theatre, known as 'Matterhorn', initially with Victors

Left: Indonesia's Lockheed C-130 Hercules and Antonov An-12 transports served with No. 31 Squadron at Halim, and they dropped men and supplies in Sarawak and in East and West Malaysia. Some sources suggest that at least one C-130 was lost to a Javelin.

Jungle resupply

The RAF made extensive use of helicopters and STOL transport aircraft in Borneo. They frequently came under hostile ground fire and some were lost. Others fell victim to accidents at the often primitive landing strips from which they operated. The combination of aircraft and experienced Gurkha jungle fighters proved devastatingly effective.

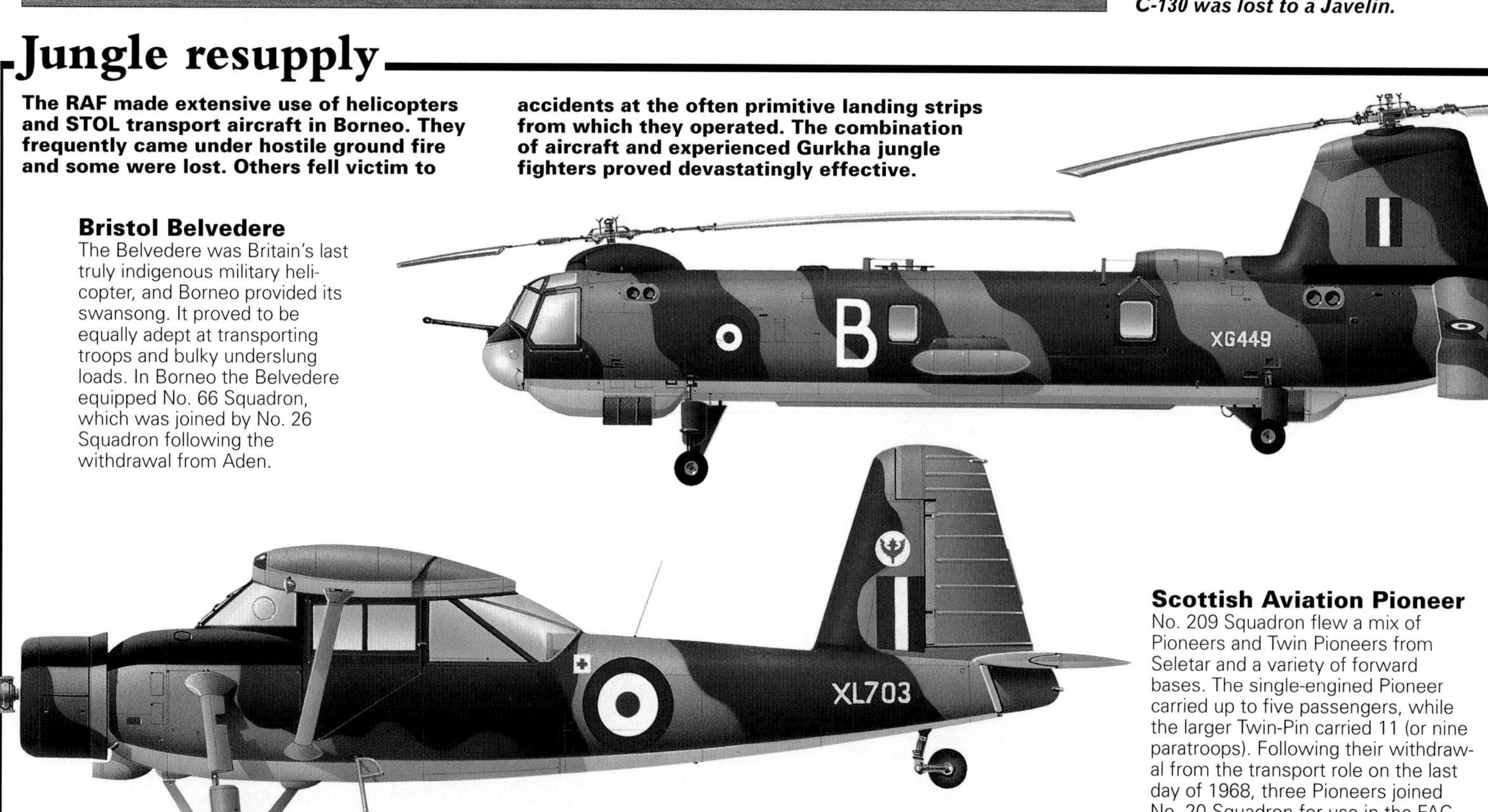

Bristol Belvedere
The Belvedere was Britain's last truly indigenous military helicopter, and Borneo provided its swansong. It proved to be equally adept at transporting troops and bulky underslung loads. In Borneo the Belvedere equipped No. 66 Squadron, which was joined by No. 26 Squadron following the withdrawal from Aden.

Scottish Aviation Pioneer
No. 209 Squadron flew a mix of Pioneers and Twin Pioneers from Seletar and a variety of forward bases. The single-engined Pioneer carried up to five passengers, while the larger Twin-Pin carried 11 (or nine paratroops). Following their withdrawal from the transport role on the last day of 1968, three Pioneers joined No. 20 Squadron for use in the FAC role, operating alongside the unit's Hunter fighter-bombers.

***Left:** With gaps in the land-based radar chain, carrierborne Gannet AEW.Mk 3s from the* **Hermes, Ark Royal, Victorious, Centaur** *and* **Eagle** *provided an invaluable addition to Britain's air-defence network in the area.*

***Below:** A Handley Page Victor B.Mk 1A of No. 57 Sqn flies over a Malayan rubber plantation during 1965. The 'Matterhorn' V-bomber detachment saw no action, but did much to deter any thoughts of escalation by the Indonesians.*

but from October 1964 consisted of Vulcan B.Mk 2s. Although for a time Victors were bombed up ready to go, the 'Matterhorn' bombers were not used in combat. In February 1964 an air-defence identification zone (ADIZ) was established, after which the Hunters and Javelins, based at Labuan and Kuching, maintained a 24-hour all-weather alert system, their pilots being authorised to engage and destroy any Indonesian aircraft entering the ADIZ.

Indonesian landings

In August of that year 100 regular Indonesian troops went ashore at three points on the west coast of the Malayan peninsula, and two weeks later an Indonesian C-130 Hercules dropped paratroops in central Johore. Although these forces had been rounded up by mid-October, there were 40 other landings and it was against these that the Hunters and Canberras of the RAF, RAAF and RNZAF were now deployed, and airborne early warning Gannets from Royal Navy carriers and shore bases were employed to patrol Malayan coastal airspace. However, the most effective counter to these cross-border raids was the rapid airlifting of troops by helicopter into the area.

Operations in Borneo waned during 1965, and by the middle of 1966 the 'confrontation' was fully over allowing the helicopters to return home from their forward-deployed bases in the jungle.

***Left:** Auster AOP.Mk 9s were deployed to Borneo with a number of units, including Nos 7 and 16 Recce Flights, and Nos 11 and 14 Liaison Flights. The aircraft was also deployed with the 4th Royal Tank Regiment's AOP Troop, and with the AOP Troop of the 1st Queen's Dragoon Guards. The AAC also deployed DHC Beavers and Scout and Sioux helicopters.*

***Above:** Royal Australian Air Force Commonwealth Sabre 32s were deployed to Labuan for air-defence duties, taking over from RAF Javelins as the confrontation came to an end with the 11 August 1966 signature of a peace treaty. The Australian Sabre used a Rolls-Royce Avon engine and was armed with a pair of 30-mm (1.2-in) cannon.*

***Right:** Troops approach a No. 5 Squadron, RAAF Bell UH-1B Iroquois. The unit was active in the confrontation from June 1964, flying from Butterworth. The white cabin top was designed to reflect heat, keeping the occupants cool. The Borneo interior had few tracks, and rivers were the primary transport routes.*

Vietnam: In-Country War

1964 - 1973

The air war in south Vietnam was unlike any other. It saw the full might of the world's greatest military and economic power pitted against an elusive but highly motivated enemy, indistinguishable most of the time from the civilian population. The enemy was equipped only with small arms, but an intimate knowledge of the terrain meant that he was no easy target.

There were many different aspects to the air war, involving aircraft ranging from World War II piston-powered bombers to Mach 2 supersonic fighters, but among the most important were the support of troops in contact with the enemy, the destruction of key Viet Cong strongholds, the defence of American and South Vietnamese bases, and the interdiction of the communist supply effort both by land and by water.

Above: The North American F-100 Super Sabre flew more combat sorties than any other warplane in Vietnam. Most were short hops to drop ordnance – like the napalm here tumbling from a low-flying 'Hun' of the 352nd TFS/35th TFW based at Phan Rang.

Right: The rotary bomb bay designed by Martin in the 1950s was finally combat-tested when the B-57 began operations in Vietnam in 1965. A license-built version of the British Canberra, the B-57 was the last USAF light bomber to fly combat sorties.

Air Support

The war against the Viet Cong was very much a short-range struggle. In a conventional war missions can be flown 'by the book'. But the Viet Cong were reading from a different script, and a whole new way of war had to be evolved. Fighters in the South were known as 'mud movers', for the simple reason that they fought down on the deck, duelling almost eye-to-eye with the insurgents on the ground.

In some cases, notably the support of American forces in close combat with the Viet Cong, it called for very great accuracy in the delivery of weaponry, occasionally to within metres of friendly troops. As a result, attacks were often pressed home at very low level.

This could be very dangerous: even though the communist insurgents lacked advanced weapons like guided missiles, they did have a lot of small arms, and low-level attacks brought the American fighters well within their range. Small arms and light anti-aircraft fire accounted for the vast majority of American aircraft losses over South Vietnam.

In a war without front lines, firebases became the key to control of territory. Strongpoints equipped with artillery, they served as bases from which patrols moved out into the country. However, they were also magnets to Viet Cong attack, and on several occasions were subjected to major assaults. In the most serious cases these required calls for air support.

Once the decision had been made to expand the war, the original adviser-flown, piston-engined machines were replaced by a full range of modern aircraft which were brought to bear against the Viet Cong. But for a fast-moving jet small targets moving beneath the jungle canopy are difficult to find, let alone attack, so forward air controllers flying low and slow in light planes were used to direct the fast jets.

Flying low and slow over the battlefield, the primary task of the forward air controller or FAC was to detect the enemy, mark his location in some way, and pass that information on to the fighters coming in to the area to provide aerial

Left: A USAF F-4 Phantom unleashes a barrage of 70-mm (2.75-in) rockets. The Phantom had set speed and altitude records before going to Vietnam and was recognized as a superb warplane, but air-to-ground work was difficult for a jet-powered 'fast mover'.

Above: The USAF deployed a new fighter, the Northrop F-5, to Vietnam during Operation Skoshi Tiger in 1965. The lightweight F-5 went on to become a major US export to developing nations, and was the backbone of South Vietnam's fighter force.

'Slow Movers'

The Cessna O-1 Bird Dog evolved into the ground commander's best friend and a major irritant to the enemy. The weathered paint on this aircraft reflects the intensity of low-level combat in harsh tropical conditions

Busy Bird Dog
Left: This Cessna O-1A Bird Dog (51-12605) of the South Vietnamese army is typical of the more than 1,000 forward air control (FAC) aircraft that flew low and slow to spot targets for bigger, faster warplanes. Bird Dog pilots inevitably flew more combat missions than anyone else: When the fighting was heavy, it was not uncommon for a FAC to fly two or three sorties per day.

Men who flew as forward air controllers were a special breed. A FAC had to be courageous and, perhaps, lucky. Not everybody could strap into an O-1 or O-2, pinpoint enemy troops with smoke rockets, and loiter overhead while the Viet Cong shot back. FACs often brought home aircraft ventilated with small-caliber bullet holes. Some died. But starting with the heroic performance of USAF Major William 'Mac the FAC' McAllister, in 1964, they made a contribution to the war that was almost too important to measure.

Right: It was called a 'war among the treetops' by one FAC, who flew 230 missions without ever getting high enough to don an oxygen mask. Fortunately, the O-1 was nimble and responsive – as it had to be to survive

Below: The twin-boomed O-2 was an 'off the shelf' Cessna 337 Skymaster. With twin push/pull engines it was more difficult to fly than the Bird Dog but had greater speed, range and endurance and could carry light ordnance.

North American F-100 Super Sabre

Hard-fighting 'Hun'
Caught up in a slugging match at treetop altitude with a lot of metal flying around, the F-100 was no longer the glamorous superstar that had set world air-speed records a decade earlier. But the Super Sabre's 75.4 kN (16,950 lb st) Pratt & Whitney J57-P-21A turbojet still gave the F-100 the ability to perform valiantly.

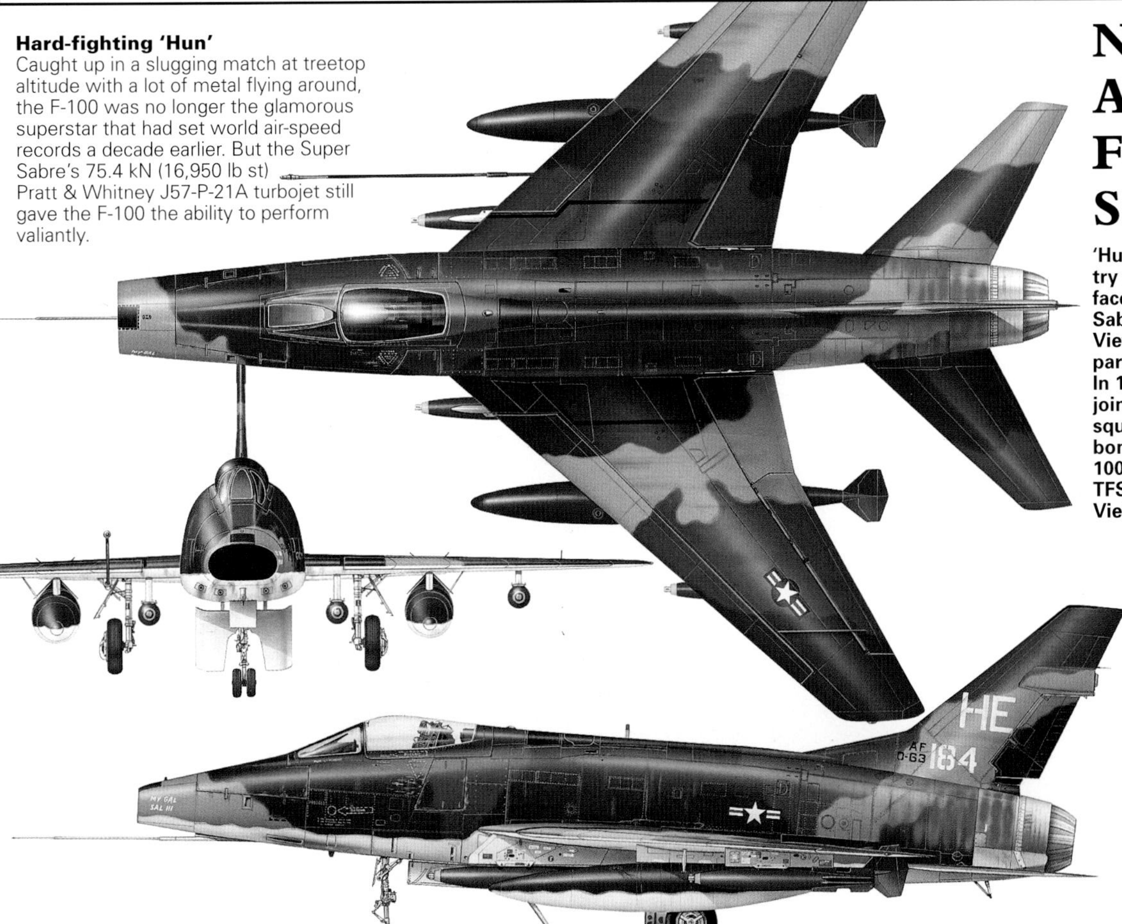

'Huns' were employed mainly for in-country missions where they did not need to face Hanoi's MiG fighters, although Super Sabres flew sorties over Laos and North Vietnam in the early phases of American participation in the war in Southeast Asia. In 1968, regular Air Force F-100 units were joined by four Air National Guard squadrons. Carrying two 340-kg (750-lb) bombs and two external fuel tanks, This F-100D-75-NA (56-3184) belongs to the 416th TFS/37th TFW at Phu Cat airfield in South Vietnam.

Armament
The F-100D Super Sabre was a potent ground attacker, with its four 20-mm Pontiac M39E cannon each with 1,200 rounds and underwing pylons for up to 3193 kg (7,040 lb) of bombs, rockets, or missiles. However, some of its weapons were less than effective: early versions of the AGM-12A/B Bullpup missile bounced harmlessly off any hard target they struck and often failed to detonate.

Below: Nothing was louder or more frightening than the sound of a B-52 blasting out a pathway in the jungle. With as many as 108 bombs from a single aircraft raining down on Viet Cong targets, the result was devastating, and could be felt as an earth tremor many miles away.

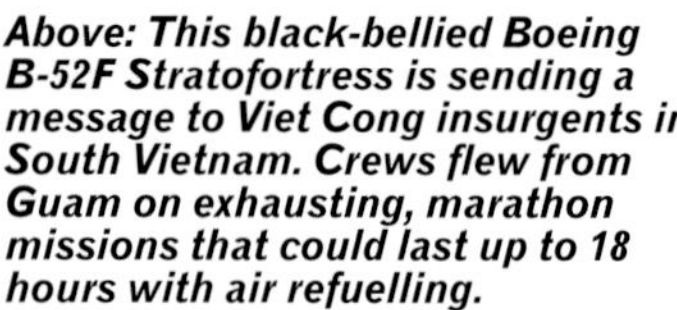

Above: This black-bellied Boeing B-52F Stratofortress is sending a message to Viet Cong insurgents in South Vietnam. Crews flew from Guam on exhausting, marathon missions that could last up to 18 hours with air refuelling.

Below: A Lockheed C-130A Hercules makes its own kind of delivery, dropping supplies to a friendly outpost. 'In-country' airlift was vital when ground access was difficult and roads often blocked by the enemy.

support and firepower. The 'slow movers' in their fragile prop-driven Cessnas played a vital part in finding the enemy, as well as identifying and marking targets.

Into the Breach

The Cessnas carried white phosphorous or smoke rockets. Forward air controllers – FACs – often flew solo, demanding the ability to control their aircraft while simultaneously hunting for the enemy and marking targets.

The FAC pilot was expected to expose himself to enemy gunfire, primarily to learn more about the target and to determine the best way of attacking.

Nobody expected the FAC to hit the target with his rockets, but he could use the smoke to give accurate instructions to fighter pilots – 'about 200 mikes [metres] uphill from the smoke,' would be a typical direction.

With bases the length of the country, American troops could rely on rapid air support: tactical aircraft could be armed and into the air within minutes of receiving any call for help.

Technology was also thrown at the problem, particularly in the night battle against the supply routes. The use of night vision and thermal sensors became widespread, along with seismic and even chemical sensors, and possible targets were engaged with pinpoint accuracy with the latest weapons.

One notable exception was the B-52 effort, where the massive Boeing bombers dropped huge tonnages of high explosive onto suspected Viet Cong positions and strongholds from high altitude. Results of these strikes, code named

Counter Insurgency

'Real' flying, some pilots insisted, was possible only in one of the light, nimble aircraft designed to keep the war very 'up close and personal'. The OV-10 Bronco had been developed with much fanfare as a 'COIN' (counter insurgency) warplane. The A-37 Dragonfly was an outgrowth of the USAF's standard primary trainer but was heavier, more powerful and could carry a useful load of bombs and rockets.

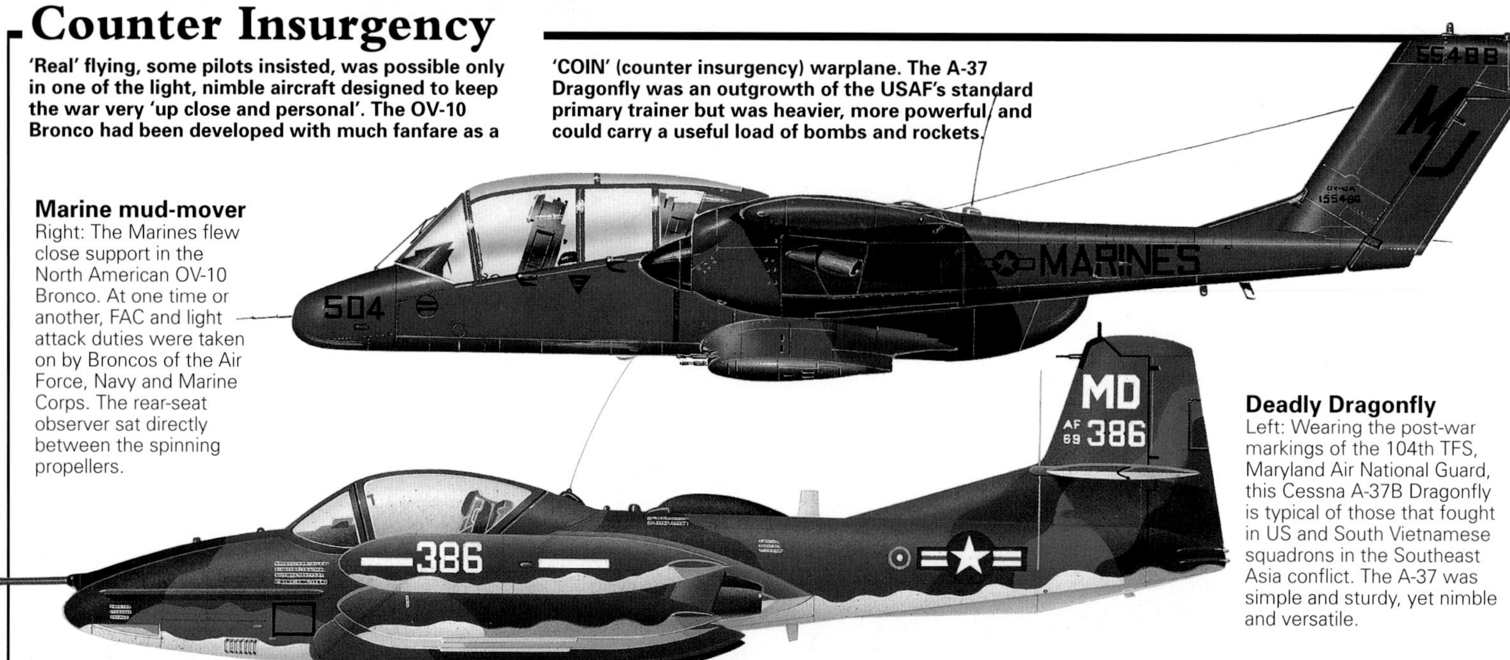

Marine mud-mover
Right: The Marines flew close support in the North American OV-10 Bronco. At one time or another, FAC and light attack duties were taken on by Broncos of the Air Force, Navy and Marine Corps. The rear-seat observer sat directly between the spinning propellers.

Deadly Dragonfly
Left: Wearing the post-war markings of the 104th TFS, Maryland Air National Guard, this Cessna A-37B Dragonfly is typical of those that fought in US and South Vietnamese squadrons in the Southeast Asia conflict. The A-37 was simple and sturdy, yet nimble and versatile.

COMBAT RESCUE

Hard-hitting 'Cowboy'
Capt Richard S. Drury of the 602nd SOS/56th SOW fires a salvo of 20-mm (2.75-in) rockets while diving his Douglas A-1H Skyraider, 'Midnight Cowboy' (BuNo. 134257) to protect a combat rescue attempt. The heavily-armed Skyraider, which could carry some 4535 kg (10,000 lb) of bombs, was the ideal escort for rescue helicopters and a welcome friend to every downed airman.

Right: This Sikorsky CH-3 is fitted with a winch above its cabin door. The better-known HH-3E 'Jolly Green Giant', was similar, but also had an in-flight refuelling probe. It was was used to rescue airmen shot down behind enemy lines.

Among the most daring of the supporting roles in Vietnam was that of rescuing downed airmen from the midst of enemy-held terrain. Heavily-armed and armoured Sikorsky HH-3 and HH-53 helicopters were used to make the actual pickups, but they did so under the protection of aging Douglas A-1 Skyraiders operating under the widely-known call-sign of 'Sandy'. The old prop-driven fighter bombers were a better performance match with the helicopters than more modern jets, and their ability both to loiter for long periods over the battlefield and to deliver a wide range of munitions made them ideal rescue escorts. To do their job effectively, 'Sandy' pilots flew some of the most dangerous missions of the conflict, often in the face of concentrated and accurate anti-aircraft fire. Their job involved making contact with the downed aircrew, drawing fire from and then destroying enemy guns and troops, laying smoke screens and supplying suppressive fire while the helicopters moved in to rescue the airmen. 'Sandy' pilots collected more than their share of gallantry medals and Purple Hearts, and many invaluable combat pilots and other aircrew owe their lives to this fearless group of men.

Right: 'Firebird' is an A-1H Skyraider flying from Nakhon Phanom, Thailand. An A-1H pilot, using the radio call-sign 'Sandy', often found himself as the mission commander at a rescue site, charged to orchestrate efforts by all involved in a pick-up attempt.

Arc Light, were debatable: when they hit the target the effect was devastating, but all too often they were bombing empty jungle.

Except for the occasional major battle such as that in the A-Shau valley or at Khe Sanh, the bulk of attacks on American positions was by troops armed with rifles, machine-guns, rockets and mortars. At Khe Sanh, however, ground-attack aircraft were faced with an enemy attacking in divisional strength, with artillery and armour. In many ways this was easier to deal with, since it provided ideal target material for massive aerial attacks by a wide variety of fighters and bombers.

The main strike effort of the US forces was augmented by many supporting missions such as aerial tanking, recovery of ditched aircraft, airborne early warning supplied by Lockheed EC-121 Warning Stars and massive airlift and ferrying involving Lockheed's C-5, C-141 and C-130, the de Havilland Canada C-7 Caribou, Douglas C-47, Boeing C-135 and numerous smaller types.

The US Navy's carriers sailing at 'Dixie Station' off the Mekong delta flew many strikes into the delta, and used these missions to work up to full strength before moving north to 'Yankee Station' in the Gulf of Tonkin, where the action was much more fierce.

Right: A McDonnell F-4B Phantom lightly armed for an air defence mission launches from the angled deck of USS Ranger (CVA-62). No serious effort was made to attack US carriers at sea near Vietnam.

Vietnam: Rolling Thunder

1965–1968

The Republic F-105 Thunderchief was the most important strike aircraft in the early years of the war against North Vietnam, and took most losses. Known as the 'Thud', it was the biggest, fastest and loudest single-seat, single-engined bomber of its time.

The initial Flaming Dart retaliation raids of 1964 were seen by the Johnson administration as the first steps in a gradual escalation of pressures on North Vietnam until the North Vietnamese decided that a Viet Cong victory was not worth the price. The policy of attacking North Vietnam only on a retaliatory basis was abandoned and Flaming Dart gave way to the sustained air campaign known as Rolling Thunder.

The air war against North Vietnam as consisting of four distinct phases – the Rolling Thunder campaign from 1965 to 1968, the bombing halt which lasted until 1972, the Linebacker campaign between May and October of that year, and the final intensive bombing of the North known as Linebacker II, which lasted for 11 days in December 1972.

Rolling Thunder, as conceived and begun, had three objectives: to reduce infiltration, to boost South Vietnamese morale and to make it clear to Hanoi that continuation of the insurgency in the South would become increasingly expensive.

In Hanoi, however, Rolling Thunder was simply seen as one more obstacle to overcome in a long struggle to remove foreign influence and unify a divided Vietnam under Vietnamese rule. No official in the North Vietnamese leadership ever saw the American air strikes as evidence that it was time to succumb.

The first USAF Rolling Thunder missions were flown on 2 March 1965, using Martin B-57s, North American F-100Ds, and Republic F-105Ds. Of the 150 aircraft available at Thai bases, 25 F-105Ds from the 12th and 67th Tactical Fighter Squadrons (both part of the 18th Tactical Fighter Wing) accompanied B-57s to an ammunition depot at Xom Bong, about 56 km (35 miles) above the DMZ (demilitarized zone) and inflicted heavy damage.

On this first raid, no fewer than five aircraft – two F-100D Super Sabres and three F-105Ds – were lost to ground fire and the first USAF pilot, Captain Hayden J. Lockhart, was taken prisoner. Already, it was clear that the idea of bombing which would quickly subdue North Vietnam required further examination.

Below: The F-4 Phantom flew beside the F-105 from the start, and took on more of the burden as the Rolling Thunder campaign progressed. Air Force, Marine, and Navy fliers all 'went north' in the F-4 from bases on land and sea.

Above: Packed with advanced electronics, Douglas EB-66s led radar-bombing missions by Thuds and Phantoms near Hanoi. The USAF lost six EB-66s in combat, a heavy toll for a craft that served in small numbers.

Muddled Strategy

From the beginning, critics of the sustained campaign against North Vietnam would argue that Rolling Thunder did not really roll and was not particularly thunderous. The planning of air strikes was a complex and unwieldy business, beginning in the Situation Room at the White House where President Johnson retained firm control over what could and could not be attacked. Decisions as routine as the choice of ordnance for a particular sortie were made at this level, thousands of miles from the fighting.

Johnson's decisions were relayed to Secretary of Defense Robert McNamara, who in turn informed the Pentagon. Directives were then passed down to CINCPAC (Commander-in-Chief, Pacific forces, in Hawaii) which then fragmented or 'fragged' the various targets among USAF, USN and – on rare occasions – South Vietnamese aircraft. The USAF headquarters in Saigon, the 2nd Air Division, made recommendations but could not choose targets.

Lt Gen Joseph Moore, who commanded 2nd Air Division, was an accomplished old fighter hand who kept making suggestions for a more effective campaign against the North Vietnamese road and rail transportation network, only to find targets approved on what seemed a random basis. The obvious targets around Hanoi and Haiphong, especially North Vietnam's air bases, were off-limits to the US forces at the time.

The most important aircraft in the early years of the war against the

North was the redoubtable Republic F-105 Thunderchief, known to most of its pilots as the 'Thud', which could lift eight 340-kg (750-lb) iron bombs and auxiliary fuel tanks. These F-105s usually attacked their targets from medium level, often on the command of a lead aircraft which was usually a Douglas EB-66 Destroyer, equipped with full electronic countermeasures (ECM) and navigation aids. Inflight refuelling was often necessary to enable the 'Thuds' to reach their targets.

ANTI-AIRCRAFT THREAT

A complicating factor was the expansion of the North Vietnamese air defences. Such losses that had been suffered in the early days were due to Soviet-supplied anti-aircraft artillery – AAA or Triple-A – which had been quickly and substantially reinforced early in 1965. Radar-directed anti-aircraft guns were a serious enough challenge to the US strike aircraft but they would soon be joined by MiGs and by guided SAMs. Northern pilots flying aged MiG-15bis fighters tended to keep well away from the US Navy Skyhawks and the USAF's F-100s. It was now that large numbers of Chinese-built MiG-17s started arriving in the North. Although not as fast as their American opponents, the MiGs were very agile, and they were to cause the Americans considerable problems in air combat. F-105s could protect themselves to some extent, and victories were scored over MiG fighters with both Sidewinder missiles and the internal 20-mm gun, but losses began to mount.

The arrival in South East Asia of the McDonnell F-4 Phantom heralded a new era as the greater range, load and speed of the aircraft enabled many more targets to be attacked. At first the F-4s were used in the bombing role, with much the same tactics as employed by the F-105s, but increasingly effective communist defences dictated a change.

The 8th Tactical Fighter Wing, known as the 'Wolf Pack' under the command of combat veteran

Route Packages

North Vietnam was divided by American mission planners into six target areas, known as Route Packages or 'Packs'.

The most heavily defended areas were those around the capital, Hanoi, and the country's major port, Haiphong. These were in Route Package Six, which because of its importance and the large numbers of targets it contained was subdivided into Pack 6A and Pack 6B.

Although there were no hard and fast divisions of responsibility, and aircraft from any service could attack any target, the Air Force generally dealt with inland targets and the Navy attacked those on the coast. Marine Corps aircraft operating out of I Corps in the north of South Vietnam were also occasionally used against North Vietnamese targets, generally in Pack 1.

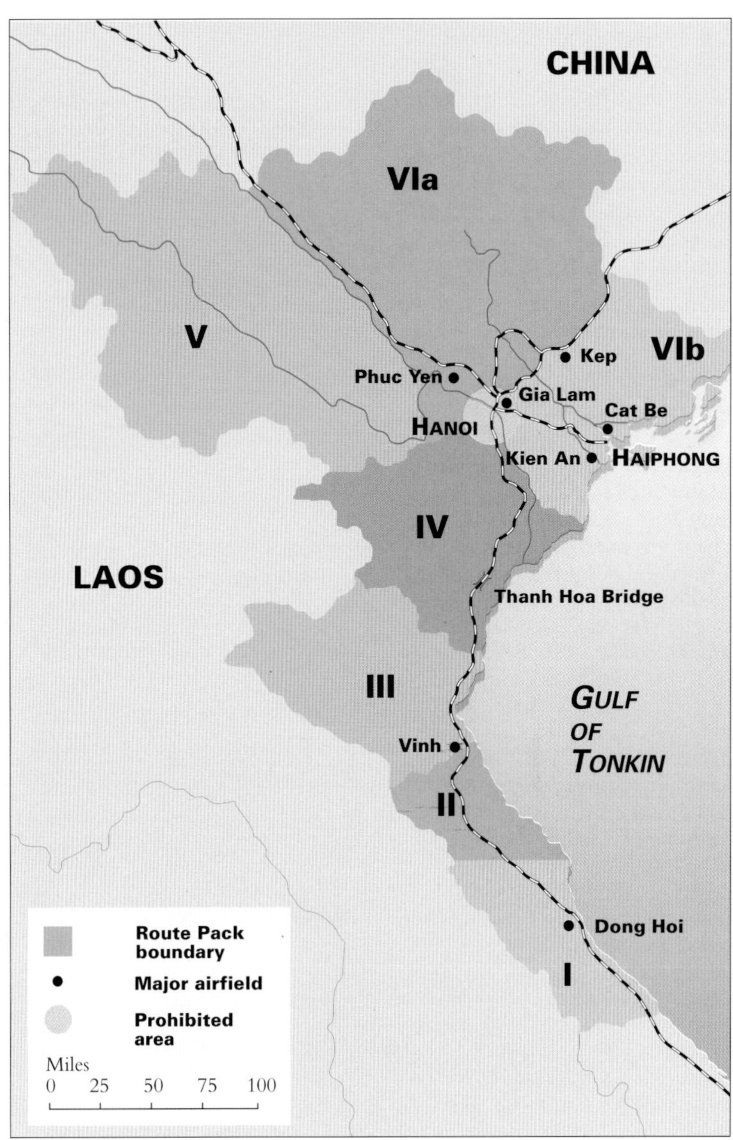

The Fighters

Americans saw air-to-air action as secondary to their bombing effort. To the North Vietnamese, every dogfight was a defence of home turf. Both sides flew state-of-the-art fighters. Hanoi relied on MiGs that were short-legged but nimble and deadly. Americans flew costlier, more complex jets with longer range that were less manoeuvrable in close quarters but, being missile-armed, lethal from afar.

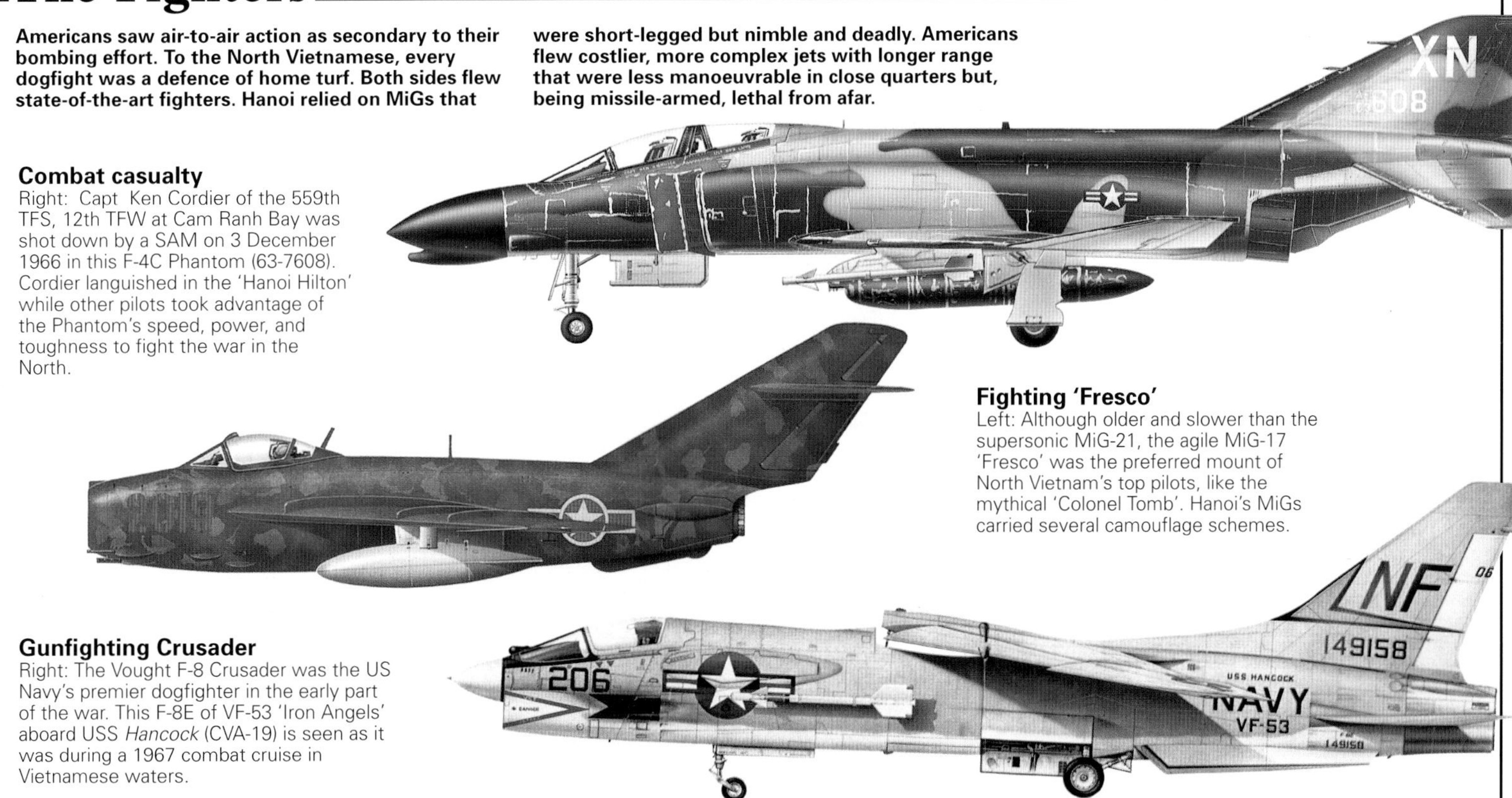

Combat casualty
Right: Capt Ken Cordier of the 559th TFS, 12th TFW at Cam Ranh Bay was shot down by a SAM on 3 December 1966 in this F-4C Phantom (63-7608). Cordier languished in the 'Hanoi Hilton' while other pilots took advantage of the Phantom's speed, power, and toughness to fight the war in the North.

Fighting 'Fresco'
Left: Although older and slower than the supersonic MiG-21, the agile MiG-17 'Fresco' was the preferred mount of North Vietnam's top pilots, like the mythical 'Colonel Tomb'. Hanoi's MiGs carried several camouflage schemes.

Gunfighting Crusader
Right: The Vought F-8 Crusader was the US Navy's premier dogfighter in the early part of the war. This F-8E of VF-53 'Iron Angels' aboard USS *Hancock* (CVA-19) is seen as it was during a 1967 combat cruise in Vietnamese waters.

Operation 'Bolo'

Life expectancy for American pilots over North Vietnam was falling fast. By 1967, growing North Vietnamese fighter and missile strength was reaping a costly harvest from the American fighter bombers. And the USAF could not strike back at the enemy airfields, forbidden by restrictive rules of engagement dictated in Washington.

Clearly something had to be done, and Colonel Robin Olds was the man to do it. World War II ace Olds commanded the 8th Tactical Fighter Wing, the 'Wolf Pack', flying F-4C Phantoms out of Ubon in Thailand. Olds was a tough, seat-of-the pants flyer of the old school. But he was a fine tactician and a superb leader.

If the 'Wolf Pack' could convince the North Vietnamese that they were bombers rather than fighters, then the MiGs might be lured into combat before they could realise their mistake. On the morning of 2 January 1967, Olds led 14 flights of Phantoms, six flights of 'Wild Weasel' defence suppression F-105s, and four flights of F-104 Starfighters, a total of nearly 100 aircraft. At least the same number of aircraft flew in supporting roles. These included EC-121 airborne radar planes, EB-66 electronic warfare platforms, more F-4Cs making diversionary sweeps, and A-1 Skyraiders, F-100s and helicopters on alert for possible rescue missions.

The Phantoms headed north along Route Package Six, the heavily defended approaches to Hanoi. The Phantoms flew at speeds and heights typical of a large-scale F-105 raid. Each of the F-4Cs was equipped with an ECM pod usually carried by Thunderchiefs, so on the North Vietnamese radar they would look like a bomber.

The first wave – three flights of four Phantoms, characteristically led from the front by Robin Olds – wheeled past Phuc Yen, an air base and major petroleum depot southwest of Hanoi. As they headed for the North Vietnamese capital, an EC-121 radar plane over the Gulf of Tonkin warned that MiGs were taking off and others were converging on the area. It looked as though the bait had been taken.

Missile fight

The MiGs bored in unsuspectingly, and Olds' flight manoeuvred to engage. Olds himself fired two Sparrows and a Sidewinder at a silver MiG, but all three missiles missed. However, Lieutenant Ralph Wettrehahn and Captain Walt Radeker, flying Olds 2 and 4 respectively, were more successful, each destroying an enemy.

It was about this time that the North Vietnamese realised what was happening, and immediately began to manoeuvre defensively. However, by now the 'Wolf Pack' was roaring. Olds barrel-rolled around another MiG before shooting it down with a Sidewinder. At the same time Captain Everett T. Raspberry was downing another.

The second Phantom flight, code-named Rambler, now arrived. Diving down on a pair of MiGs Captain John B. Stone in Rambler 1 fired two Sparrows. As one missile hit the target, Stone was attacked from behind by more MiGs. Breaking left and down with Rambler 2, Lt Lawrence Glynn, Stone brought the MiGs into the sights of Major Philip P. Combies in Rambler 4, who shot one of the enemy down. Lieutenant Glynn in Rambler 2 now turned inside the MiGs, loosed off a pair of Sparrows and destroyed a seventh North Vietnamese jet.

The MiGs broke off before any more of the 'Wolf Pack' could arrive on the scene, so there were to be no more successes that day. Olds and his men headed homewards, satisfied in the knowledge that they had downed seven of North Vietnam's best aircraft without loss to themselves. Colonel Olds had shown the way to beat the MiGs. In the following 12 months, USAF Phantoms were to shoot down another 36 North Vietnamese fighters, with the 'Wolf Pack' accounting for 23 of them. But thanks to a politically-motivated bombing halt which lasted until 1972, it was to be another four years before the US Air Force achieved similar success.

Colonel Robin Olds, laid a trap for the MiGs. Nearly 100 fighters followed exactly the same pattern as that regularly used by bombing F-105s and F-4s, but these aircraft carried only air-to-air missiles. The MiGs, under the control of excellent ground radar, soon intercepted the force and in the ensuing battle seven were destroyed without loss to the Americans, Olds himself bagging two.

Following this action, which was to remain one of the the largest aerial fights of the war, the North Vietnamese were considerably more cautious with their interceptions, especially as the Americans introduced MIGCAP fighter cover flights equipped with F-4s carrying Sidewinder and Sparrow missiles

At the same time as the MiGs were being tamed, the SAMs became an ever increasing problem as supplies of the Soviet SA-2 'Guideline' established themselves. To combat the SAMs, the USAF deployed 'Wild Weasel' F-100s and F-105s. These carried extra electronics and Shrike anti-radiation missiles (ARMs) which homed-in on the radar emissions of the 'Fan Song' guidance system of the SA-2. Under the codename Iron Hand, the 'Wild Weasels' and their naval equivalents streaked in ahead of the main attacking force to try to suppress the SAM forces before the main strike. Though partially successful, the war against the SAMs

Above: To 'sucker' Hanoi's MiG pilots, Col. Robin Olds used intelligence photos snapped by the RF-101C Voodoo. Olds later ordered that no Voodoo pilot pay for a drink at his fighter wing's bar in Ubon, Thailand.

Right: MiG-17s sheltered at an airfield in North Vietnam. For much of the war, US fliers were forbidden to bomb airfields like Kep, so their only resort was air-to-air action. It was an expensive way to fight MiGs.

F-105 Thunderchief

The Republic F-105 Thunderchief had been designed as a supersonic nuclear bomber carrying its weapons internally. In Vietnam, it was a subsonic striker, carrying ordnance externally and extra fuel in the bay. A big, powerful aircraft, the 'Thud' required excessive runway length when operating with heavy bombloads in the high ambient temperature of Southeast Asia and often required aerial refuelling to complete its missions.

Camo but no code
Thus F-105D (59-1745) wears standard T.O. 1-1-4 camouflage which was in use in 1966 but carries no tail marking.Large two-letter tail codes were in widespread use by late 1967.

Lethal bombload
This F-105D carries the standard Vietnam-era load of eight 340-kg (750-lb) bombs – six under the fuselage and two more under the wings – plus internal and external fuel. The 'Thud' was also armed with the M61A1 Vulcan 20-mm Gatling gun.

Rugged survivor
At high altitude, the F-105D had its flaws (though pilots praised the aircraft without reservation), but down 'in the weeds' where much of the war was fought, the F-105 was sturdy and could endure battle damage and bring its pilot home.

continued throughout the conflict, the Americans continuing to lose aircraft to this often unseen threat.

The first electronic countermeasures (ECM) capability to be mounted in the conflict was employed on 29 March 1965, when three RF-101C Voodoos, each carrying QRC-160 pods, flew ECM support missions accompanying a Rolling Thunder strike force to target. The QRC-160 proved unsatisfactory and was quickly withdrawn from combat, but steps were under way to develop some means of jamming or deceiving the enemy's radar defences.

Several of the low-level, small-scale strikes were controlled from a 'fast-mover FAC', an adviser sitting in the back-seat of a two-seat F-100, A-4 or TF-9 Cougar. These aircraft were able to survive the defensive fire by agility and speed, whereas more typical FAC aircraft were too slow for this hostile environment.

Overall control of the battle zone was entrusted to ships sailing in the Gulf of Tonkin and to Lockheed EC-121 Warning Star airborne early-warning aircraft circling over the sea or Thailand. Under the codename College Eye, these veteran machines used their powerful radars to co-ordinate strikes and to warn of the approach of hostile MiGs.

Many Air Force, Navy and Marines officers and pilots, who felt that their hands were tied behind their backs, considered the long air campaign to be a violation of the basic principle of combat: when you fight, you must fight to win. Men in 'Thuds' and Crusaders, Skyhawks and Phantoms believed that they had been sent against formidable defences, to attack questionable targets, under too many restrictions, with no realistic chance of waging the war in a manner that would make it possible to win.

Damage to the North

Despite all the restrictions, the on-again, off-again mood of the campaign, and the general confusion, these pilots had, in fact, done more damage to North Vietnam than is generally recognized. In the years since the conflict, a few North Vietnamese have acknowledged that at times in 1967 and 1968 the bombing was hurting badly. The diversion of resources to repair, maintain and expand bridges, roads and railways – to say nothing of infiltration routes – was a drain on an already overburdened society.

When Rolling Thunder came to an end with the bombing halt of 30 October 1968, preliminary peace talks were taking shape in Paris, though they had hardly progressed beyond such issues as the shape of the table to be used at meetings.

With the benefit of hindsight, it is clear that Rolling Thunder could have been successful only if the civilian leaders in Washington had made a policy decision to use military power effectively. Most professional airmen believed then, and still believe now, that North Vietnam could have been taken out of the war in a matter of weeks with the men and machines already located in Southeast Asia, and with no additional resources. What they felt was missing was a plan, a policy, and a coherent decision to use airmen and aircraft as they were intended to be used.

Right: The Douglas EB-66 served as a new kind of pathfinder, using its onboard electronic suite to carve out a route for fighter-bombers. On radar-directed raids, the EB-66 crew called 'Bombs away' for all.

Vietnam: The Helicopter War

1961 - 1975

***Left:** South Vietnamese troops pour from a Bell UH-1D/H Iroquois helicopter – the ubiquitous Huey – at a landing zone (LZ) in a rice paddy. Helicopter pilots had to scout out and 'secure' the LZ before landing and disgorging infantrymen.*

***Below:** An US Navy Huey gunship flies as escort to riverine patrol boats in the Mekong Delta. Helicopters and light naval forces were the only way of moving troops and firepower around the myriad of waterways of the Delta, a hotbed of Viet Cong activity.*

Helicopters had seen action in Korea, Malaya and Algeria, but it was Vietnam which was to become the first true helicopter war. Helicopters flying into 'hot' landing zones became one of the most enduring images of the war, and that was certainly the helicopter's most outstanding role, but most missions were very different. Helicopters did everything. They delivered mail and new personnel, flying men on leave and returning men full of the pleasures of Hong Kong, Tokyo or Australia. They served as taxis for the brass and television crews, and as trucks, replenishing ammunition and stores at isolated fire support bases. Other tasks included heavy lift of outsize objects, gunship fire support, combat rescue, observation, liaison and psychological warfare.

So important was the helicopter that by the end of the Vietnam War the US Army, the major user of rotary-winged machines, had become the world's third largest air force after that of the Soviet Union and the USAF. But large numbers in battle meant large numbers of casualties: in a decade of conflict, the United States lost 4,869 helicopters, of which 2,382 were destroyed by enemy action.

Helicopters were in right from the start. The first complete US Army units in action in Vietnam were the 8th and 57th Transportation Companies, which in December 1961 landed 32 twin-rotor Piasecki H-21s from the USS *Card*. Less than two weeks later they were in action, airlifting 1,000 Vietnamese paratroopers in a surprise attack on a suspected Viet Cong headquarters. The successful mission was notable as the first major use of US combat power in Vietnam, and as the beginning of a new era in air mobility.

Early in 1962 the H-21s were joined in-country by Marine Corps HUS-1 Seahorses which operated in the Mekong Delta. But the most notable arrival of the year was the US Army's 57th Medical Detachment. Its medical evacuation mission, soon to be nicknamed 'Dust Off', introduced one of the great icons of the war, the Bell UH-1 Iroquois. Known universally as the Huey, the UH-1 also equipped the Utility Tactical Transport Helicopter Company (UTTHC) based at Tan Son Nhut.

As a result of assessment of experience gained by the UTTHC, which included fitting guns and rockets, the US Army quickly adapted to the jungle conditions in Vietnam and numerous helicopter units were activated in the USA for deployment to the theatre. When American ground troops were committed to action in 1965, they came with large numbers of helicopters.

Prominent among the units which arrived in 1965 was the Air Cavalry. Since the late 1950s, the

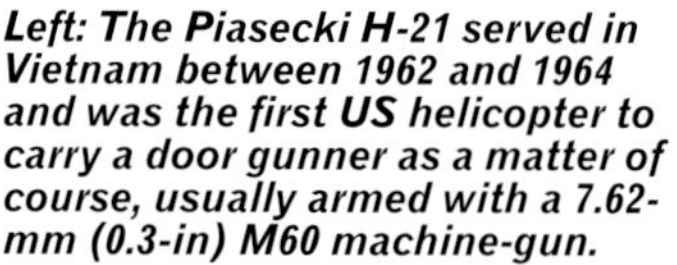

***Left:** The Piasecki H-21 served in Vietnam between 1962 and 1964 and was the first US helicopter to carry a door gunner as a matter of course, usually armed with a 7.62-mm (0.3-in) M60 machine-gun.*

***Below:** US Marine Corps Sikorsky UH-34Ds (known as HUS-1s until late 1962) were the backbone of Operation Shy Fly, the first major effort to provide helicopter 'lift' to South Vietnamese troops.*

The Ubiquitous 'Huey'

Among the most recognised flying machines in the history of aviation, the turboshaft-powered Huey revolutionised the support of combat units in the field. Transport Hueys flew men, equipment, and supplies, while gunships flew escort missions and served as a kind of flying artillery in support of troops on the ground. Hueys were used as aerial ambulances, lifting wounded soldiers from the heart of a firefight directly to medical help – in the process reducing the battlefield fatality rate in Vietnam to the lowest level in the history of warfare. The sight and distinctive sound of this great aircraft, seen on virtually every American television news broadcast of the period, became one of the great icons of the Vietnam experience.

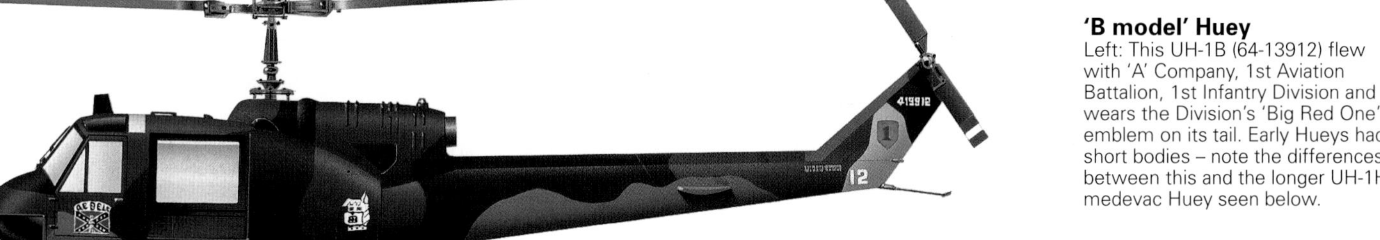

'B model' Huey
Left: This UH-1B (64-13912) flew with 'A' Company, 1st Aviation Battalion, 1st Infantry Division and wears the Division's 'Big Red One' emblem on its tail. Early Hueys had short bodies – note the differences between this and the longer UH-1H medevac Huey seen below.

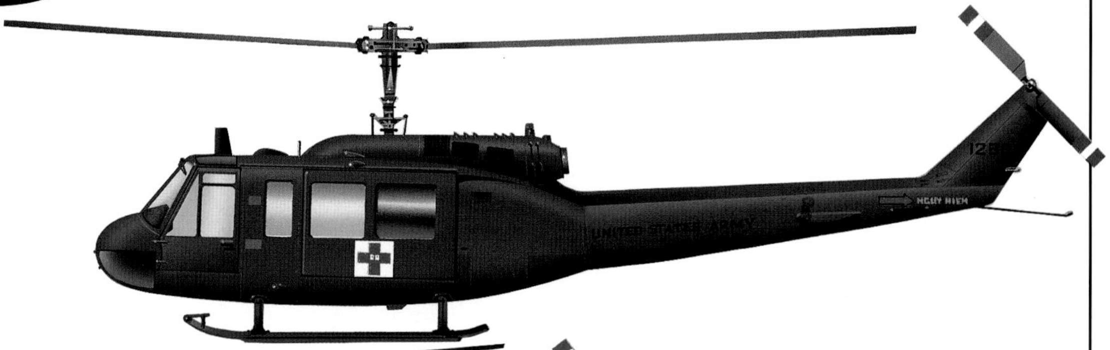

'DustOff' samaritan
Right: the UH-1D/H model, seen here with medical evacuation Red Cross markings, had a 14.63-m (48-ft) rotor and a much bigger fuselage, enabling it to carry 12 troops. On a medevac mission (universally known as 'DustOff' from the callsign of one of its early practicioners) the bigger 'D' and 'H' Hueys accommodated the pilot plus six stretchers and a medic, or up to 1814 kg (4,000 lb) of freight.

Armed to the teeth
Left: There were three essential Army Hueys – 'Slicks' (troop carriers), 'Dustoffs' (medevac machines), and heavily-armed 'Guns' or 'Hogs'. A UH-1B gunship like this 1st Air Cavalry Division example could carry 70-mm (2.75-in) rocket pods, 7.62-mm (0.3-in) multi-barrel Miniguns, 40-mm grenade launchers, and a host of other weapons.

Above: UH-1 pilots planted troops in landing zones, 'hot' with enemy action nearby or 'cold' without, and spent no more time on the ground than necessary. It took about a minute to unload troops.

Right: With a smoke grenade serving as a marker and his M16A1 rifle held aloft, this soldier is guiding a Bell UH-1 Iroquois to touchdown in an area obviously free of Viet Cong opposition.

US Army had been experimenting in using helicopters to give large units unprecedented battlefield mobility. Using large numbers of helicopters, a division-sized force could make an extremely rapid assault, seizing control of a large area of territory in a very short space of time.

The 11th Air Assault Division (Test) at Fort Benning proved the new air mobile concept to be feasible. It was seen as being ideal for Vietnam operations, so the 11th, renamed 1st Cavalry Division (Airmobile), became the first complete US Army division to be deployed to Southeast Asia. In spite of the vulnerability of the helicopter to ground fire, the Air Cav proved itself to be one of the most effective combat formations to serve in Vietnam.

A typical assault mission involving, say, about 100 troops, would require some 16-18 helicopters of which one UH-1 would be equipped as a communications command aircraft carrying the force commander and an air liaison officer whose task would be to call up any USAF support required; another UH-1 would deliver the landing zone (LZ) control party which

Air Assault

In 1965, at the height of their strength, North Vietnam's elite regulars faced inexperienced Americans of the 1st Air Cavalry Division, but thanks to helicopter assault pioneer General Hamilton Howze, the Americans brought along a new way to fight. The helicopter gave the American 'skytroopers' an unprecedented mobility: transported by large numbers of Hueys, the Cav defeated Hanoi's finest in the First and Second Battles of Ia Drang Valley. The helicopter had changed the very nature of warfare, probably forever.

Door gunner
Above: The crew chief (always a flight crew member in the US Army) often doubled as a door gunner, although climbing completely out of the Huey in mid-air was a little unusual. Scattered fire from a hand-held M60 machine-gun was unlikely to hit any Viet Cong, but it was designed not so much to hit the enemy as to force him to keep his head down, increasing the UH-1's chance of getting into and out of an LZ unscathed.

Air Cavalry
Above: Air mobility advocates viewed the helicopter not as an odd kind of flying machine but as a substitute for the Jeep, the 4x4 truck, and the armoured personnel carrier. When the 1st and 101st Air Cavalry Divisions took air mobility ideas with them to South Vietnam, they were committed to seizing the advantage every time a helicopter could help them do it. One way of doing so was in tight formation flying, which could deliver the maximum number of troops on a landing zone in the minimum possible time.

Observation
Right: With its superb visibility and ability to fly slowly or even hover, the helicopter is an unrivalled observation platform. The US Army in Vietnam used the agile Hughes OH-6A Cayuse as its standard rotary-wing spotter . The 'Loach' drew its unofficial nickname from the acronym LOH, or Light Observation Helicopter.

would land first and guide the assault force in.

Agile light observation helicopters like the Hughes OH-6A Cayuse, known as the Loach, would be used to seek out enemy forces. Support weapons too large for carriage by the assault helicopters, which included artillery up to the size of 105-mm howitzers, could be delivered as slung loads by medium- and heavy-lift helicopters.

Not unnaturally, the development of new assault weapons was accelerated, and more and more sophisticated equipment was fitted in the helicopters to bring increased firepower the US Army's airmobile companies in the field. The AH-1 HueyCobra, a potent gunship which mounted an armament mix selected from Miniguns, 20-mm cannon, automatic grenade-launchers and high-explosive rockets first, entered service in Vietnam in 1967; later, integrated television and infra-red sensors were introduced. By 1968 about 50 assault helicopter companies, equipped with between 600 and 700 HueyCobras, were based at such locations as Ban Me Thuot, Phuoc Vinh, Pleiku, Bien Hoa, Nha Trang and Tuy Hoa.

Apart from the constant and massive use of assault helicopters by the US Army, other large helicopters were also widely used for numerous heavy-lift tasks, not least of which was the recovery of downed aircraft from otherwise inaccessible locations. It has been stated that during the course of the entire Vietnam war the Boeing Vertol CH-47 Chinook alone recovered thousands of downed aircraft, worth a reputed $2.9 billion. The big twin-rotor Chinook, more than 680 examples of which had been produced by the end of the war, could carry up to 44 troops, light armoured vehicles, artillery or ten tonnes of stores on external load hooks. The bigger Sikorsky CH-54 Tarhe crane helicopter was also used and was capable of carrying items like bulldozers as slung loads.

The most powerful helicopters used in Vietnam were the variants of the Sikorsky Sea Stallion. Used as a heavy-lift troop and cargo transport by the Marines, it was selected by the US Air Force to equip the 37th Aerospace Rescue and

Left: It was inevitable that bigger helicopters would join the fray as soon as they could be built. The Boeing CH-47 Chinook, also dubbed the 'Sh--thook' by crew members, gave new size and versatility to Army rotary-wing units.

The HueyCobra in Vietnam
Powered by an 1343-kW (1,800-shp) Avco Lycoming T53-703 turboshaft engine, the HueyCobra resembled the better-known UH-1 Iroquois, or Huey, on which it was based, but had a very narrow, rakish fuselage. Designed for close-support and escort work, the AH-1G (1,126 built during the war years) fought Hanoi's PT-76 tanks in 1972.

Gunship weapons
This early example of the Bell AH-1G has an M28 chin turret with an M134 Minigun with 4,000 7.62-mm (0.3-in) rounds,. It also carries two sizes of 70-mm (2.75-in) rocket launchers. The Cobra introduced the now almost universal gunship crew layout of gunner in front, the pilot in back.

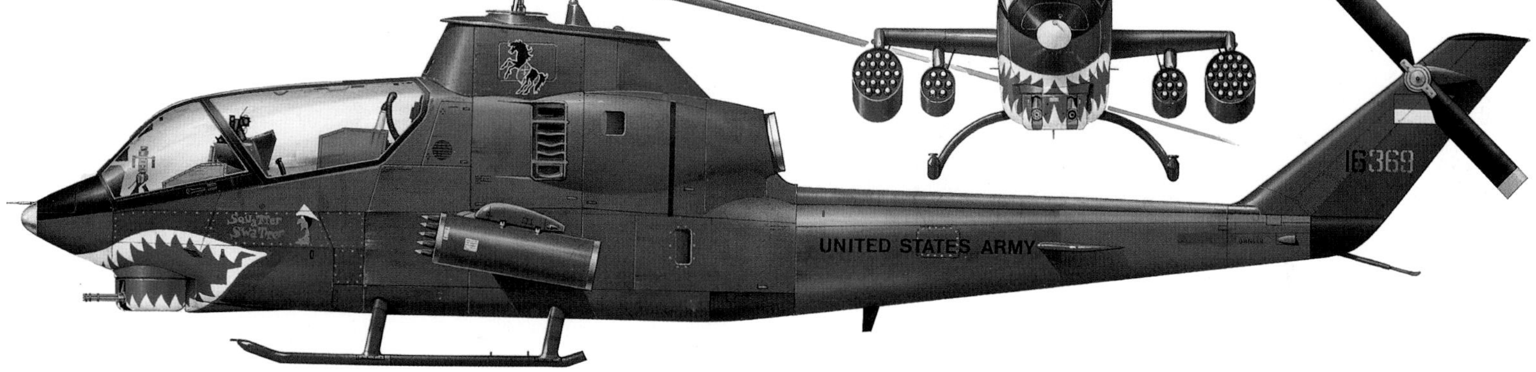

Battlefield response
The armament of the HueyCobra might have been its most obvious and important feature, but this first true battlefield helicopter was also equipped with VHF and UHF radios and associated electronics gear to enhance communication between helicopters, and between the air and the ground.

Bell AH-1 HueyCobra

The HueyCobra was developed quickly to meet urgent war needs, but the design was a superb one. While other gunship helicopters failed to reach production, the Cobra remained the standard US helicopter gunship for 18 years.

Recovery Squadron at Phu Cat later in the war. The HH-53 was heavily armed and armoured for the perilous mission of rescuing downed aircrew from hostile territory, often under intense enemy fire.

By the early 1970s, as America began to disengage from Vietnam, the process of Vietnamization saw a large number of UH-1 and CH-47 helicopters supplied to the VNAF – indeed, the number of Hueys left behind and struck off US Army charge exceeded the helicopter strength of any West European air force. The aim was to make the Vietnamese self-sufficient by the time the Americans left.

However, American financial aid did not match the massive inventory of equipment left behind, and by the time North Vietnam overran the south in 1975, most of the once powerful force was grounded and in storage for lack of operating funds.

But the helicopter still had one major role to play, being there for the end of America's Vietnam War as it had been for the beginning. As the North Vietnamese army finally took the capital in April 1975, American and Vietnamese helicopters lifted thousands of refugees to safety in the last days of Operation Frequent Wind.

Above: Sailors push a South Vietnamese UH-1H Huey over the side of USS Midway (CVA-41) during Operation Frequent Wind, the hectic April 1975 evacuation of Saigon. Dozens of aircraft were dumped.

Right: Attired for the climate, a ground crew member directs a USAF Sikorsky HH-53B/C 'Super Jolly'. The HH-53 was the largest helicopter employed for combat rescue, often penetrating deep into North Vietnamese territory..

Vietnam: War against the Trail

1963 - 1973

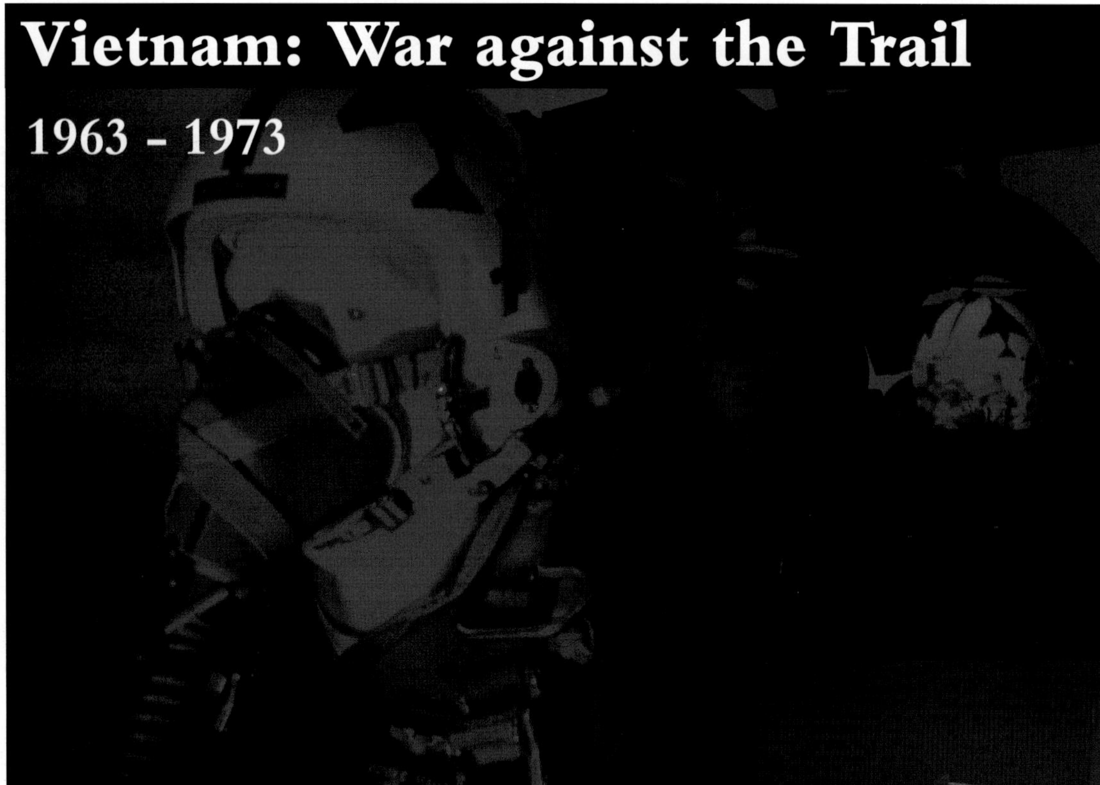

Left: Pilot Lt Victor Seavers and back seater Lt Tom Noonan flew out of Ubon, Thailand with the 497th TFS/8th TFW, part of the famous 'Wolf Pack'. Known as the 'Night Owls', the 497th pioneered night bombing work in McDonnell Douglas F-4C Phantoms, flying ultra low-level missions in pitch darkness against the Ho Chi Minh Trail and other targets.

Below: Early examples of the Martin B-57 Canberra generally attacked the trail by day, but like all warplanes in Southeast Asia they were fuelled and armed during the nocturnal hours by hard-working ground crews. B-57s gave way to fighter-bombers like the F-100 and F-4 in air-to-ground action against the Viet Cong.

Nakhon Phanom Air Base in Thailand was the centre of a major operation which was to assume ever increasing importance as the war dragged on. The North Vietnamese supplied the Viet Cong guerrillas operating in the South via the Ho Chi Minh Trail, a series of winding mud tracks running the length of Laos and Cambodia so bypassing the heavily defended area in the middle of Vietnam. The American forces went to great lengths to cut off the supply of materiel to the South by using all manner of airborne strike-power, from area bombing by B-52s to attacks by converted light aircraft such as the Cessna O-2.

As a result of their low-speed manoeuvrability, the two most successful types in the early years were the elderly Douglas A-1 Skyraider and the same company's even older B-26 Invader, both capable of carrying considerable loads and able to deliver them extremely accurately on to the truck targets hidden beneath the jungle. These were controlled by forward air controllers (FACs) which located the targets from light aircraft circling above the canopy. Favourite weapons of the attackers were unguided rockets and napalm.

A novel use of transport aircraft in Vietnam was as 'gunships', in which guns of all calibres were mounted to fire from the side while the aircraft circled an area suspected of occupation by an enemy force. After proving the concept with Douglas AC-47s, the USAF converted a number of Fairchild C-119s and Lockheed C-130s as AC-119s and AC-130 Spectres. The AC-130 was the definitive gunship, acquiring advanced night sensors to direct devastating gun batteries with deadly precision. Weapons included 7.62-mm (0.3-in) Miniguns, 20-mm Vulcan cannon, 40-mm Bofors guns and, ultimately a 105-mm (4.13-in) howitzer.

As the trail war grew, the US command invested more time and money in it and new types such as the General Dynamics F-111 were employed, this type operating with considerable success thanks to its unprecedented accuracy under blind first-pass conditions.

MOTION SENSORS

In order to monitor the traffic along the trail the Igloo White programme saw seismic sensors scattered across the trail by F-4s, C-130s and specially adapted Lockheed P-2 Neptunes of the US Navy. Tens of thousands of small devices remained inert on the ground or suspended from trees until activated by the nearby movements of a human being or vehicle; the sensor would then transmit a coded signal denoting the nature of the disturbance, its signals being received by relay drones or aircraft flying in the vicinity. The signals were processed by EC-121s and automatically relayed to the Infiltration Surveillance Center at Nakhon Phanom Air Base in neighbouring Thailand, from where target information could be

Below: Withdrawn in 1963, the Douglas B-26 Invader returned in 1967 in its B-26K variant. 56th SOS Invaders used the call-sign 'Nimrod' and harried North Vietnamese supply routes from their base at Nakhon Phanom, ('NKP' for short) in Thailand.

Above: This is a contemporary photo and map showing intense activity in th Mu Gia Pass, which led from North Vietnam into Laos. US warplanes bombed the pass relentlessly.

passed to forces alerted for a possible air or ground strike.

The US Navy also played its part against the infiltrators. Apart from operations against the trail itself, with Douglas RA-3s using camouflage detection film and real-time video cameras to find the trucks hidden beneath the triple-canopy forest, naval aircraft were also heavily involved in monitoring and intercepting junk and sampan traffic carrying war materiel.

WATCHING THE WATER

Under the name Market Time, Lockheed P-2 Neptunes and Martin P-5 Marlins plied the coasts around Vietnam, keeping watch on all movements, including Soviet supply vessels entering Haiphong harbour. These elderly aircraft were supplemented by the Lockheed P-3 Orion in the late 1960s and the maritime patrols lasted throughout the war.

Another facet of the US Navy's work was the 'brown water navy', which plied the endless creeks of the Mekong delta, policing the waterways and searching for Viet Cong guerrillas. The surface vessels were supported in the air by Bell UH-1s and OV-10 Broncos.

However, despite all the effort thrown in to the anti-infiltration war, the Viet Cong continued to be supplied and reinforced along the mass of seemingly impassable, almost undetectable tracks, and this was to seal the fate of South Vietnam as much as any other factor.

Right: An OP-2E Neptune of VO-67 dispenses electronic sensing devices on the Ho Chi Minh Trail, one of dozens of measures taken to inhibit Hanoi's well-orchestrated infiltration effort.

HO CHI MINH TRAIL

Vientiane
MU GIA PASS
Nakhon Phanom
THAILAND
Khe Sanh
Quang Tri
Hue
Da Nang
LAOS
Ubon
Kontum
Pleiku
CAMBODIA
Cam Ranh
Phnom Penh
An Loc
Saigon
MEKONG DELTA

Although the Viet Cong had roots in the south and grabbed up some of their weapons from defeated South Vietnamese troops, they relied heavily on the flow of supplies from the north to keep their war alive.
The Ho Chi Minh Trail was not really a trail but a web of supply lines. It was named not by the Ho's followers but by the Americans, who needed a simple concept to explain a complex infiltration effort. In the end, it was a perplexing target for air power, and one that air strikes could never fully take out of action.

Below: Tracer arcs down out of the night as an AC-47 gunship engages a supply column moving down the trail.

High-tech hunters

The finest science the American taxpayer could pay for was used in a spectacular response to the Viet Cong's night infiltration campaign. The C-130 'trash hauler' became an instrument-packed, nocturnal gunship. The Neptune patrol craft took on missions where infra-red sensors, and acoustic devices were principal weapons. But despite some success US air interdiction was never totally effective, and Hanoi continued to run a 'low-tech' supply effort through Laos and Cambodia.

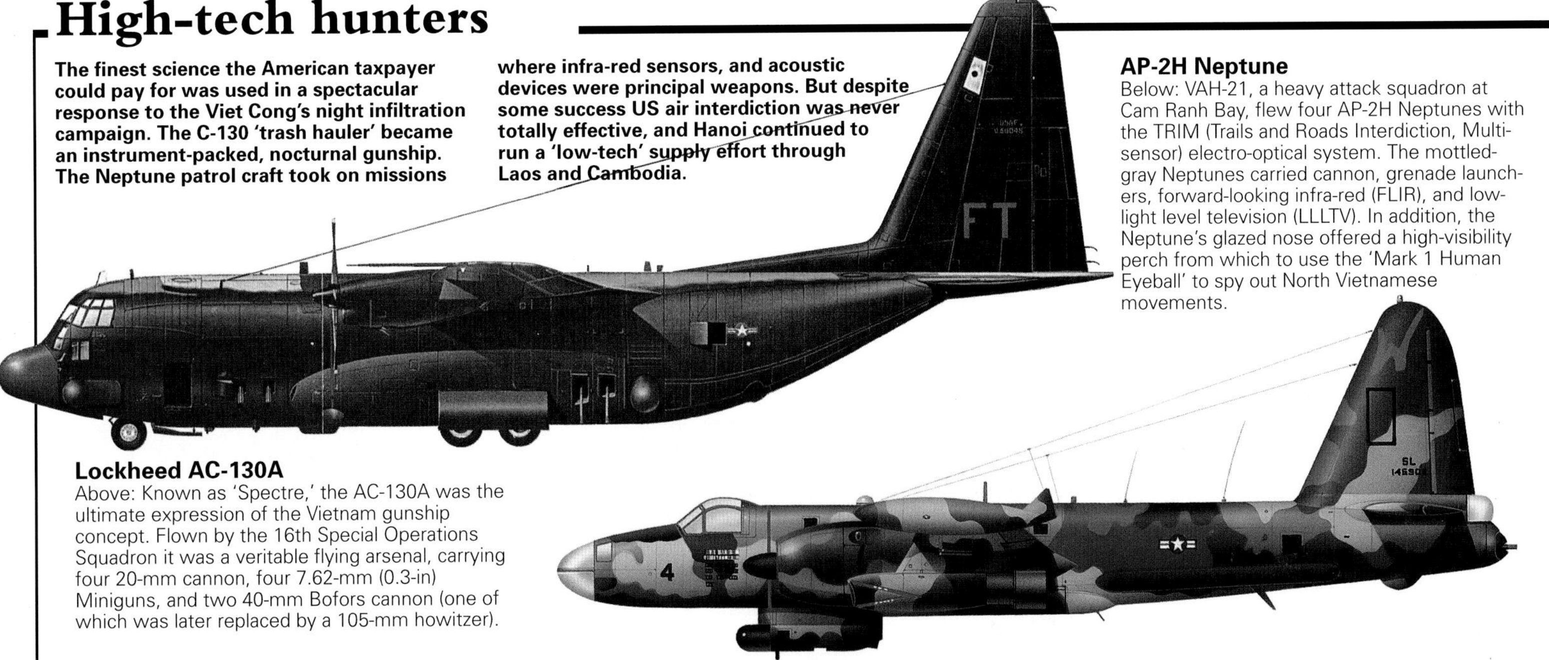

AP-2H Neptune

Below: VAH-21, a heavy attack squadron at Cam Ranh Bay, flew four AP-2H Neptunes with the TRIM (Trails and Roads Interdiction, Multi-sensor) electro-optical system. The mottled-gray Neptunes carried cannon, grenade launchers, forward-looking infra-red (FLIR), and low-light level television (LLLTV). In addition, the Neptune's glazed nose offered a high-visibility perch from which to use the 'Mark 1 Human Eyeball' to spy out North Vietnamese movements.

Lockheed AC-130A

Above: Known as 'Spectre,' the AC-130A was the ultimate expression of the Vietnam gunship concept. Flown by the 16th Special Operations Squadron it was a veritable flying arsenal, carrying four 20-mm cannon, four 7.62-mm (0.3-in) Miniguns, and two 40-mm Bofors cannon (one of which was later replaced by a 105-mm howitzer).

Vietnam: On Yankee Station

1964 - 1975

Following the Tonkin Gulf incident of 1964, the US Navy launched retaliatory strikes from the decks of the carriers *Ticonderoga* and *Constellation*. It was to be the start of the US Navy's intense involvement in combat in Southeast Asia, during which the Navy flew 52 percent of all American sorties over North Vietnam, as against 43 percent by the USAF and five percent by the Marine Corps.

Naval aviation was under the command of the 7th Fleet's Attack Carrier Striking Force, or Task Force 77. TF 77 executed raids on North Vietnam from a position known as 'Yankee Station', at the mouth of the Gulf of Tonkin, less than 320 km (200 miles) from Hanoi and Haiphong. Early in the war, however, carriers also operated from 'Dixie Station' about 160 km (100 miles) south east of Cam Ranh Bay. From there they were used to provide air support over South Vietnam until the Air Force could take on that responsibility. From that time carriers used the southern operating area primarily to work up before heading north. Between 1965 and 1973 the Navy always had four or five carriers deployed for operations in Southeast Asia. Intensive use meant that deployed carriers actually spent about 75 percent of their time at sea.

Large and small

Attack carriers or CVAs fell loosely into two categories. The large-deck carriers which could operate 80 or 90 aircraft included the 'Midway', 'Forrestal' and 'Kitty Hawk' classes as well as the nuclear-powered USS *Enterprise*. Smaller types, which had air wings of up to 60 aircraft, included the modified survivors of the wartime 'Essex', 'Ticonderoga' and 'Oriskany' classes'

The strike power of each carrier air wing was invested in a mix of fighter and attack squadrons (nominally 12 aircraft per squadron). Early in the war, small-deck types usually operated two squadrons of Vought F-8 Crusader fighters, and three attack squadrons equipped with Douglas A-4 Skyhawks and Douglas A-1 Skyraiders. Large-deck wings included two McDonnell F-4 Phantom II fighter squadrons and four A-4 attack squadrons as well as heavy attack aircraft like the Douglas A-3 Skywarrior and North American A-5 Vigilante. These last two types were soon converted to support or reconnaissance roles.

Above: Douglas A-1 Skyraiders make their contribution to the noise and fury on a carrier deck. These aging but effective propeller-driven warplanes were replaced in carrier air wings by the end of 1968, but continued to serve with the US and Vietnamese air forces ashore.

Gradually the A-1, A-4 and F-8 squadrons were phased out of service aboard the larger carriers such as *Constellation*, *Forrestal*, *Kitty Hawk* and *Midway*. However, they continued to serve on the smaller carriers such as *Bon Homme Richard*, *Hancock*, *Intrepid*, *Oriskany* and *Ticonderoga*. Aboard the big-deck vessels they were replaced by newer, vastly more capable types

Below: The McDonnell F-4 Phantom was the most important carrier-based warplane of the war. Designed as a fleet interceptor, it was used to counter North Vietnamese MiGs, but it also went into action heavily laden with air-to-surface bombs and missiles.

Right: The Douglas A-4 Skyhawk was in the fight from the beginning, and a few were still around when US involvement in the war ended. The bantamweight Skyhawk was so small it did not need folding wings on the carrier, yet it carried a heavy bombload.

Left: Although the modified World War II-vintage 'Essex' class carriers were too small to berth the F-4 Phantom, they took on a major part of the air war with lighter jet- and prop-driven warplanes.

Below: Though it had a reputation as a gunfighter, the Vought F-8 Crusader achieved all but one of its 20 aerial victories with Sidewinder missiles like the one visible during this carrier launch.

Carrier Air Wing

Life was fast and hectic on a carrier deck. A CVW (Carrier Air Wing) had two squadrons each of fighters and attack craft, plus detachments of helicopters and electronic warfare and reconnaissance ships. This 'mix' required skillful juggling during a busy flying schedule.

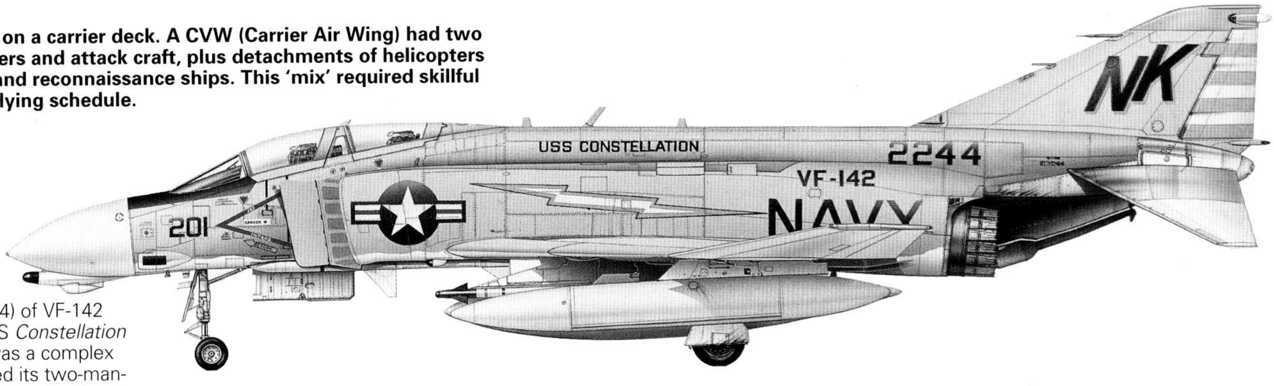

F-4B Phantom

Right: F-4B (BuNo. 152244) of VF-142 'Ghost Riders' aboard USS *Constellation* (CVA-64). The Phantom was a complex machine, which challenged its two-man-crew of pilot and radar intercept officer (RIO). But its speed, power and versatility made the F-4 the most important American warplane of the conflict.

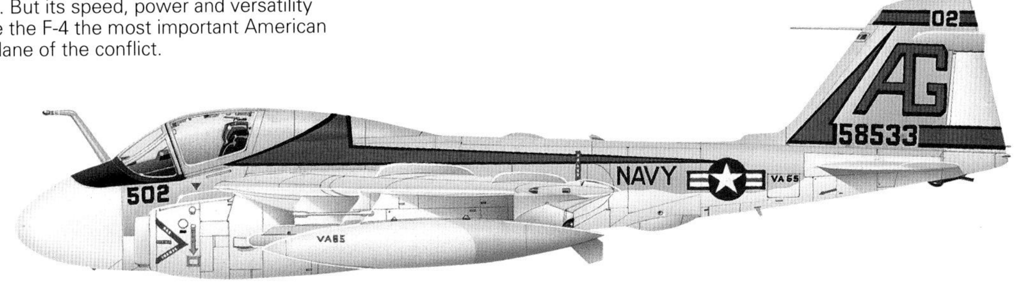

A-6 Intruder

Left: Introduced into Navy service over Vietnam in 1965, the Grumman A-6 Intruder was equipped with the world's most sophisticated radar and avionics. Until the arrival of the F-111 it was the only US warplane able to operate over North Vietnam at night, delivering accurate attacks in zero visibility.

Electronic Prowler

Right: The increasing sophistication of North Vietnam's air defences spurred the creation of specialised electronic warfare aircraft. The Grumman EA-6B Prowler, a four-seat stretched version of the Intruder, arrived late, entering combat in 1972. This sophisticated Grumman aircraft quickly became a serious nuisance to Hanoi, with its ability to jam radar signals and radio transmissions.

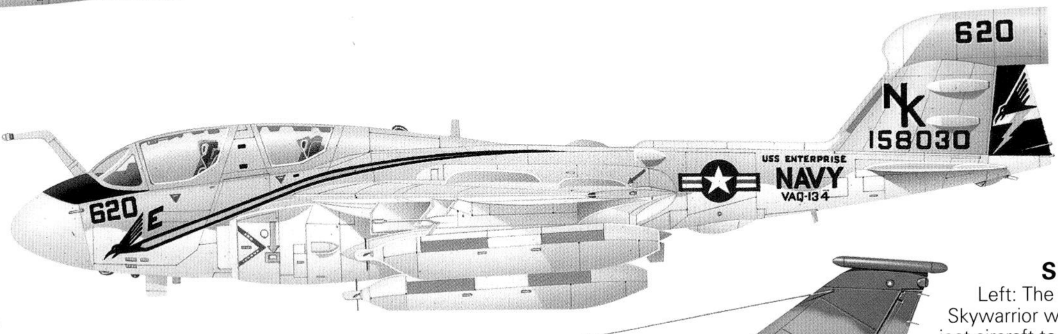

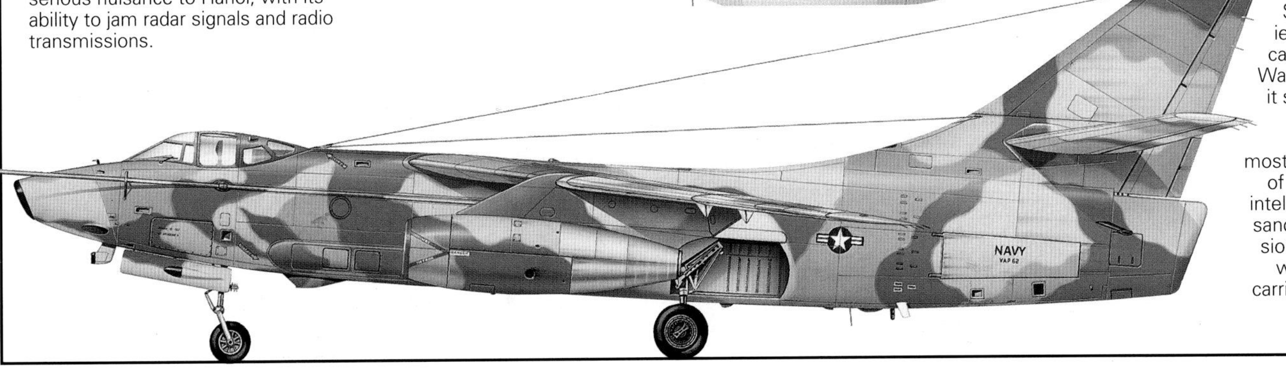

Versatile Skywarrior

Left: The Douglas A-3 Skywarrior was the heaviest aircraft to launch from carriers during the Vietnam War. Designed as a bomber, it saw only limited action in that role. However, it became one of the most important support types of the war, flying electronic intelligence, ECM, reconnaissance and aerial tanking missions. The RA-3B seen here was flown by VAP-62, and carried numerous optical and infra-red cameras.

THE FIRST VIETNAM ACES: CUNNINGHAM AND DRISCOLL

10 May 1972 saw some of the biggest air battles of the Vietnam War, during which the US Navy produced the first American aces of the conflict.

The F-4J Phantom team of Randall 'Duke' Cunningham and William 'Irish' Driscoll, flew with VF-96 from the USS *Constellation*. Both men had benefited from the new Top Gun tactical training which was revolutionising the efficiency of the US Navy's combat pilots. Although neither had been to Top Gun, both Cunningham and Driscoll had been taught by its instructors. Cunningham was at Miramar when Top Gun was just starting there, and Driscoll had been taught by Top Gun instructors in their fleet adversary role.

The resumption of missions against North Vietnam had already seen the pilot/RIO combination run up two victories against MiGs before they set off on a 10 May strike mission. VF-96 aircraft were given the callsign 'Showtime', and the aircraft flown by Cunningham and Driscoll on this mission, nominally the squadron commander's machine, was known as 'Showtime 100'.

Showtime 100 had already scored twice in the big battle southeast of Hanoi, bringing the team's victory total up to four. They were heading homewards when they encountered a superbly-flown MiG-17 – thought later to have been piloted by top North Vietnamese ace 'Colonel Tomb' though his existence has never been confirmed.

In a tightly-fought battle, neither aircraft could gain the upper hand, the Phantom having the advantage in power and speed, the MiG in agility. The two aircraft were climbing vertically, almost cockpit to cockpit, when Cunningham realised they were in a situation he had encountered several times in training with Top Gun instructors.

Chopping power suddenly and extending airbrakes, he allowed the MiG to race ahead for the first time. As both aircraft nosed down, Cunningham found himself behind the MiG. Pouring on the power, he closed to firing range and fired a Sidewinder, making his third kill of the day, and his fifth of the war. The Top Gun-trained team of Cunningham and Driscoll had just become America's first Vietnam aces.

Minutes later, Showtime 100 was hit by a surface-to-air missile. Cunningham managed to wrestle the stricken aircraft safely out to sea before the two men ejected. They were quickly picked up by helicopter and returned safely to the *Constellation*.

Left: SHOWTIME 100 was the callsign of Cunningham's F-4J, which bagged three MiGs before being downed by a SAM missile.

Above: Following the victories that made them aces on 10 May 1972, Cunningham (right) and Driscoll celebrate aboard Constellation.

like the Grumman A-6 Intruder, Grumman E-2 Hawkeye, and Vought A-7 Corsair II. A typical late-war big-deck air wing included two F-4 squadrons, two A-7 attack squadrons and one A-6 all-weather attack squadron.

All these aircraft were flown on strikes against the North with Skyraiders, Skyhawks, Intruders and Corsairs providing the teeth, with Phantoms and Crusaders providing protective combat air patrols known as MIGCAPs. F-4s were also on ground attack missions as well as flying fleet defence missions known as BARCAPs. Specially adapted A-3s and A-6s were equipped for the inflight-refuelling and ECM roles.

Initial success against the North Vietnamese MiGs was elusive, but once the Navy instituted a realistic air combat training scheme, the famous Top Gun school, the number of combat kills rose dramatically, and in 1972 the team of Randy Cunningham and Willie Driscoll flying from the *Constellation* became the first American aces of the war. However, the gun-armed A-4 and A-7 also made occasional MiG kills, and, on one historic occasion, two elderly A-1s downed a MiG-17 between them.

VERSATILE 'SPAD'

The Skyraider had started the war as the US Navy's main attack aircraft. It was already 20 years old, and it continued in fleet service until 1968 – a few surviving in the electronic warfare role beyond this date. The 'Spad' could lift phenomenal loads and absorb massive battle damage and flew many RESCAP missions in support of search-and-rescue Kaman SH-2 and Sikorsky SH-3 helicopters, in much the same way as the USAF 'Spads' supported combat rescues on land.

The A-4 Skyhawk was another brilliant Douglas design which served on the attack squadrons throughout the war, its agility enabling it to perform attacks on the most heavily defended targets. Its place was being taken by the A-7 towards the end of the conflict, an aircraft capable of carrying out the same role but with much heavier warloads. Both the A-4s and A-7s could deliver Shrike anti-radar missiles in the 'Iron Hand' defence suppression role.

Perhaps the greatest addition to the air wings was the A-6 Intruder, which at the time had the most advanced weapons delivery and navigation system in the world. It was able to deliver low-level first-pass strikes with extraordinary accuracy in weather that often prevented other aircraft from flying, let alone perform combat missions.

Reconnaissance and battle damage assessment for the fleet was provided by the RA-5 Vigilante and the RF-8 Crusader. These were often escorted by F-4s and F-8s over North Vietnam as they carried no defensive armament; additionally, though very fast, the big Vigilante was not particularly manoeuvrable.

The US Marine Corps flew large numbers of aircraft in Vietnam, mainly on short-range attacks from

Experiment with Camouflage

In 1965, the US Navy experimented with several versions of a green camouflage paint scheme on carrier aircraft. It helped little in combat, however, and created confusion on the carrier deck at night.

Green machine
Right: This F-4G Phantom wears one version of the camouflage paint scheme and carries a typical bombload for a mission 'up North'.

F-4J Phantom II 'Showtime 100'

Slammed into the air by a steam catapult that could handle the weight of a railroad box car, Cunningham and Driscoll went into North Vietnam flying a heavy, complex, costly, and powerful aircraft that was regarded as the finest in the world. Their F-4J Phantom II (BuNo. 155800) of squadron VF-96 'Fighting Falcons' was bigger than many World War II bombers and faster than a pistol bullet.

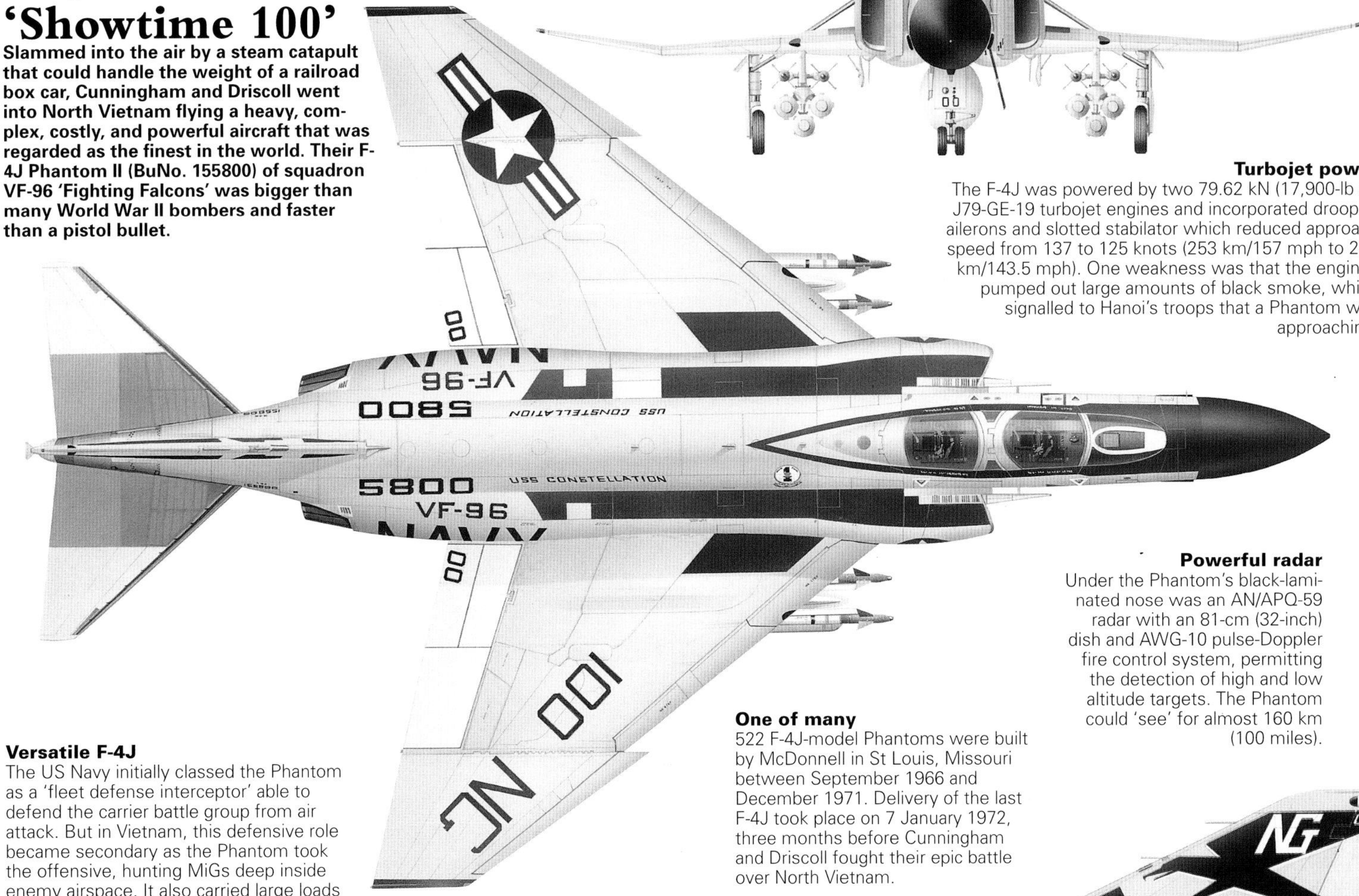

Turbojet power
The F-4J was powered by two 79.62 kN (17,900-lb st) J79-GE-19 turbojet engines and incorporated drooped ailerons and slotted stabilator which reduced approach speed from 137 to 125 knots (253 km/157 mph to 231 km/143.5 mph). One weakness was that the engines pumped out large amounts of black smoke, which signalled to Hanoi's troops that a Phantom was approaching.

Powerful radar
Under the Phantom's black-laminated nose was an AN/APQ-59 radar with an 81-cm (32-inch) dish and AWG-10 pulse-Doppler fire control system, permitting the detection of high and low altitude targets. The Phantom could 'see' for almost 160 km (100 miles).

One of many
522 F-4J-model Phantoms were built by McDonnell in St Louis, Missouri between September 1966 and December 1971. Delivery of the last F-4J took place on 7 January 1972, three months before Cunningham and Driscoll fought their epic battle over North Vietnam.

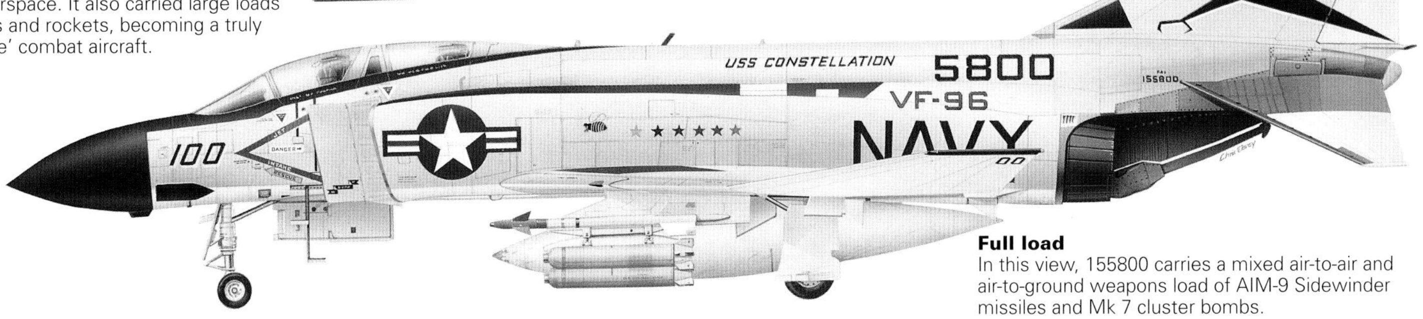

Versatile F-4J
The US Navy initially classed the Phantom as a 'fleet defense interceptor' able to defend the carrier battle group from air attack. But in Vietnam, this defensive role became secondary as the Phantom took the offensive, hunting MiGs deep inside enemy airspace. It also carried large loads of bombs and rockets, becoming a truly 'multi-role' combat aircraft.

Full load
In this view, 155800 carries a mixed air-to-air and air-to-ground weapons load of AIM-9 Sidewinder missiles and Mk 7 cluster bombs.

their bases at Chu Lai and Da Nang. Aircraft types involved were the A-4 Skyhawk, A-6 Intruder, F-4 Phantom and F-8 Crusader, used almost exclusively as ground attack 'mud-movers'.

These were controlled by 'Fast FAC' aircraft such as TA-4s and Grumman TF-9 Cougars, and an element of ECM was provided by the Douglas EF-10 Skyknight, a modified version of a Korean War-vintage jet night fighter. Rockwell OV-10s were later procured to perform light strike and FAC duties.

Following the peace talks in 1973, the last act of the US Navy in the American phase of the war was to clear Haiphong harbour under Operation End Sweep, using minesweeping Sikorsky RH-53 helicopters.

In 1975 the carriers *Enterprise*, *Midway* and *Coral Sea* provided air cover for the evacuation of Saigon, an operation notable for being the first combat deployment of the Grumman F-14 Tomcat. In the final few panic-stricken hours, helicopters were being pushed over the side as soon as they had unloaded to create landing room for further aircraft on the already overcrowded flight decks.

Right: As part of the settlement that ended the shooting, the US Navy provided Sikorsky RH-53D Sea Stallion helicopters to 'clean up' the mines in Haiphong harbor. This RH-53D tows a sled which detects mines.

Vietnam: Linebacker I and II

APRIL–DECEMBER 1972

Left: F-4D Phantoms of the 435th TFS/8th TFW head north from Ubon, Thailand. The Phantom became the backbone of the 1972 Linebacker campaign, which saw the first widespread use of precision-guided munitions (PGMs). Most of these 'smart' bombs were carried and delivered by Air Force Phantoms.

Below: Navy jets were essential to Linebacker, and Navy-Air Force cooperation was far better than in 1965-68. Here, a Shrike-armed A-4F Skyhawk prepares to take the war to Hanoi's air defences. Homing-in on the enemy's radar emitters, the Shrike and the larger Standard anti-radar missiles were vital to allow bombers to successfully penetrate Hanoi's defences.

A false calm had fallen over North Vietnam. While politicians wrangled in Paris, US prisoners in Hanoi heard no friendly warplanes overhead for more than three years. But in 1972, talk gave way to action, political speeches to a new air campaign. From land bases and from carrier decks, the jets flew north again – in the final campaign against targets north of the 17th Parallel.

In the spring of 1972 the communists unleashed a full scale military offensive against South Vietnam. American ground troops had been withdrawn from the combat zone, so it fell to air power to support the South Vietnamese fight for survival.

Allied air power had fallen dramatically from the peak years of 1968-1969. USAF assets in Vietnam, Thailand and on Guam totalled 83 B-52s, 203 F-4s, 16 F-105s, 23 A-37s, 10 B-57s, 15 A-1s and a gunship force of 15 AC-119s and 13 AC-130s. Additionally the VNAF deployed around 150 A-1s and a squadron of Northrop F-5s.

At the beginning of April, the B-52 force was put on standby for a massive operation to stem the NVA offensive. On the 6th the first break in the weather allowed fighter-bombers to go into action, initially aimed at NVA units engaged below the DMZ. The forward deployment of communist SA-2 missiles gave US aircraft their first taste of a high-threat environment within South Vietnam.

By 6 April air power started to take its toll - in one instance two cells of three B-52s destroyed an entire NVA tank battalion. In all, some 285 NVA tanks were destroyed by allied aircraft in I Corps alone during the four and a half months following the communist assault.

'BUFFS' MOVE NORTH

B-52 operations against the southern portion of North Vietnam began on 9 April, with strikes as far north as Vinh. Operations expanded over the next week to include most major target complexes from Thanh Hoa south. By 16 April the areas immediately surrounding Hanoi and Haiphong had been added to the B-52 target list.

At the outbreak of the invasion the USN had two carriers on station, the *Coral Sea* and the *Hancock*. The *Kitty Hawk* was dispatched from the Philippines, arriving on 3 April, and *Constellation* was recalled from Hong Kong. Sailing orders were also given to the *Midway* in the eastern Pacific and the *Saratoga* of the Atlantic Fleet.

Marine Air Group 15's three F-4 squadrons arrived early in May to join an A-6 squadron aboard the *Coral Sea*. Two A-4 squadrons arrived soon after, followed by another A-6 squadron and two further Phantom squadrons.

By the beginning of May there were six carriers on line at Yankee Station. They cheerfully received the news that on 8 May President Nixon had authorised the mining of Haiphong, Cam Pha, Vinh, Quang Khe, Dong Hoi, Thanh Hoa, Hon Gai, and the Red River delta. This was done, with the minimum of trouble, by 15 May.

The United States, too late in the war, was finally getting serious about hitting the North Vietnamese supply line where it hurt. The mining operation effectively cut the main overseas supply route into North Vietnam. The only way that cargo could reach Haiphong was for a ship to stop outside the mined area and offload into small boats – a process requiring up to a month for even a 5,000-ton freighter.

Left: The USAF brought the A-7D to Korat, Thailand in 1972. Never officially given the Corsair II name assigned to its US Navy counterpart, the A-7D replaced the prop-driven A-1 Skyraider in the 'Sandy' mission, escorting rescue helicopters behind the lines.

INTENSIFIED COMBAT

In the days following the mining effort, naval air operations in the Hanoi and Haiphong areas grew in intensity. North Vietnamese MiG opposition provided Lt Randy 'Duke' Cunningham and his backseater Lt Willie 'Irish' Driscoll of the *Constellation* a record three kills in one day and an overall score of five, to make them the first US ace of the war.

By 23 May, the USAF had added a further 10 fighter squadrons, an electronic warfare squadron and a couple of C-130 squadrons to Thailand, and tripled

Phantom Gunfighter

The F-4E was the first version of the Phantom armed with what pilots really wanted – an internal 20-mm cannon. Unfortunately, it arrived in the combat zone only weeks after the 'bombing halt' of October 1968. Thus, pilots had to wait until the 1972 Linebacker actions more than three years later before they got a shot at a MiG. Ironically, better radar and more reliable missiles as well as improved tactics proved more important in combat than the internal gun. Even so, the F-4E became the definitive land-based Phantom.

Fighting Phantom
This F-4E (67-0288) of the 469th TFS/388th TFW carries bombs with extended 'daisy cutter' fuses. These were designed to detonate the bombs before they dug themselves into the earth, maximising the blast effect. The shark's teeth, painted on the plane by Capt Steve Stephen with support from squadron commander Lt Col Edward Hillding, were very much non-regulation. Eventually, they were removed.

the size of the B-52 force. These reinforcements included 180 F-4s (many being improved 'E' models), 12 F-105Gs, 8 EB-66s, 32 C-130s, 124 B-52s. Also in theatre were the first Air Force examples of the Vought A-7 attack jet.

Having started bombing the north after a pause of four years, President Nixon authorised and expanded air offensive known as Linebacker. The aims of the campaign incorporated the isolation of North Vietnam from outside supply, destruction of stockpiles of materiel in the north, and interdiction of NVA supplies going south.

By mid-May, missions in the southern route packages succeeded in knocking out the pumping facilities for the Ho Chi Minh Trail pipeline which supported tank and truck operations in the South. In line with the port mining operations in May, raids against the rail lines to China reduced these supply routes to a small fraction of their former capacity.

Aircraft taking part in the renewed air offensive against North Vietnam were equipped with new weapons which had not been available during Rolling Thunder. Precision-guided weapons were used in large numbers for the first time. Two- and three-thousand pound laser-guided bombs (LGBs) and electro-optical guided bombs (EOGBs) were delivered by the Phantoms of the 8th Tactical Fighter Wing. In a three-month period the 8th TFW dropped 106 bridges all over North Vietnam, including the notorious Thanh Hoa and Paul Doumer bridges, which had shrugged off repeated and very costly conventional attacks (and even a commando raid by US Army Rangers).

Clockwise from above: The destruction of the Ninh Binh road and rail bridge, located 50 km (32 miles) north of Thanh Hoa, during the later stages of the Linebacker campaign. The first three photos are from the guidance camera of a US Navy Walleye glide bomb, and show the accuracy with which the new precision-guided weapons could strike. The larger photo records the highly effective result.

Below: A 'tall-tailed' B-52D of the kind that made up the bulk of the Linebacker II bombing force. The big bombers usually flew further apart in the danger zone.

TAIL GUNNER'S WAR
During the December 1972 bombing of North Vietnam, B-52 tail gunners claimed credit for shooting down five MiG-21 interceptors. USAF officials reviewed the claims and endorsed two of them. B-52Ds and Gs had four 12.7-mm (0.5-in) machine-guns in a manned tail turret.

B-52G MISSION
This 'short-tailed' B-52G (compare its fin shape with that of the B-52D in the photo above) typifies those that joined the fighting when Operation Linebacker II, alias the 'Eleven Day War' was unleashed on Hanoi.

HEAVY BOMBER
Until 1972, the giant B-52 Stratofotress had been employed solely against targets in the south, while fighter-bombers handled missions against military installations and industrial facilities in the north. The decision to send B-52s into North Vietnam was a major escalation of the conflict and is widely credited with persuading Hanoi's leaders to negotiate a truce.

Below: The standard B-52 formation was a 'cell' of three aircraft, in close formation in the south but more widely separated in the north. This was cited by critics as one of many tactics that made the bombers vulnerable over Hanoi in the first days of Linebacker II.

Above: During the height of the Linebacker II effort, the B-52 force had 12,000 men and women at Andersen Air Force Base, Guam, alias 'And,' or 'The Rock', located some 4675 km (2,905 miles) from their principal target, Hanoi.

North Vietnamese air bases were back on the target list, with Phuc Yen and several other fields being virtually knocked out in September along with 14 MiGs destroyed or damaged on the ground.

On 24 October, President Nixon acknowledged Hanoi's apparently genuine desire to negotiate in good faith by halting all bombing north of the 20th Parallel. Linebacker and the port mining had reduced North Vietnam's supplies to 20 percent of the levels they had enjoyed at the start.

It did not last. The North Vietnamese negotiators quickly returned to their former intransigence and by December, Nixon had had enough. He ordered a renewed bombing offensive with all the stops pulled out.

Linebacker II was conceived as a knock-out blow to the very heart of North Vietnam, namely Hanoi and Haiphong. It finally saw US air power let loose in the sort of role for which it was intended. Striking military targets within the Hanoi/Haiphong region between 18 and 29 December 1972, the heavy bombing was carried out by Boeing B-52s from U-Tapao in Thailand and Andersen AFB, Guam. A supporting cast of Navy and Air Force fighters, 'Iron Hand' and 'Wild Weasel' aircraft and ECM jamming platforms softened-up targets and hit others.

In the whole 'eleven-day war' there was only one night clear enough for good visual bombing,

Above: North Vietnamese troopers aim a Soviet-built SA-2 'Guideline' surface-to-air missile, or SAM. In December 1972, 884 SAM launches were counted by B-52 crews, and they downed 15 bombers.

Right: The anti-aircraft artillery, or Triple-A, in the region around Hanoi consisted of guns of all sizes and calibres, including many that were located adjacent to residences and office buildings.

'BUFFS' against Hanoi

The Boeing B-52 Stratofortress was active in Southeast Asia from 1965 on, but not until the Linebacker campaigns was it used against North Vietnam. The '11-day war' of Linebacker II in December 1972 was this classic bomber's finest hour: in eleven days, B-52Ds and B-52Gs flew 729 sorties against 34 targets in North Vietnam above the 20th Parallel. US assessments showed that this unfettered bombing campaign came close to obliterating Hanoi's ability to wage war.

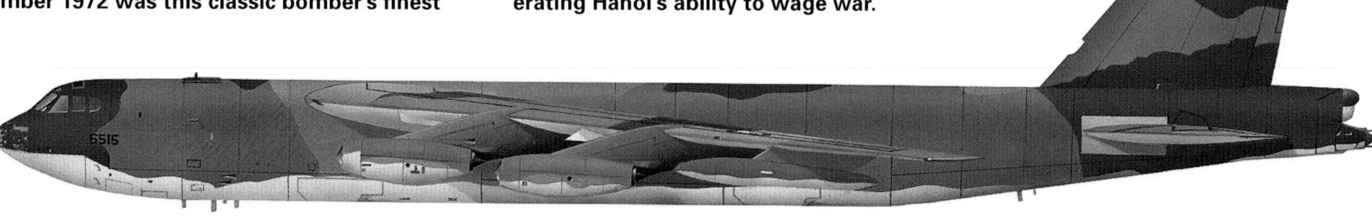

B-52G

Above: The B-52G model of the 'Big Ugly Fat Fellow' is easy to identify from its short, broad tail fin. It had integral fuel tanks in the wing giving much greater range than earlier models, but being principally a nuclear bomber lacked the heavy conventional weapons carrying capability of the B-52D.

B-52D

Below: Although older than the B-52G, the tall-tailed B-52D used in Vietnam had received a modification known as 'Big Belly', designed to increase conventional weapon capacity. A fully laden B-52D could carry 108 'iron' bombs, each nominally of 340-kg (750-lb) but actually weighing 374 kg (825 lb), for a total warload of 40392 kg (89,100 lb)

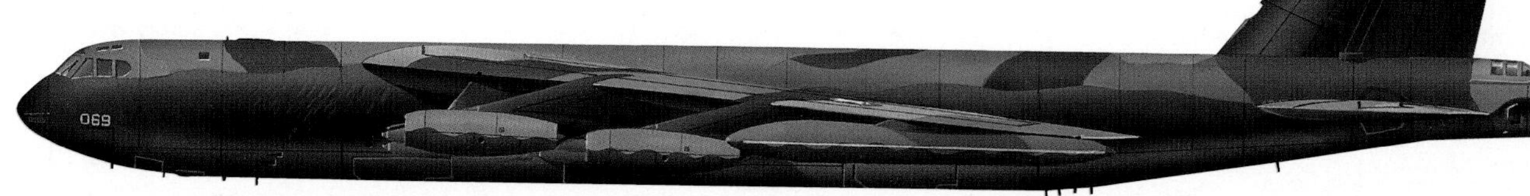

Through Hanoi's ring of steel

The high point of the Linebacker campaign came on day eight, 26 December, when 120 B-52s unloaded their bombs over the targets in the space of just 15 minutes. Colonel James R. McArthy commanded the 43rd Strategic Wing, and was also the airborne commander of the entire mission on that 'special night'.

"The flak started coming up when we made our first landfall. We were most vividly aware of the heavy, black, ugly explosions of 100-mm (3.94-in) shells, visible even at night. Since we were at a lower altitude than we'd flown before, our wave was more vulnerable to the AAA than on previous missions, and the closer we got to the initial point, the more intense it got.

"Then the SAMs really started coming. The missiles that had been tracking us lifted off and headed for the aircraft. Now that the whole force was committed and we were on the bomb run, for the moment I had nothing to do, so I decided to count the SAMs launched against us. After 26 I quit counting. They were coming up too fast to keep an accurate tally. From the cockpit, it looked like they were barraging SAMs in order to make the lead element of the wave turn from its intended course. Some were close; some were too close for comfort.

"About one hundred seconds prior to bombs away, the cockpit lit up like it was daylight. The light came from the rocket exhaust of a SAM that had come up right under our nose. The electronic warfare officer had reported an extremely strong signal, and he'd been right. That one looked like it missed us by less than 15 metres (50 feet).

"At bombs away, it looked like we were right in the middle of a fireworks factory that was in the process of blowing up. The radio was completely saturated with SAM calls and MiG fighter warnings. As the bomb doors closed, several SAMs exploded nearby. Others could be seen arcing over and starting a descent, then detonating. If the proximity fuse didn't find a target, SA-2s were set to self-destruct at the end of a predetermined time interval."

but the B-52s operated regardless ot the weather. In all, 15 B-52s were lost from a total of 729 sorties, mostly in the first days of the campaign. By the end of the period, tactics had been refined to the point where 113 B-52s were all over the target area within the space of 15 minutes and suffered no losses.

Linebacker results

The B-52 raids were immensely destructive. According to Hanoi, they killed 1,400 civilians, but even if this figure is accurate that is an astonishingly low total given the huge tonnage of bombs dropped onto targets in the middle of densely populated urban areas. The bombers were credited with destroying a quarter of Vietnam's petroleum reserves and 80 percent of the country's electricity generating capacity, as well as smashing armaments factories, military barracks, railways, roads, bridges and communications centres.

Vietnam's entire stock of several thousand surface-to-air missiles had been fired off, and since Haiphong and other major harbours had been closed off by mines, there was no prospect of resupply. Hanoi's war-making capability was at an end, smashed by US air power.

The offensive brought the North Vietnamese back to the peace talks, genuinely ready to make a deal. Linebacker II allowed America to withdraw from the Vietnam morass, recovering most of the POWs held in Northern camps. But for South Vietnam, it only put a temporary check on communist plans, and within three years, without the benefit of American air support, Saigon would finally fall.

Right: The Hanoi Thermal Power Plant was a key B-52 target. Bombs put the entire facility temporarily out of business: only the end of the 11-day war prevented the plant from being completely flattened.

Below: The US estimate was 372 pieces of rolling stock damaged or destroyed, a monstrous toll on North Vietnam's railway infrastructure. This scene is typical of the bombing results.

Below: American prisoners or war, or POWs, prepare go home. The release of the POWs was a key point in US demands, and was completed within three months after the bombing campaign.

Indo-Pakistan Wars

1965-1971

THE INDIAN NAVY AT WAR
The Sea Hawks of No. 300 Squadron played a part in both 1965 and 1971, operating from shore-bases at Jamnagar and Santa Cruz in 1965 and from the INS *Vikrant* in 1971.

Following the end of the British Raj in 1947, the Indian sub-continent was bloodily partitioned into the independent states of Moslem Pakistan and predominantly Hindu India. The British had held together a fragmented indigenous administration and a host of traditional hereditary rulers, while reconciling divided religious interests and suppressing tribal revolts. These problems now re-emerged, and on these were superimposed rival ambitions for certain disputed areas. The most important of these was the state of Jammu and Kashmir, whose ruler was a Hindu Maharajah, but whose population was overwhelmingly Moslem. The Maharajah wanted independence and refused to accede to integration with Pakistan, which funded and armed the Azad Kashmiris to carry out an insurrection. At the same time, Pathans staged an invasion. The Maharajah asked India for help, which sent troops after the state's accession. The Azad Kashmiris were supported by Pakistani artillery, across the border, and Pakistani AAA defended some Azad targets against the IAF. There was direct conflict between

Right: Many of Pakistan's victory claims were denied by India, and were later found to be unsubstantiated. Squadron Leader Mohammed Alam was credited with downing five Indian Hunters in a single engagement over Sargodha during the 1965 war, but the IAF lost only three Hunters on that day, two of them to enemy action. Two of the 'Hunter pilots' named by the PAF as victims actually flew Mystères on another strike.

Below: Both Pakistan and India inherited Douglas C-47 Dakotas from the RAF and RIAF, and these were used in the confusion of partition, and in the various small-scale conflicts which followed, in Kashmir and on the North West Frontier. Small numbers remained in use even as late as 1971.

Early conflicts

The partition of the former British Raj into independent Moslem Pakistan and predominantly Hindu India left a legacy of bitterness and rivalry, with both sides disputing certain key border areas including Jammu and Kashmir, which was predominantly Muslim but ruled by a Hindu Maharajah. In 1947 Kashmir was invaded by Pathan tribesmen and Azad 'Free Kashmiris' carried out an insurrection. These were put down by the Indian army, with air support from Spitfires and Tempests. Meanwhile Pakistani Hawker Tempests (and later Furies) were kept busy policing the troubled North West Frontier where the tribes were in open revolt.

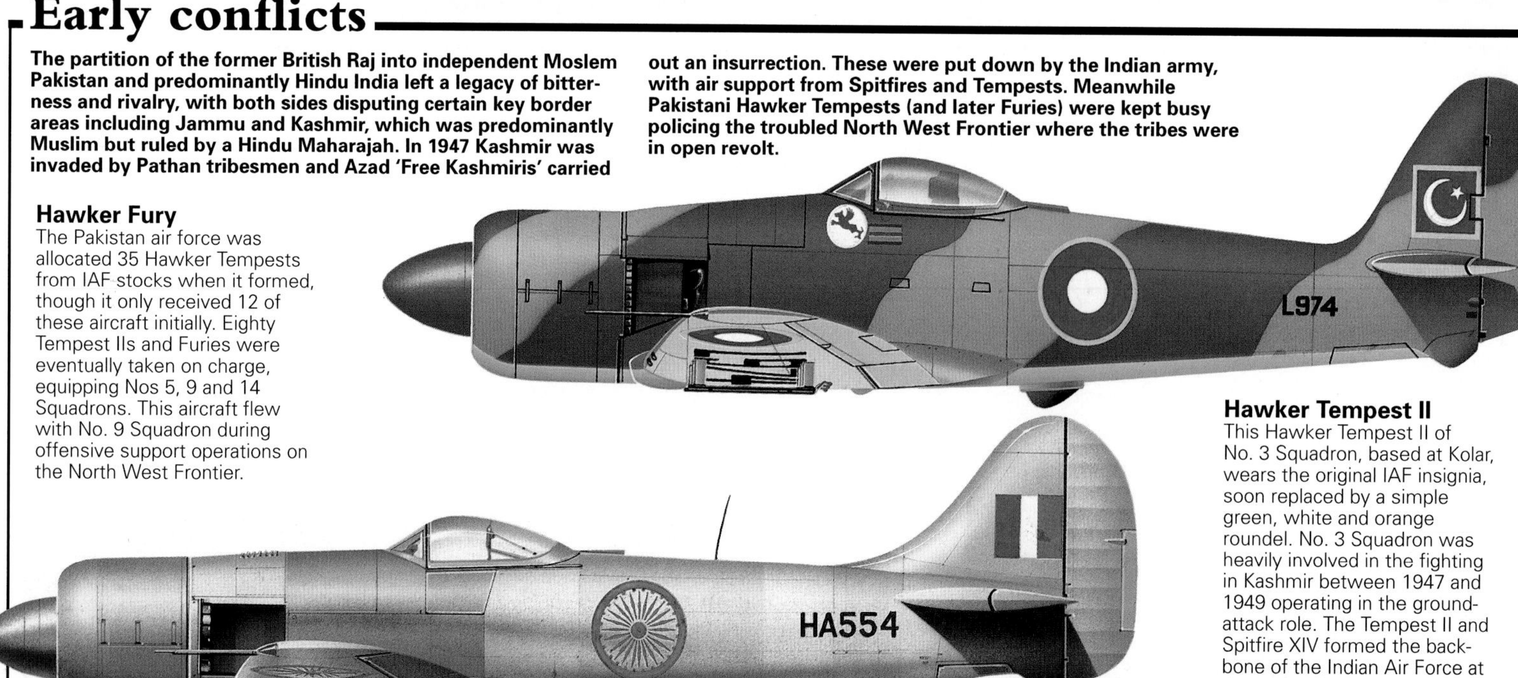

Hawker Fury
The Pakistan air force was allocated 35 Hawker Tempests from IAF stocks when it formed, though it only received 12 of these aircraft initially. Eighty Tempest IIs and Furies were eventually taken on charge, equipping Nos 5, 9 and 14 Squadrons. This aircraft flew with No. 9 Squadron during offensive support operations on the North West Frontier.

Hawker Tempest II
This Hawker Tempest II of No. 3 Squadron, based at Kolar, wears the original IAF insignia, soon replaced by a simple green, white and orange roundel. No. 3 Squadron was heavily involved in the fighting in Kashmir between 1947 and 1949 operating in the ground-attack role. The Tempest II and Spitfire XIV formed the backbone of the Indian Air Force at the end of the war.

Fighters at war, 1965

The Indo-Pakistani war of 1965 is often presented as a 'David and Goliath' struggle, though in fact, the two sides were remarkably evenly matched, since India had to keep many of its best units in the East, to guard against Chinese intervention, and these played no part in the fighting. Clever post-war propaganda by the PAF created the illusion that the war had been something of a Turkey shoot for the PAF, but while the Pakistanis enjoyed a 26:12 kill:loss ratio in air combat, they were unable to prevent offensive operations by India's bombers and fighter bombers.

NA F-86F Sabre
Pakistan claimed a kill:loss ratio of about 4:1 in the 1965 air war, crediting most victories to the Sabre, with a handful of credits for the then-new F-104 Starfighter. One individual Sabre pilot was credited with a total of nine kills (with two more probables), including five in one mission. On that sortie his real tally was two!

Hawker Hunter
At least 25 per cent of PAF Sabres were equipped to fire the AIM-9 Sidewinder AAM, whereas Indian Hunters had to rely on their four 30-mm cannon alone. The Hunter's heavy punch and high thrust made it a formidable adversary, and the type was responsible for most IAF kills. This one served with No. 7 Squadron.

India and Pakistan further north, in the Karakoram mountains, and a PAF Dakota was damaged by IAF Tempests. A UN ceasefire came into force on 31 January 1949.

Pakistan conducted its own war against insurrection on the North West Frontier, this tying down a fighter squadron from 1947 until 1960. Initially the air forces of both India and Pakistan were equipped with ex-RAF and ex-RIAF aircraft. India used Spitfires, Tempests, Liberators and Dakotas. The fledgling Pakistani air force had similar equipment, but lacked Liberators. The UK continued to supply aircraft to Pakistan (Furies, Attackers, Halifax bombers and Bristol 170 freighters) and to India (Vampires, Canberras and Hunters) although both nations also started looking for arms elsewhere. Pakistan acquired 100 F-86Fs, 12 F-104s and 24 B-57s as military aid from the USA from 1955, while India obtained Ouragan and Mystère IVA fighters from France and Il-14 and An-12 transports, Mi-4 helicopters and MiG-21 fighters from the USSR.

In 1957 Kashmir was integrated into the Indian Union despite Pakistani protests, and UN sponsored talks broke down in 1963. In February 1965 Indian troops took over a Pakistani police post in the disputed Rann of Kutch, an uninhabitable border area under water for much of the year. The post was recaptured in April, but air activity was limited. One IAF Ouregan was shot down when it strayed over the Pakistan border.

War in the Kashmir

In May 1965 Pakistan armed and trained irregulars to infiltrate Kashmir, hoping to ferment a revolution which would then topple the state into Pakistan. The insurgents were backed by Pakistani artillery, and the Pakistan army then launched a major offensive against Indian forces in the Chhamb salient. The IAF lost four obsolete Vampires to PAF Sabres in the battle, on 1 September. This led to the immediate withdrawal of the Vampire and the Ouregan from front-line use.

All-out war erupted between India and Pakistan, and during the vicious 17-day conflict the PAF flew defensive CAPs over its own bases, offensive counter-air missions against Indian airfields, and close-support and interdiction sorties, to which the Indians responded in kind. India retained much of its air force in the East, against the possibility of Chinese intervention, and as a result the air forces were

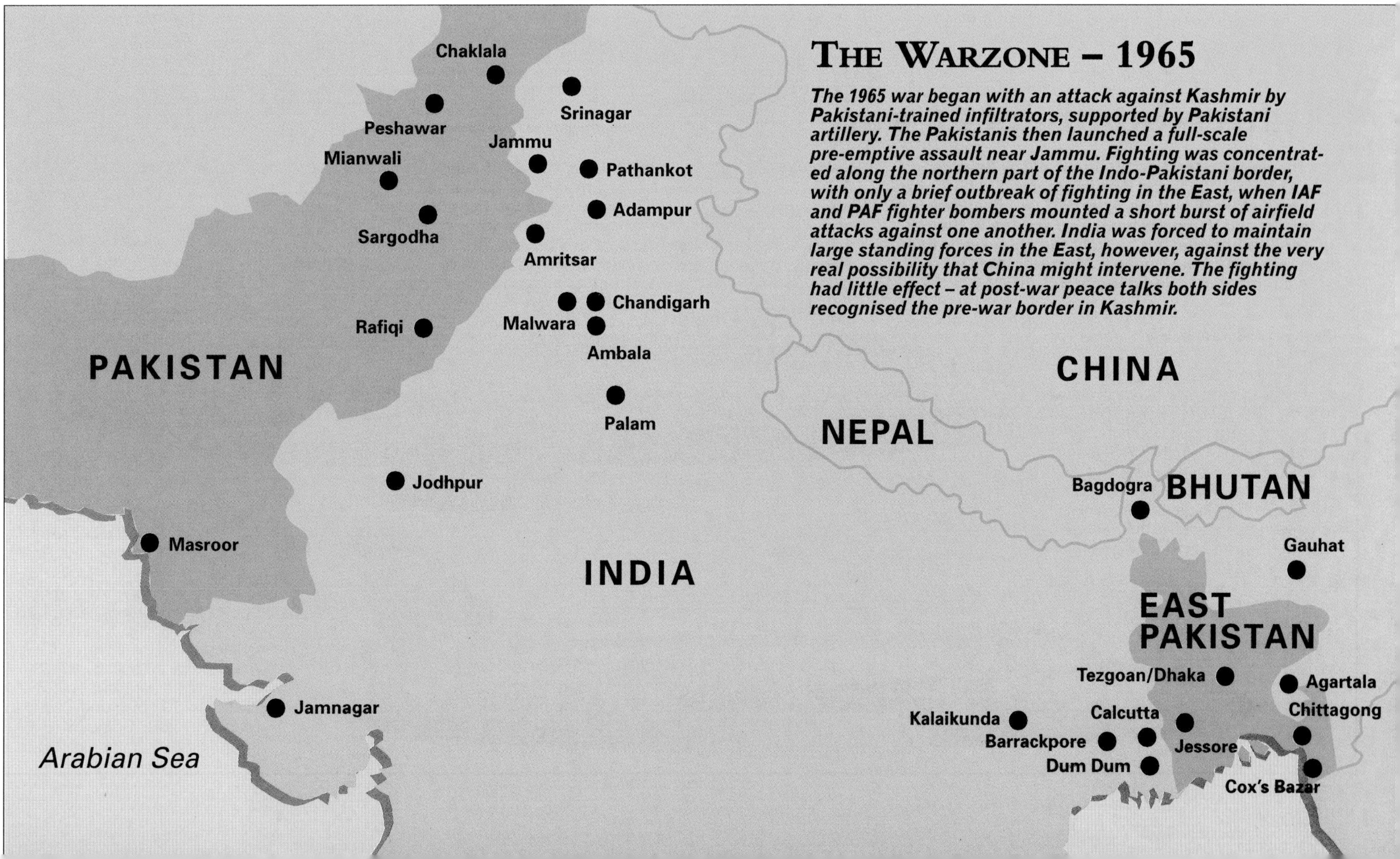

The Warzone – 1965

The 1965 war began with an attack against Kashmir by Pakistani-trained infiltrators, supported by Pakistani artillery. The Pakistanis then launched a full-scale pre-emptive assault near Jammu. Fighting was concentrated along the northern part of the Indo-Pakistani border, with only a brief outbreak of fighting in the East, when IAF and PAF fighter bombers mounted a short burst of airfield attacks against one another. India was forced to maintain large standing forces in the East, however, against the very real possibility that China might intervene. The fighting had little effect – at post-war peace talks both sides recognised the pre-war border in Kashmir.

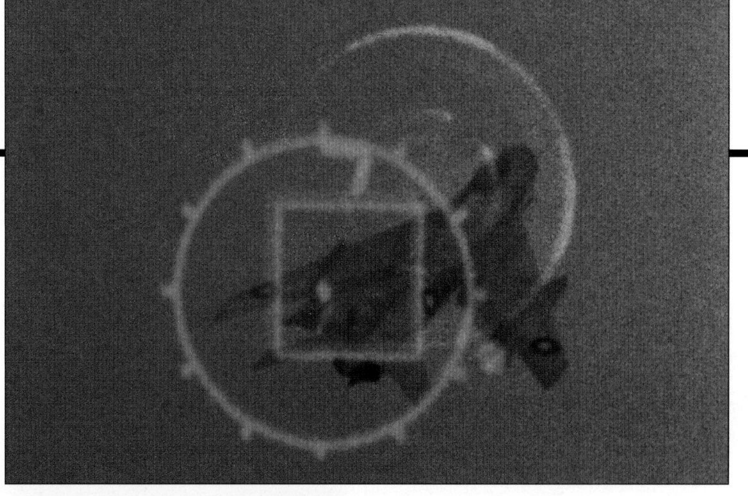

***Right:* The Chinese Shenyang F-6 formed the backbone of the PAF's fighter strength after 1965, 74 being taken on charge as Sabre replacements. These were later equipped with AIM-9 Sidewinders.**

***Below:* The Lockheed F-104 Starfighter played a part in the 1965 war, proving particularly successful in intercepting IAF Canberras at night. Three such aircraft were claimed as shot down by the F-104s.**

quite evenly balanced in the West. The PAF used skillful tactics to maintain an edge in the air, and were initially able to keep the IAF from excessive interference with Pakistan army operations, although after 6 September, little attempt was made by either side to stop fighter-bomber raids by the enemy. From this point on, the Indians flew more sorties, while the PAF tried to conserve its strength. Unfortunately, the IAF never mounted missions in strength against its key targets, sending out its aircraft in what were little better than penny packets.

Indian ground forces launched a counter-offensive which drove the Pakiștanis back across their own border in places, but generally the war became a bloody stalemate, and with 2,763 Indian dead and 6,917 Pakistani dead (and with 375 and 350 tanks destroyed, respectively) a ceasefire was declared. The pre-war borders of Kashmir were confirmed by the subsequent peace talks.

The PAF lost some 25 aircraft (11 in air combat), while the Indians lost 60 (25 in air combat). This was an impressive result, but it was simply not good enough. Pakistan ended the war having depleted 17 per cent of its front-line strength, while India's losses amounted to less than 10 per cent. Moreover, the loss rate had begun to even out, and it has been estimated that another three week's fighting would have seen the Pakistani losses rising to 33 per cent and India's losses totalling 15 per cent. Air superiority was not achieved, and were unable to prevent IAF fighter-bombers and recce Canberras from flying daylight missions over Pakistan. Thus 1965 was an expensive victory for the PAF, and one which was tainted by ridiculously exaggerated propaganda, which claimed a 4:1 or 5:1 kill:loss ratio.

Learning the lessons

India realised that its air force had been something of a glorified flying club for its pilots before 1965, and that serious effort needed to be made to improve operational readiness and training, and to provide even the most basic essentials, like camouflage netting (and even camouflage paint for some of its front-line types!). By contrast, the PAF began to believe their own propaganda, that the kill:loss ratio had been about 4:1, rather than the actual 2:1, still an impressive achievement, but simply not good enough in a war against India. They were completely unable to perceive that whatever had happened in the air, the war had ended in a draw. They also failed to realise that despite a slightly higher kill tally, the smaller size of their force meant that they could not win a war of attrition with India. Had the war lasted a little longer, the weight of Indian numbers alone might have defeated the PAF, even though India had retained more than half of its forces in the East, against the

***Right:* The survivors of Pakistan's original US-supplied F-86F Sabres were augmented post-war by 90 Canadair-built Sabres procured from West Germany, with Iran acting as a middleman. Five squadrons were still in service in 1971 when war broke out again.**

Fighter-bombers at war, 1965

The Hawker Hunter bore the brunt of the fighting in both 1965 and 1971, and was augmented in both wars by the Mystère IV and Gnat. In 1965, small numbers of Ouregans and Vampires were also serving in the fighter-bomber role, but by 1971 the older types had been retired and the Hunters, Mystères and Gnats were augmented by indigenous HAL HF-24 Maruts and Sukhoi Su-7 'Fitters'. In both wars, the short-range fighter-bombers were also augmented by Canberras operating in the interdiction role. Although the pace of operations was relatively leisurely, Indian ground-attack aircraft played their part in blunting the Pakistani ground offensive, and in contributing to Pakistan's loss of 16 per cent of its aircraft.

Dassault Mystère IVA
Inspired by the success of the Ouregan (known as Toofani in IAF service), the Indian Air Force acquired 110 Mystère IVAs between 1956 and 1958, and these equipped five squadrons, serving until 1973, latterly with a reconnaissance capability. The Mystère IVAs were heavily committed in 1965, while the older Ouregans remained on standby in the East, playing no part in the fighting.

Folland Gnat
Affectionately dubbed 'Sabre Slayer' in PAF service, the Gnat proved popular and successful in IAF service, operating in the fighter and fighter-bomber roles with equal facility. Some 23 Folland-built Gnats were followed by 20 built by HAL from Folland-supplied assemblies, and 193 built under licence by HAL. Some 89 improved Ajeets were also built.

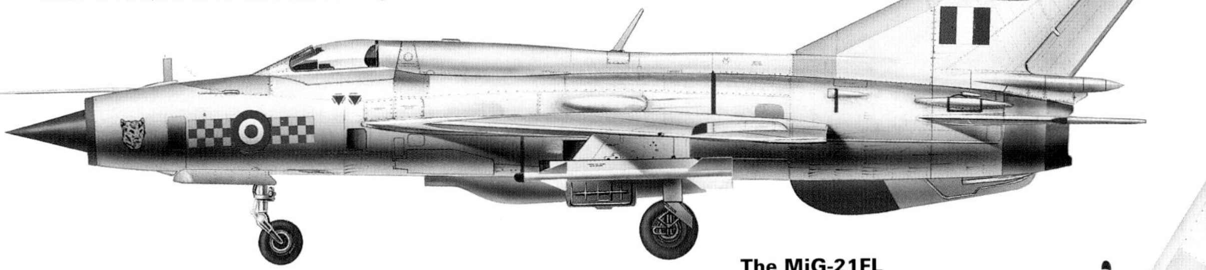

MiG-21FL

This MiG-21FL wears the Tiger's head insignia of No. 1 Squadron, the 'Tigers' who flew from Gahauti during the 1971 war. Previously a Mystère IVA operator, the squadron eventually re-equipped with the Dassault Mirage 2000.

Powerplant
The MiG-21FL was powered by a single Tumanskii R11-F2S-300 twin-spool turbojet rated at 138.26-kN (8,600-lb st) dry and 60.57 kN (13,613 lb st) with afterburning.

The MiG-21FL
The MiG-21FL was a simplified version of the MiG-21PFM, with increased fuel capacity, provision for a centreline GP-9 gun pod and with the downgraded R2L radar.

Armament
The MiG-21FL carried a pair of K-13A AAMs underwing, augmented by a centreline GP-9 gun pod containing a twin-barrelled GSh-23 cannon. Two 490-litre (108-Imp gal) tanks could be carried underwing.

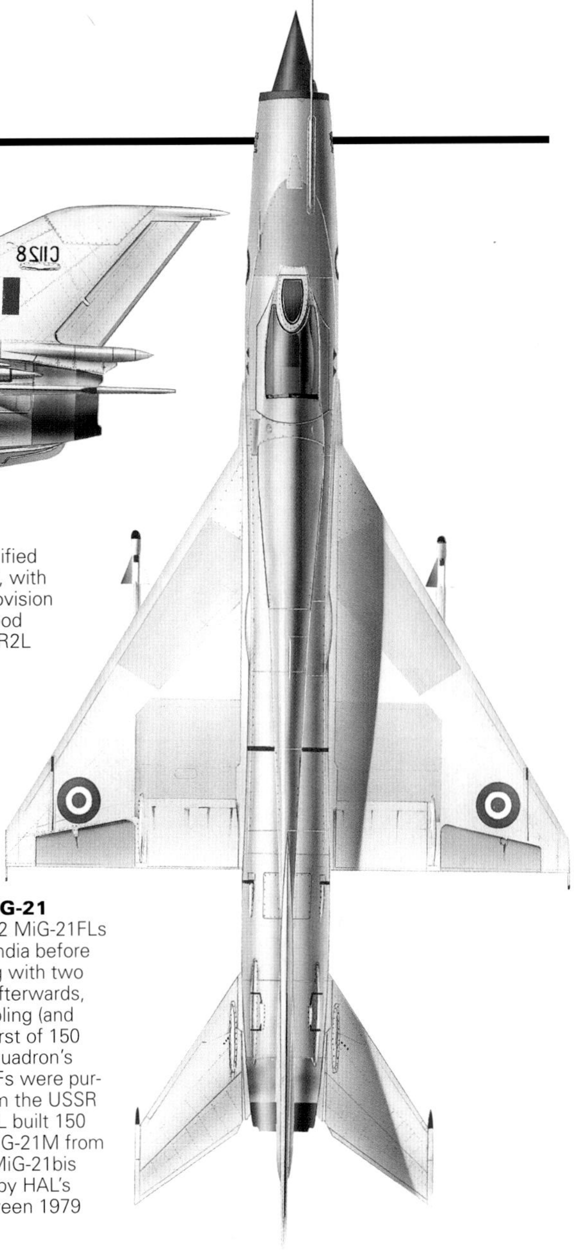

India and the MiG-21
An initial batch of 12 MiG-21FLs were delivered to India before the 1965 war, along with two PFs. Immediately afterwards, HAL began assembling (and later building) the first of 150 MiG-21FLs. Two squadron's worth of MiG-21MFs were purchased directly from the USSR in 1973, before HAL built 150 examples of the MiG-21M from 1973. Finally, 220 MiG-21bis fighters were built by HAL's Nasik division between 1979 and 1987.

Above: While the Indian Air Force used the English Electric Canberra in the bomber and reconnaissance roles, Pakistan used its US-built derivative, the Martin B-57. Both types saw service in 1965 and 1971.

threat of Chinese intervention. Had India committed its entire strength the war might have been very different. Alternatively, had India been prepared to allow the war to continue for longer, then its superior numbers would inevitably have proved telling. Finally the Pakistanis failed to take account of the extent to which they had relied on two factors which the IAF could not take for granted – complete ground-based defensive radar coverage and an adequate supply of air-to-air missiles. Much effort was expended in India to remedy these deficiencies before 1971.

With Soviet aid, India established a modern early-warning radar system, including the recently introduced 'Fansong-E' low-level radar, linked with SA-2 'Guideline' surface-to-air missiles and a large number of AA guns. By December 1971 the IAF comprised a total of 36 combat squadrons (of which 10 were deployed in the Bengal sector) with some 650 combat aircraft.

Moreover, the 1965 war resulted in the USA imposing a 10-year arms embargo on both sides. This had no effect on India, which had always looked to Britain, France and even Russia for arms, but was disastrous for Pakistan, which was forced to acquire 90 obsolete second-hand Sabres via Iran, a mere 28 Mirage IIIs from France, and 74 maintenance-intensive Shenyang F-6s. It was quite unable to replace losses among its (already weak) force of B-57s, or to acquire a modern interceptor in realistic numbers. Moreover, re-equipment and strengthening was not accorded a high priority, and the PAF was ill-prepared for war in 1971.

The 1971 war was rooted in the growing resentment in East Pakistan to rule from Islamabad, and the subsequent civil war, in

Below: Gun camera film from an Indian Hunter taken during a cannon attack against a Pakistani military train. Indian Hawker Hunters performed valiantly in both 1965 and 1971, and the type remained in IAF service in 1996.

Right: The Mil Mi-8 augmented and eventually replaced the battle-hardened and popular Mi-4 in IAF service. The Mi-8 joined the Indian Air Force in December 1971, just too late to play a part in the fighting.

PAF Fighters, 1971

When war broke out in 1971 Pakistan still relied heavily on the F-86 Sabre, with five operational squadrons. These were backed by three squadrons of F-6s and a single Mirage III squadron, together with one light bomber squadron operating the Martin B-57. This force was outnumbered by the IAF, which arguably enjoyed a qualitative edge, too.

Dassault Mirage IIIEP
The Mirage IIIEP served with No. 5 Squadron at Sargodha during the 1971 war, operating primarily in the air-defence role. Some 28 Mirages were supplied by France, and 23 were shown after the war, though six extra aircraft were said to have been supplied by a Middle Eastern ally.

Shenyang J-6
The Chinese-built copy of the MiG-19 proved extraordinarily effective, but there were too few available to make much difference to the eventual outcome. The aircraft was usually armed with US-supplied Sidewinder AAMs.

which the popular Mukhti Bahini independence movement received much aid from India. Pakistani forces were airlifted in when Bangladesh declared its independence, and when these started massacring the educated classes, India felt it had to intervene, and limited operations began in late-October. In late-November two PAF Sabres strafing Indian troops were downed by Ajeets, marking the first air combat between the two sides since 1965. On 3 December Pakistan launched what was intended to be a decisive pre-emptive strike against Indian airfields, but managed only 28 sorties, spread thinly and with insufficient accuracy to cause serious damage. The IAF hit back with retaliatory strikes which proved more successful, and at sea, the Indian Navy sank a Pakistani submarine (actually leased from the US Navy, and the only Pakistani vessel with enough range to threaten India's fleet), leaving the Bay of Bengal clear for operations by the carrier *Vikrant*. From then on Pakistan was forced on the defensive by numerically superior Indian forces.

The PAF's handful of Sabres at Tezgaon near Dacca in East Pakistan put up a useful resistance against all-out attacks by Indian fighters from 4 December. Between four and 11 of the attackers were claimed as shot down in air combat, with 17 more lost to ground fire. Five Sabres were shot down in air combat. On 6 December, an IAF attack cratered the runways at both Tezgaon and Kurmitola, effectively putting them out of action for the rest of the campaign. Apart from the IAF squadrons deployed in East Bengal, India's sole aircraft-carrier, INS *Vikrant* (with its Sea Hawk fighter-bombers and Breguet Alizé ASW aircraft) mounted attacks against the civil airport at Cox's Bazaar and Chittagong harbour. The embryo Bangladesh air force, with three DHC Otters (fitted with machine-guns) of the Mukhti Bahini Air Wing made an appearance on 7 December. Indian airborne troops, in battalion strength, made an assault on Dacca on 11 December using An-12s and Fairchild C-119Gs. This was preceded on 7 December by a heliborne infantry assault by two companies, in some nine Mil Mi-4s and Mi-8s, escorted by 'gunship' Alouettes.

Attacks on Pakistan

While India's grip on what had been East Pakistan tightened, the IAF continued to press home attacks against Pakistan itself. The campaign settled down to a series of daylight anti-airfield, anti-radar and close-support attacks by fighters, with night attacks against airfields and strategic targets by B-57s and C-130s (Pakistan), and Canberras and An-12s (India). The PAF's F-6s were employed mainly on defensive combat air patrols over their own bases, but without air superiority the PAF was unable to conduct effective offensive operations, and its attacks were largely ineffective. During the IAF's airfield attacks one US and one UN aircraft were damaged in Dacca, while a Canadian Air Force Caribou was destroyed at Islamabad, along with US military liaison chief Brigadier General Chuck Yeager's USAF Beech U-8 light twin.

Sporadic raids by the IAF continued against Pakistan's forward air bases in the West until the end of the war, and large-scale interdiction and close-support operations were maintained. The PAF played a more limited part in the operations, and was reinforced by F-104s from Jordan, Mirages from an unidentified Middle Eastern ally (probably

***Right:* A hastily-camouflaged Su-7 lands at Pathankot after a bombing attack over Pakistan, on 11 December 1971. The 'Fitter' was handicapped by its lack of payload/range capability, but proved fast at low level, and remarkably resilient.**

***Below:* Bombs explode on Cox's Bazaar airfield on 4 December 1971 during an attack by No. 300 Squadron's Sea Hawks. A low-flying Sea Hawk is just visible on the original print, by the small bend in the river at the left of the picture.**

***Left:* Sea Hawks of No. 300 Squadron (the 'White Tigers') ranged on the deck of the INS Vikrant during a lull in the 1971 fighting. The aircraft are armed with underwing rockets, in addition to their internal 20-mm (0.7-in) cannon. The 227-kg (500-lb) bomb was also used.**

Above: ***Two Canberra B(I).Mk 58s attacking harbour installations at Karachi at low level, December 1971. India placed a heavy emphasis on interdiction during the 1971 war, and this proved a successful tactic.***

Above: Indian Navy Breguet Alizés attacked and sank this ferry near the Bangladeshi port of Khulna when it attempted to run the Indian Navy's blockade. One INAS Alizé was shot down by an F-104 during the 1971 war, but overall the type gave sterling service.

Libya) and by F-86s from Saudi Arabia. Their arrival helped camouflage the extent of Pakistan's losses. Libyan F-5s were reportedly deployed to Sargodha, perhaps as a potential training unit to prepare Pakistani pilots for an influx of more F-5s from Saudi Arabia.

Hostilities officially ended at 14.30 GMT on 17 December, after the fall of Dacca on 15 December. India claimed large gains of territory in West Pakistan (although pre-war boundaries were recognised after the war), though the independence of Pakistan's east wing, as Bangladesh, was confirmed. India flew 1,978 sorties in the East and about 4,000 in the West, while the PAF flew about 30 and 2,840. More than 80 per cent of the IAF's sorties were close support and interdiction, and about 65 IAF aircraft were lost (54 losses were admitted), perhaps as many as 27 of them in air combat. Pakistan lost about 72 aircraft (51 of them combat types, but admitting only 25 to enemy action). At least 16 of the Pakistani losses, and probably 24 fell in air combat (although only 10 air combat losses were admitted, not including any F-6s, Mirage IIIs, or the six Jordanian F-104s which failed to return to their donors). But the imbalance in air losses was explained by the IAF's considerably higher sortie rate, and its emphasis on ground-attack missions. On the ground Pakistan suffered most, with 8,000 killed and 25,000 wounded while India lost 3,000 dead and 12,000 wounded. The losses of armoured vehicles were similarly unbalanced. This represented a major defeat for Pakistan.

India and Pakistan have not gone to war again, but the two nations retain their emnity, and have conducted small-scale military operations high in the Karakoram Mountains.

Below: The Alizés of No. 310 Squadron (The 'Cobras') operated from the carrier* Vikrant *and from Bombay, flying maritime patrol, ASW, minelaying and attack sorties. The Indian Navy's Sea Hawk fighter-bombers were even more heavily committed, flying some 160 sorties, mainly against airfields and harbour installations.

IAF fighter-bombers, 1971

By 1971 the IAF had several squadrons of supersonic fighter bombers (HAL Maruts and Sukhoi Su-7s), but these proved little more effective than the remaining Hawker Hunters and Canberras, though the Maruts, operating at high level, suffered no casualties and were even responsible for downing a single Sabre.

D-1224

HAL HF-24 Marut Mk 1

The HF-24 Marut entered service with No. 10 Squadron in April 1967, and with No. 220 Squadron in April 1969. Escorted by MiG-21s the Maruts attacked targets 322 km (200 miles) inside Pakistan with 454-kg (1,000-lb) bombs.

Sukhoi Su-7BMK

The Su-7 was acquired due to delays to the Marut programme. The aircraft entered service in 1968, and six squadrons were operational by 1971. These operated in the low-level interdiction and tactical reconnaissance roles. One shot down a PAF Su-7. Losses were heavy.

Southeast Asia

1975-THE PRESENT

The southern Far East region, encompassing Southeast Asia and the island states, represents a fascinating mix of nations with widely contrasting economic backgrounds and political ideologies. The ideological battle between communism and capitalism which replaced the old colonial struggles has exploded into warfare on numerous occasions, not only between nations but also within those nations. Above all, the shadow of China lies over the region, a shadow which can only grow as the most populous nation on Earth begins to flex its industrial and military muscle.

Above: After more than a decade of fighting the USAF and the US Navy during the Vietnam War, Vietnamese fighter pilots are among the most combat-ready in Southeast Asia.

Right: A Chinese Shenyang F-6 – a copy of the Soviet MiG-19 'Farmer' – lies wrecked after a dogfight with a Vietnamese MiG-21. In spite of China's relatively poor showing in the 1979 border war with Vietnam, the armed forces of the world's most populous country remain a dominant factor in the balance of power in Southeast Asia.

VIETNAM

The end of the Vietnam war saw the Republic of Vietnam fielding the most powerful military forces in the region.

In 1978 Vietnam invaded Cambodia. The Vietnamese air force, equipped with large numbers of former South Vietnamese aircraft, had little opposition. Military air activity in Cambodia had virtually ceased after the Khmer Rouge ousted the US-supported government in 1975 and began its genocidal reconstruction of the country. The Khmer Rouge's ally China supplied a few J-6 (MiG-19) fighter-bombers, but they offered little resistance.

The Northrop F-5s, Cessna A-37s and Bell UH-1s were replaced by Soviet-supplied aircraft over the next 11 years, with Mil Mi-24 'Hind' gunships seeing action against the Khmer Rouge.

Soon after the invasion, Vietnam found itself at war with a much more serious opponent. In spite of a traditional enmity dating back a thousand years or more, China had supported North Vietnam during the war with the Americans. But with the war over the unnatural alliance ceased. China invaded Vietnam on 17 February 1979 – largely in response to Vietnam's own invasion of China's ally, Kampuchea (formerly Cambodia).

85,000 troops of the People's Liberation Army (with 200,000 more in reserve) crossed the border, taking and razing the cities of Lao Cai, Cao Bang and Lang Son. The Chinese were beaten back by the Vietnamese before they could reach Hanoi. The PLA lost 62,500 troops killed or wounded, and 280 tanks. Poor weather limited air activity to a few ground attack sorties (mainly by Nanchang A-5s) and there were few clashes with the better organised, better equipped and vastly more experienced VNAF.

CAMBODIA/KAMPUCHEA

No attempt to re-organise the Kampuchean air force took place until 1984, when the government sent some pilots to the Soviet Union for training. Since then, activity has been largely confined to helicopters. At least six Mil Mi-8s and two Mi-24 'Hind' gunships have been used in army campaigns against the banished, but not vanquished, Khmer Rouge, and against other guerrilla factions opposing the Phnom Penh government. There has been little air activity in the struggle for control of the country which broke out in 1997.

THAILAND

Thailand was a major base for US combat operations in Southeast Asia. Following the US withdrawal from Thailand at the end of the Vietnam War, and the communist takeover of neighbouring Kampuchea, Thailand adopted a nominally neutral political stance. All US military aid to Thailand ended in 1978, although limited purchases of US equipment continued under the Foreign Military Sales programme.

Additional emergency aid was provided by the US State Department when Vietnamese occupation troops crossed the Thai border from Cambodia in June 1980. Arms deliveries were accelerated in April 1983 after the Vietnamese continued to pursue Cambodian Khmer Rouge anti-

Left: Thai commandos are landed in a major anti-drugs operation. Much of the world's heroin originates as opium from the 'Golden Triangle' where Burma, Laos and Thailand meet. The war against drugs has become more important as the guerrilla threat has dropped

government guerrillas into Thai territory. Guerrilla activity within Thailand has been reduced considerably, but continued unrest across the border means that Thai forces must remain alert.

MYANMAR (BURMA)

Ever since independence in 1948, the government in Rangoon has struggled to exert control over the far-flung forested uplands to the north and east known as the 'Golden Triangle'. For almost all of that time, military or military-controlled regimes have fought periodic campaigns against entrenched warlords, communist guerrillas and ethnic groups. These include the Karen and Shan, which seek independence, and in the meantime finance their insurgency by cultivating and selling opium.

Aircraft used in the long counter-insurgency war have ranged from Spitfires in the 1950s to Bell 205s, SF.260s, Pilatus PC-7s, SOKO Super Galebs and Nanchang A-5s in the 1970s and 1980s. A number of these aircraft have been lost to small-arms fire.

***Right:** Although the repressive military regime has been unable to acquire modern combat aircraft from the major exporting nations, Myanmar took delivery of six SOKO G-4 Super Galeb light attack-capable advanced trainers from Yugoslavia in 1990, just before that nation began to break apart.*

Burma was renamed Myanmar in 1989, and continues to profess strict non-alignment. It has therefore received little military aid from the major power blocs, and the repressive nature of the current government makes the provision of such aid unlikely.

PHILIPPINES

Following the end of the Huk insurrection in the mid 1950s, there was relative peace in the Philippines until 1964. It was then that ethnically Malay, religiously Muslim separatists, feeling themselves under threat from new Christian settlers, formed the Moro National Liberation Front (MNLF) and began a long guerrilla war.

Ferdinand Marcos was elected President in 1965. In 1968, a second threat to Manilla emerged with the formation of the PKP, the Philippine communist party. This formed a military wing (the New People's Army, or NPA) and began its own campaign of terrorism, initially favouring the sabotage of civilian airliners. In 1972, using the insurrections at least in part as an excuse, Marcos declared martial law, and began 14 years of dictatorial rule.

Air force units have supported the Philippine army in the long counter-insurgency war ever since, with T-28s and F-5s being augmented by AC-47 gunships, and gunship helicopters. The ageing T-28s have been replaced by SF.260s and Rockwell Broncos.

The MNLF eventually took de facto control over the Sulu archipelago and Cotabato province. Although limited regional autonomy was granted in 1977, continual wrangling has seen few of the terms of the agreement being met, and there has been a resurgence of violence in the southern portion of the Philippines in the mid 1990s.

Violence has continued, despite of the replacement of the corrupt Marcos regime by that of Cory Aquino (widow of an assassinated opposition leader) in 1986. Mrs. Aquino survived at least six coup attempts before passing power on to defence minister Ramos.

The withdrawal of US forces from Clark Air Force Base and Subic Bay has since thrown the Phillipines much more onto its own resources since 1991.

INDONESIA

The 1974 coup in Portugal resulted in a rapid withdrawal from the country's overseas possessions, one of which was East Timor. Three factions vied for control: one favoured a continuing association with Portugal, another wanted full independence, while a third wanted an association with Indonesia, which already included neighbouring West Timor. The pro-independence Fretilin took control and declared a republic on 28 November, provoking an Indonesian invasion by Marines and 1,000 paratroops (dropped by C-130Bs and C-47s), covered by F-51D Mustangs. Although the Fretilin took to the hills, they enjoy great popular support. East Timor has not been pacified, despite great repression and violence by Indonesian forces. These have fought a fierce, decades-long counter-insurgency war, supported by a wide variety of aircraft types, including OV-10 Broncos and British Aerospace Hawks.

***Below:** Although the SIAI-Marchetti SF.260 was designed as a basic trainer, its ability to deliver light weapons with accuracy in a counter-insurgency context has seen the type enter service with Myanmar, the Philippines (seen here), Singapore, and Thailand.*

Fighters and COIN

Although warfare has been endemic through Southeast Asia over the last 25 years, it has generally been of low intensity. With a couple of exceptions there has been little aerial conflict, though there has been plenty of COIN action and helicopters have become vital to the movement of troops. As a result, regional air forces have operated with a bewildering mix of combat aircraft, from former front line fighters cast off as obsolete by the major powers through armed trainers to dedicated counter-insurgency designs.

Vought F-8 Crusader
Left: Although its glory days with the US Navy were over by the end of the 1960s, the Crusader served the Philippine air force for many years after the end of the Vietnam War. The aircraft were not really suitable for the kind of action prevalent in the region, however, and were placed in storage at the end of the 1980s.

Rockwell OV-10F Bronco
Right: Designed to a US Marine Corps requirement for a counter-insurgency aircraft, the Bronco has seen extensive combat in Southeast Asia. Indonesia acquired 16 aircraft,which have been used to counter the long-running rebellion in East Timor.

Afghanistan

1980–1996

Left: *The Mil Mi-24 formed the backbone of the Soviet air effort in Afghanistan, and lessons learned in combat were incorporated to transform the aircraft's capability and survivability. Here an Mi-24P 'Hind-F' prepares to take off from an Afghan airfield.*

Below: *The Mujahideen captured a number of Afghan and Soviet aircraft, especially helicopters. Here a Taliban soldier poses in front of a captured Mi-17 'Hip'. The 'Hip' was a very versatile machine and much sought by the Mujahideen.*

Soviet and Russian interest in Afghanistan dates back many years. In the middle of the last century, this rugged, mountainous country was the scene of much tension and manoeuvring between the expanding empire of the tsars (who wanted a warm-water open-ocean port) and the Imperial might of Great Britain, determined to defend its interests in India. Soviet interest in the area intensified after World War II, hoping to see the subcontinent and Southwest Asia fall into its sphere of influence. Afghanistan and neighbouring Iran both have long, common borders with the USSR and represented useful buffers against hostile forces. Russian support for the then-Royal Afghan air force began in 1925, and Russian equipment began to predominate during the 1950s.

In 1973 the Afghan monarchy was overthrown, and a republican government under General Mohammad Daud remained on friendly terms with Moscow. The armed forces acquired large amounts of new Soviet equipment, especially the air force which by the end of the 1970s had a strength of over 180 combat aircraft, including MiG-17, MiG-19 and MiG-21 fighters, Su-7BM close-support aircraft and Il-28 bombers.

In April 1978 the army and air force led a coup which saw Daud dead and power placed in the hands of the People's Democratic Party of Afghanistan (PDPA) under Mohammad Nur Taraki. He was replaced by Hafizullah Amin, who was distrusted by the USSR because of his American education. Inflamed by a hastily enacted Marxist land-reform programme, there was a popular rebellion, to which several army elements deserted in divisional and regimental strength. March 1979 saw the rebels strong enough to seize the western city of Herat, where they massacred hundreds of government soldiers and about 50 Soviet advisers and their families.

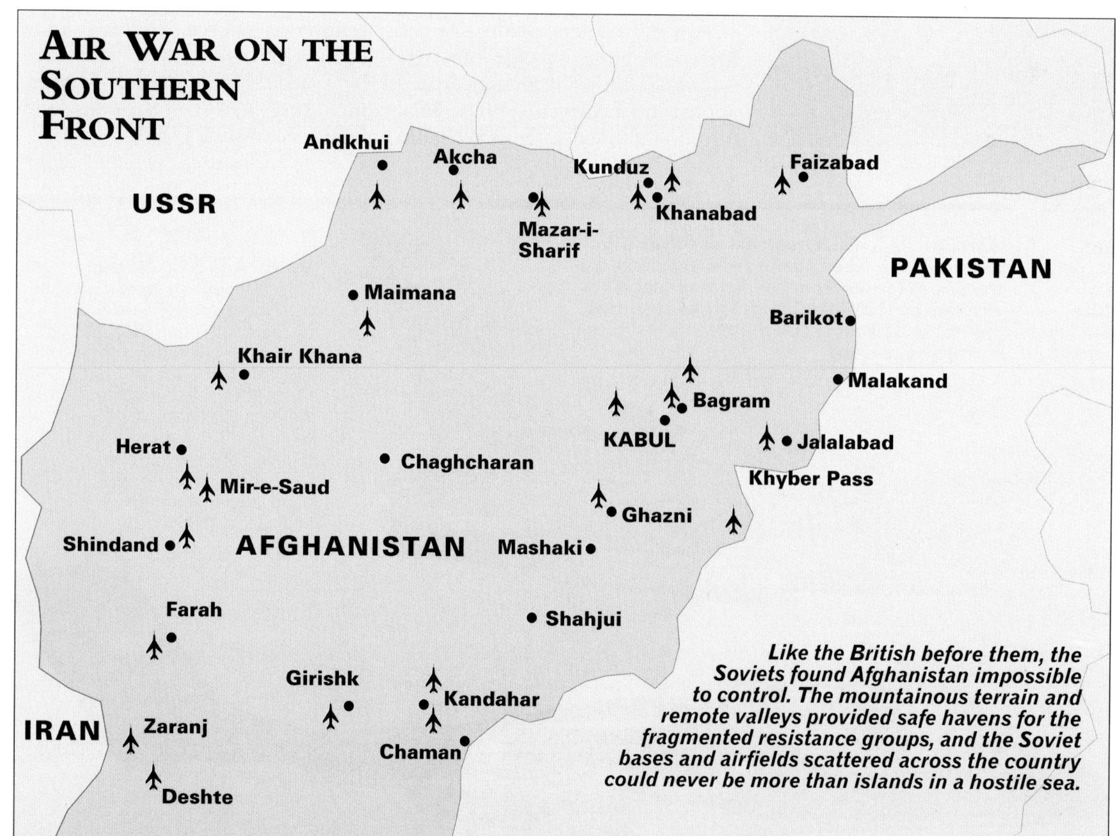

Like the British before them, the Soviets found Afghanistan impossible to control. The mountainous terrain and remote valleys provided safe havens for the fragmented resistance groups, and the Soviet bases and airfields scattered across the country could never be more than islands in a hostile sea.

Invasion preparations

With over 1,000 Soviet advisers at risk in Afghanistan, the USSR began planning to invade and restabilise the country, alarmed at the apparent resurgence of Muslim fundamentalism and keen to send warning signals to Iran and Pakistan. Army General Yepishev arranged to bolster the regime with an agreement to supply 100 T-62

Airlift into Kabul

With roads impassable, except to heavily escorted convoys, the Soviet and government forces in Afghanistan were forced to rely heavily on air transport both to bring men and material into Afghanistan, and to move it around in-country. Even the initial Soviet invasion was airborne, with 6,000 troops flown into Kabul in 300 aircraft movements.

Antonov An-26 'Curl'
The Afghan air force's own small transport element used a variety of aircraft types, of which the An-26 was the most modern. With an auxiliary turbojet in one nacelle, the An-26 enjoyed a remarkably good hot-and-high performance, and proved a useful light transport.

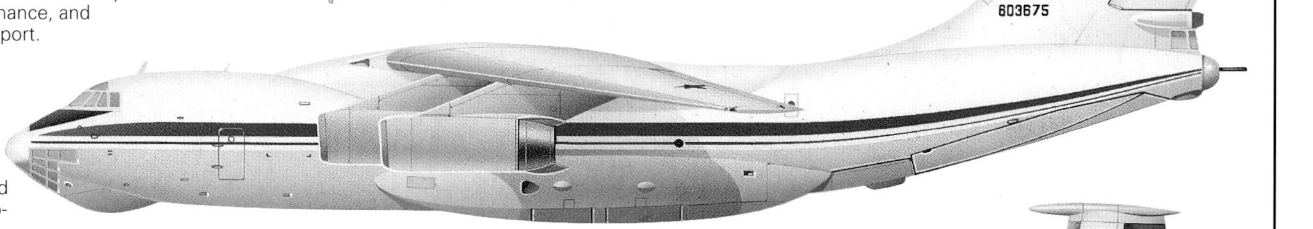

Ilyushin Il-76 'Candid'
By the time the USSR intervened in Afghanistan, the VTA had largely replaced its turboprop-powered An-12 'Cubs' with fan-engined Il-76 'Candids'. These performed the bulk of transport operations into and inside Afghanistan.

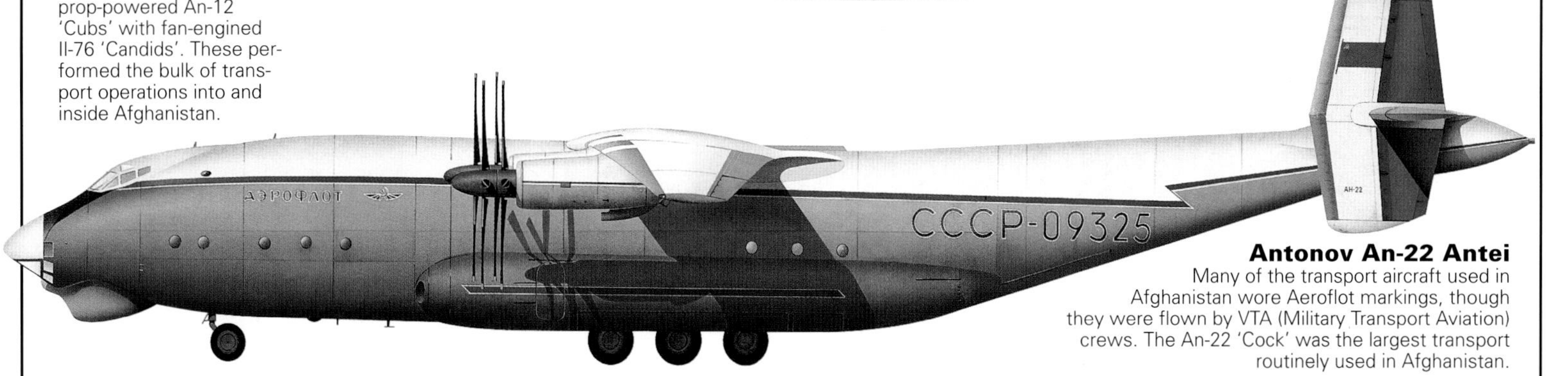

Antonov An-22 Antei
Many of the transport aircraft used in Afghanistan wore Aeroflot markings, though they were flown by VTA (Military Transport Aviation) crews. The An-22 'Cock' was the largest transport routinely used in Afghanistan.

Left: The original Mi-24 'Hind-A' saw extensive service in Afghanistan, and small numbers survived long after the introduction of later variants. The big glasshouse cockpit proved vulnerable to ground fire, while the single forward-firing gun was inadequate.

Below: The Afghan air force included a large number of MiG-17s, and these were used extensively in the ground-attack role, despite their age, poor payload and lack of advanced avionics and defensive systems. Attrition was high, however.

tanks and 18 Mi-24 'Hind' assault helicopters. Another 18 'Hinds' were supplied, including some potent 'Hind-D' gunships following further guerrilla attacks.

A Soviet-Afghan friendship treaty was signed in December 1978 and registered with the UN in September 1989. Specifically allowing either party to intervene if the security of either was threatened.

After prepositioning troops a few weeks before at the air base granted to them at Bagram and Shindand, the initial Soviet mass airlift of 6,000 combat soldiers in 300 transport aircraft movements took place over the period 24-26 December 1979, when the entire Christian world was politically and militarily impotent. The Russians attacked the Kabul regime on 27 December, installing exiled former Deputy PM, Babrak Karmal, who had 'requested the Soviet assistance' then being fraternally given.

Left: This Afghan Mujahideen soldier fires an American-supplied Stinger ground-to-air missile at Soviet or Afghan air force aircraft. The Mujahideen were very successful in downing aircraft with both the Stinger and the Shorts Blowpipe missiles, especially helicopters.

Simultaneously, up to 15,000 troops advanced from the Soviet border with armour and air support from MiG-21 fighter-bombers and Mi-24 'Hind' gunship helicopters.

The fiercely independent Afghans put up strong resistance in the country areas, declaring a Jihad, or holy war against the invaders. The USA responded by covertly arming the resistance (initially with Soviet weaponry from Egypt).

The Soviet occupation soon developed into a stalemate, in which periodic operations were mounted to clear rebel forces from specific areas, into which they generally returned as soon as the Soviets themselves withdrew. The USSR made extensive use of helicopters and air support by both in-country fighter-bombers and longer range bombers operating from Soviet bases. Tactics were

***Left:* The Mi-24D could pack a heavy punch, with its four-barrelled turret-mounted 12.7-mm (0.5-in) machine-gun. The under-wing weapons pylons were most often used for the carriage of podded 57-mm (2.2-in) unguided rocket projectiles. This one wears Afghan markings.**

***Below left:* Mujahideen fighters pose on the wreck of a downed 'Hip'. The success of the Mujahideen in downing helicopters led to improved armour, better infra-red screening of engine exhausts, and the provision of IR decoy flares.**

evolved using mobile ground forces as 'hammers' to drive guerrillas onto heli-landed 'anvils'.

Gunships in action

During the months following the invasion, the 'Hind-A' and the more heavily armed 'Hind-D' helicopters were augmented by Mi-8 'Hips' (some of them from the nominally civilian airline, Aeroflot). In order to relieve government forces under siege at Ishkashin, a paratroop force of 5,000 men was deployed.

The Afghan air force remained loyal to the pro-Moscow puppet government in Kabul, so there was no air-to-air combat over Afghanistan. Instead, Soviet and Afghan units provided close-air support for

The helicopter war

The helicopter allowed Soviet forces to respond quickly to hit-and-run attacks by Mujahideen guerrillas, and were used to mount offensive sweeps, undertake defensive patrols, and escort convoys. They became flying tanks and APCs, moving swiftly over even difficult terrain. They were immediately a priority target for the Afghan resistance.

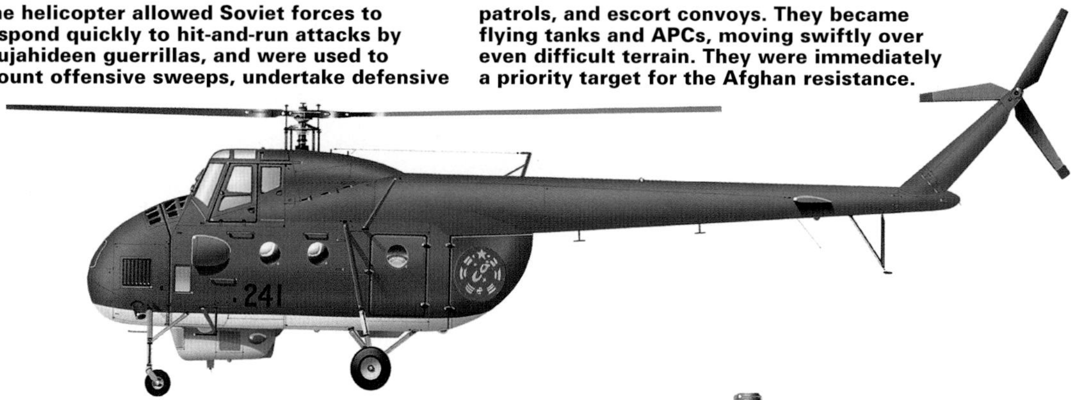

Mil Mi-4

The Afghan air force began the war with a significant number of ageing Mi-4 'Hounds' on charge. The Mi-4 was soon replaced by the larger and more versatile Mi-8 'Hip' which offered twin-engined reliability and survivability, as well as a larger cabin and higher performance.

Mil Mi-24 'Hind-A'

The original Mi-24 saw extensive service in Afghanistan, especially during the early years of the conflict. 'Hind-As' operated in both Afghan and Soviet markings, and performed rocket attacks and troop transport missions with equal facility.

Mil Mi-24D 'Hind-D'

An Afghan air force Mi-24D. The Mi-24D entered service in 1977, but was rapidly blooded in Afghanistan. Large numbers were transferred to the Afghan air force, especially after the introduction of the further improved Mi-24V 'Hind-E'.

Soviet 'Floggers' over Afghanistan

Afghanistan provided a useful proving ground for a variety of Soviet aircraft types. Among the most successful was the MiG-23ML/MLD ('Flogger-G' and 'Flogger-K'), which was a fighter but was also used in the ground-attack role in Afghanistan. The MiG-27 saw less service in Afghanistan, where the Su-25 and Su-17 were the most numerous fighter-bombers.

MiG-27D "Flogger-D'
The MiG-27 was optimised for the kind of low-level strike operations that were anticipated in Western Europe, and proved unnecessarily sophisticated for the war in Afghanistan, where robust, reliable and simple aircraft enjoyed an edge.

MiG-23ML 'Flogger-G'
Apart from occasional interference by Pakistani F-16s when Soviet fighter-bombers struck Mujahideen camps in Pakistan, the Soviet air forces in Afghanistan had no air threat to deal with. MiG-23s deployed to Afghanistan thus found themselves pressed into service as fighter-bombers.

Left: Tu-22M-3 'Backfire-C' bombers were deployed to support the Soviet withdrawal between October 1988 and January 1989. It was common practice to fire flares to distract any heat-seeking missiles fired by the Mujahideen.

Below: The supersonic MiG-21 performed surprisingly well as a fighter-bomber over Afghanistan, armed with unguided bombs and rockets. The Afghan air force lost several to ground fire, however, and at least one defected to Pakistan.

army attacks against guerrilla strongholds, often with helicopters as the prime air weapon. High-performance combat aircraft also played a limited part, though pitting a Mach 2 Su-24 'Fencer' against ragged hill tribesmen proved ineffective and costly.

Early 1980 set the pattern for subsequent years as Soviet troops conducted a major spring offensive, amid unsubstantiated claims from the USA that they were using chemical and biological weapons against the Mujahideen guerrillas. During May, Mi-24s were first seen with rearward-facing machine-guns fitted in response to the guerrilla tactic of allowing helicopters to overfly their concealed positions before opening fire.

Soviet losses

The guerrillas gained a major propaganda victory when they shot down an An-12 as it was approaching Kabul airport. At first their main anti-aircraft weapon had been the twin-barrelled 20-mm cannon, but further armament was quickly made available through Pakistan from sources as diverse as Saudi Arabia, China, Iran and particularly Egypt. The successes of the SA-7 man-portable SAM were varied, and many Soviet aircraft dispensed flares while operating close to the ground to decoy the heat-seeking missile. British Blowpipes and US Stinger SAMs were delivered later in the war, and proved harder to decoy.

By 1982, the Soviet forces were destroying crops and villages in the areas they cleared, denying their use to returning Mujahideen fighters, but further alienating the populace from the Kabul regime. Lack of co-operation between different resistance groups prevented them from exploiting Soviet weaknesses, and besieged Soviet outposts were generally able to hold out, or sometimes to break out and destroy their attackers.

Despite the growing military success of their offensives, the

Below: Equipped with intake filters and exhaust gas mixers, a Mil Mi-24V 'Hind-E' taxis at a forward airfield. The Mi-24 won its spurs in Afghanistan, and its crews won every possible award for gallantry in the face of the enemy.

Below: Despite lacking the glamour of the heavily armed Mi-24 gunships, the Mi-8 and Mi-17 'Hip' were probably more useful and versatile. Although they carried a heavier rocket load than the 'Hind', they served primarily as assault transport and support helicopters.

Soviet and Afghan strike power

The Soviets and the Afghan air force relied heavily on MiGs during the war. Both MiG-17s and -21s were used mainly in the ground-attack role. The Soviets also made use of more conventional bomber types for high-level bombing missions, including Su-24 'Fencers', Tu-16 'Badgers', Tu-22M 'Backfires' and even ancient Il-28 'Beagles'.

Mikoyan MiG-17
The Afghan air force used the MiG-17 'Fresco' to good effect in the ground-attack role, including a devastating attack in 1985 on the refugee camps in Pakistan.

Mikoyan MiG-21
The MiG-21 was one of the most common types of aircraft used by both the Russian and Afghan air forces in the ground-attack and army-support roles.

Soviets were unable to destroy the resistance movement, and in 1987 moved politically by replacing Karmal with Mohammed Najibullah, former head of the Secret Police. The new President brought some fresh allies into the fold, drawn from among disillusioned tribal chiefs.

The war against the Mujahideen intensified, especially against the forces of Ahmad Shah Massoud, an ethnic Tadjik who had achieved considerable success against the Soviets from his Panjshir Valley power base in the northeast of the country.

At the same time President Gorbachev announced a limited Soviet withdrawal, which began in October. It was soon decided that a complete withdrawal was possible, and Kabul's forces were given a massive influx of new weaponry.

Fifty per cent of Soviet forces had been pulled back into the USSR by August 1988, and the withdrawal of all Soviet forces was completed in February 1989. Russia's Vietnam was over.

The withdrawal of Soviet forces from Afghanistan did little to halt the fighting, which almost immediately degenerated into a three or more sided struggle between former factions of the resistance and the Kabul regime, which amazingly still held on to power for three years. This was in part due to the former communists sharing power with the most powerful of the Mujahideen factions.

President Najibullah was finally overthrown in April 1992, and the installation of an Islamic regime in April 1992, the new President Rabbani's forces, led by Massoud who had been appointed defence minister, went to war with the forces of the Pathan Hezb-E-Islami leader and former Prime M inister Gulbeddin Hekhmatyar.

Hekhmatyar's attempt to seize power was opposed by an alliance between Massoud and General Abdul Rashid Dostam, a former communist commander and warlord of the region around Mazar-i-Sharif in the north of the country.

The air force of the Democratic Republic of Afghanistan was Islamicised and purged. Different bases went over to different forces, with Kabul and Bagram becoming the de facto air force of Massoud, Shindand and Jalalabad going to Hekmatyar and Mazar-e-Sharif to Dostam. To further complicate the situation, tribal rivalries underly the situation, and these have often exploded into armed conflict.

Hekhmatyar's power base had been in the Afghan refugee camps in Pakistan, and it was from those camps that a far more potent force was to emerge in 1994.

Rise of the Taliban

The Taliban Islamic militia was composed primarily of religious students following the fundamentalist teaching of Mullah Mohammad Umar. Capitalizing on the unpopularity of the various warring factions, the Taliban quickly gained popular support and made rapid gains as they swept through the south of the country.

Fierce fighting continued until 28 September 1996, when Taliban forces finally seized Kabul, and it appeared that it would only be a matter of time before the north of the country followed.

But the Taleban have alienated many of their former supporters by their insistance on the world's most rigorous interpretation of Islamic law. Ahmad Shah Massoud has bounced back, leading resurgent former Mujahideen forces against a common enemy, pushing the Taleban back on Kabul.

Air force units have not been maintained to any great degree by any of the warring factions, but occasional flights (mainly by transport aircraft and helicopters) are made, and several Afghan air force fighters and at least three Mujahideen Su-20s were shot down during 1995, one by an Afghan AF MiG. The Taliban militia lost several helicopters.

It would be an incurable optimist who dared to predict the end of the long war in the troubled nation of Afghanistan.

Below: Painted in standard Soviet land forces European-style camouflage and heavily shrouded by tarpaulins, an Afghan air force 'Hind-A' gunship sits in front of a 'Hind-D' at Kabul.

The Il-76 'Candid' never fully replaced the older An-12 'Cub', which saw extensive service in Afghanistan, including participation in large-scale paratroop operations. Seen in 1988 at Kabul airport, this An-12 is participating in the withdrawal of among the last Soviet troops from Afghanistan.

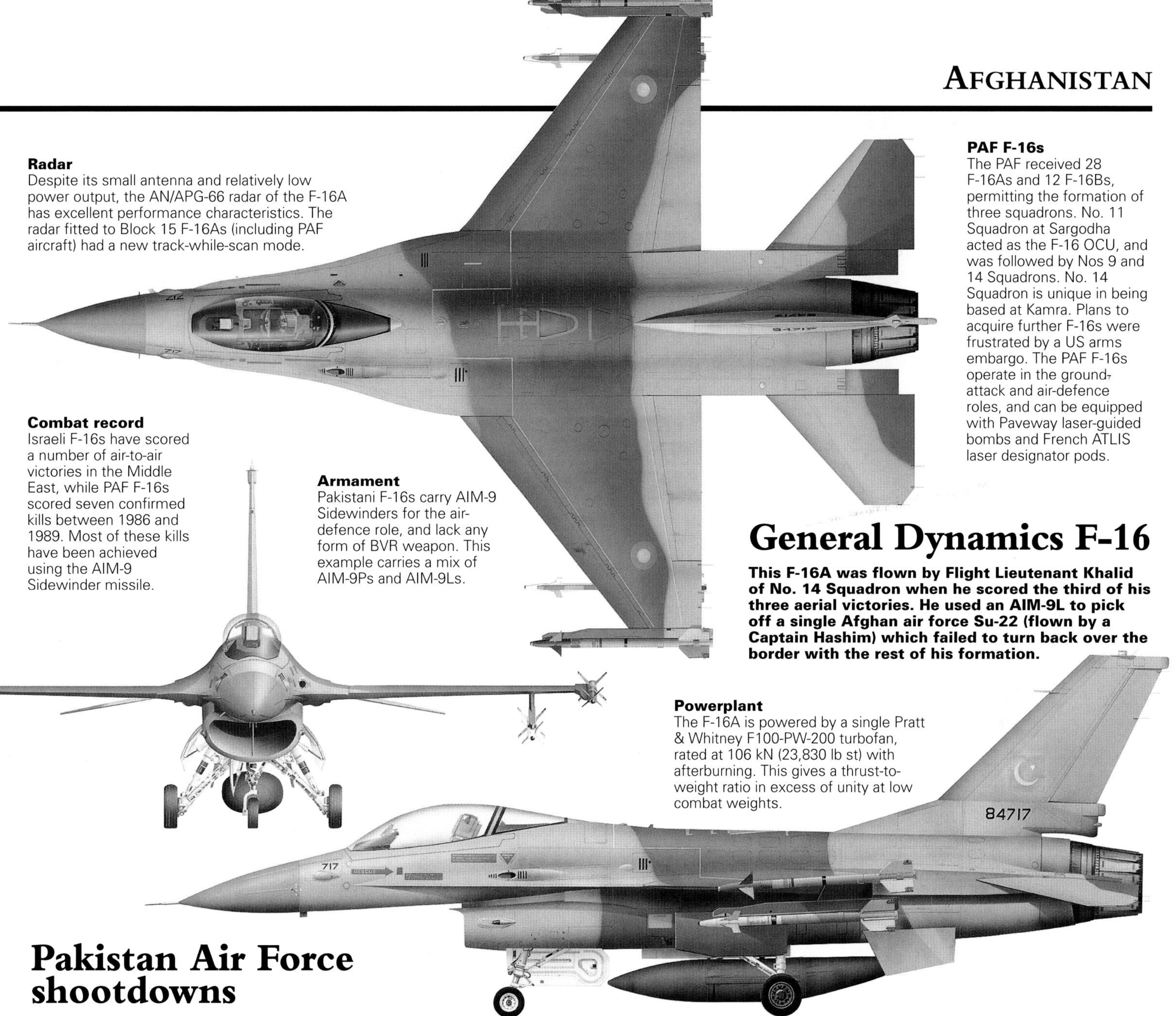

Radar
Despite its small antenna and relatively low power output, the AN/APG-66 radar of the F-16A has excellent performance characteristics. The radar fitted to Block 15 F-16As (including PAF aircraft) had a new track-while-scan mode.

PAF F-16s
The PAF received 28 F-16As and 12 F-16Bs, permitting the formation of three squadrons. No. 11 Squadron at Sargodha acted as the F-16 OCU, and was followed by Nos 9 and 14 Squadrons. No. 14 Squadron is unique in being based at Kamra. Plans to acquire further F-16s were frustrated by a US arms embargo. The PAF F-16s operate in the ground-attack and air-defence roles, and can be equipped with Paveway laser-guided bombs and French ATLIS laser designator pods.

Combat record
Israeli F-16s have scored a number of air-to-air victories in the Middle East, while PAF F-16s scored seven confirmed kills between 1986 and 1989. Most of these kills have been achieved using the AIM-9 Sidewinder missile.

Armament
Pakistani F-16s carry AIM-9 Sidewinders for the air-defence role, and lack any form of BVR weapon. This example carries a mix of AIM-9Ps and AIM-9Ls.

General Dynamics F-16

This F-16A was flown by Flight Lieutenant Khalid of No. 14 Squadron when he scored the third of his three aerial victories. He used an AIM-9L to pick off a single Afghan air force Su-22 (flown by a Captain Hashim) which failed to turn back over the border with the rest of his formation.

Powerplant
The F-16A is powered by a single Pratt & Whitney F100-PW-200 turbofan, rated at 106 kN (23,830 lb st) with afterburning. This gives a thrust-to-weight ratio in excess of unity at low combat weights.

Pakistan Air Force shootdowns

Only rarely did the Soviet presence in Afghanistan cause problems in neighbouring countries, except in Pakistan, where the effect was immediate and far-reaching. Thousands of refugees fled across the border into Pakistan, and among them were Mujahideen fighters, who established bases from which they launched attacks against Soviet forces in Afghanistan itself. With an ill-defined border between the two countries, and with the Soviets and their Afghan allies eager to hit back, border violations were inevitable, sometimes accidental and sometimes deliberate. This posed a major problem to Pakistan, which could not ignore cross-border attacks on its territory, yet which did not wish to be drawn into a war with Afghanistan or its powerful supporter.

It was soon decided that the PAF would respond to border violations, and the squadrons at Peshawar (only 24 km/15 miles from the border) and Kamra maintained an alert status in order to be able to respond. Stringent rules of engagement were enforced, including a requirement that only fighters or bombers could be attacked, and that any wreckage would have to fall inside Pakistan. Although they were scrambled many times from 1980, PAF fighters were unable to engage an intruder until May 1986.

Between then and November 1988, PAF F-16s from Nos 9 and 14 Squadrons shot down eight intruding aircraft (one classified as a probable). In the first engagement one Su-22 was downed by an AIM-9 fired by Sqn Ldr Qadri of No. 9 Squadron, while another escaped, on fire, damaged by gunfire, and classed as a probable. On 30 March 1987 Wg Cdr Razzaq (also from No. 9 Squadron) downed an An-26. On 16 April 1987 Sqn Ldr Badar of No. 14 Squadron shot down another Su-22. Things went less well on 29 April, when an F-16 was shot down while engaging six Afghan air force aircraft. The F-16 probably fell victim to his own flight lead (who claimed a kill), and the Afghan formation escaped unscathed. On 4 August 1988 No. 14 Squadron's Sqn Ldr Bokhari downed a Soviet Su-25 (flown by Alexander Rutskoi, later Russia's Prime Minister), and on 12 September Flt Lt Mahmood of No. 14 Squadron opened his score by downing two MiG-23s. The same pilot shot down an Su-22 on 3 November and on 31 January 1989 was able to watch with glee as an An-24 he was intercepting crashed while attempting to land. This was the second An-24/26 loss that winter, another having been shot down (unclaimed by the PAF) on the night of 20/21 November 1988. Soviet sources suggest that a small number of PAF fighters fell victim to Soviet fighters (a MiG-23MLD accounting for one F-16), but this cannot be confirmed.

Above: A pair of No. 9 Squadron F-16As patrols. PAF F-16s shot down seven enemy aircraft using AIM-9 Sidewinders, claimed another probable using the F-16's internal gun, and forced another manoeuvre kill. The total number of aircraft destroyed by the PAF may even be higher.

Ceylon and Sri Lanka

1958–1997

Above: ***Sri Lanka received six PT6-engined Harbin Y-12 transports in 1986. Illustrating the air force's pressing need for armed aircraft, all six were subsequently modified as makeshift bombers, each carrying a payload of 454 kg (1,000 lb).***

Left: ***Weapons at the ready, Indian para-commandos disembark from an IAF Mil Mi-8 'Hip' in Sri Lanka. With its capacious cabin and excellent payload, the Mi-8 played a major part in Indian operations in Sri Lanka. The 'Hip' could be quickly transformed from a transport into a heavily-armed assault helicopter and was used to mount rocket attacks against LTTE strongholds in the jungles of northeast Sri Lanka.***

Ceylon became independent in 1948 as the British withdrew from south Asia after World War II. The new country found itself with a potentially serious ethnic problem, in the shape of a significant Tamil minority which was mainly concentrated in the north of the island state. Small-scale Tamil riots took place in 1958, but but the first major conflict came in March 1971, when the deteriorating economic situation prompted a Sinhalese group to begin a campaign of terrorist insurgency, attacking police stations and other government targets.

The Royal Ceylon Air Force initially played a minor part in the suppression of the revolt, with the Bell JetRanger helicopters of No.4 Squadron and the de Havilland Dove and Heron transports of Nos 2 and 3 Squadrons flying resupply, reconnaissance and casevac sorties. British-supplied Jet Provosts were in storage, but were reactivated to form a new No.6 Squadron, which was immediately thrown into counter-insurgency action.

Soviet Assistance

Ceylon appealed for aid on 12 April, and a number of countries responded. Eight Alouette III helicopters were supplied by Pakistan and India (which also supplied six Bell 47s, these being shipped to Ceylon aboard RAF Argosies). More controversially, the Soviet Union supplied two Ka-26s and six MiGs: five MiG-17 fighters and one MiG-15UTI trainer. The latter joined No.6 Squadron's Jet Provosts, while the helicopters went to No.2. The rebellion was crushed in May 1971. The MiGs may have flown a few combat sorties in the hands of Soviet pilots.

Ceylon became a republic in 1972, when it became Sri Lanka. A state of emergency, aimed at containing further Sinhalese violence continued until 1977, but was by then aimed at the wrong target. The Hindu Tamil minority had suffered discrimination at the hands of the predominantly Buddhist Sinhalese since independence, and started demanding a separate state from May 1972, encouraged by the change to the *status quo* demonstrated by the founding of the republic.

The Tamil United Liberation Front spawned a militant wing, the Liberation Tigers of Tamil Eelam or LTTE. The organisation was banned in May 1978, following attacks on police stations, but the Tamil Tigers' activities increased as anti-Tamil rioting by the majority Sinhalese intensified. The Tigers blew up an Air Ceylon HS.748 in September, and in June 1981 a new state of emergency was declared.

The Sri Lanka air force began an ambitious re-equipment programme in 1985, ordering SIAI-Marchetti SF.260s and Bell 206 and

Above: ***A Mil Mi-25 of No. 125 Helicopter Unit, Indian Air Force, prepares to launch an offensive support mission from Palay. Armed with a 12.7-mm (0.5-in) rotary machine-gun, 57-mm rockets and light bombs, the 'Hind' proved to be extremely effective against LTTE positions, vehicles and even boats.***

Left: ***Known as Sutlej in Indian Air Force service, the rugged and dependable Antonov An-32 'Clines' of No.32 Squadron provided the Indian Peace-Keeping Force with most of its supplies and reinforcements. On 4 June 1987, five An-32s took off from Bangalore and carried out a relief mission over selected zones on the Jaffna peninsula, air-dropping 24 tonnes of supplies.***

Left: Four Mirage 2000s operating from the mainland, provided fighter support for the An-32s' relief operations of 4 June 1987. This early Indian air action proved to be the precursor to a massive intervention, involving up to 100,000 troops.

Below: Sri Lankan helicopters have been used extensively in the continuing conflict with LTTE separatist guerrillas. These are the three major types in operation with No. 4 Helicopter Unit at Katunayake: the Bell 206 JetRanger, Bell 212 and Bell 412. Four 212s and nine 412s are dedicated gunships. At least one gunship has been lost during operations.

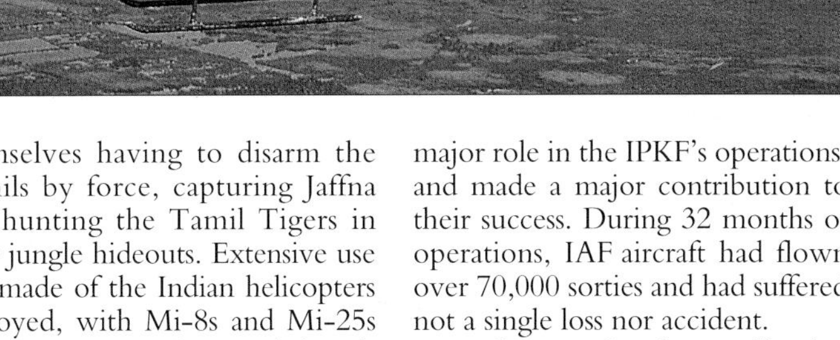

Above: Sri Lanka's response to the deteriorating situation in the Jaffna peninsula was to procure combat aircraft. Six SF.260TPs were quickly in action in the COIN role against LTTE guerillas. Two losses were made good by two attrition replacements, and by 12 further SF.260s in 1990.

212 helicopters, and these were soon in action, flying strikes against Tamil Tiger targets. The Tamil Tigers stepped up their own campaign of terrorism in response.

With the situation worsening, the government appealed to Pakistan for help in preventing arms flights to the Tamils, but in the event help was to come from a surprising quarter. India, traditionally sympathetic to the Hindu Tamils, had tried to apply pressure on the Sri Lankan government to halt its offensive against the Tamils in Jaffna, and had mounted An-32 relief-dropping flights (escorted by Mirage 2000s) from 4 June 1987.

On 29 July India and Sri Lanka signed an agreement aimed at restoring peace and 'normalcy'. India provided a massive peacekeeping force as Operation Pawan from 29 July 1987. The IPKF (Indian Peace-Keeping Force) initially consisted of 6,000 men, but numbers soon grew to 25,000 and then to 50,322 by May 1988, and eventually to over 100,000, with four full infantry divisions and their support arms.

These included two Mi-8 'Hip' and one Mi-25 'Hind' assault helicopter squadrons, and two Chetak/Cheetah-equipped light helicopter units. Although there was some surrender of arms by the Tamils, the Indians soon found themselves having to disarm the Tamils by force, capturing Jaffna and hunting the Tamil Tigers in their jungle hideouts. Extensive use was made of the Indian helicopters deployed, with Mi-8s and Mi-25s carrying out rocket and bomb attacks on the Tigers.

INDIA WITHDRAWS

India's presence helped ensure fair provincial council, presidential and parliamentary elections in 1989 and 1990, and prompted direct talks between the Tigers and the government. The IPKF began to withdraw on 28 July 1989, the withdrawal being completed in March 1990. Indian air power had played a major role in the IPKF's operations, and made a major contribution to their success. During 32 months of operations, IAF aircraft had flown over 70,000 sorties and had suffered not a single loss nor accident.

Unfortunately, the conflict has remained unresolved, and the war continues. Sri Lanka's own air force has expanded its operational arm steadily. In particular, the fixed-wing combat aircraft element has been significantly upgraded with the replacement of the 18 SF.260 and SF.260TP COIN aircraft by FMA IA-58 Pucarás, and a squadron of supersonic Chengdu F-7s, Guizhou FT-7s and Shenyang FT-5s, and most recently IAI Kfirs.

Indian helicopter support

Having committed over 100,000 troops, India's massive intervention on the Jaffna peninsula was supported by three combat helicopter squadrons, comprising the 'Hind' gunships of No. 125 Helicopter Unit and 'Hip' assault transports of Nos. 109 and 119 HUs. Indian Army Chetak and Cheetah light helicopters were backed up by the Chetaks from No. 321 Squadron, Indian Navy, which also committed a squadron of Alizé maritime patrol aircraft.

HAL Chetak

Right: Chetaks (licence-built versions of the Aérospatiale SA.316A Alouette III) of No.664 AOP Squadron, Indian Army, were used for casualty evacuation and as airborne observation posts for Mi-25 gunships. They served alongside Cheetahs, HAL versions of the Aérospatiale SA.315 Lama. The squadron was split into three operating units: Nos 10, 26 and 31 Flights.

MIDDLE EAST

The Middle East has been scarred by warfare since the dawn of recorded history, but the years since the end of World War II have seen a particularly ferocious series of conflicts. Central to the seemingly never-ending struggle has been the state of Israel, whose battles for survival against far more numerous Arab neighbours have seen this tiny country develop into a regional superpower, with one of the best trained and most efficient air forces in the world. But Arab-Israeli tension is just one of a whole series of historic ethnic and religious rivalries and hatreds, often dating back hundreds of years, which have erupted in battle since 1945.

Israel's Birth Pangs

1948-1949

Left: Avia S.199s of No. 101 Squadron (Israel's first fighter unit) taxi out for a combat patrol. Many of Israel's pilots were Jews who had fought with the USAF or RAF during the war, gaining much experience. Others were simply mercenaries or adventurers.

Below: Israel's B-17s enjoyed no more success than Egypt's hastily converted Stirling transports, though the ability to mount bombing missions was a morale booster for the Israelis.

Following the termination on 15 May 1948 of the UK's mandate in Palestine, it was almost inevitable that open strife would erupt between Jew and Arab, a situation that had been aggravated by Jewish opposition to an international (UN-approved) plan for the partition of the country into Arab and Jewish states. Neighbouring Arab states were forced to support ever-growing numbers of Palestinian refugees displaced from their lands by uncontrolled Jewish immigration.

Faced with the threat of military action by neighbouring Egypt, Iraq and Jordan, the Zionists had in November 1947 started to assemble an air arm (Shin Aleph) of the Jewish 'underground' army, the Haganah. This small force, with its collection of light aircraft, was initially confined to ground support during the civil war between the Palestinian Arabs and the Jewish immigrants.

On 15 May the state of Israel came into being, and the remaining RAF units were given orders to start dispersing to Habbaniyah in Iraq or to the Suez Canal Zone. The Royal Egyptian Air Force (REAF) possessed an expeditionary force based at El Arish in Sinai to support the Palestinians, a force that comprised a squadron of Spitfire Mk 9s, five C-47s (adapted as bombers) and a flight of Westland Lysanders. The moment the state of Israel was proclaimed it became the aim of the REAF to prevent the creation of an effective Israeli air force.

MORE ISRAELI AIRCRAFT

Israel was making frantic efforts in Europe to obtain more effective combat aircraft. The first such aircraft, Avia S.199s (a Junkers Jumo-powered development of the Messerschmitt Bf 109G), arrived from Czechoslovakia on 20 May and were first in action nine days later. On 31 May the Israeli air force (Heyl Ha'Avir) was officially established. On 3 June the S.199s forced down two Egyptian C-47s.

While the Israelis gained minor successes in the south, they suffered setbacks in the north and east where Syrian and Iraqi forces, supported by their tiny air forces, attacked Jenin, Degania and Semakh.

In the second phase of fighting, which persisted from 9 July until 18 July, Israel took the initiative, with reinforcements obtained during the ceasefire, bombing Lydda and Ramleh on the first day. On 14 July three Israeli B-17 Fortresses bombed Cairo in retaliation for an alleged attack on Old Jerusalem.

The second truce, which remained intact until 15 October, enabled Israel to greatly strengthen its air force, so that when fighting resumed it possessed five Beaufighters, three B-17s, five C-47s, six C-46s, 20 S.199s, four F-51 Mustangs, six Norsemans, three Constellations, two Hudsons, one Mosquito and nearly 50 ex-Czech air force Spitfire LF.Mk 9Es and Mk 16s.

The Syrian and Iraqi governments began to voice their reluctance to continue involvement in the war, enabling Israel to bring the great majority of its forces to bear on the Egyptian front. By December, despite being reinforced by a second Spitfire squadron at El Arish, the strength of the REAF's force in eastern Sinai had dropped so that it faced odds of almost four to one. To the north a force of 5,000 Egyptian troops was cut off at Faluja, and only sustained by air-dropped supplies. Four Egyptian Stirlings, intended as transports, were pressed into use as bombers, and made daylight attacks on an Israeli force threatening El Arish from the south; this vital forward Egyptian base fell on 29 December.

In little more than six months the neo-nationalist state of Israel had become a powerful force with which to be reckoned.

Left: Egyptian C-47s served in the transport role, but were hastily pressed into service as makeshift bombers. They operated from El Arish with No. 4 Squadron.

Spitfire versus Spitfire

Both Israel and Egypt used Supermarine Spitfires during the war of independence, in the ground-attack and fighter roles. As if this were not confusing enough, RAF squadrons (which moved from Palestine to the Canal Zone) were also Spitfire-equipped. Spitfires of the three air arms clashed on some occasions, and each lost Spitfires in air combat.

Spitfire Mk IX
Spitfires equipped a number of Egyptian air force units, including No. 2 Squadron at El Arish, and No. 6 Squadron at the same base, which included a number of older Spitfire Vs. Egyptian Spitfires played a major part in the Egyptian offensive against Israel, primarily as fighter-bombers, but reportedly scoring some air-to-air victories.

Spitfire LF.Mk IX
One of 50 Spitfires supplied to Israel by Czechoslovakia, this aircraft is seen wearing the personal markings of IDF/AF Chief of Staff Ezer Weizman. Weizman flew Spitfires in combat during Israel's war of independence.

Suez Crisis

NOVEMBER 1956

FLEET AIR ARM GROUND ATTACK
Three Royal Navy aircraft-carriers participated in Operation 'Musketeer'. Here Sea Hawks from No. 804 Squadron, operating from HMS *Bulwark*, attack Egyptian ground targets. Sea Venoms and Wyverns performed similar duties.

In 1952 Egypt's ruler King Farouk was toppled in a military coup and replaced by Colonel Gamal Abdel Nasser. Determined to end the British military presence in his country, he forced their withdrawal by 1956. That same year he nationalised the Anglo-French Suez Canal Company, seizing control of that vital waterway and thus threatening French and British trade interests with their colonies in the Middle and Far East. Britain and France decided on a military solution and gathered their forces to launch Operation 'Musketeer' in early-November 1956. The conflict ended in the humbling of the two powers that had hitherto been dominant in the Middle East.

A military plan was drawn up by Britain and France in August 1956 to seize control of the Canal. It was delayed and modified to accommodate an Israeli paratroop raid against the western end of the Mitla Pass in Sinai as retaliation for Palestinian guerrilla attacks from the Gaza Strip. On 24 October the Sèvres Agreement was signed by the UK, France and Israel, with 29 October as the planned date for the Israeli 'raid' to trigger an Anglo-French 'ultimatum'.

EGYPTIAN DEFENDERS

At the start of hostilities, the Egyptian air force had nearly 70 front-line combat aircraft. The most potent arm was provided by Soviet equipment in the form of two squadrons of MiG-15 fighters and a squadron of Il-28 bombers. Though being phased out, one squadron of Vampires and another of Meteors (both at Fayid) were still operational, with forward strips in Sinai. Supporting them were three transport squadrons (60 aircraft at Almaza and Deversoir). Six other units (84 assorted piston- and jet-engined aircraft) were non-operational, being in the process of conversion or disbandment. The Egyptian army had also withdrawn half its normal strength from Sinai to the Delta to face a British and French build-up in Malta and Cyprus. Much of the air force was also 'facing north' rather than east towards Israel.

Above: The Republic RF-84F Thunderflashes of Escadron de Reconnaissance 4/33 flew tactical reconnaissance missions from Akrotiri. Four squadrons of F-84F fighters were also involved.

ANGLO-FRENCH FORCES

France had four fighter-bomber wings (100 aircraft), three transport wings and two carriers, *Arromanches* and *La Fayette*, with F4U-7 Corsair fighters. On 23 October three French squadrons arrived in Israel. Their Mystères would defend Tel Aviv, helped by F-84s which would afterwards support the Israeli army in Sinai. The Noratlases would supply Israel's paratroops in Mitla and central Sinai. Aircraft operating over Egyptian territory were given Israeli markings. Thus, the Israeli air force's 69 jet- and 45 piston-engined fighters could be committed to Sinai, plus its B-17s and assorted transports. Mystères provided top cover, while Meteors, Ouragans, P-51s and Mosquitoes operated for ground attack, and B-17s carried out night bombing raids.

By far the most modern forces deployed were those of Britain, whose Royal Air Force moved four Valiant heavy bomber and six Canberra medium bomber squadrons to Luqa on Malta. The heaviest concentration of air power was based on Cyprus, with another 10 Canberra squadrons, four Hunter and Meteor units for air defence, four Venom squadrons for ground-attack, and six transport squadrons with Hastings and Valetta aircraft. The Fleet Air Arm deployed three aircraft-carriers – *Albion*, *Bulwark* and *Eagle* – to the Mediterranean.

Above: Fighter cover for the RAF's bombers was provided by the Sapphire-engined Hunter F.Mk 5s of Nos 1 and 34 Squadrons, which usually formed the Tangmere Hunter wing.

Right: A Canberra B.Mk 6 of No. 109 Squadron takes off from RAF Luqa, Malta, for a bombing mission. The RAF's Canberra B.Mk 2s, with their shorter range, operated from Nicosia on the island of Cyprus.

Anglo-French air power

The British and French assembled a massive tactical air armada for the assault on Egypt, with fighter-bombers and medium bombers, together with fighter and reconnaissance support. They were based on Malta and Cyprus, and aboard five aircraft-carriers and a commando carrier. Ground forces included airborne and seaborne troops with tanks; they would have seized the entire Canal Zone if the ceasefire had not been agreed.

Republic F-84F
The Republic F-84F Thunderstreaks operated with four Armée de l'Air squadrons at Suez. This one served with Escadron 3/3 at Reims, from where it was forward-deployed to Akrotiri, operating in the air-defence role. Two squadrons from the 1st Escadre at St Dizier flew ground-attack missions from Lydda, in Israel.

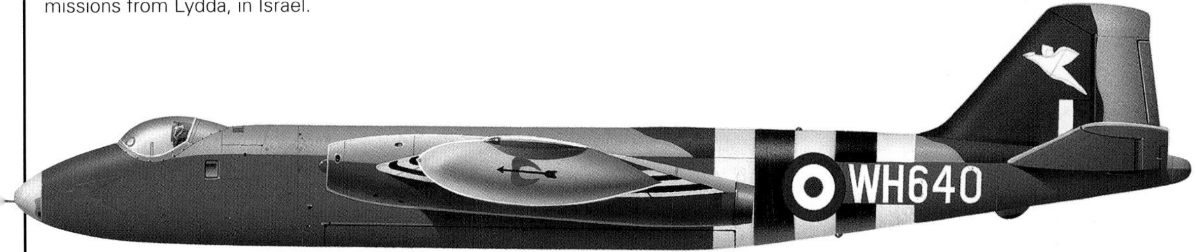

English Electric Canberra B.Mk 2
Canberra B.Mk 2s from eight RAF squadrons operated from Nicosia, Cyprus during the Suez campaign. This aircraft wears the stylised white pheasant of the Honington wing, and the red speedbird of No. 10 Squadron.

Hawker Hunter F.Mk 5
Two squadrons of Hawker Hunters were deployed to Cyprus to provide fighter support for the fighter-bomber and bomber fleets attacking Egyptian targets. With no enemy air opposition, they also flew close-support missions.

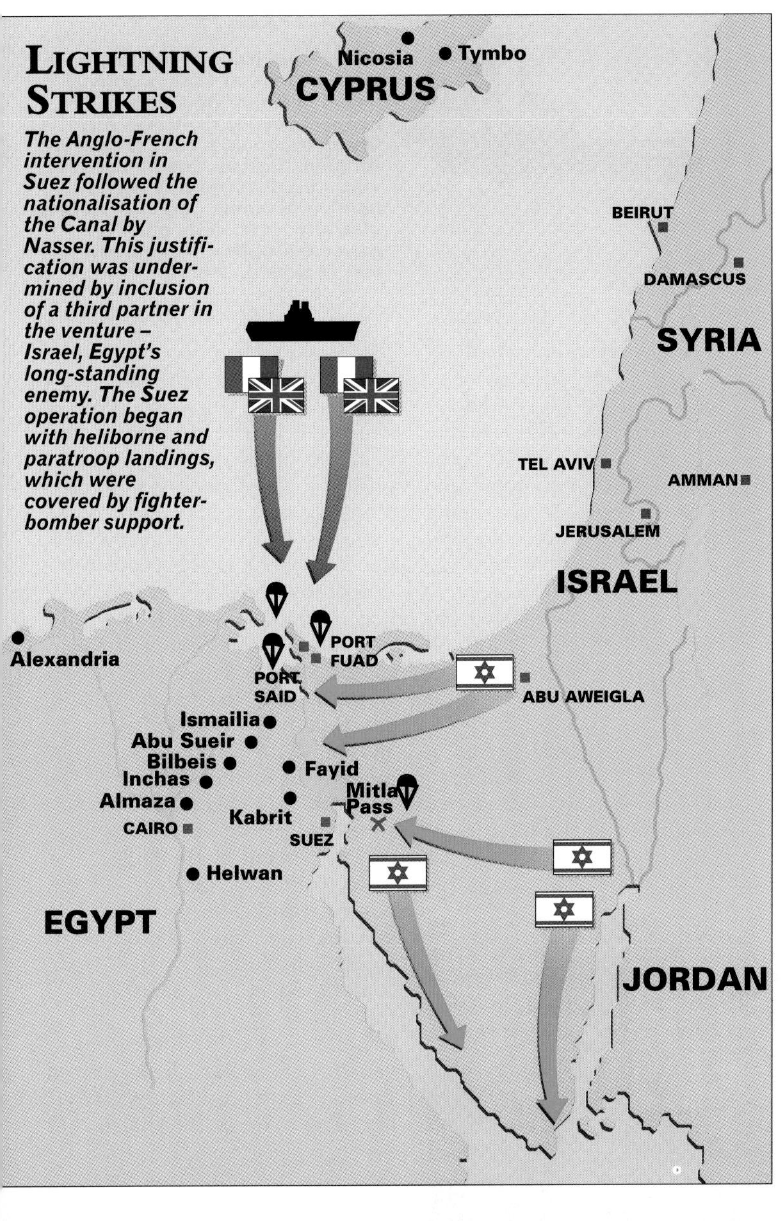

Lightning Strikes

The Anglo-French intervention in Suez followed the nationalisation of the Canal by Nasser. This justification was undermined by inclusion of a third partner in the venture – Israel, Egypt's long-standing enemy. The Suez operation began with heliborne and paratroop landings, which were covered by fighter-bomber support.

Above: Vickers Valiants from Nos 138, 148, 207 and 214 Squadrons flew conventional bombing missions from Luqa on the island of Malta.

They contributed 11 squadrons of Wyvern, Sea Venom and Sea Hawk combat aircraft.

The Suez war began late on the afternoon of 29 October when Israeli forces entered Sinai at two points. Approximately 1,600 paratroopers were then dropped from C-47s near the eastern end of the Mitla Pass while IAF Mystères patrolled central Sinai to watch for EAF reaction. By 20.00 that evening, Egyptian troops were heading across the Suez Canal towards the Mitla Pass. An hour later six French transports dropped heavy equipment to the Israeli paratroops.

At dawn on 30 October four RAF Canberras attempted a reconnaissance of Egyptian reaction in the Canal Zone. All were intercepted by MiG-15s, one being damaged. Early that same morning the Egyptian destroyer *Ibrahim al Awwal* tried to bombard Haifa harbour but was so damaged by IAF Ouragans that it had to surrender to Israeli destroyers. At almost the same moment a flight of four EAF Vampires made a reconnaissance of Israeli forces at Mitla and El

Below: The Avro Shackletons of No. 37 Squadron at Luqa flew maritime and anti-submarine patrols to protect allied shipping in the Mediterranean, but also found time to fly air transport missions in support of the British task force.

Suez stripes
Most British and French aircraft participating in Operation 'Musketeer' wore distinctive black and yellow stripes around their rear fuselage and wingroots. White paint occasionally replaced yellow, when stocks were short.

Powerplant
The Venom was powered by a single de Havilland Ghost 103 centrifugal flow turbojet, rated at 21.55 kN (4,850 lb st). This represented a 6.66 kN (1,500-lb st) increase over the most powerful Goblin-engined Vampires, which were not much lighter, and which lacked the Venom's thin wing and highly-swept leading edge. These improvements made the Venom about 161-km/h (100-mph) faster than its precursor.

Armament
Like the Vampire, the Venom had a tray of four 20-mm (8-in) Hispano cannon in the bottom of the nose, with provision for 907 kg (2,000 lb) of bombs and rockets underwing.

Wingtip tanks
The relocation of the Vampire's underwing tanks to the wingtips of the Venom brought about a considerable increase in aerodynamic efficiency, and they were seldom removed.

WR410 N

de Havilland Venom FB.Mk 4

Three squadrons of de Havilland Venoms (one of them normally based in Aden) flew close air-support sorties from Akrotiri. Another moved from the Gulf to Amman, Jordan. The Venom was a highly effective fighter-bomber, a stable gun and rocket platform, fast, agile and dependable. One Venom was lost in action.

Thamed to the east. They were followed two hours later by MiG-15s, which destroyed six vehicles and a Piper Cub on the ground. Further attacks by EAF Vampires escorted by MiGs destroyed more vehicles. A standing patrol of IAF Mystères was therefore set up over the Canal Zone. The first air combat came late in the afternoon, when six MiGs held off the six Mystères of this patrol while two EAF Meteors caused further heavy loss to the paras east of Mitla. The air battle rapidly drew in more aircraft and ended with two MiGs being destroyed for a Mystère seriously damaged.

Two Egyptian MiG-15s on a combat air patrol. The EAF performed well initially, but when the Anglo-French air attacks began it played little part since aircraft were either destroyed or fled south.

The EAF had been caught by surprise by the Israeli invasion but nevertheless managed almost 50 sorties on 30 October. The IAF flew over 100 sorties, the most effective being against Egyptian troops entering the western end of the Mitla Pass. These lost almost all their vehicles but were able to take up strong defensive positions overlooking the pass along the Heitan Defile.

At 06.00 on 31 October the British and French issued their ultimatums, demanding that both sides withdraw from the Canal Zone – which the Israelis had not reached at all. As predicted, the Egyptians refused. At dawn, four EAF Vampires attempted to attack Israeli positions at Mitla before the IAF standing patrol arrived, and were caught by six Mystères as they began their bombing runs. By pressing on the Vampires again caused serious damage but two were downed. An attempt by a solitary Il-28 to hit Lod air base failed and the aircraft dropped its bombs near Ramat Rachel.

To the east, two IAF Ouragans were sent against an isolated flight of EAF aircraft at Bir Gifgafa but were jumped by the MiG-15 top cover for EAF Meteors which had in turn just halted a column of Israeli light tanks near Bir Hasan. Both Ouragans were damaged, one subsequently force-landing in the desert, before IAF Mystères intervened. IAF aircraft then attacked Egyptian armour, which was moving south towards Bir Gifgafa, but

Right: Egypt's Ilyushin Il-28 bombers fled south to Luxor, out of range of the allied aircraft on Cyprus. They were eventually found and destroyed by French F-84Fs operating from bases in Israel.

Above: French Nord Noratlas transports dropped paratroops (including British sappers and the Guards Independent Parachute Company) on Port Said. They would have dropped paras on Ismailia, had the operation not been cancelled.

Left: Dassault Mystère IVAs from Escadre de Chasse 2 at Dijon flew air-defence missions from Haifa, freeing Israeli fighter-bombers for offensive operations. Many of the French aircraft operating within Israel wore Israeli national insignia.

were themselves intercepted by EAF Meteors, one of which was shot down. The IAF continued to strafe this Egyptian column but failed to stop it, while the EAF was similarly engaged against Israelis advancing on Bir Hama.

To the north, on 31 October the Israeli army suffered its only real defeat of the campaign, when a series of attacks on Abu Ageila was driven off with serious loss. So great were the demands now being put on the IAF that French aircraft based in Israel had to intervene against another Egyptian column advancing on Abu Ageila from the Canal Zone.

Egyptian air defences were put on full alert in the Nile Delta and Canal Zone, expecting air attack in the early hours of 31 October after the expiry of the Anglo-French ultimatum. Twenty Il-28s and 20 MiG-15s destined for the Syrian air force had already been flown to Syria via Saudi Arabia by Russian and Czech pilots. They were escorted by 20 non-operational EAF MiGs. Meanwhile, the EAF's operational and non-operational Il-28s went south to Luxor, where it was hoped they would be safe.

Until the last moment the Egyptians thought the British and French were bluffing, so there was neither black-out nor dispersal when the first bombers attacked Almaza shortly after dark.

Tasked with the destruction of the Egyptian air force, the RAF mounted a series of bombing raids later that evening. Three waves of Canberra and Valiant bombers came in from Cyprus and Malta to hit Almaza, Inchas, Abu Sueir, Kabrit and Cairo International before midnight. Bombing from 12190 m (40,000 ft), they destroyed or damaged only 14 aircraft. The EAF made only two interception attempts and only once did a Meteor NF.Mk 13 fire on a Valiant.

A pair of reconnaissance Canberras was intercepted by MiGs early on 1 November, one Canberra being damaged. They reported the limited effect of the night assault and so by day the tactics were changed. Anglo-French land- and carrier-based aircraft attacked every EAF airfield west of Sinai. The MiGs were hurriedly dispersed throughout the Delta but found it hard even to take off as each strip was under almost constant surveillance. On 2 and 3 November Bilbeis Air Academy and the Helwan repair depot were attacked, and on 6 November railway communications, barracks and anti-aircraft sites were added.

On 2 November the French carrier *Arromanches* launched its Corsairs against Alexandria harbour but was in turn attacked by the Egyptian destroyers *El Nasr* and

Below: English Electric Canberra B.Mk 6s of No. 12 Squadron lined up at RAF Luqa for operations over Egypt. Canberras performed the bulk of the bombing missions, even marking targets for the larger, more modern Valiants.

Israeli and Egyptian air power

Many on the British side were uncomfortable about operating with the Israelis, not wishing to offend Arab allies. Operation 'Cordage' was prepared for the bombing of Israeli airfields, and would have been set in motion had Israel attacked Jordan or Iraq. France and Britain had ostensibly intervened to separate Israeli and Egyptian forces and protect the Canal.

Dassault Ouragan
Israeli fighter-bombers, like this Ouragan of No. 113 Squadron, wore black and yellow Suez stripes. The sharkmouth was a unit marking.

Douglas C-47
Israel was desperately short of transport aircraft, and was forced to impress civil airliners and to rely on French Nord Noratlases to fill the gap. IDF/AF and impressed C-47s and DC-3s were used to drop Israeli paratroops.

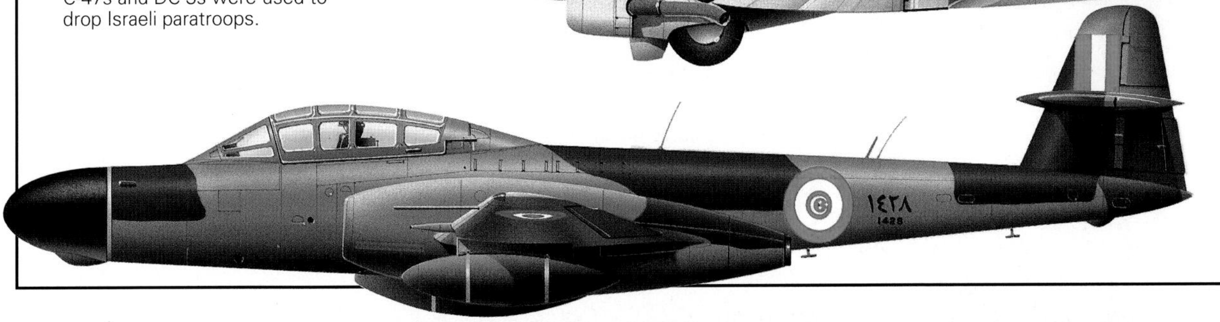

Armstrong Whitworth Meteor NF.Mk 13
Egypt's armed forces still included a great deal of British equipment, supplied when Britain and Egypt were allies. The air force included Meteor day and night fighters.

Fleet Air Arm fighter-bombers

In the absence of enemy air opposition, most of the aircraft aboard the carriers *Albion*, *Bulwark* and *Eagle* actually operated in the fighter-bomber and close-support roles. The FAA was heavily committed to supporting British paratroops after their landing at Port Said on 5 November. Two Sea Hawks and a Wyvern were lost in action.

Westland Wyvern
No. 830 Squadron aboard the *Eagle* operated in the ground-attack role, attacking targets primarily with unguided rocket projectiles. After a disastrous start, the Wyvern had proved to be a success in service, and by 1956 was a popular machine with its pilots.

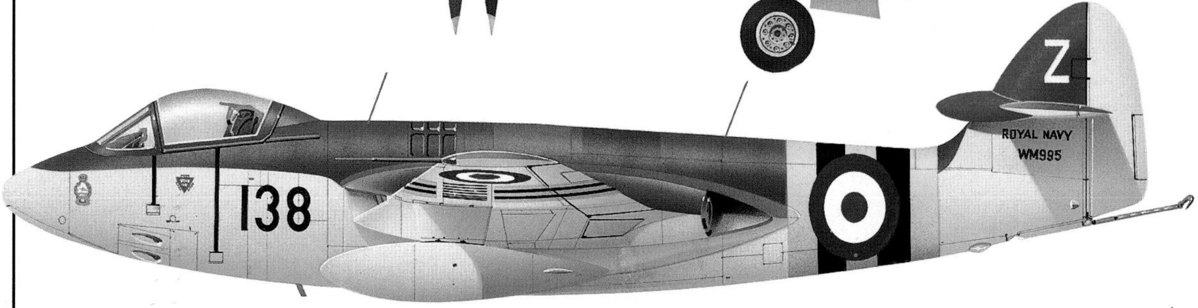

Hawker Sea Hawk FB.Mk 3
This Sea Hawk FB.Mk 3 flew from the HMS *Albion* with No. 802 Squadron. Other squadrons at Suez flew newer FGA.Mk 6s, but there was little real difference between the sub-variants, and all proved highly successful.

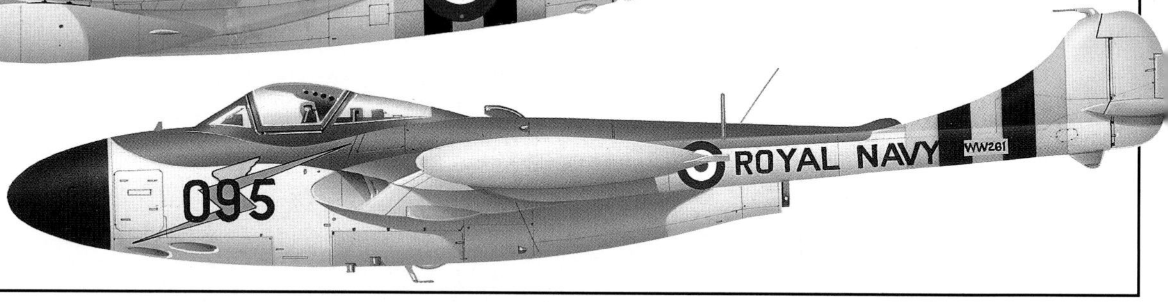

de Havilland Sea Venom FAW.Mk 21
The Fleet Air Arm deployed one squadron of Sea Venoms aboard each of its carriers at Suez, intending that they would provide air-defence cover for the fighter-bombers. In the event, they performed similar missions.

Above: French carrier Arromanches _included a detachment of TBM-3S and TBM-3W Avengers, operating in the ASW and AEW roles. The two French carriers at Suez were smaller than the British ships, with smaller, older air groups._

Tarek. These ships were forced to retire beneath a smoke-screen when the aircraft turned on them. The attacks continued on 4 and 5 November as British carrier-based aircraft hit airfields outside Alexandria in a further attempt to divert Egyptian attention away from the intended invasion of Port Said and Port Fuad. Another Canberra was damaged by a MiG near Luxor on 3 November, but Egyptian ground defences put up a more effective resistance, bringing down a Wyvern over Port Said, and a Hellcat and a Mystère over Cairo on 3 November.

The British and French air offensive against the EAF enabled the Israelis to unleash a full-scale armoured assault. It also led the Egyptians to withdraw from Sinai; they had crossed the Canal on 2 November.

Although there was only rear-guard skirmishing on the ground, the IAF and surviving units fought a bitter fight above it. Vampires from El Arish withdrew to Bir Gifgafa and Bir Rod Salim. They attacked Israeli paratroops at Mitla later in the morning of 1 November, losing one aircraft to IAF interception. Despite British and French air raids three Meteor NF.Mk 13s with an escort of MiGs appeared over Sinai in the afternoon. One MiG was downed by two IAF Mystères.

Down at Sharm el Sheikh a major battle developed from 2 November. Paratroops and their heavy equipment were dropped at El Tor on the western shore of the peninsula while other units advanced down the eastern side. The IAF, meanwhile, bombed the British frigate HMS *Crane* which, blockading Sharm, was mistaken for an Egyptian ship. On 3 November Mustangs and B-17s destroyed two of the heavy guns overlooking the Straits of Tiran at Ras Nasrani. The rest were destroyed on the night of 3/4 November by their gunners, who then retired into Sharm el Sheikh which, with its harbour and airstrip, could hope to hold out longer. Israeli troops reached Sharm from Ras Nasrani at 14.00 on 4 November. A night attack failed but a second assault backed up by Mustangs dropping napalm broke the Egyptian perimeter. Upon the arrival of Israeli paras from El Tor the garrison surrendered at 09.30 on 5 November.

Left: A Sea Venom launches from the crowded deck of HMS Albion_, the catapult strop falling away into the sea. Sea Venoms provided fighter cover for the first wave of RAF bombers, Cyprus-based Hunters lacking the range._

By now the British and French assaults had begun. At dawn on 5 November, carrier-based aircraft attacked Egyptian defensive positions and at 08.20 British paratroops hit Gamil airfield on the outskirts of Port Said. Fifteen minutes later the French dropped just south of Port Fuad. A planned British helicopter-borne raid against Canal bridges was abandoned, but further para drops reinforced the invaders. At dawn the next day, seaborne landings supported by naval bombardment and close air-support seized the waterfront. Two Sea Hawks and a Venom were lost to ground fire, and in the subsequent street fighting air supremacy meant little. It was, however, able to cover a dash down the Suez Canal in the small hours of 7 November. This reached El Kap before the ceasefire which the British and French governments had finally accepted under both domestic and international pressure. This was exerted chiefly by the US government, which had underestimated Soviet influence throughout the Middle East.

The British and French claimed to have destroyed or damaged 260 aircraft, including 207 combat jets. The EAF, however, claimed that only eight MiG-15s, seven Il-28s, nine Harvards, six C-46s, four C-47s, three civil Dakotas and a grounded Avro Lancaster were destroyed, with another 62 aircraft damaged. The Ilyushins were among those in the supposed haven of Luxor which were hit by French F-84Fs fitted with extra tanks and based in southern Israel. About 10 MiG-15s and MiG-15UTIs of the Syrian training mission were also destroyed at Abu Sueir.

Above: France's carrier-based fighter/fighter-bomber squadrons still used the veteran F4U-7 Corsair. Flottille 14F was deployed aboard the Arromanches, while 15F flew from the La Fayette.

Losses

In Sinai the EAF lost four MiGs, four Vampires, a Meteor and the Mraz Sokol. The IAF admitted the loss of one Mystère, two Ouragans, 10 Mustangs (some of which were later repaired) and two Piper Cubs. Another five damaged aircraft are believed to have crashed on their way home. The French lost only one aircraft (one of the Lydda-based F-84s), and the British four (a Canberra which crashed on landing, two Sea Hawks, a Wyvern) plus a Canberra PR.Mk 7 shot down over the Syrian-Lebanese border.

Both politically and militarily the entire Suez operation was a fruitless venture. The disarray created in the Western Bloc merely served to commit Egypt (and therefore Arab influence in the Middle East) more firmly than ever to the Soviet Union, and effectively destroyed all Western credibility in the Middle East for two decades.

Above: This Sea Venom of No. 893 Squadron made a successful wheels-up landing aboard the **Eagle** *after being damaged by flak. The aircraft was soon repaired and flying operational missions.*

Right: Sea Hawk FGA.Mk 6s are re-armed and refuelled aboard the **Albion**. *The furthest aircraft has part-finished Suez stripes, while the nearer machine still has no recognition stripes at all.*

AEW for the Task Force

The British carriers *Eagle* and *Albion*, and the two French carriers, embarked dedicated AEW aircraft. With the Egyptian air force hardly showing itself, the possibility of attacks on the carriers became increasingly remote, and the British Skyraiders and French Avengers found themselves with little to do.

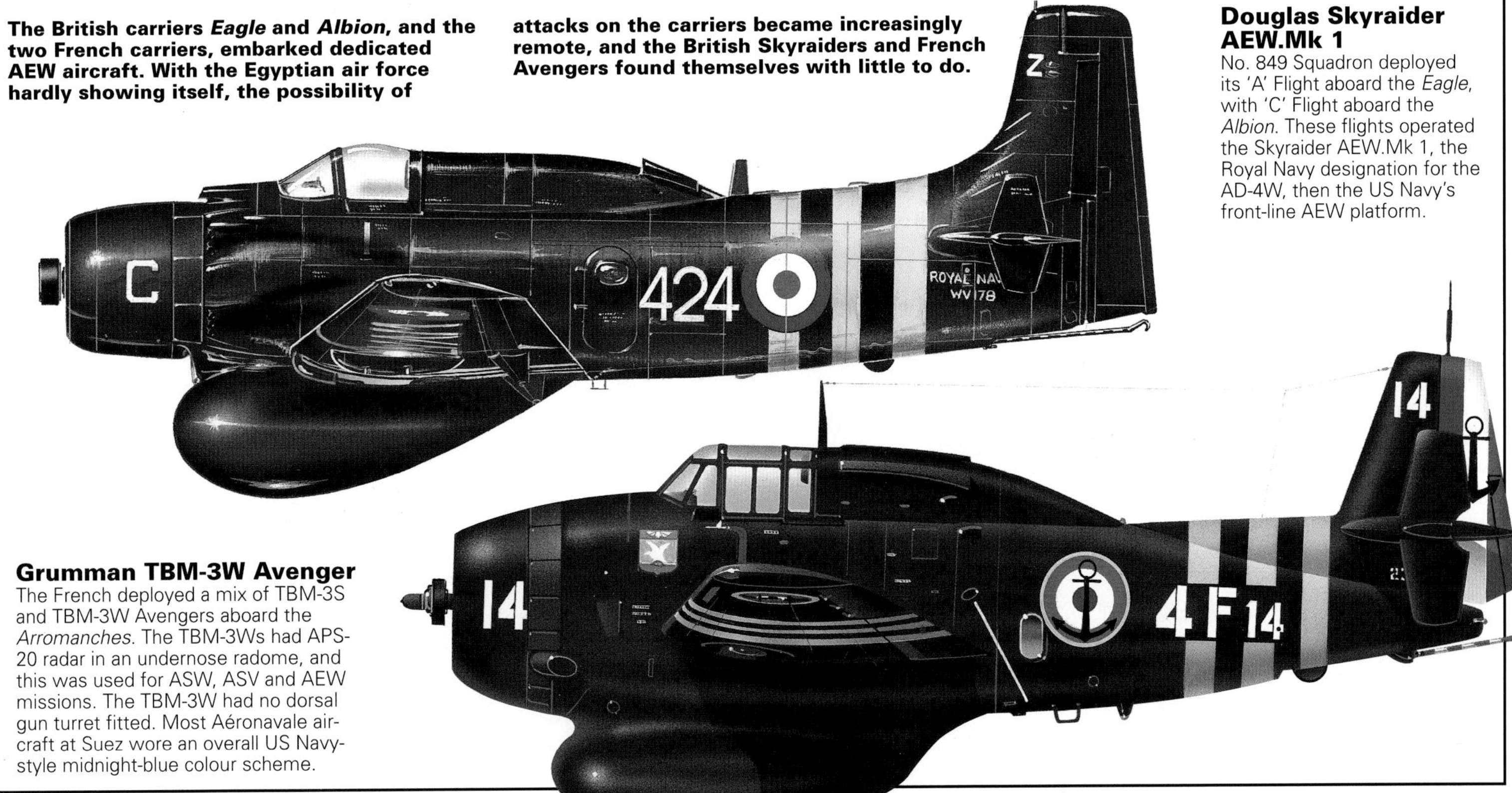

Douglas Skyraider AEW.Mk 1

No. 849 Squadron deployed its 'A' Flight aboard the *Eagle*, with 'C' Flight aboard the *Albion*. These flights operated the Skyraider AEW.Mk 1, the Royal Navy designation for the AD-4W, then the US Navy's front-line AEW platform.

Grumman TBM-3W Avenger

The French deployed a mix of TBM-3S and TBM-3W Avengers aboard the *Arromanches*. The TBM-3Ws had APS-20 radar in an undernose radome, and this was used for ASW, ASV and AEW missions. The TBM-3W had no dorsal gun turret fitted. Most Aéronavale aircraft at Suez wore an overall US Navy-style midnight-blue colour scheme.

Britain in the Middle East

1945–1975

Left: De Havilland Vampires of No. 213 Squadron on patrol over the Canal Zone, where the squadron was based until its disbandment in September 1954. Britain started to withdraw from Egypt in 1952, in the face of growing hostility.

Below: The Avro Shackletons of No. 37 Squadron flew patrols from Luqa, Malta and then, from 1957, from Khormaksar, Aden.

Left: These Royal Marine Commandos are ready to start a patrol after deplaning from a Royal Navy Wessex HAS.Mk 3. The type was hastily pressed into service as a transport helicopter during operations in the Radfan.

During World War II the RAF's Desert Air Force played a crucial role in the defeat of Rommel's Afrika Korps, and then supported the Eighth Army in its drive through Italy. After the war, RAF units returned to the area and resumed the kind of colonial policing roles they had undertaken between the wars.

The first problem faced by the British in the Middle East, following the end of the war, was the deteriorating situation in Palestine, which Britain had administered under a League of Nations Mandate since the 1920s. Massive illegal immigration by displaced Jews, along with terrorism by Jewish extremists, had to be countered until the end of the Mandate in May 1948, when Britain withdrew and the Jews and Arabs went to war, each unhappy with the partition which divided Palestine into separate Jewish and Arab states. The RAF (with massive forces stationed in the Canal Zone in neighbouring Egypt) became involved in this war by accident, when four unarmed Spitfires flying a tactical reconnaissance mission along Egypt's ill-defined border were shot down by Israeli Spitfires and ground fire. The following day a Tempest involved in the search-and-rescue operation was

Jet-powered colonial policing

During the British withdrawal from their Empire, extensive use was made of air power for demonstrating a British presence, for controlling insurgent and resistance groups, and for retaliating against attacks. Fighter-bombers, from Tempests and Hornets through Vampires, Venoms and Hunters, provided cost-effective firepower for such missions.

Gloster Meteor FR.Mk 9

The Meteor FR.Mk 9 was operated by No. 208 Squadron between 1951 and 1958, from bases in the Canal Zone, Malta and Cyprus. The squadron provided armed reconnaissance support throughout the Middle East. The aircraft retained four 20-mm (0.8-in) cannon, and had provision for underwing rockets, together with its nose-mounted cameras.

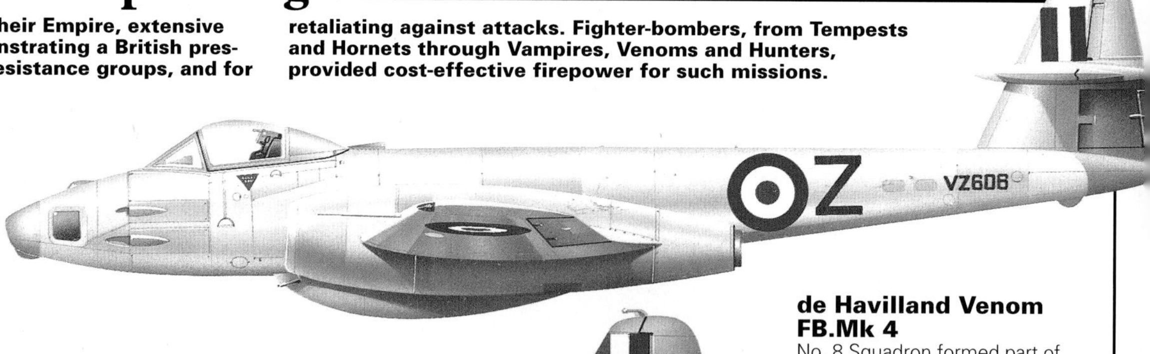

de Havilland Venom FB.Mk 4

No. 8 Squadron formed part of the British garrison in Aden from the end of the war until withdrawal in 1967. Its main role was preventing incursions by insurgents from the neighbouring Yemen. Venoms served from 1955 until 1960.

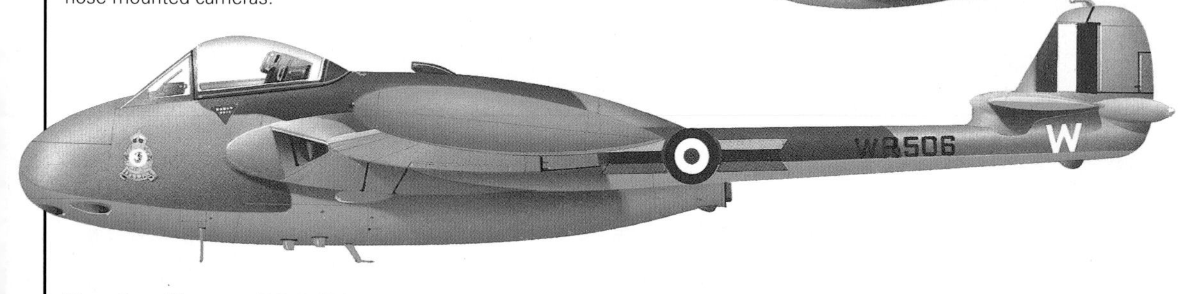

Hawker Hunter FGA.Mk 9

The Hunter FGA.Mk 9 was specifically designed as a Venom replacement for tropical use. As such, it had a braking parachute, provision for 1045-litre (230-Imp gal) underwing drop tanks and a more powerful 'big bore' Avon engine. No. 8 Squadron was the first operator of the FGA.Mk 9, using the aircraft on operations against Yemeni insurgents in Aden.

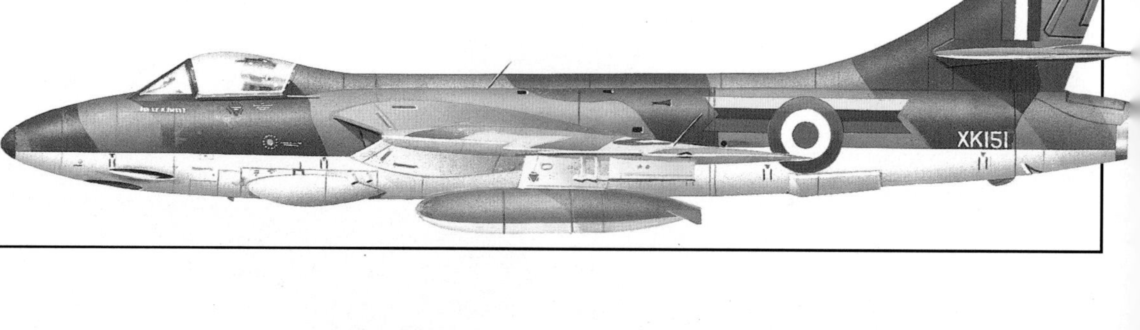

Transport support

RAF operations in what Britain referred to as the Near and Middle East required massive logistic support, and transport aircraft were permanently based in-theatre. They were frequently augmented by UK-based transport aircraft for specific operations, including the Anglo-French Suez operation in 1956 and the Kuwait operation of 1961. NEAF and MEAF transport bases provided useful stopovers for RAF aircraft en route to the Far East.

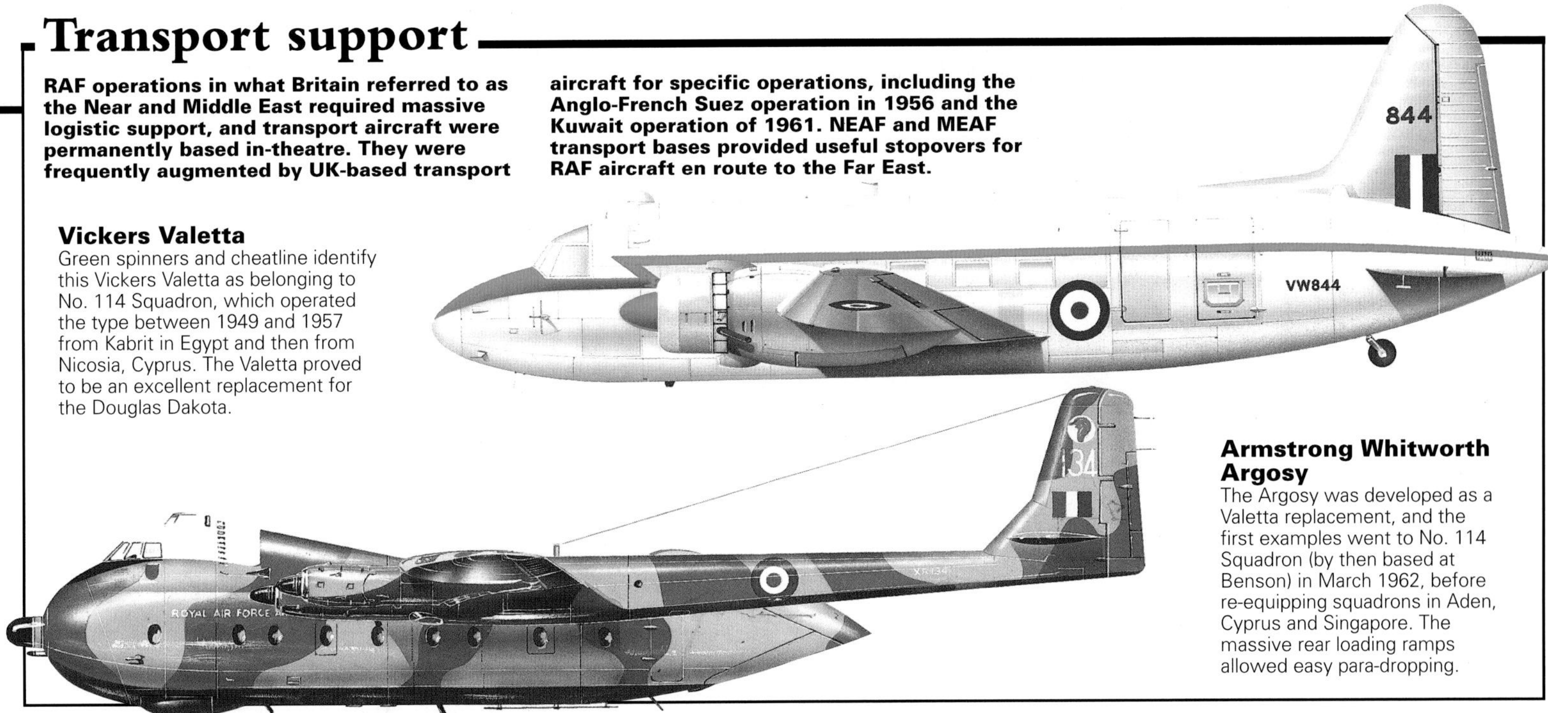

Vickers Valetta
Green spinners and cheatline identify this Vickers Valetta as belonging to No. 114 Squadron, which operated the type between 1949 and 1957 from Kabrit in Egypt and then from Nicosia, Cyprus. The Valetta proved to be an excellent replacement for the Douglas Dakota.

Armstrong Whitworth Argosy
The Argosy was developed as a Valetta replacement, and the first examples went to No. 114 Squadron (by then based at Benson) in March 1962, before re-equipping squadrons in Aden, Cyprus and Singapore. The massive rear loading ramps allowed easy para-dropping.

Above: The Scottish Aviation Twin Pioneer was a dedicated STOL transport, which needed a landing strip only 275-m (900-ft) long. Users included one squadron in Aden and two in Bahrain.

also shot down. Fortunately, only one pilot was killed.

Long-standing links

Britain already had links with the Sultanate of Oman going back more than 150 years, when it signed a new friendship treaty in December 1951. Oman called for help in late-1952, when a group of Saudis occupied an important strategic village at an oasis on the Omani-Abu Dhabi border. The RAF flew intimidatory low-level sorties over the area, then policed a blockade of routes to the oasis, eventually supporting Omani troops who moved in to expel the Saudis in July 1954. Although this problem was solved without a shot being fired, the Saudi-supported Omani Liberation Army (formed by the Imam Ghalib from rebellious tribesmen) proved a tougher nut to crack. The Imam was captured when British troops attacked his stronghold at Nizwa, but his brother Talib escaped and continued the rebellion. In 1957 rebel strongholds were attacked by Venoms from Nos 8 and 249 Squadrons (after Shackletons had dropped warning leaflets) and in January 1959 supported an SAS assault on the Jebel Akhdar. Unfortunately, Talib escaped, but the rebellion was over.

The Canal Zone initially provided a safe home for British reserves which could be deployed elsewhere in the area as required, but, as opposition to the British presence intensified, the position of the Canal Zone bases became steadily more untenable. Units moved to bases in Cyprus, Jordan and Iraq. MEAF reformed in Cyprus in December 1954, and the last flying unit left Egypt in October 1955. The Arab nationalism which prompted this withdrawal was later to force withdrawals from Iraq and Jordan, and eventually resulted in the Anglo-French invasion in 1956 – the Suez crisis.

Problems in Cyprus

Although Cyprus replaced the Canal Zone as Britain's main base in the area, it proved just as troublesome. A Crown Colony since 1925, Cyprus had a Greek majority who wished for union with Greece (Enosis), against the wishes of the substantial Turkish minority. From April 1955 to February 1959, Britain was forced to fight a vigorous anti-terrorist campaign against EOKA terrorists using Shackletons to prevent arms shipments from the mainland, Austers, Pioneers and Chipmunks for reconnaissance, and helicopters (principally Sycamores) in search-and-destroy missions.

Growing opposition to the British presence in Iraq led to a 1955 agreement to withdraw and hand over the RAF stations at Habbaniyah and Shaibah, retaining facilities at the former as a staging post. Withdrawal of based aircraft was completed in April 1956, but when RAF aircraft were prevented from using Habbaniyah following

Below: No. 26 Squadron in Aden used the Bristol Belvedere from 1963 to 1965, operating in support of Army operations in the Radfan.

Right: Blackburn Beverleys from No. 84 Sqn from Khormaksar and from squadrons based in England flew men into Kuwait in 1961 to deter an attack by Iraq. The Beverley enjoyed superb STOL performance.

Above: The Bristol Sycamore was the first British-designed helicopter in service. No. 284 Sqn's Sycamores played a major role in the war against EOKA terrorists in Cyprus.

Right: An Army Bell Sioux hovers behind a Saladin armoured car. The co-operative use of aircraft and armoured cars was pioneered in the Middle East by the RAF from 1918.

Above: De Havilland Vampire F.Mk 3s of No. 601 ('County of London') Squadron, a Royal Auxiliary Air Force squadron, are seen at an annual armament practice camp at Hal Far, Malta.

Right: A pair of English Electric Lightnings of No. 56 Squadron takes off from its Akrotiri base. Lightnings took over the fighter defence of NEAF in 1967, and finally withdrew in 1976, with the withdrawal of British forces.

the July 1958 coup and assasination of the pro-British king, remaining personnel were withdrawn.

A similar situation arose in Jordan, where the ill-considered Suez operation forced the king to rescind the 1948 treaty with Britain. The single fighter-bomber squadron at Amman withdrew to Cyprus in January 1957. The breakdown in relations with Jordan was short-lived and British forces returned briefly in July 1958, when growing instability in neighbouring Lebanon threatened the stability of the Hashemite kingdom itself.

Relations with Iraq remained strained. In 1961 matters worsened, when Iraq appeared to challenge the independence of Kuwait, with whom Britain had a longstanding (since 1899) treaty relationship. Britain (by now a major customer for Kuwaiti oil) renewed its pledge to defend the country's independence in June 1961, prompting an angry Iraq to move troops to the Kuwaiti border. Kuwait formally requested British assistance on 30 June, and Britain flew No. 45 Commando, Royal Marines, and the Hunters of Nos 8 and 208 Squadrons into Kuwait, where they were later reinforced by a parachute battalion and by Canberras from Cyprus and Germany. An Iraqi invasion was deterred, and Britain was able to withdraw its forces.

Reorganisation

With the changing centre of gravity of British forces in the area, the former Middle East Command was renamed Near East Command in March 1961, with its air element becoming the Near East Air Force instead of the Middle East Air Force. Both were headquartered in Cyprus, which steadily gained in importance as forces elsewhere withdrew (most notably in Aden and the Persian Gulf).

A coup and change of regime in the Yemen led to an increase in the campaign of propaganda and incursion mounted against the British in Aden, which had gained in impor-

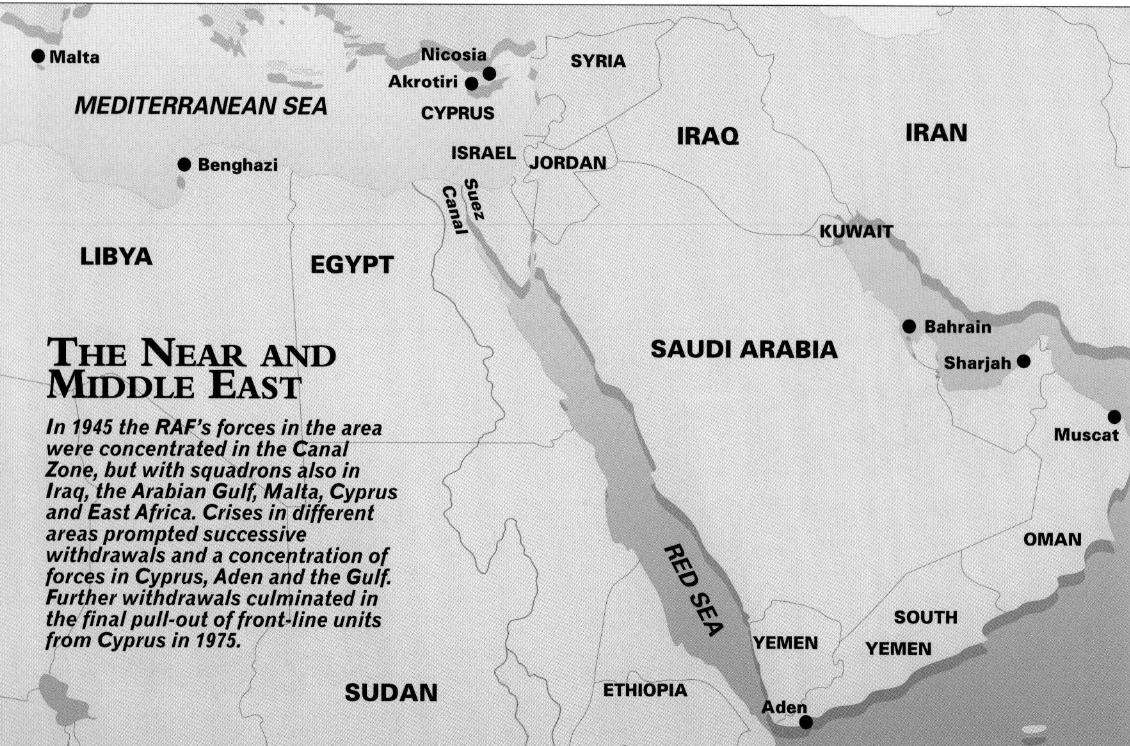

The Near and Middle East

In 1945 the RAF's forces in the area were concentrated in the Canal Zone, but with squadrons also in Iraq, the Arabian Gulf, Malta, Cyprus and East Africa. Crises in different areas prompted successive withdrawals and a concentration of forces in Cyprus, Aden and the Gulf. Further withdrawals culminated in the final pull-out of front-line units from Cyprus in 1975.

British air power on Cyprus

Cyprus fulfilled vital functions for the RAF, serving as a base for aircraft and units operating on NATO's vulnerable southern flank (usually assigned to CENTO), frustrating Russian ambitions and operations in the region. Units and aircraft in Cyprus also operated in support of British forces in the Middle East and the Gulf, supporting national interests as Britain withdrew from its Empire.

English Electric Canberra B.Mk 2
Four squadrons of English Electric Canberras formed the Akrotiri Strike Wing from 1957, replacing de Havilland Venoms. This B.Mk 2 served with No. 249 Squadron. B.Mk 2s gave way to B.Mk 6s in 1959, then B.Mk 15s and 16s from 1962. The Canberras were replaced by Vulcans in 1969.

Westland Scout AH.Mk 1
The Army Air Corps served throughout the Middle East from its formation in September 1957, with fixed-wing Austers and a variety of helicopters, including the Saro Skeeter, the Bell Sioux, and the Sud Alouette II. This Scout wears United Nations markings, signifying use by a squadron assigned to UN support duties in Cyprus.

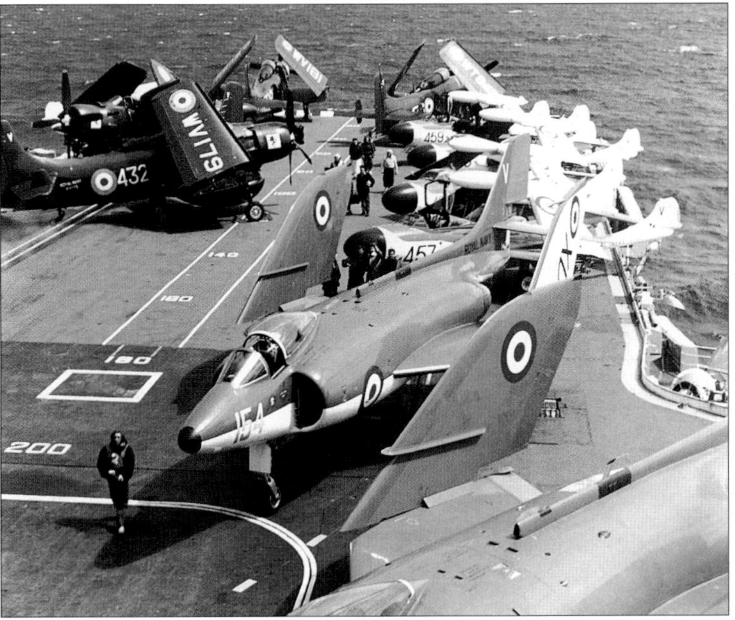

***Left: Carrier-based air power played a crucial role in augmenting RAF aircraft based in-theatre, and in reinforcing local-based forces during operations. Here Vickers Supermarine Scimitars, de Havilland Sea Venoms and Skyraiders are ranged on the deck of the HMS* Victorious.**

Right: Following Turkey's invasion of northern Cyprus, No. 84 Squadron's Westland Whirlwinds supported UN forces stationed between the Greek and Turkish front lines. The unit re-equipped with Wessexes in 1981.

tance as the home for a strategic reserve covering East Africa, the Horn of Africa and the western part of Arabia, but from which Britain had announced its intention to withdraw by 1968. The Yemeni campaign against Aden was two-pronged, with support for subversion and terrorism in Aden itself, and with similar support for dissident tribesmen who undertook their traditional activities of raiding caravans in the north of Aden, the Radfan. Successive operations (commencing in January 1964, with 'Nutcracker') by fighter-bombers and heliborne troops, and artillery eventually resulted in the capture of the last rebel point, the Jebel Huriyah, on 10 June 1964.

It was less easy to solve the problem of terrorism in the city of Aden, and difficult even to contain it. Helicopters were used to transport troops rapidly to deal with incidents, while Twin Pioneers performed reconnaissance and leaflet dropping missions. With little reason to remain, and in the face of worsening opposition, the British pulled out in late-1967, with some units relocating to the Gulf.

Withdrawal

After the ignominious withdrawal from Aden, the departure of RAF units from the Gulf was altogether more dignified. With the Gulf States able to take over the burden of their own defence (having been trained to do so by the British) the RAF was able to withdraw its two Hunter squadrons from Muharraq, and its Andovers and Wessexes from Sharjah during 1971. The two airfields closed as RAF bases in December.

The Turkish invasion of northern Cyprus brought based aircraft to a high state of readiness, but Turkish fighters and fighter-bombers avoided threatening the British Sovereign Base areas and the RAF remained on the sidelines. The invasion made training difficult for based units, and a government decision to end the declaration of forces to CENTO led to a mass withdrawal of the remaining units. NEAF was disbanded and replaced by an AHQ Cyprus within RAF Strike Command.

Mid-1976 saw only a single RAF squadron permanently based in the area, No. 84 Sqn, whose Whirlwinds performed search and rescue and UN support missions in Cyprus. An Army Air Corps flight with Alouette IIs also flew similar missions after the main withdrawal.

Closer to home, the RAF withdrew from its other Mediterranean base, RAF Luqa on the island of Malta. No. 203 Squadron disbanded in December 1977, its Nimrods returning to UK-based squadrons. No. 13 Squadron brought its Canberra PR.Mk 7s to RAF Wyton the following year, and the RAF withdrawal was completed in 1979. On Cyprus the RAF maintained its massive base at Akrotiri, which was used regularly as a destination for training flights and for armament practice camps by front-line fighter squadrons.

Right: Avro Vulcan B.Mk 2s of Nos 9 and 35 Squadrons replaced four Canberra bomber squadrons as NEAF's strike-attack element in 1969, serving until 1975. Two more Vulcan squadrons were declared to CENTO, but remained at UK bases.

The Six-Day War

JUNE 1967

Above: A Mirage IIICJ of No. 119 Squadron gets airborne from its base at Egron. The unit's distinctive battle insignia and red tail chevron were subsequently worn by F-4E Phantoms.

Antagonism in the Middle East region had blazed into full-scale war in the late-1940s and in 1956. Tension had been rising since early-April 1967 with clashes over Syria's Golan Heights. It was heightened further by the UN's decision to withdraw its peacekeeping forces from the Egypt/Israel border on 17 May 1967. This encouraged Egypt to close the Gulf of Aqaba to Israeli shipping.

At the end of May a renewed Egyptian-Syrian-Jordanian defence agreement was signed and led to the formation of the United Arab Republic Air Force. This was equipped with the latest Soviet combat aircraft – MiG-19 and -21 fighters, Su-7 ground-attack aircraft, and Il-28 and Tu-16 bombers. The main problems suffered by the Arab air force were the poor serviceability of its aircraft (20 per cent were non-operational), and the chronic shortage of qualified aircrew. Only 125 of its approximately 500 pilots could fly MiG-21s or MiG-19s, and there was no reserve pool of pilots.

PRE-EMPTIVE STRIKE

Egyptian Air Marshal Sidki and his military staff feared a pre-emptive Israeli attack in early June, and ordered an advanced state of alert. President Nasser, however, was convinced that there would be no war. He over-ruled them, and the Arab forces relaxed their posture.

Shortly after dawn on 5 June, 40 Israeli Mirage IIICJs and Super Mystères flew west, followed by two more waves, 120 in all. As usual, the Israeli aircraft dipped below the search height of Egyptian radars. Since they had been doing this regularly on training exercises, no action was taken and the Egyptian dawn fighter patrols were stood down. However, this time, the Israeli fighters turned south to cross the Egyptian coast, undetected.

At 08.45 (Cairo time), when UARAF dawn patrols had landed and most senior officers were between home and office, the airfields at El Arish, Bir Gifgafa, Cairo West, Jebel Libni, Bir Thamada, Abu Sueir, Kabrit, Beni Sueif, Inchas and, a minute or so later, Fayid, were all struck. Ten flights, each of four aircraft, made one bombing and several strafing passes, followed at 10-minute intervals by the second and third waves. An exceptionally efficient turnaround time back in Israel meant that eight waves attacked for 80 minutes. A 10-minute lull was then followed by a further 80-minute blitz. Only 12 IAF aircraft were held back to defend Israeli skies during this assault. Sixty Magister trainers, converted for ground attack, were meanwhile committed to support the Israeli army and took no part in these raids.

During this three-hour assault over 300 UARAF aircraft were destroyed or damaged, mostly on the ground. The big Tu-16

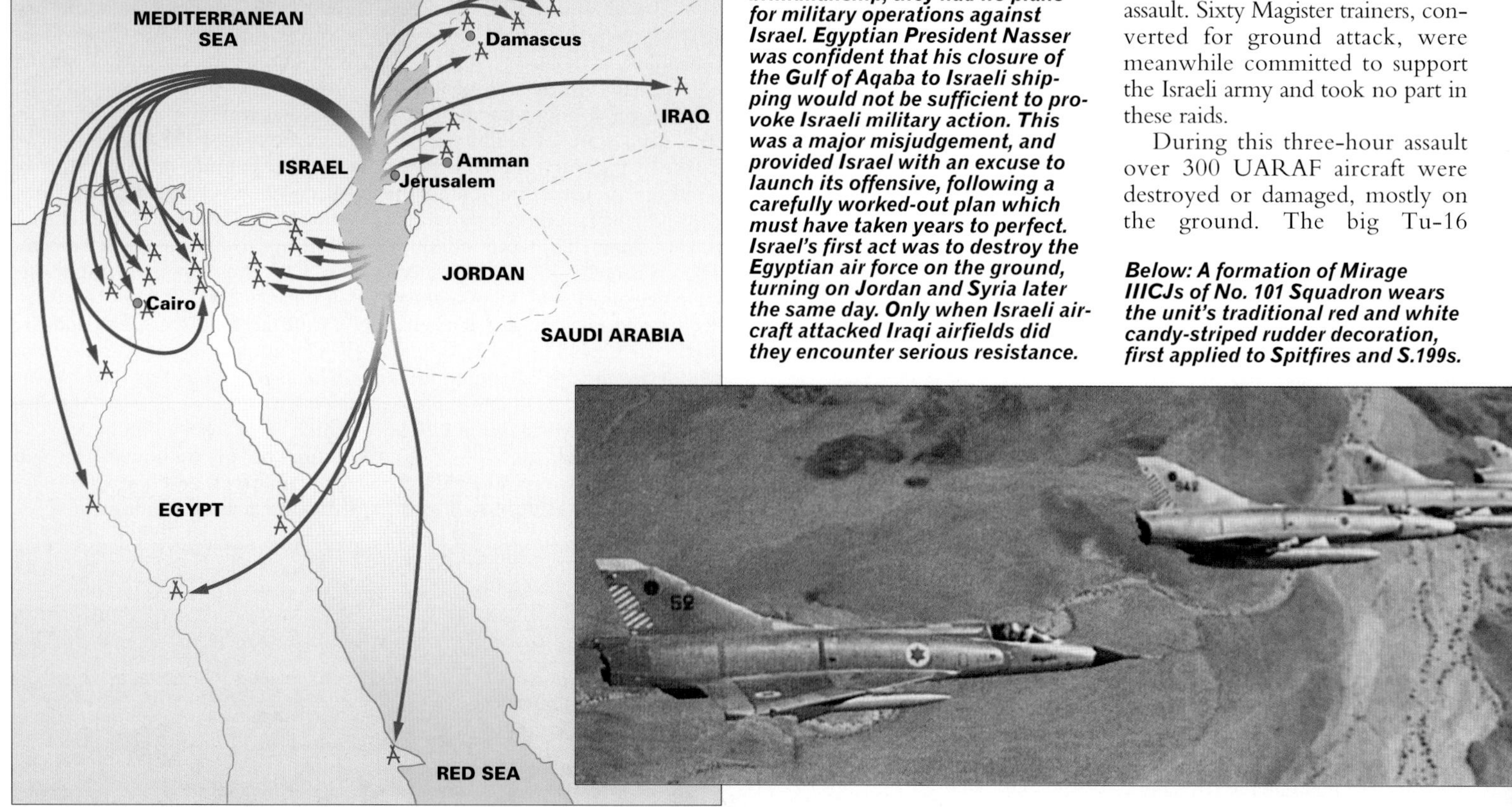

Left: Israel's strikes were claimed as being pre-emptive, but, although the Arabs were engaging in brinkmanship, they had no plans for military operations against Israel. Egyptian President Nasser was confident that his closure of the Gulf of Aqaba to Israeli shipping would not be sufficient to provoke Israeli military action. This was a major misjudgement, and provided Israel with an excuse to launch its offensive, following a carefully worked-out plan which must have taken years to perfect. Israel's first act was to destroy the Egyptian air force on the ground, turning on Jordan and Syria later the same day. Only when Israeli aircraft attacked Iraqi airfields did they encounter serious resistance.

Below: A formation of Mirage IIICJs of No. 101 Squadron wears the unit's traditional red and white candy-striped rudder decoration, first applied to Spitfires and S.199s.

bombers were considered vital targets by the IAF, because of their ability to fire large stand-off air-to-ground missiles capable of reaching Israeli towns and cities. The entire force of two squadrons of Tu-16s was destroyed. Israeli losses for these raids were 19 aircraft.

In the air, the UARAF lost four unarmed trainers near Imbaba – the first casualties of the war – and one MiG-21 as it took off from Abu Sueir. Another MiG-21 was destroyed as it attempted to land on the cratered runway after driving off four IAF Super Mystères. Three surviving MiG-21s lifted off from Inchas at 08.56 in the minutes between Israeli assaults. Ground control had collapsed, but over Cairo West they shot down an Ouragan which crashed, perhaps intentionally, into a parked Tu-16. At Abu Sueir another MiG-21 managed to take off at 10.01 and brought down a Mystère just beyond the airfield perimeter. The last two serviceable MiG-21s were then destroyed as they tried to get into the air minutes later, both hit by the same Mirage III.

The MiG-19s and -21s at Herghada flew north to help, but were jumped by 16 Mirages as they tried to land at Abu Sueir at 10.30. Four went down at once but in the dogfight that followed neither side scored additional victories. Nevertheless, all the MiGs were destroyed, either in wheels-up landings alongside shattered runways or when they ran out of fuel. The only airfield whose runways were not damaged was El Arish. Here the IAF relied on cannon-fire and a guided bomb similar to the American Bullpup to pick off parked aircraft. Only one Egyptian aircraft now remained in the air: the Ilyushin Il-14 transport carrying Air Marshal Sidki and most of the Egyptian high command had been flying over the battle zone since before the attack began. By keeping the enemy's top brass in this 'limbo', alive but out of action, the Israelis virtually paralysed Egypt's capacity to respond.

Right: Israel received 72 Mirage IIICJs and five two-seat IIIBJs, which formed the backbone of the IDF/AFs fighter force in 1967, equipping five or six squadrons. They had simplified avionics.

Below: A bombed-up Dassault Mystère IVA awaits its pilot before the first wave of attacks on Egyptian airfields. Three Mystère IVA squadrons, and one Super Mystère unit, flew the vital attack missions.

THE EASTERN FRONT

Within hours, Israel's other Arab neighbours had entered the fray in response to the attack on Egypt. Jordanian long-range artillery cratered at least one runway at Ramat David during the morning. The Israelis had, however, already moved against Jerusalem by the time the Royal Jordanian Air Force (RJAF) made its first move, an airstrike on Natanya and Kfar Sirkin by 16 Hunters.

At 14.30 (Tel Aviv time) the IAF turned its attention from the UARAF to the RJAF, attacking Mafraq and Amman air-bases and a strategic radar site at Ajlun. All but one of Jordan's 18 Hunter fighters were destroyed on the ground for the loss of one Israeli aircraft. The remaining Hunter was also damaged and two aircrew were killed, so King Hussein told his surviving Hunter pilots to place themselves under IrAF command at the Iraqi air base of H-3. Other Jordanian targets attacked by the IAF on this first day of the war included Iraqi and Palestinian units moving westwards from Mafraq, defensive positions around Jerusalem, the Jordanian HQ at Jericho, a relief column east of the Mount of Olives and the royal palace in Amman.

The SAF was also on the IAF's target list for 5 June. At 11.45 (Tel Aviv time) 12 SAF MiG-21s bombed the Haifa oil refinery and strafed Mahanayim airfield. Just over an hour later came the IAF's massive response, with strikes on the SAF bases at Damascus followed by others on Marj Rial, Dumayr

Israel strikes first

The Israeli first wave consisted of only 40 aircraft: 10 sections of four Mirages or Super Mystères which flew out over the Mediterranean, as if undertaking normal training, before swinging south to attack their targets. Once the element of surprise was lost the IDF/AF mounted an all-out offensive, rapidly turning around its attack aircraft to shuttle them back and forth to their targets.

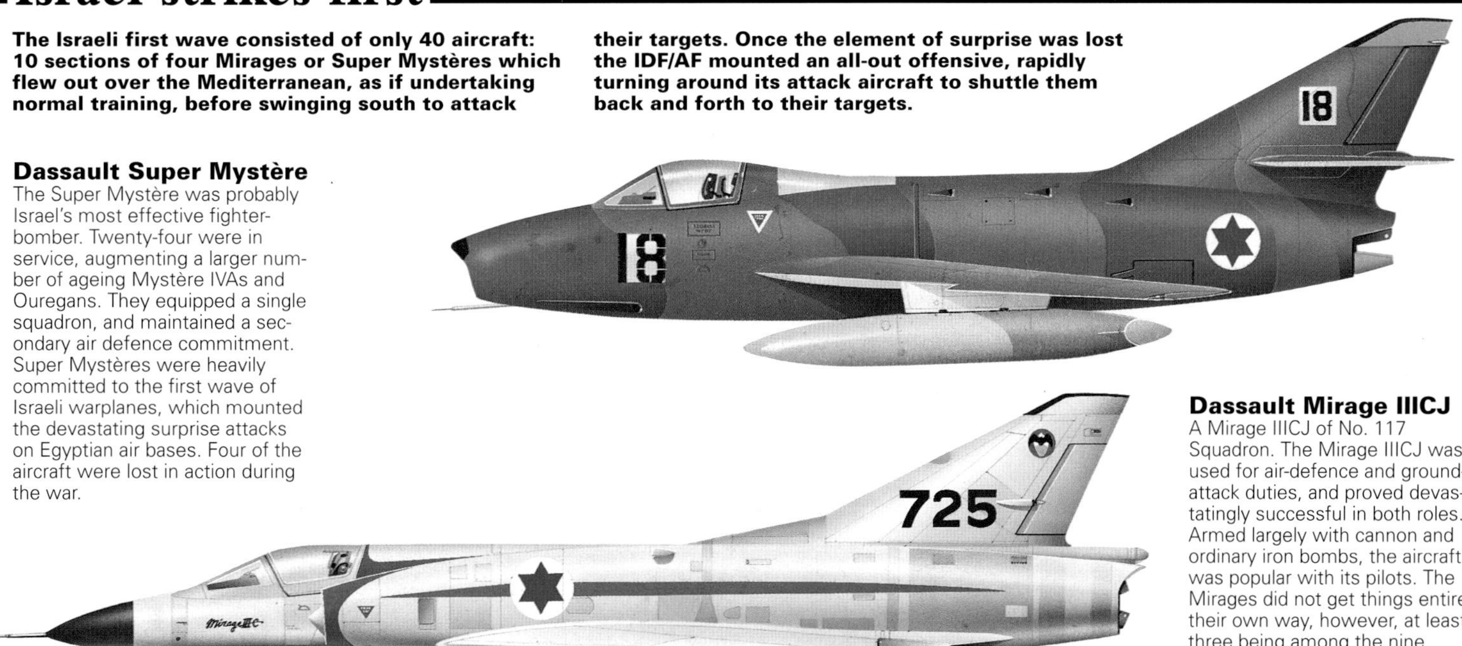

Dassault Super Mystère
The Super Mystère was probably Israel's most effective fighter-bomber. Twenty-four were in service, augmenting a larger number of ageing Mystère IVAs and Ouregans. They equipped a single squadron, and maintained a secondary air defence commitment. Super Mystères were heavily committed to the first wave of Israeli warplanes, which mounted the devastating surprise attacks on Egyptian air bases. Four of the aircraft were lost in action during the war.

Dassault Mirage IIICJ
A Mirage IIICJ of No. 117 Squadron. The Mirage IIICJ was used for air-defence and ground-attack duties, and proved devastatingly successful in both roles. Armed largely with cannon and ordinary iron bombs, the aircraft was popular with its pilots. The Mirages did not get things entirely their own way, however, at least three being among the nine aircraft downed by Hawker Hunters during the attack on Iraq's H-3 aerodrome.

Arab MiGs

The Arab air forces mainly used aircraft of Soviet origin, although the Jordanian and Lebanese air forces used only Western equipment, and Iraq's strength included three squadrons of British Hawker Hunters. Few Arab fighters survived the Israeli airfield attacks, and the handful which ventured into the air never seriously challenged Israeli air superiority.

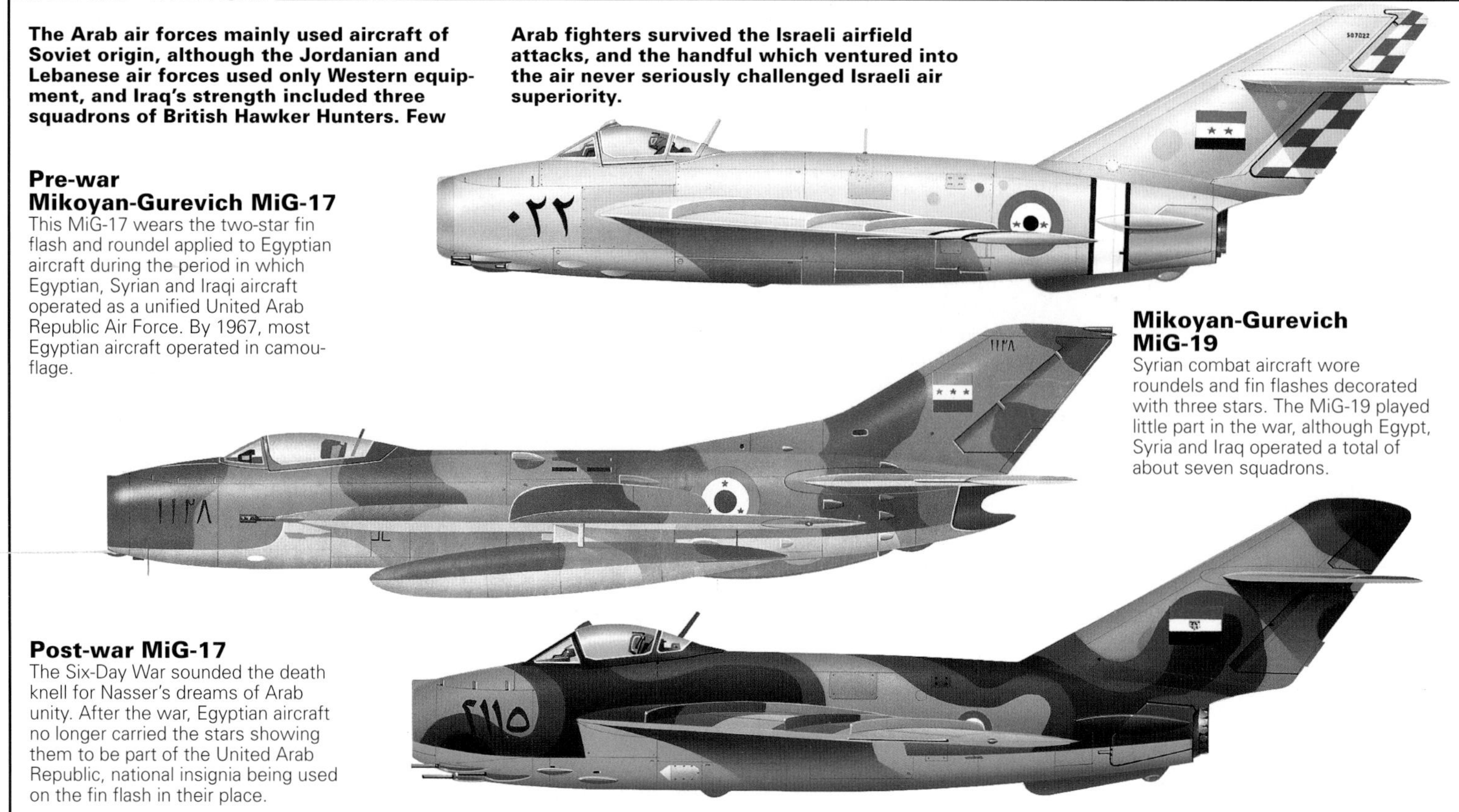

Pre-war Mikoyan-Gurevich MiG-17
This MiG-17 wears the two-star fin flash and roundel applied to Egyptian aircraft during the period in which Egyptian, Syrian and Iraqi aircraft operated as a unified United Arab Republic Air Force. By 1967, most Egyptian aircraft operated in camouflage.

Mikoyan-Gurevich MiG-19
Syrian combat aircraft wore roundels and fin flashes decorated with three stars. The MiG-19 played little part in the war, although Egypt, Syria and Iraq operated a total of about seven squadrons.

Post-war MiG-17
The Six-Day War sounded the death knell for Nasser's dreams of Arab unity. After the war, Egyptian aircraft no longer carried the stars showing them to be part of the United Arab Republic, national insignia being used on the fin flash in their place.

Left: Egypt's Il-28 light bombers played little part in the conflict. Twenty-seven were destroyed in their revetments, and the rest remained on the ground for most of the brief conflict.

and Seikal. The more distant airfield at T-4 was not struck until mid-afternoon, shortly after three Israeli aircraft had also attacked the Iraqi base at H-3. Although the SAF was not as badly damaged as the UARAF or RJAF, it did lose two-thirds of its front-line strength.

During the afternoon the IAF returned to Egypt, ranging farther afield to hit Mansura, Cairo International, Helwan, Al Minya, Bilbeis, Herghada, Luxor and Ras Banas airfields in the deep south and 23 radar sites.

Days two and three

The second day, 6 June, saw the IAF put most of its effort into supporting the Israeli army in Sinai and on the West Bank. A strike against artillery positions west of Rafah had already enabled the Israelis to successfully break through the main Egyptian defences. That night, a helicopter-borne commando attack using S-58s was made behind Jordanian lines east of Jerusalem. Another helicopter-borne attack preceded the fall of Egypt's vital Abu Agheila position near the Sinai border. Close-support attacks were made at Gaza and Bir Lahfan on 6 June, but by early morning the entire Egyptian army was already withdrawing from Sinai.

Seeing the Egyptians in full retreat, the Israelis sent a rapid force through the crumbling enemy lines to seize the Mitla and Giddi Passes. This manoeuvre succeeded and trapped a large part of the Egyptian army east of the mountains. Here it was ruthlessly bombed by the IAF, which destroyed thousands of vehicles in front of the Mitla Pass alone.

The UARAF then threw what strength it had left into a desperate attempt to break the Israeli hold on the passes. During the night of 5/6 June the UARAF managed to put together a scratch force of 50 aircraft by repairing damaged aircraft and hurriedly assembling crated equipment. The biggest blow had been to the pilot pool, over 70 of whom had been killed, with a further 200 wounded. The first sign that the UARAF still existed came at 05.36 on 6 June, when two MiG-21s were sent against an Israeli column near Bir Lahfan. Both were shot down. The same fate befell a pair of Su-7s which ran the IAF gauntlet as far as El Arish at 06.00. Egyptian Su-7s and MiG-21s twice tried to shoot down IAF helicopters. These attacks were pin-pricks compared with the pounding that the Egyptian army was receiving from the IAF.

During the night of 5/6 June the Iraqis and Jordanians had joined forces to reinforce the defences of H-3. At dawn on 6 June, an IrAF Tu-16 bombed the Natanya industrial complex in Israel but was brought down by ground fire. Not long afterwards the IAF struck again at H-3. This time it met fierce resistance from defending fighters flown by both Iraqis and Jordanians. Nine Israeli aircraft were claimed, while the IAF admitted the loss of two. The Israelis also brought down one of a pair of Lebanese reconnaissance Hunters over Galilee. Throughout 6 and 7 June the IAF blasted Jordanian positions across

Below: Jordan's Hunters were destroyed on the ground, but their pilots were then absorbed by the Iraqi Hunter wing, where several gained their revenge: one almost became an ace in a single mission.

Right: Although Egypt operated Tu-16 'Badgers', Soviet Tu-16s were also active in the Mediterranean during the 1960s and 1970s. After the Six-Day War uncamouflaged examples were based in Egypt and Syria, wearing Arab markings but retaining Soviet crews.

the West Bank. Israel also reported eight air battles on the eastern front between 6 and 9 June, mostly over H-3, where, by the end of the war, one Royal Jordanian air force Hunter pilot, Captain Ihsan Shurdom, had claimed one Mirage, two Mystères and a Sud-Ouest Vautour.

The UARAF kept up small-scale but increasingly effective strikes for the rest of the war in Sinai, although it could not alter the outcome. At dawn on 7 June four MiG-19s hit an Israeli column on the Mediterranean coastal road, though three aircraft soon went down to an IAF standing patrol. Additional United Arab Republic Air Force and Egyptian naval attacks in this sector certainly slowed the Israeli advance. The Israeli air force shot down a solitary Il-28 and a MiG at El Arish. Flights of MiG-17s sent against the Mitla Pass and southern Sinai suffered severe losses, but were sometimes able to hit back. A Super Mystère fell to MiG-17s east of Ismailia.

Right: This ex-Iraqi MiG-21F defected to Israel in August 1966, allowing the IDF/AF to comprehensively evaluate what would be its most potent foe in the Six-Day War.

The final days

By 8 June Algerian volunteers were reportedly flying alongside the Egyptians, who were also now joined by men from UARAF units in Yemen. Despite this upsurge of Egyptian air activity, IAF combat successes declined, only nine UARAF aircraft being claimed on 8 June. Late in that evening the Israelis severely damaged the USS *Liberty,* an American intelligence-gathering ship, in a still unexplained air and sea attack. The war in Sinai was, however, virtually over and Egypt accepted a UN ceasefire at 04.35 on 9 June.

Now the IAF geared itself up for another campaign, this time against Syria. Following frequent IAF attacks on the Golan defences, and finding itself alone since Egypt and Jordan had been defeated, Syria accepted a UN ceasefire on the evening of 8 June. Israel, however, did not. At 11.30 on 9 June an all-

Left: Egyptian Ilyushin Il-14 light transports were based at Almaza. About half a dozen of the 20 or so in service were destroyed on the ground, but survivors continued in use until after the Yom Kippur War.

Below: From the very first shot, the Arab air forces were at a disadvantage: an Israeli pilot's eye view of an Egyptian airbase just outside Cairo shows the carnage inflicted by the initial surprise attacks.

Israel consolidates

With Arab air power neutralised, Israel was able to operate over the battlefield with virtual impunity. Israel threw everything it had into the operation against its Arab neighbours, and this commitment, allied with a superb tactical plan and an element of good fortune, brought forth great success. Israel's initial airfield attacks were followed by an armoured push into the Sinai, which was itself supported by air power.

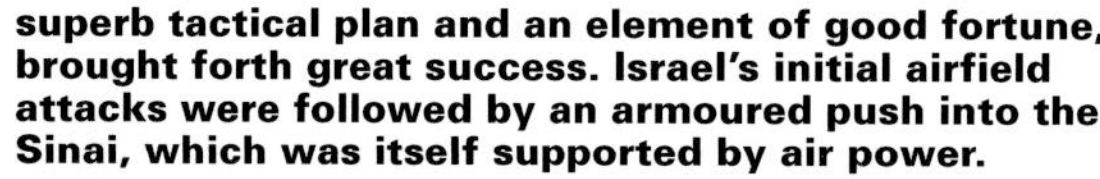

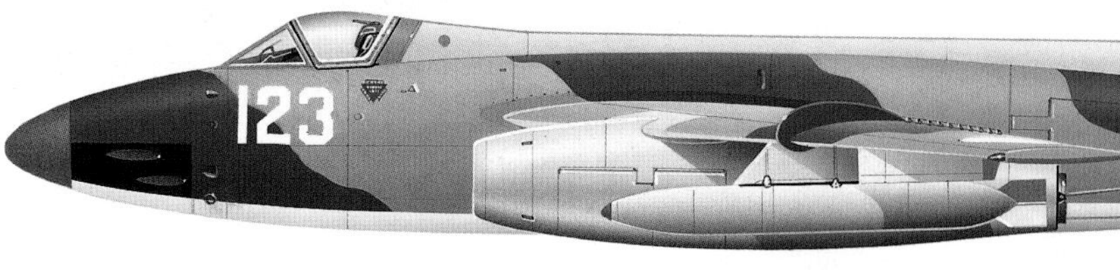

Sud Vautour
About 25 Vautours were committed to Israel's air strikes, initially operating in the medium bomber role. One was shot down by an Egyptian MiG on the first day. The aircraft were subsequently used in close-support operations, attacking Egyptian troops trapped by Israel's rapid advance. Five Vautour losses were admitted at the war's end.

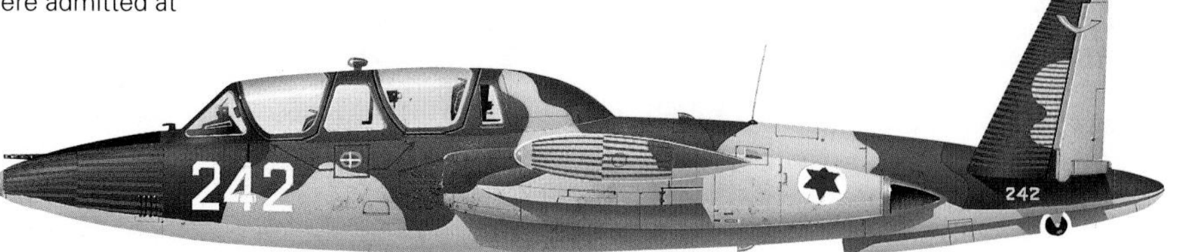

Fouga Magister
Two squadrons of Fouga Magister trainers were soon thrown into the fighting, operating mainly in the close air-support and ground-attack roles. In the almost total absence of enemy air opposition, the Magisters undertook their missions virtually unmolested.

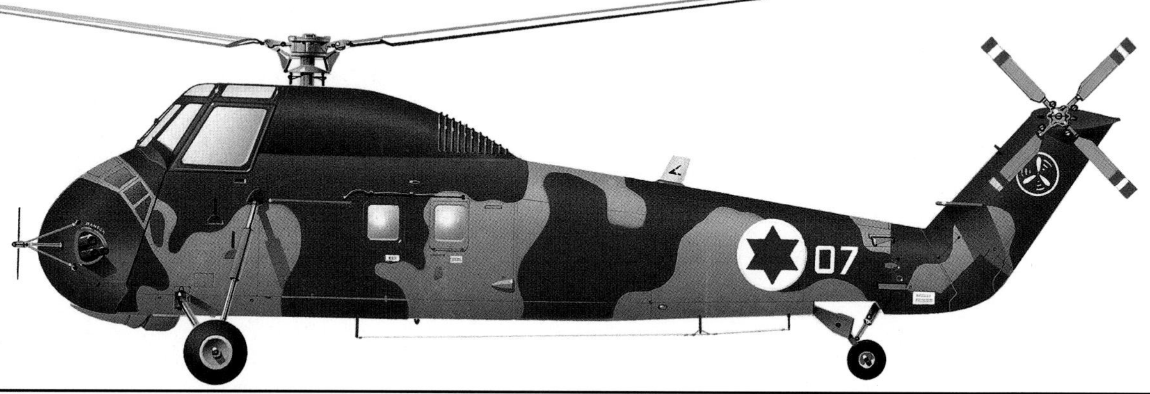

Sikorsky S-58
For the first time, the IDF/AF was able to make extensive use of helicopters to infiltrate commandos and airborne troops ahead of advancing Israeli armoured forces. Sikorsky S-58s and S-55s augmented smaller French-built Alouettes. Helicopters were also used for Casevac and SAR operations, and repeatedly proved their worth.

Above: Boeing Stratocruisers provided the IDF/AF with its only heavy transport capability. Smaller DC-3s and Noratlases formed the tactical transport force, and were used more intensively.

out attack was launched against the Golan Heights. Fighting was at first bitter but, after protesting vehemently to the UN, the Syrian government withdrew its forces to defend its capital. Air combat was minimal, although SAF and UARAF units brought down a Mystère and possibly a Vautour near Damascus. Other Israeli aircraft were hit by anti-aircraft fire. The IAF, although claiming 12 SAF aircraft in air combat during the Six-Day War, was more concerned to support its army and to seize the Golan Heights and the town of Qunaytra before the final UN ceasefire at 06.30 on 10 June.

The so-called Six-Day War was over, and Israel had won a resounding victory. The Israeli Air Force had destroyed about 286 UARAF aircraft (approximately 60 in air combat), 22 Royal Jordanian Air Force aircraft, 54 Syrian Air Force aircraft, 15 to 20 IrAF aircraft and one Lebanese machine. This had been achieved for the loss of at least 45 aircraft and probably more, about 12 of them in air combat, plus 20 pilots killed and 13 captured.

A lasting peace had failed to be imposed in the region, however. There was to be no short-term reconciliation between Arab and Jew; both sides simply set about rebuilding their forces before embarking on the next – inevitable – confrontation.

Above: An Israeli Bell UH-1 lifts off after dropping a stick of soldiers. Troop transport was one of many roles undertaken by Israeli helicopters, which played a decisive part in the brief but bloody war.

Left: The Sikorsky S-58 was the largest and most capable helicopter available to the IDF/AF in 1967. It played a vital role in the operations which resulted in the capture of the West Bank from Jordan.

Dassault Mirage IIICJ

This Mirage IIICJ wears the camouflage colours introduced during the 1970s. The Mirage IIICJ played a major role in the War of Attrition, and continued to form the backbone of Israel's air defence until the introduction of the F-4 Phantom. This aircraft wears an impressive tally of victory claims from the Six-Day War.

Armament
Although Israel's Mirage IIICJs were supplied with MATRA 530 AAMs (and later carried AIM-9 Sidewinders), all IDF/AF air-to-air victories in the Six-Day War were scored using cannon alone.

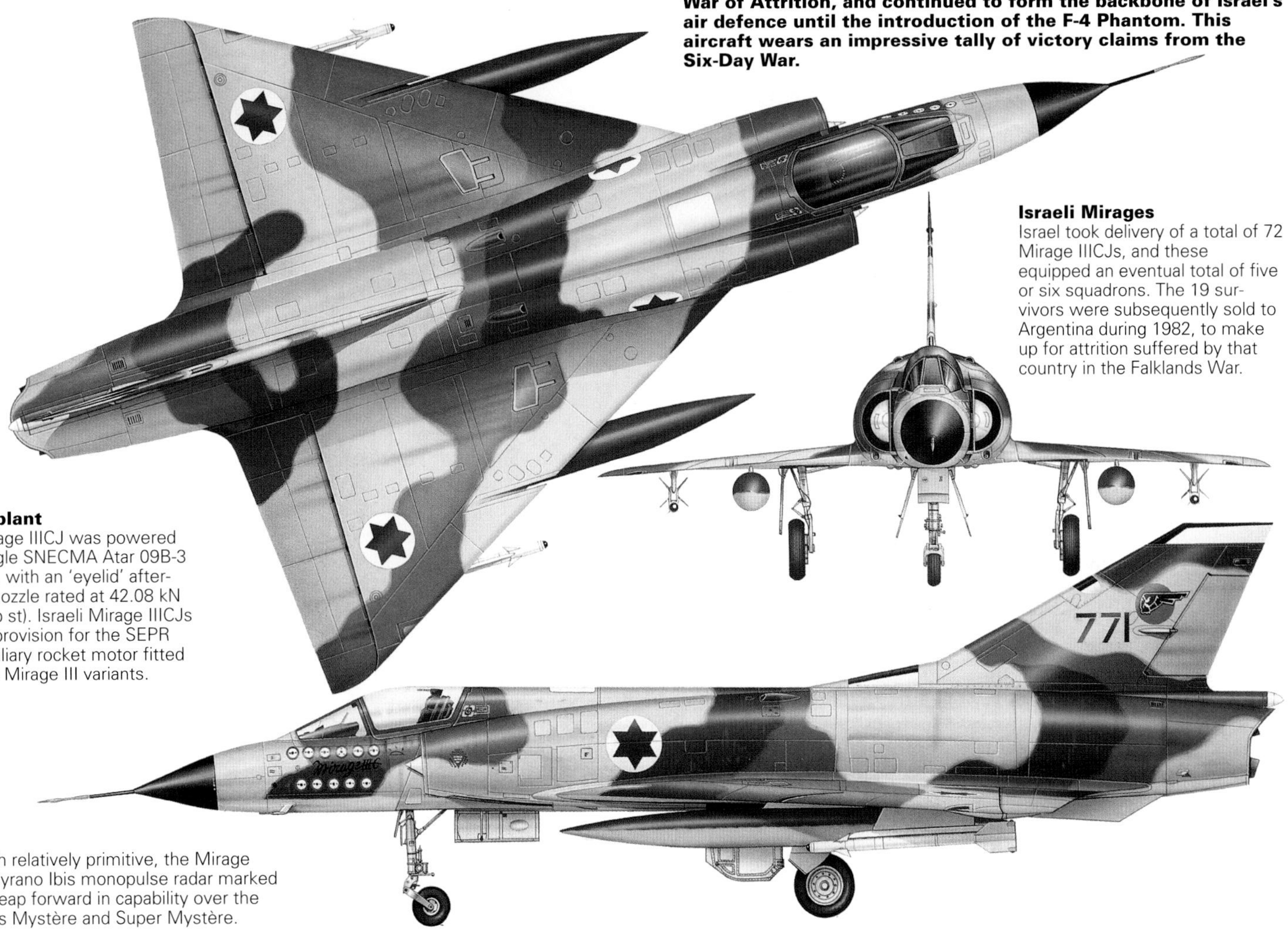

Israeli Mirages
Israel took delivery of a total of 72 Mirage IIICJs, and these equipped an eventual total of five or six squadrons. The 19 survivors were subsequently sold to Argentina during 1982, to make up for attrition suffered by that country in the Falklands War.

Powerplant
The Mirage IIICJ was powered by a single SNECMA Atar 09B-3 turbojet, with an 'eyelid' afterburner nozzle rated at 42.08 kN (9,460 lb st). Israeli Mirage IIICJs had no provision for the SEPR 841 auxiliary rocket motor fitted to many Mirage III variants.

Radar
Although relatively primitive, the Mirage IIICJ's Cyrano Ibis monopulse radar marked a huge leap forward in capability over the radarless Mystère and Super Mystère.

The War of Attrition 1969–1970

The ceasefire at the end of the Six-Day War brought about only a brief respite in the fighting between Israel and its neighbours. Just as the war of 1967 had been preceded by periodic artillery attacks, airspace intrusions (often dealt with by simply shooting down the intruder) and commando raids, so such actions continued to take place after the war. On 1 July 1967, for instance, Egyptian troops ambushed an Israeli patrol on the Eastern side of the Suez Canal, and 10 days later there were artillery duels across the canal. This prompted aerial intervention, with Israel claiming four Egyptian MiG-17s, three MiG-21s in July and four Syrian MiG-19s in October.

The French embargo on the delivery of 50 Mirage 5J fighters ordered before the war forced Israel to look elsewhere for aircraft to make good its losses and strengthen its order of battle. Fifty F-4Es and six RF-4Es were ordered from the USA, together with 25 ex-US Navy A-4Es to augment 48 A-4Hs (and two TA-4Hs) ordered before the war. The IDF/AF also took delivery of 20 Bell UH-1s in 1968.

September 1968 saw a resumption of cross-Canal shelling and, in October, Israel mounted a number of commando raids far behind Egyptian lines. Nasser announced a war of attrition in March 1969, as Israel finished its fortified Bar Lev line on the East bank of the Suez Canal. Israel responded to Egyptian artillery barrages with shelling and massive airstrikes, shooting down 21 enemy aircraft for the loss of three of its own by the end of May. By November, the IDF/AF could claim 34 enemy aircraft in air combat (of 51 EAF aircraft downed). Massive raids on 'military' targets around Cairo in January 1970 prompted the deployment of five squadrons of Soviet MiG-21s and their 'volunteer' pilots, and these proved better able to counter the IDF/AF raiders (who dropped 8000 tonnes of bombs by the end of April). From April, Egyptian fighter bombers began mounting hit-and-run raids across the Canal. Israel took a hammering in the air as well, losing five F-4Es to Soviet MiG-21s in July alone. A ceasefire was finally declared on 8 August 1970.

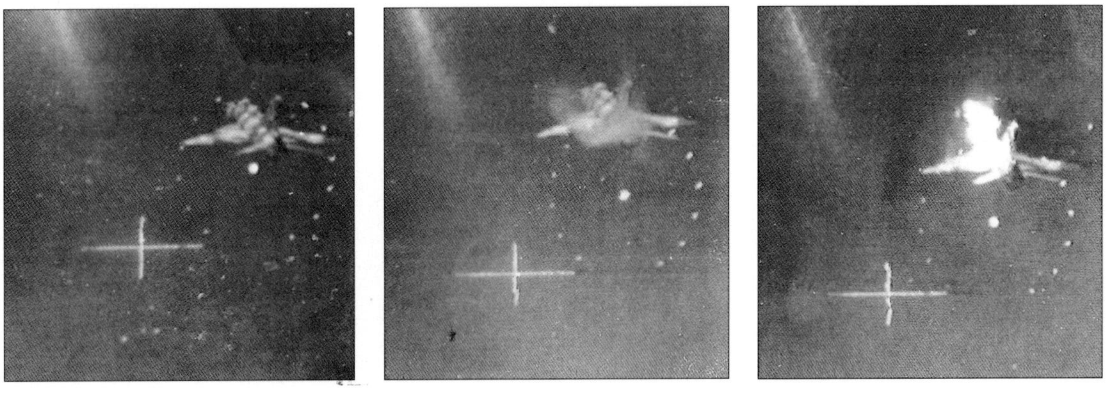

Right: A dramatic gun camera sequence records the destruction of an Arab MiG-21 by gunfire. Israel's fighter pilots enjoy a reputation second to none, the result of superb training and combat experience.

The Yom Kippur War

OCTOBER 1973

Left: Egyptian MiG-21s played a vital role in the air war, and downed a number of Israeli aircraft. Israeli losses in air combat were almost certainly higher than admitted, and most fell to the MiG-21.

Above: The IDF/AF was forced into a costly war against the Egyptian SAM system. Here an F-4E launches an AGM-45 Shrike anti-radar missile.

In 1967, the resounding victory by Israel during the Six-Day War over its historically hostile Arab neighbours had bred a dangerous complacency. Israel was a nation of 2.5 million surrounded by 100 million potential enemies. Egyptian and Syrian leaders were vowing to restore Arab pride by planning a campaign which would catch Israel completely off guard. The brutal War of Attrition had seen the gradual wearing down of Israel's air force. As the countdown to further conflict began, Israel could muster 375 combat aircraft, against 730 for Egypt and Syria. Jordan, though too weak to participate in another war, could tie down Israeli troops merely by the act of ordering mobilisation, and friendly Arab states further afield would be willing to send token forces. By October 1973, all was ready for a war which would have a profound effect on the theory and practice of air combat.

Earlier victories had confirmed Israeli opinions that the Arabs were disorganised and incapable of effective military action, despite their large, Soviet-supplied armouries. Egypt's leader, Anwar Sadat, adopted a plan in which the Arabs could win the war without winning the battlefield. A surprise two-front attack in the north (by Syria) and south (by Egypt) would be the opening move. As the Syrians retook the Golan Heights and advanced into Israeli territory, Egypt would initiate a set-piece battle across the Suez Canal.

SUCCESSFUL ASSAULT

Brought forward under the cover of training exercises, the Arab forces launched their onslaught at 14:00 on 6 October 1973. In Israel, vigilance was at its lowest for the Yom Kippur (Day of Atonement) religious holiday, as wave upon wave of Egyptian aircraft streaked over the Suez Canal to attack Israeli airfields, SAM batteries, radar sites and numerous other military positions in Sinai. In addition to 222 fighter-bombers, Egypt used 25 AS-5 'Kelt' stand-off missiles launched from Tu-16 bombers, and a number of FROG tactical SSMs.

In the north, Syrian aircraft supported a thrust forward over the Golan plateau. Low-level attack missions were flown by MiG-17s and Su-7s with top cover provided by MiG-21s. Assault troops travelled by Mi-8 'Hip' helicopter to seize key objectives, either in Sinai or on the Golan Heights.

The first Israeli aircraft to react were in the air within 30 minutes, although it was to be two hours before the IDF/AF appeared in strength. In the attack role was the A-4 Skyhawk, supported by its more capable stable-mate, the F-4 Phantom. The Mirage IIICJ, aided by the first few IAI Nesher copies built in Israel, was employed against ground targets, though both it and the F-4 were also useful in air defence. Even a dozen or so ageing Super Mystère B2s were brought in

Right: Sukhoi Su-7s supported Egyptian and Syrian ground forces, and attacked Israeli airfields and other interdiction targets. They proved highly effective, if lacking in range and endurance.

Right: An Egyptian MiG-17 flies past an exploding tank at ultra-low level over the battlefield. The MiG-17's agility and robustness gave it an edge over more modern fighter bombers.

Right: The Egyptian push over the Suez canal was spearheaded by the dropping of heliborne commandos. The robust Mil Mi-8s performed admirably, but suffered heavy losses to Israeli ground fire.

for attack. Supporting helicopters included Super Frelons and smaller UH-1s.

Though the Sinai desert acted as a buffer zone, there was no such luxury for Israel in the north. Thus, the war against Egypt was put on 'hold' and first priority given to defeating the Syrian armies only a few miles from Israeli towns and villages. The IDF just managed to hold out until reserves could be assembled and brought to bear. After three days of fighting, including a fierce tank battle, the Syrians were too weak to exploit their dearly-won gains and were forced to withdraw. At the same time (9 October) the IDF/AF replied to a FROG missile attack by bombing its opponent's HQ in Damascus and an oil refinery at Homs.

IRAQ JOINS THE FRAY

Iraq had added a squadron of Hunters to Syrian air forces on 7 October, and a unit of MiG-21s soon after this. Jordan's contribution to the air war was restricted to firing SAMs at IDF/AF aircraft coming within range of its territory. With Syrian units now falling back, air defence assumed crucial importance as the IDF/AF ranged almost as far as the Turkish border in its campaign of strategic bombing. By 12 October, the air defence network was in such disarray, with many MiG-21s destroyed or damaged, that the outclassed MiG-17 had to be diverted to interception.

Meanwhile, on the Egyptian front the situation was bleak for Israel. Within two days of the first attack, the east bank of the Suez Canal was firmly in Egyptian hands, despite no less than 23 Israeli counterattacks. IDF/AF aircraft managed to disrupt further Mi-8 commando-insertion operations and shoot down 10 helicopters on 7 October, yet the SAM screen was proving devastatingly effective, as were the anti-tank missiles defending the Egyptian-occupied strip on the ground.

IDF/AF loss returns tell almost the whole story. During the first four days, Israel lost 81 aircraft. This was two-thirds of the total it was to suffer during 19 days of conflict. In 1967, the IDF/AF had contemptuously evaded the SA-2 'Guideline' SAM, and now it suffered for its over-confidence. Stretching the whole length of the Canal on the Egyptian side were additional new

Egyptian first strikes

Egypt and Israel agreed to invade Israel simultaneously on two fronts, aiming to recover territory lost in 1967, when Israel had been the aggressor. They chose to strike on 6 October, the Jewish Day of Atonement, or Yom Kippur. Egypt's initial strikes were well planned and skillfully executed. Egyptian aircraft struck against airfields in the Sinai, as well as HAWK SAM sites and radar installations.

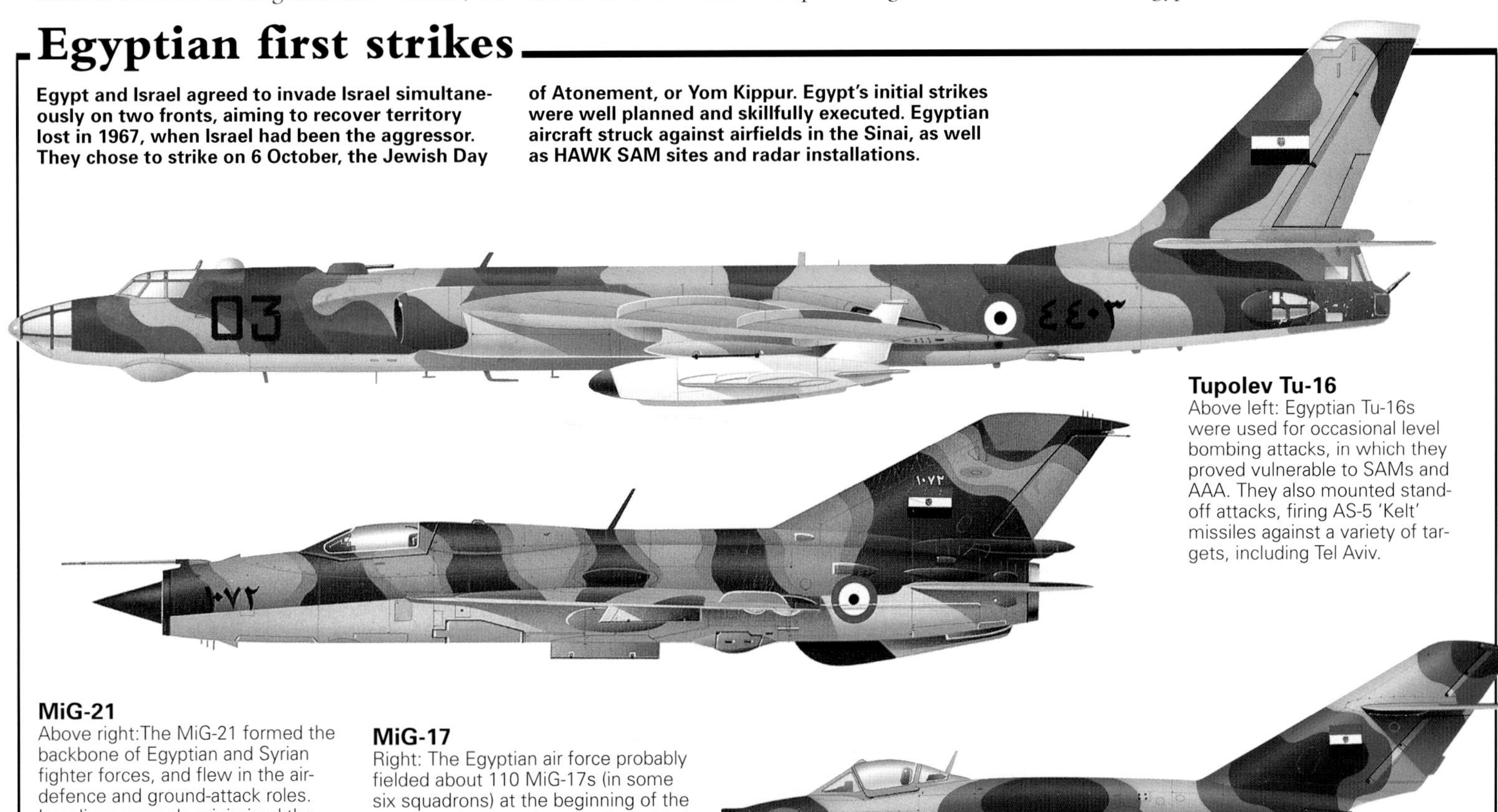

Tupolev Tu-16
Above left: Egyptian Tu-16s were used for occasional level bombing attacks, in which they proved vulnerable to SAMs and AAA. They also mounted stand-off attacks, firing AS-5 'Kelt' missiles against a variety of targets, including Tel Aviv.

MiG-21
Above right: The MiG-21 formed the backbone of Egyptian and Syrian fighter forces, and flew in the air-defence and ground-attack roles. Israeli propaganda minimised the danger presented by the MiG-21, though it now seems that the type proved an unpleasant surprise.

MiG-17
Right: The Egyptian air force probably fielded about 110 MiG-17s (in some six squadrons) at the beginning of the war, with Syria having a further 100 aircraft. These were thrown into the thick of the fighting, and proved particularly effective at strafing Israeli convoys.

Above: *An Israeli A-4 Skyhawk flashes over the top of an armoured column. With an increasing use of sophisticated SAMs and AAA by both sides, the casualty rate among the fighter bombers was high.*

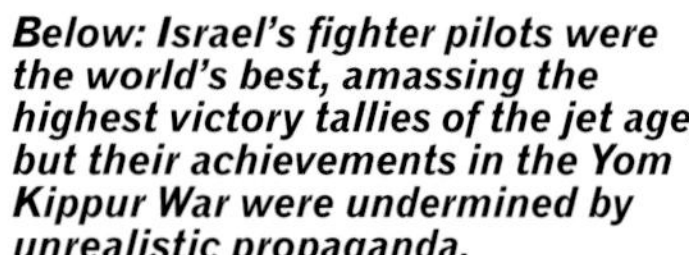

Below: Israel's fighter pilots were the world's best, amassing the highest victory tallies of the jet age, but their achievements in the Yom Kippur War were undermined by unrealistic propaganda.

SAMs: the SA-3 'Goa', SA-6 'Gainful', SA-9 'Gaskin' and shoulder-launched SA-7 'Grail' or Strela. The SA-6 was an unknown quantity in the West, and no countermeasures were known for its combined radar and electro-optical guidance system, or for the associated 'Straight Flush' target-acquisition radar.

The SAMs were set up in the classic Soviet concept of layered air defences, so that tactics to evade one known type of missile brought the IDF/AF fighters into the engagement zones of others. The SA-6, however, also proved a mixed blessing, allegedly shooting down 40 Egyptian and four Iraqi aircraft. Before the war was over, at least six SA-6 fire units had been captured and flown to the USA, where their secrets were probed and appropriate countermeasures devised.

Arab brethren

A squadron of Algerian Su-7s joined Egyptian forces on 8 October, when both sides continued the bombing of their opponent's airfields. In stark contrast with 1967, when the Arab air forces had been annihilated on the ground in the first hours of combat, not one Egyptian machine was lost in this way, though the Israelis' attempts cost them dear. Syria was less fortunate, losing a dozen in raids on three airfields during 8 October, for example. Libya committed a squadron of Mirage III/5s to the battles from 14 October, these reportedly flying 400 sorties in the hands of mercenary pilots, including Pakistanis.

Above: Heavy losses prompted massive airlifts of new supplies by the USA (to Israel) and the USSR (to its Arab clients). Here USAF C-141 Starlifters and C-5 Galaxies unload and turnaround at an Israeli base.

It was now time for both sides to be resupplied with fresh arms from their respective superpower backers. Both the USA and USSR had begun airlifting weapons on 9 October, some American aid being flown straight into Sinai airfields. Syria received about 15000 tonnes in 934 transport sorties. USAF C-141 StarLifters and C-5 Galaxies made 566 sorties with 22395 tonnes of equipment (including dismantled CH-53D helicopters) up to 15 November. El Al Boeing 707s and 747s brought a further 5500 tonnes, and there was also a sizeable seaborne effort.

Aircraft losses were restored, with the supply of 100 Soviet fighters each to Egypt and Syria, in whose air forces they entered service between 14 and 20 October. Israel had made the exaggerated claim that only four days of war supplies were left by 13 October, and this resulted in the acceleration of the previously low-key US reinforcement effort. Phantoms and Skyhawks were commandeered

Arabian follow-up

While the Egyptians hammered Israeli targets from the south and west, her allies were busy mounting attacks in the north and west. Israel's aggression in 1967 was remembered with anger and bitterness, and allowed the formation of a powerful coalition, whose main partners were Egypt, Syria, Iraq and Jordan, but which also drew support from further afield, including Algeria and even Pakistan.

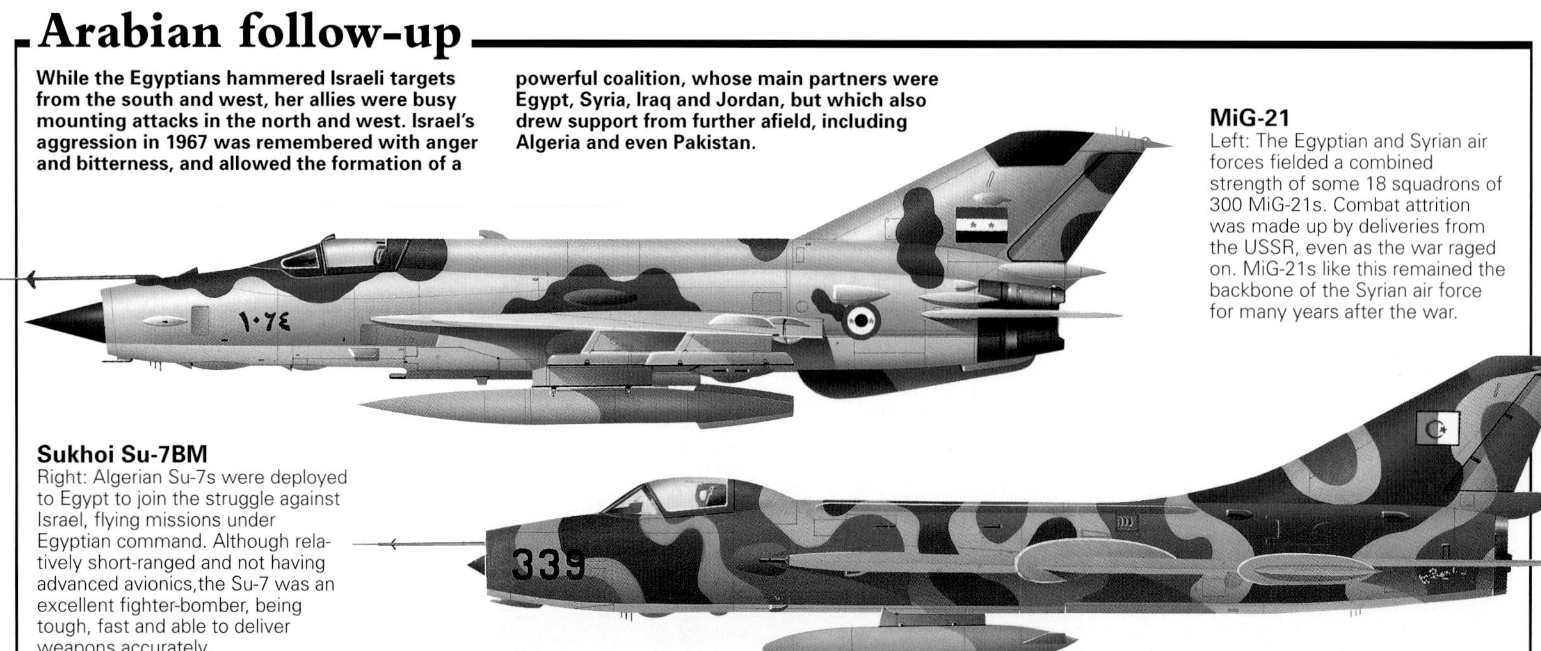

MiG-21
Left: The Egyptian and Syrian air forces fielded a combined strength of some 18 squadrons of 300 MiG-21s. Combat attrition was made up by deliveries from the USSR, even as the war raged on. MiG-21s like this remained the backbone of the Syrian air force for many years after the war.

Sukhoi Su-7BM
Right: Algerian Su-7s were deployed to Egypt to join the struggle against Israel, flying missions under Egyptian command. Although relatively short-ranged and not having advanced avionics, the Su-7 was an excellent fighter-bomber, being tough, fast and able to deliver weapons accurately.

F-4E Phantom

This F-4E wears the markings of No. 119 Squadron, based at Tel Nov during the Yom Kippur War. The squadrons flying F-4Es in 1973 were Nos 69, 107, 119 and 201. One more F-4E squadron formed after the war.

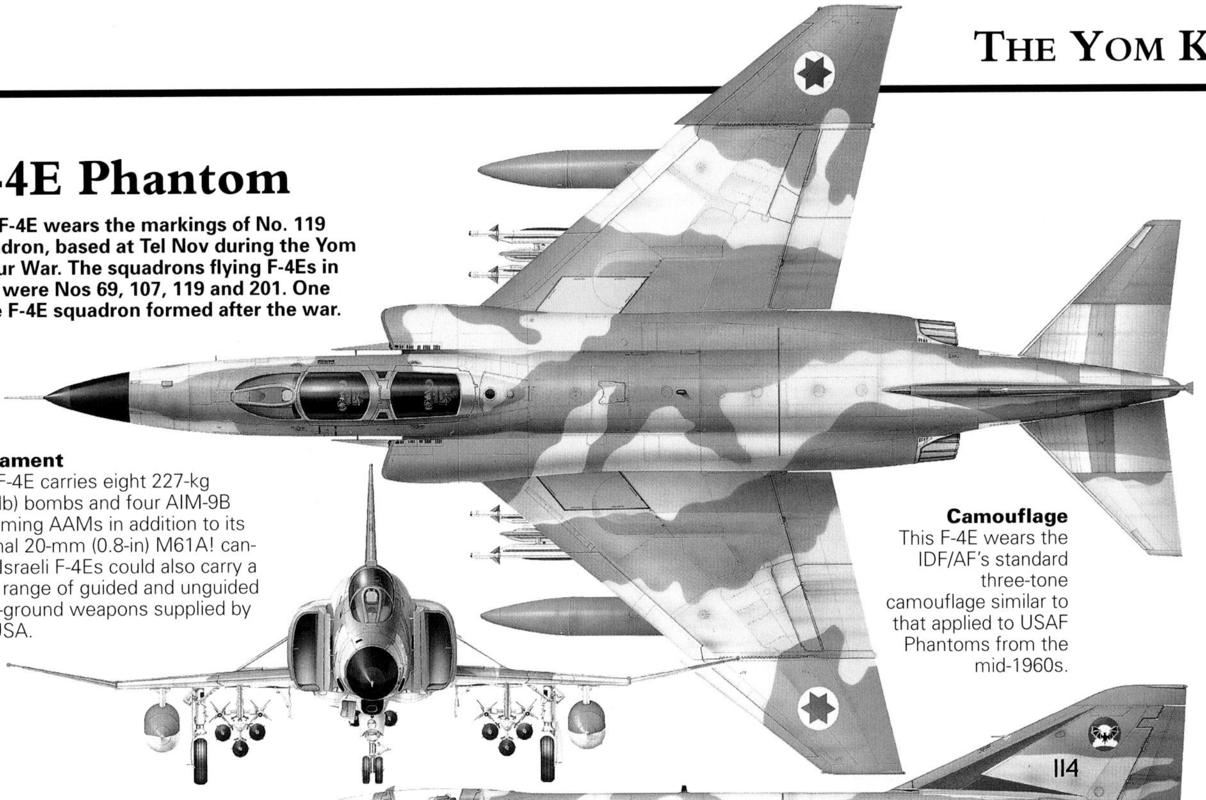

Armament
This F-4E carries eight 227-kg (500-lb) bombs and four AIM-9B IR-homing AAMs in addition to its internal 20-mm (0.8-in) M61A! cannon. Israeli F-4Es could also carry a wide range of guided and unguided air-to-ground weapons supplied by the USA.

Camouflage
This F-4E wears the IDF/AF's standard three-tone camouflage similar to that applied to USAF Phantoms from the mid-1960s.

Combat record
The IDF/AF lost six F-4Es on the second day of the war, in attacks against Syrian SAM sites, one more struggled back to Ramat David, where it landed in flames. Another F-4E was lost on 8 October, and another was downed during an attack on the Syrian army HQ in Damascus on 9 October. In airfield attacks on 11 October two F-4s fell to Egyptian MiG-21s and on 13 October one aircraft was abandoned by its crew after being hit by a SAM. On 14 October, a dogfight with two MiGs proved inconclusive, but two F-4s ran out of fuel on their way home. Another F-4 was downed over Tanta on 15 October, and five more fell to SAMs before the end of the war. Twenty-three more admitted losses have not been detailed.

Powerplant
The F-4E is powered by a pair of General Electric J79-GE-17 turbojets, with the longer 'turkey feather'-type afterburner nozzles.

Phantom at war

In the opening Egyptian attack on Ophir AB on 6 October 1973 by 28 MiG-17s and MiG-21s, a pair of IDF/AF Phantoms on QRA (Quick Reaction Alert) were able to scramble and claimed seven enemy aircraft. Elsewhere, F-4s intercepted Mi-8 'Hip' helicopters attempting to land commandos at key points in the Sinai. Five were claimed of some 40 encountered.

The next day opened with hastily planned operations against Syrian SAM sites, but these cost six Phantoms, with two aircrew killed and nine captured. At least one more F-4E was able to land back at Ramat David, in flames! Attacks against Egyptian airfields were less costly. On 8 October, the Phantoms attacked Syrian airfields and Egyptian pontoon bridges across the Sinai and mounted CAPs in various areas. Four MiG-17s were downed when they tried to attack Om Khasiba. On the debit side a single F-4E on an undisclosed mission was lost, probably shot down by a Syrian MiG-21.

On 9 October, 16 Phantoms were launched in an attack against the Syrian army HQ in Damascus. Only eight were able to attack, due to the weather, but they scored some hits. One aircraft was lost (the pilot was killed and the navigator taken prisoner) and another crawled home with several 57-mm cannon hits. Another F-4 was lost, together with its crew, during attacks on power stations and Egyptian airfields. The following day the Phantoms attacked various Egyptian and Syrian air bases suffering no losses, but in similar operations on 11 October two F-4Es fell to Egyptian MiG-21s over Banbah airfield. No losses occurred on 12 October, but the next day an F-4 was badly damaged by AAA during an attack on El Mazza airfield near Damascus. The campaign against Syrian airfields ended on 14 October, while attacks on Egypt continued. During an attack on Mansurah, two MiG-21s were claimed (but only as probables), but the MiG's resistance was sufficient that two F-4Es ran out of fuel on their way home, forcing them to land at primitive strips at Baluza and Refidim.

SAM KILLER

On 15 October, 12 Phantoms attacked Tanta airfield and downed a MiG-21, but one F-4 and its navigator was lost (the pilot becoming a PoW) and another suffered severe damage but managed to limp home without an aileron. SAM positions at Port Said were attacked on 16 October, and more SAM sites were attacked during the following two days. Unfortunately, three Phantoms were shot down and a fourth was badly damaged. Four Syrian MiG-17s were intercepted and claimed destroyed near Kuneitra on 18 October – at least one using the new indigenous Rafael Shafrir AAM. On 20 October, two more Phantoms were shot down by Egyptian SAMs.

During 11,233 IDF/AF combat sorties (by all types), 37 Phantoms were lost (including those described above) and six more were so badly damaged that they had to be written off. This attrition rate was second only to that suffered by the A-4 Skyhawk, and was a result of the difficult anti-airfield and anti-SAM missions flown by the aircraft. The losses were largely made good by the transfer of 36 USAF F-4E Phantoms during Operation 'Nickel Grass' (mainly from the 4th and 401st TFWs). These aircraft flew 200 combat missions, sometimes in USAF camouflage and with only national insignia and USAFE tail-codes overpainted. During the fighting, the four Phantom units, usually described as Nos 69, 107, 119 and 201 Squadrons, had claimed a large number (115) of enemy aircraft destroyed and had carried out devastating attacks on key enemy command centres, airfields and SAM sites.

Below: Some 43 Israeli Phantoms were destroyed during the Yom Kippur War, but these losses were largely made good with the delivery of 36 USAFE F-4Es. Israeli Phantom pilots claimed 115 aerial victories.

Israel fights back

The 1973 war was very different from that of six years previously, and the Israeli air force did not find it nearly as easy as in 1967. Fighter and fighter-bomber pilots needed all of their legendary skills to come out victorious, but other aviators also came to the fore, notably the helicopter crews whose work was becoming of increasing importance.

Aérospatiale Super Frelon
The Six-Day war showed that the reliable but aging Sikorsky S.58 was not suited to the heavy-lift jobs required of modern mobile warfare. The first step in solving the problem was to acquire some Aérospatiale Super Frelon helicopters from France. These were used to deliver commandos and to support operations in the 1973 war, and could lift five tonnes of freight or 28 troops.

Sikorsky CH-53G
Left: After the Super Frelon, the CH-53 added even more capability. The most powerful western helicopter of its time, it had already seen action in Vietnam before Israel took it to war. It can carry nearly 10 tonnes of cargo or 55 troops.

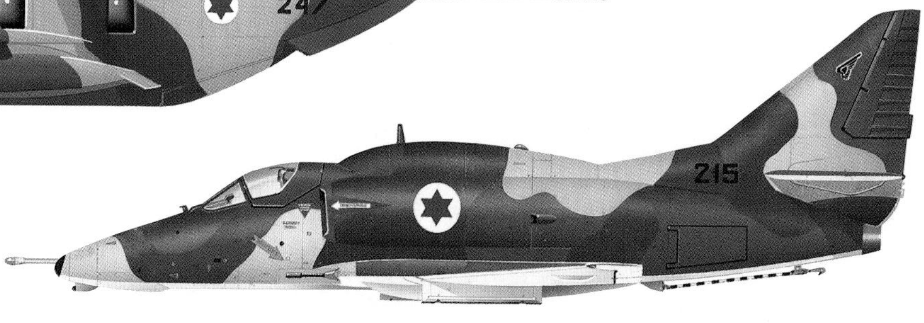

McDonnell Douglas A-4 Skyhawk
Right: One of Israel's two main strike aircraft in 1973, the A-4 bore the brunt of the ground attacks against Arab formations and their heavy missile defences. 53 were shot down, around half of all Israeli combat losses.

from US Air Force and Navy squadrons and flown out to the Middle East at short notice. The first 28 were available for combat by 17 October, followed by a further 50 on 22 October.

It was not the extra fighters which won the war for Israel, however, but the transports. Inside the USAF transports came new technology: airborne ECM kits to confuse the SA-2s and SA-3s, Walleye and HOBOS 'smart' bombs, AGM-45 Shrike air-launched anti-radar missiles, AGM-65 Maverick TV-guided missiles, Rockeye cluster bombs and TOW anti-tank missiles for the army. There were also fresh supplies of HAWK SAMs as well as AIM-9 and AIM-7 AAMs.

Turning the tide

Reinvigorated by these new weapons, Israel was well poised to exploit Egypt's tactical error of 14 October. Egyptian forces abandoned their original plan and advanced outside their extended SAM umbrella. The battle now became the fluid fight at which Israel excels, and the result was predictable. On the night of 15/16 October, as Israeli naval units, supported by helicopters, were attacking the Egyptian coast far to the west, a rift in the Egyptian front line was exploited for the insertion of Israeli troops on the opposite bank.

Air operations intensified to the extent that the northern front was sufficiently denuded of cover to allow the Syrians a rare chance to use Mi-17s and Su-7s against Israeli bases and an oil refinery. Egypt threw its Aero L-29 jet trainers into the fray, using them

Below: While Israel's pilots were feted as heroes, the achievements of the groundcrews were no less spectacular and proved just as decisive. Turnaround times were slashed, allowing the IDF/AF to maintain a high sortie rate.

Right: Yom Kippur marked the dawn of a new era of air warfare, and Egypt's sophisticated air-defence network almost carried the day. The ageing but potent SA-2 'Guideline' missile provided high-level cover to Egyptian troops.

***Above:** A formation of A-4 Skyhawks release a tumbling mass of napalm tanks during a low-level attack. The Israeli Skyhawks performed the bulk of the ground-attack missions, and large numbers were lost, including an estimated 30 in the first week alone.*

***Right:** An Israeli F-4E falls in flames. The achievement of Israel's pilots in defeating a well-trained, well-equipped and capable foe has sometimes been hidden behind inflated claims and an unwillingness to acknowledge the extent of air combat losses.*

(as expected, with little success) in the ground-attack role. Even more remarkably, Mil-8 helicopters turned bomber on 19 October in a futile attempt to disrupt Israeli Canal crossings with napalm pushed out of the hold at low level. As Israel 'rolled up' the strips of SAM sites, capturing 12 of the 40 or so installed along the Canal, the precious defensive umbrella disintegrated, leaving Egyptian air force aircraft at the mercy of the IDF/AF, not to mention the army's HAWK SAMs.

Ceasefire

As the Israeli bridgehead on the western bank of the Suez Canal was consolidated, it became clear that it was going to be Egypt which lost territory, not Israel. Now was the time for the Arabs to bring in their ultimate weapon: on 20 October, Saudi Arabia suspended oil shipments to the West. Egypt simultaneously requested a ceasefire. Under superpower pressure, this was agreed as coming into effect at 18.52 on 22 October. Israel had other ideas, though, and continued its southern drive towards Suez to encircle the Egyptian 3rd Army until the USA forced it to halt on 24 October. There was jockeying for final positions in the north, too, as Syrian and Israeli helicopters reinforced mountain-top posts under the cover of their own fighter aircraft. Helicopters and parachute troops assisted in taking the observation post atop Mt Hermon in one of Israel's final acts of the conflict.

To this day, each side disputes the other's aircraft loss admissions. What is beyond doubt is that they were staggering. Egypt and Syria suffered the destruction of some 220 machines each, to which must be added 21 Iraqi Hunters and MiG-21s, plus 30 Algerian and Libyan fighters. Israel appears to have lost 120, including at least 33 Phantoms, 52 Skyhawks and 11 Mirages or Neshers. Helicopters are excluded from the above and account for a further 42 Egyptian, 13 Syrian and six Israeli losses. Some 40 and 31 IDF/AF aircraft fell to SAMs and ground fire respectively, mainly in the opening days, whilst combined Arab losses to these causes were just 17 and 19. Air-to-air, where there were around 400 combats, only 21 IDF losses were admitted, compared with a claimed 335 (two-thirds by cannon, and the rest by AIM-9 Sidewinders or the similar IAI Shafrir AAM at close range) of the Arab air forces. 'Own goals' were Israel two, and the Arabs 58.

After the war, analysts looked for the lessons of Yom Kippur. New respect was afforded to Soviet SAM systems, and the importance of ECM equipment in increasing the likelihood of mission success was better appreciated. 'Smart' ordnance, which had already been used with success in Vietnam gained wider acceptance in view of the demonstrable effect it had upon IDF/AF attack accuracy in the latter half of the fighting. Drones and RPVs, used for data-gathering and decoy work by Israel, became an important item of equipment for any modern army.

***Left:** The Yom Kippur War saw the first appearance of the IAI Nesher, an unlicensed copy of the Mirage 5 produced after the Mirage 5Js built for Israel were embargoed by the French.*

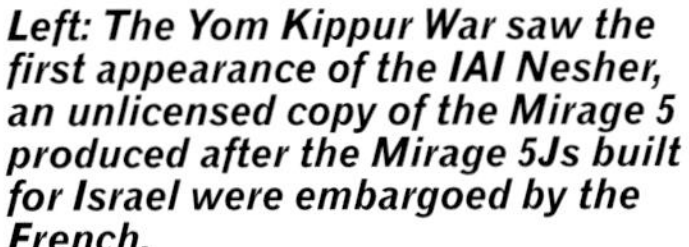

***Left:** A sharkmouthed F-4E lands after a combat sortie. Several aircraft were painted in this fashion as a disinformation exercise, intended to show that No. 113 Squadron was Phantom-equipped.*

Long-distance Israeli raids

1976-1985

In four major middle-east wars, Israel proved it had the world's best fighting air force. But in 1976 it showed for the first time that it also had the means of projecting power over long distances.

On 27 June 1976, Air France Flight 139 took off from Athens en route to Paris. Aboard the Airbus A300 were 258 passengers and crew. Among that number were four hijackers, who had transferred from a Bahrain flight at Athens. Just eight minutes after take off, the hijackers produced pistols and grenades and seized control of the aircraft. Flying first to Benghazi, it then went on to Uganda where President Idi Amin provided refuge.

The hijackers, an unholy mix of Baader-Meinhof and PLO terrorists, demanded the release of 53 'freedom fighters' from prisons in several countries. Some passengers were released, but numerous Jewish passengers were held hostage. The French crew of the aircraft elected to remain with the hostages.

Israel had long been a target for terrorist action, and immediately began planning a rescue. However, the move to Entebbe put the hijackers beyond the range of most Israeli aircraft. Nevertheless, a daring mission was put into effect with breakneck speed. It was given the codename Operation Thunderbolt

On Saturday 3 July, three heavily laden C-130s took off from Ophir, at the tip of occupied Sinai and Israel's southernmost airfield. Along with a Boeing 707 which provided airborne control and communications for the mission, the force flew over Ethiopia and Kenya. Bypassing Nairobi, where a second 707 – a hospital aircraft – had already landed, the flight approached Uganda's airport at Entebbe. Israeli agents had already infiltrated the airport and reported that the hijacked plane was parked next to the old terminal, where the hostages were being held.

The three C-130s landed just after midnight. The first moved openly to the terminal building and disgorged a black Mercedes (identical to Amin's, even down to the numberplate). It was escorted by Land Rovers driven by men in Palestinian clothing and carrying AK-47 rifles. The Ugandan guards saluted what they thought was their president, before being shot down by the disguised Israeli commandos.

Above: The entry into service of advanced new fighters like the General Dynamics F-16A Fighting Falcon gave the Israeli air force of the early 1980s the ability to strike hard over very long distances.

More commandos rushed from the other aircraft entering the terminal building shouting, 'We're Israelis, get down.' Another unit assaulted the control tower and destroyed its radios, but not before Lt Colonel Yehonatan Netanyahu, the strike force commander, had been killed by a sniper. Others destroyed eleven MiG fighters – almost the entire combat-worthy Ugandan air force – to forestall any aerial pursuit

Within minutes, the terrorists had been shot and the hostages were being rushed to a fourth, empty C-130 which had just landed. Unfortunately, three hostages were killed in the crossfire.

The C-130s took off, leaving the dead hijackers, as well as 20 dead and over 100 wounded Ugandan soldiers. Landing in Kenya, they refuelled, the wounded were transferred to the waiting hospital plane, and the formation continued on to Israel and a triumphant recepton at Tel Aviv's Ben Gurion airport.

OSIRAK

Five years later, Israel made another long-range strike, but of a very different nature.

Iraq had long been suspected of having a secret nuclear weapons programme, for which the Osirak nuclear plant was the key. It was being built with French and Italian assistance in the desert some 19 km (12 miles) southeast of Baghdad.

Israeli intelligence had reported that the power station would be in operation by September of 1981, and that enriched uranium and weapons grade plutonium would

Rescue at Entebbe

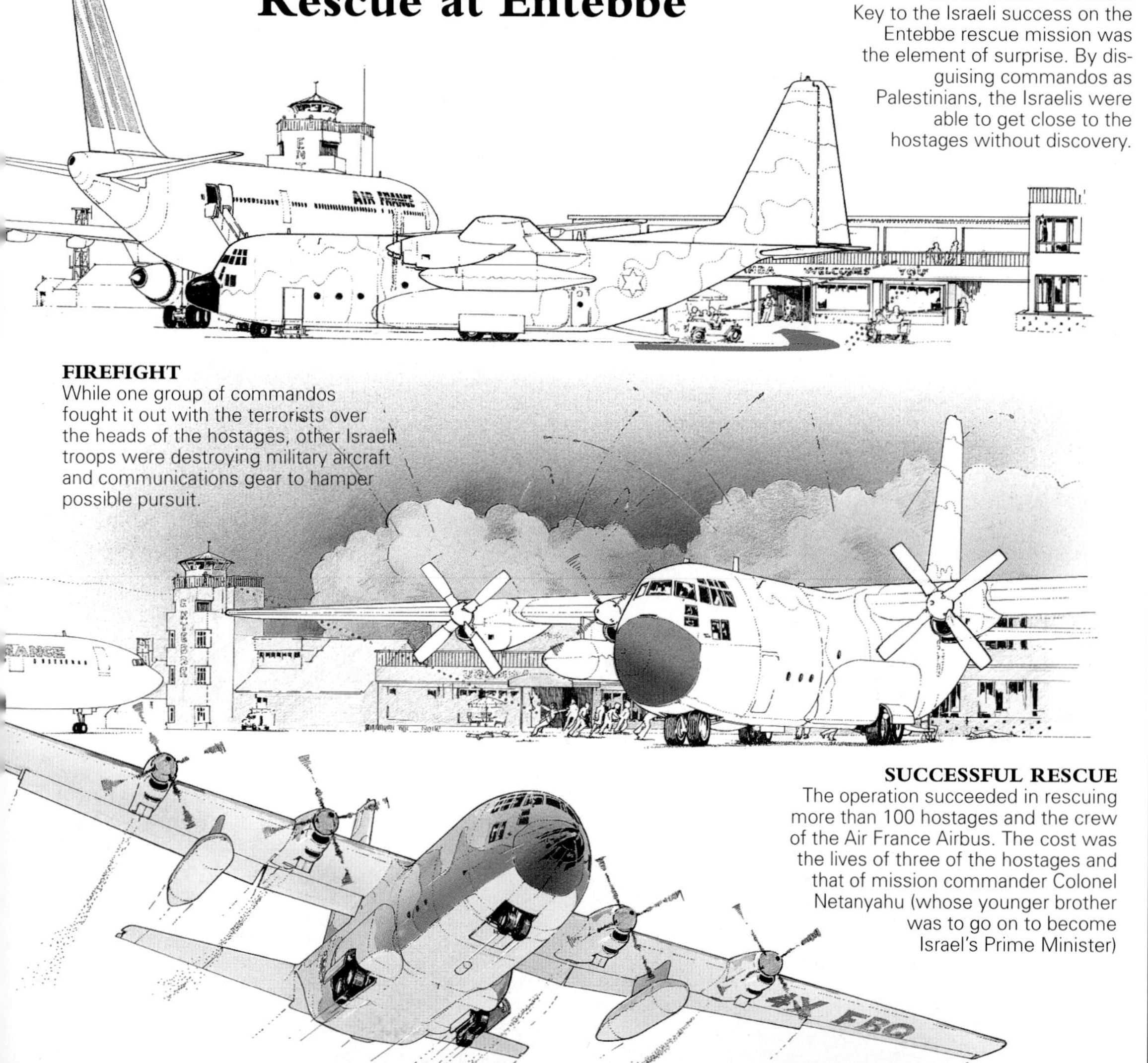

SURPRISE ATTACK
Key to the Israeli success on the Entebbe rescue mission was the element of surprise. By disguising commandos as Palestinians, the Israelis were able to get close to the hostages without discovery.

FIREFIGHT
While one group of commandos fought it out with the terrorists over the heads of the hostages, other Israeli troops were destroying military aircraft and communications gear to hamper possible pursuit.

SUCCESSFUL RESCUE
The operation succeeded in rescuing more than 100 hostages and the crew of the Air France Airbus. The cost was the lives of three of the hostages and that of mission commander Colonel Netanyahu (whose younger brother was to go on to become Israel's Prime Minister)

be produced soon after. This was looked on with misgivings by all of Iraq's neighbours. But it was Israel which would have been the prime target, and it was Israel's decision to attack the reactor from the air.

It would not be easy. Baghdad is more than 1100 km (685 miles) from Israel. However, Israel had recently acquired American-built F-15 and F-16 fighters, which could carry out such a long mission.

After meticulous preparation, which included Israel's best pilots flying rehearsals against full-scale mock-ups of the target, the mission was given the go-ahead. The pilots were briefed by General Rafael Eitan, the IDF's chief of staff, who stated that it was vital for them to succeed since, "the alternative is our destruction".

On Sunday 6 June 1981, six F-15 Eagles, which were to provide fighter cover, and eight F-16 Fighting Falcons, each armed with two 1000-kg (2,205-lb) bombs, took off from Etzion air base.

Flying a low-level course across deserted portions of Jordan and Saudi Arabia, the Falcons reached their target some 80 minutes later. Popping up from their low level flight, the F-16s quickly acquired the distinctive dome shape of the reactor and made their attacks. It is believed that all 16 bombs hit the target, although one failed to go off.

Above: Israel uses the F-15 in the air defence role, but it was the big fighter's long range which decided its use in the long overwater raid on the PLO headquarters in Tunis.

Iraqi air defences woke up, but it was too late. Even as the anti-aircraft guns opened fire, the Israeli jets were heading homewards.

The attack aroused great public anger in the Arab world (and possibly some secret satisfaction at Iraq's set back) but it also demonstrated that the Israelis had both the ability and the will to strike hard and far in what they saw as their own interest.

That was again made plain in 1985.

Entebbe had been a rescue. Osirak had been a strategic strike. But the raid on the PLO headquarters was a classic example of Israel's firm belief that terrorist acts should not go unpunished.

Raid on Tunis

On 25 September 1985, three Israelis were brutally murdered aboard a yacht at Larnaca in Cyprus. The perpetrators werre identified as Force 17, a terrorist organization linked with the PLO.

Israel decided to retaliate by striking at the PLO's headquarters in Tunis. The challenge was the distance: almost 2000 km (nearly 1250 miles) there and back called for the longest strike mission in Israeli history. Planners decided to use McDonnell Douglas F-15 Eagles for the mission, refuelling from a Boeing 707 tanker en route.

The target was the PLO complex at Hamam-al-Shatt, which included Yasser Arafat's office and those of his senior advisers, as well as PLO operations, communications and public relations centres. The complex was also reported to house Force 17.

The raid was launched on 1 October, and the air-to-air refuelling went without a hitch. The only worry was the weather: the Gulf of Tunis was covered in cloud. However, as the fighters approached the coast the weather cleared, and the F-15 pilots were able to identify and fix their targets, attacking with complete surprise and with deadly effect. All targets were damaged or destroyed. Arafat's headquarters took a direct hit, as did the Force 17 barracks.

Israel had once again shown that she would retaliate for any actions against her or her people – no matter what the cost politically or in world opinion.

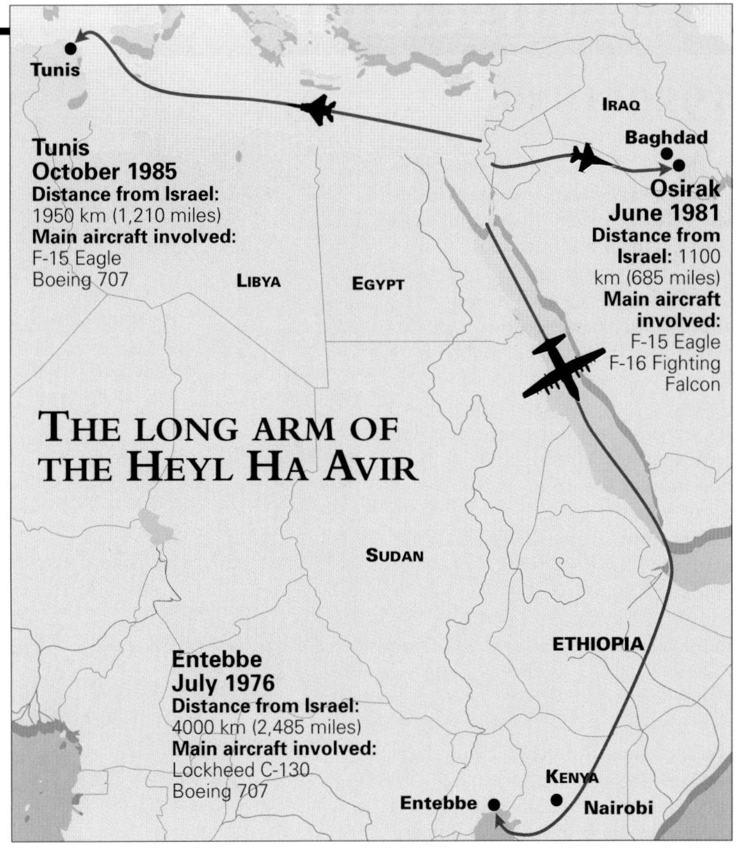

Israel's air force, the Heyl Ha'Avir, has always had fast reactions, since nowhere in the tiny country is more than a few minutes flying time from the border. But the missions to Entebbe, Baghdad and Tunis called for very different skills, involving long-distance navigation and the ability to find a target after long hours in the cockpit.

Israel's aerial spearhead

The superb skills and training of Israel's pilots have given them a considerable advantage in their long struggle with hostile neighbours. But for the last 18 years, they have had the further advantage of being equipped with better aircraft than their opponents – particularly in the shape of the supremely agile Fighting Falcon and Eagle. Israel was one of the the first export customers for both of these types, taking them into service soon after the US Air Force, and giving both types their baptisms of fire.

General Dynamics F-16A Fighting Falcon

Left: The first of an initial order for 75 single-seat F-16As and two-seat F-16Bs were delivered to Israel in July 1980. Known as *Netz* or Hawk in Heyl Ha'Avir service, they have since been joined by large numbers of improved F-16Cs and Ds, which are called *Barak* or Lightning by the Israelis.

McDonnell Douglas F-15A Eagle

Right: The Eagle has been the world's best fighter for more than two decades. It has been used primarily as an air superiority fighter by the Heyl Ha'avir, in whose hands the type has shot down more than 60 enemy aircraft without loss since its first victory in 1979.

The First Gulf War

1980-1989

An American military official famously concluded his briefing on the early days of the Iran/Iraq War by saying, "It's a pity they can't both lose." America's public antipathy and hostility towards Iran was provoked by the fact that its new Islamic government had overthrown a loyal US ally, seized American hostages in the US embassy in Teheran and roundly denounced the USA as 'the Great Satan'. At the same time, the USA had no more time for Iran's enemy, Iraq, whose Marxist regime enjoyed close links with the USSR and which had threatened US allies including Israel, Saudi Arabia and Kuwait, as well as threatening the political stability of the conservative part of the Arab world. Behind the scenes, the USA was later forced to offer some support to Iran, providing arms in return for the release of its hostages, following the failure of the USA's ambitious hostage rescue plan, Operation 'Eagle Claw'.

War between Iran and Iraq became inevitable following the Islamic revolution in Iran. The Mullahs loudly declared their intent to export their fundamentalist revolution to neighbouring nations which had turned away from Islam. Iraq also feared that the new regime would renounce the 1975 agreement which placed the border of the two nations along the Shatt al Arab, and feared for the future of the tiny strip of land which gave it access to the Persian Gulf.

Political pressure on Iran to withdraw from a number of islands

***Above:** Iraqi pilots have a last-minute briefing behind their Mirage F1EQ fighter-bombers. There have been reports that some of the F1s were flown by mercenaries, and even that the aircraft operated from Dhahran in Saudi Arabia.*

***Above:** Iran's Boeing 747Fs were capable of refuelling in flight from the IRIAF's fleet of 14 Boeing 707-3J9C tankers. Iran's fleet of US-supplied aircraft was handicapped by the shortages of spares caused by sanctions.*

***Right:** Iran managed to keep a high proportion of its F-4D and F-4E Phantom fleet serviceable with Israeli assistance, and with covert CIA assistance supplied in return for the release of hostages.*

The American Embassy hostage rescue attempt

The US forces participating in Operation 'Eagle Claw' primarily consisted of the air wings of the carriers *Nimitz* and *Kitty Hawk*, with a force of Special Operations Hercules operating from Masirah in Oman, and a squadron of converted RH-53Ds to insert and recover the rescue teams and the hostages. All fixed-wing aircraft wore broad black-edged red bands on their wings. The mission was aborted due to helicopter unserviceability, and ended in tragedy as one of the RH-53Ds collided with its EC-130H tanker on the ground at Desert One, killing eight aircrew.

***Left:** The RH-53D was selected for the hostage rescue mission primarily because it did not look out of place on the deck of a carrier.*

***Above:** F-14s, A-6s, A-7s (seen here) and USMC F-4s, supported by EA-3B Skywarriors and E-2C Hawkeyes, would have provided top cover and fighter-bomber support for the hostage rescue mission.*

Iranian air power

Under the Shah, Iran was one of the best customers for American weapons and systems; he was determined to build himself a truly modern air force and was able to pay in cash. When the Shah was toppled, the revolutionary Islamic regime which took over had to operate a host of American weapons systems without US support, and in the face of strict sanctions.

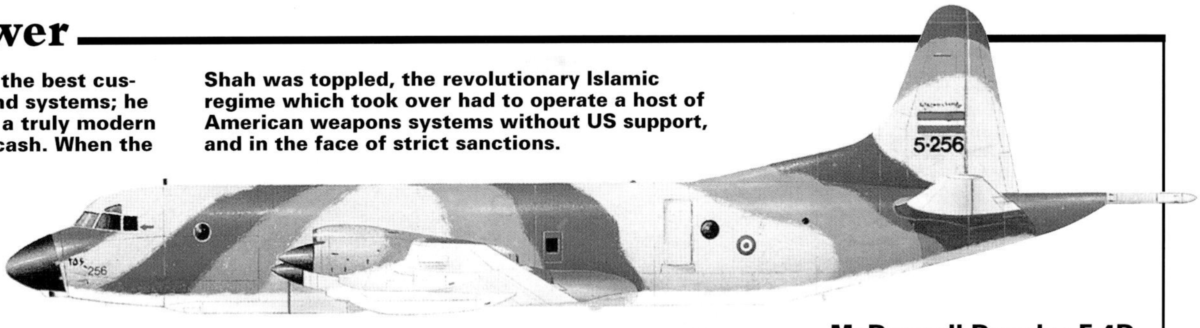

Lockheed P-3F Orion
The IRIAF used its fleet of P-3F Orions for maritime patrol duties, but also pressed the aircraft into service as AWACS and battle management platforms. The five survivors served with a squadron based at Bandar Abbas.

McDonnell Douglas F-4D Phantom
Iran was able to keep more of its US-supplied aircraft operational than was supposed at the time, thanks in no small measure to Israel (which was happy to help any opponent of Iraq), and to the CIA, which mounted a covert if unwilling assistance programme.

Northrop F-5E
Before the fall of the Shah, Iran fielded seven F-5 squadrons, most of which were kept operational with assistance from Vietnam and Israel, and (after the Arms for Hostages deal) the CIA. An estimated 50 F-5s were lost in action during the early years of the war.

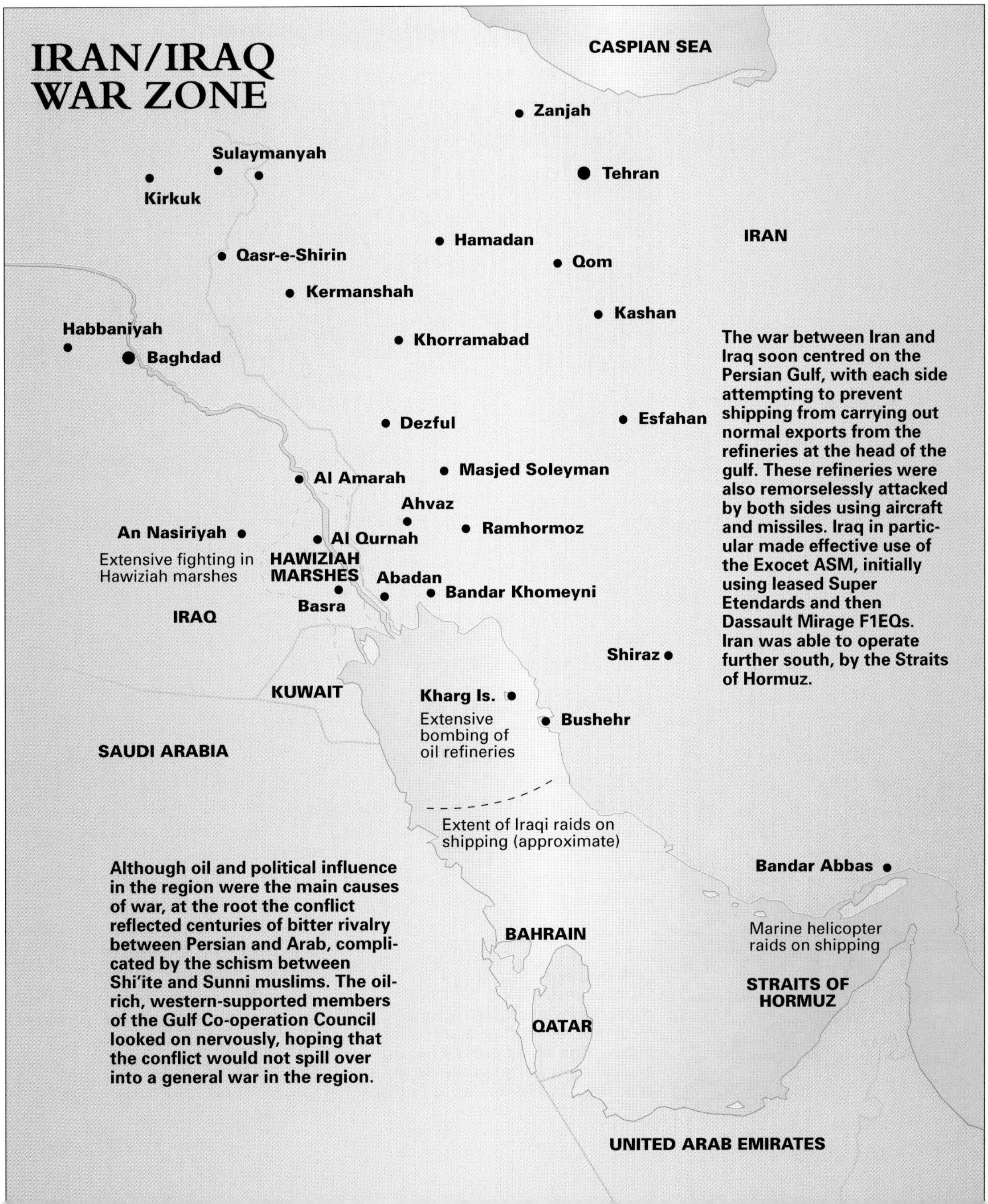

IRAN/IRAQ WAR ZONE

The war between Iran and Iraq soon centred on the Persian Gulf, with each side attempting to prevent shipping from carrying out normal exports from the refineries at the head of the gulf. These refineries were also remorselessly attacked by both sides using aircraft and missiles. Iraq in particular made effective use of the Exocet ASM, initially using leased Super Etendards and then Dassault Mirage F1EQs. Iran was able to operate further south, by the Straits of Hormuz.

Although oil and political influence in the region were the main causes of war, at the root the conflict reflected centuries of bitter rivalry between Persian and Arab, complicated by the schism between Shi'ite and Sunni muslims. The oil-rich, western-supported members of the Gulf Co-operation Council looked on nervously, hoping that the conflict would not spill over into a general war in the region.

in the Shatt drew little response, apart from some desultory artillery shelling of frontier positions on 4 September 1980. Iraq pre-empted further action by launching an attack on Iran. On 22 September Iraqi aircraft ineffectively attacked 10 Iranian airfields, and on the next day Iraqi troops invaded on several fronts. Iraqi aircraft mounted additional raids, and Iranian F-4 Phantoms and F-5E Tiger IIs attacked Baghdad, Kirkuk and a number of airfields. Eight of Iraq's Tu-22 'Blinders' bombed Teheran on 28 September, flying on to sanctuary in Riyadh. Both sides had large air forces but air activity was limited, although inflated kill claims suggested otherwise. Iraq claimed 140 enemy aircraft, and Iran 68.

Nature of the war

Iraq hoped that its attack would prompt a new revolution in Iran, expecting that the Iranian armed forces would have little loyalty to the new regime. When they met fierce resistance, it became clear that the war would become a grinding battle of attrition. For its part, Iran bombed targets in Kurdestan, hoping to provoke a Kurdish uprising against the Baath party regime in Baghdad.

After the initial weeks of the war, further sporadic air activity was largely restricted to the battle zone by a mutual undeclared agreement, with attacks on enemy troops and oil installations by aircraft and surface-to-surface missiles, with some strategic raids against power stations and command facilities.

There was intermittent air activity in support of the regular offen-

Iraqi air power

Iraq's air force was primarily built around Soviet-built aircraft types, augmented by some new French-built combat aircraft and helicopters, plus a handful of surviving aircraft from the 1950s and early-1960s when the country enjoyed closer links with Britain. Attrition during the war was made up from the USSR, France and China, which supplied aircraft and weapons to both sides.

Aero L-39ZO Albatross
The Aero L-39ZO was a dedicated weapons trainer with four underwing hardpoints and a simple bombsight. Two squadrons of these aircraft operated in the light ground-attack role, based at Mosul and Kirkuk.

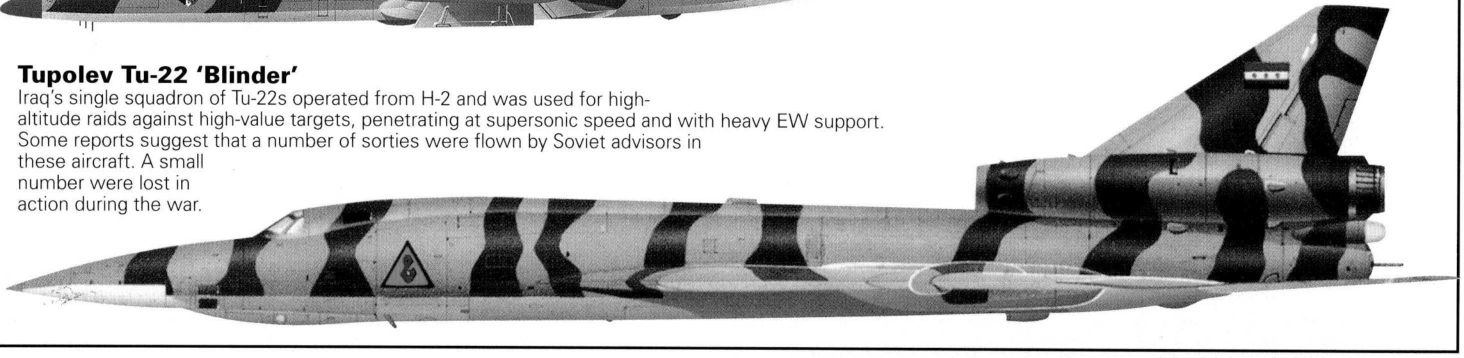

Dassault Mirage F1EQ
Iraq took delivery of 108 Mirage F1s, of 128 ordered. Delivery of the remainder was halted because Iraq was having problems paying for them; they were then embargoed following the 1990 invasion of Kuwait. Thirty-eight of the Iraqi Mirages were F1EQ-5s and 6s, with Agave radar for compatibility with the Exocet.

Tupolev Tu-22 'Blinder'
Iraq's single squadron of Tu-22s operated from H-2 and was used for high-altitude raids against high-value targets, penetrating at supersonic speed and with heavy EW support. Some reports suggest that a number of sorties were flown by Soviet advisors in these aircraft. A small number were lost in action during the war.

sives and counter-offensives. Helicopter gunships were used more often than fixed-wing close-support aircraft, even when Iran mounted a major armoured counter-attack at Susangerd in January 1981.

FIGHTER COMBAT

Some fighter combat occurred in early-1981 in the fighting around Qasr-e-Shirin – in which Iraqi MiG-21s scored some kills with French Magic AAMs and Iranian F-14s saw combat as they countered Iraqi raids – but this was exceptional. Ground-attack aircraft occasionally flew intensive close-support operations, with the Iraqi air force generating 400-500 sorties per day at peak times. In mid-1983 Iraq admitted to the loss of 85 aircraft (including about 35 MiG-19s and MiG-21s, and six Mirage F1s) since the beginning of hostilities, two years earlier.

Right: An AM39 Exocet anti-ship missile is loaded under an Iraqi Dassault Mirage F1EQ. Many of the Mirage F1s capable of delivering the missiles were delivered with dark-grey topsides to suit them to over-water operation.

Bombing raids on cities (notably by high-flying Tu-22 'Blinders') had been restricted to 'nuisance raids' by one or two pairs of aircraft.

The war soon assumed a predictable pattern. Iran used its Revolutionary Guards (or Pasdaran) to launch impressive (but ultimately futile) human wave assaults on Iraq's defensive positions, often in a massive spring offensive intended finally to finish the war. In March 1982 the push was from Dezful, and in February 1983 across the marshes towards Al Amarah. In May 1982 the Iranians recaptured Khorramshahr, but a massive offensive in July was unable to take Basra. In March 1984, Iran pushed across the Hawizah marsh, intending to drive a wedge between the defenders of Al Amarah and Basra.

Left: Iraq replaced its ageing Mi-4s with Mil Mi-8 'Hip' helicopters and operated these on transport, assault and anti-tank duties. The Mi-8s proved robust and reliable. Large numbers were acquired, and losses were heavy.

IRANIAN OFFENSIVES

In February 1986 Iran successfully captured Al Faw after crossing the Shatt. Encouraged by this success it launched another major offensive against Sulamaniyah. Tanks massing at Dezful were prevented from launching a third push only by a massive Iraqi fighter-bomber operation, involving more than 50 MiG-23BNs alone. The January 1987 Karbala 5 offensive against Basra (with a second front against Sumar) threatened to break Iraq, and both Jordan and Saudi Arabia offered to send F-5s and pilots to help stem the Iranian push, which was halted for the loss of at least 50 Iraqi aircraft. Further offensives were launched against Kurdestan in March, and Basra in April.

There was no Iranian offensive in 1988, with Iraq attacking and retaking the Faw peninsula, pushing on until both sides were left where they had been in 1980. There was little more fighting on the ground.

From late-1983 it had become clear that Iraq enjoyed a measure of superiority in the air, but could not make a serious impact on the ground. Merely halting Iranian attacks required extreme measures, and Iraq began using napalm and chemical weapons. On the other side, the Iranian air force was ham-

Below: The Iranian army acquired 68 Italian-built Elicotteri Meridionali (Boeing Vertol) CH-47C Chinooks, and used these intensively during the long war with Iraq. Serviceability proved good.

Right: The Bell 214A 16-seat utility helicopter was developed specifically to meet an Imperial Iranian Army requirement, and was named Isfahan in Iranian service. Iraq used gunship-configured 214STs.

pered by the poor serviceability of its aircraft and a lack of experienced pilots. Serviceability improved as Israel began covert support, but the release of imprisoned aircrew to fight had mixed effects, many taking the opportunity to defect in their F-4s to Turkey and Saudi Arabia. With stalemate at the front, both sides looked to continue the war elsewhere, launching strategic attacks on each other's cities and also against oil targets and shipping in the gulf.

The Iraqi air force began attacking Iranian population centres during late-1983, in an effort to undermine civilian morale and perhaps provoke revolt. Iran responded with similar attacks on Iraqi cities. The offensive petered out, but was resumed in December 1986, when Iran launched 'Scuds' against Baghdad, with Iraq retaliating with air strikes. Iraq mounted 200 sorties against Iranian cities from January 1987, losing two Tu-16s in the process. In February 1988 there was another round of city attacks, with Iraq firing 40 SS-12s at Teheran and the holy city of Qom.

TANKER WAR

The oil industry was of such vital economic importance to both nations that it was always a key strategic target. Iraq attacked the oil production plant at Abadan within a month of the war starting, while Iran attacked Kuwaiti oil facilities

Grumman F-14A Tomcat

Iran took delivery of 79 of the 80 F-14As it purchased, the final aircraft being embargoed before delivery. After experiencing some difficulties in keeping the Tomcats serviceable, a significant number of F-14s were maintained in service. They were used in mixed fighter force tactics, often acting as mini-AWACS platforms. The F-14 scored some victories but it was not invulnerable; at least one fell to an Iraqi Mirage F1.

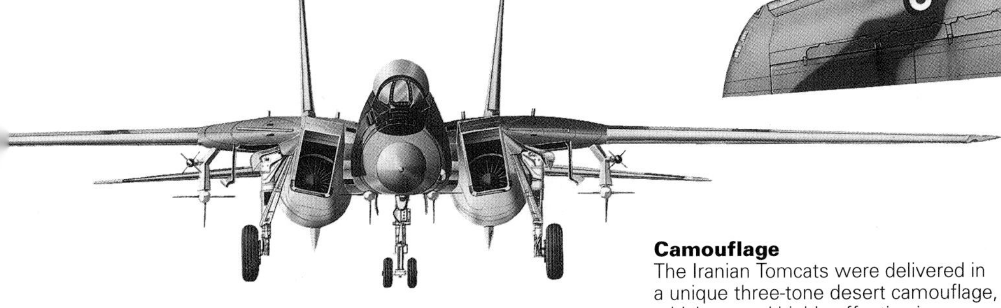

Radar
Imperial Iran was one of a tiny handful of nations considered safe enough to receive AN/AWG-9 technology, which remains impressive even by today's standards. F-14A can track 24 targets, and can engage six of them simultaneously.

Fuel
The Tomcat's impressive endurance and unrefuelled range is made possible by generous internal fuel tankage. Integral tanks in the outer wings and centre-section contain a total of 9029 litres (2,385 US gal). Internal tankage can be augmented by a pair of 1011-litre (267-US gal) tanks below the intakes.

Armament
The Tomcat was designed to carry the Hughes AIM-54 Phoenix. This weapon was delivered to and used by Iran, although stocks were carefully husbanded, and AIM-7 Sparrows (which were cheaper and easier to replace) were the Iranian Tomcat's primary BVR weapon. For close-in engagements, the F-14 carried a pair of AIM-9 Sidewinder AAMs, and an internal 20-mm (0.8-in) M61A1 cannon.

Camouflage
The Iranian Tomcats were delivered in a unique three-tone desert camouflage, which proved highly effective in overland operations.

Above: Both sides made heavy use of helicopter gunships. Iran took delivery of 202 Bell AH-1J Cobras, many of which were equipped with nose-mounted TOW missile sights. All featured the more powerful engine of the AH-1T, which gave much improved hot-and-high capability.

Above: An Iraqi Mi-24 'Hind' gunship flies over the battlefield. The heavily-armed Mi-24 was Iraq's most capable combat helicopter, and played a decisive part in supporting Iraqi army offensives.

(on the basis that they were handling Iraqi oil) during 1981. Iraqi aircraft using Exocet missiles attacked Iran's main oil terminal at Kharg Island from 1983, sinking a Greek tanker there on 22 November 1983, and a British tanker in February 1984. Iran began to retaliate by attacking tankers leaving Kuwaiti and Saudi ports, since they were believed to be exporting Iraqi oil. F-4Es firing AGM-65 Maverick missiles were Iran's weapon of choice for its tanker attacks. Two F-4Es were shot down by Saudi F-15s on 5 June, but the pace of attacks increased steadily.

Kharg Island target

In 1985 Iraq concentrated on attacking the main terminal at Kharg Island, while Iran began mounting attacks on tankers in the lower gulf, using missile-armed AB 212 helicopters operating from a floating platform. Iraqi attacks were so effective that the use of Kharg Island virtually halted, and supertankers instead unloaded at Sirri, further down the gulf, where the oil was transferred to lower-value ships which shuttled to Kharg and to Larak.

Both Sirri and Larak had been outside the range of Iraqi strike aircraft, but the introduction of An-12 tankers (and the alleged use of Dhahran in Saudi Arabia) allowed Mirage F1EQs to attack both targets in 1986.

Right: Iraq's helicopter inventory at the start of the war included 11 Aérospatiale Super Frelons. They were used for anti-shipping, transport and SAR operations, and suffered some losses.

Opposing helicopters

Iran's reliance on 'human wave' tactics – throwing into battle thousands of young men, all intent on becoming martyrs – threatened to overwhelm Iraq's professional army, and great reliance had to be placed on high-technology weapons to counter Iran's numerical superiority in men. Attack helicopters proved an effective way of countering Iranian offensives.

Aérospatiale Gazelle
Iraq took delivery of 40 Aérospatiale SA 342M Gazelles, armed with Euromissile HOT anti-tank missiles and equipped with a roof-mounted sight. They augmented the larger Russian-built Mi-24s and proved devastatingly effective against Iranian armour.

Bell 214A Isfahan
The Iranian army also made considerable use of helicopters, with more than 400 Bell 214s and Bell AH-1s on charge when the war began. The Bell 214 had been developed specifically to meet Iranian requirements.

Above: A crude-oil tanker lists and burns fiercely after being fatally struck by an Exocet missile. Some reports suggest that mercenary pilots flew the long-range Mirage F1/Exocet sorties. A total of 37 tankers were hit and sunk by both Iran and Iraq during the conflict, while a further 23 were badly damaged.

1987 saw the tanker war intensify further, with Iranian Revolutionary Guard speedboats planting mines and machine-gunning ships, and with the stationing of HY-2 'Silkworm' anti-ship missiles at Bandar Abbas. Iraqi Mirages continued to attack tankers near Iranian oil terminals, and the terminals themselves, but generally avoided attacking neutral shipping. It damaged the US frigate *Stark* on 17 May, but Iraq quickly apologised for the damage and the 37 deaths.

It was also the year in which the tanker war widened to draw in new combatants. Kuwait reflagged some of its tankers (re-registering them as Soviet or American ships) and called on the US Navy for protection. From July the US Navy began escorting convoys of reflagged tankers up and down the gulf and deployed mine-clearing helicopters to the region. Britain and France also deployed warships (carrying helicopters) to the gulf, Britain increasing a presence which dated from 1980. From late 1987, the US began attacking Iranian vessels, using USMC AH-1 Cobras and US Army OH-58Ds. On 3 July 1988 the USS *Vincennes* engaged what it thought was a hostile Iranian F-14 with two standard SAMs, then found it had shot down an unarmed Iran Air A300 Airbus. Although the shootdown was a mistake, it was also a potent declaration of intent.

On 19 July 1988 two Iranian F-14As were shot down over the gulf by Iraqi fighters (possibly the newly delivered MiG-29s). In an unconnected move on the same day, Iran accepted UN Resolution 598 calling for a ceasefire. The war was over.

Above: As the tanker war intensified, Western nations were forced to intervene, clearing mines and escorting neutral ships in the Persian Gulf. Although the bulk of the protection force was provided by the US Navy, Britain also had traditional interest in the region. As a result, a succession of Royal Navy warships, each with Lynx or Sea King helicopters, was deployed to the region for what was known as the 'Armilla Patrol'.

Right: As an interim solution to acquiring its own fixed-wing maritime strike capability, Iraq leased five Dassault Super Etendards, along with a large number of AM39 Exocet missiles, pending the delivery of its own Exocet-capable Mirage F1EQs.

Above: Operation 'Prime Chance' saw US Army OH-58Ds operating against Iranian patrol boats attacking tankers transitting the Persian Gulf. They could carry Stinger and Hellfire missiles, as well as gun and rocket pods.

Left: As the oil war intensified, Saudi Arabia and Kuwait began to be drawn into the conflict, and with them came western allies. The US Navy together with Britain and France deployed warships to protect the tankers and oil platforms. Here, a rig used as a base by Iranian Revolutionary Guard speedboats burns after an attack by US Navy SEALs, backed by US Army Special Forces helicopters and naval gunfire.

MIDDLE EAST

Air War over the Beka'a

JUNE 1982

Above: This bombladen IAI Kfir-C7 is from No. 144 Squadron. Used primarily in the fighter-bomber role, the Kfir also enjoyed some success as an air-to-air fighter. In the 1982 fighting, the IDF/AF's Kfirs were used primarily for attacking Syrian SAM and radar sites.

Following the realignment by Egypt with the West after the historic Camp David agreement in 1978, Israel's principal Arab antagonist automatically became Syria. This Arab country had for many years championed the cause of the Palestinians in their continuing efforts to secure their own formally recognised state. Opposition to the peace pact between Israel and Egypt came in the form of cross-border attacks by Palestine Liberation Organisation (PLO) guerrillas operating from bases in southern Lebanon. In retaliation, PLO bases had been bombed by strike aircraft of the Israeli Defence Force/Air Force (IDF/AF).

SYRIAN FORCES

Syria had moved its troops into neighbouring Lebanon in what was ostensibly a gesture to halt the Lebanese civil war. The Syrian force was not to be seen as one of occupation, so it left its air cover and large SAM units behind. Many of the latter were stationed in the border regions where they could counter any Israeli aircraft seeking to attack Damascus.

Parallel with the border, running southwards from Rayak to the Israeli-occupied Golan Heights, is the Beka'a valley. Israel mounted an intense reconnaissance effort to gain intelligence on these Syrian positions and lost several Firebee RPVs (Remotely Piloted Vehicles) to Syrian ground fire.

IDF/AF clashes with the Syrian air force between 1979 and June 1982 led to the loss of at least 12 Syrian MiGs, including two MiG-25s shot down while attacking RF-4E reconnaissance aircraft.

Above: Israel's F-16s were in action from soon after their delivery in July 1980. From the start, the F-16s were used as fighter-bombers and as air superiority fighters, escorting bombladen F-4Es or conducting sweeps or CAPs. Israeli F-16s claimed 44 kills over the Beka'a.

Above: A flight of F-15s overflies the fortress at Masada. The F-15 has been Israel's primary air-defence fighter since 1976, opening its tally in June 1977 with four Syrian MiG-21s. In 1982, they despatched many of the IDF/AF's claimed 92 victories.

CYPRUS
Akrotiri
MEDITERRANEAN SEA
LEBANON
Bhamdun
Beirut
Damur
SHUF MTS.
Sidon
ANTI-LEBANON MTS
BEKA'A VALLEY
Damascus
DAMASCUS HIGHWAY
GOLAN HEIGHTS
SYRIA
Ramat David
JORDAN
ISRAEL
Tel Aviv

OPERATION 'PEACE FOR GALILEE'

The attempted assassination of Israel's ambassador in London was used as justification for Israel's 1982 invasion of neighbouring Lebanon. This was aimed at throwing the PLO out of its bases in the Lebanon, from where it had been mounting a number of pinprick raids and shelling and mortar attacks against Israel itself. The Lebanon was already in the throes of a civil war between Israeli-backed Christian forces and an ad hoc alliance of Moslem and PLO groups supported by the Syrians.

By mid-1982, Israel had been planning for some time an armoured thrust into Lebanon to remove the threat posed by the PLO. In order to lessen international reprobation, the onslaught was to be presented initially as revenge for a PLO atrocity and thus the *casus belli* became the attempted assassination of the Israeli ambassador in London on 3 June.

At 15.15 on the following

Syria's defenders

Syria invaded the Lebanon on the last day of May 1976 in an effort to enforce a peace between the warring factions. Israeli forces themselves occupied part of southern Lebanon (up to the Litani river) in March and April 1978. The IDF/AF periodically attacked targets inside the Lebanon thereafter, often drawing a response from Syrian air forces.

MiG-25
Despite its breathtaking performance, the MiG-25 proved to be ineffective as a fighter, hampered by poor agility and above all by its undue reliance on GCI control. Nevertheless, Arab sources suggest that the type achieved some success.

MiG-23MLD
Cold War propaganda and a lack of hard information wrote off the MiG-23 as a typically crude, primitive and ineffective fighter. When Israelis evaluated a MiG-23MLD which defected from Syria, they judged it to be a better aircraft than expected. It is likely that some of the IDF/AF aircraft officially lost to SAMs actually fell to 'Floggers'.

Left: Israeli Hughes 500MDs operated principally in the anti-tank role, using their TOW missiles to devastating effect. The Israeli gunship helicopters (operating alongside AH-1 Cobras) had their day on 10 June, going into action when Syrian armour attempted to stop an Israeli armoured column.

afternoon, seven waves of A-4s, F-4s and F-16s of the Israel Defence Force/Air Force streaked over Beirut, the Lebanese capital, attacking the Palestinian refugee camps. During the next morning, Beirut, the coast road and a PLO stronghold were hit from the air; a Skyhawk fell to an SA-7 as the IDF/AF's first casualty.

Full-scale invasion

Not until 6 June was the full scale of Israel's plans apparent. Ground forces, with helicopter support, began a northward thrust through the coastal area which was eventually to lead almost to the gates of Beirut. The claimed objective of the full-scale invasion was to establish a demilitarised buffer zone in front of Israel. PLO resistance was swept aside, obliging Syria, as an ally, to provide assistance. The SAF first appeared on 7 June in a limited attempt to intercept F-16s over Beirut and Damur, losing two MiGs as a result. To protect its flanks, Israel used CH-53 heavy helicopters to airlift a strong force into the Shouf mountains (southeast of Beirut) on the following day. This threatened to outflank the Syrian positions in the Beka'a valley and cut communications between Beirut and Damascus, so Syria reacted with an attack by Gazelle helicopter gunships. Syrian strike aircraft penetrated farther into Lebanese airspace to attack Israeli armour near the port of Sidon.

By now, it was clear to the Israelis that the Syrians would have to be prevented from interfering with the anti-PLO operations being undertaken on the coastal plain. IDF/AF freedom of action was being hampered by the Beka'a valley SAM sites, and, since more missiles were reportedly being installed, early action was advisable.

At this time there were 19 SAM sites in the Beka'a valley, and in four closely-spaced raids on 9 June at least 17 of the sites were put out of action by 90 aircraft. First, soon after 14.00, a force of 26 F-4s launched AGM-65 Maverick air-to-surface missiles and AGM-45 and AGM-78 Standard anti-radar missiles against both the SAM bases and their control posts. This was supported by Ze'ev short-range SSMs fired by the Israeli ground forces, and resulted in 10 sites being rendered inoperative in the first 10 minutes. Almost completely blinded, the Syrian air-defence organisation was delivered a body-blow by 40 F-4s, A-4s and Kfirs which went for the weapons themselves, using more TV-guided Mavericks, together with cluster bombs and GBU-15 guided bombs to rip apart the missile positions. This second phase was completed at 14.35, and was followed by a back-up wave which in the third phase attacked other Syrian positions on the front, plus any SAM sites which had escaped.

Higher above, the top-cover component of IDF/AF F-16s and F-15 Eagles was involved in large-scale clashes with Syrian fighters. Forces of MiG-21s and MiG-23s were severely mauled, resulting in IDF/AF claims of 22 shot down plus seven damaged, for no loss. Syria admitted 16, but claimed 26: the majority of these were probably RPVs.

The end of the SAMs

On 10 June, the remaining two SAM sites were destroyed, leaving the SAF as the only weapon which could challenge Israel in the air. In more fierce fighting, Israel claimed 28 aircraft including three helicopters shot down. The latter resulted from Syrian attempts to

Right: The McDonnell Douglas F-4E was arguably the most important IDF/AF type engaged in Operation 'Peace for Galilee'. They flew close-support, interdiction, and anti-SAM sorties, as well as CAPs and reconnaissance flights.

Israel's strike force

Israeli fighter-bombers operated in huge waves during Operation 'Peace for Galilee' (30 to 90 aircraft per wave), closely escorted by F-16s and F-15s. Phantoms armed with AGM-78 Standard ARMs and AGM-45 Shrikes took out Syrian SAM and GCI radar sites, while Kfirs attacked using free-fall and cluster bombs. Syrian air defences were effectively blinded within a day.

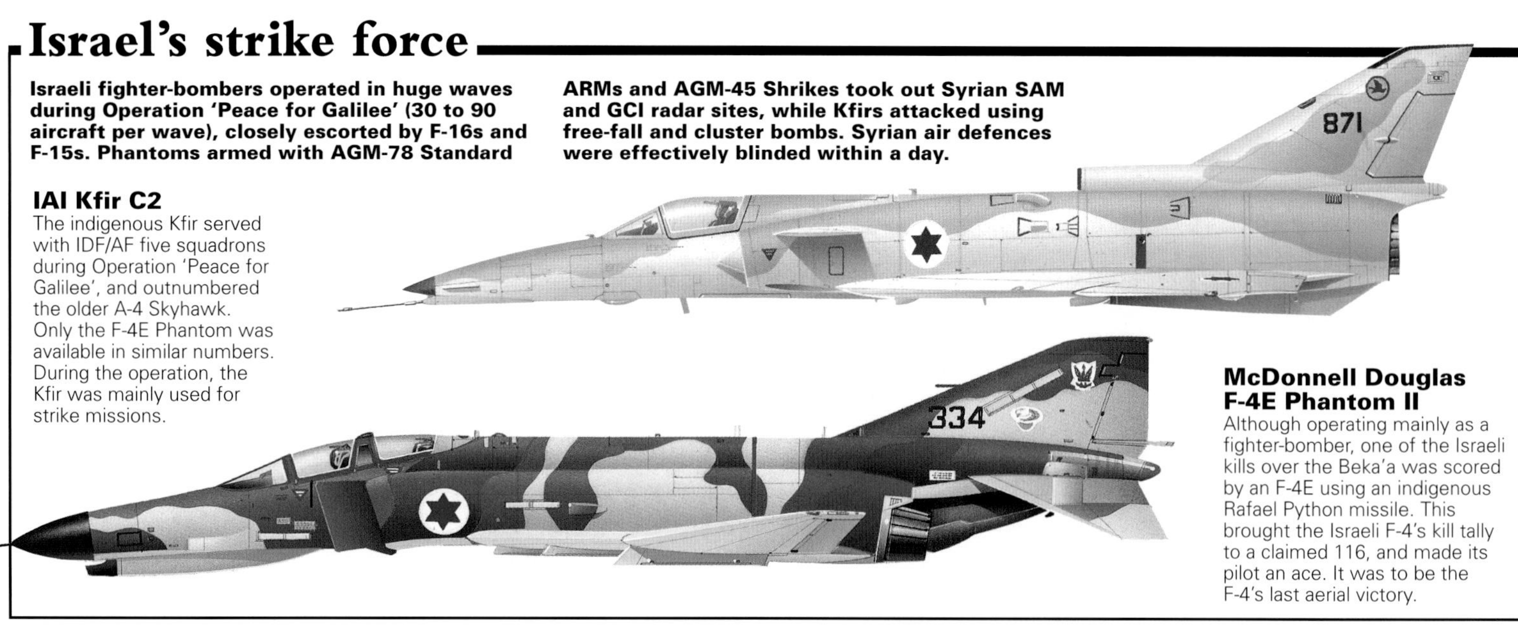

IAI Kfir C2
The indigenous Kfir served with IDF/AF five squadrons during Operation 'Peace for Galilee', and outnumbered the older A-4 Skyhawk. Only the F-4E Phantom was available in similar numbers. During the operation, the Kfir was mainly used for strike missions.

McDonnell Douglas F-4E Phantom II
Although operating mainly as a fighter-bomber, one of the Israeli kills over the Beka'a was scored by an F-4E using an indigenous Rafael Python missile. This brought the Israeli F-4's kill tally to a claimed 116, and made its pilot an ace. It was to be the F-4's last aerial victory.

***Left:* Laden with a centreline tank and six 454-kg (1,000-lb) bombs, an F-4E of No. 105 Squadron sets out on a mission. The F-4E has continued to be involved in raids on targets in Lebanon since the end of Operation 'Peace for Galilee'.**

halt an Israeli column penetrating the Beka'a valley, while Israel responded with its own force of AH-1 Cobra and Hughes 500MD Defender gunships. On the next day (11 June) similar battles took place when Syria attacked a force which appeared to be intent on cutting the road from the Beka'a valley to Beirut. This cost the SAF 18 more aircraft, according to Israeli accounts, before an intermittent ceasefire was arranged. It was, in effect, the end of the air war, although more strikes were made by the IDF/AF. Israeli helicopters were kept busy in the days and months afterwards supporting the Israeli forces occupying the southern part of Lebanon.

Air supremacy

Israeli supremacy over the SAF was absolute and owed much to the support elements. The key element was Israel's multi-faceted Air Battle Management System, one of whose major components was the newly acquired E-2C Hawkeye airborne early warning aircraft. During operations, two of the four available E-2s were kept on station off the coast. Syria later admitted that all its aircraft were detected almost as soon as they left base, robbing them of any possibility of the surprise attack. The E-2s were backed up by a number of Westinghouse low-altitude surveillance radar systems (essentially an AN/TPS-63 tactical radar slung beneath a tethered balloon). Tactical reconnaissance was provided by RF-4E Phantoms. One was lost to ground fire and, because of the sensitive nature of its avionics and sensors (some of which were of Israeli origin), the IDF/AF mounted a raid to destroy the wreckage. This raid arrived in time to catch a group of 11 Soviet personnel in the act of removing some of the 'black boxes', but was pressed home regardless. Remotely piloted vehicles (RPVs) were widely used throughout the Beka'a fighting, both for decoy and reconnaissance work. The Israeli forces used Firebee drones backed up by propeller-driven IAI Scouts. The latter were equipped with both TV and wide-angle film cameras and provided immediate post-attack intelligence.

When attacking the SAM sites, the IDF/AF planned its moves carefully. The first wave kept well clear of the opposition (about 35

Israeli tank killers

Although Israel decisively defeated Egyptian and Syrian tanks during the 1973 Yom Kippur War, the conflict illustrated the shortcomings of fixed-wing fast-jet fighter-bombers as tank killers, and set Israel on the path of acquiring dedicated anti-tank helicopters. The latter first saw service in Operation 'Peace for Galilee', and largely justified the faith which had been placed in them.

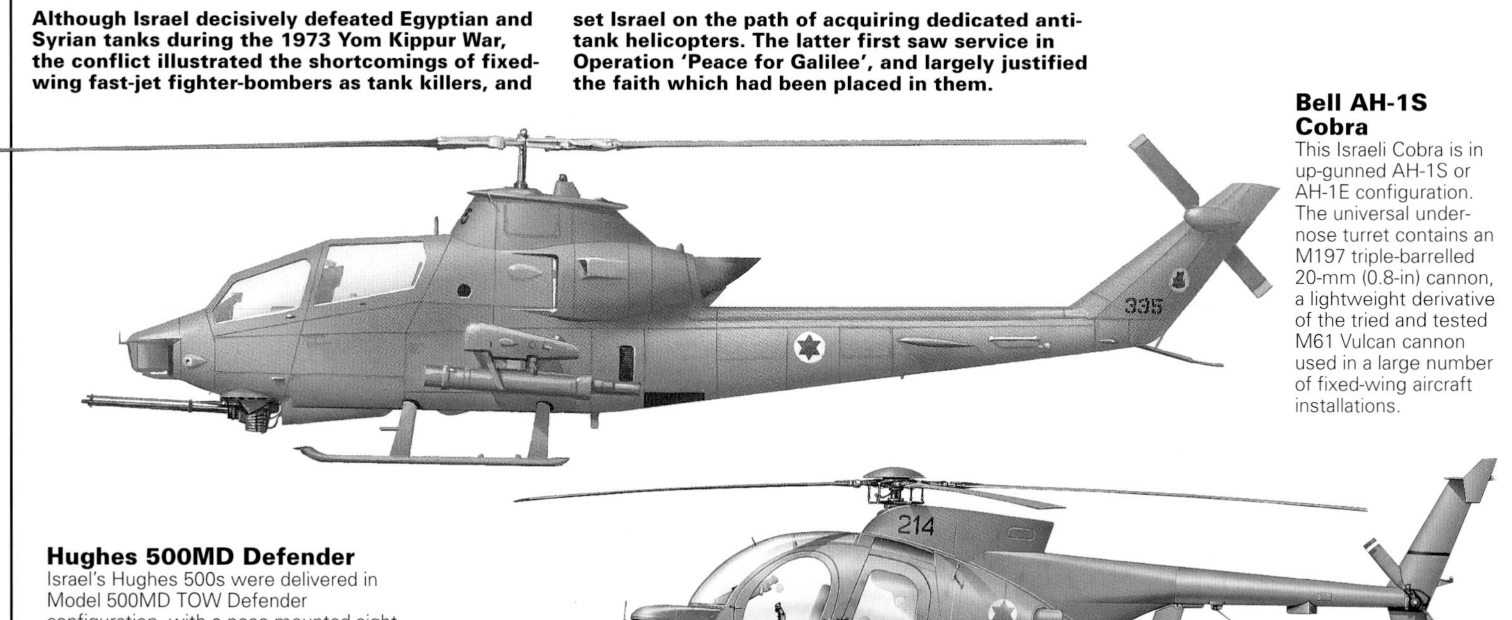

Bell AH-1S Cobra
This Israeli Cobra is in up-gunned AH-1S or AH-1E configuration. The universal under-nose turret contains an M197 triple-barrelled 20-mm (0.8-in) cannon, a lightweight derivative of the tried and tested M61 Vulcan cannon used in a large number of fixed-wing aircraft installations.

Hughes 500MD Defender
Israel's Hughes 500s were delivered in Model 500MD TOW Defender configuration, with a nose-mounted sight (similar to that fitted to the AH-1) and with provision for two (or exceptionally four) TOW (Tube-Launched Optically-Tracked Wire-Guided) anti-armour missiles on each outrigger pylon.

McDonnell Douglas F-15A Eagle

This F-15A wears the markings of Israel's No. 133 Squadron, based at Tel Nov, and carries four victory markings claimed during Operation 'Peace for Galilee'. The nickname *Skyblazer* is carried on the nose, in Hebrew.

Powerplant
The F-15A is powered by a pair of Pratt & Whitney F100-PW-100 turbofans, each rated at 111.2 kN (25,000 lb st) with afterburning.

Radar
Although the Eagle is extremely fast and remarkably agile, at the heart of its success is a superb weapon system, built around the Hughes AN/APG-63 I/J-band pulse-Doppler radar.

Internal armament
The F-15A is fitted with a single 20-mm (0.8-in) M61A1 six-barrelled cannon in the starboard wingroot, and carries 940 rounds of ammunition in a drum in the centre fuselage, below the airbrake.

Missile armament
Israeli F-15s can carry the same mix of AIM-9 Sidewinder and AIM-7 Sparrow AAMs as their USAF counterparts (as seen here), but may also carry the indigenous Shafrir, or Python IR-homing missiles.

km/22 miles) as it launched its missiles. They were intended for pinpoint attack against the nerve-centres of the SAM network, and so comprised TV-guided Mavericks as well as AGM-45 Shrike and AGM-78 Standard anti-radar weapons. With their nerve centres inoperative, the SAM sites could be attacked from closer quarters and torn apart with cluster bombs and high explosive. Phantoms undertook much of this work.

Also active before and during the attacks were the IDF/AF's Boeing 707s, much modified versions of the airliner. Fitted with side-looking radar for surveillance, they also undertook stand-off jamming of the SAM radar, as well as jamming the SAF's fighter control and navigation aid networks.

In all, 40 SAF aircraft, equally divided between MiG-21s and MiG-23s, were claimed by the 37 F-15 Eagles then in IDF/AF service (bringing that aircraft's air-fighting score to 58 for no losses). The McDonnell Douglas stable was credited with an additional victory by an F-4E. The remaining 44 SAF losses claimed by Israel went to the 72 F-16s, and again comprised MiG-21s and MiG-23s in about equal numbers.

Syria admitted the loss of 60 aircraft and 'less than 30' SAM sites. Israel claimed 92 aircraft including five Gazelle helicopters, of which 85 were fighters shot down in air-to-air combat. After initially high estimates Syria settled for a claim of 19 Israeli aircraft, of which just three were conceded: a Skyhawk and two helicopters. True IDF/AF losses seem to be two Skyhawks, a Phantom, a probable F-16, seven other aircraft (which may have been technical write-offs after returning home), and two shootdowns by the PLO (an AH-1 Cobra and a Bell 212).

Israeli aerial victory

The inevitable wrangle over shootdowns must not be allowed to obscure the fact that Israel won a resounding victory in fighter-versus-fighter combat over the Beka'a valley. Even the Syrian loss figures do not seek to deny that truth, questioning only the margin of Israel's superiority.

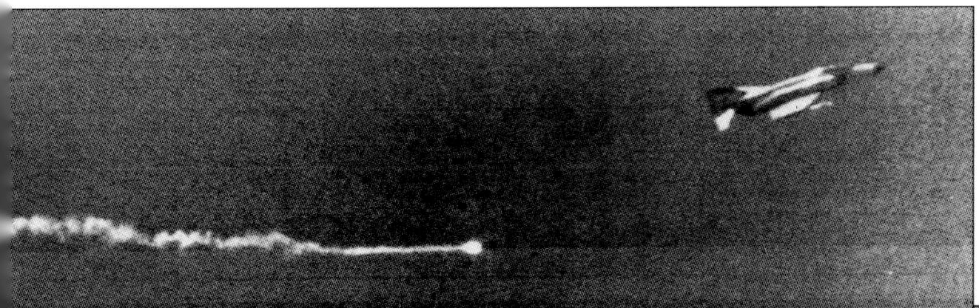

***Above:** An IDF/AF F-4E Phantom dispenses IR-decoy flares in a low-level attack. By 1982, Israeli Phantoms were equipped with comprehensive defensive systems, and had warning systems and countermeasures adequate for the modern battlefield.*

***Right:** F-16 claimed almost half of Israel's 92 claimed victories over the Beka'a. At least one contributed to 13 admitted IDF losses. Israel maintained that all its losses were to SAMs; Syrian fighters claimed at least 21 air-to-air victories and admitted to 40 air combat losses.*

Peacekeepers in Lebanon

DECEMBER 1983

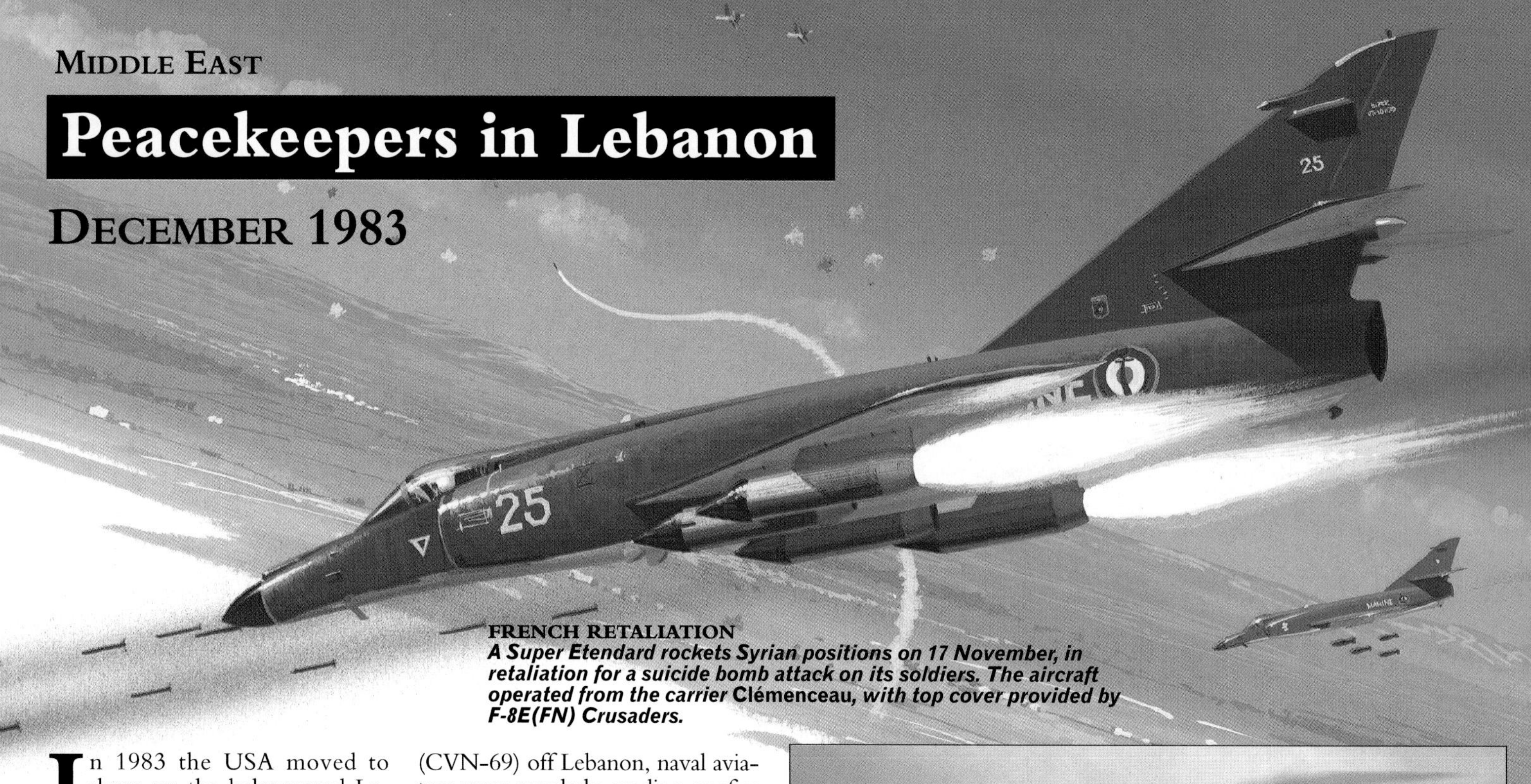

FRENCH RETALIATION
A Super Etendard rockets Syrian positions on 17 November, in retaliation for a suicide bomb attack on its soldiers. The aircraft operated from the carrier* Clémenceau*, with top cover provided by F-8E(FN) Crusaders.

In 1983 the USA moved to shore up the beleaguered Lebanese government by stationing Marines in Beirut and keeping the Sixth Fleet on alert nearby. Lebanon's fragile ethnic and religious balance had been torn asunder by the Israeli invasion and partial occupation, by Syrian partial occupation, and by the stirrings of an indigenous home-grown revolution. The US effort at peacekeeping was opposed on all sides.

The American presence was first challenged by two bombings of the US embassy in Beirut. On 24 October the US Marines compound in Beirut was struck by a suicide truck-bomb which killed 242 men. Syrian and Druze artillery positions took regular pot-shots at American ships offshore.

By September 1983, with the USS *Dwight D. Eisenhower* (CVN-69) off Lebanon, naval aviators were regularly evading gunfire while carrying out reconnaissance missions, but the *Eisenhower* was replaced before her pilots could have retribution. By October USS *John F. Kennedy* (CV-67) was the carrier on 'Bagel Station', and was soon joined by USS *Independence* (CV-62), which reached the Mediterranean after a detour to Grenada.

On 3 December the Syrians directed no fewer than 10 SAMs at a pair of TARPS-equipped VF-32 Tomcats. This was sufficient provocation for both carriers to launch an Alpha Strike of 12 A-7E Corsairs and 16 A-6E Intruders, with two F-14s providing MiGCAP above them. The A-6Es attacked Syrian gun positions and munitions sites at Falouga and Hammana, some 16-km (10-miles) north of the highway linking Beirut and Damascus. One A-6E was shot down while rolling in on a SAM radar site at Hammana. The pilot died soon after ejecting, but his bombardier-navigator ejected, and was captured.

The Corsairs, laden with cluster bombs, struck at Jabal al Knaisse and Mghite 31-km (19-miles) east of Beirut. After hitting his target, *Independence*'s carrier air wing commander (CAG) Commander Edward T. Andrews, led a SAR effort to recover the downed A-6E crew. He was shot down, but ejected safely. His parachute was carried out to sea, where he was quickly picked up by a US Navy helicopter. The two losses were perhaps inevitable, after the decision was made to send the strike aircraft into battle without organic ECM support, failing to make use of the electronic warfare capabilities of the carrier's EA-6Bs and E-2s.

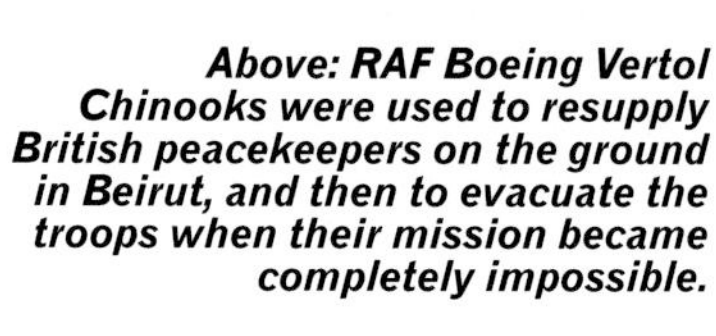

Above: RAF Boeing Vertol Chinooks were used to resupply British peacekeepers on the ground in Beirut, and then to evacuate the troops when their mission became completely impossible.

The 4 December 1983 mission failed to reinforce the US presence in Lebanon, and actually intensified hostility to that presence, and even to US influence. The Marines were soon withdrawn, leaving only a residual US presence which thereafter fell prey to hostage-taking and hijacking.

EUROPEAN PEACEKEEPERS

As foreign peacekeepers assumed the perilous and thankless task of attempting to separate warring factions in West Beirut, they brought with them their own air support. France had begun the practice of rooftop 'showing the flag' when *Foch* arrived in Lebanese waters on 6 September. Included in the air group were three Flotilles of Super Etendards, plus reconnaissance-tasked Etendard IVPs.

Below: US Marines are delivered to Beirut by a Sikorsky CH-53E Super Stallion. The Marine positions around the airport were vulnerable to artillery fire from the nearby Chouf mountains, but suicide truck bombers proved to be a far more devastating threat.

Farther to the rear, at the British sovereign base of Akrotiri, the RAF deployed three Chinooks and six Buccaneer S.Mk 2Bs between 7 and 9 September. These helicopters were tasked with re-supply flights to Beirut. The Buccaneers' were retasked from maritime strike to overland attack and were maintained on alert at all times, loaded with 454-kg (1,000-lb) bombs. They announced their arrival on 11 September with a low-level beat-up of Beirut, but thereafter kept a discreet distance. Six Aeritalia F-104S Starfighters of the Italian air force were also deployed to Akrotiri, and were similarly circumspect.

US carrier aircraft were used to strike at Lebanese artillery threatening the Marine positions in Beirut. One A-6 and one A-7 were lost to SAMs.

Hunters in action

On 16 September the Lebanese Air Force (LAF) undertook its first combat action for a decade. Operating from a motorway airstrip 30-km (19-miles) north of Beirut, five Hunters struck at Druze militia positions in the Chouf mountains. One was badly hit by 23-mm AAA fire, forcing the pilot to eject into the sea, from where he was rescued by a USN helicopter. One more Hunter suffered damage and two more diverted to Akrotiri. On 19 September, a Bulldog trainer used as an observation aircraft was shot down by ground fire.

In response to an attack on its troops, France launched a reprisal raid on 22 September, sending four Aéronavale Super Etendards to bomb four Druze gun batteries, some 20-km (12-miles) east of Beirut. F-8E(FN) Crusaders provided top cover, and Etendard IVMs undertook pre- and post-raid reconnaissance. The air group transferred to *Foch*'s newly-arrived sister ship *Clémenceau* early in October. In a further attack on 17 November (mounted in retaliation for a suicide 'lorry bomb' which killed 58 French soldiers) 14 Super Etendards made two largely unsuccessful raids against Shia militia barracks close to the Syrian border. Also active was the IDF/AF, which had raided targets near Baalbek on 16 November. It returned to strike Palestinian guerrilla bases in three Lebanese towns on 20 November, losing a Kfir to a Syrian missile near Bhamdoun. Another Israeli mission on 3 December coincided with the US Navy Alpha Strike.

Withdrawal

The other would-be peacekeepers had fared no better than the United States. France, Italy and the UK all withdrew their troops during March and April 1984 when it became apparent that their task was impossible. Royal Navy Sea King HC.M 4s were used to extract the British contingent from Lebanon. On 14 February, the LAF was back in action when two Hunters fired rockets at Druze militia. Four sorties failed to prevent the Druze linking up with the Shia forces then controlling south and west Beirut, and supporting US naval gunfire was equally unsuccessful. Israel returned to the fray on 19 February, launching its fighter-bombers against the southern port of Damour and the towns of Aley and Bhamdoun southeast of Beirut.

As the multi-national peacekeeping force completed its withdrawal, Israel and Syria were left alone to resume their strategy of playing off the rival Lebanese factions against each other, backed by the periodic IDF/AF air raids against alleged Palestinian guerrilla targets. Israel long ago learned that keeping its hostile neighbours fighting amongst themselves can be an effective means of deterring direct attacks.

***Left:* A detachment of six Blackburn Buccaneers of Nos 12 and 208 Squadron flew low-level flag-waving sorties over Beirut and stood ready to mount retaliatory air strikes. Fortunately, the order to attack never came.**

Ageing warriors

Peacekeeping operations over the Lebanon provided an opportunity for a number of elderly aircraft types to prove their mettle. The French carrier air groups included Etendard IVP reconnaissance aircraft and Crusader fighters, while the RAF deployed Buccaneers to its base on the island of Cyprus. Lebanon's own air force used its ancient Hawker Hunters.

Hawker Hunter F.Mk 70

Left: While Lebanon's Mach 2 Mirage fighters remained in storage, a flight of Hawker Hunters was thrown into the fighting, attacking militia targets with accuracy and daring. One of the Hunters was shot down, but the credibility of the Lebanese armed forces was enhanced.

LTV F-8E(FN) Crusader

Right: Both the *Foch* and the *Clémenceau* deployed F-8E(FN) Crusaders from Flotille 12F for air-defence duties. These flew CAP and escort missions, but were not called upon to engage hostile aircraft.

US-Libyan confrontations

1981-1989

During the 1980s, the USA found itself clashing with Colonel Khadaffi's Libya on a number of occasions, a war of words boiling over into military action several times. Both the USA and Britain maintained bases in Libya until 1967, when growing nationalism prompted the Libyan government to ask for the two foreign nations to withdraw. In 1969 the government (and King Idris) were overthrown by the young Colonel Khadaffi, a revolutionary nationalist and devout Muslim who was implacably opposed to Imperialism. Within two years of seizing power, Khadaffi had established links and military aid agreements with the USSR, and in 1972 nationalised British oil interests in the country.

In October 1973 Libya unilaterally expanded its territorial waters to latitude 32°30' N, enclosing the Gulf of Sidra (also known as the Gulf of Sirte). A USAF Hercules flying in the general area was inconclusively attacked by Libyan fighters shortly afterwards.

As he consolidated power, Khadaffi became more active internationally, lending support to forces fighting against what he saw as Imperialism, from the PLO to the IRA (most of the rest of the world seeing this support as being tantamount to the state sponsorship of terrorism). As a convinced Pan Arab he was bitterly opposed to Egypt's rapprochement with Israel, and instigated a brief border war with Egypt in 1977 aiming to discourage peace initiatives. In 1980 Libyan-backed rebels operating from within Libya attacked neighbouring Tunisia. But Khadaffi was willing to confront the USA directly, and not just its client states.

Above: F-14A Tomcats provided fighter cover for the strike force. It has been suggested that an F-14 was responsible for the loss of the single F-111 which failed to return.

Left: An A-6E Intruder of VMA-533 'Hawks' launches from the USS Saratoga, passing a parked VMAQ-2 'Playboys' EA-6B. Each of the three carriers involved in Operation 'El Dorado Canyon' carried a single squadron of A-6s, with a detachment of EA-6Bs.

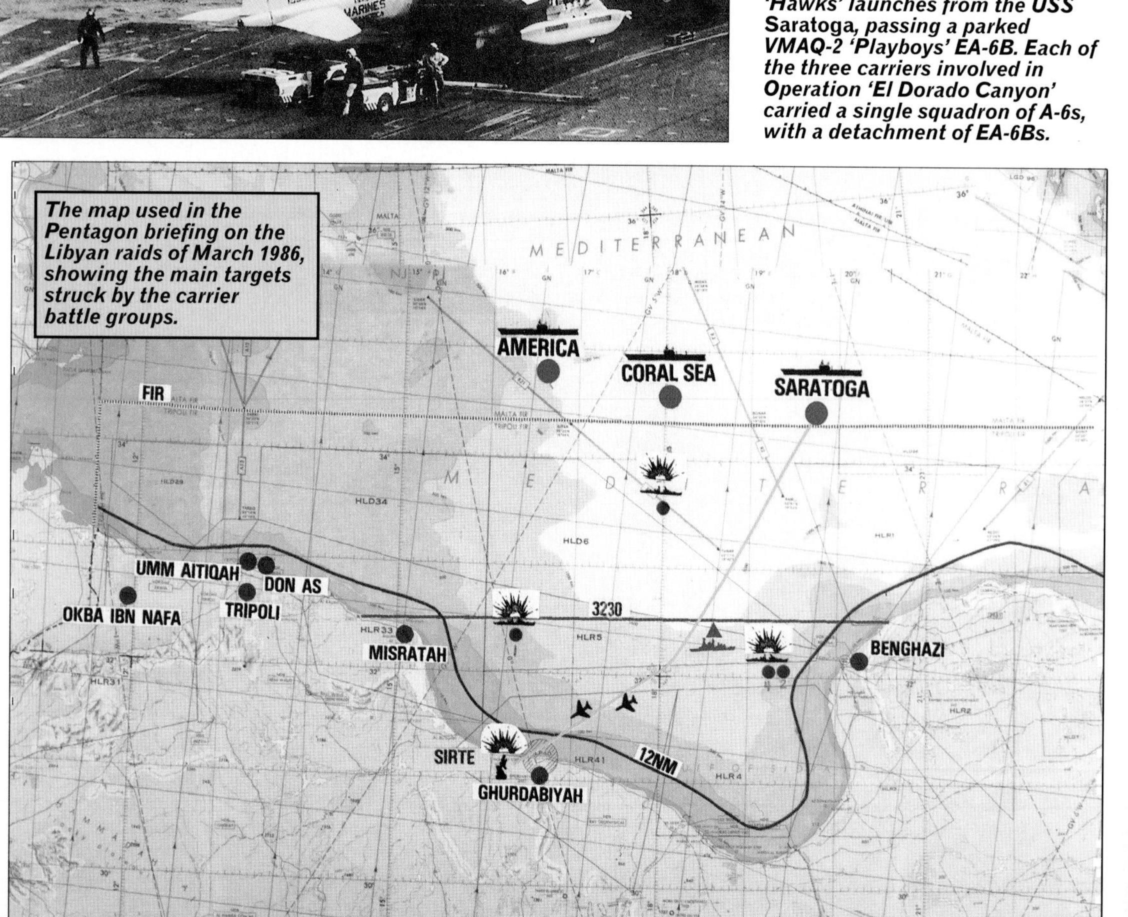

The map used in the Pentagon briefing on the Libyan raids of March 1986, showing the main targets struck by the carrier battle groups.

The USA had never recognised Libya's unilateral extension of its territorial waters, and units from the Mediterranean-based Sixth Fleet regularly exercised in the Gulf of Sidra, ostensibly undertaking 'Freedom of Navigation' exercises, but also demonstrating America's military power and Libya's inability to prevent such manoeuvres. US Navy aircraft participating in such exercises frequently found themselves intercepting or being intercepted by a mix of Libyan fighters, from French-supplied Mirage F1s to Mikoyan MiG-25s. Rules of engagement were strict, and initially neither side fired upon the other.

FIRST KILLS

All that changed on 19 August 1981, when two F-14 Tomcats of

Below: Final preparations are made to an A-7E Corsair of VA-81 aboard the USS Saratoga. The aircraft carries a single fuel tank, two Rockeye cluster bombs and a single HARM missile, with two AIM-9s.

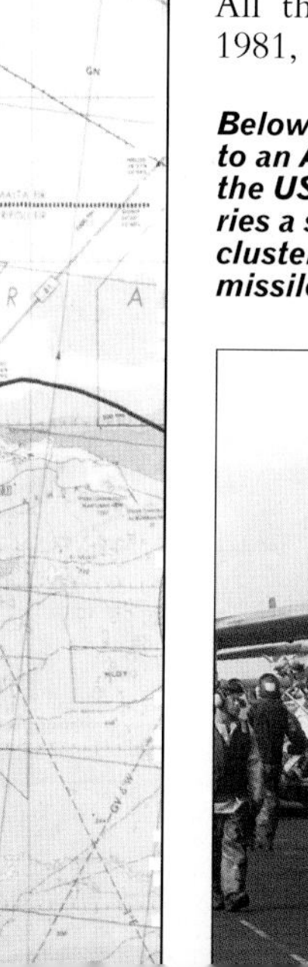

The USAF in El Dorado Canyon

Many US military operations in the 1980s were planned to involve as many of the four armed services as possible, since none wanted to be left out and all wanted a share in the glory. This proved fatal in Operation 'Eagle Claw', when helicopter pilots were selected to involve the USMC, rather than for their suitability. El Dorado Canyon could have been undertaken solely by carrier-based aircraft, but the USAF ensured that it was not left out.

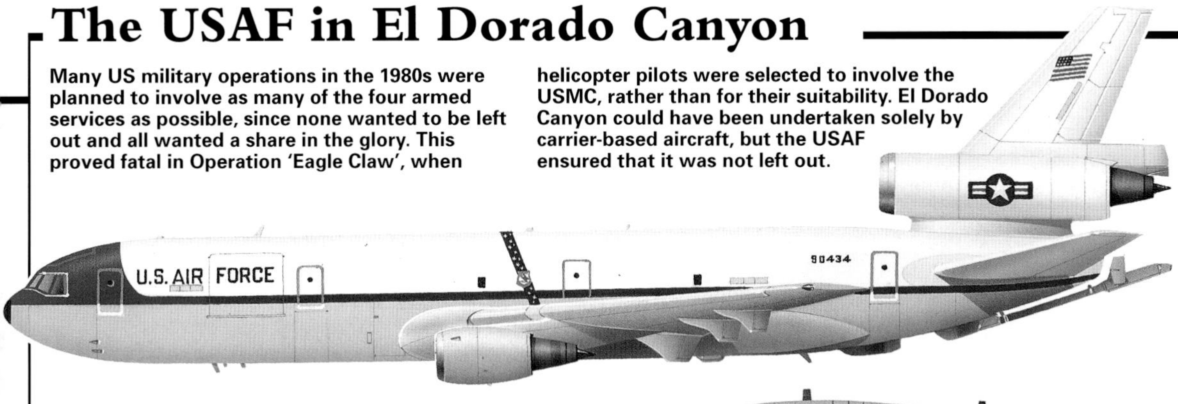

McDonnell Douglas KC-10A
Left: The flight of 24 F-111Fs (including six back-up aircraft which turned back after one inflight refuelling) and six EF-111As (one of which turned back) from Britain to Libya required massive tanker support. KC-10As from three units were involved.

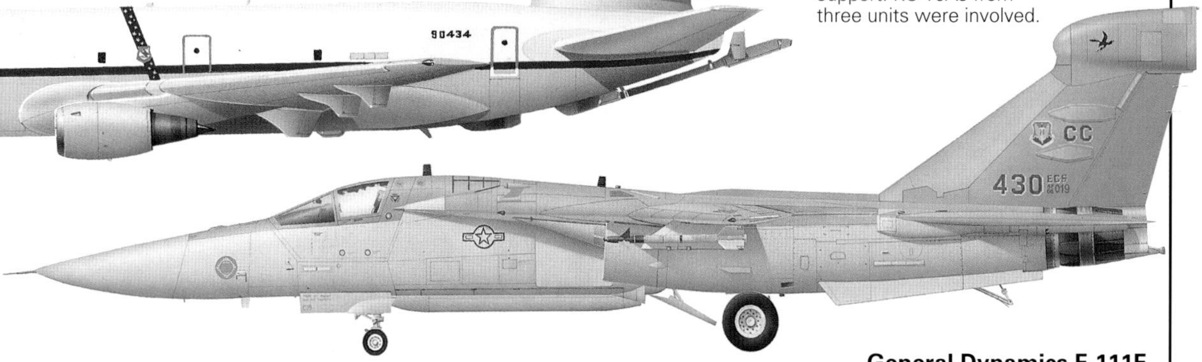

Grumman/General Dynamics EF-111A Raven
Right: Six EF-111As from the 42nd Electronic Combat Squadron took off from RAF Upper Heyford fin England or Operation 'El Dorado Canyon'. Two were spares, one of which turned back after the first refuelling, while the other went all the way to the target. The EF-111As provided electronic warfare support for the F-111Fs, jamming Libyan air defence and SAM guidance radars.

General Dynamics F-111F
Left: Some 24 F-111Fs took off from Lakenheath for El Dorado Canyon, the six air spares dropping out as planned after the first refuelling over the Bay of Biscay. Unfortunately, five of the remaining 18 strike aircraft aborted before reaching their targets. Eight attacked Khadaffi's HQ at Al Aziziyah, and the barracks at Sidi Bilal, while the other five attacked Tripoli airport's military ramps.

VF-41, based aboard the USS *Nimitz*, were intercepted by a pair of Sukhoi Su-22 'Fitter-Js'. These non-radar fighter-bombers were occasionally used as fighters by the Libyans, and had been encountered carrying AA-2 'Atoll' IR-homing missiles, so did represent a threat, of sorts. As he manoeuvred to try to get on the tails of the Sukhois, one of the F-14 pilots thought he saw a missile being fired at him (perhaps a missile which failed to track, perhaps only an external fuel tank being jettisoned), and under the Rules of Engagement, this allowed him to fire back. Both of the Libyan fighters were despatched in short order, one pilot bailing out successfully.

Prairie fire

Increasing Libyan support for terrorism (and especially for the PLO) prompted a 1985 Washington declaration that terrorist actions would meet with a strong military reaction, and it was made clear that Libya itself might be targeted. Khadaffi responded by declaring a 'Line of Death' across the Gulf of Sidra. This was an open invitation for the Sixth Fleet to conduct more 'Freedom of Navigation' exercises, and the carriers *Saratoga* and *America* (with *Coral Sea*) entered the Gulf of Sidra. This marked the start of Operation 'Prairie Fire', which was specifically aimed at drawing a Libyan reaction that would itself justify US military action. On 24 March 1986 Libya responded to the provocation by launching SA-5 SAMs at USN aircraft, and this in turn drew a response, with A-7Es from VA-83 attacking the SAM site with HARM missiles. When Libyan navy vessels threatened US Navy ships they were attacked, with a Combattante II patrol boat being sunk by a pair of VA-34 Intruders, and with another patrol boat and a Nanuchka II Corvette falling victim to more A-6Es that evening and the next day. Another patrol boat was sunk by the USS *Yorktown*.

A terrorist attack on a Berlin disco on 5 April 1986 killed a US soldier, and was thought to have had Libyan backing, and the USA decided to react more strongly, justifying its actions by its 'inherent right of self defence, recognised in Article 51 of the UN Charter'. Plans were made for a massive co-ordinated air attack by the USAF and the USN on Libya, aimed at Libyan military targets

Above: Il-76s at Tripoli airport seen through the AN/AVQ-26 Pave Tack laser designator of one of the attacking F-111Fs. Six Il-76s, a Boeing 737 and a G.222 were destroyed in the attack.

Left: A bombladen A-6E Intruder taxies forward onto the catapult. The A-6Es were capable of precision strikes, using their Norden AN/APQ-148 radars and AN/AAS-33 TRAM packages of EO sensors and laser designators.

Below: Lakenheath's F-111Fs attacked their targets with GBU-10 Paveway 907-kg (2,000-lb) laser-guided bombs. Each carried four of these weapons, designating targets with its underfuselage AN/AVQ-26 Pave Tack pod. The F-111s achieved superb accuracy, but there was heavy collateral damage.

Above: Cluster bombs are wheeled out to waiting F/A-18A Hornets aboard the USS Coral Sea. CVW-13 embarked four instead of the usual two Hornet attack squadrons, including two Marines Corps units.

(including Khadaffi himself), and terrorist training facilities. Ironically, while the USA was launching what it liked to describe as a decisive blow against terrorism, it was itself conducting an arms-for-hostages deal with another sponsor of terrorism, Iran.

PREPARATIONS UNDERWAY

Boeing RC-135s based in Greece, augmented by Rota-based EA-3Bs and EP-3Es flew intensive Elint missions against Libya, while Cyprus-based TR-1As and SR-71s from RAF Mildenhall flew photo-reconnaissance missions over possible targets.

France and Spain were not prepared to allow aircraft involved in an attack on Libya to overfly their territory, but the participation of USAF F-111s based in Britain was felt to be essential, and a 8047-km (5,000-mile) round trip around France and Spain then through the Straits of Gibraltar and along the north-African coast by these aircraft was accepted willingly. This necessitated the provision of massive tanker support, and 32 KC-10A Extenders and 34 KC-135 Stratotankers were deployed to British bases!

On 15 April 1986, Operation 'El Dorado Canyon' was launched. The 18 F-111Fs (plus six air-spares) of the 48th TFW took off from Lakenheath at about 18.30 BST (20:30 in Libya), at about the same time as three EF-111As (plus two air-spares) took off from Upper Heyford. With all of the designated attack aircraft fully-serviceable, the six spare F-111Fs, and one of the spare EF-111As, turned back after the first refuelling, over the Bay of Biscay. A small fleet of support aircraft, protected by a HVACAP of US Navy F-14s arrived on station at about 00:30 (local). These included an EC-135E from the 7th ACCS, an E-3A of the 960th AWCS, E-2Cs from VAW-123 and VAW-127 and EA-3Bs from VQ-2.

Several of the USAF F-111s had started to experience problems, and by the time they reached Libya, five had been forced to abort. This left a group of eight aircraft (instead of the planned 12) to attack Khadaffi's headquarters at Al Aziziyah barracks, and the Sidi Bilal training camp. The remaining five (instead of the planned six) attacked the military area of Tripoli airport, destroying six Il-76s, a Boeing 737 and a G.222 on the ground. The F-111s attacked at high speed (400 kts +) and low level (61 m/200 ft), using their AN/AVQ-26 Pave Tack equipment to designate for their GBU-10 907-kg (2,000-lb) Paveway laser-guided bombs. One F-111F crashed into the sea on its egress, possibly shot down by a SAM or groudfire, or even by a US Navy F-14.

While the USAF attacked targets in the west of Libya, around Tripoli, the Navy took targets in the east, around Benghazi. Eight A-6Es from VA-196 (with a single EA-6B) aboard the USS *Coral Sea* attacked Benina airfield, supported by six F/A-18s from VFA-132 and

Above: F/A-18s from the Coral Sea used AGM-88A HARM missiles for defence suppression, and cluster bombs to attack vulnerable radar arrays. CVW-13's Hornet units were backed up by a medium attack-squadron with eight A-6E Intruders.

Below: Pylons empty, an F-111F approaches a tanker on its long journey home. Poor serviceability detracted from the F-111Fs success, with five aircraft failing to attack their targets.

MCDONNELL DOUGLAS F/A-18A HORNET

USS Coral Sea (CV-43) arrived on station with the Sixth Fleet carrying an experimental Air Wing with no less than 48 F/A-18s in four squadrons. The F/A-18 was still very new, and the cruise was the aircraft's first. While a US carrier force gathered off Libya, Hornets flew Combat Air Patrols to protect their battle group from threat. Libyan interceptors came out to pry around and the F/A-18A pilots found themselves intercepting, challenging and escorting MiG-25s, Su-22s and Mirages. The Hornet proved versatile and dependable during subsequent combat operations and began what was to be a highly successful US Navy career.

Defence suppression mission
The Hornet made its combat debut carrying out the SEAD (Suppression of Enemy Air Defences) role, using its comprehensive onboard RHAWS equipment and AGM-88A HARM defence suppression weapons. F/A-18s participating in Operation 'Prairie Fire' used HARMs to knock out SA-5 SAM sites at Sirte. One month later, HARMs were used once again with devastating effect against Libyan air defence radars around Benina airfield during 'El Dorado Canyon'.

Markings
For operations aboard the *Coral Sea*, VMFA-314's normal 'VW' tailcode was replaced by the 'AK' tailcode normally allocated to CVW-13.

Hornet deployment
The two Navy Hornet squadrons, VFA-131 'Wildcats' and VFA-132 'Privateers' were augmented by two Marine Corps units; VMF(A)-314 'Black Knights' and VMFA-232 'Death Ratters' for combat operations over Libya. Although USMC F/A-18 squadrons are regularly deployed today aboard Navy carriers, in 1986 such deployments were rare.

The Tomcat draws blood

The USA has made extensive use of carrier-based aircraft to challenge and intimidate Libya when it has attempted to extend its territorial waters. Libyan and US Navy fighters have met over the Gulf of Sidra regularly, and on two separate occasions, in 1981 and 1989, pairs of Libyan fighters have been shot down by US Navy F-14 Tomcats. In both instances all particpants were flying 'swing-wing' fighters: F-14s, Su-22s and MiG-23s.

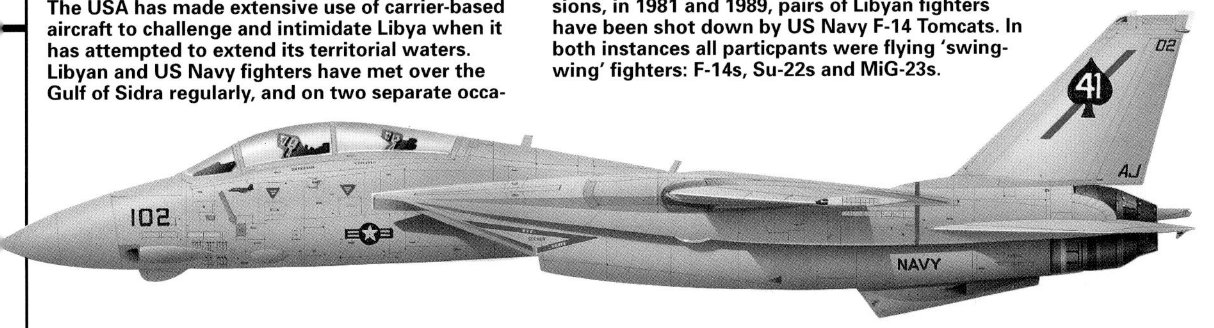

Grumman F-14A Tomcat
Left: This F-14A of VF-41 (callsign 'Fast Eagle 107' was flown by Cdr Hank Kleeman in the 19 August 1981 engagement which resulted in the downing of two Libyan Su-22 'Fitters'. Kleeman himself downed one of the enemy aircraft, the other falling to an AIM-9 Sidewinder fired by his wingman, Lt Harry ('Music') Muczynski.

Mikoyan MiG-23MF 'Flogger-B'
Right: Two Libyan MiG-23s were shot down on 4 January 1989, after making what the US Navy claimed was a threatening approach. Images from the Tomcats' Television Camera System were released purporting to show that the aircraft were 'Flogger-Bs' armed with R-23 (AA-7 'Apex') semi-active radar-homing AAMs, whereas others maintained that they were 'Flogger-Es' with only close-in R-60 (AA-8 'Aphid') IR-homing AAMs.

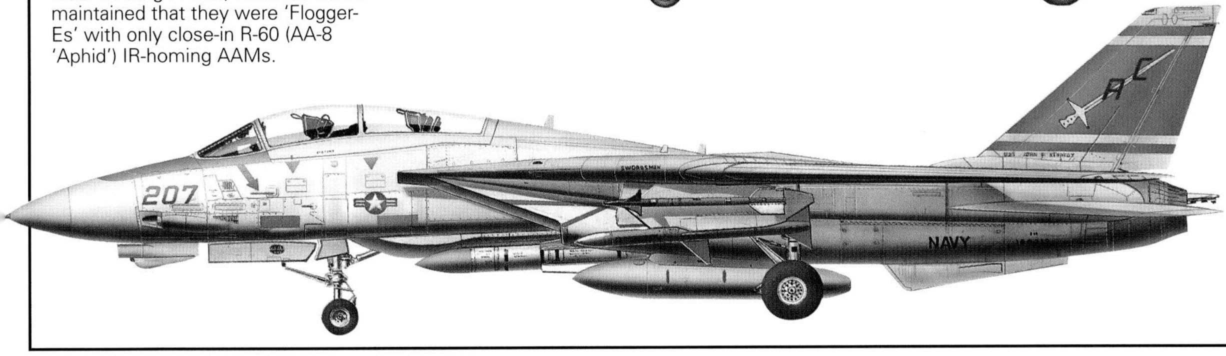

Grumman F-14A Tomcat
Left: On 4 January 1989 two Libyan MiG-23s kept turning in towards two F-14s from VF-32 'Swordsmen' as the latter manoeuvred to get on the MiGs' tails. This was construed as hostile and Cdr. Joseph B.Connolly, flying the lead F-14, fired two AIM-7s and an AIM-9 to down the two enemy aircraft. The MiG pilots ejected, but were reportedly not rescued by Libyan SAR forces.

VMFA-323 and by six VA-46 and VA-72 A-7Es from the USS *America*, armed with HARM and Shrike missiles. Four MiG-23s, two Mi-8s and two F27s were destroyed at Benina, and many more aircraft were damaged. Six A-6Es from VA-34, and a single EA-6B from VAQ-135 aboard the *America* attacked Al Jamahiriyak Barracks. The A-6Es dropped conventional 227- and 340-kg (500- and 750-lb) dumb bombs.

More kills for the F-14

The 1986 airstrikes did not resolve the situation between the USA and Libya. On 4 January 1989 two F-14s of VF-32, operating from the *John F. Kennedy*, (carrying out Freedom of Navigation operations in the Gulf of Sidra), felt threatened by a pair of Libyan MiG-23s. Rules of Engagement did not require the F-14s to be fired upon, and the Libyan fighters were shot down. By 1988, the USA was more concerned with Iran (attempting to deny the Persian Gulf to shipping), and the 1990 invasion of Kuwait elevated Saddam Hussein's Iraq to the status of 'Public Enemy No. 1', while the peace deal between Israel and the Palestinians has dramatically reduced the impact of terrorism against US interests. But it would be premature to believe that the tension between Libya and the USA is over.

Below: Other Libyan aircraft regularly intercepted by US Navy fighters during the 1980s were MiG-25P 'Foxbat-As' and MiG-25PD 'Foxbat-Es'. Some were rumoured to have been flown by Soviet pilots.

Above: Libyan Su-20 and Su-22 'Fitters' are used for air-defence duties, as well as fulfilling their intended ground-attack role. Two were shot down by US Navy F-14As on 19 August 1981.

Right: One of 16 radar-equipped Mirage F1EDs delivered to Libya from January 1978, alongside 16 Mirage F1AD fighter bombers and six F1BD two-seat trainers. All are based at Okba ibn Nafa.

Gulf War: Desert Shield

AUGUST 1990-JANUARY 1991

The F-15C Eagles of the USAF's 1st Tactical Fighter Wing were the first warplanes to deploy to the Gulf, making a 17-hour flight with numerous air refuellings.

The Iraqi invasion of Kuwait in August 1990 was the culmination of a long dispute between two neighbouring but very different Arab states. Both were oil producers, but Iraq was a brutal dictatorship fielding the fourth-largest army in the world, while Kuwait was a more benign totalitarian state whose native population was outnumbered by resident Palestinians and guest workers drawn from all over the Arab and Muslim world.

After the conclusion of his war with Iran, Saddam Hussein turned his attention towards Kuwait. The ruler of Iraq accused the Kuwaitis of 'slant-drilling' oil wells from their own territory to steal oil from the Iraqi fields around Basra. This, together with the allegation that Kuwait and the Saudis had kept oil prices low in order to hurt Iraq, provided the pretext for invasion. An unspoken, but probably very important, reason for military action was Iraq's lack of an unrestricted port on the Gulf, without which its trade would always be at the mercy of the Iranians or the members of the Gulf Co-operation Council.

Iraq began massing troops on the Kuwaiti border. April Glaspie, the American ambassador to Iraq, in a meeting two weeks before the invasion of Kuwait, informed Saddam Hussein that the USA had no interest in internal affairs of the Gulf region. Saddam took this to mean that there would be no opposition to his annexation of Kuwait.

On 2 August 1990, overwhelming Iraqi forces overran Kuwait. At a stroke, Saddam Hussein had seized control of the world's second-largest oil reserves, and threatened the world's largest, just over the border in Saudi Arabia. His troops immediately began a reign of terror, seizing anything valuable and shipping their ill-gotten gains back to Baghdad.

WORLD REACTION

The world community, led by the United States, immediately took action in response to this threat to vital oil resources. Large American air and naval forces together with elements of the 82nd Airborne Division were deployed to the Gulf in an operation called Desert Shield, with the intention of defending the Saudi oil fields.

First into the breach, in a powerful display of the strategic mobility of air power, were 48 F-15C/D Eagles of the USAF's 1st Tactical Fighter Wing. Deploying from Langley Air Force Base on 7 August, less than a day after King Fahd of Saudi Arabia requested assistance, they flew armed and ready to fight their way in on the possibility that Saddam had not stopped at Kuwait. They were on the Kuwaiti border 16 hours later.

At the same time the USS *Dwight D. Eisenhower* entered the Red Sea, the first element of the most powerful carrier force ever deployed, which would include six carrier air wings by the time war broke out. B-52 bombers were

Left: A Tornado under guard. Given Saddam Hussein's 'grab' of Kuwait, an Iraqi march onward to Saudi oilfields and air bases looked imminent. The first members of the Coalition to arrive had little real security but protected their aircraft as well as they could.

Below: Kuwait's principal combat aircraft in 1990 was the Douglas A-4KU Skyhawk. Some of these, with their pilots, escaped the takeover of their country by Iraqi forces. Exiled, they became part of the forces of 'Free Kuwait', in the growing anti-Saddam coalition.

deployed to Diego Garcia in the Indian Ocean, and forces from other nations began to arrive in the region. These included a squadron of air defence Tornados from Britain's Royal Air Force deployed alongside similar Saudi machines, a Jaguar squadron in Oman, and the initial elements of France's rapid reaction force. By the end of August large numbers of US Marine F/A-18 Hornets and AV-8B Harriers were in-theatre. And for the first time, the Lockheed F-117 Nighthawk – the 'stealth fighter' – was openly committed to battle, the first 22 examples of the type arriving on 21st August.

American diplomatic pressure nudged the United Nations into action with unprecedented speed, resolutions being passed which demanded immediate Iraqi withdrawal and implementing economic sanctions against the aggressor.

In November, US President George Bush decided to double the size of American forces deployed to the Gulf. Along with contributions from other nations, including the United Kingdom, France, Egypt, Syria and the Gulf states, the anti-Saddam Coalition now had more than enough power to defend Saudi Arabia from any threat. In fact, Coalition forces were now strong enough to undertake the expulsion of the Iraqis from Kuwait if necessary. Further United Nations resolutions gave Saddam Hussein until 15 January to get out of Kuwait; should he not do so, the Coalition was authorised to go to war.

Iraq intends to stay

Far from withdrawing, the Iraqis moved massive reinforcements into Kuwait, and began digging a formidable series of fortifications along the Kuwaiti/Saudi border. Media pundits talked knowledgeably about the Iraqi 'berms', or sand-walls, backed by anti-tank ditches and minefields, which with entrenched troops and large quantities of dug-in armour and artillery would make any frontal assault ruinously expensive in terms of human lives. But the war did not start on the ground, and the extensive Iraqi fortifications did them no good at all.

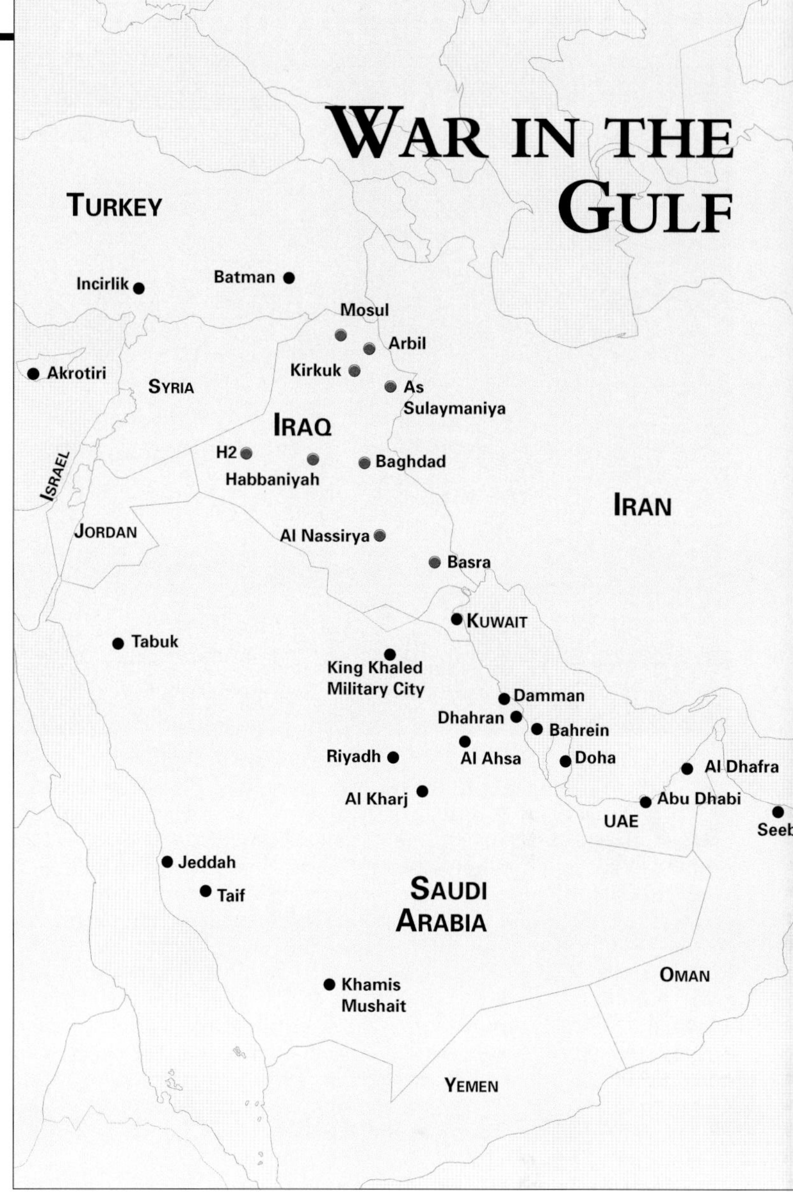

Left: American troops poured into Saudi Arabia and the Gulf states. First on the scene was the US 82nd Airborne Division, which always keeps at least one battalion ready for instant rapid deployment. Soon, more troops with heavier equipment bulwarked the Coalition as war grew more likely.

Above: Oil-rich Kuwait was a tempting prize for Iraq's Saddam Hussein, who apparently expected to seize a neighbour's turf and get away with it. The Coalition allies' first task was to mount a defence of Saudi Arabia, and then to get the Iraqis out of Kuwait, by force if necessary.

Oil defenders

A US Air Force pilot stepped out of his F-15 Eagle in Dhahran after the 17-hour trip, looked around, and was relieved to see the airfield still in friendly hands. For tense days and weeks beginning in August 1990, no one knew how long that situation would prevail, and F-15C Eagle and Tornado F.Mk 3 ADV (Air Defence Variant) interceptors flew patrols to keep Iraqi warplanes from crossing the line.

Victorious 'Spirit'
Left: 'Gulf Spirit' was the F-15C Eagle piloted by 33rd TFW wing commander Col Rick Parsons, who claimed two aerial victories when the buildup became a conflict. Crew chief on this Eagle was Staff Sergeant Craig Sniff.

Saudi ADV
Right: Saudi Arabia integrated its 24 Tornado F.Mk 3 ADV interceptors into the Coalition air defence network, which also included British ADVs. These aircraft scored no combat 'kills' once the shooting started, but a Saudi pilot in one of that country's F-15C Eagles got two victories on one mission.

Gulf War: Desert Storm

JANUARY 1991

Above: It was the first war which started live on worldwide television. In Baghdad, journalists hunkered down in their hotel rooms and continued broadcasting while Iraqi anti-aircraft fire lit up the night skies. Some of the shooting was aimed at American F-117s and cruise missiles, but much of it was fired blind, and had no affect on the attackers.

On the night of 16/17 January, the skies of Baghdad lit up as Iraqi gunners blasted at targets they could not see. Explosions ripped through the night, as American F-117A 'stealth fighters' and BGM-109 Tomahawk cruise missiles hit with pinpoint accuracy at Iraqi command and communications targets. Operation Desert Shield had now become Operation Desert Storm.

The F-117 had not covered itself in glory on its first combat outing, over Panama in 1989, but any doubts about its utility were resolved in the Gulf, where the stealth fighter proved to be an outstanding success. Its unique facetted construction scattered radar energy away from enemy transmitters, making it next to impossible for defenders to get a radar 'fix'.

Its low observability meant that the F-117 could orbit in the general area of a target, giving its pilot plenty of time to locate targets with forward-looking and downward-looking infra-red sensors. With much less time pressure than in conventional aircraft, the pilot could also concentrate more on the delivery of its weapons. Over Baghdad the 'Black Jet' showed phenomenal accuracy, being able to deliver 907-kg (2,000-lb) GBU-24 laser guided bombs through doorways and down ventilation holes to destroy underground bunker.

In parallel with the knock-out blow against Saddam Hussein's ability to command his armies, the Coalition air forces also made a determined effort to obliterate Iraq's air defences, in order to deny the enemy the skies. American defence suppression aircraft, which included McDonnell Douglas F-4G 'Wild Weasels', F/A-18 Hornets, General Dynamics/Grumman EF-111 'Sparkvaarks', Grumman A-6 Intruders and EA-6 Prowlers, targetted Iraqi air defence radars and missile sites with powerful electronic jamming systems and HARM anti-radiation missiles.

Iraq's air facilities came under particularly heavy attack. Strike aircraft like the Anglo-French Jaguar, the F-16 Fighting Falcon and the F/A-18 Hornet mounted heavy raids with conventional bombs and cluster munitions against the major airfield complexes. British and Saudi Tornados used their JP233 runway-denial munitions against runways and taxiways, though thanks to their low-level tactics British losses were relatively high. However the real knock-out blows came when the allies attacked the Iraqis in their hangars.

Iraq made extensive use of the hardened aircraft shelter or HAS, based on those used in Europe at the end of the Cold War. Each

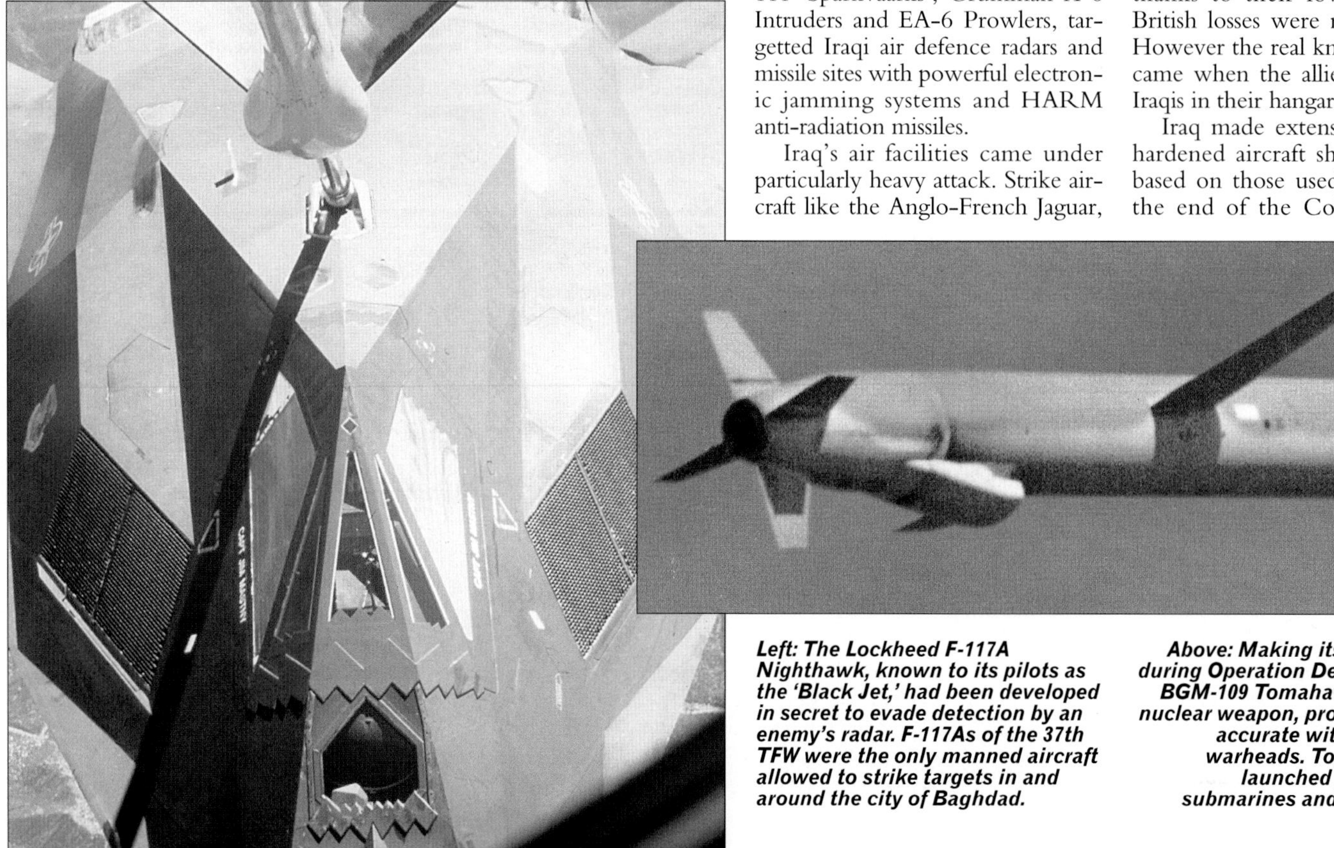

Left: The Lockheed F-117A Nighthawk, known to its pilots as the 'Black Jet,' had been developed in secret to evade detection by an enemy's radar. F-117As of the 37th TFW were the only manned aircraft allowed to strike targets in and around the city of Baghdad.

Above: Making its combat debut during Operation Desert Storm, the BGM-109 Tomahawk, originally a nuclear weapon, proved stunningly accurate with conventional warheads. Tomahawks were launched from warships, submarines and B-52 bombers.

The 'Black Jet'

The Lockheed F-117A Nighthawk was slow, ugly, and many considered it to be limited in its military application, but it captured the imagination like no other aircraft of the 1990s. Never before had an aircraft been developed in such secrecy, nor had any aircaft been designed from the outset to employ 'stealth,' to defeat an enemy's radar. When war came in the Persian Gulf region, the F-117A flew sedately and invisibly through the intensive air defences of Baghdad, dropped their bombs precisely, and emerged unscathed. The F-117 represented only 2.5 per cent of the shooters in theatre on the first day of the war, yet hit over 31 per cent of the targets. During the war, 45 F-117s and about 60 pilots flew 1,271 combat sorties, dropped over 2,000 tons of bombs, flew over 6,900 hours, and – as the US Air Force described it – 'demonstrated accuracy unmatched in the history of air warfare'.

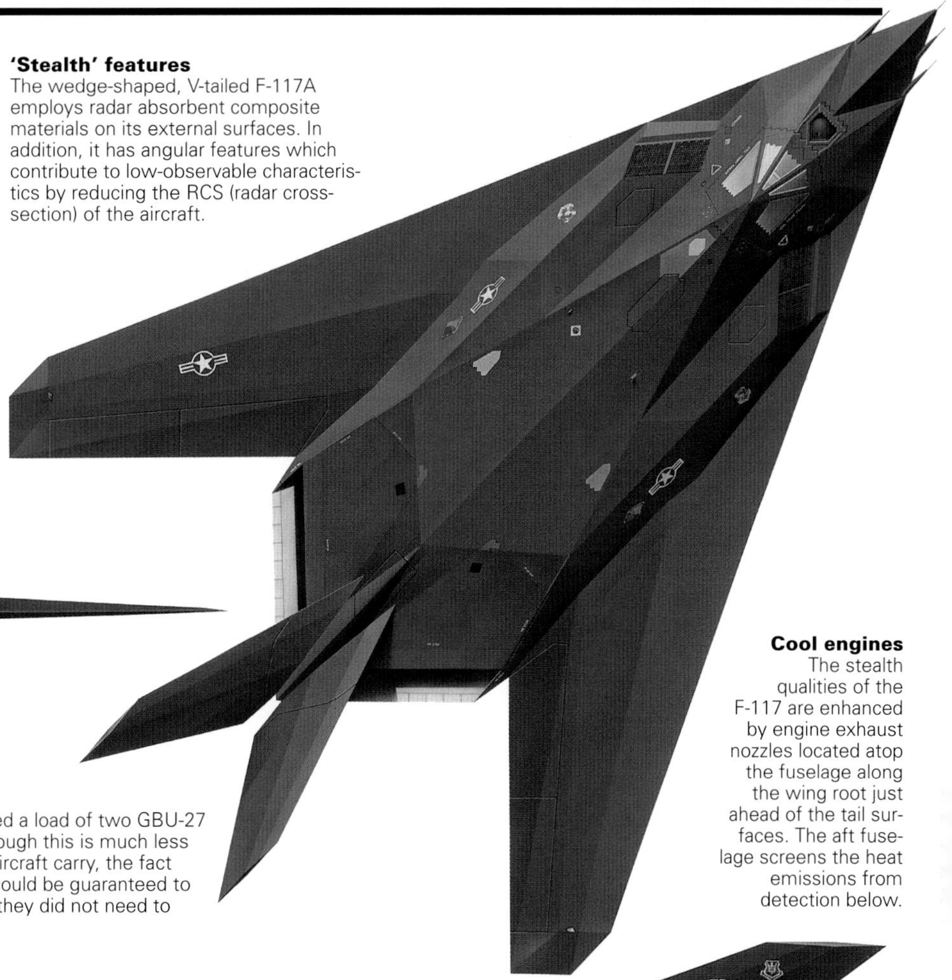

'Stealth' features
The wedge-shaped, V-tailed F-117A employs radar absorbent composite materials on its external surfaces. In addition, it has angular features which contribute to low-observable characteristics by reducing the RCS (radar cross-section) of the aircraft.

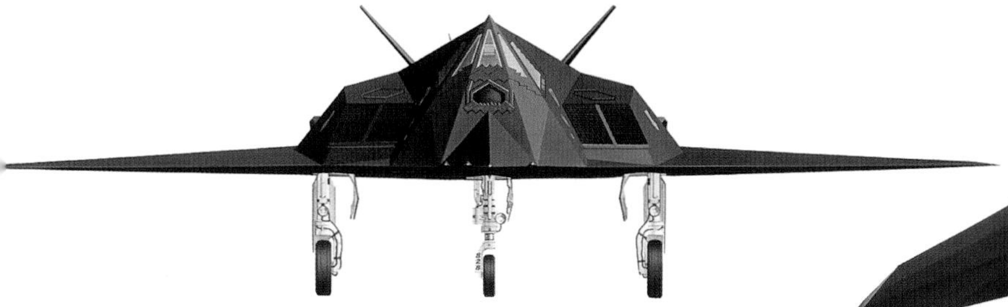

Cool engines
The stealth qualities of the F-117 are enhanced by engine exhaust nozzles located atop the fuselage along the wing root just ahead of the tail surfaces. The aft fuselage screens the heat emissions from detection below.

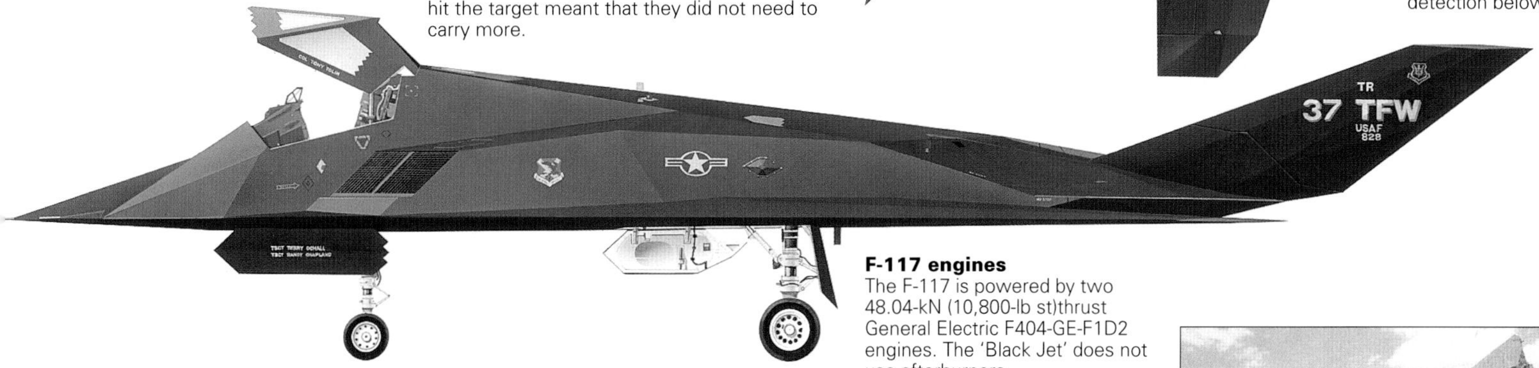

Expert crews
The 37th TFW which flew the 'Black Jet' in the Gulf was manned by some of the most experienced pilots in the US Air Force.

Weapons
The F-117 generally carried a load of two GBU-27 laser-guided bombs. Although this is much less than more conventional aircraft carry, the fact that almost every bomb could be guaranteed to hit the target meant that they did not need to carry more.

F-117 engines
The F-117 is powered by two 48.04-kN (10,800-lb st)thrust General Electric F404-GE-F1D2 engines. The 'Black Jet' does not use afterburners.

HAS was a strong concrete structure often covered with a thick layer of earth, and was intended to withstand almost any strike in less than nuclear strength.

But the safety they provided was illusory. No matter how tough a building is, it still needs large doors to allow aircraft in and out, and doors are a weakness. Coalition precision-guided weapons like the French AS.30L laser-guided missile were accurate enough to attack the doors directly. And the supposedly bomb-proof construction was also less effective in reality.

Coalition aircraft like the McDonnell Douglas F-15E and the F-111 dropped large numbers of laser-guided bombs onto Iraqi airfields. The 2,000-pound high-explosive GBU-24 was dropped onto taxiways and hard stands, to prevent Iraqi aircraft from being moved around. And the steel-cased GBU-27 was solid enough to penetrate the thick concrete of the

***Right:** Iraq's airfield hangars were heavily reinforced, but were nearly all above ground. Standard 907-kg (2,000-lb) bombs were more than capable of destroying most of these structures, but as the war progressed, the Coalition developed even more potent weapons to deal with high-value targets buried deep underground.*

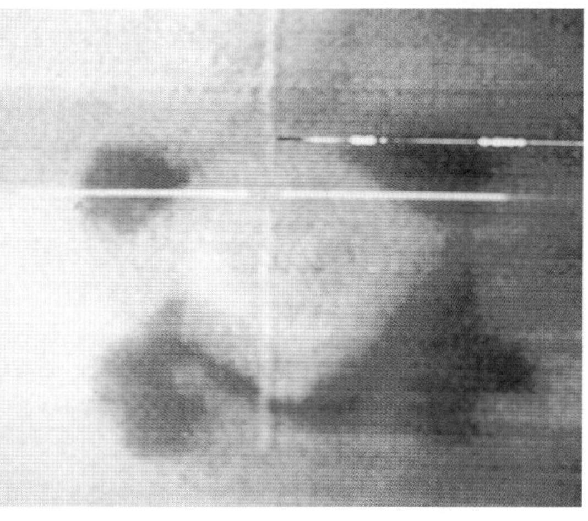

***Right:** The accuracy of precision-guided weapons is demonstrated in this strike on a building that hits exactly on the mark. A coalition spokesman said, with little exaggeration, that allied warplanes were able to 'put a bomb down an elevator shaft'.*

Iraq's MiG threat

Iraq began the desert war with the world's fourth largest army and a formidable air arm that included Mirage F1s, MiG-23 'Floggers' and a small number of the spectacular, Soviet-built MiG-29 'Flanker' fighters (below) that were among the most agile and lethal warplanes in the world. But in spite of their great potential, the MiGs were never to prove a real threat. Iraq's command structure, communications system and air defence network were smashed by Coalition air power on the first night of the war, and the training and committment of the Iraqi air force's pilots proved inadequate when they mattered most, in combat.

Iraqi MiG-29

Above: The MiG-29 failed to up to its promise. At least four were shot down by F-15C Eagles and not one 'Fulcrum' pilot was able to seriously threaten a Coalition aircraft, let alone turn the tables and achieve an aerial victory.

hangar roofs before exploding within, destroying any aircraft inside.

Starting from the first night of the war, raids were repeated every night for weeks. The effect was obvious: in spite of a sortie rate of more than 2,000 missions per day, Coalition air losses were under one-tenth of one per cent.

But no aerial campaign against ground targets is ever completely effective, and the Iraqis still had fighters available. At the start of the war, the Iraqi air force had about 200 modern combat aircraft. These included two squadrons of Soviet-supplied MiG-29 'Fulcrums', one of the most agile fighters ever built. The Coalition could field 350 air superiority fighters, including McDonnell Douglas F-15C Eagles, Grumman F-14 Tomcats, Panavia Tornado ADVs and Dassault Mirage 2000s. On top of that there were also more than 500 dual-purpose fighter-bombers available, including General Dynamics F-16 Fighting Falcons and McDonnell Douglas F/A-18 Hornets.

The allies were superior to the Iraqis in numbers, control, quality and training. Thanks to the sophisticated, long-range radar and advanced command and control capabilities of the Boeing E-3 AWACS, Coalition pilots knew exactly what was going on in the skies over the war zone, which was much more than their opponents knew. When Iraqi pilots tried to make a fight of it, they were knocked out of the sky, primarily by the F-15 Eagles of the US Air Force.

At least 120 USAF Eagles participated in the Gulf War, together with four Saudi squadrons. Eagles scored 35 out of a total of 41 Coalition aerial victories in the Gulf, including the only two non-American kills – by an Eagle of the Royal Saudi Air Force's No.13 Squadron. The most successful unit was the 58th Tactical Fighter Squadron of the 33rd Tactical Fighter Wing, normally based at Eglin AFB in Florida, but operating out of Tabuk.

Eagles carry a variety of weaponry, including a Vulcan cannon and up to four AIM-9 Sidewinders. However, in spite of its long-standing reputation for unreliability, the majority of enemy aircraft destroyed in combat were brought down by AIM-7 Sparrow radar-guided missiles.

The result of all the attention by Coalition assets both on the ground and in the air meant that the Iraqi air force played very little part in the battle, and indeed a large proportion of its most modern aircraft was flown to internment in Iran to escape destruction.

Above: US Navy carrier air wings relied on the Grumman F-14 Tomcat for the air-to-air mission, and for defence of the fleet. They had no chance to test themselves against Iraqi fighters: unlike the Air Force's Eagles, the Tomcats were tied down on the escort mission and could not go hunting MiGs. One F-14 was shot down. Its back-seater, Lt Lawrence Slade of VF-103 became the only downed airman to be rescued from enemy territory during the war.

Left: Four French Dassault Mirage 2000C air defence fighters were among the first allied combat aircraft to reach the Gulf. They were on station at Al Ahsa, 370 km (230 miles) south of Kuwait, three months before the war started.

Eagles Triumphant

The F-15's domination of the Gulf air war is recalled by Captain Anthony Schiavi of the 58th TFS, USAF. On 26 January 1991 he was on the wing of Captain Rhory Draeger on patrol over western Iraq. After failing to intercept four Iraqi jets – they were too far away – they were warned by fighter controllers aloft in an AWACS radar plane of three more enemy fighters closer to hand

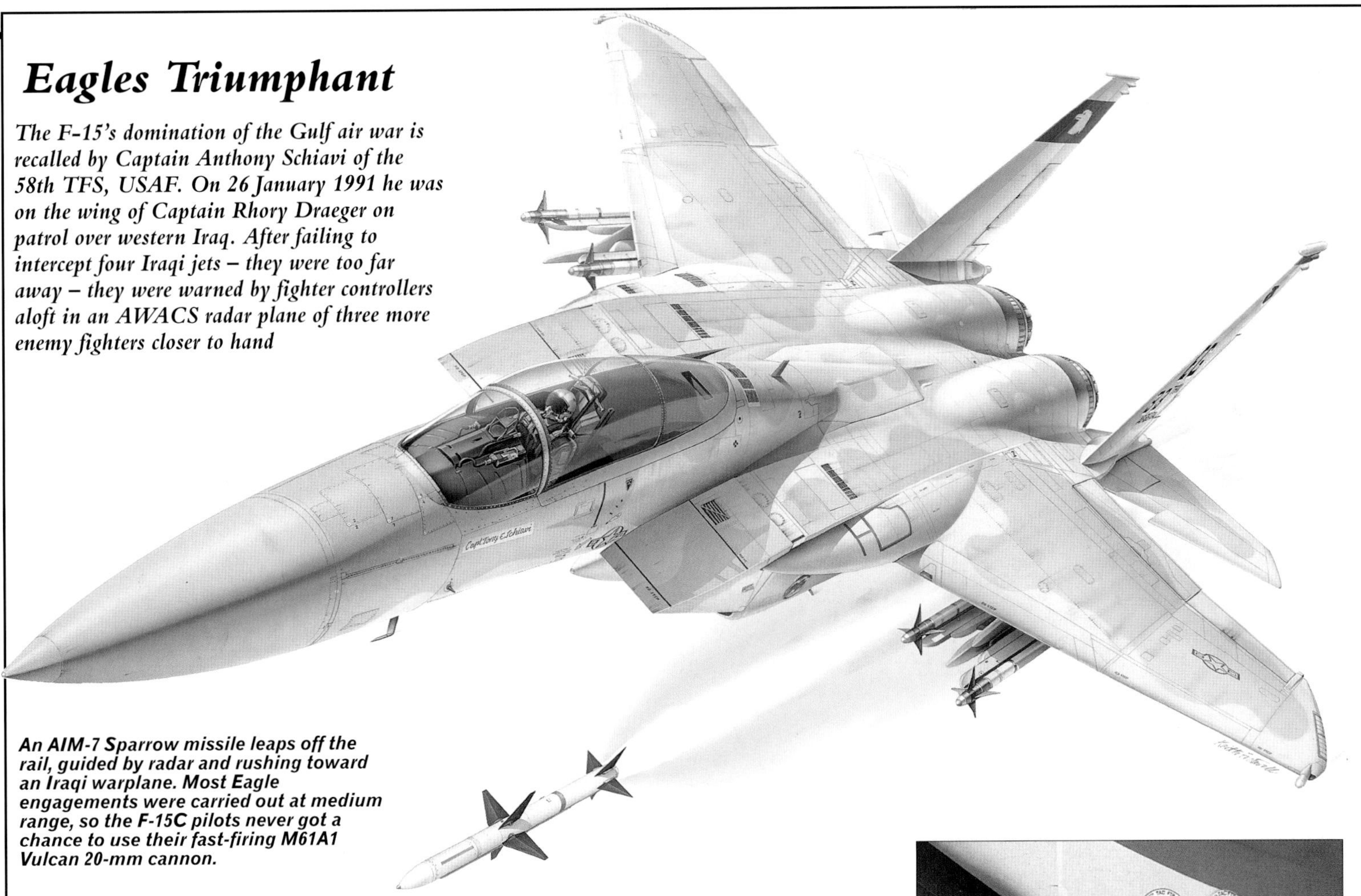

An AIM-7 Sparrow missile leaps off the rail, guided by radar and rushing toward an Iraqi warplane. Most Eagle engagements were carried out at medium range, so the F-15C pilots never got a chance to use their fast-firing M61A1 Vulcan 20-mm cannon.

"We'd been up on CAP for about an hour and a half, and had just gone down to a tanker to refuel. As we were coming off the tanker, AWACS called and said 'Hey, we've got Bandits taking off from H2, a whole group of them heading northeast.'"

The Eagles turned northeast to intercept. H2 was an airfield in the desert of western Iraq, not far from the borders with Jordan and Syria. It was too far from Iran for the Iraqis to be fleeing there for safety, so they were probably just moving from airfield to airfield, as they had been doing for several days in an attempt to avoid destruction. But they were more than 100 miles away, heading on the same course as the Eagles, and as the old saying goes, 'a tail chase is a long chase'.

"I'm thinking, 'There's no way we're going to catch these guys. We're starting to cut them off, but it's going to take a lot of a time and more gas than we've got.'"

The Eagles had closed the gap to about 130 km (80 miles), but were fast approaching the point where low fuel meant that they would have to turn back. Then four more Iraqi jets took off from H2, and this time the F-15s were ideally placed to bounce them. But Schiavi was worried. Could it be an Iraqi trap? There was only one way to find out.

To increase their manoeuvrability, the F-15s dropped their wing tanks, keeping only the centreline tank. Diving down from 7620 m (25,000 feet) they accelerated through the speed of sound. The American pilots could not see the ground or their targets through the overcast, so once they fired their missiles the best they could expect would have been a glow as they hit.

Captain Draeger locked on to the enemy leader. He knew that the other Iraqis were probably concentrating on keeping formation, not bothering much about navigation, and he was working on the well-tried tactic of 'kill the leader, and the rest will panic'. Schiavi took the fighter trailing to the northwest, leaving the remaining enemy to the other two Eagles. Schiavi's AIM-7 Sparrow missiles soon locked on, and he was ready to fire.

"We're now well inside 20 miles [32 km]. I see Captain Draeger's missile come off then I see it guiding. I shoot next, just a couple of seconds later. Because Bruce and Rico [Captain Bruce Till and Captain Cesar Rodriguez, flying the other two F-15s] are offset from us they have to wait a little longer."

As the Sparrows accelerated rapidly away, a big hole opened up in the weather. The Eagles dived through, and immediately sighted the enemy, three MiG-23 'Floggers' running fast and low across the desert.

"Captain Draeger's missile hits his man, which is so low that you can see dust kick up around it. He calls 'Splash'. Then he looks again: the airplane has flown right through the fireball and out the other side! He had been hit and is burning, but is not knocked out. Draeger goes to a heater [prepares to fire a heat-seeking Sidewinder missile], but before he can shoot the fire reaches the wingroot of the target and it suddenly explodes in a huge fireball. I'm so busy watching this guy blow up that I've almost forgotten my own missile.

Above: Capt Tony Schiavi of the 33rd TFW leans on the radome of an AIM-7 Sparrow medium-range radar-guided missile. The F-15C carrying the weapon is marked with the emblems of the wing's combat squadrons.

"After the first guy blows up, the other two do a hard right hand turn, right into us. Whether they've picked up a visual on us, I don't know, but what they are doing is too late. Right about then, my missile hits my guy. I call a second 'Splash' and there's another big fireball. Number four's missiles are maybe two seconds late, so number three – Captain Rodriguez – gets the third kill.

"There was a road right underneath them; I think they were navigating along it. The first guy blows up on one side, and the other two go down the other side, three fireballs in a row!"

This was to be a scene repeated every time Iraqi and American pilots met in battle. The combination of good pilots and a superb aeroplane proved to be a winner. There might be faster jets, there might be more manoeuvrable machines, but when it comes to the combat crunch, a well-handled F-15 is still the world's best fighter.

Gulf War: Strategic Campaign

JANUARY–FEBRUARY 1991

A heavily-laden Boeing B-52G Stratofortress lifts off the wintery runway of RAF Fairford in England, en route to contribute to the round-the-clock punishment being inflicted on Iraq's Republican Guard. B-52s also flew the longest combat missions in the history of warfare, when aircraft from Barksdale AFB, Louisiana were used to launch cruise missile attacks on key targets in Iraq and occupied Kuwait.

Air superiority makes it much simpler to win a ground offensive. Having smashed the Iraqi air defences on the ground and in the air, taking out the radar network and airfields with precision-guided munitions and airfield denial weapons, the Coalition could move on to other matters.

Iraq's ability to reinforce and resupply its troops became the target of a concentrated bombing campaign involving tactical fighters, all-weather strike fighters, fighter-bombers and giant B-52 bombers operating from bases as far apart as Lousiana, the United Kingdom and the island of Diego Garcia in the Indian Ocean. Power stations, command centres, communications systems and government buildings were struck on the first night of the war. Other important targets included nuclear and chemical

Below: Precision-guided munitions like these Paveway bombs aboard an F-111 dramatically enhanced the effectiveness of air-to-ground attacks. Although ten times more expensive than conventional bombs, they were far more than ten times as effective.

Right: The Boeing E-3 Sentry AWACS kept watch on activity by aircraft on both sides. Most air-to-air victories were made possible when alert AWACS crews told Coalition fighter pilots where the enemy was, where he was going, and how best to make an intercept.

Aardvark in action

Colonel Tom Lennon commanded the 66 F-111Fs of the 48th Tactical Fighter Wing deployed to Saudi Arabia for the Gulf War. With its range, speed, bombload, advanced night-flying capability and above all its highly effective Pave Tack target acquisition and designation system, the veteran F-111F proved to be one of the most important combat aircraft of the conflict.

"Initially we were tasked against the strategic targets, because of the size of the threat. This was the fourth largest army in the world. Airfields, command and control centers, chemical storage sites all had to be kept under control. We worked the strategic targets for the first 30 days of the war and then shifted over to softening up the battlefield, going against tanks and artillery.

"For me it was the first time I'd got to lead a large F-111 strike package. On the first night we had 54 aircraft leaving Taif, with six EF-111s as EW support. The target I selected was a large airfield north of Baghdad. To save fuel I'd planned to go about half way to Baghdad at medium altitude before dropping down, but about 30 miles [48 km] inside Iraq we started getting a lot of indications that people were looking at us and locking onto us, so we were forced to descend a lot earlier than planned. Going across the Euphrates you could see all the lights on, and the blink-blink of people shooting at us. About abeam of Baghdad we saw an aircraft, but it looked like he couldn't do a conversion on us. We were running at about 650 kt [1200 km/750 mph] on the TF (Terrain Following radar) at 200 ft [60 m], and we just accelerated on out. We swung north around Baghdad, heading west for our target area. I've never seen any defenses like it. The sky was red with triple-A.

"I was the first one in, aiming to drop a GBU-15 on a hangar. We came to release point, hit the pickle button and for some reason the bomb didn't come off. We went into our turn and came back but the triple-A, even though it was an unaimed barrage for the most part, tended to follow me - they were using the sound of the jet. We had three missiles launched at us just as we released the second weapon, which had to be negated.

"We ended up dropping back down to 200 ft on the TF, rolling out, hitting a tanker and coming back to our field, only to find it just like the UK, socked-in with fog! Tankers were scrambled and we stayed around until the sun opened up a little hole and we could start landing. Out of 53 aircraft launching that night, 26 of them got into Taif, the others having to divert to other bases for fuel. We got them home and still launched 40 aircraft that night.

"Two other missions stand out for me. One was where we had absolutely no defenses against us, and we took a five-ship in with four bombs each. We took out 20 aircraft shelters that night. The other one was when I was involved in the concept validation of dropping PGMs against tanks and armored vehicles, which we did the last 12 days of the war and at which we ended up being very, very successful - something like 920 tanks and armored vehicles.

"We used 500-lb (227-kg) GBU-12 laser-guided munitions against the tanks, but for other targets it was mostly 2,000-lb (907-kg) munitions. We also dropped a lot of mines, sub-munitions from CBU-89 dispensers, to keep people out of areas at, for instance, chemical storage areas or airfields. We did a little bit of 'Scud' hunting and were partially successful. It was very difficult to find the mobile launchers: the F-111F and Pave Tack is much better against fixed targets. If we could preplan our mission we'd have very high success rates: if it was a catch-can, we were not as successful."

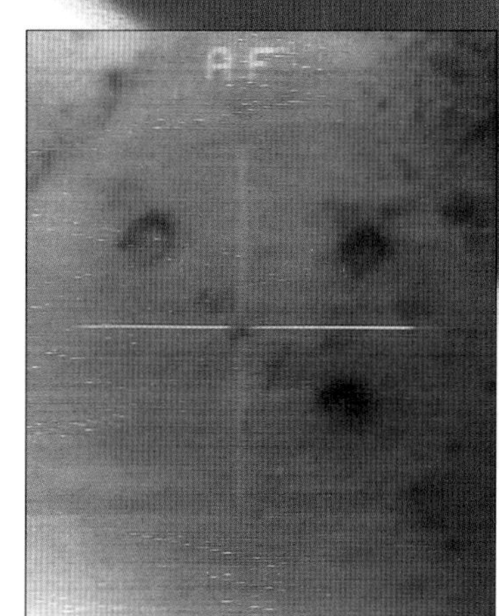

Above: Although primarily an interdiction platform, the F-111 proved to be a successful tank killer, picking up enemy armoured formations on its Pave Tack system and destroying vehicles with small laser-guided bombs.

weapons facilities, ammunition stores, military barracks, military manufacturing centres, weapons dumps, as well as railways, roads, and bridges. Command and control of the air offensive was provided by American and Saudi E-3 AWACS aircraft, while the new and still experimental J-STARS battlefield control system, mounted in Boeing E-8s, kept a close watch on enemy ground movements.

GUIDED MUNITIONS

One of the abiding images of the war is that of American guided bombs entering doorways and plunging down air shafts of strategic targets in Iraq. The accuracy demonstrated in those early attacks was confirmed in the campaign to destroy Iraq's communications network, when the majority of the road and rail bridges across the Tigris and Euphrates rivers were dropped in precision attacks. Weapons in use included Paveway laser-guided bombs, designed to home in on the reflected 'sparkle' of a laser beam held on the target by an airborne or ground-based Special Forces designator, and electro-optical bombs and missiles. These have infra-red TV sensors in their noses and can be computer-guided onto targets, whatever the light or weather.

The General Dynamics F-111F was among the most successful of all

Right: Two F-111F Aardvarks of Col Tom Lennon's 48th TFW in flight over the Middle East just before the Gulf War. The combat performance of the F-111F – probably the best of the war – was largely overlooked by the press.

Left: F-15E Strike Eagles and F-16C Fighting Falcons celebrate the end of the war with a joint sortie over oil field fires in newly liberated Kuwait.

Above: Iraq claimed that allied bombs were falling on schools, hospitals, even a children's milk factory. Only certain selected journalists were shown the rubble.

Coalition warplanes, although at the time its performance was overshadowed by other, more glamorous machines. Flown by the 48th Tactical Fighter Wing out of the Saudi base at Taif, the 'Aardvarks' went everywhere – even to the outskirts of Baghdad, which was otherwise reserved for F-117s and cruise missiles. F-111s destroyed bridges, airfields, radio transmitters, tanks, artillery, pumping stations and 'anything that would hold still long enough for us to put a bomb on it!'

In 2,500 sorties, the 66 F-111s deployed to the Gulf destroyed 2,203 targets, all claims being backed up by videotaped proof taken from the Pave Tack sensor carried by each of the big fighter-bombers. These including 252 artillery pieces, 245 hardened aircraft shelters, 13 runways and 12 bridges (with another 52 seriously damaged. More than 8,000 precision-guided munitions were dropped by the USAF during the war: F-111s accounted for 4,660 of them.

'Scud' attacks

On 18 January the Iraqis dramatically widened the scope of the war when they started firing extended-range 'Scud' surface-to-surface missiles at Israel and Saudi Arabia. Although of little consequence militarily, politically they were highly dangerous. Should Israel retaliate, the Arab members of the anti-Iraqi coalition might withdraw. Allied air forces were diverted into an all-out

Left: The two Boeing E-8A Joint STARS prototypes were rushed into use during Operation Desert Storm to direct fighter-bombers in attacks on Iraqi tanks and troop formations pinpointed by the E-8A's sophisticated belly-mounted radar system. Like the E-3 Sentry AWACS aircraft which directs aerial action, the ground-monitoring E-8A is based on the Boeing 707-320B airliner.

Panavia Tornado GR.Mk 1

'MiG Eater' was one of the most heavily used of the RAF's Tornado bombers. Based at Tabuk, in northwestern Saudi Arabia, it flew some 40 missions into hostile territory. The Tabuk force was led by No. 16 Squadron, but included elements of Nos 2, 9, 13, 14, 20 and 617 Squadrons.

Below: 'Sky Pirates' Buccaneer S.Mk 2Bs joined the fighting on 2 February 1991 and enhanced the accuracy of the Tornado strike force by designating targets for 'smart' bombs.

Sky Shadow
The ARI 23246/1 Sky Shadow electronic countermeasures system is an autonomous ECM pod which incorporates both active and passive electronic warfare systems, using an integral transmitter/receiver and a powerful signal processor.

Weapons
With all wing pylons occupied by pods or fuel tanks, the Tornado's offensive weaponry was carried almost exclusively under the fuselage. Weapons carried included bombs, JP233 airfield denial weapons, and ALARM missiles.

Performance
The Tornado's small, variable-geometry wing gives its two-man crew a very comfortable ride in most flight regimes, especially during the high-speed, low-level mission for which it was designed. The RB.199 engines are also optimised for low-level work: so much so, in fact, that when Tornados switched to medium-level bombing in the Gulf they had problems reaching altitude with a full load of bombs and tanks.

Radar warning
The tip of the Tornado's large tail houses a VHF communications aerial, with a pair of GEC-Marconi passive radar-warning receivers projecting fore and aft beneath.

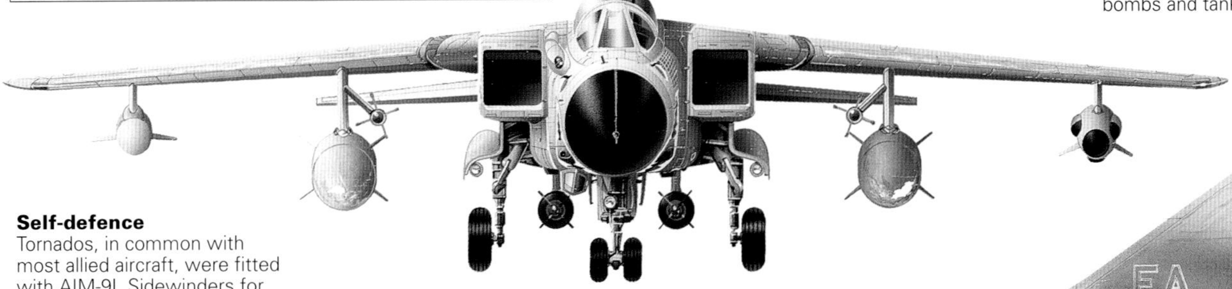

Self-defence
Tornados, in common with most allied aircraft, were fitted with AIM-9L Sidewinders for self-defence against Iraqi air attack. Two missiles were carried, one on the inside of each inner wing pylon.

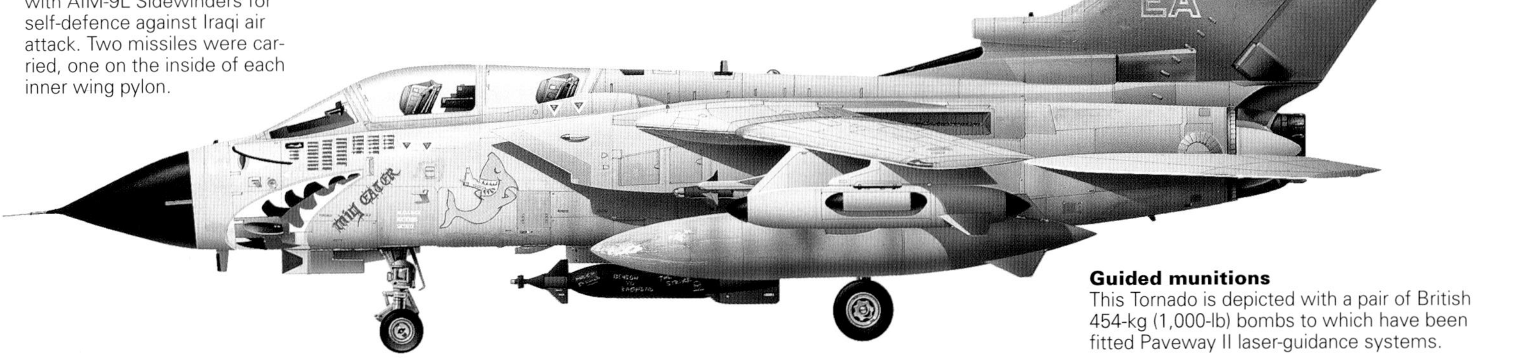

Guided munitions
This Tornado is depicted with a pair of British 454-kg (1,000-lb) bombs to which have been fitted Paveway II laser-guidance systems.

Radar
The Tornado's multi-mode, terrain-following, ground-mapping radar is its primary attack/navigation system. A chin-mounted sensor contains the windows for a Ferranti laser-range finder/marked target seeker, which enables the Tornado to drop LGBs onto designated targets.

Right: Saudi Arabia's Panavia Tornado IDS (Interdictor/Strike) aircraft flew alongside the RAF's similar GR.Mk 1 Tornados in low-level strikes on airfields and other strategic targets deep inside Iraq.

Carrier Strikers

The first aircraft carrier on the scene following Iraq's 1990 invasion of Kuwait was USS *Independence* (CV-62), followed by the USS *Dwight D. Eisenhower* (CVN-69). Both had been nearing the end of their cruises when Iraq invaded Kuwait, and both had been relieved by the time Desert Shield had become Desert Storm. Ultimately, the US Navy had six carrier battle groups in the war zone: The USS *Saratoga* (CV-60), *America* (CV-66), *John F. Kennedy* (CV-67) and *Theodore Roosevelt* (CVN-71) in the Red Sea, and the USS *Ranger* (CV-61) and *Midway* (CV-41) in the Persian Gulf itself. Navy carriers maintained continuous air operations on both sides of the Arabian peninsula. Although Iraq launched some attacks on Coalition vessels, none came near the carriers.

Above: Carrier air wings have their own tankers, but these proved too limited to handle the intense scale of operations in the Gulf, and Navy jets relied heavily on land-based tankers like this USAF KC-135.

Left: 'Ike' was within range of Iraqi missiles when it passed through the Suez Canal during the Desert Shield build-up, but its passage proved uneventful. The ability to position forces quickly in the region was the key to the allies' success when fighting began.

search for the missile-launchers.

Special Forces patrols were inserted deep into hostile territory by helicopter, to locate and occasionally destroy transporter-erector-launchers (although more often they would designate targets for allied strike aircraft. Reconnaissance aircraft like the RAF's infra-red-equipped Tornado GR.Mk 1A, quartered vast areas of desert looking for the elusive 'Scuds'. J-STARS aircraft looked for missile launchers on the move, while AWACs radar planes located the missiles after launch. Target data was passed to Coalition strike aircraft, though one of the few systems capable of responding fast enough to trap a mobile launcher before it could move was the brand new F-15E Eagle. Receiving target information via datalink while on patrol over Iraq, the Eagle could be delivering weaponry on target within minutes.

CONTINUING THREAT

However, in spite of destroying a number of missile sites, the Coalition was never able to eliminate the 'Scud' threat completely. Defence against incoming 'Scuds' was the responsibility of the US Army's Patriot missile batteries. Designed to take out aircraft, the Patriot's radars and computer software had been upgraded in an attempt to deal with tactical ballistic missiles. Never more than a temporary stop-gap, the Patriot system destroyed some incoming missiles in flight, but had nothing like the success claimed at the time.

At sea, aircraft from six of the US Navy's carrier battle groups played their part in the air war. In addition to conventional gun, bomb and rocket attacks, Grumman A-6 intruders made the first combat firings of the SLAM missile. This is a variant of the Harpoon anti-ship weapon equipped with an imaging infra-red seeker head, designed to attack land targets in all weathers.

The threat offered by the Iraqi navy to the hundred-strong allied fleet in the Gulf was limited. Already in a poor state after the Iran-Iraq war, the Iraqis were in no position to challenge the carrier battle groups, battleships, cruisers, destroyers and frigates of the coalition navies. Nevertheless, on some occasions they did come out of port, led by TNC 45 fast patrol craft captured from Kuwait.

Multi-mission Hornet

With a position for a back-seater who provided an extra pair of eyes and ears, the McDonnell F/A-18D Hornet suddenly took on new missions, including battlefield surveillance and forward air control (FAC) duty. Two-seat Hornets do not operate from shipboard, but land-based F/A-18Ds flown by Marine pilots and observers became, in effect, tools of the ground commander, who used them to keep tabs on Iraqi movements and to guide strike aircraft, artillery, and ground movements.

Versatile F/A-18D
This F/A-18D Hornet of VMFA(AW)-121 'Moonlighters' carries external fuel tanks and rocket pods, the latter being the ideal weapon in 'Fast FAC' work.

Defeating Saddam's Navy

The upper reaches of Persian Gulf was deemed too confining for aircraft carriers, but other Coalition ships plied the waterway despite an ever-present threat. Iraq's modest-sized navy included some missile-armed fast attack craft as well as several craft seized from Kuwait, that could have challenged the Coalition's frigates and destroyers.

However, Iraq had nothing to compare to the American Sikorsky SH-60B Sea Hawk, the British Lynx HAS Mk 3, and other aircraft and helicopters. These gave extended range and versatility to the Coalition's warships, and destroyed or damaged most of Iraq's fleet.

Above: An Exocet-armed TNC-45 fast attack craft. Iraq captured several of these missile boats when it occupied Kuwait, but never made effective use of them.

Below: The ten Lynx helicopters that flew from HMS Gloucester and six other vessels in the Gulf used Sea Skua surface-skimming anti-ship missiles to engage fast-moving Iraqi patrol craft.

Below: An Iraqi patrol boat burns after being disabled by a hit from a Lynx-launched Sea Skua missile. This kind of hit left a vessel dead in the water even if it never sank.

The Iraqis did not do very well. Some were sunk by Royal Navy Lynx helicopters firing Sea Skua missiles. Others were destroyed by rockets, cluster munitions and gunfire from aircraft like the US Navy's A-6 Intruder and the Anglo-French Jaguar.

When they had had enough, many vessels tried to flee from Basra to Iran, but few managed to complete the trip. The only Iraqi success was the damaging of the assault ship USS *Tripoli* and the 'Aegis' class cruiser *Princeton* by mines, but coalition mine-countermeasures, which included US Navy MH-53 helicopters in adition to more conventional minesweepers and minehunters, managed to clear enough of the Gulf to allow the fleet to operate without further damage.

New weapons

Modern weaponry was a vital ingredient in Coalition success with many advanced systems making their combat debuts from Day 1 of the conflict. The list includes Panavia Tornados with JP233 runway-cratering munitions, F-15E strike fighters, and the improved AV-8B Harrier II. Another missile making its combat debut was the Tomahawk. The US Navy lifted the usual veil of secrecy that it keeps over submarine operations to announce that USS *Louisville* had successfully made a submerged launch of a Tomahawk against Iraqi targets from a position in the Red Sea. Less widely publicised was the fact that B-52s from Barksdale AFB in Louisiana attacked Iraqi targets with conventional warhead air-launched cruise missiles, in the process making by far the longest bombing raids in history.

Other weapons which had seen brief or unsuccessful outings in previous conflicts were used much more extensively and with considerable success in the Gulf. These included McDonnell Douglas F/A-18 Hornets with HARM missiles, British Aerospace Sea Skua light anti-ship missiles, AH-64 Apache helicopters, A-10A Thunderbolt II tank-busters, and, above all, the US Air Force's F-117A 'stealth' fighter.

Below: The Grumman EA-6B Prowler was the nemesis of Iraqi air defense system. In 332 combat sorties, some 30 Navy and Marine Prowlers jammed, confused and confounded enemy radar transmitters, and attacked SAM sites with HARM missiles.

Gulf War: Winning the Ground War

FEBRUARY–MARCH 1991

The commander of Coalition forces, General Norman Schwartzkopf, called it "Preparing the battlefield". He knew that neither intense diplomatic efforts nor the condemnation of the United Nations were likely to persuade Iraq to leave Kuwait voluntarily. The problem would be decided by military action, and ultimately by battles on the ground.

The Coalition could call on some of the toughest and best-trained troops in the world, but the Iraqis promised to be a hard nut to crack. Possessed of the fourth largest army in the world, and equipped with large numbers of modern tanks and artillery, they needed to be softened up.

This is where air power was brought into play with such devastating effect. From the start of the shooting in January 1991, Iraq's invasion forces were subject to incessant attack. And by the end of the month, as the interdiction campaign progressively smashed Iraq's air power, command and control networks, communications and industry, more and more Coalition air assets were free to be turned against Iraq's troops, artillery positions, rear supply centres, and lines of communication, destroying their effectiveness for the land battles to come.

Above: The hard-fighting Fairchild A-10 Thunderbolt II, the 'Warthog' to its pilots, had a key role as the Coalition launched its ground offensive. The A-10 supported friendly troops, hunted 'Scud' sites, and stalked Iraqi vehicles on the 'Highway of Death'.

CONSTANT ATTACK

Ground-attack fighters were in action day and night, pounding Iraqi troops, artillery positions, rear base areas and supply centres. Giant B-52 bombers unloaded thousands of tons of explosive on Iraq's best troops, the Republican Guard, which was being held back as a mobile reserve. The army's communications with Baghdad were also primary targets, and coalition aircraft using laser- and TV-guided missiles destroyed many of which

Above: With 251 examples in the war zone, the F-16 Fighting Falcon was the most numerous 'shooter' in the Coalition's air arm. Dust, sand, and haze fouled the infra-red sensor pods employed by some F-16s, but their overall performance was good.

'Wild Weasel'

The F-4G Advanced Wild Weasel was the ultimate weapon against Iraqi SAM sites. The USAF deployed 35 of these modified Phantoms to the Gulf, flying hundreds of sorties with the loss of only one aircraft. The two-man crew of pilot and electronic warfare officer used the AN/APR-47 system to detect and seek out hostile radars. Part of the system was located in the nose, part in the rounded 'football' atop the fin. Using its 'black boxes', the F-4G found SAM sites, shut them down with HARM missile shots, enabling other warplanes to get through to their targets safely.

AGM-88 HARM

Developed by Texas Instruments, the AGM-88A HARM (High-speed Anti-Radiation Missile) had a 66-kg (146-lb) warhead designed to explode into 25,000 pre-formed fragments. The 360-kg (800-lb) missile 'locked on' to emissions from an Iraqi radar unit and homed in on it. At times, forcing the enemy to shut down his radar was as effective as achieving a 'kill' of a radar site.

Fighting F-4G

This F-4G Phantom II (69-7244) belongs to the 52nd TFW, Spangdahlem Air Base, Germany. The 52nd deployed aircraft like this to the Gulf where they became part of the 35th TFW (Provisional). They were painted in standard USAF tactical grey and carried 'mission markers' astride the engine air intakes.

Right: France's role in the Coalition was considerable, but one of the the Armée de l'Air's main combat aircraft could not play as active a part as its pilots might have liked. Dassault Mirage F.1 fighters were flown by the Iraqi air force as well as the French, and considerable effort had to be spent to keep the Allies from mistaking one for the other. Here, a Mirage F.1CR of Escadre de Reconnaissance 33 flies with a Sepecat Jaguar. The reconnaissance Mirages served as 'pathfinders' for the Jaguars, by virtue of their more comprehensive navigation equipment.

had survived the strategic campaign.

In spite of the pounding being received by his country, Saddam Hussein showed no signs of withdrawing from Kuwait. Allied air forces were destroying his armies, and artillery duels were being fought across the Saudi/ Kuwaiti frontier. The Multiple Launch Rocket System operated by the US and British armies was striking hard at Iraqi positions up to 30 km (18.5 miles) across the border. Specialist tank-killers like the AH-1 Cobra and AH-64 Apache helicopters, and the AV-8B Harrier, A-10 'Warthog' and SEPECAT Jaguar close support aircraft were hammering enemy front-line positions.

Clearly, the Coalition ground offensive was coming, but without aerial reconnaissance the Iraqis could not know when or where. And when the offensive steamroller did get into action, the survival of the Iraqi army in the face of overwhelming armour, artillery and tactical air superiority was to be measured in hours and days.

Before the allies moved into the ground war, the commanders wanted the Iraqi army to be at least half-destroyed. Armed with cluster bombs, rocket pods and laser or TV-guided missiles, the attack air-

Right: These Vought A-7E Corsair IIs of squadrons VA-46 'Clansmen' and VA-72 'Blue Tail Flies' aboard USS John F. Kennedy (CV-67) were fighting their final war. The Corsair made its combat debut in Vietnam, and was finally withdrawn from service on 23 May 1991, only weeks after the end of the Gulf War.

Above: Continuing a tradition from World War II, Coalition aircrew painted bomb silhouettes on their aircraft to 'count' successful combat missions. This B-52G Stratofortress has completed 24 missions, and has picked up a piece of non-regulation nose art in the process.

Right: The AV-8B Harrier II 'jump jet' operated from bases close to the front line, providing quick-reaction support to Marines on the ground. But with its jet pipes near the centre of the fuselage, it proved a little vulnerable to heat-seeking missiles, and four were lost to Iraqi SAMs.

craft were guided onto the target by forward air controllers in scout helicopters, or observers on the ground with laser designators. Apache helicopters also joined the attack.

The priority targets were the Republican Guard, the elite of the Iraqi army. Roving at will over the battlefield in the absence of Iraqi air opposition, the ground-attack aircraft hammered home their attacks on enemy troops already demoralised by weeks of round-the-clock bombing.

IRAQIS HELPLESS

The Iraqi forces could do little to interrupt the constant bombardment, as their battlefield air defence system had been reduced to limited numbers of missiles and obsolete gun systems. Although a small number of allied aircraft were shot down or damaged, the devastation of Iraq's army was complete.

When the Coalition moved, it moved fast. The assault burst upon the Iraqi army on 24 March. US Marine, US Army, Saudi, Kuwaiti, Egyptian, Syrian and other Arab forces poured into Kuwait through engineer-blasted gaps in the Iraqi defences. Far to the west, American airborne and air assault troops in company with a French light armoured division were racing north through the Iraqi desert, heading for the Euphrates, with the aim of cutting off all Iraqi forces in the Kuwaiti theatre of operations.

In the centre came the main punch. The US Army's VII Corps, a heavily-armoured five-division force including the British 1st Armoured Division, drove along the Kuwait/Iraq border outflanking the main defence lines and engaged the Republican Guard. Iraqi troops, already demoralised by weeks of bombing, gave themselves up by the thousand.

Close support aircraft were one of the starring features of the land war. McDonnell Douglas AH-64 Apaches were involved in battle from the start of the war when they eliminated an air defence centre to allow tactical aircraft to launch their strikes into Iraq. In the quickening tempo of operations before the land war was launched, Apaches even managed to capture Iraqi ground troops, holding them under guns and missiles until larger helicopters could come and transport the prisoners to the rear. The Apache's Hellfire missile system proved lethal to enemy tanks in the last days of the war.

Helicopters were everywhere in the Gulf. Apache and Cobra gunships tore out the heart of Iraqi armoured forces and proved dab hands at taking out bunkers.

Above: The Sikorsky UH-60 Black Hawk was the US Army's standard utility helicopter and greatly aided the mobility of Coalition ground forces. The Black Hawk was powered by two 1,261-kW (1,690 shp) General Electric T700-GE-700/701 turboshaft engines. Heat, sand and bad weather were a challenge to the UH-60, as they were to other aircraft, but it proved itself a tough and reliable combatant.

Ground attack

There was little glory or glamour in it, but pilots who flew air-to-ground missions had the riskiest job of the Desert Storm war. Even after the air campaign had weakened it, the Iraqi army was able to 'throw up a tremendous amount of flying metal,' as one pilot described the shells, bullets, and missiles that swirled upward from the ground. Even so, remarkably few ground attack aircraft were lost to ground fire.

Desert Jaguar
Right: SEPECAT Jaguar GR.Mk 1A (XZ364/Q) 'Sandman' was one of two RAF Jaguars that flew 47 missions during the Gulf War. Note the AIM-9L Sidewinder missiles on overwing pylons, carried for self-defense early in the fighting.

Marine Machine
Left: AV-8B Harrier II (Bu.no. 163668) of VMA-311 'Tomcats.' The squadron was home-ported at MCAS Yuma, Arizona but took up station during the conflict at King Abdul Aziz air base, later moving closer to the Kuwaiti border. Harriers in the Gulf carried a variety of weapons, including the 12 bombs and two Sidewinders shown.

Warrior 'Warthog'
Right: This Fairchild A-10 Thunderbolt II (80-0186), 'Tiger 1,' belonged to the wing commander of the 23rd TFW and was deployed to Saudi Arabia from England AFB, Louisiana. Under its inboard pylons, this 'Warthog' carries a pair of Hughes AGM-65A/B Maverick missiles. Note also the two bombs, ECM pod, and twin AIM-9 Sidewinder air-to-air missiles.

Above: AH-64 Apache helicopters at a Forward Air Refueling Point, or FARP. As the 101st Airborne Dvision drove ahead, the Apaches stayed with the main ground force. One group of Iraqi soldiers actually surrendered to an AH-64.

Apache Rampage

Colonel William Bryan commanded the AH-64s of the US Army's 2nd Battalion, 229th Aviation Regiment, attached to the 101st Airborne Division in the Gulf. The Apaches were a key feature in the initial Coalition attacks.

"The sector we were in was far to the west of the main Iraqi troop concentrations. It was lightly defended and lightly populated. We reached the Euphrates, about 50 km [31 miles] north of the division's forward base, that first day of the ground offensive.

"The Iraqis we did see realised that they were about to be bypassed, and they tried to run north. Once they saw the armed helicopters appear they would get out of their vehicles and take cover. We destroyed the vehicles.

"When we came across a convoy, one company would attack, one was about 30 km [18.5 miles] back in a holding area, and one 50 km [31 miles] back at the FARP [Forward Area Refueling Point] at the division's forward operating base. Each company would attack in turn, ensuring the enemy was being engaged continuously. If you really want to pile them all in, you can, but then there's going to be a break in the action when everybody goes back to re-arm and refuel.

"Companies normally operate in two teams. The light team of two Apaches will usually be the first to engage, then the heavy team of three or four helicopterswill take up the fight.

"In Europe we were taught to mask, to use the terrain as cover from behind which we launch attacks. In the desert, you can't hide. It should have been extremely dangerous, since some of their anti-aircraft missile systems outranged us, but the Iraqis showed little or no desire to fight.

"Had the Iraqis been an armoured force we would have made stand-off attacks, but in this case we shot them with 30-mm cannon fire to get them stopped and the people dismounted. Then we fired three Hellfires, which took out the three lead vehicles. From that point we were able to finish them off with 30-mm and 2.75-inch [70-mm] high-explosive rockets.

"Our greatest concerns were the Iraqi shoulder-fired air-defense weapons. We could get around the long-range systems by flying low and letting the ground clutter mask our signature. But with the man-pack SAMs one person in a hole in the ground can take you out. We also knew that the enemy had over 5,000 armored vehicles, each with a heavy anti-aircraft machine-gun, and he had large numbers of 23-mm and 57-mm cannon. But as long as we stayed more than 3 km [just under 2 miles] away we were generally out of range. In any case we were usually flying at a height of 10 metres [33 feet] or less.

McDonnell Douglas AH-64A Apache

Developed as a 'state-of-the-art' anti-tank weapon during the Cold War, where it was intended to counter the threat of a massive Soviet armoured attack on Western Europe, the Apache is an immensely tough helicopter. Equipped with powerful weapons and advanced all-weather sensors, it devastated Iraqi vehicles and troops during the final phases of Operation Desert Storm. It proved surprisingly reliable for such a complex machine, in spite of the harsh desert operating conditions.

High-power helicopter
The Apache's two 1285-kW (1,723-shp) General Electric T700-GE-701 turboshaft engines drive a four-blade rotor with a diameter of 14.63-m (48 ft). The engine exhaust is via McDonnell Douglas's 'Black Hole' infra-red suppression system, consisting of nozzles which reduce the temperature of exhaust gases, reducing vulnerability to heat-seeking missiles.

Gun
The AH-64's fixed armament consists of one 30-mm M230E-1 Chain Gun automatic cannon. It is mounted in a hydraulically-operated turret which traverses 110 degrees either side of the centerline, with 11 degrees of elevation and 60 degrees of depression.

Missiles
Seen firing two 19-round pods of 70-mm (2.75-inc) Folding-Fin Aircraft Rockets or FFAR, this Apache also carries eight Hellfire laser-guided heavy anti-tank missiles.

Battlefield survival
The Apache was designed to withstand fire from weapons of up to 23-mm. Its structure is stressed to absorb and to withstand a vertical impact of 12.80-m (42 ft) per second.

Left: The AH-64 Apache cut a swath through retreating Iraqi forces. Like all allied combat aircraft, the AH-64 was challenged more by bad weather and harsh desert conditions than by Saddam Hussein's army, but it performed well despite obstacles.

General-purpose battlefield helicopters in use included Sikorsky UH-60 Black Hawks, Bell UH-1 'Hueys', British Lynxes, and French-built Gazelles. Heavy lift was provided by Boeing Helicopters CH-47 Chinooks, Sikorsky CH-53 Super Stallions, and Anglo-French Pumas and Super Pumas.

Close support

Fixed-wing close support was provided in the main by Air Force F-16s, A-10s and Marine Corps AV-8Bs. The A-10's huge gun and powerful weapons load ripped through Iraqi artillery and armour with ease: two A-10s established a record at the end of the war by destroying 35 tanks in a day. Other aircraft used for close support included British and French Jaguars, US Navy Hornets and Free Kuwaiti A-4 Skyhawks. Curiously, one of the most successful tank killers of the war was the long-range F-111, which had been heavily engaged on strategic missions in the early part of the battle. The big swing-wing bombers used small laser-guided bombs to 'plink' tanks to deadly effect.

Normally, one would expect

Left: US Marine Corps commanders are great believers in helicopter mobility. Four squadrons of Marine UH-1N Huey helicopters (foreground) were used to support troops in the field, while CH-53D/E Sea Stallion heavy lifters from six squadrons provided heavy logistics support from land bases and from amphibious vessels offshore.

Below: A Kuwaiti SA.342 Gazelle helicopter herds surrendered Iraqi soldiers into captivity. Once feared for their numbers and their supposed fighting prowess, the Iraqis wilted under relentless pounding by Coalition air power and quickly folded once the hard-hitting ground campaign began.

that with so much complicated machinery being used en masse under combat conditions for the first time, there would have been teething troubles. The astonishing thing about the war was the fact that most things worked as advertised, or even better than expected.

Iraqi failure

On the other side, there was little to cheer about. The Iraqi air force hardly took to the skies, and its best aircraft fled ignominiously to internment in Iran well before the end of the war. The army's artillery included some of the best equipment in the world, but without air cover it proved a sitting duck to allied air power. Iraqi armour was present in huge numbers, and while most of its tanks were inferior to Coalition vehicles, they could have proved a major threat had they been used effectively. After all, the Germans beat the French in 1940 with smaller numbers of less well-protected and armed tanks than those of the French army. Unfortunately for Saddam Hussein his generals had no real grasp of modern mobile warfare, and the armour proved no more effective in the face of overwhelming Coalition air power than had the Iraqi air force or navy.

Those who stood and fought were no match for the state-of-the-art armour fielded by the powerful Coalition forces. The final impetus to surrender came when the close support aircraft brought the battle to a close by annihilating the massive Iraqi column fleeing from Kuwait along the Basra road. In under 100 hours, the half-million strong Iraqi force in Kuwait and southern Iraq was finished, and Kuwait could be liberated.

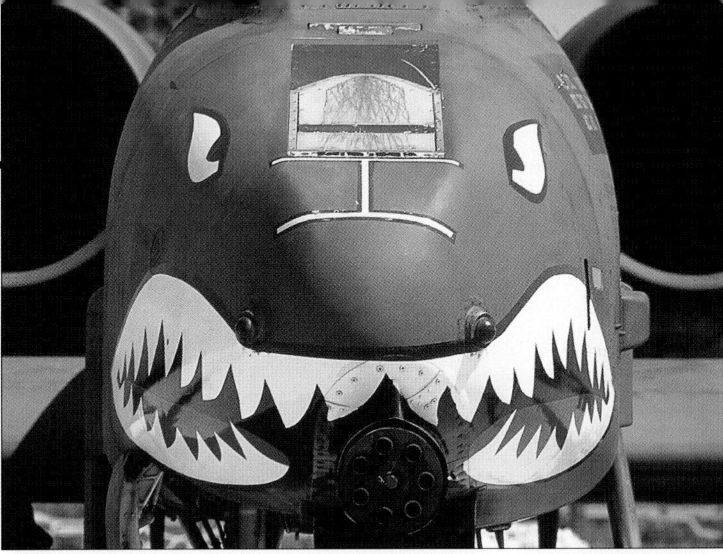

Right: The business end of an open-jawed, angry-eyed Fairchild A-10 Thunderbolt II was a sight that repeatedly confronted Iraqi tanks, vehicles, and troops as the Coalition pressed ahead with the ground war.

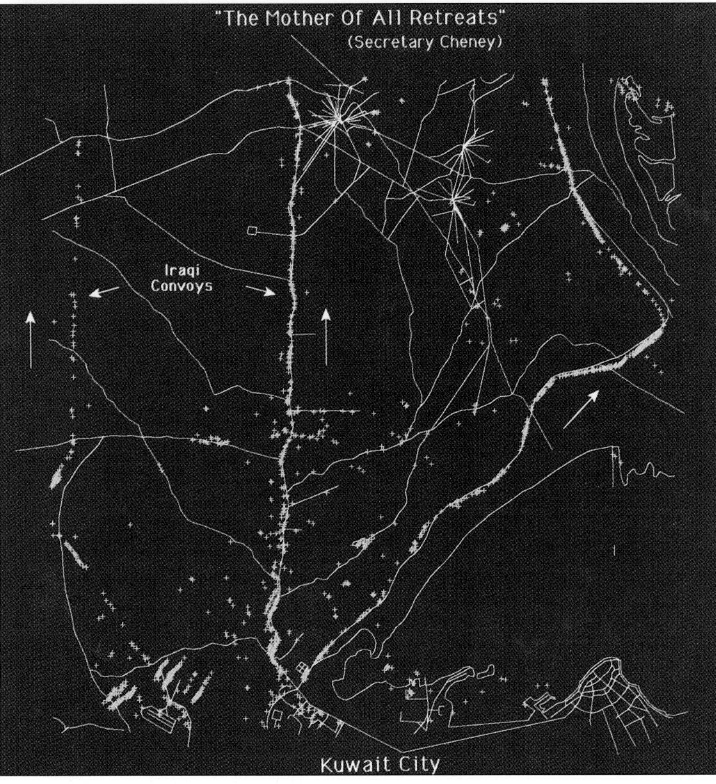

Right: US Secretary of Defense Richard Cheney was stating the obvious when he pointed out that the collapsing Iraqi army was performing the 'mother of all retreats'. The moving target imagery from a J-STARS aircraft shows the routes followed by Saddam Hussein's forces as they withdrew from Kuwait – routes that were to become a killing ground.

After the Storm

In large measure, the end of the Persian Gulf war signalled a new era for military affairs and for air warfare. There was now a 'New World Order', said US President George Bush in 1991.

Western nations would increasingly find themselves in smaller, shorter wars, with more elusive enemies – not merely Third World tyrants but rebels, renegades, and terrorists. Special operations forces might become more important than strategic bombers. Instead of practising the delivery of nuclear warheads, air forces would rehearse unconventional fighting deep into potentially hostile territory. Typical of the new kind of military endeavour was Operation Provide Comfort, begun in April 1991 and continued by the USA, Britain and other allies until December 1996. A Combined Task Force was assembled to enforce the 'no-fly' zone in northern Iraq (above the 36th Parallel) and to support Coalition humanitarian relief operations in the region, in particular providing protection, foods and medicine to the Kurdish settlements that had been a focus of repression by the Iraqi regime.

The air effort to police the Desert Storm truce included helicopter missions hauling food to the Kurds, reconnaissance and surveillance flights, and combat air patrols. Almost immediately, it became clear that Iraq might challenge the results of the hard-fought war. For example, the first 'post-war' aerial victory came on 20 March 1991 when an Iraqi Sukhoi Su-22 'Fitter' was shot down by 36th TFW F-15C Eagle pilot Captain Thomas N. Dietz. Two days later, another F-15C downed an Su-22. An accompanying Iraqi Pilatus PC-7 prop-driven trainer was taken under attack but its pilot bailed out before a shot was fired, creating a weaponless 'kill.'

Operation Southern Watch

A similar 'no-fly' zone was established in August 1992, south of the 32nd Parallel. Operation Southern Watch was set up to monitor UN Security Council Resolution 688, calling for Saddam Husssein to cease air and ground attacks on insurgents in south east Iraq.

The Iraqis began challenging the zone late in 1992, and a US F-16 shot down an intruding MiG-23. In January 1993, Southern Watch aircraft attacked Iraqi air defence sites, and US Navy missiles destroyed the Zaafaraniyah nuclear fabrication facility.

Above: The Union Jack emblazoned on its tail, an RAF Chinook HC.Mk 1 helicopter puts in heavy lifting duty during humanitarian relief operations in the northern part of Iraq, where Kurdish opposition groups suffered under Saddam Hussein's tyranny.

In October 1994, Operation Vigilant Warrior saw coalition troops deploy to Kuwait and the Gulf States in response to aggressive Iraqi troop movements in southern Iraq. Operation Vigilant Sentinel a year later followed the same pattern. Meanwhile, as Operation Desert Storm receded, other conflicts around the world demonstrated that times had indeed changed, that air power would now face a new era, and that training, tactics, and technology would become more important than ever.

AFRICA

As with many of the wars in Asia, much of the conflict in Africa since 1945 has been associated with the withdrawal of the European imperial powers from their colonies. But the liberation struggles of the 1950s and 1960s did not bring the rewards of peace so many had hoped for, with the first generation of African leaders often proving to be despots of the worst order. Bloody internal struggles – often driven by religious or tribal rivalries – have continued all over the continent into the 1990s. The relatively peaceful transition to majority rule in South Africa, where diplomacy has replaced active-military intervention in neighbouring states, is a sign of hope, however. But there is still a long way to go.

Kenya

1951–1955

***Left:** Avro Lincoln heavy bombers were used extensively against the Mau Mau. The Lincolns operated from November 1953 to July 1955, bombing Mau Mau concentrations in the Aberdare mountains and around Mount Kenya.*

***Below:** A detachment of Vampire FB.Mk 9 ground attack jets was deployed from Aden to Kenya in April 1954. The aircraft supported Operation Anvil, a major sweep in and around Nairobi which led to the detention of more than 16,000 suspected Mau Mau supporters.*

At the end of World War II more than 85 per cent of Africa was distributed between the empires of the UK, France, Belgium and Portugal, or about to be administered by these nations under United Nations trusteeship. Within 30 years the entire continent, comprising almost 50 states, had divested itself of the trappings of colonial rule and was to a great extent independent of its traditional imperial parents. A more insidious style of imperial domination emerged, based on the strategic interests and embracing the world ambitions of the superpowers, the Soviet Union, the United States and communist China. But in varying degrees (depending on the relations that existed at the time of independence) many emergent states opted to retain defence agreements with their former colonial parents in exchange for economic and cultural aid.

In Kenya, a British crown colony since 1920, Jomo Kenyatta, British-educated president of the Kenya African Union and a long-standing nationalist, was arrested on charges of inciting an uprising in the Kikuyu tribal area in 1952. His removal did not end the rebellion and the British authorities declared an emergency, detained suspected leaders, organised Kikuyu loyalists and isolated the rebels in the forests. Between 1952 and 1955 11,000 casualties were inflicted for the loss of 95 white lives. Initial involvement by air forces began in April 1953 when 12 North American Harvard trainers were flown up from Rhodesia to operate as light ground-attack aircraft; within a year these had flown 2,000 sorties, fired 750,000 rounds of 7.7-mm (0.303-in) ammunition and dropped 15,000 8.6-kg (19-lb) fragmentation bombs. In November 1953 Avro Lincoln heavy bombers of No. 49 (Bomber) Squadron arrived at Eastleigh on a three-month detachment from the UK, being relieved in turn by Lincolns of Nos 110 and 214 Squadrons during 1954. Middle East Air Force sent a small number of de Havilland Vampires and photo-reconnaissance Gloster Meteors, while support of the ground forces was undertaken by Vickers Valettas, Hunting Pembrokes, Auster AOPs and Bristol Sycamore helicopters. The use of aircraft proved decisive in quelling the rebellion, which ended in 1955, but the uprising by the Mau Mau (the Kikuyu secret society involved) demonstrated the inadequacy of colonial political structures, and Kenya was to become independent within the British Commonwealth eight years later, and a republic in 1965.

***Above:** The Mau Mau was a secret Kikuyu rebel group, poorly armed and equipped. But they knew the country, and it was hard for ground troops to catch them. The use of air power was something the rebels could not deal with, however.*

***Right:** It was difficult for the authorities to gather information about Mau Mau movements or to gauge the effect of air strikes. To help in the process, a detachment of photo-reconnaissance Meteors was sent to Kenya in August 1954.*

Anti-Mau Mau Lincoln strike

Foreshadowing America's use of B-52s in Vietnam more than a decade later, the Royal Air Force's Lincoln bombers were used to mount pattern bombing attacks on suspected Mau Mau hideouts in the heavily-forested highlands of Kenya. A typical Lincoln load consisted of five 454-kg (1,000-lb) bombs and up to nine 227-kg (500-lb) bombs or 159-kg (350-lb) cluster bombs, with attacks often flown at low level because of low tropical clouds.

Avro Lincoln B.Mk II
Left: A long-range evolution of the classic World War II Lancaster, the Lincoln was swiftly rendered obsolete by the rapid postwar development of jet bombers. Powered by four Rolls-Royce Merlin piston engines, the Lincoln could carry a six-tonne bomb load over a combat radius of 2500 km (1,500 miles) at a maximum speed of 475 km/h (295 mph).

Algeria

1954–1962

North American T-6Gs played an important light-attack role during France's involvement in Algeria. Some 700 were delivered to the escadrilles d'aviation légère d'appui (light-attack squadrons) in Algeria. They equipped 38 squadrons, with a peak total of 21 squadrons active within Groupe d'Aviation Légère d'Appui 72. They were armed with two 7.5-mm (0.3-in) gun pods, napalm, 10-kg (22-lb) bombs or rockets.

Above: The vulnerability of the T-6G to ground fire led to the introduction of the North American T-28 Trojan and the Douglas AD-4N Skyraider. The Skyraiders equipped the three squadrons of Escadre de Chasse 20, and were redeployed to French Somalia (now Djibouti) and Madagascar after the withdrawal.

Coming within months of the humiliating defeat in Indochina, the rebellion in Algeria – a state that was closer to being a *département* of metropolitan France than a colony – carried profound portents. Only the authoritarian grasp of President Charles de Gaulle, to whom that nation turned for leadership in 1958, prevented the horror of open revolution at home from becoming a reality.

As in Indochina, the armed Algerian nationalists – the Front de Libération Nationale – possessed no air arm but, having intimate familiarity with the local terrain, preferred to conduct guerrilla

Below: The Douglas B-26 Invader equipped four bomber escadrilles (one a dedicated night-attack unit) in Algeria, with a fourth unit operating in the recce role. The bombers served until 1962, and the recce aircraft left in December 1963.

Below: Escadre de Chasse 6 used the Sud Est Mistral (the Nene-engined French-built Vampire) until the unit withdrew from Algeria in December 1960. Several other units in Algeria also used the Mistral, operating primarily in the air-defence and ground-attack roles.

War against the FLN

Algeria was actually part of metropolitan France, and the French government had to contend with both Muslim separatists (who wanted independence), and a significant European population who were prepared to fight for the status quo, and who mounted an abortive coup and a campaign of terrorism when de Gaulle 'sold out'.

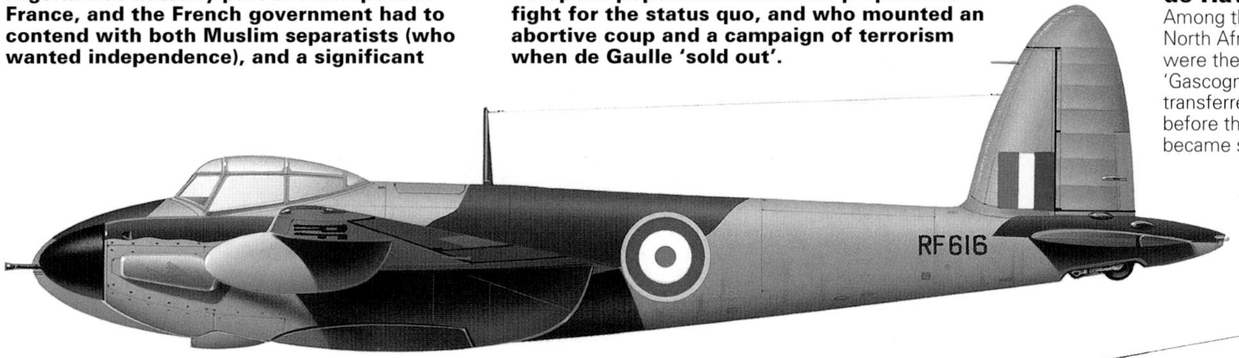

de Havilland Mosquito
Among the aircraft stationed in North Africa at the end of the war were the Mosquitoes of GC 19 'Gascogne', but they were transferred to Indochina in 1949 before the troubles in Algeria became serious.

Republic P-47N Thunderbolt
At the end of the war in Europe, the Armée de l'Air included four units equipped with P-47 Thunderbolts. They were retained until they could be replaced in the air-defence role by the Mistral, and were then used for close-support duties until replaced by the Skyraider. This one wears the markings of EC 20 'Lorraine'.

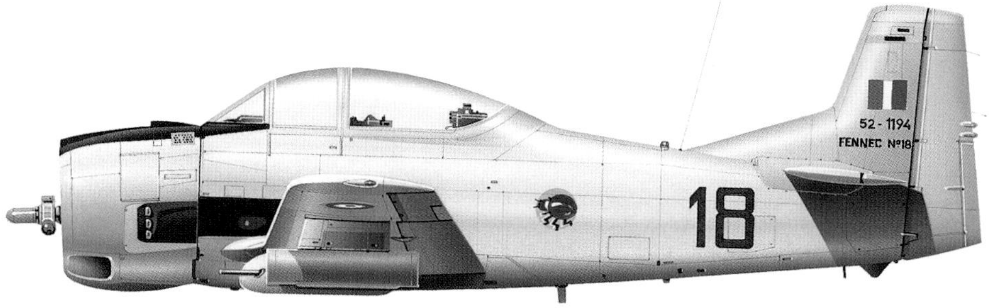

North American T-28D-52
Known as the Fennec in French service, the T-28 replaced the T-6G in service with some of the light-attack squadrons serving in Algeria. The aircraft was simple to fly, simple to service and cheap, but lacked the punch and survivability of the Skyraider, which became the Armée de l'Air's weapon of choice in colonial warfare.

Douglas AD-4N
The Armée de l'Air received 113 Skyraiders between February 1960 and March 1962, sending them to North Africa for service with EC 20. When the French withdrew from Algeria, the aircraft went to EAA 21 in French Somalia and Madagascar, and later to EAA 22 in Chad. The last were retired in 1975.

warfare. Despite the commitment of almost one million troops against them, they proved not only highly proficient but eventually persuaded France that, once again, no military solution was attainable. And in 1962, despite everything that sophisticated weaponry could achieve, Algeria won its independence under the erstwhile nationalist leader Ahmed Ben Bella.

At the beginning of the war in November 1954 the French air force in Algeria comprised a squadron of S.E.535 Mistral jet interceptors (licence-built Vampires) and a training squadron flying aged F-47 Thunderbolts, as well as a hotch-potch of obsolete second-line aircraft and trainers. None of these aircraft was in any way suitable for operations in the desert against fleet, mobile guerrilla forces whose tactics were based on lightning strikes and instant dispersal.

Below: The SIPA 111A was a French-built Arado 396, and was known as the S.10, S.11, S.111 or S.12 in French service. Three squadrons saw service in Algeria during the mid-1950s.

Above: The Dassault Flamant was a common sight in Algeria, for not only was it the Armée de l'Air's standard light transport and liaison aircraft, but some served in the bomber and navigation training roles. This aircraft was a six-seat MD312 transport.

Small COINs

As a matter of expediency, therefore, the local French commanders ordered a host of light aircraft and trainers into operational use, hurriedly modified with machine-guns and light bomb racks. Quite fortuitously, they had hit upon an ideal counter-insurgency weapon and one that was to sire a whole new operational philosophy employing dedicated COIN aircraft. Such aircraft as the North American T-6 Texan became synonymous with the world's mounting problem of anti-guerrilla operations.

Observation and recce

The Armée de l'Air has used a variety of aircraft types in the observation and light reconnaissance roles. Such aircraft played a vital role in Algeria, helping ground forces to react quickly to incursions and terrorist incidents, and helping to patrol Algeria's least populated areas. With an absence of enemy air opposition, such aircraft could also fulfil a limited close-support role.

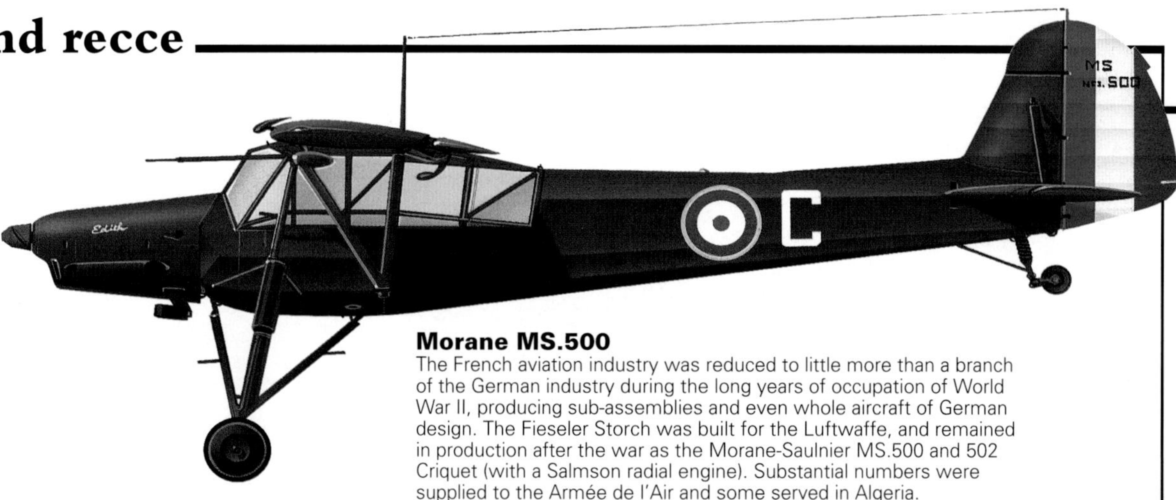

Morane MS.500
The French aviation industry was reduced to little more than a branch of the German industry during the long years of occupation of World War II, producing sub-assemblies and even whole aircraft of German design. The Fieseler Storch was built for the Luftwaffe, and remained in production after the war as the Morane-Saulnier MS.500 and 502 Criquet (with a Salmson radial engine). Substantial numbers were supplied to the Armée de l'Air and some served in Algeria.

Thus, in 1955, as the regular squadrons of conventional fighters retained their normal air defence tasks, the first escadrilles d'aviation légère d'appui (EALA, or light support squadrons) equipped with Morane-Saulnier MS.500s and 733s became operational. The following year they were joined by a groupe, GALA 72, of four escadrilles with T-6 Texans, and three of SIPA S.111s and 112s (the latter distributed between Tunisia, Morocco and Algeria).

More significant was the introduction of the Max Holste Broussard, the first aircraft formally customised for the counter-insurgency role and capable of lifting small numbers of troops to remote areas of local trouble. Following de Gaulle's resumption of command of the state in 1958, General Maurice Challe was given the task of crushing the Algerian rebellion and undertook a complete overhaul and reorganisation of the air force. One of his first priorities was to replace the excellent but aged T-6s which had hitherto flown the majority of operations against the rebel forces. An adaptation of the T-28 Trojan, itself a modern derivative of the T-6, was selected (being named the Fennec in French service).

Above: Between 1959 and 1961 EC 1/3 operated its F-100Ds on bombing raids over Algeria, though the aircraft operated from their Rheims base, refuelling at Istres in the south of France on their return journeys. The F-100's primary role was one of nuclear strike.

Above: A white cabin top and upper centre section were added to Broussards in Algeria to reduce cabin and fuel-tank temperatures. The type performed liaison and observation duties in Algeria, supplanting aircraft like the MS.500.

Crosshead please

Major weapon in the counter-insurgency arsenal was the helicopter, the Armée de l'Air having formed its first light helicopter squadron in Algeria in 1955 with Bell 47Gs and Sikorsky H-19s (S-55s). Pioneer operations by this escadrille had quickly demonstrated the flexibility of the helicopter, as much for casualty evacuation as delivery of troops into combat, and by the end of 1956 the 12-man Sikorsky H-34 was in service in the assault role. Within a year the French forces in Algeria possessed a total of 250 helicopters, of which the army flew 139, the Armée de l'Air 90 and the Aéronavale 18. In due course the French gave some of their helicopters a 'ground-attack' capability by mounting guns of 7.5-mm (0.3-in), 12.7-mm (0.5-in) and 20-mm (0.8-in) calibre, as well as rockets. Among the army helicopters were such troop-carrying aircraft as the Vertol-Piasecki H-21.

Left: Probably the most important transport aircraft flying resupply missions to French forces in Algeria was the Nord 2501 Noratlas. Some 426 were built, in France and Germany, and the type was widely exported. It equipped two escadres des transports, with three escadrons being based in North Africa.

Increased commitment

As the war dragged on, and the rebel forces (far from acknowledging defeat) stepped up their operations, so the French brought greater pressure to bear in Algeria, not least in the air. Two medium-attack bomber groups with B-26 Invaders were deployed in Algeria, together with a growing number of ex-US Navy AD-4 Skyraiders (of which France had ordered 113 from the USA in 1956).

The latter proved to be a highly-effective COIN aircraft, capable of delivering a very heavy punch in the ground-attack role and suppressing ground opposition during helicopter assaults.

Effective as Challe's 'steamroller' campaign was – forcing the rebels to revert to isolated guerrilla tactics by the end of 1960 – the mounting

Below: T-28 Trojans, called Fennec in French service, replaced T-6Gs in the close air support and COIN roles, but were themselves soon replaced by AD-4N Skyraiders.

Right: France received 135 Sikorsky H-34s built in the United States, and 130 built by Sud Aviation. The type served with GMH 57 in Algeria, and with six Algeria-based escadrilles of EH 22 and EH 23 and their forerunners. The H-34 proved to be the most successful of the French helicopters deployed in Algeria.

Below: Piasecki (Vertol) H-21s were used by both the Aéronavale and the Aviation Légère de l'Armée de Terre in Algeria. This H-21C wears the markings of GH 2, which was based at Sétif during early-1962.

cost of the war and the depradations imposed on French society by increasing terrorist activities in metropolitan France combined to sap the enthusiasm for an apparently fruitless continuation of the war. In 1962 de Gaulle was forced to accept terms for Algerian independence.

Militarily, whatever else the war in Algeria demonstrated, it illustrated the impotence of a conventional air force, equipped and organised for air defence, when it tried to operate in an environment of concerted guerrilla warfare. The lessons were there for the US to digest when, just two years later, it faced a similar threat in Vietnam. Ironically, it took 10 years for the United States to arrive at no less a humiliating political defeat than the French had suffered in Algeria.

Below: Probably the most effective of all the ground-attack aircraft that were used by the French air force was the ex-United States Navy Douglas AD-4N Skyraider. Large numbers served with the escadrons de chasse (fighter squadrons).

Helicopters in support

The war in Algeria probably cost one million lives, including 17,456 French servicemen. It also provoked massive political unrest in France, and damaged France's reputation overseas. But, at the same time, the war provided an excellent training ground for the French armed forces, which operated with great flexibility and with a high degree of inter-service co-operation. Nowhere was this more apparent than in the use of helicopters, aircraft from all three services being jointly tasked to perform troop transport, assault, observation and liaison duties.

Sikorsky S-55
The Sikorsky S-55 (sometimes referred to by the US military designation H-19) was used by all three services in Algeria, giving way to the H-34 in Armée de l'Air service, and to the HSS-1 in Aéronavale squadrons. ALAT H-19s remained active until the end of the war in Algeria.

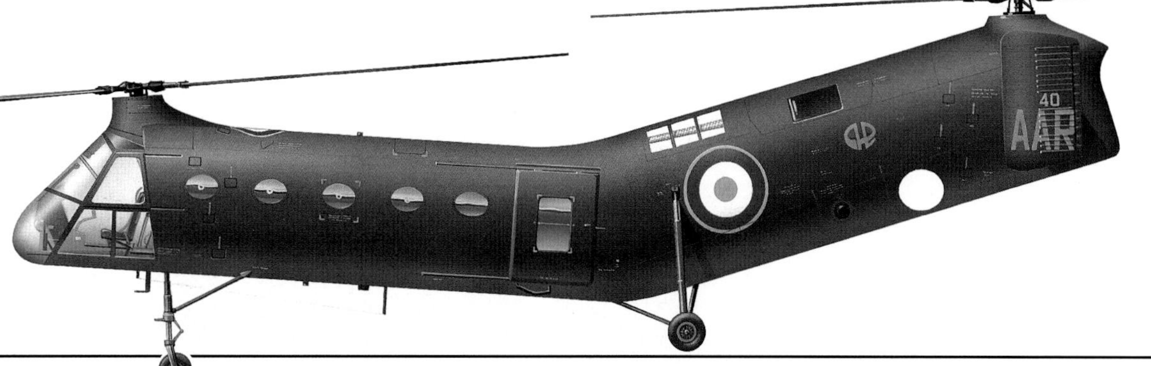

Piasecki (Vertol) H-21C
The H-21C saw service with the ALAT's GH 2, and also with the Aéronavale's Flottille 31F. The aircraft's ungainly appearance belied its effectiveness, the aircraft proving able to transport 20 fully-armed troops.

Central Africa

1960-1997

***Left:** To see Swedish warplanes in action outside Swedish airspace is an extremely rare occurrence, but the Congo emergency of the 1960s saw Saab J29 fighters flying support missions for UN troops on the ground.*

***Below:** Also forming part of the United Nations force, the Indian contingent was centred on a detachment of English Electric Canberra bombers, which often flew missions alongside the Swedish fighters.*

***Bottom:** Flygflottij 22 was a volunteer unit, flying both fighter bomber and reconnaissance versions of the barrel-like J29. The photo-ships wore camouflage, while the standard combat aircraft were overall natural metal.*

Belgium had for many years adopted a much more exploitative attitude than the other European colonial powers in Africa. When native peoples in British and French territories started campaigning for self-determination, Belgium hoped to prevent such demands spreading to the Congo. It quickly became obvious that such hopes would prove vain, and Belgium reversed its policy overnight and offered immediate political independence in 1960. Civil war of a tribalist nature broke out almost immediately and continued intermittently for seven years. During this period, numerous acts of atrocity were carried out against Belgian nationals who had chosen to remain in the former colony.

The immediate threat to peaceful transition to independence was posed when Moise Tshombe led a movement for the separation of the Katanga region from Kinshasa, and when the United Nations charter was invoked to provide a peacekeeping force there were immediate difficulties in selecting forces from member nations that had no colonialist connotations and were thus acceptable in an area seething with violently anti-imperialist hatred.

In due course Sweden, Canada, India and Ethiopia contributed air force elements, of which Sweden's Flygflottij 22 Voluntary Air Component with Saab J29s provided the most significant part, together with a number of de Havilland Canada Otters and de Havilland Canada Beavers; ground crews were also provided by Norway and Denmark. A particularly remarkable aspect of F22's contribution was the fact that the Swedish air force was not equipped, organised or trained for prolonged operation overseas, yet served with ONUC (Organisation Nations-Unies au Congo) from 1961 until 1963; moreover when called on to fly operations the unit maintained a consistent 90 per cent serviceability rate.

SWEDISH J29S IN ACTION

Based in turn at Luluabourg and Kamina, the nine J29Bs and two J29C reconnaissance versions undertook numerous gun and

India's Peacekeeper

The establishment of an armed United Nations presence in the Congo called for forces from non-aligned countries, calculated to be seen as less likely to be partisan in the vicious civil struggle. India, Ethiopia, Italy and Sweden sent combat aircraft to provide air support for UN forces, as they began to take a more active role in the ground fighting, and they soon began flying missions against the Katangan separatists.

English Electric Canberra B(I).Mk 58
India's Canberras were equivalent to the British B(I).Mk 8. They were night intruder versions of the Canberra bomber, stressed for low-level agility and able to carry a wide variety of weaponry, including a powerful belly-mounted cannon pack.

French Workhorse

Although Belgium was the major colonial power in central Africa, it is the French, whose imperial possessions tended to be further to the north, who have been most active in military rescues in the region. French forces have intervened at least 30 times since the 1960s, primarily with troops on the ground but supported by Armée de l'Air logistics squadrons. On occasion, French paratroopers have made combat drops in the course of their duties, almost invariably from the cargo compartment of Transall C.160 transports.

Transall C.160
Smaller than the American C-130 Hercules, the Franco-German C.160 entered service in the late 1960s, and has been one of France's main transport assets since that time. It can take a payload of up to 16 tonnes, 88 fully-equipped paratroops or more than 90 conventional troops.

Above: Paratroopers descend from a C.160 Transall as the African sun sets. Western powers have been involved in central Africa since colonial days, primarily in protecting their interests and personnel, but occasionally in the thankless peacekeeping role.

Right: Foreign Legion Paratroopers check passers-by on a road in Katanga. The 1978 crisis was distinguished by singularly brutal behaviour on the part of the rebels, and only the airborne troopers could be inserted fast enough to protect innocent foreigners.

rocket attacks and reconnaissance sorties, often in company with Indian air force English Electric Canberras. The Swedes' most significant operations were the surprise attacks of December 1962-January 1963 against the base at Kolwezi, where almost the entire Katangese air strength was eliminated by the J29s. The precision of this series of attacks had such a profound psychological effect upon the white mercenaries of the Katangese air force that many promptly defected and escaped to Angola.

Katanga revisited

The Republic of Zaire, as the former Belgian Congo became, was not to have an easy existence. In March 1977 President Mobutu declared a state of emergency when foreign mercenaries invaded the southern province of Shaba with the intention of supporting the establishment of an independent state of Katanga. France and Morocco answered his appeal for military assistance and, in Operation 'Verveine', 13 Armée de l'Air Transall C-160 transports airlifted 1,500 Moroccan troops to the air base at Kolwezi. With the addition of limited military aid from the United States, and after increased efforts by Mirage IIIs and Aermacchi M.B.326s of the Force Aérienne Zaïroise, the initial invasion was repulsed. A second invasion in May 1978 was better supported by air defence weapons, however, and only after about 10 FAZ aircraft had been lost (including six M.B.326s) was this attack defeated with the help of French and Belgian paratroops.

Left: Zaire's MB.326 trainers should have been of some advantage in the counter-insurgency fighting that has erupted in the last two decades, but poor maintenance and poor training meant that they never played a major part in the final struggle for the country.

Great lakes wars

One area which has seen more than its share of warfare in the last two decades has been around the great lakes of central Africa. Idi Amin's Uganda was a brutal dictatorship which was eventually overthrown by tribal rebels. Although Amin had received a number of MiGs from Warsaw Pact countries, they played little part in the war, which was largely fought out on the ground. Amin's successor, Milton Obote, was in turn overthrown.

Further south, Rwanda and Burundi have long been on the brink of (and some time over the edge of) bitter tribal violence between the majority Hutus and the formerly dominant Tutsis. Massacres in the 1970s and 1980s were made to seem as nothing in the 1990s as the tribal communities in each country tore each other apart. Once again, air power played little part in the fighting, although it was the death of the president of Rwanda in a plane crash in Burundi which was the spark to the worst violence. But air power was vital in getting relief supplies to the millions of people fleeing the horrors which had overwhelmed their homes.

Mobutu's fall

The violence in Rwanda and Burundi spilled over into Zaire, where the ailing President Mobutu's long time grip on power was starting to slacken. Guerrilla forces under the control of Laurent Desiré Kabila advanced towards the capital, and the collapse of central government led to yet another multi-national evacuation, with European and Americans being airlifted to safety. Mobutu fled to Morrocco, where he died of cancer, while the new government renamed Zaire. It is now the Democratic Republic of Congo.

Rhodesian bush wars

1965-1979

For much of the period of African decolonisation one state sought to resist the granting of independence on terms unacceptable to its minority white administration. In 1965 Southern Rhodesia unilaterally declared itself independent from the United Kingdom. Despite efforts at mediation by the UK, international sanctions were imposed by the United Nations on Rhodesia.

The predominantly white-staffed Royal Rhodesian Air Force (RRAF) had a long and honourable tradition which stretched back to before World War II. In the post-war years the RRAF had continued to maintain a small number of squadrons, equipped with British aircraft, and by the time of the unilateral declaration of independence (UDI) this force was spearheaded by a squadron of Hawker Hunters and one of English Electric Canberras. Despite sympathies among members of the RAF, Rhodesia found herself without many allies and the UN sanctions were fairly effective in preventing a significant build-up of the RRAF.

EVADING SANCTIONS

The air force's immediate task was supporting the Rhodesian army, and consisted mainly of supply missions and limited patrol and reconnaissance duties. Ten Aermacchi AL.60-F5 transports were obtained covertly in 1967. With the 1969 proclamation of a republic, the 'Royal' prefix was dropped by the air force, which now amounted to seven squadrons of Hunters, Canberras, de Havilland Vampires, Trojans, Douglas Dakotas and other assorted transports.

Above: the essence of bush warfare is tracking down lightly-armed, mobile guerrillas in largely trackless terrain. Aircraft and helicopters provide the mobility necessary to flush targets out of the long grass.

Right: Rhodesian Alouette IIIs, known as 'G-Cars', usually carried 12.7-mm (0.5-in) door guns. Some, known as 'K-Cars', were fitted with 20-mm cannon or quadruple 'fifties' for the escort role.

Frustration by neighbouring black states at the failure of sanctions to bring down the administration under Ian Smith led to an escalation of infiltration of 'Patriotic Front' terrorists into Rhodesian territory from bases in Botswana, Mozambique and Zambia. These were the guerrillas of ZANU and ZAPU, led respectively by Joshua N'komo and Robert Mugabe.

By 1972 the role of the RhAF hardened to one of active counter-guerrilla operations, with hot-chase, airborne landings by the Rhodesian Special Air Service and commando-style units in the outlying bush country, as well as rocket and bomb attacks by Hunters and Canberras on terrorist bases.

In 1976 17 Reims Cessna F337s were obtained by covert means for counter-insurgency tasks and around 34 Aérospatiale (Sud) Alouette III helicopters were supplied by South Africa. In the transport role the aged Dakotas were joined by a dozen ex-civil Britten-Norman Islanders, and in 1978 about 20 SIAI-Marchetti SF.260W Warriors were also obtained by clandestine means.

RhAF aircraft were frequently deployed on 'externals' over Mozambique, and to a smaller extent over Zambia and Botswana, the last posing the least threat. The only air opposition encountered by the RhAF came from a Botswana Defence Force Britten-Norman Defender, flown by a British pilot, which attacked ground troops during a raid near Francistown but was itself shot down by a 'K-Car' heli-

Rhodesian attack jets

The Royal Rhodesian Air Force had a long and distinguished history stretching back to the years before World War II. At the time of Ian Smith's unilateral declaration of independence, it was one of the most powerful air forces in southern Africa, with an all-jet strike force. Not strictly suitable for a counter-insurgency bush war, the aircraft were kept flying by a variety of means, and were used on many of the longer cross-border raids against guerrilla camps in neighbouring countries.

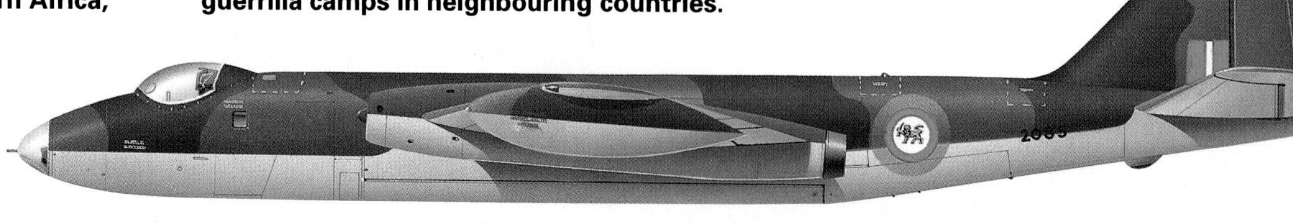

English Electric Canberra B.Mk 2
Above right: The Canberra was one of the first truly successful jet bombers. The Royal Rhodesian Air Force took delivery of 15 B.Mk 2 bombers and three T.Mk 4 trainers before UDI, and survivors continued to operate with No.5 Squadron into the 1990s. Canberras were used both for counter-insurgency work and in attacks on guerrilla camps in Angola and Mozambique, two being lost over the latter country.

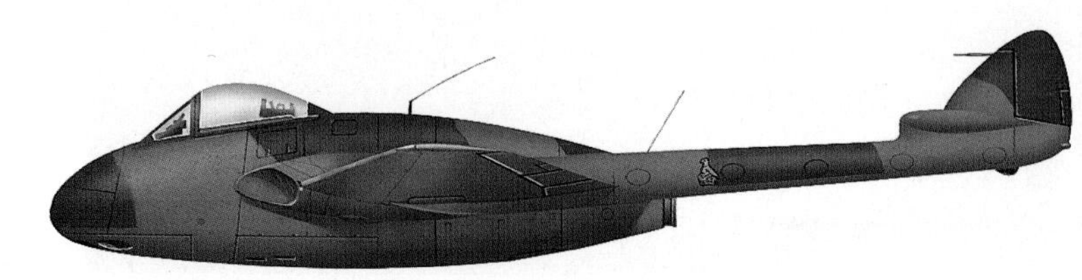

de Havilland Vampire FB.Mk 9
Right: The Royal Rhodesian Air Force operated 25 Vampires when the former colony broke with Britain in 1965. Used primarily for ground attack, they served through the civil war, and some trainers were still flying with Zimbabwe in the 1980s.

Equipped with full blind-flying instrumentation, the Lynxes also carried out night casualty evacuation and a limited amount of reconnaissance. Flare dropping was carried out over farms in isolated areas that were being attacked by terrorists.

Fire Force

A total of 17 Reims Cessna 337s acquired clandestinely in 1976 were quickly transformed into hard-hitting Lynxes and became among the most important RhAF combat aircraft during Rhodesia's long bush war. The Lynxes were armed with two 7.7-mm (0.303-in) machine-guns above the cabin, and typically carried two 37-mm rocket pods and 15 boosted HE rockets underwing.

The loss over Mozambique of two AL.60s to SA-7 Strela SAMs made the Rhodesian Air Force highly SAM-conscious. On the Lynx both engine exhausts were covered with heat shields to reduce their infra-red signature to missiles.

Combat equipment

The aircraft were also given comprehensive nav/com equipment, and during 'external operations', they were used frequently as an airborne communications relay stations between the ground forces, fast jets and helicopters, this task being codenamed Telstar. This system was also used extensively at night in support of external paradrops from Dakotas, Douglas DC-7s and INS-equipped Bell Model 205s.

Most Lynx sorties were mounted in support of the Fire Force, for rapid-response highly mobile anti-terrorist operations. On Fire Force missions the Lynx would usually operate with up to three 'K-Car' Alouette III gunships, and as many 'G-Cars' (troop-carrying Alouettes) or 'Cheetahs' (Bell Model 205 troop carriers) that could be gathered together. Even the troop-carrying 'choppers' were armed, with a pair of side-firing Browning 7.7-mm (0.303-in) machine-guns. A 'Para-Dak' (Douglas C-47 Dakota) with 16-20 paratroopers, and a 'Skyshout' (Cessna 185) 'Kiwit' or Britten Norman Islander could accompany the Fire Force. These 'Skyshout' psychological warfare aircraft were equipped with a powerful loudspeaker system, used to spread government propaganda to encourage the 'Terrs' or terrorists to surrender.

Another Lynx role was forward air control, generally in support of the fast jet force. A 'jet effort' was usually laid on against targets too heavily defended for Fire Force action. Using a high dive profile the Lynx would mark the target area with 37-mm smoke or phosphorus rockets, or frangible (napalm) fuel bombs. The Lynx pilot would then direct the jets, usually controlling pairs of Hunters, Vampires or Canberras.

copter (Aérospatiale Alouette IIIs configured as gunship with 20-mm cannon). Zambian MiGs were sometimes scrambled against the Rhodesian raiders but usually arrived too late.

Fuel starvation

One of the potential dangers always faced by the RhAF was a possible drying-up of fuel supplies following imposition of oil sanctions, and alongside the Royal Navy Britain's RAF undertook a limited patrol task with Avro Shackletons based in Madagascar to keep watch for sanction-breaking tankers from the Middle East attempting to land their cargoes on the African coast.

Despite the presence of communist-supplied SAMs to neighbouring black states, the RhAF continued to operate highly effectively both over and beyond Rhodesian territory right up to the point at which an internal settlement of the country's future administration was reached in 1979. However, with Marxist support of the ZANU and ZAPU, which had by 1979 reached substantial proportions, there is no doubt that the cost of military operations by the Rhodesian security forces was biting deep into the state's economy.

Yet throughout the 14 years in which the country lay in the economic wilderness, the RhAF's adaptability and determination saw it survive as an efficient counter-insurgency force.

Right: The most advanced aircraft available to the Rhodesian air force at UDI were the Hawker Hunter FGA.Mk 9s of No. 1 Squadron, which with the notable exception of South Africa outclassed anything used by other air forces in the region at that time.

Below: Jets are not the best way to counter insurgents in the bush. Rhodesia managed to clandestinely acquire Cessna 337s and SIAI-Marchetti SF.260s which were much more suitable for COIN operations.

Right: The end of the civil war saw the transformation of Rhodesia into Zimbabwe. The new state was free to acquire modern aircraft, and the first BAe Hawk armed trainers were ordered in 1982.

Portugal in Africa

1959-1975

Left: Portugal was one of the biggest users of the Fiat G91, which saw extensive service in the later stages of the country's colonial wars in Africa. G91Rs were sent to Mozambique in 1969, and were also used in Angola from 1963 to 1975.

By the early 1960s, Portugal's surviving colonial possessions in Africa began to reject Portuguese authority, the first armed rebellion emerging in Portuguese Guinea. Fighting broke out in August 1959 with the PAIGC (Partido Africano de Independencia da Guiné e Capo Verde). At first only a handful of T-6 Texans of the FAP (Força Aérea Portugesa – Portuguese air force) were available to deal with the emergency, until supplemented by Republic F-84G Thunderjets in 1963. FAP presence increased to match the rebel activity and in 1967, Esq. 121 'Tigres' with eight G91R-4s was set up at Bissalau, along with additional T-6s and Do 27 liaison aircraft. The G91s flew in support of Portuguese troops and against the PAIGC's supply trails near the Senegalese and French Guinean borders. Five of the type were lost to enemy action, at least two of them shot down by SA-7 missiles.

In May 1968 General Antonio de Spinola was appointed governor, and he ordered 12 Alouette III helicopters, which were essential for operations in a country that was comprised largely of marsh and soft terrain. The Alouette IIIs were part of Esq. 121, as was a flight of Nord Noratlas transports which undertook all local supply flights.

By 1970 the campaign had taken on a much tougher approach and the FAP was using napalm and defoliants against PAIGC targets. The PAIGC received limited air support from a number of diverse sources. Conakry-based Nigerian MiG-17s were used for reconnaissance flights, while Soviet-supplied Mi-4s carried out supply flights in the east of the country. Several FAP aircraft were lost to SA-7s and AAA fire: PAIGC claimed to have shot down 21 aircraft in seven years.

The PAIGC declared an independent republic in September 1973. Seven months later, the military seized power in Portugal in a nearly bloodless coup and established a provisional military government which installed Spinola as president. As a result, independence was granted to Guinea-Bissau on 10 September 1974. The FAP undertook the withdrawal of most military and civilian personnel by 15 October.

ANGOLA

While the situation in Portuguese Guinea was worsening, trouble flared up farther south in Angola. The actions of the Marxist Movimento Popular de Libertação de Angola (MPLA) forced the stationing of FAP C-47s and PV-2 Harpoons at Luanda to support the army. Several major towns soon came under MPLA siege and the small Portuguese army element in Mozambique was stretched to breaking point. A number of civilian aircraft, such as Piper Cubs, were pressed into service as light transports to resupply outlying settlements, while DC-3s and Beech 18s were used as makeshift bombers. These and the other FAP aircraft were joined in June 1961 by F-84Gs. A substantial paratroop-dropping effort was sustained, first by the C-47s and later by Noratlases, to relieve several towns under siege. Fighting continued, mostly in the north of the country, and the Noratlas detachment made regular parachute drops with the 21st Battalion of the Regimento de Caçadores Paraquedistas to garrison towns.

Although Portugal was the subject of a US arms embargo due to its African conflicts, seven B-26s were sold to the FAP in 1965 to supplement the PV-2s. These helped to compensate for the F-84G losses, which stood at five (mostly through accident rather than action) and growing Soviet support for the MPLA. Yet another guerrilla group materialised in 1966, when a breakaway MPLA group established itself as the Uniao Naçional de Independençia Total de Angola (UNITA), under the

Piston veterans at war

Portugal was the first of Europe's maritime powers to establish an overseas colonial empire, but by the 1950s it was becoming more and more difficult for one of the poorest nations in Europe to maintain its position in Africa. Air power was important to the struggle with independence movements, but the aircraft used were often aging and unreliable veterans of World War II.

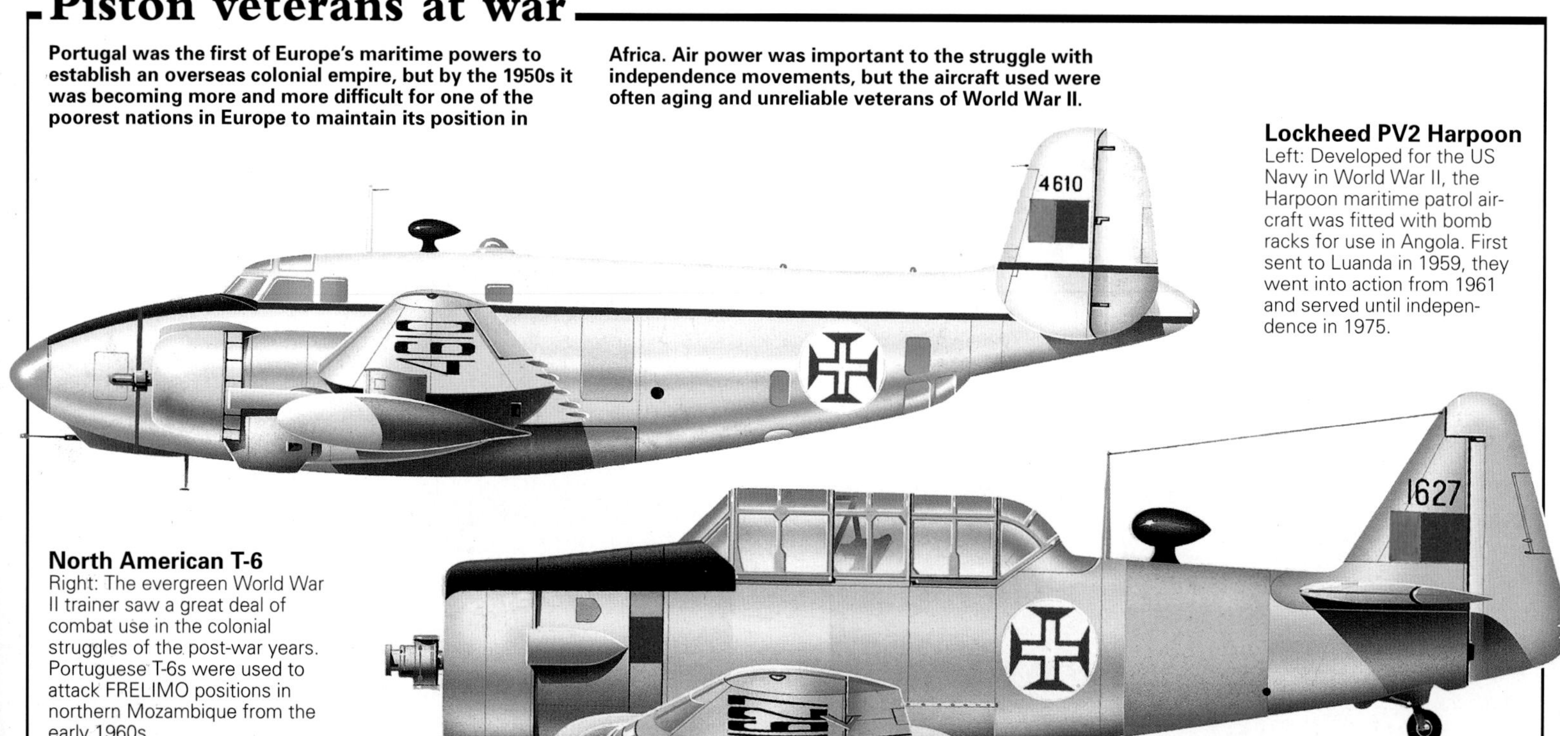

Lockheed PV2 Harpoon
Left: Developed for the US Navy in World War II, the Harpoon maritime patrol aircraft was fitted with bomb racks for use in Angola. First sent to Luanda in 1959, they went into action from 1961 and served until independence in 1975.

North American T-6
Right: The evergreen World War II trainer saw a great deal of combat use in the colonial struggles of the post-war years. Portuguese T-6s were used to attack FRELIMO positions in northern Mozambique from the early 1960s.

Portuguese air power in Angola

The war in Angola began in the early 1960s. In the beginning, Portugal had complete control of the air in its fight with the MPLA, the FNLA and Unita. However, by the end of the 1960s the guerrilla movements began to receive heavier weapons from neighbouring countries, and the first shoot down occurred in 1967, when the MPLA destroyed a Do 27. Several helicopters were shot down in 1968.

Aeritalia (Fiat) G91R-4

Right: During its African combat career, the 'Gina' proved to be a reliable and sturdy fighter-bomber and reconnaissance platform, operating mostly in adverse conditions. All active aircraft were forward deployed during operations and rearmed and refuelled as close to their operational areas as possible. In at least one instance Esq. 121 engaged MiG-17s from Guinea-Bissau, but with inconclusive results.

Aérospatiale Alouette III

Left: The essence of counter insurgency operations is the rapid deployment of troops directly into the operational area. From the middle of the 1960s, Portugal began to rely more and more heavily on its helicopter force to fill that function, initially with Alouette IIs but later with the more capacious Alouette III, which could carry up to six troops.

Right: The independence wars in Africa placed great strain on Portugal's transport capability. In 1962 the air force acquired the Nord Noratlas for parachute operations and for supplying outlying areas.

leadership of Jonas Savimbi. FAP aircraft maintained constant attacks against the MPLA, which was advancing inexorably westward towards the capital.

The arrival of G91R-4s in 1972 (some coming from FAP units stationed in neighbouring Mozambique) boosted the FAP's combat power. Helicopters also became an increasingly important part of operations. The Alouettes were used to move troops rapidly to trouble spots and by 1969 they had been joined in country by the first Pumas. F-84Gs, B-26s, T-6Gs and even armed Do 27s which kept up a constant cycle of air attacks on rebel positions.

However, the strain of fighting across Africa was proving too much for Portugal. The coup heralded the end of Portugal's involvement in Angola, which was offered independence on 1 July 1974.

Mozambique

The third chapter of Portugal's African wars concerned Mozambique. Following the other colonies' struggle for independence, Mozambique saw the rise of Eduardo Mondlan's Frente de Libertação de Moçambique (FRELIMO) movement in 1962. Again, only small numbers of FAP C-47s and T-6s were on hand when serious trouble broke out in 1964. In a short space of time, 16,000 troops had arrived in the country and additional T-6s, PV-2s (eight), Do 27s (12) and some Alouette IIIs were despatched to support them. FRELIMO operated from bases in Tanzania and later Zambia.

The FAP commitment to Mozambique became larger than that in either Guinea or Angola, though combat operations did not begin in earnest until 1968. A network of new air bases was set up as a result at Beira (T-6Gs, PV-2s, Auster D.5s and Noratlas transports) and at Tete (T-6Gs, Do 27s, Auster D.5s, Alouette IIIs and G91R-4s). Additional G91s were based at Nacala. Nova Freixo was occupied by T-6s, Austers and Alouettes while C-47 transports were based Lourenço Marques.

Now under the command of Samora Machel (later to become president), FRELIMO began vigorous operations against the Portuguese from 1970. South African-registered crop-sprayers were used to spray herbicides over FRELIMO's border strongholds, in an attempt to deny them food. These aircraft departed the country prematurely, after AAA fire shot down escorting T-6s and one of the crop-sprayers.

Once again Portugal found itself fighting a losing battle with a conscript army. The G91s returned to Portugal in 1974 in anticipation of an offer of full independence. Mozambique gained independence on 25 June 1975 and took possession of several T-6s and Noratlases for its own use.

Left: Very tough and with excellent short-field ability, the Dornier Do 27 saw extensive service in Africa. Portuguese Do 27s were used for liaison, to support T-6s operating deep in the bush and, rarely, to carry and deliver weapons.

South African Bush Wars

1975-1996

The political circumstances by which South Africa slid into isolation in the 1960s and 1970s are well documented, but resulted from the desire of the minority white population to retain political power, which was achieved by the maintenance of a system of separate development – Apartheid – for the different races. This became increasingly unacceptable to the international community, especially after America had put its own house in order by abolishing segregation and discouraging discrimination.

A culture in which politicians advocated a 'total onslaught' against minority white regimes soon began to prevail in those nearby countries which had black majority governments. Initially, however, the presence of white-ruled Rhodesia and Portuguese Angola insulated South Africa itself, and provided alternative targets for potential enemies.

Above: The South African Defence Force was the major military power in sub-Saharan Africa. The Blackburn Buccaneer was seen as a key element of that power, being able to fly interdiction missions far beyond South Africa's borders.

Over a period of time, South Africa found itself becoming increasingly involved in a counter-insurgency war in the territory then known as South West Africa. This started in the early 1960s, when the South West Africa People's Organisation (SWAPO), began its infiltration of what it called Namibia.

South African forces had conquered the territory from the Germans during World War I, and South Africa had been awarded the

Right: The Aérospatiale Alouette III was the South African Air Force's first modern helicopter. Entering service in 1962 it remains in use in a number of roles, including liaison and mountain rescue.

Helicopter mismatch

The essence of counter-insurgency warfare, especially in the bush, is the rapid movement of small units at great speed. The helicopter is in many ways the ideal bush war weapon, and South Africa used helicopters extensively in Namibia and Angola. However, they are vulnerable to modern weapons, and as the war went on and more advanced Soviet weaponry began to appear, a number were lost to anti-aircraft fire and to surface-to-air missiles.

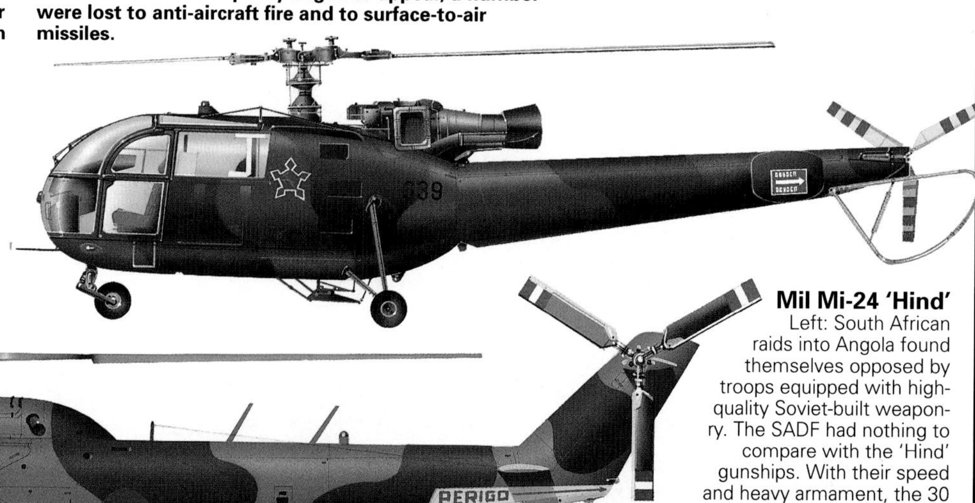

Aérospatiale Alouette III

Right: Although the basic design dates back to the 1950s, the French-built Alouette III is a highly effective light general purpose helicopter, with excellent 'hot and high' performance. South Africa had as many as 60 on strength through the period of the Bush War, in spite of supplying a number to Rhodesia. The Alouette III can carry up to five troops in addition to the pilot, and in the operational area was used as an assault transport as well as for command, liaison and search and rescue.

Mil Mi-24 'Hind'

Left: South African raids into Angola found themselves opposed by troops equipped with high-quality Soviet-built weaponry. The SADF had nothing to compare with the 'Hind' gunships. With their speed and heavy armament, the 30 delivered to the MPLA could have been a major threat, but fortunately for the SADF they were never used to their best effect.

Right: France became the major supplier of military equipment to South Africa after political differences arose with Britain in the 1960s. The South African Air Force took delivery of a variety of new French weapons in the 1960s and 1970s, before mandatory United Nations sanctions made France cease trading with the Apartheid regime. First delivered in 1969, the Aérospatiale SA.330 Puma is the country's most important transport helicopter, and its 3-tonne or 16-man payload was vital to the success of SADF operations in Namibia and Angola.

League of Nations mandate to administer the area. The United Nations did not recognise the mandate, and this consequently put South Africa at odds with the international community.

Cross-border raids

The first SWAPO incursion into Ovamboland in northern South West Africa took place in September 1965. South African police units retaliated by attacking a SWAPO camp at Ongulumbashe, arriving there by Alouette III helicopter. For most of the 1960s and early 1970s, the conflict in Namibia remained at a low intensity, with the Alouettes active in the counter-insurgency role.

A direct result of the 1974 Portuguese revolution and the ensuing withdrawal from Angola was SWAPO's freedom to establish bases, with backing from the de facto rulers of the former colony, the Marxist MPLA. The situation was deemed serious enough for direct military involvement by South Africa.

The resulting Bush War saw South African Defence Force units, supported by the SAAF, involved in numerous operations in southern

Right: Helicopters are vulnerable on the ground, so South African troops learned to embark and disembark in a hurry. On one occasion a Puma picked up a squad while under fire from a Cuban tank!

Above: South African Mirage IIIs gave the SAAF unmatched regional air-to-air capability in the 1960s. But by the time that South African forces became embroiled in Angola in the late 1970s and 1980s, the opposition included Cuban-piloted MiG-23s and Sukhoi Su-22s, and only superior training gave the Mirages the edge.

Right: First entering South African service in 1963, the Canberra was intended to provide bombing experience for Buccaneer crews. But the Canberra is a potent warplane in its own right, and it was used with some success in preparatory strikes against SWAPO base areas before major ground operations.

Angola between 1974 and 1987. The protracted conflict began on the 23 August 1976 when C-130Bs flew troops to South West Africa to occupy the strategic waterworks at Calueque, a few kilometres into Angola. Eight SAAF Alouette IIIs assisted with the actual occupation. The water plant had been built with South African funding during the Portuguese administration of Angola, and provided much-needed irrigation water to the farmlands in the north of South West Afica. This was the beginning of Operation Savannah, which saw South African forces, supported by SAAF helicopter, transport and reconnaissance missions, penetrate Angola right up to the outskirts of Luanda. The aim of Operation Savannah was to help the pro-Western FNLA and UNITA liberation movements against the Cuban-backed Marxist MPLA. The MPLA aimed to take over the country before the elections which would accompany Angolan independence on 11 November 1975. The South Africans were forced to withdraw when US support for the initiative failed to materialise.

ANGOLAN BASES

With the end of Operation Savannah, the MPLA formed the new government, actively supporting SWAPO and giving it sanctuary in southern Angola. South Africa's quarrel was essentially with SWAPO, but because of the active Angolan support for SWAPO's Peoples Liberation Army/PLAN, South African forces found themselves involved in clashes with Angolan government (FAPLA) forces during their incursions into southern Angola.

Operation Reindeer began on 4 May 1978 and saw the SAAF attack SWAPO training bases at Cassinga and Chetequera in response to a dramatic SWAPO incursion into South West Africa. The air attack was initiated by Mirages, which were followed by Buccaneers. On completion of the raid, ground forces were evacuated using Pumas and Super Frelons. By now there were permanent detachments of Pumas and Alouette IIIs to Ondangwa, Mpacha and Rundu, with a Super Frelon detachment at Mpacha. During Operations Rekstok and Safraan, mounted during March 1979, Impala Mk IIs, Mirage IIIEZs, Bosboks and Kudus made their operational debut in the combat area, with Impala and Mirage detachments at Ondangua, and an Impala detachment at Mpacha in the Caprivi Strip. Operation Safraan was mounted against SWAPO training camps near the Caprivi strip, while Operation Rekstok consisted of air strikes and heliborne raids on

The Atlas Kudu is a tough utility aircraft developed from an Italian Aermacchi design. Kudus were often flown on route navigation missions and as communications relay aircraft during operations in Namibia – essential given the flat, featureless nature of the terrain .

Ground attack

South African external operations into Angola initially met with very little aerial opposition, and SAAF aircraft could concentrate on their main function, which was the support of troops on the ground. Aircraft used ranged from high-performance jets to light utility aircraft, and targets varied from individual guerrillas in the bush to large, well-protected SWAPO base camps protected by surface-to-air missiles and anti-aircraft guns.

Canberra B(I).Mk 12
Above: Designed in the 1950s as a high-level night intruder/bomber, South African Canberras were switched to low-level operations in the 1970s. Normal combat radius in bush operations was 1300 km (808 miles), with a bombload of 2720 kg (6,000 lb) internally and a further 454-kg (1,000 lb) weapon under each wing.

Mirage F.1
Above right: The Mirage F.1CZ, South Africa's main interceptor in the 1980s, was the also a capable ground attacker. It served alongside the F.1AZ attack variant, which was delivered with improved navigation equipment and better air-to-surface fire-control systems.

Atlas Impala Mk.II
Right: Based on the single-seat light strike variant of the MB326 trainer, the Impala is a no-frills combat aircraft which was used with great success in the operational area. Armed with two 20-mm cannon, it can also carry 1814 kg (4,000 lb) of bombs or rockets on six underwing hard points.

Above: Lieutenant Adriano Bomba of the Mozambique air force defected to South Africa on 8 July 1981. His well-maintained MiG-17 was escorted into Hoedspruit air base by SAAF Mirage F.1AZs. South African pilots took the opportunity to make a thorough evaluation of the fighter before it was returned to its owners in November.

Right: The first real opposition to to South African fighters over Angola came from MiG-21s flown by Cuban and East German pilots. This aircraft force landed in South Africa after a defection attempt. Repaired and flown by the South African Air Force, it was thoroughly evaluated before finding a home in the SAAF museum.

SWAPO camps in southern Angola. While performing a low-level air attack on 14 March 1979, in southern Angola, the SAAF suffered its only Canberra loss, when the pilot was wounded by small arms fire and was unable to maintain control of his aircraft.

Operation Sceptic saw the largest SADF mechanised infantry assault since World War II. It was launched on 20 May 1980 against SWAPO bases and its southern headquarters. The operation commenced on 7 June with attacks by 12 Mirages and four Buccaneers on the southern HQ, and by 16 Mirages on the main SWAPO HQ at Lubango. Two of these Mirages were damaged by SA-3 missiles but returned safely, landing at Ruacana and Rundu. Three days later two further air strikes followed. Eighteen Mirages attacked the southern HQ with eight 250-kg (551-lb) bombs each, while four Buccaneers attacked a SWAPO camp at Mulola with eight 450-kg (992-lb) bombs each.

Helicopter assaults

Operation Sceptic lasted for three weeks and saw the extensive use of Pumas and Alouette IIIs in support of ground forces. During this operation the SAAF suffered its first loss by an surface-to-air missile when an Alouette III was shot down. During this period, three Impala Mk II pilots were killed after being shot down in separate incidents. A month later, Alouette III gunships, armed with side-firing 20-mm cannon, were first reported in Operation Klipklop performing an attack on the SWAPO transit point at Chitado.

During Operation Protea, which was initiated in August 1981, a major SAAF attack was made on 23 August against Angolan air defence installations, and these were seriously damaged – although the main objective of Protea was to attack the SWAPO North Western and Northern Front headquarters at Xangongo and Ongiva. An Alouette III was shot down on 25 August. In November 1981, Operation Daisy was launched against SWAPO bases at Bambi and Cheraqurera, which were captured by ground troops following an SAAF attack. On 6 November 1981 an SAAF Mirage F1CZ flown by Major Johann Rankin, shot down an Angolan Air Force MiG-21 using its 30-mm cannon, the first SAAF dogfight kill since World War II.

Left: Mil-24 'Hind-Es' sit in front of of Mi-8 and M-17 transports. Although fitted with launch rails for anti-tank missiles, UV-32-57 rocket pods were a more common weapons load. Angolan 'Hinds' rarely carried a full weapons load, probably because of the hot climate which reduced performance.

Early in 1982 a SAAF Puma was shot down, and later in May 1982 an Impala Mk II was downed near Cuvelai. During an attack on Cassinga (Operation Mebos) a SAAF Puma was shot down, killing all 15 on board. A Bosbok was also lost in July, killing both crew. Whilst escorting a recce mission in southern Angola during December 1982, two Mirage F.1CZs were jumped by four Angolan MiG-21s. In the ensuing engagement, one of the MiGs was shot down by Major Rankin (the same pilot responsible for the first kill, again using the Mirage's 30-mm cannon). This added to six air-to-air victories scored by SAAF Impalas during the Bush War.

During Operation Askan, the SAAF mounted a major attack on Angolan air defences. During this, on 22 December 1983 an Impala Mk II was hit by a SAM which failed to explode. The warhead of a new SAM-9 was identified stuck in the rudder of the Impala. It was now clear that Angola had acquired the very latest air defence systems, and this was a source of grave concern.

Attempted peace negotiations in 1985 produced a Joint Angolan South African Monitoring Commission which aimed to oversee the withdrawal of South African forces from Angola, but SWAPO could not be persuaded to take part and the conflict continued. An SAAF Dakota was hit in the tail by an SA-7 on 1 May 1986 but the pilot made an exceptionally skilful landing at Ondangua without further damage to the aircraft. During Operation Egret in September 1985, aimed at preventing a major SWAPO infiltration into SWA, the Angolan air force took an increasingly offensive stand, and in addition to MiG-21s the SAAF encountered MiG-23s, although engagements were inconclusive.

Right: The MiG-23 'Flogger' has replaced the older MiG-21 in the fighter role in Angola. Surprisingly the Angolans were given the late-model MiG-23ML 'Flogger-G' by the Soviets. This was considerably more capable than the earlier variants used by some Warsaw Pact air forces of the day.

FINAL BATTLES

During Operation Moduler, which took place in the latter half of 1987, the SAAF was faced with what was arguably the most sophisticated air defence system of Soviet origin outside the WarPac countries, but fortunately there were no losses. Moduler was followed by Operation Hooper, the last major SADF offensive. This opened on 13 January 1988 with an attack north-east of Cuito Cuanavale. By now the South African forces were not only operating against SWAPO, but were actively supporting the pro-Western Angolan UNITA forces against the government's own armed forces.

The SAAF played a major part in this and follow up attacks, but was restricted by a loss of air supremacy. The Mirage F.1AZs of No. 1 Squadron flew 683 sorties, supporting ground forces, and delivering 3,068 bombs. Most of these sorties had to be flown low, under Angolan MiG-23 CAPs and avoiding FAPLA radar defences. One F.1AZ was shot down and another was lost in an landing accident at Rundu following a missile hit. The small Buccaneer contingent from No. 24 Squadron, by now reduced to five operational aircraft, delivered 701 bombs during 99 sorties, without loss.

By this time, the politicians had succeeded in negotiating a withdrawal of Cuban forces from Angolan soil, in exchange for South African withdrawal from Angola, the granting of independence to Namibia, and the ultimate withdrawal of South African forces from Namibia itself. During August 1988, the last South African forces left Angola. Peace had finally arrived – at least in the air. In Angola itself, the civil war continued to be fought out with savage ferocity well into the 1990s. However, a shaky United Nations-brokered peace has gradually taken hold in the war-torn former Portuguese colony.

Angola's quiet air war

One of the more interesting sidelights on the long civil war in Angola has been the key role played by a South African firm, Executive Outcomes. South Africa had been a long-time supporter of UNITA guerrillas, one of the three main groups struggling for control of the former Portuguese colony. However, in 1993 this privately run firm, staffed by ex-South African military personnel, was contracted to train the armed forces of Angola's MPLA government – the very people who many of the South Africans concerned had been fighting (and winning) against for more than a decade – to beat UNITA.

The aerial portion of the contract saw extremely experienced former SAAF pilots flying combat missions in support of EO-trained ground troops. After quick and somewhat primitive familiarisation courses, the South Africans found themselves going into action in Angolan air force Mil Mi-17 helicopters, armed Pilatus PC-7 trainers and even MiG-23 'Floggers'.

Left: Executive Outcomes pilots first went into action in armed PC-7 trainers. They were ideal platforms for fast-moving counter-insurgency warfare, but they were also vulnerable to ground fire.

Below: The South African pilots were very experienced. Colonel 'P' was a former Mirage and Cheetah instructor who also had more than 2,000 hours on Impalas, including combat time over Angola.

Up until that point, the Angolans had been fighting along the rigid lines dictated by their previous Warsaw-Pact style training and had not been doing well. In 28 months, the EO advisers and a handful of pilots turned the situation around. Applying their own hard-won bush war experience, they trained the MPLA to first hold UNITA's advances, and then begin to force them back. By the time EO left Angola in 1995, UNITA had sued for peace, and, somewhat reluctantly, joined the government to forge a new fragile peace agreement.

NEW COMBAT AIRCRAFT DESIGNS

South Africa's political and military isolation began in the 1960s, as international condemnation of the racist Apartheid system grew. As a United Nations arms embargo began to bite, sources of modern weaponry began to to dry up.

At the same time South Africa felt that it was under increasing threat from a ring of neighbouring Marxist- and Communist-inspired African governments. By the early 1980s, the escalation of the bush war in Namibia and Angola had left the South African Air Force (SAAF) hard-pressed to counter the sophisticated Soviet-supplied aircraft and SAM systems deployed against it, and the search began for new and better combat aircraft.

South Africa's state-owned Atlas Aerospace already had experience in assembling the Impala Mk 1 jet trainer and Impala Mk 2 light attack aircraft (licence-built versions of the Aermacchi M.B.326M/K).

From 1975 onwards Atlas had assembled the SAAF's Mirage F1AZ fighters and also built Puma and Alouette III helicopters. It was Atlas's experience with the Mirage, and the SAAF's large but ageing fleet of Mirage IIIs, that would allow the South African firm to proceed with a series of upgrades to the French jets that would ultimately provide the SAAF with one of the most capable combat aircraft in the world.

However, South Africa could not embark on such an ambitious programme completely alone. It needed a little help from its friends – and that help came from Israel. Drawing on IAI experience with the Kfir upgrade, Atlas developed the two-seat Cheetah D attack aircraft, based on the Mirage IIIDZ, which appeared in 1986. Next came the single-seat Cheetah E fighter, but this was only a stepping stone to the Cheetah C, the ultimate Mirage upgrade. Cheetah C boasts a new multi-mode radar and cockpit avionics, advanced ECM and self-protection systems, much expanded weapons capability and a refuelling probe. The Cheetah C was a highly secret programme , which only became known in the early 1990s. Mystery still surrounds the source of the upgraded airframes, as all of the SAAF's existing Mirage IIIs are believed to be accounted for as either crashed, withdrawn from use or converted to Cheetah E/D standard. The Cheetah D and C are now the front-line combat jets in South Africa's air force.

Bush war experience also drove the requirement for a dedicated attack helicopter, a type greatly missed by the SAAF, which had to field armed transport helicopters instead. Development of this new aircraft began in 1981 and, in 1990, the prototype of what became the Rooivalk (Red Falcon) attack helicopter was flown. Rooivalk is now in the final development stage and is on the verge of entering SAAF squadron service. Atlas are also hoping for export sales as the new political situation in South Africa frees them to show their work to the rest of the world.

Above: The Atlas-developed Cheetah E was a stop-gap conversion of the SAAF's single-seat Mirage IIIEZs, that closely resembled Israel's Kfir C.7

The Rooivalk helicopter is armed with a 20-mm cannon under the nose, laser-guided Atlas Swift anti-tank missiles, 68-mm rockets and Darter or Viper air-to-air missiles.

Atlas Cheetah C

The Cheetah C emerged in a relative blaze of publicity in 1995 when the wraps were taken off what had hitherto been South Africa's most secret aviation project. Earlier Cheetahs had been the result of a mid-life update programme for elderly Mirage IIIs. The Cheetah C is a significantly more capable aircraft, probably owing much to Israeli engineering experience with the Kfir although this has never been officially confirmed.

Weapons
The primary air-to-air weapon for the Cheetah is the Kentron V3C Darter all-aspect infra-red guided missile. Developed from the V3B Kukri, it can acquire targets from the pilot's helmet-mounted sight.

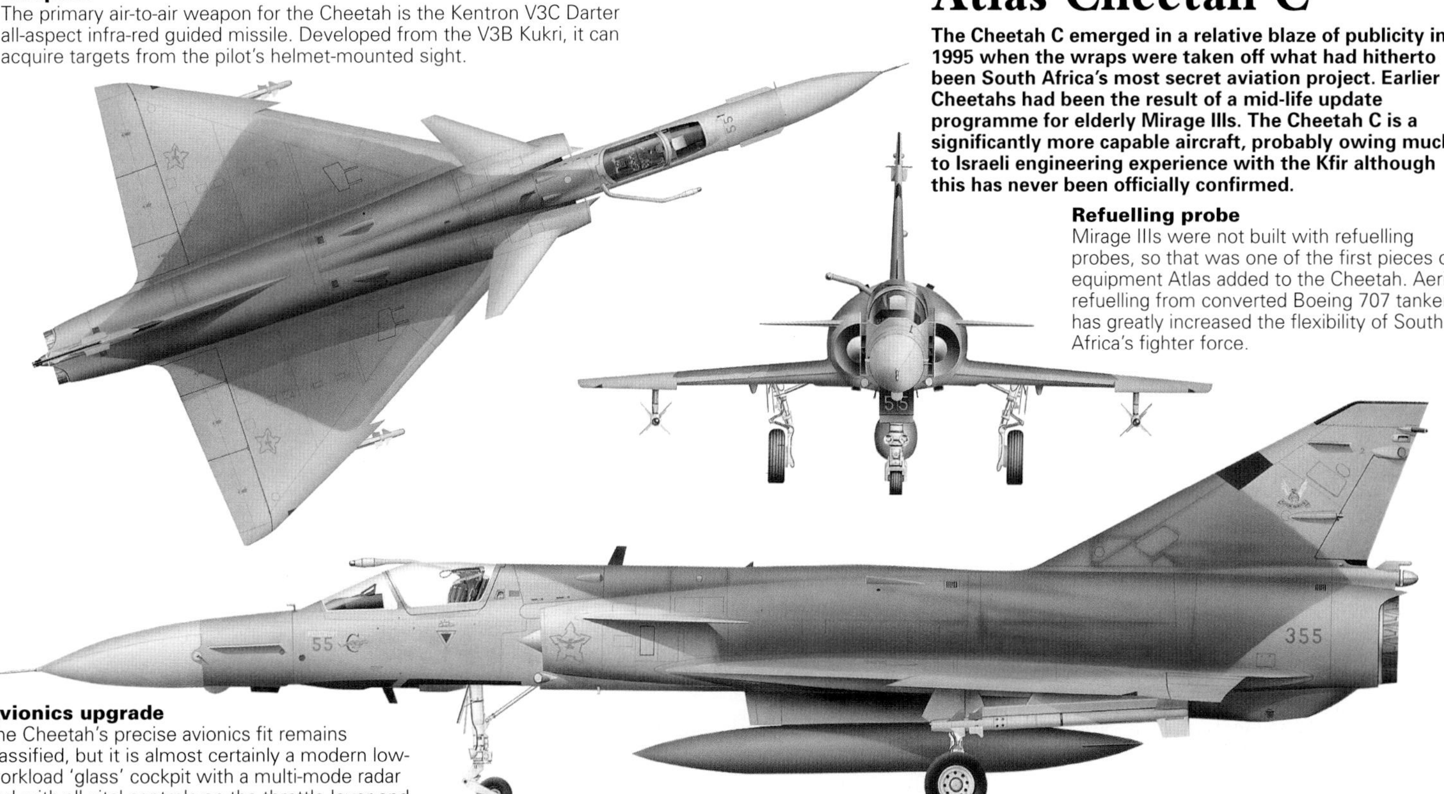

Refuelling probe
Mirage IIIs were not built with refuelling probes, so that was one of the first pieces of equipment Atlas added to the Cheetah. Aerial refuelling from converted Boeing 707 tankers has greatly increased the flexibility of South Africa's fighter force.

Avionics upgrade
The Cheetah's precise avionics fit remains classified, but it is almost certainly a modern low-workload 'glass' cockpit with a multi-mode radar and with all vital controls on the throttle lever and joystick.

Morocco and Chad

1976-1986

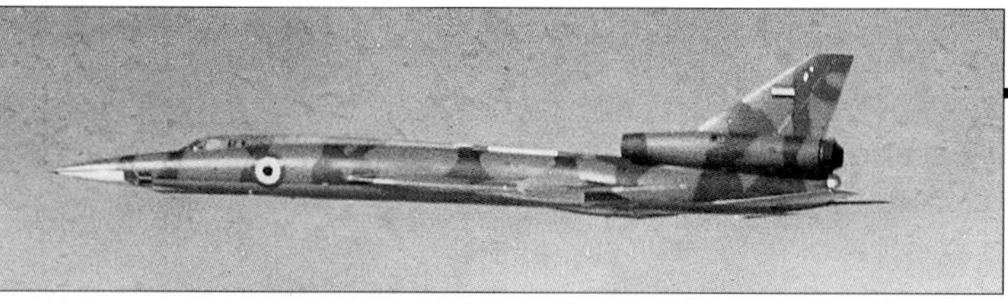

***Above:** In retaliation for the **Ouadi Doum** strike, Libyan **Tu-22s** mounted at least two missions against **N'Djamena** airport. The first, on 24 February 1986, was successful, putting the airport out of action for two days, while the **Crotale SAMs** sat idle, unable to engage such a high-flying target. On 7 September a **Tu-22** was downed over **N'Djamena** by a **HAWK SAM**.*

***Left:** BAP-100 anti-runway bombs dropped by **Armée de l'Air Jaguar As** rain down on the Libyan airfield at **Ouadi Doum** in illegally-occupied northern Chad. Mounted in February 1986, the strike severely damaged the runway.*

Chad, which gained independence from France in 1960, was left with a minority Christian government ruling over a majority Muslim population. French forces returned to Chad in 1968 to help fight the Islamic Front de Libération Nationale de Tchad, withdrawing in 1975 after a coup installed an Islamic government.

Libyan leader Colonel Gaddafi was always enthusiastic to support other Islamic movements, and Libyan interest in Chad was further sharpened by the possibility of mineral resources in the disputed Aouzou strip in the extreme north of Chad.

Libya occupied the strip in 1973, shortly before the French withdrawal. In 1978 the new Muslim government invited French forces back to eject the Libyans, but the regime proved precarious and in 1980 civil war broke out between the factions of the men who had previously shared power, Habré and Oueddi. Habré was ousted, retiring to the Sudanese border area, where he formed the Forces Armées du Nord (FAN). Oueddi invited Libyan forces into Chad, which attacked FAN bases in Chad and Sudan (mainly using SIAI-Marchetti SF.260WLs). By 1981, however, Habré controlled most of the east and centre of the country, including the capital, and his FAN became the Forces Armées Nationales Tchadiennes (FANT). A peacekeeping force from Nigeria, Senegal and Zaïre replaced the Libyans, and Oueddi fled north to raise the Libyan-backed Armée de Liberation Nationale (ALN).

For the next decade the FANT (with support from French and Zairean forces) fought off Libyan air attacks and ALN military action. In 1983 French forces established a red line roughly along the 15th Parallel, from Torodum to Oum Chalouba, which became the bor-

French Jaguars in Chad and Morocco

France's defence links with her former colonies saw French combat aircraft commited to combat operations over North Africa during the 1970s and 1980s. Jaguar As of the Armée de l'Air's 11e Escadre de Chasse (three squadrons of which are assigned to the Force d'Intervention) have been responsible for most overseas interventions, supported by personnel, and sometimes aircraft, from EC 7. The first action took place in December 1977 after Jaguars had been deployed to Dakar, Senegal (Operation Lamantin) for raids on Polisario Front guerillas attacking Mauritanian territory in the former Spanish Sahara. Two Jaguars were shot down in December and another on 3 May 1978 during the fourth French air strike.

During Operation Tacaud, the Dakar detachment sent eight Jaguars to Chad in April 1978. Operating from N'djamena, the Chad flight lost a Jaguar to an SA-7 SAM on 31 May 1978 while supporting French troops. Another crashed on a recce flight on 8 August; two were lost in separate collisions in August and October. By then the guerrillas had formed a coalition government and French forces began a withdrawal completed in May 1980. France maintained regular detachments at Bangui/M'poko airport in the Central African Republic under the title of *Eléments Français d'Assistance Opérationelle* for assisting its former colonies and the help of these units was requested in 1983 when civil war again erupted. Operation Manta, the establishment of a 'red line' between the warring factions in Chad, included arrivals of Jaguars at N'djamena on 21 august. Regular patrols were flown with tanker support from Boeing C-135Fs and Transall C.160NGs, but no action was seen until 25 January 1984, when one Jaguar was shot down by 23-mm cannon while attacking a rebel convoy. Another was lost in an accident on 16 May, but a stalemate allowed the French to withdraw, and the Jaguar flight, mostly of aircraft from EC 4/11, left N'djamena on 3 October. Libya built a major air base at Ouadi Doum in illegally-occupied northern Chad to support a further rebel offensive. Requested to assist, France launched eight Jaguars, supported by C-135Fs, from Bangui on 16 February 1986, and in a five-hour round trip, they seriously damaged the runway. This mission was part of Operation Epervier during the course of which a Jaguar accidentally crashed near Bangui on 27 March 1986. The aircraft undertook regular surveillance flights punctuated by a further attack on Ouadi Doum on 7 January 1987. Launched from N'djamena, 10 Jaguars attacked radar installations with Martel ARMs. This was the Jaguars' last offensive action of Operation Epervier.

SEPECAT Jaguar A

Based at Toul/Rosières, two *escadrons* of EC 11, 3/ 11 and 4/11, were attached to the Force d'Action Eteriuere for overseas intervention and were extensively committed to operations in north Africa. Wearing a two-tone camuflage scheme of sand and chocloate brown, this Jaguar A of EC 4/11 carries the secretary bird emblem of its first *escadrille*, SPA158, on the port side of its fin.

Moroccan COIN air power

Morocco's annexation in November 1975 of the Western Sahara territory vacated by Spain embroiled it in a little-reported war with Algerian- and Libyan-backed Polisario guerillas.

Rockwell OV-10 Bronco
First seeing combat with US forces in Southeast Asia, the Rockwell OV-10 is one of the few aircraft currently in service which was designed from the outset as a counter-insurgency platform. The Moroccan air force received six refurbished former USMC OV-10As in 1981. Three have been lost.

Dassault-Dornier Alpha Jet E
The major Moroccan re-equipment programme of the 1980s saw the air force acquire 24 examples of the Franco-German Alpha Jet. Primarily used as an advanced trainer, it can also carry more than 2500 kg of ordnance in the light attack role.

Below: Among the Libyan air force aircraft captured in Chad were SF.260s and Mi-25 gunships. A few of these 'Hinds' were passed on to NATO air forces by France for further evaluation. The Ispanka infra-red jammer and faded camouflage are noteworthy.

der between the government and rebel forces. French forces withdrew in the Autumn of 1984, but Libyan forces remained, and built a massive base at Ouadi Doum. The ALN crossed the red line in February 1986, supported by Libyan aircraft from Ouadi Doum. French forces returned to Chad and counter-attacked, putting the airfield out of action. Libya responded with a high-level bombing raid on N'Djamena by Tu-22s. Fighting broke out again in early-1987, with intensive bombing raids by both sides. French aircraft supported an infantry attack against the north, and Ouadi Doum was captured on 22 March. Aouzou was recaptured on 8 August, and on 5 September Chad invaded Libya, destroying 22 aircraft at Sara airfield before withdrawing. Both sides then accepted a ceasefire, though Libyan overflights have continued sporadically.

Moroccan war

Following the 1974 Spanish withdrawal from Spanish Sahara, Morocco and Mauretania agreed to partition the territory. This was opposed by the Algerian-backed and based Polisario (Popular Front for the Liberation of Saguiet el-Hamra and Rio de Oro) resistance. Fighting broke out in the spring of 1976 and Morcco received substantial help from France, including French equipment and deployments of French combat aircraft. Moroccan air force Mirage F1s, Alpha Jets and F-5s (together with Mauretanian BN Defenders) were supported by French Jaguars and Mirage F1s deployed to Dakar. Morocco's F-5A/E force was based at Kenitra and initially bore the brunt of air operations (along with a squadron of Magisters). Mauretania agreed a ceasefire with the Polisario in 1978, following a coup, and the Polisario were then able to operate from bases in the southern part of Spanish Sahara. However, Morocco's war with the Polisario intensified, and many warplanes fell to Polisario SAMs during subsequent operations. Several F-5s were lost to SA-7s in 1978. Polisario surface-to-air defences were strengthened during the mid-1980s with the supply of SA-6 batteries and these claimed several Moroccan aircraft, including two F-5Es in 1985 and 1987. An uneasy peace was finally bought to to the region in 1991 when a transitional period with UN forces preparing the region for a referendum on its future.

Above: Moroccan F-5A/Es were heavily committed in the ground-attack role against Polisario guerillas and many were downed by SAMs and groundfire. Losses were offset by the delivery of surplus Aggressor F-5Es from the USA in 1980 and 1989 funded by Saudi Arabia

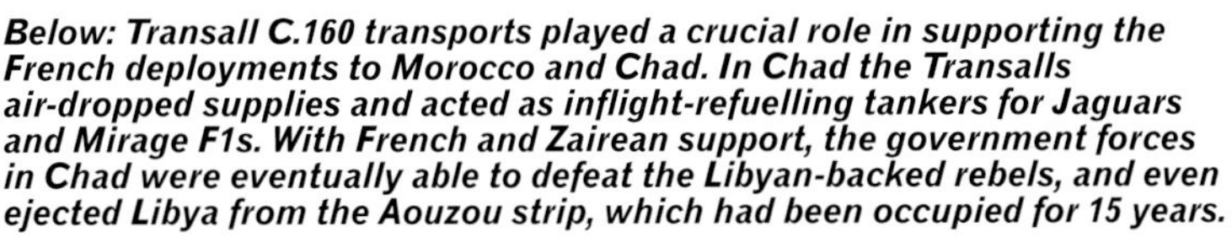

Below: Transall C.160 transports played a crucial role in supporting the French deployments to Morocco and Chad. In Chad the Transalls air-dropped supplies and acted as inflight-refuelling tankers for Jaguars and Mirage F1s. With French and Zairean support, the government forces in Chad were eventually able to defeat the Libyan-backed rebels, and even ejected Libya from the Aouzou strip, which had been occupied for 15 years.

Morocco's Mirages at war

From 1978 Morcco received 50 Mirage F1s comprising 30 F1CHs, 14 F1EHs and six F1EH-200s. These are all based in hardened air shelters at Sidi Slimane, from where detachments were made to El Aïoune for combat operations against Polisario guerillas in Western Sahara until Morocco relinquished its territorial claims in August 1988. F1EHs have undertaken attack and reconnaissance operations (using an indigenously-developed recce pod) during which several were lost to Polisario groundfire. Documented instances include two on 13 October 1981 and aother on 14 January 1985. The first pair was hit be SAMs during a rebel attack on the garrison at Gelta Zemmour, at least one of the aircraft being at 30,000 ft (9145 m) when struck. The 1985 loss was also to a SAM – apparently fired from Algerian territory – during a clash with Polisario forces which claimed to have destroyed three Moroccan aircraft of unknown type.

Horn of Africa

1970- THE PRESENT

Above: The sight of an aircraft delivering relief supplies in the Horn of Africa has become one of the staples of news reports over the last two decades. But drought and famine are only part of the region's tragedy: continual warfare has heightened the almost unbearable misery of the people.

Political allegiances of the nations of the so-called Horn of Africa have become so blurred in the past 25 years that it has often been hard to say where civil wars ended and wars with neighbouring states began. What is clear is the fact that a quarter of a century of fighting has managed to inflict the worst horrors of war on a drought-stricken civilian population which would have had to struggle to survive at the best of times.

Soviet military influence in the area dates back to 1963 when, following the creation of independent Somalia out of the unification of British and Italian Somalilands in 1960, Russia supplied MiG-15s and MiG-17s in return for use of a number of sea and air bases in the country. The Soviet aim was to influence the southern approaches to the oil-rich Gulf states; later a modest strike potential was added by the arrival of a number of Ilyushin Il-28 bombers. In 1969 this influence was extended to the Sudan, where a left-wing coup was followed by the arrival of Chinese and Soviet technicians to organise a squadron of MiG-17s, later supplemented by MiG-21s.

Ethiopia and Eritrea

By the early 1970s the Western-backed but domestically fragile nation of Ethiopia was almost entirely surrounded by potentially hostile communist-backed states. For some years an almost mediaeval administration, headed by the veteran Emperor Haile Selassie, had been propped up by half-hearted American military and economic aid, and as the plight of Ethiopia became all too obvious a $100 million military equipment order, including Northrop F-5s and Cessna A-37 strike aircraft (to bolster previous deliveries), was negotiated with the USA. In 1974, however, the emperor was overthrown by a cabal of middle-ranking military officers known as the Derg. After three years of internecine fighting Mengistu Haile Mariam emerged as the dominant power and began leading the country down the road to Marxism.

To complicate the situation a guerrilla war broke out between the Soviet-backed government forces and the Arab-backed Eritrean Liberation Front in northern Ethiopia, while Ethiopian royalist forces conducted a guerrilla war using bases in the Sudan, a situation which at one time threatened to erupt into open war between the two Soviet-equipped countries. The Eritrean secessionists were joined by a highly active rebel group in Tigre, while further groups were active in the south.

By the late 1980s, the country was suffering from famine and economic collapse. The government's refusal to deal with the former, together with its misappropriation of international aid, led to worldwide condemnation and provided an even greater spur to the rebels, who continued to gain ground.

In 1990, Eritrean forces surrounded and took the government stronghold of Asmara in spite of being subject to cluster bomb attacks by MiG-23 'Floggers', and also captured the port of Masawa. A year later, Ethiopian air force personnel fled with their aircraft as rebels closed in on the capital, but not before several MiGs had been shot down by rebels armed with captured ZSU-23-4 anti-aircraft guns. Government forces were on the brink of defeat.

A ceasefire on May 27 1991 resulted in the overthrow of the Derg, and the establishment of the free and independent state of Eritrea.

Somalia

Power in Somalia, independent since 1960, was seized by Major General Muhammad Siyad Barre in 1969. The socialist, centralised regime established close ties with Moscow, but droughts and famine in the mid-1970s hit hard.

Barre took Somalia into war with Ethiopia in 1977, primarily in support of ethnic Somali rebels liv-

Left: Ethiopia and its air force were largely Western-influenced in the quarter of a century following World War II. But after the Marxist overthrow of Emperor Haile Selassie aircraft like this Canberra lost in combat with Somalia were replaced by Soviet-built machines.

ing in the Ogaden region. Attrition among Ethiopia's surviving Canberras and F-5As had been exceptionally high, and, both opposing air forces operated Soviet-supplied MiG-17s, MiG-21s, Il-28s, Mil helicopters and Antonov transports.

In the course of the first six months' fighting, when Cuban mercenaries were flying Ethiopian MiG-21s, as well as some newly delivered MiG-23s, Somalia suffered the loss of at least 20 MiGs.

FAMINE AND PESTILENCE

Inevitably, in an area almost entirely populated by scattered peoples seeking to scratch a meagre living in an environment scarcely capable of supporting crops and livestock, the ferocity of modern warfare and weapons left large numbers of helpless civilians starving and without water. Disease and hunger killed huge numbers of people whose plight was largely ignored in the bitterness of war.

Before long, however, the attrition among aircraft and other military equipment on both sides convinced the Moscow authorities of the futility of this conflict and, following Somalia's discontinuation of all ties with the Soviet Union in November 1977, a ceasefire was agreed in March 1978.

Armed opposition to Siyad Barre, largely inspired by clan loyalties, began to surface in 1988. By 1990 government control was slipping, and the president fled in January 1991. Fighting then broke out between rival warlords, disrupting all economic activity and when this was exacerbated by drought, within 18 months a third of all Somalis faced starvation, and more than one million had become refugees.

International relief agencies attempted to give aid, but to no avail. Military assistance was sought, and Operation Provide Relief saw four USAF C-130s begin flying in aid to a gravel airstrip at Belet Huen, 400 km (250 miles) north of Mogadishu. These were joined by two British C-130 Hercules.

In December 1992, Operation Restore Hope got under way as a

WAR ZONE: HORN OF AFRICA

Red Sea
SAUDI ARABIA
YEMEN
PEOPLE'S DEMOCRATIC REPUBLIC OF YEMEN
Khartoum
Masawa
Asmara
Sana
ERITREA
Aden
TIGRE
SUDAN
DJIBOUTI
SOMALIA
Addis Ababa
ETHIOPIA
OGADEN
Mogadishu
Indian Ocean

It would be easy to blame the almost continual warfare which the Horn of Africa has suffered over the last half century on the artificial borders drawn by the old imperial powers without reference to the situation on the ground, but that is only part of the story. Rather, conflict has been the product of a devil's brew of ethnic, tribal, political and religious differences, combined with endemic famine and drought. Tensions in the area have been exacerbated further by the intervention of the superpowers playing for influence in this strategically-located region. Any alliances in the area are purely a matter of expediency, founded upon perceptions of a common enemy rather than any recognition of common causes.

Left: Designed mainly to provide small, technologically backward air forces with a simple, easy-to-maintain combat jet, the Northrop F-5 equipped a number of countries in north and east Africa, including Ethiopia and the Sudan.

Below: China's burgeoning arms export business has seen its F-7 fighter – a copy of the Soviet MiG-21 'Fishbed' – enter service in many countries. The new Muslim government in Sudan has acquired the type via Iran.

United Nations peacekeeping force led by 2,000 US Marines was sent to restore order enough to allow the relief agencies to do their jobs. The food airlift into refugee camps ceased on 28 February, road convoys by then having become safe. American troops officially handed over the peacekeeping effort to the 3,500-strong UNOSOM (United Nations Operations in Somalia) force on 4 May, though the 17,700 men of the US Joint Task Force in Somalia remained on station but not under UN control.

However, failure to disarm the warring factions proved to be a critical error as the period of relative peace was used primarily to re-arm. The warlords also looted aid supplies, and extorted money from the aid agencies in order to fill their war chests. Fighting soon broke out again, and over the next two years some 50,000 people were killed in factional violence, with an estimated 300,000 dying from starvation.

SOMALI FIREFIGHTS

UN and US peacekeepers began to be drawn involuntarily into the fighting. In June 1993, a Pakistani unit engaged in collecting weapons was ambushed by Somali militiamen loyal to Mohammed Farah Aidid, the most powerful of the warlords, and 21 were killed. In August four US military policemen were killed by a mine. In September militiamen attacked Nigerian peacekeepers, and the US responded by sending a Special Forces unit known as Task Force Ranger into action, with the aim of hunting down Aidid and his Lieutenants.

During September Aidid's militia group became the target for sustained operations, with heliborne US troops supported by Marine AH-1 Cobra gunship helicopters mounting numerous operations. On 25 September one helicopter was shot down and its three crew killed, with more casualties taken in the ensuing rescue attempt.

The most notable battle took place on 3 October, when six senior militia commanders were captured in a raid. Two UH-60s were shot down during the withdrawal, and troops on the ground came under heavy attack. In the fierce fight which lasted through the night and into 4 October, at least 300 Somalis were killed, while American losses totalled 18 dead and 81 wounded. Aidid was not captured, however, and he remained a dominant figure until his death in 1996. The only result of the fighting was to convince President Clinton to pull US troops out of Somalia.

The withdrawal began in March 1994. Cobras covered a heli-borne evacuation to US Navy assault ships off shore, while C-130s, C-141s and C-5 Galaxies lifted troops and heavy equipment out of Mogadishu. The USAF also discontinued fixed-wing gunship operations: four AC-130H Spectres had been flying out of Mombasa in Kenya since 1993.

Although attempts have been made to find a negotiated peace, Somalia remains an armed camp.

OTHER CONFLICTS

Sudan gained independence from a joint Egyptian and British protec-

***Above:** For much of the time, fighting in Somalia made surface transportation of relief supplies nothing less than suicide. Aircraft were the only means of distributing aid, and the aircraft most often used was the Lockheed C-130 Hercules. This is an American Air National Guard example of the type delivering supplies at Mogadishu.*

***Below:** Sudan's relations with the Soviet Union deteriorated in the 1970s, and after a ten-year gap the country acquired a number of western aircraft, including six C-130s. But the rise of Islamic fundamentalism in the 1980s and America's belief that Sudan was a terrorist sponsor meant that the rapprochement was short-lived.*

Offshore support

The fighting in September and October 1993 saw the US presence at sea beefed up to cover a possible withdrawal from Somalia. The USS *Abraham Lincoln* carrier battle group joined amphibious ready groups centred on the USS *New Orleans* and *Guadalcanal*, each of which could deploy a brigade-sized Marine Expeditionary Unit. In the event, they were not required, but US troops began withdrawing from the region early in 1994.

***Right:** A Marine Corps CH-53E ferries supplies between the US Navy's amphibious task force in the Indian Ocean and the Marine Corps peacekeepers ashore in Somalia.*

***Below:** In addition to their force of Marines, the assault ships of the US Navy's amphibious ready groups also operated Marine Corps AH-1, CH-46 and CH-53 helicopters and AV-8B STOVL attack jets.*

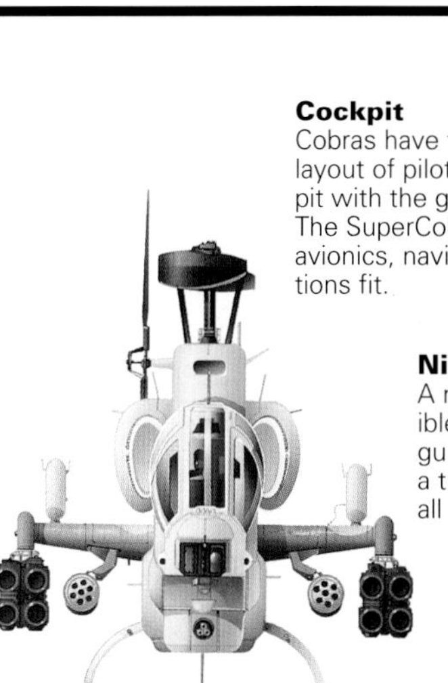

Cockpit
Cobras have the near standard gunship layout of pilot high up in the rear cockpit with the gunner low down in front. The SuperCobra has a completely new avionics, navigation and communications fit.

Night vision
A new pilot head-up display is compatible with night vision goggles. The gunner's TOW sight now incorporates a thermal imaging systems for use in all weathers.

Bell AH-1W SuperCobra

Used extensively by American forces in Somalia, the 'Whiskey Cobra' is the most advanced variant of the pioneering helicopter gunship. It originated as the AH-1T+, an upgrade of existing aircraft with improved weapons systems and more power. Subsequent new-build aircraft were given the AH-1W designation.

Missions
Marine Cobras in Somalia were used for convoy escort, fire support and armed reconnaissance missions.

Weapons
This aircraft carries the standard USMC fit of eight BGM-71 TOW anti-tank missiles, two LAU-68 seven-round rocket pods and an M197 20-mm cannon. Hellfire laser-guided missiles can also be used.

Powerplant
The SuperCobra is powered by two General Electric T700 turboshafts, each rated at 1211 kW (1,625 shp). The exhaust jetpipes are each fitted with an infra-red suppressor.

torate in 1954. This vast country saw military coups in 1958, 1969, 1985 and 1989. Since then, General Omar Hassan Ahmed al Bashir and his 15-member Revolutionary Council have transformed Sudan into a Muslim state.

However, this has exacerbated traditional religious and tribal rivalries between the Muslim north and the Christian south, and for much of the 1990s the Sudanese People's Liberation Movement has been has been fighting against the fundamentalist regime in Khartoum. The government has responded by attacking rebel positions with Chinese-built Chengdu F-7 fighters, apparently supplied by Iran.

Djibouti was granted independence from France in 1981. Led by Hassan Gouled, the one-party state fought a low-key guerrilla war against pro-democracy rebels, though this was brought to a negotiated settlement in 1994. France maintains a strong presence in the region, and used Djibouti as a staging post in moving aircraft, helicopters, troops and equipment into the region during the Gulf War.

Yemen civil war

Not part of the Horn of Africa, but separated by less than 32 km (20 miles) across the mouth of the Red Sea, the Yemen has also been infected by internecine struggles. Britain's withdrawal from Aden and the closure of the Suez Canal in 1967 brought the economy to the verge of ruin. Rivalry between the Yemen Arab Republic to the north and the People's Democratic Republic of Yemen to the south saw the two states fight short border wars in 1972, 1978 and 1979. By 1990, however, political differences had apparently been settled, and the two countries combined at least notionally, as the Republic of Yemen.

In April 1994 fighting erupted as the Southern government refused to merge with the North. All-out war followed on 5 May, when both sides launched air attacks. The increasing pace of the war, together with a number of SS-1 'Scud' attacks by both sides saw a mass evacuation of foreigners from Aden. Aircraft used included a British Airways DC-10 and two RAF Hercules flying from Cyprus.

The advantage lay with the South, which had some 70 combat aircraft – MiG-17s, MiG-21s and Su-22s – against around 35 similar aircraft plus a few Northrop F-5s in the North. By the end of May, 30 aircraft were reported to have been shot down on both sides. In June, the South deployed the MiG-29 'Fulcrum', 12 of which had been bought from Moldova with Saudi funds. One was shot down, and six were destroyed on the ground.

Despite its aerial advantage, the South was no match for the Northern army on the ground, and by the beginning of July Northern columns were closing on Aden. The capture of the airport and the fall of the city on July 7 brought the war to an end.

Left: Originally supplied to South Yemen by the former Soviet state of Moldova, the MiG-29 'Fulcrum' fighters of the Republic of Yemen air force are the most capable combat aircraft in the region.

Right: French army Pumas land aboard the carrier* Clemenceau *after exercising ashore in Djibouti. France used the small African country as a staging post for its forces involved in the Gulf War.

West Africa

1966–1997

Granted independence in 1960, Nigeria seemed set on a course of peacefui transition until 1966 when the first federation's central government collapsed followed by appalling massacres of the Ibo people in the Northern Region. Colonel Ojukwu, military ruler of the Eastern Region, declared independence for his area, homeland of the Ibo tribe. For three years a bloody civil war raged between the rebel state of Biafra and forces of the central government. The federal government obtained its first combat equipment in the form of 16 MiG-17 fighters and MiG-15UTI trainers from communist bloc countries (followed later by 28 further MiG-17s). These were later joined by five Ilyushin Il-28 bombers, flown by Egyptians and other mercenaries. About a dozen Czech Aero L-29 Delfin strike trainers were also purchased. Ojukwu's air force comprised a motley collection of ancient aircraft (some of them of World War II vintage) flown almost exclusively by white mercenaries; his cause nonetheless gained diplomatic recognition by several African states, notably Zambia and Tanzania. In the air war itself only one jet aircraft was lost in combat by the government forces. The Nigerian Civil War ended in January 1970 with the collapse of the secessionist government as Ojukwu fled to the Ivory Coast. More recently a military coup in July 1975 resulted in considerable modernisation of the Nigerian air

Above: A United Nations Sikorsky S-58 takes off from the airport at Port Harcourt, past an Ilyushin Il-28 bomber of the Federal air force. Before the war, Nigeria had no air arm to speak of: by the end it was operating jet fighters and bombers.

Below: The plight of the starving in Biafra saw the world's charities mobilised in an attempt to provide relief to the helpless and seriously wounded in the war zone. This DC-6 is a flying ambulance, chartered by the Swedish Red Cross.

Aid and Weapons

Both sides in the Biafran war had need of weaponry, supplies and armaments, and the Biafrans had the added problem of having hundreds of thousands of starving people to feed. Modern weapons arrived, and aid was flown in in large quantities, but aid flights into Biafra were often attacked: they had to operate by night and the Federal forces could not tell which aircraft were bringing in guns and which were bringing in food, clothing and medicines.

Ilyushin Il-28 'Beagle'

Left: One of the earliest successful jet bombers, the Il-28 was sold to Soviet client states around the world. Nigeria acquired six via Egypt. Flown by Egyptian and Czech crews, the 'Beagles' mounted an indiscriminate bombing campaign against Biafran villages, killing at least 2,000 people between May and October 1968.

Boeing C-97G

Right: This ex-USAF freighter owned by Balair was one of many cargo aircraft employed by charitable organisations delivering aid to the war zone. 20 tonnes of aid was being flown into Biafra each night, but at great risk – one Red Cross flight was shot down by a MiG-17.

Left: A Nigerian Air Force MiG-17 stands on the tarmac at Enugu with a Dornier Do 27 in the background. The arrival of such relatively sophisticated weaponry gave the Federal forces the edge over the poorly-equipped Biafrans.

Above: Six Swedish-built MFI-9B trainers were fitted with Matra rocket pods and used by the Biafrans for light attack duties. Known as Minicons, the tiny aircraft were used primarily in attacks on the Nigerian oil industry.

force, and the East/West balance of aircraft procurement has been maintained by purchases from the UK, France, South Africa, West Germany, the USA and the Soviet Union.

Elsewhere in West Africa there has been considerable political and military turmoil, but in general air power has played only a minor part in conflicts in the region.

LIBERIA

Founded in 1847 by freed American slaves, the Republic of Liberia has suffered violent changes since 1980, when native Liberians under Samuel K. Doe overthrew the ruling American-descended oligarchy. Doe paid lip-service to democracy but kept power for the next decade.

In 1989, opposition factions under Charles Taylor and Prince Johnson rebelled, and after a year of fighting overthrew Doe – who was tortured to death. US Marines had to mount a rescue operation as the country descended into anarchy, the start of six years of bitter fighting that was to lead to more than 200,000 deaths.

There has been little air action in the fighting: apart from rescue missions the only aircraft flying have been those of the peacekeepers flown in by the Nigerian-dominated Economic Community of West Africa. Supposedly in place to unite the warring factions, they have had little effect – indeed, as fighting reached new heights in 1996 they even took part in looting the capital Monrovia. Meanwhile, the USA airlifted more than 1,400 foreigners to safety in nearby Sierra Leone. But this was not to remain a safe haven for long.

SIERRA LEONE

Since 1991 the National Provisional Ruling Council, the military junta controlling Sierra Leone, had been fighting the Revolutionary United Front or RUF. Led by former corporal Alfred Foday Sankoh and supplied with arms by Liberian warlord Charles Taylor, the RUF had waged a terror campaign which peacekeeping troops sent from the West African Economic Community Monitoring Group (ECOMOG) in neighbouring Liberia could do little to control. By 1995 the RUF were threatening the capital, Freetown.

The government contracted Executive Outcomes, the South African company which had been so successful in Angola. EO provided high-quality tactical leadership to the government troops, and flew air support in three Mil Mi-17 'Hips' and one Mil Mi-24 'Hind' gunship.

By the beginning of 1997 EO's professional skills had made a considerable difference. A ceasefire was holding, and a democratically elected government was in power. But in May, things went from hopeful to awful.

Middle-ranking officers, led by Major Johnny Paul Koroma but backed by the RUF, overthrew the government of President Ahmed Tejan Kabbah. US Marines evacuated hundreds of foreigners, lifting them to the assault ship USS *Kearsarge* and then on to Conakry in Guinea.

The United Nations and the Organisation of African States condemned the coup. Nigeria went further, however, ordering its ECOMOG contingent into battle. So far, the powerful Nigerian air force has played little part in the increasingly fierce conflict, which has been fought out with small arms, mortars and artillery, though helicopters have provided most of ECOMOG's communications. But along with the Nigerian navy it is helping to enforce a tight sea and air blockade of Sierra Leone.

Above: Sierra Leone goverment troops unload mortar ammunition from an Executive Outcomes 'Hip' helicopter. The ammunition will be used in a successful assault on a RUF strongpoint 25 km (16 miles) south of Koidu.

Below: A door gunner's view as Sierra Leone's Mi-24V 'Hind' gunship flies in formation with a Mil Mi-17 transport helicopter, en route from Koidu to Kailahun. The helicopters gave the government a serious advantage over the RUF.

THE AMERICAS

Dominated by the mighty presence of the United States, the Americas have presented rather a different pattern of combat than has been common in the rest of the world since 1945. Even though the Cuban missile crisis was in many ways the zenith of the Cold War, most conflicts have been internal, although there have been a few border skirmishes, and American troops have been active in the region several times on peace-keeping duties. One notable exception was the Falklands War, which was probably the last major conflict of the European colonial era.

Latin America

1955-1995

Latin America has largely avoided the cataclysmic wars which have raged throughout the world through much of the 20th century. That is not to say that the continent has been a stranger to violence, however. There have been numerous relatively minor border clashes between neighbouring nations, but by far the majority of conflicts have been internal, and rebellions, coups and counter-insurgency campaigns have been endemic in most of the region since World War II.

Above: Early Latin American wars were distinguished by the use of weaponry long discarded from the armouries of the major powers. But by the 1980s, many South American air forces were equipped with modern high-performance aircraft like these Ecuadorian Kfirs.

ARGENTINA

After the death of Eva Peron in 1955, the right-wing dictatorship of Juan Domingo Peron lost popular support. In June a naval mutiny saw Government House bombed. In September, a more serious naval uprising saw several Meteor fighters seized and used against government troops. Strikes were also flown by such unlikely types as navy PBYs, SNJs, AT-11s and J2Fs. In response, air force Meteors attacked the naval base at Rio Santiago, damaging two destroyers but losing one aircraft to anti-aircraft fire. A Meteor is also reported to have downed a navy SNJ in combat. Air force Lincoln bombers made demonstration flights, but are not thought to have been used in action.

Many troops switched sides after the navy began shelling coastal installations, and by the end of June Peron had been forced into exile and a military junta took power.

In a two-day rising in April 1963, naval aircraft supported the rebels, while the air force supported the government. Navy F4Us, F9Fs, PBYs, SNJs were used on ground - attack strikes against army formations; one SNJ and one F9F were shot down. Air force Meteors, MS.760s, F-86Fs, and Lincolns were used on bombing raids before the rebellion was defeated on 3 April. Two years later, in a border dispute with Chile, one F4U was lost but there was no aerial combat.

In 1975 an air force revolt saw Mirage IIIs fly a number of threatening sorties. Navy A-4 Skyhawks attacked rebels in Buenos Aires

BOLIVIA

Che Guevara instigated a 1965 revolt against right-wing dictator General Barrientos. Bolivian air force F-51s, T-28s and T-6s were used against guerrilla positions with limited success. Aircraft were also used as communications relays and H-19 helicopters moved troops in the successful hunt for Che, who was killed in October 1967.

Barrientos was killed in a helicopter accident in 1969, and the air force played a part in a series of military coups over the next decade. The most notorious incident was in 1971, when F-51 Mustangs were used to strafe protesting students occupying the university quarter of the capital, La Paz.

CHILE

In September 1973 a military coup led by General Augusto Pinochet Ugarte overthrew democratically

Below: Argentina is one of the few nations to have used heavy bombers in anger. During a 1963 coup attempt by elements of the navy, ageing Avro Lincolns of the Fuerza Aerea Argentina mounted attacks on rebel positions.

South America broke away from Spanish and Portuguese control in the 19th Century. But freedom brought its own problems, and since that time, it has been a continent in turmoil. Some countries have seen long periods of democratic government, but military juntas and right-wing dictatorships have been the general rule into the 1980s.

Above: South American air forces have given many great aircraft their last exposure to combat, but it has not always been an honorable usage. In 1971, Bolivian Mustangs were used to strafe demonstrating students in the capital, La Paz.

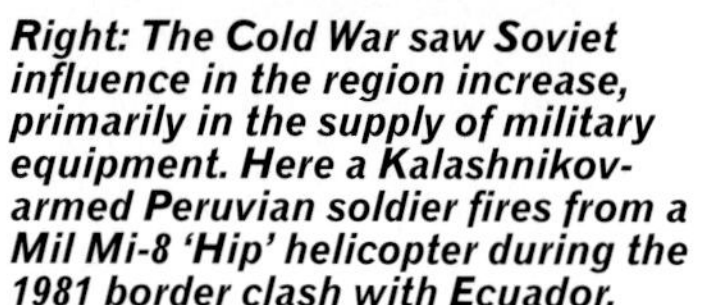

Right: The Cold War saw Soviet influence in the region increase, primarily in the supply of military equipment. Here a Kalashnikov-armed Peruvian soldier fires from a Mil Mi-8 'Hip' helicopter during the 1981 border clash with Ecuador.

elected Marxist President Salvador Allende. Hawker Hunters were used to bomb the presidential palace just before Allende's surrender and subsequent death – which was claimed as suicide by the military but thought to be murder by the socialists.

COLOMBIA

A continuous civil war known as La Violencia lasted from 1948 to 1958. The air force used AT-6s and F-47Ds in COIN operations.

In the 1970s and 1980s the air force was in action in two different campaigns: in countering the flourishing cocaine trade and in operations against numerous left-wing guerrilla groups. Air force A-37s were used to strike at guerrilla strongpoints, and in 1986 air attacks drove rebels out of the town of Morales which they had captured.

ECUADOR AGAINST PERU

In 1981 a minor and inconclusive border conflict with Peru saw Cessna T-37s, Mirage F.1Es and Jaguars flying armed reconnaissance sorties.

A more serious clash occurred in the Cordillera del Condor region in 1995. Ecuadorian Mirage F.1JAs claimed to have shot down two Peruvian Sukhoi Su-22 'Fitters' on 10 February. A Cessna A-37 was shot down by an Ecuadorian Kfir on the same date. Three Peruvian Mil Mi-8 helicopters were also claimed destroyed by Ecuadorian Blowpipe SAMs or ground fire on 30 January and 7 February, while similar hits, with unknown results, were reported on two FAE Kfirs and an A-37B on 12 February.

PARAGUAY

Converted transports bombed Asuncion in a 1947 army revolt. In 1959 exiles invaded from Bolivia to attempt the overthrow of fascist dictator General Alfredo Stroessner. The air force used T-6s and C-47s fitted with bomb racks to support troops used to crush rebellion

PERU

A long-lasting counter-insurgency struggle against numerous rebel groups has been under way since the 1980s, most notably against the Maoist movement known as Sendero Luminoso, or Shining Path. Air force strikes have been used to support army operations against the guerrillas and against Colombian cocaine cartel-backed drug traffickers, during which Mil Mi-8 and Mil Mi-24 helicopters have provided troops with the ability to make surprise assaults on revolutionary positions.

VENEZUELA

In 1958 The arrest of the army commander and his chief of staff, Colonel Leon, led to an uprising, initially by the air force followed by the navy and parts of the army. Vampires and Sabres were used to strafe the presidential palace and the defence ministry, and to bomb the National Security headquarters. They had little support from the populace, however, and the coup leaders fled or surrendered. Leon was released however, and went into exile in Colombia. In 1960, he led a further rebellion, which was put down when rebel units were bombed by loyal air force Canberras.

Canberras were used to bomb rebel troops in 1961, and again in 1962 when a Marine battalion mutinied. A month later air force Vampires strafed rebel buildings after an unsuccessful naval rebellion at Puerto Cabello.

Reacting to violations of its air space by Ecuadorian Mirage 5s, Venezuelan troops supported by F-16 fighters and Tucano COIN aircraft were moved to the border region as a deterrent in 1987. The confrontation concerned a territorial dispute over parts of the Gulf of Venezuela.

In 1992 a failed coup by army paratroopers in February was followed in November by an uprising of parts of the air force. The government's F-16 wing remained loyal, however, and played a major part in putting the rebellion down.

CENTRAL AMERICA

For decades, most of countries in Central America have been wracked by internal strife. The civil war in El Salvador and the attempt to bring down the left-wing Sandinista revolutionary government of Nicaragua by right-wing, US-backed guerrillas were perhaps the bloodiest conflicts, but few areas escaped unscathed.

Guerrilla subversion was endemic in Guatemala from the 1960s, in a bloody war which saw the death of over 100,000 people. At the

Ecuadorian dogfighter

Ecuador originally agreed to buy ex-Israeli Kfirs in the late 1970s, but the sale was initially embargoed by the US who would not agree to the re-export of the J79 engines. After a long delay the sale was approved, and 12 aircraft were delivered in 1982. The Kfirs featured strongly in Ecuador's border clash with Peru in 1995, where one of the type was credited with shooting down a Peruvian Cessna A-37.

IAI Kfir C2

Left: Developed by Israel Aircraft Industries from the Dassault Mirage III, the Kfir features a more powerful American-designed General Electric J79 engine than the original French Atar powerplant. Ecuadorian aircraft are nominally Kfir C2s, but feature many of the avionics upgrades fitted to the later Kfir C7. The aircraft depicted is flown by Escuadron de Combate 2113, part of Grupo 211 based at Taura.

Coup attempt in Venezuela

By comparison to other nations in the region, Venzuela has enjoyed a relatively stable government. The Fuerza Aérea Venezolana suffered from a long period of limited funding which had left a number of units in non-operational state, but in the 1980s this situation was rectified with the delivery of modern equipment such as F-16As and upgraded Mirages.

In spite of this seemingly progressive situation within the air force, a failed coup attempt was made on 4 February 1992 by the paratroopers of Grupo de Parcaidistas 'Aragua' led by Lt Col Chavaz. Athough quashed, feelings within the air force apparently remained high and at dawn on 27 November a further coup attempt was made by elements of the FAV led by Brigadier General Visconti, the air force logistic service inspector.

Under the cover of Air Force Day preparations, Visconti contrived to move forces sympathetic to Chavaz to the El Libertador Air Base, Palo Negro, Aragua. These included one NF-5B, five T-2Ds, three OV-10Es, six OV-10As and two A-27s, which, together with units stationed within the complex, gave him a very commanding situation.

Visconti seized control of the base at 0330 on the morning of 27 November. He was supported by the bulk of the 10th Special Operations Group which operates most of the FAV's helicopters and by Grupo de Caza 11.

The crews from the FAV's F-16 wing, Grupo de Caza 16, refused to join the rebellion and managed to scramble the two 'QRA' aircraft which fled to Barquisimeto. This base appears to have remained loyal to the president. The remainder of Grupo 16 were either captured or managed to retreat under fire to the administrative compound.

At the same time , other personnel took control of nearby Mariscal Sucre air base, in Boca Del Rio, Maracay, This houses the FAV's training wing, operating EMB-312 Tucano and T-34A trainers.

REBEL ATTACKS

At first light three Mirage 50EV fighters of Grupo 11 strafed army barracks in Caracas while a mixed formation of a dozen aircraft including Broncos, Tucanos and a single Buckeye attacked the presidential palace, the Presidential Guard barracks, the foreign ministry and police headquarters.

The two F-16s that had escaped to Barquisimeto returned over the city at around 0700 and chased away the rebel Broncos and Tucanos, going on to attack El Libertador with their 20-mm cannon. Meanwhile, loyal troops holding out at both Sucre and El Libertador were subjected to repeated attacks by rebel helicopters and aircraft. In the process one Bronco was downed by small arms and AAA fire.

Rebel Mirages and Broncos in turn attacked the air base at Barquisimeto to prevent further sorties being flown in support of the government, destroying three stored CF-5As. A civilian MD-80 airliner was also hit by cannon fire.

Grupo de Caza 12 managed to scramble its sole NF-5A, and one of the F-16s got airborne to shoot down two of the attacking OV-10s. The few defending fighters kept up the struggle against the rebel forces but the only other kill was an A-27 Tucano brought down by an F-16. A further Bronco was lost over Caracas when it was either hit by small arms fire or had an engine problem. Both crewmen ejected, the aircraft crashing by the La Carlota runway.

By 1300 La Carlota air base was secured against the remaining limited resistance and both El Libertador and Sucre followed shortly afterwards when tanks and paratroops entered the bases.

This followed the departure of Brigadier General Visconti and 92 officers in a Grupo 6 C-130H Hercules to Peru, where they sought asylum. Two of the four Grupo 11 Mirage 50EVs escaped to the Dutch island of Aruba and an OV-10 Bronco was flown to Curaçao. One thousand FAV officers and NCOs were reportedly arrested, which no doubt created a major setback to the FAV in its struggle to become an integrated front-line force once again.

Above: The Venezuelan F-16 units remained loyal to the President, and played a significant part in defeating the rebels.

Below: OV-10s taxi down the apron at El Libertador. At least four rebel Broncos were shot doen in the coup attempt, two by F-16s.

Below: Mirage 50EVs started the air portion of the rebellion, shooting up government troops with their powerful 30-mm cannon.

same time Guatemalan claims on Belize brought the country into confrontation with British troops and warplanes sent to protect the former colony. Relatively tranquil Honduras, which fought a brief but nasty little war with El Salvador in 1969, and pacifist Costa Rica, which had abolished its army 20 years earlier, were both threatened by an overspill of violence from their neighbours. Hovering in the background was Latin America's most formidable military power, Fidel Castro's Cuba.

El Salvador

Although the Salvadorean army was victorious in the 10-day 'Football War' against Honduras in 1969, the Honduran air force gained control of the air from an early stage of that slightly bizarre conflict. During the following years El Salvador engaged in a concentrated build-up of its armed forces and in particular of its air force, which by the late 1970s was marginally stronger than that of its neighbour and former enemy.

The final ratification of a peace treaty between El Salvador and Honduras in 1980 coincided with the escalation of internal violence in El Salvador into something approaching a full-scale civil war, and from 1980 onwards the attention of the Salvadorean armed forces became increasingly focused on internal security. It was a brutal war marked by the activities of death squads who seemed beyond the control of any leaders.

At this time the 1,000-man Salvadorean air force consisted of a fighter squadron equipped with 18 Dassault Ouragans purchased from Israel five years earlier, a light strike squadron equipped with nine

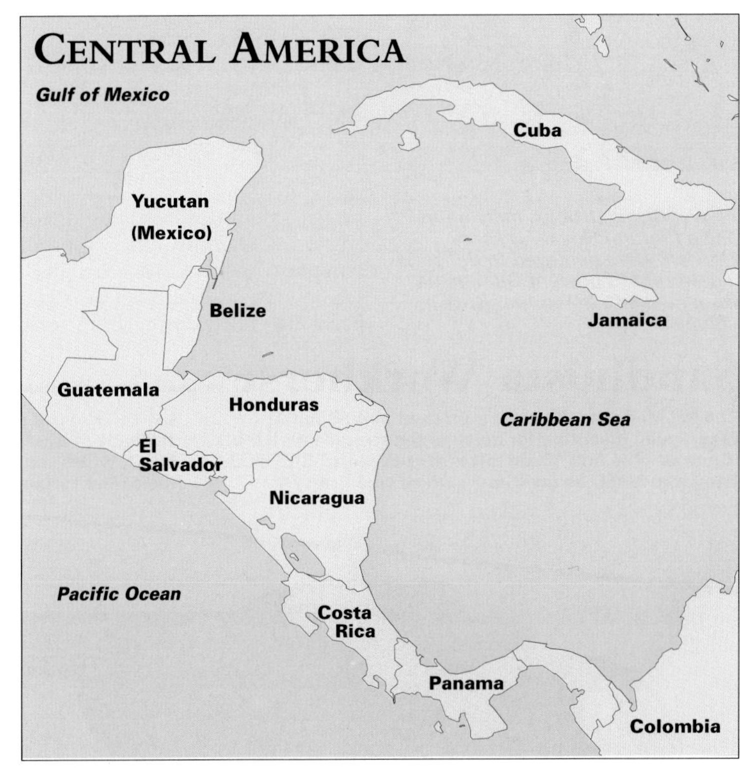

Right: Central America has seen more than its share of violence over the last three decades, with border tensions and territorial claims contributing in part. But much of the bloodshed has been internal, with both right and left-wing regimes countering rebels backed by Cuba or the United States respectively.

The Football War

The Mustang's last air-to-air conflict was the El Salvador/Honduras 'Soccer War' (Guerra de Futbol) of July 1969. It erupted after the two nations played three bitterly contested matches in the World Cup. Behind it lay other grievances. Spurred by riots against Salvadorean immigrants (who formed one-eighth of the Honduran population) and by long-standing territorial ambitions, El Salvador opened hostilities on 14 July 1969 after alleged mistreatment of its national football team. A ceasefire took effect four days later but El Salvador continued spradic military operations until the Organisation of American States threatened sanctions on 29 July. The 'Soccer War' is listed in one encyclopedia as 'costing thousands of lives' but the actual number may be as few as a dozen; a peace treaty was not signed until 1980.

Honduras' air arm consisted mainly of Vought F4U Corsairs, while El Salvador possessed Goodyear FG-1D Corsairs and a handful of C-47 transports pressed into service as bombers, in addition to its new fleet of Mustangs. Another F-51D had been a pristine warbird owned by a local businessman and engineer, which was impressed into combat service. On a typical mission, Salvadorean C-47s and FG-1Ds carrying bombs were escorted by 'clean' F-51D Mustangs performing escort duty like that at which they had excelled during World War II missions over Europe. Ranges were short, however, and the Mustangs went into battle with minimal fuel loads, except for the occasional deep strike to Tegucigalpa. The FAS had help from some colourful mercenaries who flew a number of the Mustang sorties. Documentation is lacking, but it appears that five Mustangs were lost in action in a conflict which saw virtually all aircraft hit by friendly and hostile fire. Two Mustangs were lost in a mid-air collision, and two to fuel starvation. No Salvadorean pilot claimed an air-to-air victory while flying an F-51, but at least one FAS F-51D was shot down by a Honduran F4U Corsair – and some sources say two were. These marked the final instance of air combat between World War II fighters. The final Mustang ever to be lost in an air-to-air engagement was piloted by FAS Captain Humberto Varela and was shot down on 17 July 1969 by an F4U-5 flown Honduran Major Soto, who also downed an FG-1D.

Both sides in the Football War employed Vought Corsairs, the El Salvador version being the Goodyear-built FG-1.

Right: With very few aircraft able to perform ground attack missions, both El Salvador and Honduras pressed Douglas C-47 transports into service as make-shift bombers. Salvador lost four aircraft in the war, while Honduras lost eight, including two C-47s.

Above: British troops, helicopters and a flight of Royal Air Force Harriers were deployed to Belize as a deterrent to prevent Guatemala from invading the former British colony.

Fouga Magisters also used for advanced training, and assorted transports, trainers and helicopters. US military assistance, which had been suspended during the Carter administration, began again in 1981 with the delivery of at least 12 Bell UH-1H helicopters together with advisory help.

The air force's principal task was in flying strike missions against elusive guerrillas, redeploying infantry to points often inaccessible by land (mainly in its tired transport force of C-47s), inserting small units of special forces into areas of high guerrilla activity, and evacuating casualties.

But it was a war of attrition, with a notable guerrilla success occuring in 1982 with an immensely destructive attack on the Ilopango air base on 27 January 1982. Within weeks, however, the USA had delivered another 12 UH-1Hs, eight Cessna A-37B light strike aircraft, four Cessna O-2A forward air control aircraft and three Fairchild C-123 transports as replacements for the lost materiel.

During the closing months of 1983 the civil war acquired a new dimension with the creation of a 'strategic brigade' by the guerrillas, who engaged elements of the 1st and 3rd Brigades of the Army and the ATLACATL and ATONAL immediate-reaction battalions in conventional military operations in the north and east of the country, causing grave casualties which in turn heavily stressed the air force's casevac capabilities.

Although the Salvadorean fixed-wing aircraft continued to fly ground support and transport missions, the helicopter had (as in Vietnam) already proved to be the most useful type of aircraft in the continuing war against an elusive enemy. The helicopter arm therefore continued to enjoy a fairly spectacular growth although there was attrition through guerrilla ground fire and accidents.

The Salvadorean air force car-

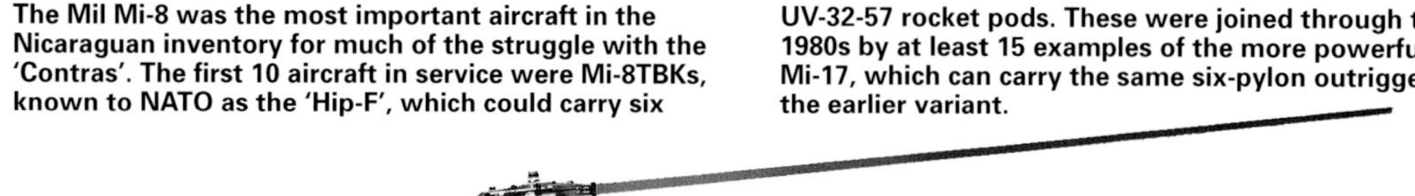

Sandinista Workhorse

The Mil Mi-8 was the most important aircraft in the Nicaraguan inventory for much of the struggle with the 'Contras'. The first 10 aircraft in service were Mi-8TBKs, known to NATO as the 'Hip-F', which could carry six UV-32-57 rocket pods. These were joined through the 1980s by at least 15 examples of the more powerful Mil Mi-17, which can carry the same six-pylon outrigger as the earlier variant.

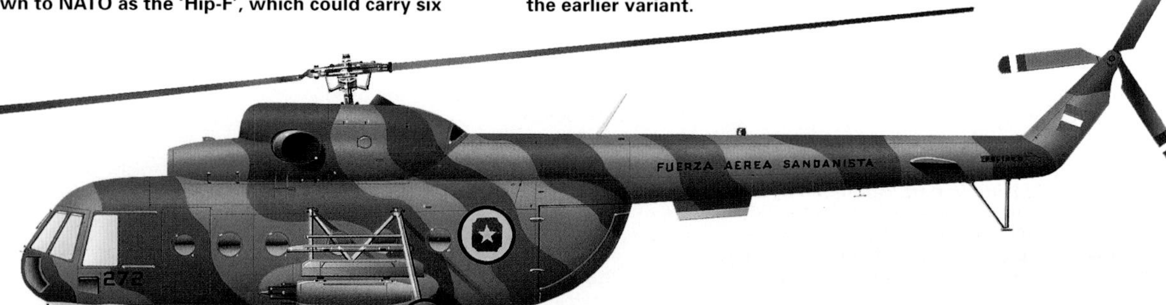

Mil Mi-8 'Hip'

Left: One of the greatest helicopter designs in history, the rugged Mil Mi-8 'Hip' has seen combat in Africa, Asia and South America since its first flight in 1961. Twin turbine-powered, the 'Hip' can carry up to 28 troops or a heavy load of weaponry on outrigger pylons. Improved versions with uprated engines are designated Mi-17.

A rocket-armed Cessna Skywagon of the Sandinista air arm is seen on a dirt airstrip in Nicaragua with a Mil Mi-8 and an Antonov An-2 transport biplane.

ried out 227 air strikes against the guerrillas in 1983 and 158 more strikes during the first six months of 1984 (74 of them in June alone). Although plans for the transfer of a number of Douglas AC-47 gunships were shelved two of the existing C-47 transport aircraft were armed with 12.7-mm (0.5-in) machine-guns which effectively transformed them into similar weapons platforms.

Government forces now totalled approximately 40,000, with the guerrillas, who had united under Cuban and Nicaraguan auspices as the Farabundo Marti National Liberation Front, or FMLN, being less than a third as strong. Even so, they retained control of almost 30 per cent of the republic, principally in the north and northeast, and had by now raised a second 'strategic brigade' for conventional military operations against the government forces.

The election of Jose Napoleon Duarte in 1984, the first freely elected president in 50 years, signalled a change. Although the war of attrition continued, politicians were now talking about dialogue, and Alfredo Christiani, who defeated Duarte in an election in 1989, strove to come to terms with the guerrillas. The FMLN had other ideas, however, and in November of that year launched a bloody offensive which killed thousands.

At the instigation of other central American leaders, UN mediation was called for. A peace agreement was signed in 1991, with the conclusion of decades of struggle coming on 15 December 1992.

NICARAGUA

To the south, the left-wing Sandinista revolutionary government of Nicaragua had toppled the corrupt Somoza dictatorship in 1979. In 1981 the Sandinistas were seen by newly elected US President Reagan as a major threat to stability in the region, and determined American-backed efforts to overthrow it were made by CIA-trained groups of right-wing guerrillas based in neighbouring Honduras and Costa Rica. These were composed both of emigré Nicaraguans and mercenaries colloquially as 'Contras'. They were supported by their own helicopters and by the Honduran air force.

Air power did not play much part in the Nicaraguan war, although the reported presence of a dozen Mikoyan-Gurevich MiG-21s, supposedly transferred to Nicaragua from Cuba during 1981 but never actually confirmed, loomed large in American thinking at the time.

As the Sandinistas had very few serviceable fixed-wing aircraft, the burden of ground support in the war against the guerrillas fell mainly on the helicopter arm, which suffered several casualties to 'Contra' ground fire. Three Mi-24 'Hind' gunship helicopters were delivered, to join a growing fleet which by 1984 included a dozen Mi-8s in addition to two Alouette IIIs and a miscellaneous collection of US-built types which had survived the civil war which overthrew the Somoza dictatorship.

The majority of the military Mi-8s seemed to have been acquired from the second half of 1983 onwards and appear to be employed in the gunship configuration, photographs of them in this role having appeared in the Cuban press as early as May 1984.

Although Sandinista president Daniel Ortega won a fair popular election in 1984, the civil war and US attempts to topple the government continued until 1990, when the Sandinistas were defeated in the polls and Violeta Chamorro came to power.

Above: The only air assets available to the Sandinistas after they came to power in Nicaragua were a few light attack types like this T-28 Trojan. T-28s were also used by the opposition Contras, some having been flown into exile in 1979. A T-28 based in Costa Rica attacked Managua airport in 1983, destroying one C-47 before being shot down.

Helicopters played a major part in the civil war in Nicaragua. Soviet-built Mil Mi-8 and Mi-17 'Hip' transports, escorted and supported Mi-24 'Hind' gunships, proved vital in giving mobility to Sandinista troops fighting the American-backed 'Contra' guerrillas.

Falklands Invaded

APRIL 1982

***Above:* A Lynx hovers over the deck of HMS Invincible, having dropped an underslung load of stores. The despatch of the Task Force was a triumph of logistics, and intensive use was made of helicopters during all phases of the operation.**

The Falklands have been a British possession since 1833, when the Royal Navy evicted newly-arrived Argentinian settlers and claimed the islands for Britain. They are bleak and inhospitable, but have served as a useful base for whaling, as a strategic naval base, and have given Britain an internationally recognised 'share' of Antarctica. The islands' inhabitants regard themselves as British, and fiercely oppose any transfer of sovereignty to Argentina, which has long claimed the islands as the Malvinas.

A military government was established in Argentina in 1976, and in 1977 a British naval task force was sent to the area after reports that an occupation of nearby South Georgia was likely. This signalled that Britain would maintain sovereignty over the islands, but doubt resurfaced when a new Conservative government came to power. It announced cuts in defence expenditure, including the planned withdrawal, without replacement, of the Antarctic survey vessel HMS *Endurance*, the area's *de facto* garrison ship.

To many this was an indication that an Argentinian invasion of the Malvinas might not be opposed militarily. Argentinian scrap metal workers landed on South Georgia on 19 March 1982, and began dismantling the disused whaling station. Such an action was almost certainly intended to gauge how Britain might react to a full-scale invasion. Britain landed observation teams and Royal Marines from the *Endurance* on 23 and 31 March, while nuclear submarines headed south on 25 March. Had more publicity been given to these responses the Argentinians might have reconsidered their decision to proceed with an invasion, taken on 23 March. Two Argentinian Task Groups set sail on 28 March.

***Left:* HMS Antrim's obsolescent Wessex HAS.Mk 3 played a significant role in the war, recovering an SAS patrol from South Georgia (and the crews of the two Wessex HU.Mk 5s originally sent to do the job) and later attacking the Argentine submarine Santa Fé.**

ARGENTINE ASSAULT

Meanwhile, on 2 April, 2,800 Argentinians landed on the Falklands. The 80-strong British garrison surrendered after brisk fighting, on the orders of the island's governor, Sir Rex Hunt. South Georgia was invaded the following day, by a third Argentinian task group. The Royal Marine defenders put up fierce resistance, even downing an Argentine Puma, with a Carl Gustav anti-tank rocket and a support Allouette was damaged by machine-gun fire before the Marines surrendered and followed their comrades into captivity. Argentina installed an AN/TPS43F radar and established a control centre at Port Stanley, providing an integrated air defence for the islands.

Having failed to deter the Argentine invasion, Britain assembled a task force to retake the islands, under the codename Operation 'Corporate'. The surface ships committed to the operation became TF.317, while the submarines already despatched became TF.324. RAF air traffic control staff were sent to Wideawake airfield (a facility built by the USA to support a tracking station and normally run by Pan Am) on the British island of Ascension, to prepare it for its potential role as a staging post to the Falklands. Victor tankers and

***Right:* The normally quiet airfield at Ascension was soon packed with RAF aircraft, including Hercules transports, Nimrod ASW aircraft and virtually the RAF's entire fleet of Victor tankers. Fourteen Victors can be seen in this view alone, along with a single Vulcan.**

Above: A Sea Skua-armed Lynx of No. 815 Squadron flies off the coast of South Georgia. Similarly-armed Lynxes were deployed aboard the 'Sheffield'-, 'Broadsword'- and 'Amazon'-class ships, and one from **Brilliant** *torpedoed the submarine* **Santa Fé** *after it had been depth-charged by the* **Antrim's** *Wessex.*

Right: Argentine ground crew load a Pucará with unguided rockets. Argentina deployed only light-weight attack aircraft to the Falklands, instead of laying a PSP runway from which Skyhawks could operate. This was probably a factor in costing Argentina the war.

Nimrod maritime patrol aircraft soon began flying operations.

The task force commander, Rear-Admiral John 'Sandy' Woodward, sailed from Gibraltar for Ascension on 2 April, aboard HMS *Glamorgan*, accompanied by four destroyers, five frigates and three support vessels assembled for exercises in the Mediterranean. The carriers *Hermes* and *Invincible*, with the assault ship *Fearless*, four support ships, two frigates and four landing ships sailed from Portsmouth on 5 and 6 April. The hastily requisitioned liner *Canberra* set sail from Southampton on 9 April, with 2,000 troops drawn from 40 and 42 Commandos and from 3 Para. These caught up with Woodward as he paused at Ascension.

On 7 April Britain declared a 322-km (200-mile) Maritime Exclusion Zone around the Falklands, to become effective on 14 April, after which shipping in the area would be liable to attack without warning. From 21 April, a small element of the task force retook South Georgia. SAS and SBS soldiers were inserted and then recovered after the weather deteriorated before Wessex, Lynx and Wasp helicopters attacked and beached the submarine *Santa Fé* on 23 October. Troops landed to take advantage of the surprise this caused, and the Argentine garrison surrendered without a fight after a 235-shot naval bombardment.

Below: This Fuerza Aérea Argentina Boeing 707 was the aircraft which discovered the Task Force as it sailed south, confirming to the Junta that the British meant business.

Argentine garrison

Argentina's invasion of the Falklands was primarily seaborne, although a small number of helicopters did participate. However, once the British garrison surrendered, the Argentinians brought in Pucarás, T-34Cs and MB.339s for light attack duties, Short Skyvans for communications and patrol, and a mixed bag of helicopters from the army, air force and Prefectura.

Agusta A 109 Hirundo

Two A 109s were used by the Combat Aviation Battalion 601 of the Army Aviation Command in the Falklands. These were later captured by the British Forces and flown in Royal Marine markings. They still serve today as ZE411 and 412 with 7 Regiment (8 Flight) AAC in support of the SAS.

Aermacchi MB.339A

The Argentinian navy deployed six Aermacchi MB.339As to Port Stanley from their mainland base. They operated in the light-ground-attack role, and participated in attacks on British shipping, despite their inadequate armament and lack of defensive avionics.

Lockheed C-130E Hercules

The C-130Es and C-130Hs of GTA.1 were augmented by Fokker F27s and F28s on the air bridge between their base at Comodoro Rivadavia and Port Stanley. One C-130 was lost during the war, shot down by a Sea Harrier.

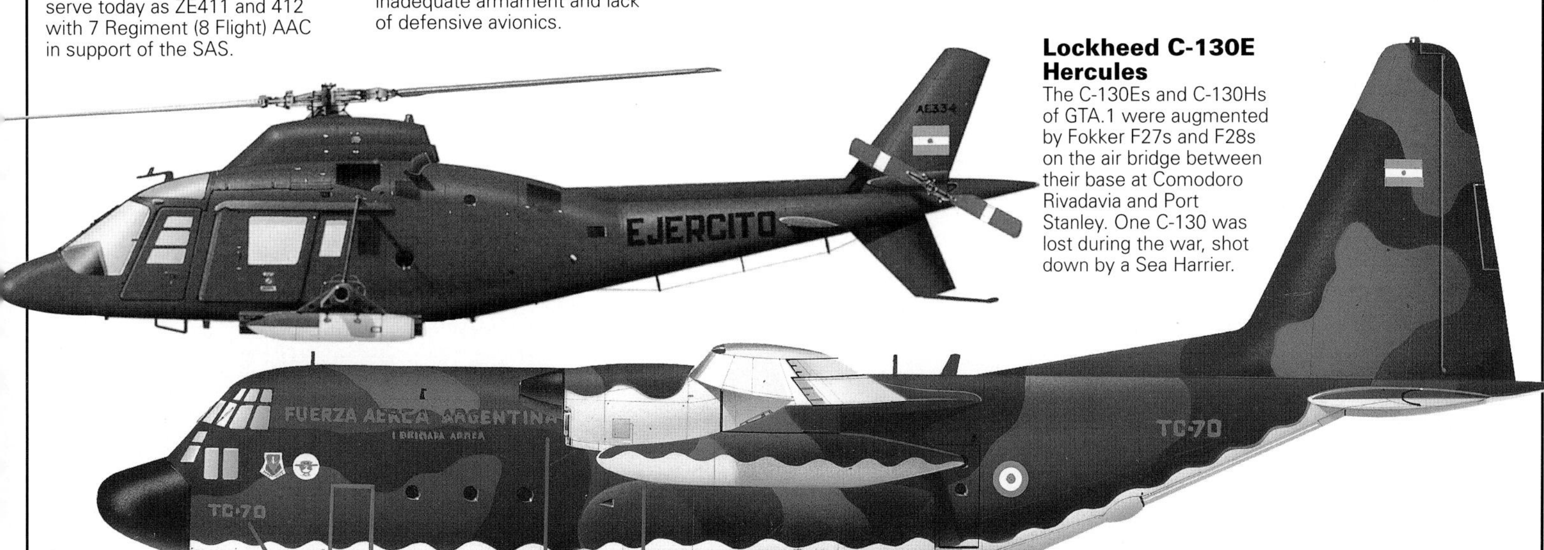

Falklands First Strikes

1 May – 20 May 1982

Left: Vulcan XM607 lands at Wideawake airfield, Ascension Island, after the first Black Buck bombing mission on 30 April 1982. The aircraft carried 14 454-kg (1,000-lb) bombs for this mission, but only one clipped the Port Stanley runway.

Above: The first of the Black Buck Vulcans refuels in flight from a Victor K.Mk 2 tanker during one of its three successful bombing raids against the airfield at Port Stanley. Another Vulcan flew two successful anti-radar missions, and two Vulcan missions were aborted.

As the British task force sailed south, it was reinforced by men and materiel (later including the Harrier GR.Mk 3s of No. 1 Squadron, and aircraft from a third Sea Harrier squadron) flown to Ascension and then helicoptered or flown on to the waiting ships, while other elements of the British force got into position. Canberra PR.Mk 9s and Nimrod R.Mk 1s flew reconnaissance and Elint sorties from a still undisclosed location (perhaps in Chile, or even Brazil), while maritime Nimrods and radar reconnaissance Victors operated from Ascension. Back in the UK, the MoD requisitioned the *Queen Elizabeth II* to carry 3,500 Welsh Guards, Scots Guards and Gurkhas to the Falklands.

On the Falkland Islands, the Argentine garrison prepared defensive positions, and by late-April had its own detachment of 24 Pucaras for close-support, six naval MB-339As and four T-34Cs, alongside a disparate group of army and air force helicopters. Port Stanley and Goose Green airfields were well defended by Roland SAMs and 20- and 35-mm AAA.

Above: Britain's operation to recapture the Falklands would have been impossible without its pair of carriers, **Hermes** (shown) and **Invincible**. These allowed the task force to fly south with its own organic air-defence and close air-support/ground-attack assets.

Right: An Argentine pilot's target view. The Dagger and Skyhawk pilots pressed home their attacks at very low level: so low, in fact, that their bombs frequently failed to fuse before they hit their targets.

Left: Argentina's five Dassault Super Etendards had an importance far beyond that suggested by their limited numbers. They were the launch aircraft for Argentina's five AM-39 Exocet anti-ship missiles, which destroyed two task force vessels.

Argentine attackers

While Argentina's ageing Canberras were never likely to prove too much of an embarrassment to the Sea Harrier, the British jet's superiority over the supersonic Mirage III and IAI Dagger came as a pleasant surprise to some senior officers, who had not thought that agility and the all-aspect Sidewinder would provide quite such an edge over the Argentine fighters and fighter bombers.

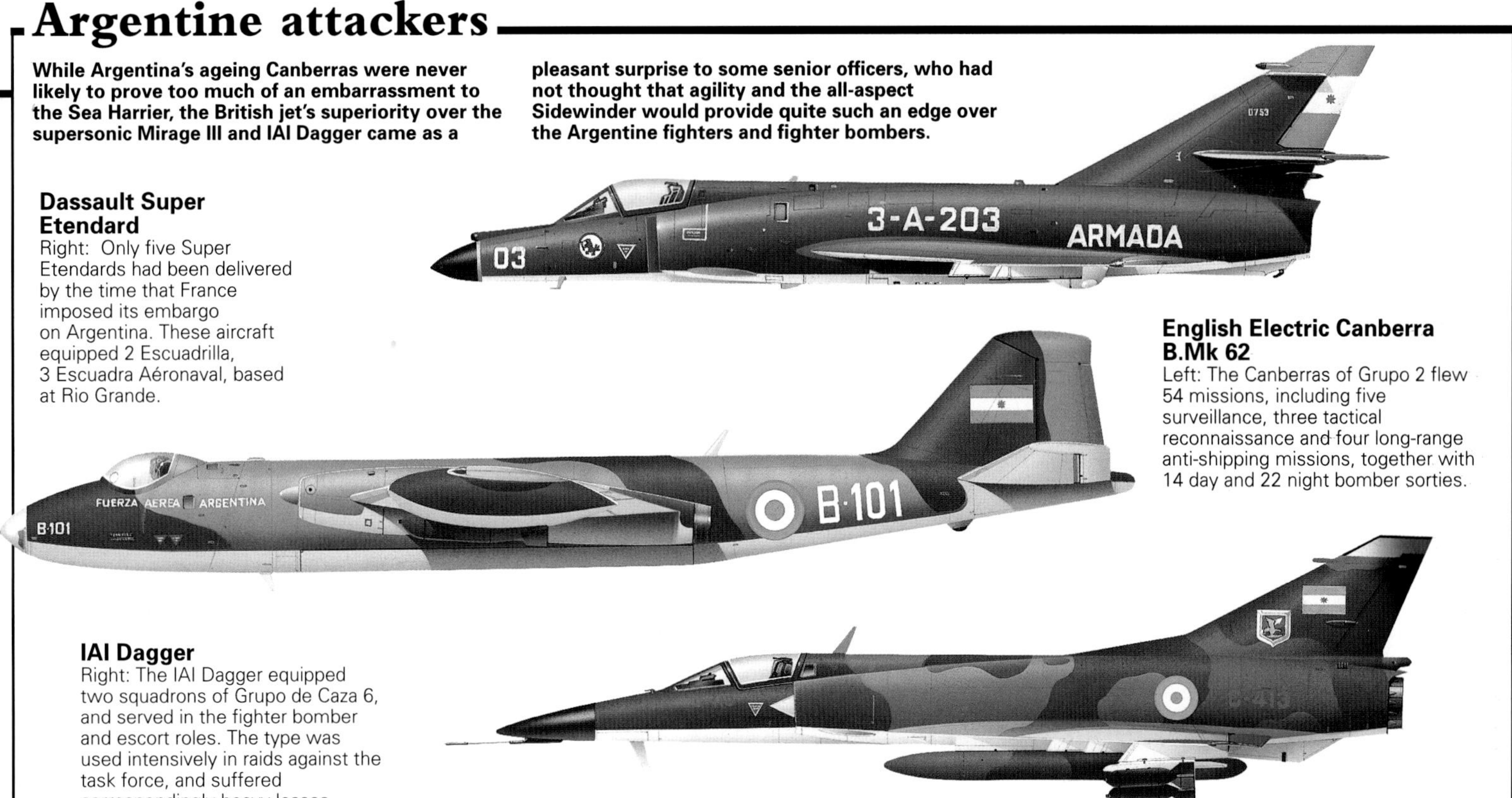

Dassault Super Etendard
Right: Only five Super Etendards had been delivered by the time that France imposed its embargo on Argentina. These aircraft equipped 2 Escuadrilla, 3 Escuadra Aéronaval, based at Rio Grande.

English Electric Canberra B.Mk 62
Left: The Canberras of Grupo 2 flew 54 missions, including five surveillance, three tactical reconnaissance and four long-range anti-shipping missions, together with 14 day and 22 night bomber sorties.

IAI Dagger
Right: The IAI Dagger equipped two squadrons of Grupo de Caza 6, and served in the fighter bomber and escort roles. The type was used intensively in raids against the task force, and suffered correspondingly heavy losses.

Left: Harriers and Sea Harriers cocooned on the deck of the **Atlantic Conveyor*****. The aircraft boarded the ship at Ascension, and were transported down to the Falklands, where they were flown off before the vessel was sunk.***

The Task Force was located by an Argentine Boeing 707 on 21 April before being escorted from the scene by a Sea Harrier. On 30 April, with diplomatic moves to find a solution exhausted, Britain transformed its Maritime Exclusion Zone into a Total Exclusion Zone, while the USA formally endorsed Britain's position.

Long-range bombing

On 1 May a single Vulcan bombed Port Stanley, dropping a stick of bombs obliquely across the runway, and also sending a clear signal that no Argentine target could be deemed safe from potential air attack. Later that morning, the airfields at Port Stanley and Goose Green were attacked by Sea Harriers. From midday, warships began bombarding military positions in and around Port Stanley. The Fuerza Aerea Argentina (FAA) responded by launching attacks against the task force, damaging a handful of ships but losing two Mirage IIIs, a Dagger, and a Canberra to patrolling Sea Harriers.

On 2 May the Argentine cruiser *Belgrano* was sunk by a British submarine, and Lynxes from *Glasgow* and *Coventry* damaged a patrol craft as SAS parties were landed on the islands, while the night of 3/4 May saw the second Black Buck Vulcan raid against Port Stanley. There was also a second Sea Harrier airfield attack, one aircraft falling to a Tigercat SAM. Later on 4 May two Super Etendards struck back by attacking RN ships on picket duty, fatally damaging HMS *Sheffield* (which sank while under tow six days later) and killing 26 of its crew. One Sea Harrier was shot down by AAA during an attack on Goose Green. Air attacks by both sides were mounted as the weather permitted, with Argentine losses

Right: The British had a range advantage over the Falklands. The much more numerous Argentine aircraft had to fly between 700 and 950 km (435/590 miles) to reach the combat zone. Sea Harriers, on the other hand, were flying off carriers less than 160 km (100 miles) to the east of the Falklands.

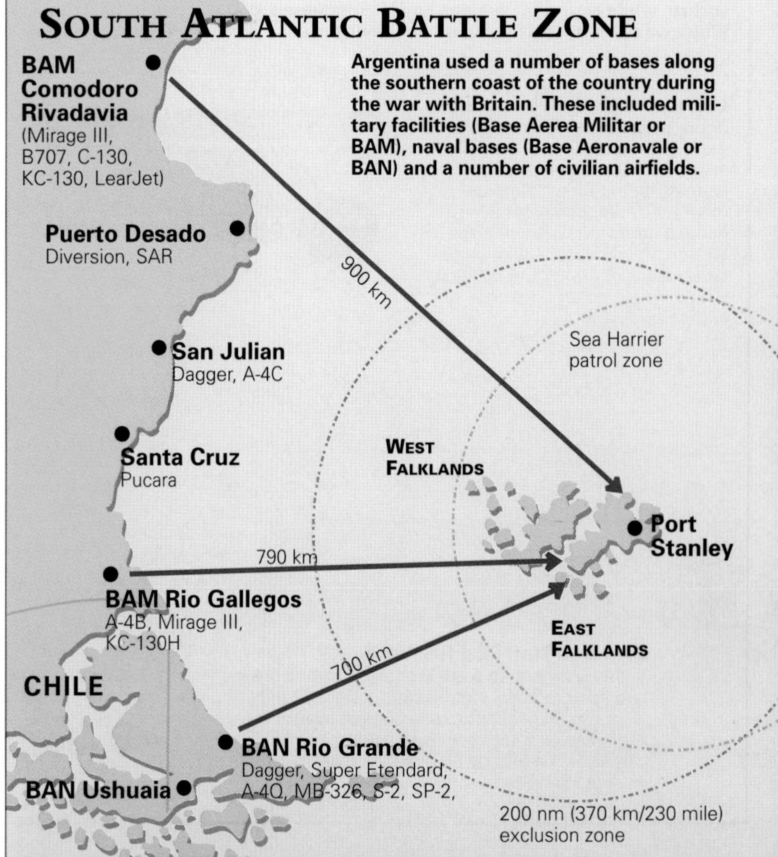

Argentina used a number of bases along the southern coast of the country during the war with Britain. These included military facilities (Base Aerea Militar or BAM), naval bases (Base Aeronavale or BAN) and a number of civilian airfields.

Above: Bomb racks and fuel tanks nearly empty, a Skyhawk refuels as it heads homewards for Argentina, after an anti-shipping strike over the Falklands.

Below: A Harrier GR.Mk 3 from No. 1 Squadron RAF is seen at Ascension Island before setting off on the long flight to the task force in the South Atlantic.

mounting steadily to the weather, Sea Harriers and SAMs. On 9 May SBS soldiers dropped from Sea Kings boarded the Argentine intelligence gatherer *Narwal* after it had been attacked by Sea Harriers. A raid by Skyhawks on 12 May against RN ships bombarding Port Stanley put the *Glasgow* out of action, though the bomb which hit the ship fortunately failed to explode. A planned third Vulcan raid was aborted due to high winds over the target on 13 May, but an SAS raid destroyed six Pucaras, a Skyvan and four Mentors at Pebble Island on 14 May. Task force helicopter losses continued to mount to birdstrikes, and accidents, while on 17 May a Sea King was burned by its crew at Agua Fresca, near Punta Arenas in Chile, after an SAS insertion mission. The SAS and SBS teams inserted before the invasion spotted for naval guns.

While SAS and SBS units made diversionary attacks on Goose Green and Darwin, the full-scale British landings (Operation Sutton) began at San Carlos under cover of mist and darkness , before dawn on 21 May. The FAA made a series of spirited attacks on the invasion fleet, damaging several ships for the loss of five Daggers, two Pucaras, and five Skyhawks. The Argentine pilots won the respect of their adversaries, flying their attacks with reckless bravery and some degree of accuracy. One of the Falklands-based MB.339s even entered the fray, making an accurate if relatively ineffective attack against the *Argonaut*, which suffered minor damage. Had Argentine bombs been better fused, or had the FAA been able to sustain a higher sortie rate, many ships might have been worse damaged than they were. Nevertheless, one of the damaged ships sank the following day. The British lost a Harrier GR.Mk 3 to a Blowpipe SAM, and two Gazelles to small arms fire. But at the end of the day, the British were able to land forces ashore, and consolidated their position the following day, when bad weather prevented further attacks.

Right: The Mirage IIIEAs of Grupo de Caza 8 were mainly retained at Comodoro Rivadavia for air defence duties, though they flew a handful of long-range escort sorties over the Falklands, losing a number of aircraft to Royal Navy Sea Harriers.

The empire strikes back

The ships of the British task force were accompanied and supported by a wide range of aircraft performing a variety of roles. Sea Harriers and Harriers aboard the two carriers flew air defence, attack and reconnaissance sorties, while Nimrods, Vulcans and Victors based at at Wideawake on Ascension Island flew maritime reconnaissance, ASW, bomber, SEAD, tanker and radar reconnaissance missions. It is believed that Canberra PR.Mk 9s and Nimrod R.Mk 1s flew intelligence-gathering sorties from a South American base, possibly in Chile or even Brazil, but this has never been confirmed by the Ministry of Defence.

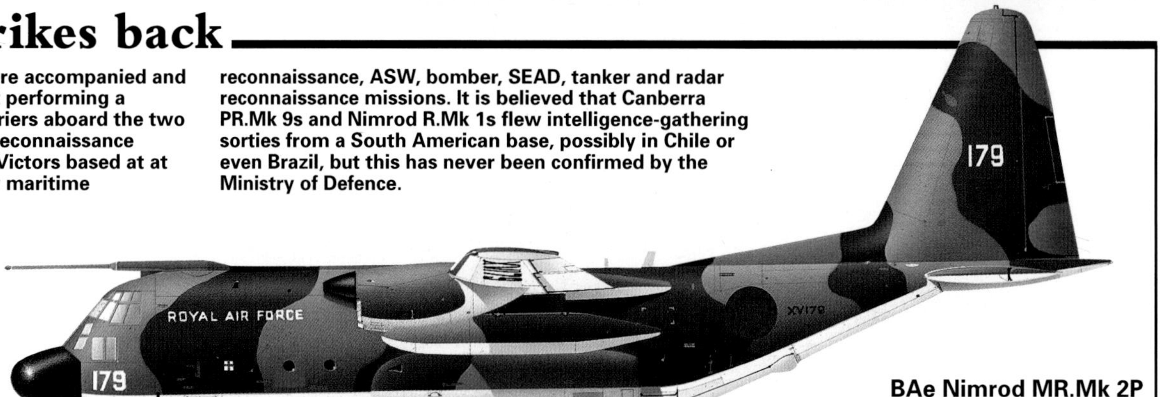

Lockheed C-130 Hercules

Right: Some 25 RAF Hercules were given refuelling probes to allow them to make the long journey south to the task force, where they dropped urgently-needed items to task force ships. Six aircraft were also equipped to serve as inflight-refuelling tankers, with a simple hose-and-drogue unit in the rear fuselage.

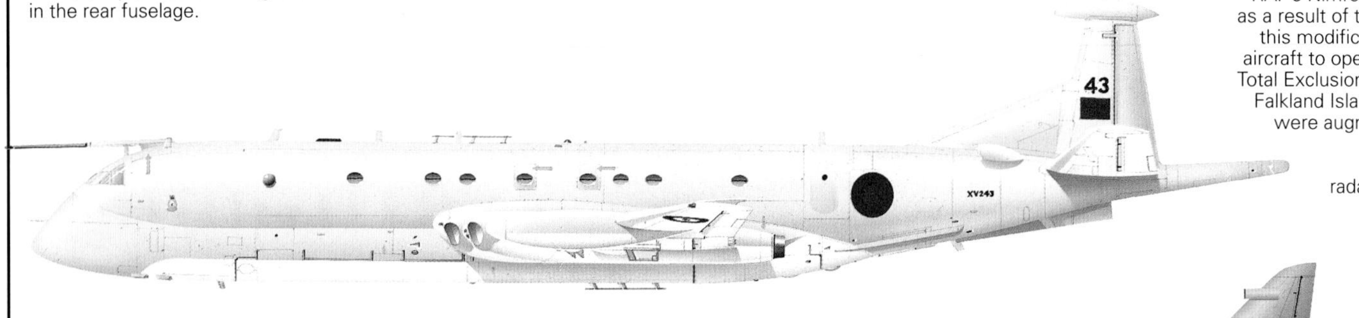

BAe Nimrod MR.Mk 2P

Left: The programme to fit inflight-refuelling probes to the RAF's Nimrods was expedited as a result of the Falklands War, this modification allowing the aircraft to operate right into the Total Exclusion Zone around the Falkland Islands. The Nimrods were augmented by Victors operating in the maritime radar reconnaissance role.

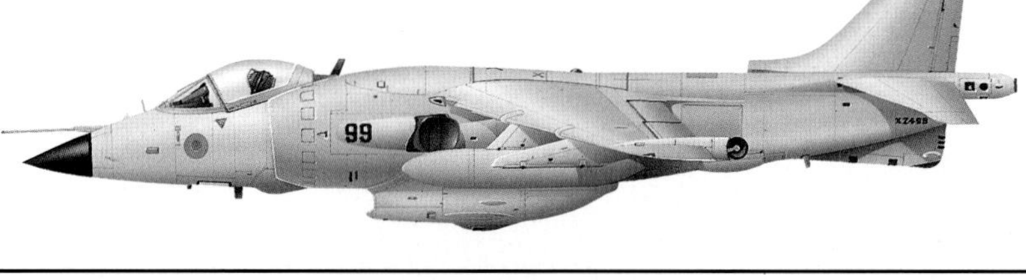

BAe Sea Harrier FRS.Mk 1

Right: Sea Harriers were embarked aboard the two carriers, HMS *Hermes* and *Invincible* and were the first aircraft to see combat against the Argentine air force. The Sea Harrier became known as 'La Muerta Negra' (The Black Death) to its Argentine opponents.

Sea Harrier in the Falklands
Of 28 Sea Harriers deployed, two were shot down by ground fire, and four more were lost in accidents. They flew 1,100 CAPs and 90 offensive support sorties, logging 2,088 deck landings.

Powerplant
The corrosion-resistant 95.55-kN (21,500-lb st) Pegasus Mk.104 made extensive use of magnesium components, but was otherwise similar to the engine fitted to the RAF's land-based Harrier GR.Mk 3.

Armament
The first-generation Harrier's normal armament of two 30-mm Aden cannon in underfuselage pods could be augmented by two, or later four, AIM-9L Sidewinder AAMs, though the twin-rail launcher did not enter service until after the end of the fighting in the Falklands.

Radar
The Sea Harrier FRS.Mk 1 was fitted with a Ferranti Blue Fox pulse-modulated I-band radar, developed from the Lynx helicopter's Seaspray.

BAe Sea Harrier

This Sea Harrier FRS.Mk 1 of No. 899 Squadron, bears two Mirage or Dagger kill markings and one Skyhawk kill marking. Task Force Sea Harriers claimed large numbers of Argentine aircraft during the conflict while none were lost to enemy fighters. The aircraft's overall dark-grey colour scheme earned it the nickname 'Black Death'.

First Harrier victory

Flight Lieutenant Paul Barton, an experienced Harrier pilot seconded to the Royal Navy, was leading Lieutenant Steve Thomas in a pair of 801 Squadron Sea Harriers on patrol west of the Task Force on 1 May 1982. Port Stanley had been bombed, the Argentines were coming out in strength, and one of the warships on radar picket had detected incoming enemy fighters. Thomas was first to make radar contact.

"We were running in towards each other, head-on. I was doing about 400 kt [740 km/460 mph], Paul accelerated to about 550 kt [1020 km/635 mph] and pulled away to the right, to try and get around the back of them. I locked my radar on to their leader, then I began looking for the others – I couldn't believe that a pair of fighters would come in alone like that. Their formation was poor, what the Americans call 'welded wing', flying very close together."

The incoming aircraft were Mirage IIIs from Grupo 8, the Argentine air force's only dedicated interceptor unit. Capt Garcia Cuerva was leading the pair, with Lt Carlos Perona as wing man.

"This is the sort of thing one learns not to do on Day 1 at the Tactical Weapons Unit." Paul Barton recalled, drily. "We would never dream of flying that sort of formation, so it was mildly surprising when they did."

"My job now was to act as 'shooter', to get round behind the bogeys and attack if they proved hostile. I accelerated to maximum speed, locking my radar on to the No. 2. I dived down, visually acquiring the bogeys at about five miles [8 km]."

By now the Argentine fighters had almost reached Thomas. Hurtling toward the Mirages at a combined closing speed of over 1600 km/h (1,000 mph), he eased back on his stick to pass over the top of them, then dropped his right wing and pulled into a turn. As he did so the enemy fighters passed close underneath him. The Mirages continued in their shallow turn to port, oblivious to the presence of Paul Barton who was now moving rapidly into a firing position behind Perona's aircraft. The Sea Harrier pilot was sure he had still not been seen. Had either of the enemy pilots known where he was they would have pulled their turn far tighter to try to shake him off.

Barton eased forward on his stick to descend a little and silhouette the Mirage against the cold background of the powder-blue sky, to give the Sidewinder the best possible chance. Then he squeezed the firing button and the missile roared off the starboard launcher leaving a trail of grey smoke as it accelerated away.

"At first I thought it had failed. It came off the rail and ducked down. I had not fired a 'winder before so its behaviour at launch was new to me. I was surprised not to see it home straight in – to see it duck down was disconcerting. I'd begun to wonder if it was a dud. It took about half a mile for it to get its trajectory sorted out, then it picked itself up and for the last half mile it just homed straight in. The missile flight time was about four seconds, then the Mirage exploded in a brilliant blue orange and red fireball."

So it was that Perona gained the dubious distinction of being the first pilot ever to be shot down by a 'jump' jet. Although at the time Barton was convinced that nobody could have survived from the blazing Mirage, in fact the Argentine pilot was able to eject to safety. Like so many of those shot down in fighter-versus-fighter combat, he never saw the aircraft that hit him.

Left: A Sea Harrier FRS.Mk 1 takes off from the ski jump, streaming spray from its undercarriage. Weather conditions in the South Atlantic were often very poor indeed, and three Sea Harriers were probably lost directly due to the poor conditions.

Falklands, Final Victory

21 MAY – 14 JUNE 1982

An FAA Skyhawk receives damage during an attack on the HMS* Fearless. *The FAA's Skyhawks were the most destructive aircraft fielded by Argentina, and proved a formidable foe, although they were very vulnerable to fighters and SAMs.

Above: The Argentine pilots pressed home their attacks at very low level. One of Grupo 6's Daggers is visible behind the assault ship HMS* Fearless, *flying past the main mast at bridge level only a few feet above the deck. The landing ships and support vessels were vulnerable to air attack, yet remarkably all survived the landings at San Carlos.

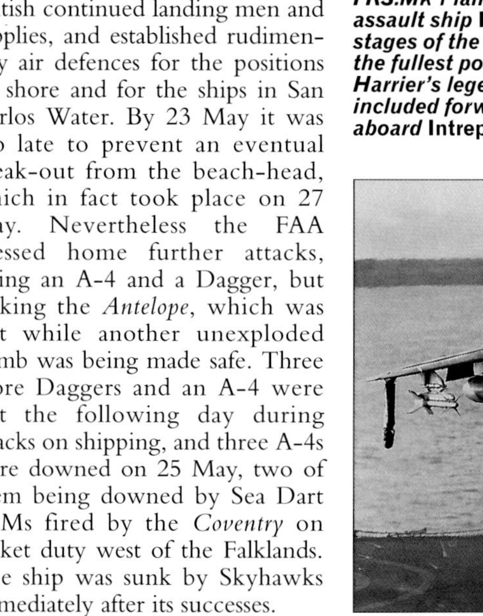

The Falklands War entered its third and final phase with the success of the British landings at San Carlos. Argentine air attacks had failed to prevent a beach-head from being established on 21 May, and bad weather prevented the FAA from intervening on 22 May, while the British continued landing men and supplies, and established rudimentary air defences for the positions on shore and for the ships in San Carlos Water. By 23 May it was too late to prevent an eventual break-out from the beach-head, which in fact took place on 27 May. Nevertheless the FAA pressed home further attacks, losing an A-4 and a Dagger, but sinking the *Antelope*, which was lost while another unexploded bomb was being made safe. Three more Daggers and an A-4 were lost the following day during attacks on shipping, and three A-4s were downed on 25 May, two of them being downed by Sea Dart SAMs fired by the *Coventry* on picket duty west of the Falklands. The ship was sunk by Skyhawks immediately after its successes.

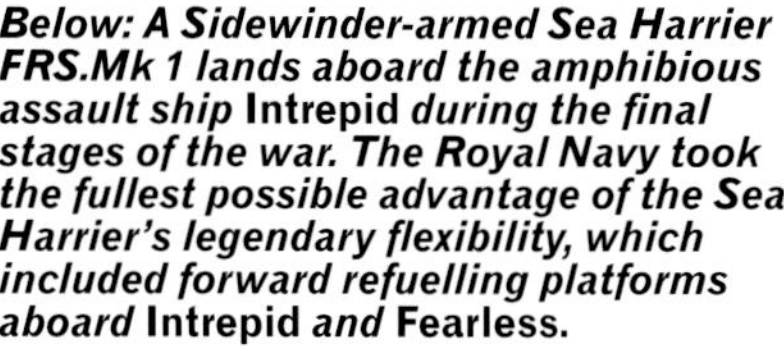

***Below: A Sidewinder-armed Sea Harrier FRS.Mk 1 lands aboard the amphibious assault ship* Intrepid *during the final stages of the war. The Royal Navy took the fullest possible advantage of the Sea Harrier's legendary flexibility, which included forward refuelling platforms aboard* Intrepid *and* Fearless.**

A Sea King and a Type 21 frigate come to the assistance of HMS* Plymouth, *burning in San Carlos Water after being hit by bombs. The frigate survived, thanks to the faulty fusing of the Argentine weapons.

On the same day the CANA fired the third and fourth of its five Exocet missiles, one of these accounting for the *Atlantic Conveyor* and its cargo of spares, supplies, and Wessex and Chinook helicopters, only one of the latter escaping the catastrophe.

GROUNDFIRE LOSSES

On 27 May, an RAF Harrier was lost to groundfire while the Argentines resisted the British advance, losing an A-4, an MB-339 and two Pucaras in the process. The next day Pucaras made an unsuccessful attack using napalm, but fortunately this was the only occasion on which this horrific weapon was used. The fourth Vulcan raid (intended as an anti-radar sortie using Shrike missiles) was aborted when one of the Victor tankers went unserviceable. Air activity continued unabated as the British

Supporting the advance

While the Royal Navy's Sea Harriers won the glory, other aircraft were more directly involved in supporting the Army's rapid advance across the Falklands. RAF Harrier GR.Mk 3s provided expert close air support, while helicopters from all four services played their part in resupply, transport and casevac missions. The sole Chinook to escape the catastrophic sinking of the *Atlantic Conveyor* was used especially intensively, though the larger number of Sea Kings available played a more important role.

BAe Harrier GR.Mk 3
Left: The RAF Harrier GR.Mk 3s of No. 1 Squadron deployed with the task force were originally intended as attrition replacements for the Sea Harriers, and were armed with AIM-9s. Losses were lower than anticipated, though, and the RAF Harriers were used almost exclusively in the ground-attack role.

Boeing Vertol Chinook HC.Mk 1
Right: Known by its twin letter code, 'Bravo November' was the sole Chinook to escape the destruction of the *Atlantic Conveyor*. The aircraft lacked spares, manuals and equipment and no-one expected it to be serviceable for long, but remarkably the helicopter remained airworthy for the rest of the war, performing a number of spectacular transport missions.

Westland Sea King HC.Mk 4
Left: British versions of the troop-carrying Commando served with No. 846 Squadron, and were augmented by stripped examples of the ASW HAS.Mk 2 and HAS.Mk 5. Three squadrons in the Falklands still used the ancient Wessex HU.Mk 5. The peacetime rulebook was thrown away by helicopter squadrons in the Falklands. Aircraft frequently flew at very high weights, and the usual servicing intervals were often stretched.

infantry pushed eastwards towards Port Stanley, with both sides suffering losses. Another Sea Harrier fell victim to an accident on 29 May, and another was shot down by a Roland SAM on 1 June. Sea Harriers shot down a C-130 Hercules on the same day. The Argentines lost a Dagger on 29 May, and two A-4s on 30 May, all to Rapier or Sea Dart SAMs. The A-4s were reportedly supporting the CANA's final Exocet attack, the fifth missile apparently having been successfully decoyed away from its target, the *Invincible*. Poor weather limited air activity until 8 June, one RAF Harrier being lost on 30 May after groundfire severed a fuel line. The pilot was forced to eject when he could not reach the *Hermes*.

The Harrier's reliance on the carriers (which had to stand off out of range of Argentine aircraft) was eased on 2 June, with the completion of 'Sid's strip', a temporary airfield at San Carlos where aircraft could be refuelled and re-armed. The Vulcan flew an unsuccessful fifth mission on 31 May, but followed this with a third anti-radar mission on 3 June, damaging a Skyguard radar in the process. Unfortunately the aircraft was forced to divert to Rio de Janeiro after its refuelling probe broke on the journey home, and it was detained until the end of the war. During the poor weather, the FAA mounted a number of Canberra night-bombing raids, and a reconnaissance Learjet was downed by a Sea Dart SAM on 7 June.

When the weather cleared on 8 June, the Argentines were faced with plum targets as the assault ships *Fearless* and *Intrepid*, together with the landing ships *Sir Galahad* and *Sir*

Above: Army and Royal Marines Gazelles saw extensive service in the observation and reconnaissance, liaison, casevac and gunship roles, but proved very vulnerable to small arms fire.

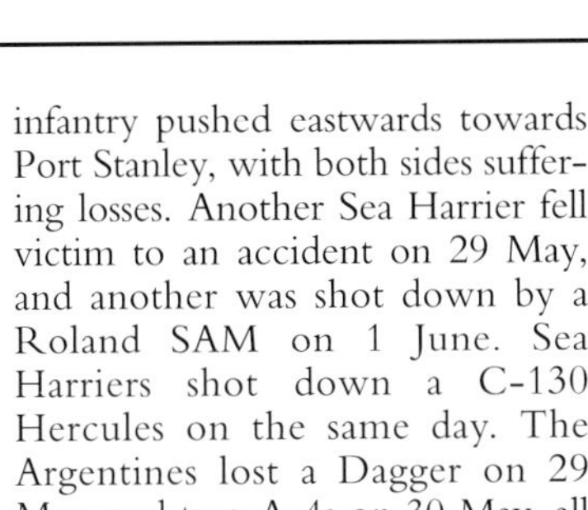

Above: Wessex HU.Mk 5s flew with five flights of No. 845 Squadron, four of No. 848 Squadron and with No. 847 Squadron. These operated detachments onboard a variety of support ships, and onshore.

Right: Sea Kings were among the most useful aircraft available to task force commanders, capable of lifting heavy underslung loads.

Above: Napalm tanks were among the weapons used by the Argentine Pucaras during the Falklands campaign. However they were dropped on only one mission – without success – and were then dumped.

Tristram, which were busy moving troops from San Carlos to Fitzroy Cove in preparation for the final push on Port Stanley. The FAA mounted a raid by five A-4Bs and six Daggers (with four Mirages making a diversionary raid on San Carlos to draw off the Sea Harriers). *Sir Galahad* and *Sir Tristram* were badly damaged, and 43 Welsh Guardsmen and seven seamen were killed. Outbound, the Daggers crippled HMS *Plymouth*, and all the FAA aircraft returned to base safely.

Sea Harrier revenge

Things went less well for the second wave of Argentine attack aircraft that afternoon. Three Skyhawks were destroyed by Sea Harriers after sinking a landing craft. The temporary landing strip was put out of action when a Harrier made a heavy landing.

12 and 13 June saw some of the heaviest fighting of the war, as the Paras fought to take Mount Longdon and Wireless Ridge, being supported by SS.11-firing Westland Scouts in the latter attack. *Glamorgan* was hit by a ground-launched Exocet that day (losing her Wessex helicopter) and soon afterwards, the Vulcan force launched its seventh and final mission, dropping airburst bombs on Port Stanley airfield. A final air attack came when a single Wessex HU.Mk 5 attacked Port Stanley Town Hall with an AS.12 missile, aiming to hit a major conference taking place there. One missile hit the neighbouring police station, and the second missed altogether.

Below: An armed Gazelle hovers over a forward position, while a Wessex flies in another load of ammunition. The effective use of support helicopters was crucial to the success of the task force.

On 13 June, Argentine Skyhawks attacked the British Brigade HQ on Mount Kent, and a Canberra was shot down in the type's final

'Black Buck'

The five Vulcans deployed to Wideawake flew seven missions under the codenames Black Buck 1 to Black Buck 7. Two primary Vulcans flew all five successful missions. Plans to disband No. 44 Squadron were put on hold, and the squadron flew a number of realistic conventional bombing exercises over Scotland before the first aircraft was deployed to Ascension Island. The Vulcans had not used inflight refuelling for some years, and a massive search had to be mounted for serviceable inflight-refuelling probes, to the extent of salvaging probes from aircraft already retired to museums. The five aircraft selected for Black Buck were all aircraft once intended to carry Skybolt, so had attachment points for underwing pylons. These were used for the carriage of a Westinghouse AN/ALQ-101(V)-10 ECM pod under the starboard wing, with two or four Shrike ARMs for Black Bucks 4, 5 and 6. Drop tests of the 454-kg (1,000-lb) laser-guided bomb were undertaken before the deployment, using a laser designator in the bomb-aimer's undernose cupola, but this weapon was not deployed operationally. The most important result of the Vulcan raids was that they raised a real fear that the RAF could attack targets on the mainland, forcing the FAA to retain its best fighters for air defence.

Left: Bombs were loaded in clips of seven, two such clips being carried for Black Buck missions.

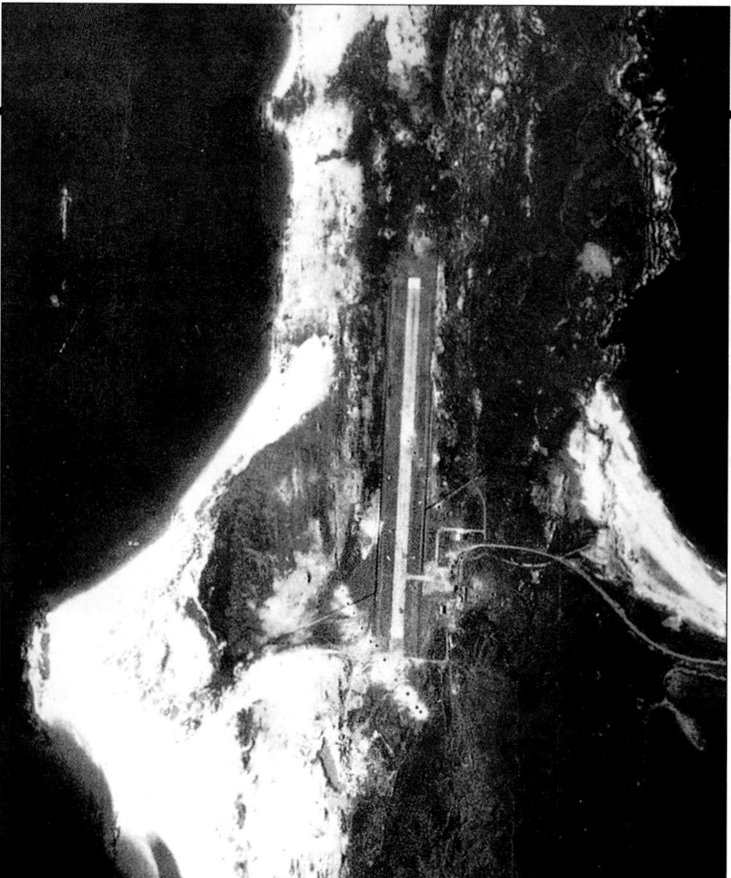

Above: Bombs damage at Port Stenley airfport. Two parallel strings of craters marking Vulcan attacks can be seen, one of which comes to an end with a crater in the centre of the runway.

Left: A hastily camouflaged AGM-45 Shrike anti-radar missile under the wing of XM597 before Black Buck 4, the first abandoned Shrike mission. Black Buck 5, flown two nights later, was more successful. Before they deployed to Wideawake the Vulcans conducted trials and live firings with the AS.37 Martel as well as the AGM-45 Shrike. Six Shrikes were fired during the war.

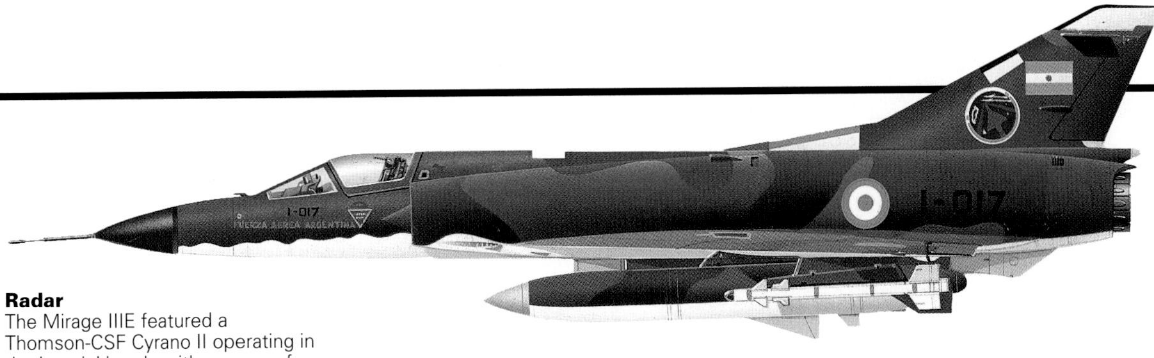

Powerplant
The Mirage IIIE was powered by a single SNECMA Atar 09C-3 engine, with a conventional petal-type afterburner nozzle replacing the eyelid-type nozzle fitted to the Mirage IIIC's Atar 9B-3. Provision was made for the fitting of a SEPR 844 rocket booster engine, but few customers actually specified this as an option.

Radar
The Mirage IIIE featured a Thomson-CSF Cyrano II operating in the I- and J-bands with a range of air-to-air and air-to-ground modes. Although designed as a multi-role fighter-bomber, the Mirage IIIRA was used by Argentina as a pure air-defence aircraft.

Dassault Mirage IIIEA

This Mirage IIIEA was one of 17 delivered to Argentina from France during 1973. It wears the markings of I Escuadrón de Caza, Grupo 8 de Caza. The squadron had detachments at Rio Gallegos and Comodoro Rivadavia during the Falklands War, and lost two aircraft in action, both falling to Sea Harriers. The squadron remains in service today, flying from Tandil.

Armament
The Mirage IIIE carried a pair of internal 30-mm cannon, and augmented these with underwing R.550 Magic IR-homing close-range missiles. The Argentine Mirage IIIEA differed from the basic Mirage IIIE in being equipped to fire the BVR Matra R.530 AAM.

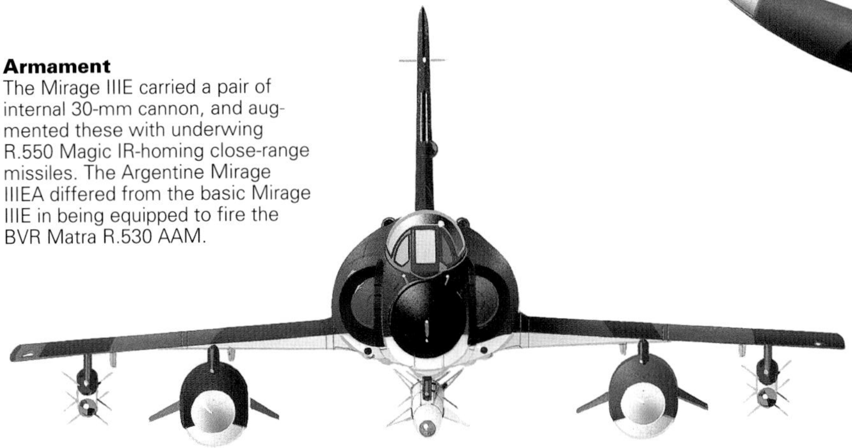

appearance over the Falklands. Although LGB attacks had begun on 10 June, designation problems had rendered them unsuccessful. On 13 June everything came right, and Harriers successfully bombed a company HQ at Tumbledown and a 105-mm (4.13-in) gun at Moody Brook.

On 14 June two Harriers took off for an LGB attack against Sapper Hill, but were recalled because white flags were already flying in Port Stanley. An Argentine surrender was signed at one minute before midnight.

Britain had recovered the Falklands at minimal cost, with an apparently decisive victory which did much to enhance the reputation of its armed forces. The war also brought the government much-needed popularity (despite the fact that the war had been caused by its own defence cuts and inability to foresee their consequences), and an early election was called, bringing a victory which many ascribed to the 'Falklands Factor'. The disparity in losses hid the fact that the war had been a close-run thing at several points, while it was seldom recognised that Britain's continuing defence cuts would have made the operation impossible to carry out only a few months later. Useful lessons were learned from the conflict, and it also led to the rapid development and deployment of a number of key systems, perhaps the most important being the AEW Sea King, which was just too late to see front-line service in the war itself.

Argentina has not lost its ambitions to gain sovereignty over what it calls the Malvinas, but has been prevented from attempting further military adventures by a much enlarged British military presence on the Falklands, and by the construction of a major international airport, which would allow rapid reinforcement by air, and which houses a permanent detachment of Tornado fighters.

Above: Four of the 10 RAF Harrier GR.Mk 3s deployed to the Falklands were lost in action. Modifications included the addition of AIM-9 Sidewinders, and Tracor AN/ALE-40 chaff/flare dispensers.

Below: Wrecked Pucaras lie beside the runway at Port Stanley after the war, as an RAF Hercules makes its final approach. Some 29 aircraft were captured at Port Stanley alone, though few were flyable.

US police actions: Grenada, Panama and Haiti

1983-1995

Having been under British rule since 1763, Grenada was granted full independence in February 1974 with a democratic government being formed under Sir Eric Gairy. Five years later following a nearly bloodless coup d'etat, a People's Revolutionary Government (PRG) was organised by Maurice Bishop and his left-wing New Joint Endeavour for Welfare, Education and Liberation (JEWEL) movement.

The Cuban presence in Grenada quickly grew with the building a new airport which had potential military application in spite of its avowed commercial purpose, and became a source of concern for the US government over its potential use for Cuban military operations in Central America.

TURMOIL IN GRENADA

Then, in October 1983, Prime Minister Bishop and several members of his cabinet were arrested and subsequently executed by elements of the People's Revolutionary Army (PRA). The emerging leaders – General Hudson Austin of the PRA and the former Deputy Prime Minister, Bernard Coard – benefitted from the support of about 50 military advisers of Cuba's Fuerzas Armadas Revolucionarias (FAR), several hundred Cuban civilian advisers and construction workers, and a small number of Soviet military personnel from the Spetsnaz.

Chaos set in, and the lives of US and other foreign nationals were thought to be endangered. Still, there was no legal ground for US intervention until 23 October ,when six eastern Caribbean nations together with Jamaica and Barbados issued a formal request for assistance by the United States. Shortly thereafter, a letter from Governor General Sir Paul Scoon, the Queen's representative in Grenada, requested outside intervention and provided a legitimate cover for military action. Earlier US plans for a non-combat rescue evacuation of Americans from the island were discarded and preparations for full military operations were initiated. Urgent Fury was under way.

To carry out the assignment, CINCLANT – the US Navy's Commander-in-Chief, Atlantic – was given operational control over Air Force, Army and Marine units in addition to his own forces. Land operations were to be conducted by Army special forces, two Ranger battalions and the 82nd Airborne Division, Navy SEAL special forces, and Marines of the 22nd Marine Amphibious Unit. Transportation and paradrop of Army troops was to be performed by USAF C-130 Hercules, heavy-lift support coming from C-141B StarLifters and giant C-5A Galaxy aircraft. The Marines, escorted by AH-1T Cobra attack helicopters, were to be taken ashore by CH-46Es and CH-53Ds based aboard the assault ship USS *Guam* (LPH-9) and by four landing ships of Phibron (Amphibious Squadron) Four.

Air support for Joint Task Force 120, as the combined service force was called, was to be provided by

The Lockheed AC-130 Spectre gunship, much-improved and upgraded since the Vietnam war, was the ideal weapon for Grenada, a setting where the other side had little or no anti-aircraft weaponry.

Grenada was the first big US effort since Vietnam, so it was the baptism of fire for the Sikorsky UH-60 Black Hawk, the helicopter which had replaced the ubiquitous UH-1 Huey in the US Army's inventory.

Below: A Bell AH-1T Cobra of US Marine Corps squadron HMM-261 runs up its engines as deck crews on the USS **Guam** ***(LPH-9) top off its fuel tanks for an assault on Grenada's Pearls Airport.***

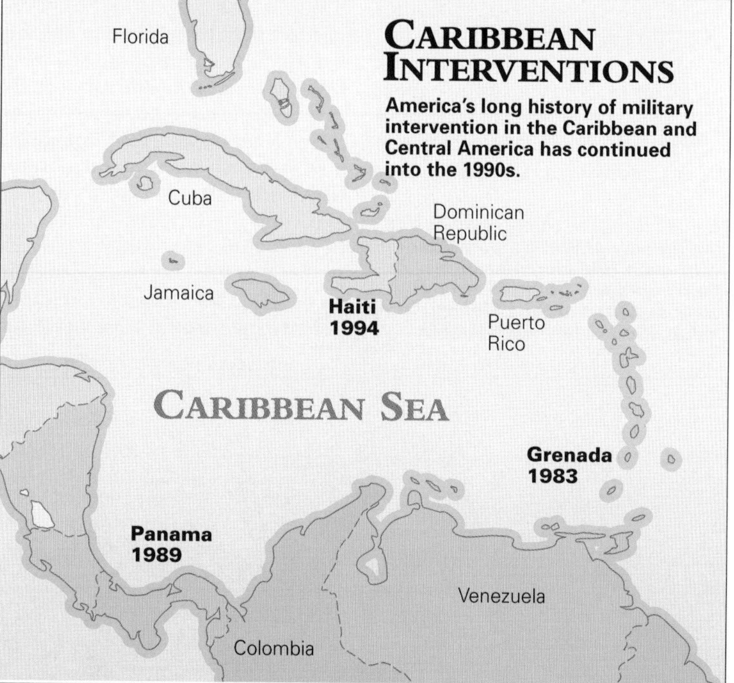

Marine Corps helicopters

The Marine Corps was always out in front in introducing helicopters to combat. In Korea in 1950, they fielded the Sikorsky HRS-1 thirty months before the US Army flew the equivalent H-19. In Vietnam in 1965, the Marines were flying the Sikorsky CH-53A Sea Stallion more than a year before other service branches introduced their own versions. Helicopters were vital to the Grenada operation, which was itself a harbinger of the post-Cold War world.

Bell AH-1T Cobra
Right: A development of the Vietnam-era AH-1J (and a predecessor of the AH-1W of the 1990s), this Marine AH-1T typifies dozens that covered the landing in Grenada. The small nose-mounted turret above the twin-barreled M197 20-mm cannon houses a stabilized sight for use with TOW wire-guided anti-tank missiles. The larger white cylinders house 70-mm (2.75-in) FFAR rockets.

Boeing-Vertol CH-46E Sea Knight
Left: The predominant aircraft type in HMM-261's inventory during the Grenada assault was the CH-46E, twelve of which were operated in the medium transport role. Much-loved, versatile, but long in the tooth, the Sea Knight is expected to remain the principal transport helicopter of the Marine Corps until the expected arrival of the V-22 Osprey early in the 21st century.

AC-130H gunships of the 1st Special Operations Wing and by three attack squadrons of Carrier Air Wing Six from the USS *Independence* (CV-62).

Mapping Grenada

No adequate maps were available and the Army's 63rd Engineer Company was forced to use a Grenadian Chamber of Commerce map to develop a grid system and produce the maps used by Army forces in the assault. Even less factual were the limited data on the likely strength of the enemy opposition: Intelligence estimated that the 600 PRA regular troops were supplemented by some 2,500 auxiliaries including the ill-disciplined and ineffectually-trained People's Revolutionary Militia (PRM) and the police. Cuban strength on the island was estimated at 50 military advisers and some 700 armed construction workers. Precious little was known of weapons and precise locations of this motley opposition

As finally drawn, plans called for nearly simultaneous insertions of Marines near Pearls Airport and Rangers at the Point Salines Airport, the first Marines being brought in by CH-46Es from the *Guam* and the first Rangers being para-dropped by C-130. Reinforcements at Point Salines were to be air landed after the Rangers secured the partially completed runway, while those at Pearls were to be taken ashore by landing ships.

After the go-ahead for the intervention was given by President Reagan during the evening of 23 October, Vice Admiral Joseph Metcalf III and his JTF-120 staff aboard the *Guam* set the operation into motion.

***Left:* Operation Urgent Fury was successful in part because of the Sikorsky CH-53D Sea Stallion, by far the largest helicopter used by US forces during the attack. Four of these were assigned to HMM-261, which covered the Marines' landing on the island.**

***Below:* The only aircraft lost during the Grand Anse rescue operation was this battered Marine CH-46E Sea Knight. This helicopter was disabled by ground fire during the initial insertion of the Ranger rescue force and was then abandoned on Grand Anse beach.**

Two platoon-size SEAL teams went ashore the next night, where they discovered that reefs rendered the scheduled amphibious assault impractical. The location of one of the proposed helicopter landing sites also had to be moved as the SEALs found anti-aircraft defences at Pearls Airport to be heavier than expected.

Gunship leads the way

First into the fray was an AC-130H of the 16th Special Operations Squadron. It flew over the Point Salines Airport during the early hours of 25 October using its advanced sensors to scan the area for anti-aircraft weapons and runway obstructions. Attracting much AAA fire, the gunship radioed back valuable information in time for field commanders to revise plans for the initial assault.

The Marines were first inserted by Sea Stallion helicopters near Pearls Airport at 0520 on 25 October, and 16 minutes later Rangers began jumping from Air Force C-130s over Point Salines. The fight was on.

The principal Navy fixed-wing aircraft used during Urgent Fury were the Vought A-7E Corsair IIs and Grumman A-6E Intruders of Air Wing Six operating from the USS *Independence*. In general, the Corsair proved effective in providing air support for the ground forces, but the type was also involved in two unfortunate incidents. In the afternoon of 25 October, an A-7 caused numerous Grenadian civilian casualties when after taking AAA fire from the direction of a large building, it bombed the suspected area; unfortunately, this building turned out to be a mental hospital. Two days later, due to poor communications yet another A-7E accidentally strafed an outpost of the 82nd Airborne Division; the accident, in which one GI was killed and 15 others wounded, was blamed on poor co-ordinates having been

Airlift of troops

The biggest operator of aircraft during the Grenada invasion was the US Air Force's Military Airlift Command (MAC), which kept C-130s, C-5s, and C-141s flowing to the island. After the initial assault from the sea and parachute assault from C-130s, most long-range troop movements were handled by civil airliners flown by contract companies. MAC's main function was the movement of huge amounts of supplies and equipment, though airlifters like the C-141 also transported hundreds of soldiers and Marines to the island from bases in the USA.

Lockheed C-141B Starlifter

Left: Enlarged by a 'stretching' programme that lengthened its fuselage and increased its carrying capacity, the C-141B was the workhorse of the Grenada campaign. The rear-loading ramp and 'roll on, roll off' capability of the Starlifter enabled it to haul a variety of cargoes including many large vehicles.

Above: American military aircraft are seen alongside civil transport on the ramp at Pearls Airport, Grenada. Although the invasion received mixed reaction abroad, the general feeling on Grenada was one of satisfaction at the restoration of democracy.

given to the pilot.

As part of its reinforced complement, HMM-261 had four Bell AH-1T Cobra attack helicopters aboard the *Guam*. These four machines saw much action, and two were shot down by the PRA during the fighting for Fort Frederick on 25 October. The last two remained in the thick of the fight until the final Urgent Fury actions.

Boeing-Vertol CH-46E Sea Knights, the main Marine Corps transport helicopters, performed well from the assault against Pearls and Grenville in the early morning hours of 25 October until the last Marine operation, the taking of Carriacou Island on 1 November. One CH-46E was shot down on 26 October during the rescue of American students at the Grand Anse campus of the Medical School.

Another type making its combat debut during Urgent Fury, the Sikorsky UH-60A Black Hawk earned praises on account of its reliability and, thanks to its twin-engined configuration, its ability to be ferried over long overwater distances (ie from Barbados to Grenada). However, three were shot down or damaged beyond repair, one heavily damaged, and two lightly damaged. Other helicopter losses included one Hughes 500 Defender shot down on 25 October during operations against the Richmond Hill Prison and one OH-58C Kiowa receiving major damage.

Above: The compound for the Cuban airport construction workers had a distinctly military look, with its perimeter security fencing, vehicle storage sheds and a military-style assault course.

Casualty bill

American casualties during Urgent Fury included 19 dead and 116 wounded; Cuban casualties were 25 dead and 59 wounded, while Grenadian casualties, including civilians, were 45 dead and 350 wounded.

Although successful, Urgent Fury raised numerous political questions, both in the United States and abroad, and lent credence to doubts expressed in many quarters about the combat use of helicopters in the face of determined and well-armed opponents. On the other hand, the happy conclusion of the intervention in Grenada did much to boost the confidence of the American public in its armed forces and helped the latter to regain most of the pride which had been lost 10 years earlier in the Vietnamese quagmire, and lessons learned during the operation were put to good use in Panama and Haiti over the next decade.

Haiti: Operation Uphold Democracy

The military junta of General Raoul Cedras held on to power in Haiti in spite of elections won by Jean-Bertrand Aristide. A full-scale US invasion to restore democracy was averted when a last-minute agreement was brokered by former US President Jimmy Carter. General Cedras agreed to stand down with effect from 15 October 1994 and permit exiled President Aristide to assume power the following day.

On 19 September 2,000 US troops, most of whom were from the 10th Mountain Division (Light) at Fort Drum, NY were airlifted ashore from ships of Joint Task Force 190 located off the Haitian coast. US Army UH-60s ferried the troops to Haiti while AH-1 Cobras flew protective air cover. The helicopters operated from the aircraft carrier USS *Eisenhower* (CVN-69).

This was the first occasion in which the Adaptive Joint Force Package concept, involving the integration of various services, had been employed operationally. In excess of 50 US Army helicopters were embarked on the US Navy aircraft-carrier for the operation.

US Air Force aircraft played a supporting role, with the majority forward-deployed to the naval station at Roosevelt Roads, Puerto Rico. E-3 Sentries of the 552nd ACW from Tinker AFB, Oklahoma monitored the skies above Haiti as well as the air space around Cuba.

Twenty-four F-15Cs of the 33rd FW from Eglin AFB, Florida were stationed at Roosevelt Roads along with nine KC-135s, as a precautionary measure to perform combat air patrols if needed. In the event, the Eagles were not required when the invasion was cancelled and they returned home after only four days.

Other USAF types included three EC-130Es of the 42nd ACCS, 355th Wing from Davis-Monthan AFB, Arizona which performed airborne battlefield management. AC-130H Spectre gunships were on hand to provide firepower if necessary, while RC-135 Rivet Joint aircraft monitored communications.

The initial complement of 2,000 US Army forces was boosted to 15,000 within a week to ensure the country remained stable during the transition back to democracy.

Right: US Army helicopters use the broad flight deck of the USS* Dwight D. Eisenhower *as a mobile base from which to launch the Haitian peacekeeping force.

Panama: Operation Just Cause

Panama's leader, General Manuel Noriega, had been needling the United States for years. He had been indicted in an American court for drug offences, and after surviving a failed coup d'état went so far as to 'declare war' on the US on 15 December 1989. He had pushed the Americans too far and they decided to take action against him.

Hints of impending action in Panama began on 16 December when a US Marine Corps lieutenant was murdered by Panamanian soldiers at a roadblock, and a US Navy officer and his wife were detained and mistreated.

Action begins

Operation Just Cause began in the early hours of Wednesday 20 December 1989, when US Navy SEALs attacked Paitilla Airport, where Noriega kept a possible getaway LearJet. Four SEALs were killed confronting unexpectedly heavy resistance before the aerodrome was secured and the LearJet destroyed.

AC-130H Spectre gunships of the 16th Special Operations Squadron attacked key targets, including the Panama Defense Forces fortress known as the Comandancia, as well as the Puma Battalion barracks just outside Omar Torrijos Airport. US artillery already deployed at the US Army base of Fort Amador opened up on PDF barracks nearby.

The initial assault made use of 7,000 of the 22,500 American troops eventually deployed for the operation, divided into five groups. The first wave of 77 C-141B StarLifters, 22 C-130 Hercules, and 12 C-5 Galaxies made a total of 84 air drops, followed by a second wave of 40 C-141Bs and 13 C-5s. These airlifted troops from the 82nd Airborne Division, the 7th Infantry Division and other Army units.

Task Force Bayonet, including light tanks and infantry, assaulted and destroyed the Comandancia. Other troops were helicoptered from Howard Air Force Base to reinforce friendlies and block the PDF at Fort Amador. Bayonet included the SEAL assault at Paitilla.

Task Force Red made a parachute assault on Torrijos Airport and the Puma barracks, spearheaded by an Army Ranger battalion and 82nd Airborne troopers. A second Ranger battalion parachuted into Rio Hato where some of Noriega's most loyal units were based, seizing an armoury after fierce fighting.

Task Force Pacific brought 20 C-141B loads of additional troops, who formed a second wave parachuting into Torrijos Airport and then blocked a bridge over the Pacora River to prevent PDF forces from advancing into Panama City from the east.

Task Force Semper Fidelis, made up of US Marines and a light armoured infantry company, seized the Bridge of the Americas, the only access into Panama City from the west. Task Force Atlantic, consisting of 82nd Airborne and 7th Light Infantry troopers, took the electrical powerplant at Sierra Tigre, the Madden Dam and Gamboa Prison.

Stealth emerges

In retrospect, the most noteworthy event was the first combat use of the Lockheed F-117A Nighthawk 'stealth fighter'.Flying nonstop from Nevada, with the aid of air refuelling, two F-117As from the 37th TFW dropped 907-kg (2,000-lb) LGBs in a field next to the barracks to frighten the troops and to destroy an anti-aircraft position defending the airfield.

After the first day, fighting was sporadic and scattered, though some PDF continued to resist. Noriega took refuge in the Vatican ambassador's residence, before surrendering on 3 January. He was flown on a US Army UH-60A Black Hawk to Howard, then taken aboard an MC-130E Combat Talon I to Florida to be arraigned on a drug indictment. Once Noriega was gone, resistance collapsed and by 22 January 1990 the 82nd Airborne could return to the US.

Operation Just Cause's casualties included 23 American and 200 Panamanian combatants killed, as well as 202 Panamanian civilian fatalities. A number of Panamanian aircraft were destroyed or damaged. Numerous US aircraft were damaged, including 11 C-130s, and US Army losses included one OH-58 and three AH-6s.

Above: Noriega sought asylum in the Vatican Embassy, which was immediately surrounded. A Special Forces Sikorsky MH-53J lands on a football pitch nearby while in the foreground an American soldier keeps watch on the Embassy.

Left: The less than stellar performance of the Lockheed F-117 Nighthawk in Panama evoked some controversy. US officials had a hard time demonstrating that the high-ticket 'stealth' jet was really worth the money.

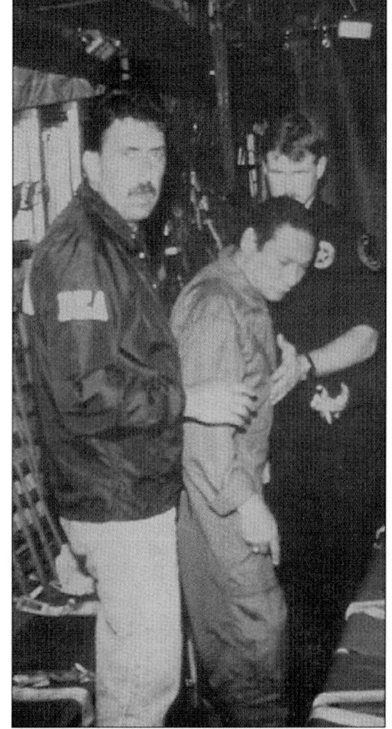

Right: Panama's Manuel Noriega, carried to the US aboard a C-130, became the United States' only prisoner of war. He was charged with and in a Florida court trial convicted of a string of narcotics offences.

Drug Wars

1970–THE PRESENT

Left: Colombian commandos, advised by agents from the US Drug Enforcement Agency (DEA), set off in a US-supplied Bell UH-1 on a raid against a jungle cocaine processing site. Helicopter mobility has been essential in the campaign by Colombian law-enforcement units against the ever-spreading tentacles of the drug barons.

In most countries, dealing with the drug trade is a job for the police, but in the United States it is a war. The drug problem on America's streets is so serious that the full weight of the government has been thrown into the struggle to terminate supplies. Apart from the Drug Enforcement Agency, the president's anti-drug task force can call on the Department of Defense, the Coast Guard, the State Department, the Department of Justice, the US Customs Service, the FBI, and the Bureau of Alcohol, Tobacco and Firearms.

The South American trade is a little different from the heroin trails of Asia. Cocaine is the big money-maker in Colombia, and the producers have established the drug business in a big way. Despite the best efforts of the Colombian government and judiciary, which have seen the virtual elimination of the Medellin cartel and the imprisonment or death of many of the leaders of the Cali cartel, they remain multi-billion dollar businesses, corrupting everyone from local judges and policemen to entire Central American and Caribbean governments.

STOPPING THE SOURCE

The war against drugs is being fought on several fronts. Drugs can be stopped at source by bringing political pressure to bear on the supplier countries. This can take the form of economic assistance, given when the local government makes serious efforts to stop the trade, or military assistance, in the form of weapons and Special Forces training teams.

Most of the coca leaf from which cocaine is produced is actually grown in Peru and Bolivia. Hundreds of tonnes of cocaine base are shipped into Colombia where it is converted in clandestine laboratories into cocaine hydrochloride, the finished drug. From there it is exported to the target markets of the United States and Europe.

The military has a number of options in dealing with the trade at source. The first step is to destroy the coca leaves on the trees, using aircraft to spray herbicides. This is not entirely effective, as it also destroys legitimate crops and arouses hostility in the peasantry. The second option is to destroy the processing centres by direct attack. This generally involves helicopter assaults supported by ground attack aircraft. But the country is rugged, and even when one jungle factory is raided the producers can simply set up in some other valley.

If one cannot control the drugs at source, one must try to stop them in transit. Cocaine from Colombia

Right: Peru uses armed EMBRAER Tucano trainers in an aggressive programme of interdiction. Drug flights are intercepted and ordered to land: should they fail to do so then they are shot down. More than 50 drug-laden aircraft have been taken out by the Peruvian and Colombian air forces since 1994.

Left: the US Customs Service operates an airborne early warning version of the Lockheed P-3 Orion maritime patrol aircraft to monitor sea and air traffic in the Caribbean and the Gulf of Mexico.

Above: US Military airborne radar in the shape of the E-3 AWACS and E-2 Hawkeye (seen here) are also used in the war against drugs. Each aircraft can monitor thousands of square miles of the surface.

Above: Suspicious flights are shadowed by aircraft from one of the many agencies involved. Once the suspected drugs runner has landed, customs and DEA agents use Sikorsky Black Hawk helicopters to move in, hopefully catching the criminals in possession of illicit drugs.

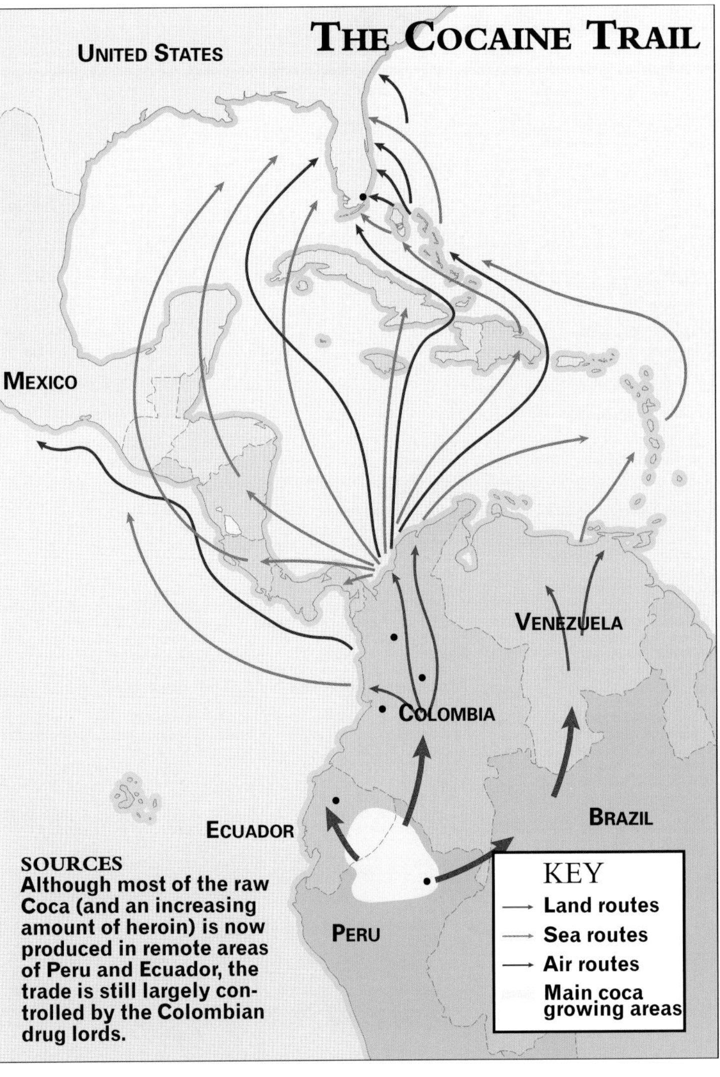

Above: Aerial interdiction by key South American nations has forced a considerable change on the patterns of the traffickers. The risk of being shot down has cut the use of aircraft within South America by at least half. The drugs barons are now shipping the raw material by land for conversion to cocaine, which is then transhipped via a bewildering variety of routes through central America and the Caribbean. Anti-drug efforts resulted in the seizure of at least 250 tonnes of cocaine in 1995 – but that was only a third of the estimated production for that year, and had little effect on the amount of the drug on the streets. It is clear that there is still a long way to go.

is shipped via neighbouring Brazil, Peru, Venezuela and Ecuador, and increasingly via Mexico.

Cocaine is a high-value, low-bulk product, so a light plane can carry a valuable load quite easily. Indeed, when moving a couple of suitcases worth a million dollars or so, the $50,000 it costs to buy a second-hand plane is an incidental expense, and the plane is very definitely expendable. In the past, the drugs were flown from jungle airstrips to transhipment points, but aggressive actions on the part of the governments of Peru and Brazil, in particular, have seen a large number of drug flights shot down over the jungle, most often by armed trainers like the EMBRAER Tucano.

However, drugs still reach shipping ports, and they are still exported across the Caribbean in a variety of ways.

Stopping the trade involves cutters from the US Coast Guard, often supported by larger US Navy vessels, up to and including aircraft carriers. Navy, Air Force and US Customs Service airborne early warning aircraft keep track of air and surface movements by day or night, supported by tethered aerostats - unmanned airships carrying radar.

If there is a suspicion that a ship is running drugs, it can be boarded and searched. However, it is difficult to search an aircraft unless one forces it down, so suspect aircraft are shadowed. This can be done by radar, using airborne early warning planes, or it can involve physically trailing the aircraft.

INTERDICTION

High-performance military jets are not necessarily the best aircraft to follow a piston-engined plane flying low and slow, so the US Customs Service has a number of light aircraft – often confiscated from drug-runners – fitted with extra tanks and low-light vision gear to do the job. Other aircraft which have been used for the job include the awesome AC-130 gunships of the US Air Force, whose highly sophisticated night vision devices are ideal for the purpose.

But no matter how good the sensors, it can be like looking for a needle in a haystack. A hundred or more light planes make the crossing between the Bahamas and Florida every day, and cabin cruisers and powerboats are just as common in the 85-km (53-mile) wide Florida Strait. Aircraft making directly for Miami airport will probably be honest, but those making for some point in the Everglades are probably intending to land drugs, and are worth checking out.

Drug runners might risk a direct flight into an airfield deep in the Florida swamps, particularly when confederates can make a rapid pick-up. Helicopters are the best means of dealing with these deliveries, as they are able to drop in and catch the smugglers in the act.

Joint Interagency Task Forces

As the struggle to control the drugs trade has come to resemble warfare, the US military found it necessary to establish co-ordinating bodies to make most effective use of the high-tech (and high-cost) resources available. Established in April 1994, the three Joint Interagency Task Forces are just what their titles proclaim: international, interagency bodies which coordinate the operational aspects of the drugs war.

JIATF East, based at NAS Key West, is the largest. Reporting to the Commander-in-Chief, US Atlantic Command, it has representatives from the Federal Bureau of Investigation, Defense Intelligence Agency, Drug Enforcement Agency, US Coast Guard and allied militaries. JIATF West, based at Alameda in California, is responsible for West Coast and Mexican border operations. JIATF South is the third operational unit, headquartered with US Southern Command at Howard AFB, Panama.

The control centre at JIATF-E monitors the primary sea- and air-borne approaches to the USA across the Caribbean and the Gulf of Mexico.

INDEX

Page numbers in **bold** refer to an illustration

INDEX

INDEX

Picture acknowledgments

The publishers would like to thank the following organisations for their help in providing photographs for this volume.

Aerospace Collection
Aérospatiale
Associated Press
Dassault Aviation
Robert F. Dorr
Peter Foster
Gamma Liaison
Imperial War Museum
MacClancy Collection
Peter March
Herman Potgeiter
Tim Ripley
Royal Air Force
Royal Navy
Frank Spooner Pictures
UK Ministry of Defence
US Air Force
US Customs Service
US Department of Defense
US Navy
US Marine Corps